Cisco Networking Academy

Copyright© 2014 Cisco Systems, Inc.

Published by:
Cisco Press
800 East 96th Street
Indianapolis, IN 46240 USA

Printed in the United States of America

Fourth Printing: May 2015

Library of Congress Cataloging-in-Publication data is on file.

ISBN-13: 978-1-58713-316-9

ISBN-10: 1-58713-316-4

Warning and Disclaimer

This book is designed to provide information about the Cisco Networking Academy Introduction to Networks course. Every effort has been made to make this book as complete and as accurate as possible, but no warranty or fitness is implied.

The information is provided on an "as is" basis. The authors, Cisco Press, and Cisco Systems, Inc. shall have neither liability nor responsibility to any person or entity with respect to any loss or damages arising from the information contained in this book or from the use of the discs or programs that may accompany it.

The opinions expressed in this book belong to the author and are not necessarily those of Cisco Systems, Inc.

Publisher
Paul Boger

Associate Publisher
Dave Dusthimer

**Business Operation
Manager, Cisco Press**
Jan Cornelssen

Executive Editor
Mary Beth Ray

Managing Editor
Sandra Schroeder

Development Editor
Ellie C. Bru

Project Editor
Mandie Frank

Copy Editor
John Edwards

Technical Editor
Aubrey Adams

Editorial Assistant
Vanessa Evans

Designer
Mark Shirar

Composition
Studio Galou, LLC

Indexer
Larry Sweazy

Proofreader
Debbie Williams

Cisco Networking Academy

Cisco Press

800 East 96th Street

Indianapolis, Indiana 46240 USA

Trademark Acknowledgements

All terms mentioned in this book that are known to be trademarks or service marks have been appropriately capitalized. Cisco Press or Cisco Systems, Inc., cannot attest to the accuracy of this information. Use of a term in this book should not be regarded as affecting the validity of any trademark or service mark.

Corporate and Government Sales

The publisher offers excellent discounts on this book when ordered in quantity for bulk purchases or special sales, which may include electronic versions and/or custom covers and content particular to your business, training goals, marketing focus, and branding interests. For more information, please contact:

U.S. Corporate and Government Sales
1-800-382-3419
corpsales@pearsontechgroup.com

For sales outside the United States, please contact:

International Sales
international@pearsoned.com

Feedback Information

At Cisco Press, our goal is to create in-depth technical books of the highest quality and value. Each book is crafted with care and precision, undergoing rigorous development that involves the unique expertise of members from the professional technical community.

Readers' feedback is a natural continuation of this process. If you have any comments regarding how we could improve the quality of this book, or otherwise alter it to better suit your needs, you can contact us through email at feedback@ciscopress.com. Please make sure to include the book title and ISBN in your message.

We greatly appreciate your assistance.

Americas Headquarters
Cisco Systems, Inc.
170 West Tasman Drive
San Jose, CA 95134-1706
USA
www.cisco.com
Tel: 408 526-4000
800 553-NETS (6387)
Fax: 408 527-0883

Asia Pacific Headquarters
Cisco Systems, Inc.
168 Robinson Road
#28-01 Capital Tower
Singapore 068912
www.cisco.com
Tel: +65 6317 7777
Fax: +65 6317 7799

Europe Headquarters
Cisco Systems International BV
Haarlerbergpark
Haarlerbergweg 13-19
1101 CH Amsterdam
The Netherlands
www-europe.cisco.com
Tel: +31 0 800 020 0791
Fax: +31 0 20 357 1100

Cisco has more than 200 offices worldwide. Addresses, phone numbers, and fax numbers are listed on the Cisco Website at www.cisco.com/go/offices.

©2007 Cisco Systems, Inc. All rights reserved. CCVP, the Cisco logo, and the Cisco Square Bridge logo are trademarks of Cisco Systems, Inc.; Changing the Way We Work, Live, Play, and Learn is a service mark of Cisco Systems, Inc.; and Access Registrar, Aironet, BPX, Catalyst, CCDA, CCDP, CCIE, CCIP, CCNA, CCNP, CCSP, Cisco, the Cisco Certified Internetwork Expert logo, Cisco IOS, Cisco Press, Cisco Systems, Cisco Systems Capital, the Cisco Systems logo, Cisco Unity, Enterprise/Solver, EtherChannel, EtherFast, EtherSwitch, Fast Step, Follow Me Browsing, FormShare, GigaDrive, GigaStack, HomeLink, Internet Quotient, IOS, IP/TV, iQ Expertise, the iQ logo, iQ Net Readiness Scorecard, iQuick Study, LightStream, Linksys, MeetingPlace, MGX, Networking Academy, Network Registrar, Packet, PIX, ProConnect, RateMUX, ScriptShare, SlideCast, SMARTnet, StackWise, The Fastest Way to Increase Your Internet Quotient, and TransPath are registered trademarks of Cisco Systems, Inc. and/or its affiliates in the United States and certain other countries.

All other trademarks mentioned in this document or Website are the property of their respective owners. The use of the word partner does not imply a partnership relationship between Cisco and any other company. (0609R)

About the Contributing Authors

Mark A. Dye

Mark is the lead network engineer for Kwajalein Range Services at Ronald Reagan Ballistic Missile Defense Test Site on Kwajalein, Marshall Islands. He is responsible for the network team that provides design, deployment, and operation of all the missile test range data networks across ten islands as well as three continental U.S. locations.

He has previously worked as subject matter expert and content team lead for the Cisco Academy Program as well as an author for multiple Cisco Network Academy Fundamentals online courses. He worked to develop and review courseware and assessments for both the Academy and certification programs.

For more than 20 years, Mark served as technology manager for The Bevill Center for Advanced Manufacturing Technology of Alabama Technology Network. He developed and implemented comprehensive network strategies for intranet and Internet, including policies, administrative procedures, network security, and interconnectivity. He also implemented and taught Cisco Networking Academy Fundamentals of Wireless LANs, Fundamentals of Network Security, and CCNA and CCNP courses at The Bevill Center for instructors and students.

Allan D. Reid

Allan is a professor and program supervisor at Centennial College in Toronto, Ontario, Canada, where he teaches courses in networking, network security, virtualization, and cloud computing. He is the lead for the Centennial College ASC/ITC and has been teaching the academy curriculum since one of the earliest versions.

Allan has authored multiple books and online courses for the Cisco Academy program, where he is a subject matter expert and content team lead. He works as part of the core team to develop state-of-the-art assessments and courseware.

Outside of his academic responsibilities, Allan has been active in the computer and networking fields for more than 30 years and is currently a principal in a company involved in the design, installation, and management of network solutions for small- to medium-sized companies.

Contents at a Glance

Contents

Syntax Conventions

Router Wireless Router PIX Firewall Left Router with Firewall Workgroup Switch

Route/Switch Processor Firewall Firewall Appliance Printer File/Application Server

PC Laptop IP Phone Satellite Satellite Dish

Telephone Switch Hub Tablet House Small Business

Headquarters Cloud Internet Line: Ethernet Line: Serial Wireless Connectivity

The conventions used to present command syntax in this book are the same conventions used in the IOS Command Reference. The Command Reference describes these conventions as follows:

- **Boldface** indicates commands and keywords that are entered literally as shown. In actual configuration examples and output (not general command syntax), boldface indicates commands that are manually input by the user (such as a **show** command).

- *Italics* indicate arguments for which you supply actual values.

- Vertical bars (|) separate alternative, mutually exclusive elements.

- Square brackets ([ ]) indicate an optional element.
- Braces ({ }) indicate a required choice.
- Braces within brackets ([{ }]) indicate a required choice within an optional element.

Introduction

Introduction to Networks Companion Guide is the official supplemental textbook for the Cisco Network Academy CCNA Introduction to Networks course. Cisco Networking Academy is a comprehensive program that delivers information technology skills to students around the world. The curriculum emphasizes real-world practical application, while providing opportunities for you to gain the skills and hands-on experience needed to design, install, operate, and maintain networks in small- to medium-sized businesses, as well as enterprise and service provider environments.

As a textbook, this book provides a ready reference to explain the same networking concepts, technologies, protocols, and devices as the online curriculum. This book emphasizes key topics, terms, and activities and provides some alternate explanations and examples as compared with the course. You can use the online curriculum as directed by your instructor and then use this Companion Guide's study tools to help solidify your understanding of all the topics.

Who Should Read This Book

This book is intended for students in the Cisco Networking Academy CCNA Routing and Switching Introduction to Networks course. The book, as well as the course, is designed as an introduction to data network technology for those pursuing careers as network professionals as well as those who need only an introduction to network technology for professional growth. Topics are presented concisely, starting with the most fundamental concepts and progressing to a comprehensive understanding of network communication. The content of this text provides the foundation for additional Cisco Academy courses, and preparation for the CCENT and CCNA Routing and Switching certifications.

Book Features

The educational features of this book focus on supporting topic coverage, readability, and practice of the course material to facilitate your full understanding of the course material.

Topic Coverage

The following features give you a thorough overview of the topics covered in each chapter so that you can make constructive use of your study time:

- **Objectives:** Listed at the beginning of each chapter, the objectives reference the core concepts covered in the chapter. The objectives match the objectives stated in the corresponding chapters of the online curriculum; however, the question format in the Companion Guide encourages you to think about finding the answers as you read the chapter.

How To 🔍

- **"How-to" feature:** When this book covers a set of steps that you need to perform for certain tasks, the text lists the steps as a how-to list. When you are studying, the icon helps you easily refer to this feature as you skim through the book.

- **Notes:** These are short sidebars that point out interesting facts, timesaving methods, and important safety issues.

- **Chapter summaries:** At the end of each chapter is a summary of the chapter's key concepts. It provides a synopsis of the chapter and serves as a study aid.

- **Practice:** At the end of each chapter there is a full list of all the Labs, Class Activities, and Packet Tracer Activities to refer back to for study time.

Readability

The following features have been updated to assist your understanding of the networking vocabulary:

- **Key terms:** Each chapter begins with a list of key terms, along with a page-number reference from inside the chapter. The terms are listed in the order in which they are explained in the chapter. This handy reference allows you to find a term, flip to the page where the term appears, and see the term used in context. The Glossary defines all the key terms.

- **Glossary:** This book contains an all-new Glossary with almost 200 terms.

Practice

Practice makes perfect. This new Companion Guide offers you ample opportunities to put what you learn into practice. You will find the following features valuable and effective in reinforcing the instruction that you receive:

- **Check Your Understanding questions and answer key:** Updated review questions are presented at the end of each chapter as a self-assessment tool. These questions match the style of questions that you see in the online course. Appendix A, "Answers to the 'Check Your Understanding' Questions," provides an answer key to all the questions and includes an explanation of each answer.

- **Labs and activities:** Throughout each chapter, you will be directed back to the online course to take advantage of the activities created to reinforce concepts. In addition, at the end of each chapter, there is a "Practice" section that collects a list of all the labs and activities to provide practice with the topics introduced in this chapter. The labs and class activities are available in the companion *Introduction to Networks Lab Manual* [ISBN 978-1-58713-312-1]. The Packet Tracer Activities PKA files are found in the online course.

- **Page references to online course:** After headings, you will see, for example, (1.1.2.3). This number refers to the page number in the online course so that you can easily jump to that spot online to view a video, practice an activity, perform a lab, or review a topic.

Lab Manual

The supplementary book *Introduction to Networks Lab Manual*, by Cisco Press (ISBN 978-1-58713-312-1), contains all the labs and class activities from the course.

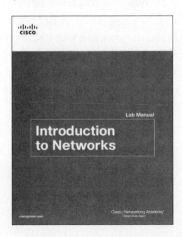

Practice and Study Guide

Additional Study Guide exercises, activities, and scenarios are available in the new *CCENT Practice and Study Guide* (978-158713-345-9) and *CCNA Routing and Switching Practice and Study Guide* (978-158713-344-2) books by Allan Johnson. Each Practice and Study Guide coordinates with the recommended curriculum sequence—the CCENT edition follows the course outlines for *Introduction to Networks* and *Routing and Switching Essentials*. The CCNA edition follows the course outlines for *Scaling Networks* and *Connecting Networks*.

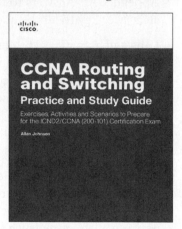

Packet Tracer
☐ Activity

About Packet Tracer Software and Activities

Interspersed throughout the chapters you'll find many activities to work with the Cisco Packet Tracer tool. Packet Tracer allows you to create networks, visualize how packets flow in the network, and use basic testing tools to determine whether the network would work. When you see this icon, you can use Packet Tracer with the listed file to perform a task suggested in this book. The activity files are available in the course. Packet Tracer software is available only through the Cisco Networking Academy website. Ask your instructor for access to Packet Tracer.

How This Book Is Organized

This book corresponds closely to the Cisco Networking Academy Introduction to Networks course and is divided into 11 chapters, one appendix, and a glossary of key terms:

- **Chapter 1, "Exploring the Network":** Introduces the concept of a network and provides an overview of the different types of networks encountered. It examines how networks impact the way we work, learn, and play. This chapter also examines new trends in networks such as video, cloud computing, and BYOD, and how to help ensure that we have a robust, reliable, secure network to support these trends.

- **Chapter 2, "Configuring a Network Operating System":** Introduces the operating system used with most Cisco devices: the Cisco IOS. The basic purpose and functions of the IOS are described as well as the methods to access the IOS. The chapter will also present maneuvering through the IOS command-line interface as well as basic IOS device configuration.

- **Chapter 3, "Network Protocols and Communications":** Examines the importance of rules or protocols for network communication. It explores the OSI reference model and the TCP/IP communication suite, examining how these models provide the necessary protocols to allow communication to occur on a modern converged network.

- **Chapter 4, "Network Access":** Introduces the lowest layer of the TCP/IP model: the transport layer. This layer is essentially the equivalent of the OSI data link layer and the physical layer. The chapter discusses how this layer prepares network layer packets for transmission, controls access to the physical media, and transports the data across various media. This chapter includes a description of the encapsulation protocols and processes that occur as data travels across the LAN and the WAN as well as the media used.

- **Chapter 5, "Ethernet":** Examines the functionality of one of the most common LAN protocols in use today. It explores how Ethernet functions and interacts with the TCP/IP protocol suite to provide high-speed data communications.

- **Chapter 6, "Network Layer":** Introduces the function of the network layer—routing—and the basic device that performs this function—the router. The important routing concepts related to addressing, path determination, and data packets for both IPv4 and IPv6 will be presented. The chapter also introduces the construction of a router and the basic router configuration.

- **Chapter 7, "Transport Layer":** Introduces Transmission Control Protocol (TCP) and User Datagram Protocol (UDP) and examines how each transports information across the network. It explores how TCP uses segmentation, the three-way handshake, and expectational acknowledgements to ensure reliable delivery of data. It also examines the best-effort delivery mechanism provided by UDP and describes when this would be preferred over TCP.

- **Chapter 8, "IP Addressing":** Focuses on IPv4 and IPv6 network addressing, including the types of addresses and address assignment. It describes how to use the address mask or prefix length to determine the number of subnetworks and hosts in a network. This chapter also introduces Internet Control Message Protocol (ICMP) tools, such as ping and trace.

- **Chapter 9, "Subnetting IP Networks":** Examines how to improve network performance by optimally dividing the IP address space based on network requirements. It explores the calculation of valid host addresses and the determination of both subnet and subnet broadcast addresses. This chapter examines subnetting for both IPv4 and IPv6.

- **Chapter 10, "Application Layer":** Introduces some protocols of the TCP/IP application layer, which also relates to the top three layers of the OSI model. The chapter focuses on the role of the application layer and how the applications, services, and protocols within the application layer make robust communication across data networks possible. This will be demonstrated by examining some key protocols and services including HTTP, DNS, DHCP, SMTP/POP, Telnet, and FTP.

- **Chapter 11, "It's a Network":** Reexamines the various components found in a small network and describes how they work together to allow network growth. Network security and performance issues are examined, along with some of the commands that can be used to examine the configuration of devices and the performance of the network. Router and switch file systems are also examined, along with methods for backing up and restoring their configuration files.

- **Appendix A, "Answers to the 'Check Your Understanding' Questions":** This appendix lists the answers to the "Check Your Understanding" review questions that are included at the end of each chapter.

- **Glossary:** The glossary provides you with definitions for all the key terms identified in each chapter.

CHAPTER 1

Exploring the Network

Objectives

Upon completion of this chapter, you will be able to answer the following questions:

- How do networks affect the way we interact, learn, work and play?

- How do networks support communication?

- What is a converged network?

- What are the four basic requirements of a reliable network?

- What are the uses of various network devices?

- How do the devices and topologies found in a LAN compare to those found in a WAN?

- What is the basic structure of the Internet?

- How do LANs and WANs connect to the Internet?

- What impact do BYOD, online collaboration, video, and cloud computing have on a business network?

- How are networking technologies changing the home environment?

- What are some basic security threats and solutions to both small and large networks?

Key Terms

This chapter uses the following key terms. You can find the definitions in the Glossary.

Introduction (1.0.1.1)

We now stand at a critical turning point in the use of technology to extend and empower our ability to communicate. The globalization of the *Internet* has succeeded faster than anyone could have imagined. The manner in which social, commercial, political, and personal interactions occur is rapidly changing to keep up with the evolution of this global network. In the next stage of our development, innovators will use the Internet as a starting point for their efforts—creating new products and services specifically designed to take advantage of the network capabilities. As developers push the limits of what is possible, the capabilities of the interconnected networks that form the Internet will play an increasing role in the success of these projects.

This chapter introduces the platform of data networks upon which our social and business relationships increasingly depend. The material lays the groundwork for exploring the services, technologies, and issues encountered by network professionals as they design, build, and maintain the modern network.

The Networking Academy curriculum has a new component: modeling activities! You will find them at the beginning and end of each chapter.

Some activities can be completed individually (at home or in class), and some will require group or learning-community interaction. Your instructor will be facilitating so that you can obtain the most from these introductory activities.

These activities will help you enhance your understanding by providing an opportunity to visualize some of the abstract concepts that you will be learning in this course. Be creative and enjoy these activities!

The Introduction to Networks Lab Manual contains all the labs and class activities from the course. You can access the full instructions in the course itself or in this printed lab manual.

Here is your first modeling activity:

Class Activity 1.0.1.2: Draw Your Concept of the Internet

In this activity, you will draw and label a map of the Internet as you interpret it now. Include your home or school/university location and its respective cabling, equipment, devices, and so on. Some items you might want to include are as follows:

- Devices/equipment
- Media (cabling)
- Link addresses or names
- Sources and destinations
- Internet service providers

Upon completion, be sure to save your work in a hard-copy format, as it will be used for future reference at the end of this chapter. If it is an electronic document, save it to a server location provided by your instructor. Be prepared to share and explain your work in class.

For an example to get you started, please visit www.kk.org/internet-mapping.

Globally Connected (1.1)

Networks are all around us. They provide us with a way to communicate and share information and resources with individuals in the same location or around the world. This requires an extensive array of technologies and procedures that can readily adapt to varying conditions and requirements.

Networking Today (1.1.1)

For most individuals, the use of networks has become a daily occurrence. The availability of these networks has altered the way in which we interact with each other.

Networks in Our Daily Lives (1.1.1.1)

Among all the essentials for human existence, the need to interact with others ranks just below our need to sustain life. Communication is almost as important to us as our reliance on air, water, food, and shelter.

The methods that we use to communicate are constantly changing and evolving. Whereas we were once limited to face-to-face interactions, breakthroughs in technology have significantly extended the reach of our communications. From cave paintings to the printing press to radio and television, each new development has improved and enhanced our ability to connect and communicate with others.

The creation and interconnection of robust *data networks* has had a profound effect on communication, and has become the new platform on which modern communications occur.

In today's world, through the use of networks, we are connected like never before. People with ideas can communicate instantly with others to make those ideas a reality. News events and discoveries are known worldwide in seconds. Individuals can even connect and play games with friends separated by oceans and continents.

Networks connect people and promote unregulated communication. Everyone can connect, share, and make a difference.

Video **Video 1.1.1.1:** View the video in the online course for an understanding of how the network impacts our daily lives.

Technology Then and Now (1.1.1.2)

Imagine a world without the Internet. No more Google, YouTube, instant messaging, Facebook, Wikipedia, online gaming, Netflix, iTunes, and easy access to current information. No more price-comparison websites, avoiding lines by shopping online, or quickly looking up phone numbers and map directions to various locations at the click of a mouse. How different would our lives be without all of this? That was the world we lived in just 15 to 20 years ago. But over the years, data networks have slowly expanded and been repurposed to improve the quality of life for people everywhere.

In the course of a day, resources that are available through the Internet can help you

- Post and share your photographs, home videos, and experiences with friends or with the world

- Access and submit school work

- Communicate with friends, family, and peers using email, instant messaging, or Internet phone calls

- Watch videos, movies, or television episodes on demand

- Play online games with friends

- Decide what to wear using online current weather conditions

- Find the least congested route to your destination, displaying weather and traffic video from webcams

- Check your bank balance and pay bills electronically

Innovators are figuring out ways to use the Internet more every day. As developers push the limits of what is possible, the capabilities of the Internet and the role the Internet plays in our lives will expand broader and broader. Consider the changes that have happened over the last 25 years, as depicted in the Figure 1-1. Now consider what changes will happen within the next 25 years. This future holds the *Internet of Everything (IoE)*.

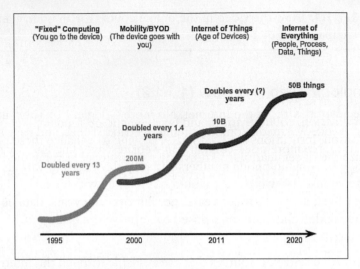

Figure 1-1   Evolution of the Network

The IoE is bringing together people, process, data, and things to make networked connections more relevant and valuable. It is turning information into actions that create new capabilities, richer experiences, and unprecedented economic opportunity for individuals, businesses, and countries.

What else do you think we will be able to do using the network as the platform?

The Global Community (1.1.1.3)

Advancements in networking technologies are perhaps the most significant change agents in the world today. They are helping to create a world in which national borders, geographic distances, and physical limitations become less relevant, and present ever-diminishing obstacles.

The Internet has changed the manner in which social, commercial, political, and personal interactions occur. The immediate nature of communications over the Internet encourages the creation of global communities. Global communities allow social interaction that is independent of location or time zone. The creation of online communities for the exchange of ideas and information has the potential to increase productivity opportunities across the globe.

Cisco refers to this as the human network. The human network centers on the impact of the Internet and networks on people and businesses.

How has the human network affected you?

Networks Support the Way We Learn (1.1.1.4)

Networks and the Internet have changed everything we do, from the way we learn, to the way we communicate, to how we work, and even how we play.

Changing the Way We Learn

Communication, *collaboration*, and engagement are fundamental building blocks of education. Institutions are continually striving to enhance these processes to maximize the dissemination of knowledge. Traditional learning methods provide primarily two sources of expertise from which the student can obtain information: the textbook and the instructor. These two sources are limited, both in the format and the timing of the presentation.

Networks have changed the way we learn. Robust and reliable networks support and enrich student learning experiences. They deliver learning material in a wide range of formats including interactive activities, assessments, and feedback. As shown in Figure 1-2, networks now

- Support the creation of *virtual classrooms*

- Provide on-demand video

- Enable collaborative *learning spaces*

- Enable *mobile learning*

Figure 1-2   Networks Support the Way We Learn

Access to high-quality instruction is no longer restricted to students living in proximity to where that instruction is being delivered. Online distance learning has removed geographic barriers and improved student opportunity. Online (e-learning) courses can now be delivered over a network. These courses can contain data (text, links), voice, and video available to the students at any time from any place. Online discussion groups and message boards enable a student to collaborate with the instructor, with other students in the class, or even with students across the world. Blended courses can combine instructor-led classes with online courseware to provide the best of both delivery methods.

Video

Video 1.1.1.4: Click the second graphic in the online course to view a video that illustrates the way networks have expanded the classroom.

In addition to the benefits for the student, networks have improved the management and administration of courses as well. Some of these online functions include student enrollment, assessment delivery, and progress tracking.

Networks Support the Way We Communicate (1.1.1.5)

Networks eliminate geographic and time-zone boundaries, allowing us to easily communicate with individuals from around the world.

Changing the Way We Communicate

The globalization of the Internet has ushered in new forms of communication that empower individuals to create information that can be accessed by a global audience.

Some forms of communication include

- **Instant messaging (IM)/texting:** IM and texting both enable instant real-time communication between two or more people. Many IM and texting applications incorporate features such as file transfer. IM applications can offer additional features such as voice and video communication.

- **Social media:** Social media consists of interactive websites where people and communities create and share user-generated content with friends, family, peers, and the world.

- **Collaboration tools:** Collaboration tools give people the opportunity to work together on shared documents. Without the constraints of location or time zone, individuals connected to a shared system can speak to each other, often across real-time interactive video. Across the network they can share text and graphics, and edit documents together. With collaboration tools always available, organizations can move quickly to share information and pursue goals. The broad distribution of data networks means that people in remote locations can contribute on an equal basis with people at the heart of large population centers.

- **Weblogs (blogs):** Weblogs are web pages that are easy to update and edit. Unlike commercial websites, which are created by professional communications experts, blogs give anyone a means to communicate their thoughts to a global audience without technical knowledge of web design. There are blogs on nearly every topic one can think of, and communities of people often form around popular blog authors.

- **Wikis:** Wikis are web pages that groups of people can edit and view together. Whereas a blog is more of an individual, personal journal, a wiki is a group creation. As such, it can be subject to more extensive review and editing. Like blogs, wikis can be created in stages, and by anyone, without the sponsorship of a major commercial enterprise. Wikipedia has become a comprehensive resource—an online encyclopedia—of publicly contributed topics. Private organizations and individuals can also build their own wikis to capture collected knowledge on a particular subject. Many businesses use wikis as their internal collaboration tool. With the global Internet, people of all walks of life can participate in wikis and add their own perspectives and knowledge to a shared resource.

- **Podcasting:** Podcasting is an audio-based medium that originally enabled people to record audio and convert it for use. Podcasting allows people to deliver their recordings to a wide audience. The audio file is placed on a website (or blog or wiki), where others can download it and play the recording on their computers, laptops, and other mobile devices.

- **Peer-to-peer (P2P) file sharing:** Peer-to-peer file sharing allows people to share files with each other without having to store and download them from a central server. The user joins the P2P network by simply installing the P2P software. This lets the user locate and share files with others in the P2P network. The widespread digitization of media files, such as music and video files, has increased the interest in P2P file sharing. P2P file sharing has not been embraced by everyone. Many people are concerned about violating the laws of copyrighted materials.

What other sites or tools do you use to share your thoughts?

Networks Support the Way We Work (1.1.1.6)

Networks provide fast, reliable access to business resources regardless of the geographic location of the employee.

Changing the Way We Work

In the business world, data networks were initially used by businesses to internally record and manage financial information, customer information, and employee payroll systems. These business networks evolved to enable the transmission of many different types of information services, including email, video, messaging, and telephony.

The use of networks to provide efficient and cost-effective employee training is increasing in acceptance. Online learning opportunities can decrease time-consuming and costly travel yet still ensure that all employees are adequately trained to perform their jobs in a safe and productive manner.

There are many success stories illustrating innovative ways that networks are being used to make us more successful in the workplace. Some of these scenarios are available through the Cisco website at www.cisco.com.

Networks Support the Way We Play (1.1.1.7)

Networks allow us to locate and interact with others who share common interests.

Changing the Way We Play

The widespread adoption of the Internet by the entertainment and travel industries enhances the ability to enjoy and share many forms of recreation, regardless of location. It is possible to explore places interactively that previously we could only dream of visiting, as well as to preview the actual destinations before making a trip. Travelers can post the details and photographs from their adventures online for others to view.

In addition, the Internet is used for traditional forms of entertainment. We listen to recording artists, preview or view motion pictures, read entire books, and download material for future offline access. Live sporting events and concerts can be experienced as they are happening, or recorded and viewed on demand.

Networks enable the creation of new forms of entertainment, such as online games. Players participate in any kind of online competition that game designers can imagine. We compete with friends and foes around the world in the same manner as if they were in the same room.

Even offline activities are enhanced using network collaboration services. Global *communities* of interest have grown rapidly. We share common experiences and hobbies well beyond our local neighborhood, city, or region. Sports fans share opinions and facts about their favorite teams. Collectors display prized collections and get expert feedback about them.

Online markets and auction sites provide the opportunity to buy, sell, and trade all types of merchandise.

Whatever form of recreation we enjoy in the human network, networks are improving our experience.

Figure 1-3 illustrates some of the ways that networks support the way that we play. How do you play on the Internet?

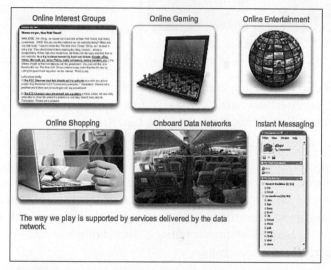

Figure 1-3 Networks Support the Way We Play

 Lab 1.1.1.8: Researching Collaboration Tools

In this lab, you will research and explore various collaborative tools. You will share documents, explore conferencing and web meetings, and create a wiki page.

Providing Resources in a Network (1.1.2)

To efficiently provide resources to end users, networks occur in many sizes and forms.

Networks of Many Sizes (1.1.2.1)

Networks come in all sizes, as shown in Figure 1-4. They can range from simple networks consisting of two computers to networks connecting millions of devices.

Figure 1-4   Networks Come in Many Sizes

Simple networks installed in homes enable sharing of resources, such as printers, documents, pictures, and music between a few local computers. Home networks are also used to connect several devices to the Internet.

Home office networks and small office networks are often set up by individuals who work from a home or remote office and need to connect to a corporate network or other centralized resources. Additionally, many self-employed entrepreneurs use home office and small office networks to advertise and sell products, order supplies, and communicate with customers. Communication over a network is usually more efficient and less expensive than traditional forms of communication, such as regular mail or long-distance phone calls.

In businesses and large organizations, networks can be used on an even broader scale to allow employees to provide consolidation, storage, and access to information on network servers. Networks also allow rapid communication such as email, instant messaging, and collaboration among employees. In addition to internal organizational benefits, many organizations use their networks to provide products and services to customers through their connection to the Internet. These networks can have many locations with hundreds or thousands of interconnected computers.

The Internet is the largest network in existence. In fact, the term *Internet* means a "network of networks." The Internet is literally a collection of interconnected private and public networks, such as the ones described previously. Businesses, small office networks, and even home networks usually provide a shared connection to the Internet. The Internet connects hundreds of millions of computers worldwide.

It is incredible how quickly the Internet has become an integral part of our daily routines.

Clients and Servers (1.1.2.2, 1.1.2.3)

All computers connected to a network that participate directly in network communication are classified as hosts or end devices. Hosts can send and receive messages on the network. In modern networks, end devices can act as a client, a server, or both. The software installed on the computer determines which role the computer plays.

Servers are hosts that have software installed that enable them to provide information, like email or web pages, to other hosts on the network. Each service requires separate server software. For example, a host requires web server software to provide web services to the network.

Clients are computer hosts that have software installed that enable them to request and display the information obtained from the server. An example of client software is a web browser, like Windows Internet Explorer. This client software accesses web pages that are stored on a web server. Other common client software includes Microsoft Outlook, used to access email on a web server, and Windows Explorer, used to access files stored on a file server.

A computer with server software can provide services simultaneously to one or many clients.

Additionally, a single computer can run multiple types of server software. In a home or small business, it might be necessary for one computer to act as a file server, a web server, and an email server.

A single computer can also run multiple types of client software. There must be client software for every service required. With multiple clients installed, a host can connect to multiple servers at the same time. For example, a user can check email and view a web page while instant messaging and listening to Internet radio.

Peer-to-Peer (1.1.2.4)

Client and server software usually runs on separate computers, but it is also possible for one computer to carry out both roles at the same time. In small businesses and homes, many computers function as the servers and clients on the network. This type of network is called a peer-to-peer network and is illustrated in Figure 1-5.

Figure 1-5   Peer-to-Peer Network

The simplest peer-to-peer network consists of two directly connected computers using a wired or wireless connection.

Multiple PCs can also be connected to create a larger peer-to-peer network, but this requires a network device, such as a hub, to interconnect the computers.

Peer-to-peer networks are easy to set up, are less complex, and can be created at lower cost than client-server networks because network devices and dedicated servers might not be required. These networks can be used for simple tasks such as transferring files and sharing printers. Peer-to-peer networks have no centralized administration, are not as secure or scalable as client-server networks, and often suffer from host performance issues if they are acting as both a client and a server at the same time.

In larger businesses, because of the potential for high amounts of network traffic, it is often necessary to have dedicated servers to support the number of service requests.

LANs, WANs, and the Internet (1.2)

Many different components are required to allow a network to provide services and resources. These various components work together to ensure that resources are delivered in an efficient manner to those requiring the services.

Components of a Network (1.2.1, 1.2.1.1)

The *network infrastructure* contains three categories of network components—devices, media, and services—as shown in Figure 1-6.

The path that a message takes from source to destination can be as simple as a single cable connecting one computer to another or as complex as a network that literally spans the globe. This network infrastructure is the platform that supports the network. It provides the stable and reliable channel over which our communications can occur.

Figure 1-6   Components of the Network Infrastructure

Devices (Figure 1-6a) and media (Figure 1-6b) are the physical elements, or hardware, of the network. Hardware is often the visible components of the network platform such as a laptop, PC, switch, router, wireless access point, or the cabling used to connect the devices. Occasionally, some components might not be so visible. In the case of wireless media, messages are transmitted using invisible radio frequency or infrared waves without requiring any physical connecting media.

Network components are used to provide services and processes (Figure 1-6c). These are the communication programs, called software, that run on the networked devices. A network service provides information in response to a request. Services include many of the common network applications people use every day, like email-hosting services and web-hosting services. Processes provide the functionality that directs and moves the messages through the network. Processes are less obvious to us but are critical to the operation of networks.

End Devices (1.2.1.2)

The network devices that people are most familiar with are called end devices, or hosts. These devices form the interface between users and the underlying communication network.

Some examples of end devices are

- Computers (work stations, laptops, file servers, web servers)
- Network printers
- *VoIP* phones
- *TelePresence* endpoints
- Security cameras
- Mobile handheld devices (such as smartphones, tablets, PDAs, and wireless debit/credit card readers and bar-code scanners)

A host device is either the source or destination of a message transmitted over the network. To distinguish one host from another, each host on a network is identified by an address. When a host initiates communication, it uses the address of the destination host to specify where the message should be sent. Data originates with an end device, flows through the network, and arrives at an end device. Messages can take alternate routes through the network between end devices.

Intermediary Network Devices (1.2.1.3)

Intermediary devices interconnect end devices. These devices provide connectivity and work behind the scenes to ensure that data flows across the network. Intermediary devices connect the individual hosts to the network and can connect multiple individual networks to form an internetwork.

Examples of intermediary network devices are

- Network access (switches and wireless access points)
- Internetworking (routers)
- Security (firewalls)

The management of data as it flows through the network is also a role of the intermediary devices. Intermediary devices direct the path of the data but do not generate or change the data content. These devices use the destination host address, in conjunction with information about the network interconnections, to determine the path that messages should take through the network.

Processes running on the intermediary network devices perform these functions:

- Regenerate and retransmit data signals

- Maintain information about what pathways exist through the network and internetwork

- Notify other devices of errors and communication failures

- Direct data along alternate pathways when there is a link failure

- Classify and direct messages according to quality of service (QoS) priorities

- Permit or deny the flow of data, based on security settings

Network Media (1.2.1.4)

Communication across a network is carried on a medium. The medium provides the channel over which the message travels from source to destination.

Modern networks primarily use three types of media to interconnect devices and to provide the pathway over which data can be transmitted. As shown in Figure 1-7, these media are

- Metallic wires within cables

- Glass or plastic fibers (fiber-optic cable)

- Wireless transmission

Figure 1-7   Network Media

The signal *encoding* that must occur for the message to be transmitted is different for each medium type. On metallic wires, the data is encoded into electrical impulses that match specific patterns. Fiber-optic transmissions rely on pulses of light, within either infrared or visible light ranges. In wireless transmission, patterns of electro-magnetic waves depict the various bit values.

Different types of network media have different features and benefits. Not all network media have the same characteristics and are appropriate for the same purpose. The criteria for choosing network media are

- The distance the medium can successfully carry a signal
- The environment in which the medium is to be installed
- The amount of data and the speed at which it must be transmitted
- The cost of the medium and installation

Network Representations (1.2.1.5)

When conveying complex information such as displaying all the devices and media in a large internetwork, it is helpful to use visual representations. A diagram provides an easy way to understand the way the devices in a large network are connected. Such a diagram uses symbols to represent the different devices and connections that make up a network. This type of "picture" of a network is known as a *topology* diagram.

Like any other language, the language of networking uses a common set of symbols to represent the different end devices, network devices, and media, as shown in

Figure 1-8. The ability to recognize the logical representations of the physical networking components is critical to being able to visualize the organization and operation of a network. Throughout this course and labs, you will learn both how these devices operate and how to perform basic configuration tasks on these devices.

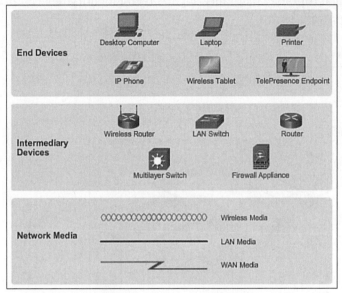

Figure 1-8   Network Symbols

In addition to these representations, specialized terminology is used when discussing how each of these devices and media connect to each other. Important terms to remember are

- **Network interface card (NIC):** A NIC, or LAN adapter, provides the physical connection to the network at the PC or other host device. The medium connecting the PC to the networking device plugs directly into the NIC.

- **Physical port:** A connector or outlet on a networking device where the medium is connected to a host or other networking device.

- **Interface:** Specialized ports on an internetworking device that connect to individual networks. Because routers are used to interconnect networks, the ports on a router are referred to as *network interfaces*.

Topology Diagrams (1.2.1.6)

Topology diagrams, as shown in Figure 1-9, are mandatory for anyone working with a network. They provide a visual map of how the network is connected.

There are two types of topology diagrams:

- **Physical topology diagrams (Figure 1-9a):** Identify the physical location of intermediary devices, configured ports, and cable installation.

- **Logical topology diagrams (Figure 1-9b):** Identify devices, ports, and IP addressing scheme.

a

b

Figure 1-9   Network Topologies

Interactive
Graphic

Activity 1.2.1.7: Network Component Representation and Functions

Go to the course online to perform this practice activity.

LANs and WANs (1.2.2)

Network infrastructures can vary greatly in terms of

- Size of the area covered
- Number of users connected
- Number and types of services available

For this reason, networks are often classified into various types based on a number of characteristics.

Types of Networks (1.2.2.1)

Figure 1-10 illustrates the two most common types of network infrastructures:

- **Local-area network (LAN):** A network infrastructure that provides access to users and end devices in a small geographical area.
- **Wide-area network (WAN):** A network infrastructure that provides access to other networks over a wide geographical area.

Figure 1-10   LANs and WANs

Other types of networks include

- **Metropolitan-area network (MAN):** A network infrastructure that spans a physical area larger than a LAN but smaller than a WAN (for example, a city). MANs are typically operated by a single entity such as a large organization.

- **Wireless LAN (WLAN):** Similar to a LAN but wirelessly interconnects users and endpoints in a small geographical area.

- **Storage-area network (SAN):** A network infrastructure designed to support file servers and provide data storage, retrieval, and replication. It involves high-end servers, multiple disk arrays, and Fibre Channel interconnection technology.

Local-Area Networks (1.2.2.2)

Local-area networks (LAN) are a network infrastructure that spans a small geographical area. Specific features of LANs include

- LANs interconnect end devices in a limited area such as a home, school, office building, or campus.

- A LAN is usually administered by a single organization or individual. The administrative control that governs the security and access control policies are enforced on the network level.

- LANs provide high-speed bandwidth to internal end devices and intermediary devices.

Wide-Area Networks (1.2.2.3)

Wide-area networks (WAN) are a network infrastructure that spans a wide geographical area. WANs are typically managed by service providers (SP) or Internet service providers (ISP).

Specific features of WANs include

- WANs interconnect LANs over wide geographical areas such as between cities, states, provinces, countries, or continents.

- WANs are usually administered by multiple service providers.

- WANs typically provide slower-speed links between LANs.

The Internet (1.2.3, 1.2.3.1)

Although there are benefits to using a LAN or WAN, most individuals need to communicate with a resource on another network, outside of the local network within the home, campus, or organization. This is done using the Internet.

As shown in Figure 1-11, the Internet is a worldwide collection of interconnected networks (internetworks or internet for short), cooperating with each other to exchange information using common standards. Through telephone wires, fiber-optic cables, wireless transmissions, and satellite links, Internet users can exchange information in a variety of forms.

LANs and WANs may be connected into internetworks.

Figure 1-11   Internet

The Internet is a conglomerate of networks and is not owned by any individual or group. Ensuring effective communication across this diverse infrastructure requires the application of consistent and commonly recognized technologies and standards as well as the cooperation of many network administration agencies. There are organizations that have been developed for the purpose of helping to maintain the structure and standardization of Internet protocols and processes. These organizations include the Internet Engineering Task Force (IETF), the Internet Corporation for Assigned Names and Numbers (ICANN), and the Internet Architecture Board (IAB), plus many others.

Note

The term *internet* (with a lowercase *i*) is used to describe multiple interconnected networks. When referring to the global system of interconnected computer networks, used by services such as the World Wide Web, the term *Internet* (with a capital *I*) is used.

Intranet and Extranet (1.2.3.2)

There are two other terms that are similar to the term *Internet*:

- Intranet

- Extranet

Intranet is a term often used to refer to a private connection of LANs and WANs that belongs to an organization, and is designed to be accessible only by the organization's members, employees, or others with authorization. Intranets are basically an internet that is usually only accessible from within the organization.

Organizations can publish web pages on an intranet about internal events, health and safety policies, staff newsletters, and staff phone directories. For example, schools can have intranets that include information on class schedules, online curricula, and discussion forums. Intranets usually help eliminate paperwork and speed workflows. The intranet can be accessible to staff working outside of the organization by using secure connections to the internal network.

An organization can use an extranet to provide secure and safe access to individuals who work for a different organization, but require company data. Examples of extranets include

- A company providing access to outside suppliers/contractors

- A hospital providing a booking system to doctors so that they can make appointments for their patients

- A local office of education providing budget and personnel information to the schools in its district. Figure 1-12 shows how intranets, extranets, and the Internet relate.

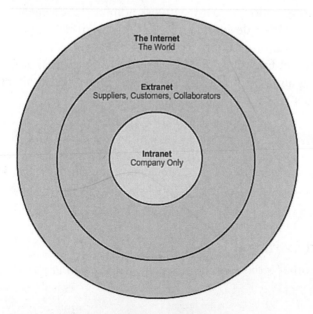

Figure 1-12   Intranets, Extranets, and the Internet

Lab 1.2.3.3: Researching Converged Network Services

Convergence in the context of networking is a term used to describe the process of combining voice, video, and data communications over a common network infrastructure. In this lab, you will survey your understanding of convergence and research ISPs that offer converged services. Based on your understanding of convergence, you will also select the best local ISP that offers converged services and research a local company that uses converged services.

Internet Access Technologies (1.2.4.1)

There are many different ways to connect users and organizations to the Internet.

Home users, teleworkers (remote workers), and small offices typically require a connection to an Internet service provider (ISP) to access the Internet. Connection options vary greatly between ISP and geographical location. However, popular choices include broadband cable, broadband digital subscriber line (DSL), wireless WANs, and mobile services.

Organizations typically require access to other corporate sites and the Internet. Fast connections are required to support business services, including IP phones, video-conferencing, and data center storage.

Business-class interconnections are usually provided by service providers (SP). Popular business-class services include business DSL, leased lines, and Metro Ethernet.

Connecting Remote Users to the Internet (1.2.4.2)

Figure 1-13 illustrates some common connection options for small office and home office users, which include

- **Cable:** Typically offered by cable television service providers, the Internet data signal is carried on the same coaxial cable that delivers cable television. It provides a high-bandwidth, always-on connection to the Internet. A special cable modem separates the Internet data signal from the other signals carried on the cable and provides an Ethernet connection to a host computer or LAN.

- **DSL:** Provides a high-bandwidth, always-on connection to the Internet. It requires a special high-speed modem that separates the DSL signal from the telephone signal and provides an Ethernet connection to a host computer or LAN. DSL runs over a telephone line, with the line split into three channels. One channel is used for voice telephone calls. This channel allows an individual to receive phone calls without disconnecting from the Internet. A second channel is a faster download channel, used to receive information from the Internet. The third channel is used for sending or uploading information. This channel might be slower than the download channel. The quality and speed of the DSL connection depends mainly on the quality of the phone line and the distance from your phone company's central office. The farther you are from the central office, the slower the connection.

- **Cellular:** Cellular Internet access uses a cell phone network to connect. Wherever you can get a cellular signal, you can get cellular Internet access. Performance will be limited by the capabilities of the phone and the cell tower to which it is connected. The availability of cellular Internet access is a real benefit in those areas that would otherwise have no Internet connectivity, or for those constantly on the move.

- **Satellite:** Satellite service is a good option for homes or offices that do not have access to DSL or cable. Satellite dishes require a clear line of sight to the satellite, so service might be difficult in heavily wooded areas or places with other overhead obstructions. Speeds will vary depending on the contract, though they are generally good. Equipment and installation costs can be high (although check the provider for special deals), with a moderate monthly fee thereafter. The availability of satellite Internet access is a real benefit in those areas that would otherwise have no Internet connectivity.

- **Dialup telephone:** An inexpensive option that uses any phone line and a modem. To connect to the ISP, a user calls the ISP access phone number. The low bandwidth provided by a dialup modem connection is usually not sufficient for large data transfer, although it is useful for mobile access while traveling. A modem dialup connection should only be considered when higher-speed connection options are not available.

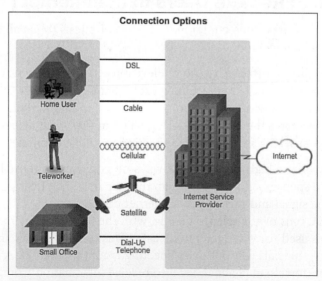

Figure 1-13   Common Internet Connection Options

Many homes and small offices are now being connected directly with fiber-optic cables. This enables an Internet service provider to provide higher bandwidth speeds and support more services such as Internet, phone, and TV.

The choice of connection varies depending on geographical location and service provider availability.

What are your options for connecting to the Internet?

Connecting Businesses to the Internet (1.2.4.3)

Corporate connection options differ from home user options. Businesses often require higher bandwidth, dedicated bandwidth, and managed services. Connection options available differ depending on the number of service providers located nearby.

Figure 1-14 illustrates common connection options for organizations, which include

- **Dedicated leased line:** This is a dedicated connection from the service provider to the customer premises. Leased lines are actually reserved circuits that connect geographically separated offices for private voice and/or data networking. The circuits are typically rented at a monthly or yearly rate, which tends to make them expensive. In North America, common leased line circuits include T1 (1.54 Mbps) and T3 (44.7 Mbps), while in other parts of the world, they are available in E1 (2 Mbps) and E3 (34 Mbps).

- **Metro Ethernet:** Metro Ethernet is typically available from a provider to the customer premises over a dedicated copper or fiber connection providing bandwidth speeds of 10 Mbps to 10 Gbps. Ethernet over Copper (EoC) is more economical than fiber-optic Ethernet service in many cases, is widely available, and reaches speeds of up to 40 Mbps. However, Ethernet over Copper is limited by distance. Fiber-optic Ethernet service delivers the fastest connections available at an economical megabit-per-second price. Unfortunately, there are still many areas where this service is unavailable.

- **DSL:** Business DSL is available in various formats. A popular choice is symmetric digital subscriber lines (SDSL), which are similar to asymmetric digital subscriber lines (ADSL), but provide the same upload and download speeds. ADSL is designed to deliver bandwidth at different rates downstream than upstream. For example, a customer getting Internet access might have downstream rates that range from 1.5 to 9 Mbps, whereas upstream bandwidth ranges are from 16 to 640 kbps. ADSL transmissions work at distances up to 18,000 feet (5,488 meters) over a single copper twisted pair.

■ **Satellite:** Satellite service can provide a connection when a wired solution is not available. Satellite dishes require a clear line of sight to the satellite. Equipment and installation costs can be high, with a moderate monthly fee thereafter. Connections tend to be slower and less reliable than its terrestrial competition, which makes it less attractive than other alternatives.

The choice of connection varies depending on geographical location and service provider availability.

Figure 1-14   Internet Connectivity Options for Businesses

Packet Tracer Activity 1.2.4.4: Network Representation

Packet Tracer is a fun, take-home, flexible software program that will help you with your Cisco Certified Network Associate (CCNA) studies. Packet Tracer allows you to experiment with network behavior, build network models, and ask "what if" questions. In this activity, you will explore a relatively complex network that highlights a few of Packet Tracer's features. While doing so, you will learn how to access Help and the tutorials. You will also learn how to switch among various modes and workspaces. Finally, you will explore how Packet Tracer serves as a modeling tool for network representations.

The Network as a Platform (1.3)

The network has become a platform for distributing a wide range of services to end users in a reliable, efficient, and secure manner.

The Converging Network (1.3.1.1)

Modern networks are constantly evolving to meet user demands. Early data networks were limited to exchanging character-based information between connected computer systems. Traditional telephone, radio, and television networks were maintained separately from data networks. In the past, every one of these services required a dedicated network, with different communication channels and different technologies to carry a particular communication signal. Each service had its own set of rules and standards to ensure successful communication.

Consider a large school in the early 1990s. Back then, classrooms were cabled for the public announcement network, the telephone network, a video network for televisions, a data network, and perhaps a security network. These separate networks were disparate, meaning that they could not communicate with each other, as shown in Figure 1-15a.

Advances in technology are enabling us to consolidate these different kinds of networks onto one platform, referred to as the *converged network*. Unlike dedicated networks, converged networks are capable of delivering voice, video streams, text, and graphics among many different types of devices over the same communication channel and network structure, as shown in Figure 1-15b. Previously separate and distinct communication forms have converged onto a common platform. This platform provides access to a wide range of alternative and new communication methods that enable people to interact directly with each other almost instantaneously.

Figure 1-15   Multiple Networks Versus Converged Networks

In a converged network, there are still many points of contact and many specialized devices, such as personal computers, phones, TVs, and tablet computers, but there is one common network infrastructure. This network infrastructure uses the same set of rules, agreements, and implementation standards.

Planning for the Future (1.3.1.2)

The convergence of the different types of communications networks onto one platform represents the first phase in building the intelligent information network, as shown in Figure 1-16. We are currently in this phase of network evolution. The next phase will be to consolidate not only the different types of messages onto a single network but to also consolidate the applications that generate, transmit, and secure the messages onto integrated network devices.

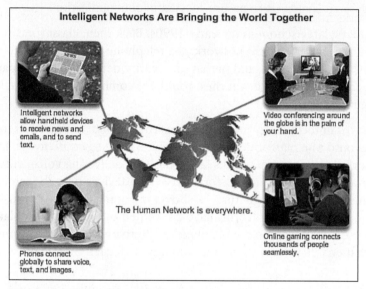

Figure 1-16   Intelligent Information Network

Not only will voice and video be transmitted over the same network, but the devices that perform the telephone switching and video broadcasting will also be the same devices that route the messages through the network. The resulting communications platform will provide high-quality application functionality at a reduced cost.

The pace at which the development of exciting new converged network applications is occurring can be attributed to the rapid growth and expansion of the Internet. With only about 10 billion of potentially 1.5 trillion things currently connected globally, there is vast potential to connect the unconnected through the IoE. This expansion has created a wider audience for whatever message, product, or service can be delivered.

The underlying mechanics and processes that drive this explosive growth have resulted in a network architecture that is both capable of supporting changes and able to grow. As the supporting technology platform for living, learning, working, and playing in the human network, the network architecture of the Internet must adapt to constantly changing requirements for a high quality of service and security.

Lab 1.3.1.3: Mapping the Internet

In this lab, you will test network connectivity using ping and Windows tracert. Additionally, you will use web-based and software tools to trace a route to a remote server.

The Supporting Network Architecture (1.3.2.1)

Networks must support a wide range of applications and services, as well as operate over many different types of cables and devices, which make up the physical infrastructure. The term *network architecture*, in this context, refers to the technologies that support the infrastructure and the programmed services and rules, or protocols, that move messages across the network.

As networks evolve, we are discovering that there are four basic characteristics, as shown in Figure 1-17, that the underlying architectures need to address in order to meet user expectations:

- Fault tolerance (Figure 1-17a)

- Scalability (Figure 1-17b)

- Quality of service (QoS) (Figure 1-17c)

- Security (Figure1-17d)

Figure 1-17 Characteristics of a Reliable Network

Fault Tolerance in Circuit-Switched Networks (1.3.2.2)

With our reliance on networks, certain precautions must be taken to ensure that the network functions as designed, even if things go wrong.

Fault Tolerance

The expectation is that the Internet is always available to the millions of users who rely on it. This requires a network architecture that is built to be fault tolerant. A fault-tolerant network is one that limits the impact of a failure so that the fewest number of devices are affected by it. It is also built in a way that allows quick recovery when such a failure occurs. These networks depend on multiple paths between the source and destination of a message. If one path fails, the messages can be instantly sent over a different link. Having multiple paths to a destination is known as *redundancy*.

Circuit-Switched Connection-Oriented Networks

To understand the need for redundancy, we can look at how early telephone systems worked. When a person made a call using a traditional telephone set, the call first went through a setup process. This process identified the telephone switching locations between the person making the call (the source) and the phone set receiving the call (the destination). A temporary path, or circuit, was created for the duration of the telephone call. If any link or device in the circuit failed, the call was dropped. To reconnect, a new call had to be made, with a new circuit. This connection process is referred to as a *circuit-switched process* and is illustrated in Figure 1-18.

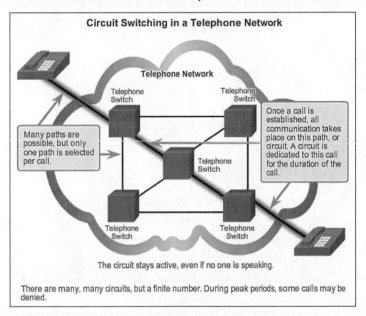

Figure 1-18   Circuit Switching in a Telephone Network

Many *circuit-switched* networks give priority to existing circuit connections at the expense of new circuit requests. After a circuit is established, even if no communication is occurring between the persons on either end of the call, the circuit remains connected and resources used until one of the parties disconnects the call. Because there are only so many circuits that can be created, it is possible to get a message that all circuits are busy and a call cannot be placed. The cost to create many alternate paths with enough capacity to support a large number of simultaneous circuits, and the technologies necessary to dynamically re-create dropped circuits in the event of a failure, is why circuit-switched technology was not optimal for the Internet.

Fault Tolerance in Packet-Switched Networks (1.3.2.3)

Because of the technical issues and cost associated with building a fault-tolerant circuit-switched network, network designers turned their attention to packet-switched technologies.

Packet-Switched Networks

In the search for a network that was more fault tolerant, the early Internet designers researched *packet-switched* networks. The premise for this type of network is that a single message can be broken into multiple message blocks, with each message block containing addressing information to indicate the origination point and final destination. Using this embedded information, these message blocks, called *packets*, can be sent through the network along various paths, and can be reassembled into the original message when reaching their destination, as illustrated in Figure 1-19.

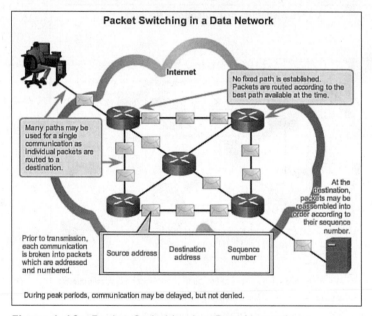

Figure 1-19   Packet Switching in a Data Network

The devices within the network itself are typically unaware of the content of the individual packets. Only visible is the address of the final destination. These addresses are often referred to as *IP addresses*, which can be represented in a dotted-decimal format, such as 10.10.10.10. Each packet is sent independently from one location to another. At each location, a routing decision is made as to which path to use to forward the packet toward its final destination. This would be like writing a long message to a friend using ten postcards. Each postcard has the destination address of the recipient. As the postcards are forwarded through the postal system, the destination address is used to determine the next path that postcard should take. Eventually, they will be delivered to the address on the postcards.

If a previously used path is no longer available, the routing function can dynamically choose the next best available path. Because the messages are sent in pieces, rather than as a single complete message, the few packets that might be lost can be retransmitted to the destination along a different path. In many cases, the destination device is unaware that any failure or rerouting occurred. Using our postcard analogy, if one of the postcards is lost along the way, only that postcard needs to be mailed again.

The need for a single, reserved circuit from end to end does not exist in a packet-switched network. Any piece of a message can be sent through the network using any available path. Additionally, packets containing pieces of messages from different sources can travel the network at the same time. By providing a method to dynamically use redundant paths, without intervention by the user, the Internet has become a fault-tolerant method of communication. In our mail analogy, as our postcard travels through the postal system, it will share transportation with other postcards, letters, and packages. For example, one of the postcards might be placed on an airplane, along with lots of other packages and letters that are being transported toward their final destination.

Although packet-switched connectionless networks are the primary infrastructure for today's Internet, there are some benefits to a connection-oriented system like the circuit-switched telephone system. Because resources at the various switching locations are dedicated to providing a finite number of circuits, the quality and consistency of messages transmitted across a connection-oriented network can be guaranteed. Another benefit is that the provider of the service can charge the users of the network for the period of time that the connection is active. The ability to charge users for active connections through the network is a fundamental premise of the telecommunication service industry.

Scalable Networks (1.3.2.4)

Not only must a network be fault tolerant, but it must also be able to grow to accommodate new users and services.

Scalability

Thousands of new users and service providers connect to the Internet each week. For the Internet to support this rapid amount of growth, it must be scalable. A scalable network can expand quickly to support new users and applications without impacting the performance of the service being delivered to existing users. Figure 1-20 shows the structure of the Internet.

The fact that the Internet is able to expand at the rate that it is, without seriously impacting the performance experienced by individual users, is a function of the design of the protocols and underlying technologies on which it is built. The

Internet has a hierarchical layered structure for addressing, for naming, and for connectivity services. As a result, network traffic that is destined for local or regional services does not need to traverse to a central point for distribution. Common services can be duplicated in different regions, thereby keeping traffic off the higher-level backbone networks.

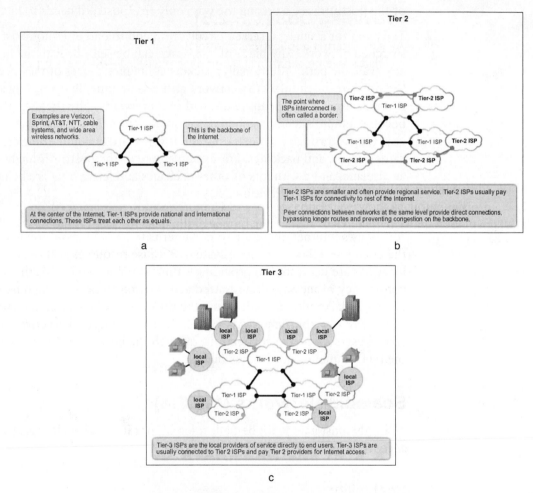

Figure 1-20   Internet as a Scalable Network

Scalability also refers to the ability to accept new products and applications. Although there is no single organization that regulates the Internet, the many individual networks that provide Internet connectivity cooperate to follow accepted standards and protocols. The adherence to standards enables the manufacturers of hardware and software to concentrate on product development and improvements in the areas of performance and capacity, knowing that the new products can integrate with and enhance the existing infrastructure.

The current Internet architecture, while highly scalable, might not always be able to keep up with the pace of user demand. New protocols and addressing structures are under development to meet the increasing rate at which Internet applications and services are being added.

Providing QoS (1.3.2.5)

As new Internet applications and services are added, it becomes increasingly apparent that some mechanism is required to handle the different types of traffic encountered in a converged network.

Quality of Service

Quality of service (QoS) is an ever-increasing requirement of networks today. New applications available to users over internetworks, such as voice and live video transmissions as shown in Figure 1-21, create higher expectations for the quality of the delivered services. Have you ever tried to watch a video with constant breaks and pauses?

Figure 1-21   Types of Traffic Found in a Converged Network

Networks must provide predictable, measurable, and at times, guaranteed services. The packet-switched network architecture does not guarantee that all packets that comprise a particular message will arrive on time and in their correct order, or even that they will arrive at all.

Networks also need mechanisms to manage *congested* network traffic. Network bandwidth is the measure of the data-carrying capacity of the network. In other words, how much information can be transmitted within a specific amount of time? Network bandwidth is measured in the number of bits that can be transmitted in a single second, or bits per second (bps). When simultaneous communications are attempted across the network, the demand for network bandwidth can exceed its availability, creating network congestion. The network simply has more bits to transmit than what the bandwidth of the communication channel can deliver.

In most cases, when the volume of packets is greater than what can be transported across the network, devices queue, or hold, the packets in memory until resources become available to transmit them, as shown in Figure 1-22. *Queuing* packets causes delay because new packets cannot be transmitted until previous packets have been processed. If the number of packets to be queued continues to increase, the memory queues fill up and packets are dropped.

Figure 1-22   Using Queues to Prioritize Communication

Achieving the required QoS by managing the delay and packet loss parameters on a network becomes the secret to a successful end-to-end application quality solution. One way that this can be accomplished is through classification. To create QoS classifications of data, we use a combination of communication characteristics and the relative importance assigned to the application, as shown in Figure 1-23. We then treat all data within the same classification according to the same rules. For example, communication that is time sensitive, such as voice transmissions, would be classified differently from communication that can tolerate delay, such as file transfers.

Figure 1-23   Importance of Quality of Service (QoS)

Examples of priority decisions for an organization might include

- **Time-sensitive communication:** Increase priority for services like telephony or video distribution

- **Non-time-sensitive communication:** Decrease priority for web page retrieval or email

- **High importance to organization:** Increase priority for production control or business transaction data

- **Undesirable communication:** Decrease priority or block unwanted activity, like peer-to-peer file sharing or live entertainment

Providing Network Security (1.3.2.6)

As new users and services are added to the network, it becomes important that measures be taken to ensure that information access is strictly controlled.

Security

The Internet has evolved from a tightly controlled internetwork of educational and government organizations to a widely accessible means for transmission of business and personal communications. As a result, the security requirements of the network have changed. The network infrastructure, the services, and the data contained on network-attached devices are crucial personal and business assets. Compromising the integrity of these assets could have serious consequences, such as

- Network outages that prevent communications and transactions from occurring, with consequent loss of business

- Intellectual property (research ideas, patents, or designs) that is stolen and used by a competitor

- Personal or private information that is compromised or made public without the users' consent

- Misdirection and loss of personal or business funds

- Loss of important data that takes significant labor to replace or is irreplaceable

There are two types of network security concerns that must be addressed: network infrastructure security and information security.

Securing a network infrastructure includes the physical securing of devices that provide network connectivity and preventing unauthorized access to the management software that resides on them.

Information security refers to protecting the information contained within the packets being transmitted over the network and the information stored on network-attached devices. Security measures taken in a network should

- Prevent unauthorized disclosure

- Prevent theft of information

- Prevent unauthorized modification of information

- Prevent denial of service (DoS)

To achieve the goals of network security, there are three primary requirements, as shown in Figure 1-24:

- **Ensuring confidentiality:** Data *confidentiality* means that only the intended and authorized recipients—individuals, processes, or devices—can access and read data. This is accomplished by having a strong system for user authentication, enforcing passwords that are difficult to guess, and requiring users to change the passwords frequently. Encrypting data, so that only the intended recipient can read it, is also part of confidentiality.

- **Maintaining communication integrity:** Data *integrity* means having the assurance that the information has not been altered in transmission, from origin to destination. Data integrity can be compromised when information has been corrupted—willfully or accidentally. Data integrity is made possible by requiring validation of the sender as well as by using mechanisms to validate that the packet has not changed during transmission.

- **Ensuring availability:** *Availability* means having the assurance of timely and reliable access to data services for authorized users. Network firewall devices, along with desktop and server antivirus software, can ensure system reliability and the robustness to detect, repel, and cope with such attacks. Building fully redundant network infrastructures, with few single points of failure, can reduce the impact of these threats.

Figure 1-24   Importance of Network Security

Activity 1.3.2.7: Reliable Networks

Go to the course online to perform this practice activity.

The Changing Network Environment (1.4)

The network environment continues to evolve, providing new experiences and opportunities for end users. The network is now capable of delivering services and applications in a manner that was once only dreamed about.

Network Trends (1.4.1)

Just as the way we work, play, and learn impacts the network, the availability of a robust reliable network has an impact on our daily lives.

New Trends (1.4.1.1)

When you look at how the Internet has changed so many of the things people do daily, it is hard to believe that it has only been around for most people for about

20 years. It has truly transformed the way individuals and organizations communicate. For example, before the Internet became so widely available, organizations and small businesses largely relied on print marketing to make consumers aware of their products. It was difficult for businesses to determine which households were potential customers, so businesses relied on mass print marketing programs. These programs were expensive and varied in effectiveness. Compare that to how consumers are reached today. Most businesses have an Internet presence where consumers can learn about their products, read reviews from other customers, and order products directly from the website. Social networking sites partner with businesses to promote products and services. Bloggers partner with businesses to highlight and endorse products and services. Most of this product placement is targeted to the potential consumer, rather than to the masses.

There are many predictions about the Internet in the near future, including the following:

- By 2014, traffic from wireless devices will exceed traffic from wired devices.

- By 2015, the amount of content traversing the Internet annually will be 540,000 times time the amount that traveled in 2003.

- By 2015, 90 percent of all content on the Internet will be video based.

- By 2015, a million video minutes will traverse the Internet every second.

- By 2016, the annual global IP traffic will surpass the zetabyte threshold (1,180,591,620,717,411,303,424 bytes).

- By 2016, the number of devices connected to IP networks will be nearly three times as high as the global population.

- By 2016, 1.2 million minutes of video content will cross the network every second.

- By 2020, 50 billion devices will be connected to the Internet.

As new technologies and end-user devices come to market, businesses and consumers must continue to adjust to this ever-changing environment. The role of the network is transforming to enable the connections of people, devices, and information. There are several new networking trends that will effect organizations and consumers. Some of the top trends include

- Any device, to any content, in any way

- Online collaboration

- Video

- Cloud computing

These trends are interconnected and will continue to build on one another in the coming years. The next couple of topics will cover these trends in more detail.

But keep in mind, new trends are being dreamed up and engineered every day. How do you think the Internet will change in the next 10 years? 20 years?

Video

Video 1.4.1.1: Click the second graphic in the online course to view a video that outlines some Cisco thoughts on future developments of the Internet.

Bring Your Own Device (BYOD) (1.4.1.2)

The concept of any device, to any content, in any way is a major global trend that requires significant changes to the way devices are used. This trend is known as *Bring Your Own Device (BYOD)*.

BYOD is about end users having the freedom to use personal tools to access information and communicate across a business or campus network. With the growth of consumer devices, and the related drop in cost, employees and students can be expected to have some of the most advanced computing and networking tools for personal use. These personal tools include laptops, netbooks, tablets, smartphones, and e-readers. These can be devices purchased by the company or school, purchased by the individual, or both.

BYOD means any device, with any ownership, used anywhere. For example, in the past, a student who needed to access the campus network or the Internet had to use one of the school's computers. These devices were typically limited and seen as tools only for work done in the classroom or in the library. Extended connectivity through mobile and remote access to the campus network gives students tremendous flexibility and more learning opportunities for the student.

BYOD is an influential trend that has or will touch every IT organization.

Online Collaboration (1.4.1.3)

Individuals want to connect to the network, not only for access to data applications but also to collaborate with one another. Collaboration is defined as "the act of working with another or others on a joint project."

For businesses, collaboration is a critical and strategic priority. To remain competitive, organizations must answer three primary collaboration questions:

■ How can they get everyone on the same page with a clear picture of the project?

■ With decreased budgets and personnel, how can they balance resources to be in more places at once?

■ How can they maintain face-to-face relationships with a growing network of colleagues, customers, partners, and peers in an environment that is more dependent on 24-hour connectivity?

Collaboration is also a priority in education. Students need to collaborate with assist each other in learning, to develop team skills used in the workforce, and to work together on team-based projects.

One way to answer these questions and meet these demands in today's environment is through online collaboration tools. In traditional workspaces, and with BYOD environments alike, individuals are taking advantage of voice, video, and conferencing services in collaboration efforts.

The ability to collaborate online is changing business processes. New and expanding collaboration tools allow individuals to quickly and easily collaborate, regardless of physical location. Organizations have much more flexibility in the way they are organized. Individuals are no longer restricted to physical locations. Expert knowledge is easier to access than ever before. Expansions in collaboration allow organizations to improve their information gathering, innovation, and productivity.

Collaboration tools give employees, students, teachers, customers, and partners a way to instantly connect, interact, and conduct business, through whatever communications channels they prefer, and achieve their objectives.

Video Communication (1.4.1.4)

Another trend in networking that is critical in the communication and collaboration effort is video. Video is being used for communications, collaboration, and entertainment. Video calls are becoming more popular, facilitating communications as part of the human network. Video calls can be made to and from anywhere with an Internet connection, including from home or at work.

Video calls and videoconferencing are proving particularly powerful for sales processes and for doing business. Video is a useful tool for conducting business at a distance, both locally and globally. Today, businesses are using video to transform the way they do business. Video helps businesses create a competitive advantage, lower costs, and reduce the impact on the environment by reducing the need to travel. Figure 1-25 shows the trend of video in communication.

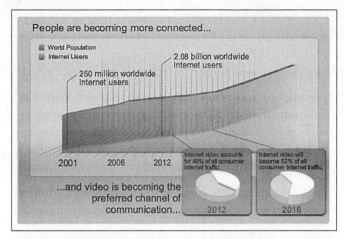

Figure 1-25   Trend of Video in Communication

Both consumers and businesses are driving this change. Video is becoming a key requirement for effective collaboration as organizations extend across geographic and cultural boundaries. Video users now demand the ability to view any content, on any device, anywhere.

Businesses are also recognizing the role of video to enhance the human network. The growth of media, and the new uses to which it is being put, is driving the need to integrate audio and video into many forms of communication. The audioconference will coexist with the videoconference. Collaboration tools designed to link distributed employees will integrate desktop video to bring teams closer together.

There are many drivers and benefits for including a strategy for using video. Each organization is unique. The exact mix, and the nature of the drivers for adopting video, will vary from organization to organization, and by business function. Marketing, for example, might focus on globalization and fast-changing consumer tastes, while the chief information officer's (CIO) focus might be on cost savings by reducing travel costs of employees needing to meet face to face.

Some of the drivers for organizations to develop and implement a video solution strategy include

- **A global workforce and need for real-time collaboration:** Create collaborative teams that span corporate and national boundaries and geographies.

- **Reducing costs and green IT:** Avoiding travel reduces both cost and carbon emissions.

- **New opportunities for IP convergence:** These include converging video applications, such as high-definition video collaboration, video surveillance systems, and video advertising signage onto a single IP network.

- **Media explosion:** The plummeting cost of video cameras and a new generation of high-quality, low-cost devices have turned users into would-be movie producers.

- **Social networking:** The social networking phenomenon can be as effective in business as it is in a social setting. For example, employees are increasingly filming short videos to share best practices with colleagues and to brief peers about projects and initiatives.

- **Demands for universal media access:** Users are demanding to be able to access rich-media applications wherever they are and on any device. Participation in videoconferencing, viewing the latest executive communications, and collaborating with coworkers are applications that will need to be accessible to employees, regardless of their work location.

Video

Video 1.4.1.4: Click the third graphic in the online course for a closer look at how TelePresence using video can be incorporated into everyday life and business.

Another trend in video is video on demand and streaming live video. Delivering video over the network lets us see movies and television programs when we want and where we want.

Cloud Computing (1.4.1.5)

Cloud computing is the use of computing resources (hardware and software) that are delivered as a service over a network. A company uses the hardware and software in the cloud and a service fee is charged.

Local computers no longer have to do all the "heavy lifting" when it comes to running network applications. The network of computers that make up the cloud handles them instead. The hardware and software requirements of the user are decreased. The user's computer must interface with the cloud using software, which can be a web browser, and the cloud's network takes care of the rest.

Cloud computing is another global trend that is changing the way we access and store data. Cloud computing encompasses any subscription-based or pay-per-use service, in real time over the Internet. Cloud computing allows us to store personal files and even back up our entire hard drive on servers over the Internet. Applications such as word processing and photo editing can be accessed using the cloud.

For businesses, cloud computing extends IT's capabilities without requiring investment in new infrastructure, training new personnel, or licensing new software. These services are available on demand and delivered economically to any device anywhere in the world without compromising security or function.

The term *cloud computing* really refers to web-based computing. Online banking, online retail stores, and online music downloading are all examples of cloud computing. Cloud applications are usually delivered to the user through a web browser. Users do not need to have any software installed on their end device. This allows many different kinds of devices to connect to the cloud.

Cloud computing offers the following potential benefits:

- **Organizational flexibility:** Users can access the information anytime and anyplace using a web browser.

- **Agility and rapid deployment:** The IT department can focus on delivering the tools to mine, analyze, and share the information and knowledge from databases, files, and people.

- **Reduced cost of infrastructure:** Technology is moved from on-site to a cloud provider, eliminating the cost of hardware and applications.

- **Refocus of IT resources:** The cost savings of hardware and applications can be applied elsewhere.

- **Creation of new business models:** Applications and resources are easily accessible, so companies can react quickly to customer needs. This helps them set strategies to promote innovation while potentially entering new markets.

There are four primary types of clouds: private, public, hybrid, and custom. A private cloud offers applications and services intended only for a specific organization or entity such as the government. A private cloud can be set up using the organization's private network, though this can be expensive to build and maintain. A private cloud can also be managed by an outside organization with strict access security.

Cloud-based services offered in a public cloud are made available to the general population. Services can be free or are offered on a pay-per-use model, such as paying for online storage. The public cloud uses the Internet to provide services.

Hybrid clouds are made up of two or more clouds (for example part custom and part public), where each part remains a distinctive object, but both are connected using a single architecture. Individuals on a hybrid cloud would be able to have degrees of access to various services based on user access rights.

Custom clouds are built to meet the needs of a specific industry, such as healthcare or media. Custom clouds can be private or public.

Data Centers (1.4.1.6)

Cloud computing is possible because of data centers. A data center is a facility used to house computer systems and associated components, including

- Redundant data communications connections

- High-speed virtual servers (sometimes referred to as server farms or server clusters)

- Redundant storage systems (typically use SAN technology)

- Redundant or backup power supplies

- Environmental controls (for example, air conditioning and fire suppression)

- Security devices

A *data center* can occupy one room of a building, one or more floors, or an entire building. Modern data centers make use of cloud computing and virtualization to efficiently handle large data transactions. Virtualization is the creation of a virtual version of something, such as a hardware platform, operating system (OS), storage device, or network resources. While a physical computer is an actual discrete device, a virtual machine consists of a set of files and programs running on an actual physical system. Unlike multitasking, which involves running several programs on the same OS, *virtualization* runs several different OSs in parallel on a single CPU. This drastically reduces administrative and cost overheads.

Data centers are typically very expensive to build and maintain. For this reason, only large organizations use privately built data centers to house their data and provide services to users. For example, a large hospital might own a separate data center where patient records are maintained electronically. Smaller organizations, which cannot afford to maintain their own private data center, can reduce the overall cost of ownership by leasing server and storage services from a larger data center organization in the cloud.

Video 1.4.1.6: View the video in the online course to learn about the growing use of cloud computing and data center services.

Technology Trends in the Home (1.4.2.1)

Networking trends are not only affecting the way we communicate at work and at school, but they are also changing just about every aspect of the home.

The newest home trends include "smart home technology." This is technology that is integrated into everyday appliances, allowing them to interconnect with other devices, making them more "smart" or automated. For example, imagine being able to prepare a dish and place it in the oven for cooking prior to leaving the house for the day. Imagine that the oven was "aware" of the dish it was cooking and was connected to your calendar of events so that it could determine what time you should be available to eat, and adjust start times and length of cooking accordingly.

It could even adjust cooking times and temperatures based on changes in schedule. Additionally, a smartphone or tablet connection gives the user the ability to connect to the oven directly, to make any desired adjustments. When the dish is "available," the oven sends an alert message to a specified end-user device that the dish is done and warming.

This scenario is not far off. In fact, smart home technology is currently being developed for all rooms within a house. Smart home technology will become more of a reality as home networking and high-speed Internet technology becomes more widespread in homes. New home networking technologies are being developed daily to meet these types of growing technology needs.

Powerline Networking (1.4.2.2)

Powerline networking is an emerging trend for home networking that uses existing electrical wiring to connect devices, as shown in Figure 1-26. The concept of "no new wires" means the ability to connect a device to the network wherever there is an electrical outlet. This saves the cost of installing data cables and adds no cost to the electrical bill. Using the same wiring that delivers electricity, powerline networking sends information by sending data on certain frequencies similar to the technology used for DSL.

Figure 1-26   Powerline Networking

Using a HomePlug standard powerline adapter, devices can connect to the LAN wherever there is an electrical outlet. Powerline networking is especially useful when wireless access points cannot be used or cannot reach all the devices in the home. Powerline networking is not designed to be a substitute for dedicated cabling for data networks. However, it is an alternative when data network cables or wireless communications are not a viable option.

Wireless Broadband (1.4.2.3)

Connecting to the Internet is vital in smart home technology. DSL and cable are common technologies used to connect homes and small businesses to the Internet. However, wireless can be another option in many areas.

Wireless Internet Service Provider (WISP)

A wireless Internet service provider (WISP) is an ISP that connects subscribers to a designated access point or hot spot using similar wireless technologies found in home wireless local-area networks (WLAN). WISPs are more commonly found in rural environments where DSL or cable services are not available.

Although a separate transmission tower might be installed for the antenna, it is common that the antenna is attached to an existing elevated structure such as a water tower or a radio tower. A small dish or antenna is installed on the subscriber's roof in range of the WISP transmitter. The subscriber's access unit is connected to the wired network inside the home. From the perspective of the home user, the setup isn't much different than DSL or cable service. The main difference is that the connection from the home to the ISP is wireless instead of using a physical cable.

Wireless Broadband Service

Another wireless solution for the home and small businesses is wireless broadband. This uses the same cellular technology used to access the Internet with a smartphone or tablet. An antenna is installed outside the house, providing either wireless or wired connectivity for devices in the home. In many areas, home wireless broadband is competing directly with DSL and cable services.

Security Threats (1.4.3.1)

Network security is an integral part of computer networking, regardless of whether the network is limited to a home environment with a single connection to the Internet, or as large as a corporation with thousands of users. The network security implemented must take into account the environment, as well as the tools and requirements of the network. It must be able to secure data while still providing the quality of service that is expected of the network.

Securing a network involves protocols, technologies, devices, tools, and techniques to secure data and mitigate threats. Many external network security threats today are spread over the Internet. The most common external threats to networks include

- **Viruses, worms, and Trojan horses:** Malicious software and arbitrary code running on a user device

- **Spyware and adware:** Software installed on a user device that secretly collects information about the user

- **Zero-day attacks, also called zero-hour attacks:** An attack that occurs on the first day that a vulnerability becomes known

- **Hacker attacks:** An attack by a knowledgeable person to user devices or network resources

- **Denial of service attacks:** Attacks designed to slow or crash applications and processes on a network device

- **Data interception and theft:** An attack to capture private information from an organization's network

- **Identity theft:** An attack to steal the login credentials of a user to access private data

It is equally important to consider internal threats. There have been many studies that show that the most common data breaches happen because of internal users of the network. This can be attributed to lost or stolen devices, accidental misuse by employees, and in the business environment, even malicious employees. With the evolving BYOD strategies, corporate data is much more vulnerable. Therefore, when developing a security policy, it is important to address both external and internal security threats.

Security Solutions (1.4.3.2)

No single solution can protect the network from the variety of threats that exist. For this reason, security should be implemented in multiple layers, using more than one security solution. If one security component fails to identify and protect the network, others still stand.

A home network security implementation is usually rather basic. It is generally implemented on the connecting host devices, as well as at the point of connection to the Internet, and can even rely on contracted services from the ISP.

In contrast, the network security implementation for a corporate network usually consists of many components built into the network to monitor and filter traffic. Ideally, all components work together, which minimizes maintenance and improves security.

Network security components for a home or small office network should include, at a minimum:

- **Antivirus and antispyware:** To protect user devices from malicious software.

- **Firewall filtering:** To block unauthorized access to the network. This can include a host-based firewall system that is implemented to prevent unauthorized access to the host device, or a basic filtering service on the home router to prevent unauthorized access from the outside world into the network.

In addition to the these items, larger networks and corporate networks often have other security requirements:

- **Dedicated firewall systems:** To provide more advanced firewall capability that can filter large amounts of traffic with more granularity

- **Access control lists (ACL):** To further filter access and traffic forwarding

- **Intrusion prevention systems (IPS):** To identify fast-spreading threats, such as zero-day or zero-hour attacks

- **Virtual Private Networks (VPN):** To provide secure access to remote workers

Network security requirements must take into account the network environment, as well as the various applications and computing requirements. Both home environments and businesses must be able to secure their data while still providing the quality of service that is expected of each technology. Additionally, the security solution implemented must be adaptable to the growing and changing trends of the network.

The study of network security threats and mitigation techniques starts with a clear understanding of the underlying switching and routing infrastructure used to organize network services.

Interactive Graphic

Activity 1.4.3.3: Network Security Terminology

Go to the course online to perform this practice activity.

Cisco Network Architectures (1.4.4.1)

The role of the network has changed from a data-only network to a system that enables the connections of people, devices, and information in a media-rich, converged network environment. For networks to function efficiently and grow in this type of environment, the network must be built upon a standard network architecture.

The network architecture refers to the devices, connections, and products that are integrated to support the necessary technologies and applications. A well-planned network technology architecture helps ensure the connection of any device across any combination of networks. While ensuring connectivity, it also increases cost efficiency by integrating network security and management, and improves business processes. At the foundation of all network architectures, and in fact, at the foundation of the Internet itself, are routers and switches. Routers and switches transport data, voice, and video communications, as well as allow wireless access and provide security.

Building networks that support our needs of today and the needs and trends of the future starts with a clear understanding of the underlying switching and routing infrastructure. After a basic routing and switching network infrastructure is built, individuals, small businesses, and organizations can grow their network over time, adding features and functionality in an integrated solution.

CCNA (1.4.4.2)

As the use of these integrated, expanding networks increases, so does the need for training for individuals who implement and manage network solutions. This training must begin with the routing and switching foundation. Achieving Cisco Certified Network Associate (CCNA) certification is the first step in helping an individual prepare for a career in networking.

CCNA certification validates an individual's ability to install, configure, operate, and troubleshoot medium-size route and switched networks, including implementation and verification of connections to remote sites in a WAN. The CCNA curriculum also includes basic mitigation of security threats, introduction to wireless networking concepts and terminology, and performance-based skills. This CCNA curriculum includes the use of various protocols, such as IP, Open Shortest Path First (OSPF), Serial Line Interface Protocol, Frame Relay, VLANs, Ethernet, access control lists (ACL), and others.

This course helps set the stage for networking concepts and basic routing and switching configurations and is a start on your path for CCNA certification.

Lab 1.4.4.3: Researching IT and Networking Job Opportunities

In this lab, you will research the current networking jobs and hiring trends in IT/networking. You will also examine the value of career certifications, especially those offered by Cisco Systems.

Summary (1.5)

Class Activity 1.5.1.1: Draw Your Concept of the Internet Now

In this activity, you will use the knowledge you have acquired throughout Chapter 1 and the modeling activity document that you prepared at the beginning of this chapter. You can also refer to the other activities completed in this chapter, including Packet Tracer activities.

Draw a map of the Internet as you see it now. Use the icons presented in the chapter for media, end devices, and intermediary devices.

In your revised drawing, you might want to include some of the following:

- WANs
- LANs
- Cloud computing
- Internet service providers (tiers)

Save your drawing in hard-copy format. If it is an electronic document, save it to a server location provided by your instructor. Be prepared to share and explain your revised work in class.

Networks and the Internet have changed the way we communicate, learn, work, and even play.

Networks come in all sizes. They can range from simple networks consisting of two computers to networks connecting millions of devices.

The Internet is the largest network in existence. In fact, the term *Internet* means a "network of networks." The Internet provides the services that enable us to connect and communicate with our families, friends, work, and interests.

The network infrastructure is the platform that supports the network. It provides the stable and reliable channel over which communication can occur. It is made up of network components including end devices, intermediate devices, and network media.

Networks must be reliable. This means that the network must be fault tolerant, be scalable, provide quality of service, and ensure security of the information and resources on the network. Network security is an integral part of computer networking, regardless of whether the network is limited to a home environment with a single connection to the Internet or as large as a corporation with thousands of users. No single solution can protect the network from the variety of threats that exist. For this reason, security should be implemented in multiple layers, using more than one security solution.

The network infrastructure can vary greatly in terms of size, number of users, and number and types of services that are supported on it. The network infrastructure must grow and adjust to support the way the network is used. The routing and switching platform is the foundation of any network infrastructure.

This chapter focused on networking as a primary platform for supporting communication. The next chapter will introduce you to the Cisco Internet Operating System (IOS), which is used to enable routing and switching in a Cisco network environment.

Practice

The following activities provide practice with the topics introduced in this chapter. The labs and class activities are available in the companion *The Introduction to Networking Lab Manual* (ISBN 978-1-58713-312-1). The Packet Tracer Activities PKA files are found in the online course.

Class Activities

- Class Activity 1.0.1.2: Draw Your Concept of the Internet
- Class Activity 1.5.1.1: Draw Your Concept of the Internet Now

Labs

- Lab 1.1.1.8: Researching Collaboration Tools
- Lab 1.2.3.3: Researching Converged Network Services
- Lab 1.3.1.3: Mapping the Internet
- Lab 1.4.4.3: Researching IT Networking Jobs and Hiring Trends in IT/ Networking

Packet Tracer Activities

Packet Tracer
☐ Activity

- Packet Tracer Activity 1.2.4.4: Network Representation

Check Your Understanding

Complete all the review questions listed here to test your understanding of the topics and concepts in this chapter. The appendix, "Answers to the 'Check Your Understanding' Questions," lists the answers.

1. What is a group of web pages that groups of individuals can edit and view together called?

   A. Podcasting

   B. Wiki

   C. Weblog (blog)

   D. Instant messaging

2. Which of the following are disadvantages of peer-to-peer networking? (Choose two.)

   A. Expensive to set up and maintain

   B. No centralized administration

   C. Complex configuration

   D. Scalability

3. Which devices would be considered end devices on a network? (Choose four.)

   A. Switch

   B. Printer

   C. IP phone

   D. Server

   E. Tablet computer

   F. Wireless access point

4. What type of information would be found on a logical topology diagram?

   A. Location of departmental printer

   B. Length and type of all cable runs

   C. IP addressing scheme

   D. Location of departmental switch

5. What is a network infrastructure that provides access to other networks over a wide geographic area?

    A. LAN

    B. WLAN

    C. MAN

    D. WAN

    E. SAN

6. Which of the following are business-class Internet connection technologies normally supplied by a service provider? (Choose two.)

    A. Leased lines

    B. Broadband cable

    C. Metro Ethernet

    D. Mobile services

    E. Cellular

7. Which technology would be best to provide a home user with a high-speed, always-on Internet connection?

    A. Dialup

    B. DSL

    C. Satellite

    D. Cellular

8. What is a converged network?

    A. A network that makes use of both fiber-optic and copper connections

    B. A network where voice, video, and data move over the same infrastructure

    C. A network that makes use of both wired and wireless technology

    D. A network that makes use of both satellite and terrestrial connections to move data

9. What is a fault-tolerant network?

    A. A network that can provide priority treatment of voice and video traffic

    B. A network that offers secure transactions

    C. A network that can reroute traffic in case of device failure

    D. A network that is incapable of failing

10. What is true of Tier 3 ISPs?

  A. They act as local providers of service directly to end users.

  B. They connect directly to Tier 1 ISPs.

  C. They interconnect with other Tier 1 ISPs.

  D. They provide high-speed redundant services to other ISPs.

11. Which type of traffic must receive the highest priority from QoS?

  A. Web traffic

  B. Email

  C. VoIP

  D. Order processing

12. What are the primary requirements of information security? (Choose three.)

  A. Confidentiality

  B. Integrity

  C. Availability

  D. QoS

  E. Scalability

13. List four current network trends.

14. Describe some common everyday uses of a modern-day network.

15. In what ways has the network transformed the way we learn?

CHAPTER 2

Configuring a Network Operating System

Objectives

Upon completion of this chapter, you will be able to answer the following questions:

- What is the purpose of Cisco IOS?

- How is the Cisco IOS accessed and navigated?

- What is the command structure of the Cisco IOS Software?

- How are host names configured on Cisco IOS devices using the CLI?

- How is access to device configuration limited on Cisco IOS devices?

- How is the running configuration saved on Cisco IOS devices?

- How do devices communicate across network media?

- How are Cisco IOS devices configured with an IP address?

- How is connectivity between two end devices verified?

Key Terms

This chapter uses the following key terms. You can find the definitions in the Glossary.

Introduction (2.0.1)

This chapter will reference a basic network topology, consisting of two switches and two PCs, to demonstrate the use of Cisco IOS.

Introduction to Cisco IOS (2.0.1.1)

Home networks typically interconnect a wide variety of end devices including PCs, laptops, tablets, smartphones, smart TVs, Digital Living Network Alliance (DLNA)–compliant network media players (such as the Xbox 360 or PlayStation 3), and more.

All of these end devices are usually connected to a home router. Home routers are actually four devices in one:

- **Router:** Forwards data packets to and receives data packets from the Internet
- **Switch:** Connects end devices using network cables
- **Wireless access point:** Consists of a radio transceiver capable of connecting end devices wirelessly
- **Firewall appliance:** Secures outgoing traffic and restricts incoming traffic

In larger business networks with significantly more devices and traffic, these devices are often incorporated as independent, standalone devices, providing dedicated service. End devices, such as PCs and laptops, are connected to network switches using wired connections. To send packets beyond the local network, network switches connect to network routers. Other infrastructure devices on a network include wireless access points and dedicated security devices, such as firewalls.

Each device is very different in hardware, use, and capability. However, in all cases, the operating system enables the hardware to function.

Operating systems are used on virtually all end-user and network devices connected to the Internet. End-user devices include devices such as smartphones, tablets, PCs, and laptops. Network devices, or intermediary devices, are devices used to transport data across the network and include switches, routers, wireless access points, and firewalls. The operating system on a network device is known as a network operating system.

The *Cisco Internetwork Operating System (IOS)* is a generic term for the collection of network operating systems used on Cisco networking devices. Cisco IOS is used for most Cisco devices regardless of the type or size of the device.

Class Activity 2.0.1.2: It Is Just an Operating System!

In this activity, imagine that you are employed as an engineer for a car manufacturing company. The company is currently working on a new car model. This model will have selected functions that can be controlled by the driver giving specific voice commands.

Design a set of commands used by this voice-activated control system, and identify how they are going to be executed. The functions of the car that can be controlled by voice commands are

- Lights
- Wipers
- Radio
- Telephone set
- Air conditioning
- Ignition

IOS Boot Camp (2.1)

This section will provide a concise overview of the Cisco IOS.

Cisco IOS (2.1.1)

This section will introduce the operating system used in most Cisco devices.

Operating Systems (2.1.1.1)

All end devices and network devices connected to the Internet require an operating system (OS) to help them perform their function.

When a computer is powered on, it loads the OS, normally from a disk drive, into RAM. The portion of the OS code that interacts directly with the computer hardware is known as the kernel. The portion that interfaces with the applications and user is known as the shell. The user can interact with the shell using either the *command-line interface (CLI)* or *graphical user interface (GUI)*.

When using the CLI, the user interacts directly with the system in a text-based environment by entering commands on the keyboard at a command prompt. The system executes the command, often providing textual output. The GUI interface allows the user to interact with the system in an environment that uses graphical images, multimedia, and text. Actions are performed by interacting with the images on screen. GUI is more user friendly and requires less knowledge of the command structure to utilize the system. For this reason, many individuals rely on the GUI environments. Many operating systems offer both GUI and CLI.

Figure 2-1 represents the user interface to an operating system. As can be seen, the user does not interact directly with the hardware. This system hardware is protected by layers of software and/or firmware. The user interface allows users to request specific tasks from the system. These requests are made through the CLI or GUI. The kernel provides communications between the hardware and software of the computer system as well as manages hardware resources. The hardware consists of the physical electronic components such as CPU and memory.

Figure 2-1   User Interface to an Operating System

Most end-device operating systems are accessed using a GUI, including MS Windows, Mac OS X, Linux, Apple iOS, Android, and more.

The operating system on home routers is usually called firmware. The most common method for configuring a home router is using a web browser to access an easy-to-use GUI. Most home routers enable the update of the firmware as new features are developed or security vulnerabilities are discovered.

Intermediate network devices, also called infrastructure network devices, use a network operating system. As previously presented, the network operating system used on Cisco devices is called the Cisco Internetwork Operating System (IOS). The most common method of accessing these devices is using a CLI.

This chapter will focus on a small business network switch topology. The topology consists of two switches and two PCs that will be used to demonstrate the use of Cisco IOS using the CLI.

Purpose of OS (2.1.1.2)

Network operating systems are in many ways similar to the operating systems of PCs. An operating system performs a number of technical functions "behind the scenes" that enable a user to

- Use a mouse

- View output on a monitor

- Enter text commands

- Select options within a dialog box window

- Manage hardware processes

The shell functions for switches and routers are very similar. These shell functions of the IOS on a switch or router, which take place "behind the scenes," provide the network technician with an interface. The technician can enter commands to configure, or program, the device to perform various networking functions. The IOS operational details vary on internetworking devices, depending on the purpose of the device and the features supported.

There are many distinct variations of Cisco IOS:

- IOS for switches, routers, and other Cisco networking devices

- IOS numbered versions for a given Cisco networking device

- IOS feature sets, providing distinct packages of features and services

Just as a PC might be running Microsoft Windows 8 and a MacBook might be running OS X, a Cisco networking device runs a particular version of the Cisco IOS. The version of IOS is dependent on the type of device being used and the required features. While all devices come with a default IOS and feature set, it is possible to upgrade the IOS version or feature set to obtain additional capabilities.

In this course, you will focus primarily on Cisco IOS Release 15.x.

Location of the Cisco IOS (2.1.1.3)

The IOS file itself is several megabytes in size and is stored in a semipermanent memory area called *flash*. Flash memory provides nonvolatile storage. This means that the contents of the memory are not lost when the device loses power. Although the contents of flash are not lost during a loss of power, they can be changed or overwritten if needed. This allows the IOS to be upgraded to a newer version or to have new features added without replacing hardware. Additionally, flash can be used to store multiple versions of IOS software at the same time.

In many Cisco devices, the IOS is copied from flash into *random-access memory (RAM)* when the device is powered on. The IOS then runs from RAM when the device is operating. RAM has many functions, including storing data that is used by the device to support network operations. Running the IOS in RAM increases performance of the device; however, RAM is considered volatile memory because data is lost during a power cycle. A power cycle is when a device is purposely or accidentally powered off and then powered back on.

The quantity of flash memory and RAM required for a given IOS varies significantly. For the purposes of network maintenance and planning, it is important to determine the flash and RAM requirements for each device, including the maximum flash and RAM configurations. It is possible that the requirements of the newest versions of IOS could demand more RAM and flash than can be installed on some devices.

IOS Functions (2.1.1.4)

Cisco IOS routers and switches perform functions that network professionals depend upon to make their networks operate as expected. Major functions performed or enabled by Cisco routers and switches include

- Providing network security

- IP addressing of virtual and physical interfaces

- Enabling interface-specific configurations to optimize connectivity of the respective media

- Routing

- Enabling quality of service (QoS) technologies

- Supporting network management technologies

- Frame switching and/or packet forwarding

Each feature or service has an associated collection of configuration commands that allow a network technician to implement it.

The services provided by the Cisco IOS are generally accessed using a CLI.

Video

Video 2.1.1.5: View the video in the online course for an introduction to Cisco.com.

Accessing a Cisco IOS Device (2.1.2)

This section investigates the methods of accessing the CLI environment of the Cisco IOS.

Console Access Method (2.1.2.1)

There are several ways to access the CLI environment. The most common methods are

- Console

- Telnet or SSH

- AUX port

Console

The console port is a management port that provides out-of-band access to a Cisco device. Out-of-band access refers to access through a dedicated management channel that is used for device maintenance purposes only. The advantage of using a console port is that the device is accessible even if no networking services have been configured, such as when performing an initial configuration of the networking device. When performing an initial configuration, a computer running terminal emulation software is connected to the console port of the device using a special cable. Configuration commands for setting up the switch or router can be entered on the connected computer.

The console port can also be used when the networking services have failed and remote access of the Cisco IOS device is not possible. If this occurs, a connection to the console can enable a computer to determine the status of the device. By default, the console conveys the device startup, debugging, and error messages. After the network technician is connected to the device, he can perform any configuration commands necessary using the console session.

For many IOS devices, console access does not require any form of security, by default. However, the console should be configured with passwords to prevent unauthorized device access. In the event that a password is lost, there is a special set of procedures for bypassing the password and accessing the device. The device should also be located in a locked room or equipment rack to prevent unauthorized physical access.

Telnet, SSH, and AUX Access Methods (2.1.2.2)

While a console connection provides a method of locally accessing the IOS CLI, there are methods for remotely accessing the CLI. This section introduces some of these methods.

Telnet

Telnet is a method for remotely establishing a CLI session of a device, through a virtual interface, over a network. Unlike the console connection, Telnet sessions require active networking services on the device. The network device must have at least one active interface configured with an Internet address, such as an IPv4 address. Cisco IOS devices include a Telnet server process that allows users to enter configuration commands from a Telnet client. In addition to supporting the Telnet server process, the Cisco IOS device also contains a Telnet client. This allows a network administrator to telnet from the Cisco device CLI to any other device that supports a Telnet server process.

SSH

The *Secure Shell (SSH)* protocol provides a remote login similar to Telnet, except that it uses more secure network services. SSH provides stronger password authentication than Telnet and uses encryption when transporting session data. This keeps the user ID, password, and the details of the management session private. As a best practice, use SSH instead of Telnet whenever possible.

Most versions of Cisco IOS include an SSH server. In some devices, this service is enabled by default. Other devices require the SSH server to be enabled manually. IOS devices also include an SSH client that can be used to establish SSH sessions with other devices.

AUX

An older way to establish a CLI session remotely is through a telephone dialup connection using a modem connected to the auxiliary (AUX) port of a router. Similar to the console connection, the AUX method is also an out-of-band connection and does not require any networking services to be configured or available on the device. In the event that network services have failed, it might be possible for a remote administrator to access the switch or router over a telephone line.

The AUX port can also be used locally, like the console port, with a direct connection to a computer running a terminal emulation program. However, the console port is preferred over the AUX port for troubleshooting because it displays startup, debugging, and error messages by default.

The location of the AUX and Console port on a Cisco 1941 is shown in Figure 2-2.

Figure 2-2 AUX and Console Port of a Cisco Router

Terminal Emulation Programs (2.1.2.3)

There are a number of *terminal emulation* programs available for connecting to a networking device either by a serial connection over a console port or by a Telnet/ SSH connection. Some of these include

- PuTTY
- Tera Term
- SecureCRT
- HyperTerminal
- OS X Terminal

These programs allow you to enhance your productivity by adjusting window sizes, changing font sizes, and changing color schemes.

Interactive Graphic

Activity 2.1.2.4: Accessing Device

Go to the course online to perform this practice activity.

Navigating the IOS (2.1.3)

To configure, test, and troubleshoot Cisco network devices, technicians need to have a working knowledge of the Cisco IOS. This section introduces the fundamentals of the method and modes of the Cisco IOS.

Cisco IOS Modes of Operation (2.1.3.1)

After a network technician is connected to a device, it is possible to configure it. The network technician must navigate through various modes of the IOS. The Cisco IOS modes are quite similar for switches and routers. The CLI uses a hierarchical structure for the modes.

In hierarchical order from most basic to most specialized, the major modes are

- *User executive (user EXEC) mode*

- *Privileged executive (privileged EXEC) mode*

- *Global configuration mode*

- Other specific configuration modes, such as interface configuration mode

Descriptions and the appropriate prompts of the IOS modes are shown in Table 2-1.

Table 2-1   IOS Primary Modes

Mode	Description	Prompt
User EXEC mode	Limited examination of router. Remote access.	Router>
Privileged EXEC mode	Detailed examination of router. Debugging and testing. File manipulation. Remote access.	Router#
Global configuration mode	Global configuration commands.	Router (config)#
Other configuration modes	Specific service or interface configurations	Router (config-mode)#

Each mode has a distinctive prompt and is used to accomplish particular tasks with a specific set of commands that are available only to that mode. For example, global configuration mode allows a technician to configure settings on the device that affects the device as a whole, such as configuring a name for the device. However, a different mode is required if the network technician wants to configure security settings on a specific port on a switch, for example. In this case, the network technician must enter interface configuration mode for that specific port. All configurations that are entered in interface configuration mode apply only to that port.

The hierarchical structure can be configured to provide security. Different authentication can be required for each hierarchical mode. This controls the level of access that network personnel can be granted.

Primary Modes (2.1.3.2)

The two primary modes of operation are user EXEC mode and privileged EXEC mode. As a security feature, the Cisco IOS Software separates the EXEC sessions into two levels of access. The privileged EXEC mode has a higher level of authority in what it allows the user to do with the device.

User EXEC Mode

The user EXEC mode has limited capabilities but is useful for some basic operations. The user EXEC mode is at the most basic level of the modal hierarchical structure. This mode is the first mode encountered upon entrance into the CLI of an IOS device.

The user EXEC mode allows only a limited number of basic monitoring commands. This is often referred to as view-only mode. The user EXEC level does not allow the execution of any commands that might change the configuration of the device.

By default, there is no authentication required to access the user EXEC mode from the console. However, it is a good practice to ensure that authentication is configured during the initial configuration.

The user EXEC mode is identified by the CLI prompt that ends with the > symbol. An example of this prompt can be seen in Table 2-1.

Privileged EXEC Mode

The execution of configuration and management commands requires that the network administrator use the privileged EXEC mode or a more specific mode in the hierarchy. This means that a user must enter user EXEC mode first, and from there, access privileged EXEC mode.

The privileged EXEC mode can be identified by the prompt ending with the # symbol. An example of this prompt can also be seen in Table 2-1.

By default, privileged EXEC mode does not require authentication. It is a good practice to ensure that authentication is configured.

Global configuration mode and all other more specific configuration modes can only be reached from the privileged EXEC mode. In a later section of this chapter, we will examine device configuration and some of the configuration modes.

Global Configuration Mode and Submodes (2.1.3.3)

Global configuration mode and interface configuration modes can only be reached from the privileged EXEC mode.

Global Configuration Mode

The primary configuration mode is called global configuration or global config mode. From this mode, CLI configuration changes are made that affect the operation of the device as a whole. The global configuration mode is accessed before accessing specific configuration modes.

The following CLI command is used to take the device from privileged EXEC mode to the global configuration mode and to allow entry of configuration commands from a terminal:

```
Switch# configure terminal
```

After the command is executed, the prompt changes to show that the switch is in global configuration mode.

```
Switch(config)#
```

Specific Configuration Modes

From the global configuration mode, the user can enter different subconfiguration modes. Each of these modes allows the configuration of a particular part or function of the IOS device. The following list shows a few of them:

- **Interface mode:** To configure one of the network interfaces (Fa0/0, Gi0/0/0, Te0/0, S0/0/0)

- **Line mode:** To configure one of the physical or virtual lines (console, AUX, VTY)

To exit a specific configuration mode and return to global configuration mode, enter **exit** at a prompt. To leave configuration mode completely and return to privileged EXEC mode, enter **end** or use the key sequence **Ctrl-Z**.

Command Prompts

When using the CLI, the mode is identified by the command-line prompt that is unique to that mode. By default, every prompt begins with the device name. Following the name, the remainder of the prompt indicates the mode. For example, the default prompt for the global configuration mode on a switch would be

```
Switch(config)#
```

As commands are used and modes are changed, the prompt changes to reflect the current context.

Navigating Between IOS Modes (2.1.3.4, 2.1.3.5)

The section will demonstrate the methods of moving from one IOS mode to another at the CLI.

Moving Between the User EXEC and Privileged EXEC Modes

The **enable** and **disable** commands are used to change the CLI between the user EXEC mode and the privileged EXEC mode, respectively.

To access the privileged EXEC mode, use the **enable** command. The privileged EXEC mode is sometimes called the enable mode.

The syntax for entering the **enable** command is

```
Switch> enable
```

This command is executed without the need for an argument or keyword. After the Enter key is pressed, the prompt changes to

```
Switch#
```

The # at the end of the prompt indicates that the switch is now in privileged EXEC mode.

If password authentication is configured for the privileged EXEC mode, the IOS prompts for the password.

For example:

```
Switch> enable
Password:
Switch#
```

The **disable** command is used to return from the privileged EXEC to the user EXEC mode.

For example:

```
Switch# disable
Switch>
```

The **enable** command is used on both the Cisco router and Cisco switch accessing the privileged EXEC mode. Similarly, the **disable** command is used on both the Cisco router and Cisco switch for returning to the user EXEC mode.

Moving from and to Global Configuration Mode and Submodes

To quit from the global configuration mode and return to the privileged EXEC mode, enter the **exit** command.

Note that entering the **exit** command in privileged EXEC mode causes the console session to be ended. That is, upon entering **exit** in privileged EXEC mode, you will be presented with the screen that you see when you first initiate a console session. At this screen, you have to press the Enter key to enter user EXEC mode.

To move from any submode of the global configuration mode to the mode one mode higher in the hierarchy of modes, enter the **exit** command. For example, to return to user EXEC mode from privileged EXEC mode, type the **exit** command. Similarly, the **exit** command is used to return to the global configuration mode from interface configuration mode.

To move from any mode within the privileged EXEC mode to the privileged EXEC mode, enter the **end** command or press the key combination **Ctrl-Z**. Additionally to move directly from any submode of the global configuration mode to another submode of the global configuration mode, enter the corresponding command that is normally entered from global configuration mode. For example, in Example 2-1, the router mode is changed directly from the line configuration mode to the interface configuration mode by issuing the **interface Gi0/0** command. Notice that there was no **exit** command issued to return to the global configuration mode before the **interface Gi0/0** command was issued.

Example 2-1   Moving Directly from Line Configuration Mode to Interface Configuration Mode

```
Router> enable
Router# configure terminal
Enter configuration commands, one per line.  End with CNTL/Z.
Router(config)# line vty 0 4
Router(config-line)# interface Gi0/0
Router(config-if)# end
Router#
```

Video

Video 2.1.3.6: View the video in the online course for a demonstration of navigation through the different CLI command modes of both a router and a switch using Cisco IOS.

The Command Structure (2.1.4)

The Cisco IOS, like other programming, uses commands that have a specific structure. To configure an IOS device, a network technician needs to understand this structure. This section will introduce the IOS command structure.

IOS Command Structure (2.1.4.1)

A network technician cannot memorize every possible command. Understanding the general structure of the IOS commands can help the technician enter the commands. This section introduces the structure and written representation of the IOS commands.

Basic IOS Command Structure

A Cisco IOS device supports many commands. Each IOS command has a specific format or syntax and can only be executed at the appropriate mode. The general syntax for a command is the command followed by any appropriate keywords and arguments. Some commands include a subset of keywords and arguments that provide additional functionality. Commands are used to execute an action, and the keywords are used to identify where or how to execute the command.

As shown in Figure 2-3, the command is the initial word or words entered in the command line following the prompt. The commands are not case sensitive. Following the command are one or more keywords and arguments. After entering each complete command, including any keywords and arguments, press the Enter key to submit the command to the command interpreter.

The keywords describe specific parameters to the command interpreter. For example, the **show** command is used to display information about the device. This command has various keywords that must be used to define what particular output should be displayed. For example:

```
Switch# show running-config
```

The command **show** is followed by the keyword **running-config**. The keyword specifies that the running configuration is to be displayed as the output.

Figure 2-3   Basic IOS Command Structure

IOS Command Conventions

A command might require one or more arguments. Unlike a keyword, an argument is generally not a predefined word. An argument is a value or variable defined by the user. To determine the keywords and arguments required for a command, refer to the command syntax. The syntax provides the pattern or format that must be used when entering a command.

For example the syntax for using the **description** command is

```
Switch(config-if)# description string
```

As shown in Table 2-2, boldface text indicates commands and keywords that are typed as shown, and italic text indicates an argument for which you supply the value. For the **description** command, the argument is a string value. The string value can be any text string of up to 80 characters.

Therefore, when applying a description to an interface with the **description** command, enter a line such as this:

```
Switch(config-if)# description MainHQ Office Switch
```

The command is **description** and the user-defined argument is **MainHQ Office Switch**.

The following examples demonstrate some conventions used to document and use IOS commands.

For the *ping* command:

Syntax:

```
Switch> ping IP-address
```

Example with values:

```
Switch> ping 10.10.10.5
```

The command is **ping** and the user defined argument is the **10.10.10.5**.

Similarly, the syntax for entering the *traceroute* command is

Syntax:

```
Switch> traceroute IP-address
```

Example with values:

```
Switch> traceroute 192.168.254.254
```

The command is **traceroute** and the user defined argument is the **192.168.254.254**.

Table 2-2 IOS Conventions

Convention	Description
Boldface	Boldface text indicates commands and keywords that are entered literally as shown.
Italics	Italic text indicates arguments where the user supplies values.
[X]	Square brackets enclose an optional element (keyword or argument). A vertical line (|), as shown in the following cells, indicates a choice within an optional or required set of keywords or arguments.
[X	Y]	Square brackets enclosing keywords or arguments separated by a vertical line indicate an optional choice.
{X	Y}	Braces enclosing keywords or arguments separated by a vertical line indicate a required choice. The italicized value, in the previous example the correct IP address, is a value that the person configuring the router must provide.

Cisco IOS Command Reference (2.1.4.2)

The Cisco IOS Command Reference is a collection of online documentation that describes in detail the IOS commands used on Cisco devices. The Command Reference is the ultimate source of information for a particular IOS command, similar to how a dictionary is the ultimate source for information about a particular word.

The Command Reference is a fundamental resource that network engineers use to check various characteristics of a given IOS command. Some of the more common characteristics are

- **Syntax:** The most detailed version of the syntax for a command that can be found

- **Default:** The manner in which the command is implemented on a device with a default configuration

- **Mode:** The configuration mode on the device where the command is entered

- **History:** Descriptions of how the command is implemented relative to the IOS version

- **Usage guidelines:** Guidelines describing specifically how to implement the command

- **Examples:** Useful examples that illustrate common scenarios that use the command

To navigate to the Command Reference and find a particular command, follow these steps:

How To

Step 1.   Go to www.cisco.com.

Step 2.   Click **Support.**

Step 3.   Click **Networking Software** (IOS & NX-OS).

Step 4.   Click **15.2M&T** (for example).

Step 5.   Click **Reference Guides.**

Step 6.   Click **Command References.**

Step 7.   Click the particular technology that encompasses the command you are referencing.

Step 8.   Click the link on the left that alphabetically matches the command you are referencing.

Step 9.   Click the link for the command.

For example, the **description** command is found in the *Cisco IOS Interface and Hardware Component Command Reference*, under the link for the alphabetic range *D through E.*

Note

Complete PDF versions of the command references for a particular technology can be downloaded from links on the page that you reach after completing Step 7 in the previous list.

Context-Sensitive Help (2.1.4.3)

The IOS has several forms of help available:

- Context-sensitive help

- Command syntax check

- Hot keys and shortcuts

Context-Sensitive Help

The context-sensitive help provides a list of commands and the arguments associated with those commands within the context of the current mode. To access context-sensitive help, enter a question mark, **?**, at any prompt. There is an immediate response without the need to press the Enter key.

One use of context-sensitive help is to get a list of available commands. This can be used when you are unsure of the name of a command or if you want to see whether the IOS supports a particular command in a particular mode.

For example, to list the commands available at the user EXEC level, enter a question mark, **?**, at the Switch> prompt.

Another use of context-sensitive help is to display a list of commands or keywords that start with a specific character or characters. After entering a character sequence, if a question mark is immediately entered, without a space, the IOS will display a list of commands or keywords for this context that start with the characters that were entered.

For example, enter **sh?** to get a list of commands that begins with the character sequence **sh**.

A final type of context-sensitive help is used to determine which options, keywords, or arguments are matched with a specific command. When entering a command, enter a space followed by a **?** to determine what can or should be entered next.

As shown in the Table 2-3, after typing the command **clock set 19:50:00**, we can enter the **?** to determine the additional options or keywords available for this command.

Table 2-3   Context-Sensitive Help

Convention	Description
Switch# **cl?** clear clock Switch# **cl**	Command options; displays commands or keywords that start with the characters **cl**.
Switch# **clock set ?** hh:mm:ss Current Time Switch# **clock set**	Command explanation; displays the command arguments or variables and an explanation of each.
Switch# **clock set 19:50:00 ?** <1-31> Day Of the month MONTH Month of the year Switch# **clock set 19:50:00**	Command explanation with more than one argument or variable option.
Switch# **clock set 19:50:00 27 June 2013** Switch#	Completed and accepted command.

Command Syntax Check (2.1.4.4)

When a command is submitted by pressing the Enter key, the command-line interpreter parses the command from left to right to determine what action is being requested.

Tip

The IOS generally only provides negative feedback. If the interpreter understands the command, the requested action is executed and the CLI returns to the appropriate prompt. However, if the interpreter cannot understand the command being entered, it will provide feedback describing what is wrong with the command.

Table 2-4 uses the **clock set** command to show some of the command syntax check help messages. The three different types of error messages shown are

- Ambiguous command
- Incomplete command
- Incorrect command

Table 2-4   Command Syntax Check Help

Error Message	Meaning	Example	How to Get Help
%Ambiguous command: 'command'	Not enough characters were entered for the IOS to recognize the command.	Switch# c %Ambiguous command: 'command'	Reenter the command followed by a question mark (**?**) with no space between the command and the question mark. The possible keywords that you can enter with the command are displayed.
%Incomplete command	Not all the required keywords or arguments were entered.	Switch# **clock set** %Incomplete command	Reenter the command followed by a question mark (**?**) with a space after last word. The required keywords or arguments are displayed.

Error Message	Meaning	Example	How to Get Help
%Invalid input detected at ^marker	Command was entered incorrectly. The error occurred where the caret mark (^) appears.	Switch# **clock set 19:50:00 25 6** $\mid\wedge\mid$ %Invalid input detected at $\mid\wedge\mid$ marker	Reenter the command followed by a question mark (**?**) with a space after last word. It might also need to have the last keyword(s) or argument(s) deleted.

Hot Keys and Shortcuts (2.1.4.5)

The IOS CLI provides hot keys and shortcuts that make configuring, monitoring, and troubleshooting easier.

Table 2-5 shows most of the CLI shortcuts. The following are worthy of special note:

- **Down arrow:** Allows the user to scroll forward through former commands
- **Up arrow:** Allows the user to scroll backward through former commands
- **Tab:** Completes the remainder of a partially typed command or keyword
- **Ctrl-A:** Moves to the beginning of the line
- **Ctrl-E:** Moves to the end of the line
- **Ctrl-R:** Redisplays a line
- **Ctrl-Z:** Exits the configuration mode and returns to privileged EXEC
- **Ctrl-C:** Exits the configuration mode or aborts the current command
- **Ctrl-Shift-6:** Allows the user to interrupt an IOS process such as ping or traceroute

Table 2-5   Hot Keys and Shortcuts

CLI Line Editing	
Shortcut	**Description**
Tab	Completes a partial command name entry.
Backspace	Erases the character to the left of the cursor.

CLI Line Editing

Shortcut	Description
Ctrl-D	Erases the character at the cursor.
Ctrl-K	Erases all characters from the cursor to the end of the command line.
Esc-D	Erases all characters from the cursor to the end of the word.
Ctrl-U or Ctrl-X	Erases all characters from the cursor to the beginning of the command line.
Ctrl-W	Erases the word to the left of the cursor.
Ctrl-A	Moves the cursor to the beginning of the command line.
Left-arrow key or Ctrl-B	Moves the cursor one character to the left.
Esc F	Moves the cursor forward one word to the right.
Right-arrow key or Ctrl-F	Moves the cursor one character to the right.
Ctrl-E	Moves the cursor to the end of the command line.
Up-arrow key or Ctrl-P	Recalls command in the history buffer, beginning with the most recent commands.
Ctrl-R, Ctrl-I, or Ctrl-L	Redisplays the system prompt and command line after a console message is received.

At the --More—Prompt

Shortcut	Description
Enter key	Displays the next line.
Spacebar	Displays the next screen.
Any other alphanumeric key	Returns the EXEC prompt.

Break Keys

Shortcut	Description
Ctrl-C	When in any configuration mode, ends the configuration mode and returns to privileged EXEC mode. When in setup mode, aborts to the command prompt.
Ctrl-Z	When in any configuration mode, ends the configuration mode and returns to privileged EXEC mode.
Ctrl-Shift-6	All-purpose break sequence. Used to abort DNS lookups, traceroutes, and pings.

Note

Delete, the key to erase to the right of the cursor, is not recognized by terminal emulation programs. To use control shortcuts, press and hold the **Ctrl** key and then press the specified letter key. For escape sequences, press and release the **Esc** key and then press the letter key.

The following sections examine some of these in more detail.

Tab

Tab complete is used to complete the remainder of abbreviated commands and parameters if the abbreviation contains enough letters to be different from any other currently available commands or parameters. When enough of the command or keyword has been entered to appear unique, press the **Tab** key and the CLI will display the rest of the command or keyword.

This is a good technique to use when you are learning because it allows you to see the full word used for the command or keyword.

Up and Down Arrows

Previous command keys will recall the history of commands entered. The Cisco IOS Software buffers several past commands and characters so that entries can be recalled. The buffer is useful for reentering commands without retyping.

Key sequences are available to scroll through these buffered commands. Use the **up-arrow** key (**Ctrl-P**) to display the previously entered commands. Each time this key is pressed, the next successively older command will be displayed. Use the **down-arrow** key (**Ctrl-N**) to scroll forward through the history to display the more recent commands.

Ctrl-R

Redisplaying the line will refresh the line just typed. Press **Ctrl-R** to redisplay the line. For example, you might find that the IOS is returning a message to the CLI just as you are typing a line. You can press **Ctrl-R** to refresh the line and avoid having to retype it.

In this example, a message regarding a failed interface is returned in the middle of a command.

```
Switch# show mac-
16w4d: %LINK-5-CHANGED: Interface FastEthernet0/10, changed state to down
16w4d: %LINEPROTO-5-UPDOWN: Line protocol on Interface FastEthernet0/10, changed
    state to down
```

To redisplay the line that you were typing, press **Ctrl-R**:

```
Switch# show mac
```

Ctrl-Z

Exit configuration mode will leave any configuration mode and return to privileged EXEC mode. Because the IOS has a hierarchical mode structure, you might find yourself several levels down. Rather than exit each mode individually, press **Ctrl-Z** to return directly to the privileged EXEC prompt at the top level.

Ctrl-C

This interrupts the entry of a command and exits the configuration mode. This is useful after entering a command that needs to be canceled.

Ctrl-Shift-6

The escape sequence will interrupt any running process. When an IOS process is initiated from the CLI, such as a **ping** or **traceroute**, the command runs until it is complete or is interrupted. While the process is running, the CLI is unresponsive. To interrupt the output and interact with the CLI, press **Ctrl-Shift-6**.

Abbreviated Commands or Keywords

Commands and keywords can be abbreviated to the minimum number of characters that identify a unique selection. For example, the **configure** command can be abbreviated to **conf** because **configure** is the only command that begins with **conf**. An abbreviation of **con** will not work because more than one command begins with **con**.

Keywords can also be abbreviated.

As another example, the **show interfaces** command can be abbreviated like this:

```
Switch# show int
```

You can abbreviate both the command and the keywords, for example:

```
Switch# sh int
```

IOS Examination Commands (2.1.4.6)

To verify and troubleshoot network operation, we must examine the operation of the devices. The basic examination command is the **show** command.

There are many different variations of this command. As you develop more skill with the IOS, you will learn to use and interpret the output of the **show** commands. Use the **show ?** command to get a list of available commands in a given context, or mode.

A typical **show** command can provide information about the configuration, operation, and status of parts of a Cisco switch or router.

In this course, we focus on mostly basic **show** commands.

A very commonly used **show** command is **show interfaces**. This command displays statistics for all interfaces on the device. To view the statistics for a specific interface, enter the **show interfaces** command followed by the specific interface type and slot/port number. For example:

```
Switch# show interfaces GigabitEthernet 0/1
```

Some other **show** commands frequently used by network technicians include

- **show startup-config:** Displays the saved configuration located in NVRAM.

- **show running-config:** Displays the contents of the currently running configuration file.

The More Prompt

When a command returns more output than can be displayed on a single screen, the **--More--** prompt appears at the bottom of the screen. When a **--More--** prompt appears, press the **spacebar** to view the next portion of output. To display only the next line, press the **Enter** key. If any other key is pressed, the output is canceled and you are returned to the prompt.

The show version Command (2.1.4.7)

One of the most commonly used commands on a switch or router is

```
Switch# show version
```

This command displays information about the currently loaded IOS version, along with hardware and device information. If you are logged in to a router or switch remotely, the **show version** command is an excellent means of quickly finding useful summary information about the particular device to which you are connected. Some of the information points shown from this command are

- **Software version:** IOS software version (stored in flash)

- **Bootstrap version:** Bootstrap version (stored in boot ROM)

- **System uptime:** Time since last reboot

- **System restart info:** Method of restart (for example, power cycle or crash)

- **Software image name:** IOS filename stored in flash

- **Router type and processor type:** Model number and processor type

- **Memory type and allocation (shared/main):** Main processor RAM and shared packet I/O buffering

- **Software features:** Supported protocols/feature sets

- **Hardware interfaces:** Interfaces available on the device

- **Configuration register:** Sets bootup specifications, console speed setting, and related parameters

Example 2-2 displays the output of the **show version** command for a Cisco 1941 ISR.

Example 2-2   Output of the **show version** Command

```
Router# show version
Cisco IOS Software, C1900 Software (C1900-UNIVERSALK9-M), Version 15.1(4)M4, RELEASE
  SOFTWARE (fc2)
Technical Support: http://www.cisco.com/techsupport
Copyright (c) 1986-2007 by Cisco Systems, Inc.
Compiled Wed 23-Feb-11 14:19 by prod_rel_team


ROM: System Bootstrap, Version 15.1(4)M4, RELEASE SOFTWARE (fc1)
cisco1941 uptime is 1 minutes, 38 seconds
System returned to ROM by power-on
System image file is "flash0:c1900-universalk9-mz.SPA.151-1.M4.bin"
Last reload type: Normal Reload


This product contains cryptographic features and is subject to United States and
  local country laws governing import, export, transfer and use. Delivery of Cisco
  cryptographic products does not imply third-party authority to import, export,
  distribute or use encryption.
```

```
Importers, exporters, distributors and users are responsible for compliance with
  U.S. and local country laws. By using this product you agree to comply with
  applicable laws and regulations. If you are unable to comply with U.S. and local
  laws, return this product immediately.

A summary of U.S. laws governing Cisco cryptographic products may be found at:

http://www.cisco.com/wwl/export/crypto/tool/stqrg.html


If you require further assistance please contact us by sending email
  toexport@cisco.com.
Cisco CISCO1941/K9 (revision 1.0) with 491520K/32768K bytes of memory.
Processor board ID FTX152400KS
2 Gigabit Ethernet interfaces
DRAM configuration is 64 bits wide with parity disabled.
255K bytes of non-volatile configuration memory.
249856K bytes of ATA System CompactFlash 0 (Read/Write)


License Info:
License UDI:
----------------------------------------------------------
Device#    PID                   SN
----------------------------------------------------------
*0         CISCO1941/K9          FTX1524A699


Technology Package License Information for Module:'c1900'
-----------------------------------------------------------------------
Technology      Technology-package           Technology-package
                Current          Type        Next reboot
-----------------------------------------------------------------------
ipbase          ipbasek9         Permanent   ipbasek9
security        none             none        none
data            none             none        none


Configuration register is 0x2102
Router#
```

Packet Tracer Activity: 2.1.4.8: Navigating the IOS

In this activity, you will practice skills necessary for navigating the Cisco IOS, including different user access modes, various configuration modes, and common commands you use on a regular basis. You also practice accessing the context-sensitive help by configuring the **clock** command.

Lab 2.1.4.9: Establishing a Console Session with Tera Term

In this lab, you will complete the following objectives:

- Part 1: Access a Cisco Switch Through the Serial Console Port

- Part 2: Display and Configure Basic Device Settings

- Part 3: (Optional) Access a Cisco Router Using a Mini-USB Console Cable

Getting Basic (2.2)

Before devices can be used in a network, they will require configuration. This section introduces the basic configuration of Cisco IOS devices.

Host Names (2.2.1)

An important part of the basic device configuration is assigning the device a name. This section will discuss the naming of Cisco IOS network devices.

Why the Switch (2.2.1.1)

As discussed, Cisco switches and Cisco routers have many similarities. They support a similar modal operating system, support similar command structures, and support many of the same commands. In addition, both devices have identical initial configuration steps when implementing them in a network.

However, a Cisco IOS switch is one of the simplest devices that can be configured on a network. This is because there are no configurations that are required prior to having the device function. At its most basic, a switch can be plugged in with no configuration, and it will still switch data between connected devices.

A switch is also one of the fundamental devices used in the creation of a small network. By connecting two PCs to a switch, those PCs will instantly have connectivity with one another.

For these reasons, the remainder of this chapter will focus on the creation of a small, two-PC network connected through a switch configured with initial settings. Initial settings include setting a name for the switch, limiting access to the device configuration, configuring banner messages, and saving the configuration.

Device Names (2.2.1.2)

When configuring a networking device, one of the first steps is configuring a unique device name, or host name. Host names appear in CLI prompts, can be used in various authentication processes between devices, and should be used on topology diagrams.

Host names are configured on the active networking device. If the device name is not explicitly configured, a factory-assigned default device name is used by Cisco IOS. The default name for a Cisco IOS switch is "Switch."

Imagine if an internetwork had several switches that were all named with the default name "Switch." This could create considerable confusion during network configuration and maintenance. When accessing a remote device using SSH, it is important to have confirmation that you are connected to the proper device. If all devices were left with their default names, it would be difficult to determine that the proper device is connected.

By choosing names wisely, it is easier to remember, discuss, document, and identify network devices. To name devices in a consistent and useful way requires the establishment of a naming convention that spans the company or, at least, the location. It is a good practice to create the naming convention at the same time as the addressing scheme to allow continuity within an organization.

Some guidelines for naming conventions are that names should

- Start with a letter
- Contain no spaces
- End with a letter or digit
- Use only letters, digits, and dashes
- Be less than 64 characters in length

The host names used in the device IOS preserve capitalization and lowercase characters. Therefore, it allows you to capitalize a name as you ordinarily would. This contrasts with most Internet naming schemes, where uppercase and lowercase characters are treated identically.

Host Names (2.2.1.3)

Host names allow devices to be identified by network administrators over a network or the Internet.

Applying Names Example

Let's use an example of three switches connected together in a network, spanning three different floors. To create a naming convention for switches, take into consideration the location and the purpose of the devices. For example, these three switches could be named Sw-Floor-1, Sw-Floor-2, and Sw-Floor-3. This would identify these devices as switches and on which floor they are located.

In the network documentation, we would include these names, and the reasons for choosing them, to ensure continuity in our naming convention as devices are added.

After the naming convention has been identified, the next step is to apply the names to the devices using the CLI.

Configuring Host Names (2.2.1.4)

This section will demonstrate how to configure device names from the CLI.

Configure IOS Host Name

From the privileged EXEC mode, access the global configuration mode by entering the **configure terminal** command:

```
Switch# configure terminal
```

After the command is executed, the prompt will change to

```
Switch(config)#
```

In the global configuration mode, enter the host name:

```
Switch(config)# hostname Sw-Floor-1
```

After the command is executed, the prompt will change to

```
Sw-Floor-1(config)#
```

Notice that the host name appears in the prompt. To exit global configuration mode, use the **exit** command.

Always make sure that your documentation is updated each time a device is added or modified. Identify devices in the documentation by their location, purpose, and address.

Note

To undo the effects of a command, preface the command with the **no** keyword.

For example, to remove the name of a device, use:

```
Sw-Floor-1(config)# no hostname
Switch(config)#
```

The **no hostname** command caused the switch to revert to the default host name of "Switch."

Example 2-3 shows the complete process to configure a host name on a switch.

Example 2-3   Configuring Host Name

```
Switch> enable
Switch# configure terminal
Enter configuration commands, one per line.  End with CNTL/Z.
Switch(config)# hostname SW-Floor-1
SW-Floor-1(config)# end
SW-Floor-1#
%SYS-5-CONFIG_I: Configured from console by console

SW-Floor-1#
SW-Floor-1# copy running-config startup-config
Destination filename [startup-config]?
Building configuration...
[OK]
SW-Floor-1#
```

Limiting Access to Device Configurations (2.2.2)

To help ensure the security of a network, access to the network devices should be protected. This section will examine the basics of limiting device access.

Securing Device Access (2.2.2.1)

Physically limiting access to network devices by placing them in closets and locked racks is good practice; however, passwords are the primary defense against unauthorized access to network devices. Every device, even home routers, should have locally configured passwords to limit access. Later, we will introduce how to strengthen security by requiring a username along with a password. For now, we will present basic security precautions using only passwords.

As discussed previously, the IOS uses hierarchical modes to help with device security. As part of this security enforcement, the IOS can accept several passwords to allow different access privileges to the device.

The passwords introduced here are

- *Enable password*: Limits access to the privileged EXEC mode

- *Enable secret*: Encrypted, limits access to the privileged EXEC mode

- **Console password:** Limits device access using the console connection

- **VTY password:** Limits device access over SSH or Telnet

As good practice, use different authentication passwords for each of these levels of access. Although logging in with multiple and different passwords is inconvenient, it is a necessary precaution to properly protect the network infrastructure from unauthorized access.

Additionally, use strong passwords that are not easily guessed. The use of weak or easily guessed passwords continues to be a security issue in many facets of the business world.

Consider these key points when choosing passwords:

- Use passwords that are more than eight characters in length.

- Use a combination of uppercase and lowercase letters, numbers, special characters, and/or numeric sequences in passwords.

- Avoid using the same password for all devices.

- Avoid using common words such as *password* or *administrator*, because these are easily guessed.

Note

Most of the labs associated with this companion guide use simple passwords such as **cisco** or **class**. These passwords are considered weak and easily guessable and should be avoided in a work environment. These passwords are used for convenience in a classroom setting or to illustrate configuration examples.

Securing Privileged EXEC Access (2.2.2.2)

To secure privileged EXEC access, use the **enable secret** *password* command. An older, less secure variation of this command is the **enable password** command. Although either of these commands can be used to establish authentication before access to privileged EXEC (enable) mode is permitted, it is recommended to use the **enable secret** command. The **enable secret** command provides greater security because the password is encrypted.

Example command to set passwords:

```
Switch(config)# enable secret class
```

Example 2-4 illustrates how a password is not requested when first using the **enable** command. Next, the **enable secret class** command is configured and now privileged EXEC access is secured. Notice that for security reasons, the password is not displayed when it is being entered.

Example 2-4 Configuring **enable secret** Password

```
SW-Floor-1> enable
SW-Floor-1#
SW-Floor-1# configure terminal
Enter configuration commands, one per line.  End with CNTL/Z.
SW-Floor-1(config)# enable secret class
SW-Floor-1(config)# exit
SW-Floor-1#
%SYS-5-CONFIG_I: Configured from console by console

SW-Floor-1# disable
SW-Floor-1>
SW-Floor-1> enable
Password:
SW-Floor-1#
```

Securing User EXEC Access (2.2.2.3)

The console port of network devices must be secured, at a bare minimum, by requiring the user to supply a strong password. This reduces the chance of unauthorized personnel physically plugging a cable into the device and gaining device access.

The following commands are used in global configuration mode to set a password for the console line:

```
Switch(config)# line console 0
Switch(config-line)# password cisco
Switch(config-line)# login
```

From global configuration mode, the **line console 0** command is used to enter line configuration mode for the console. The zero is used to represent the first (and in most cases only) console interface.

The second command, **password cisco**, specifies a password for the console line.

The **login** command configures the switch to require authentication upon login. When login is enabled and a password set, the console user will be prompted to enter a password before gaining access to the CLI.

VTY Password

The *vty* lines allow access to a Cisco device through Telnet. By default, many Cisco switches support up to 16 vty lines that are numbered 0 to 15. The number of vty lines supported on a Cisco router varies with the type of router and the IOS version. However, five is the most common number of vty lines configured. These lines are numbered 0 to 4 by default, though additional lines can be configured. A password needs to be set for all available vty lines. The same password can be set for all connections. However, it is often desirable that a unique password be set for one line to provide a fall-back for administrative entry to the device if the other connections are in use.

Example commands used to set a password on vty lines:

```
Switch(config)# line vty 0 15
Switch(config-line)# password cisco
Switch(config-line)# login
```

By default, the IOS includes the **login** command on the vty lines. This prevents Telnet access to the device without authentication. If, by mistake, the **no login** command is set, which removes the requirement for authentication, unauthorized persons could connect across the network to the line using Telnet. This would be a major security risk.

Example 2-5 illustrates the securing of the user EXEC access on the console and virtual terminal lines.

Example 2-5   Configuration to Secure User EXEC Access

```
SW-Floor-1# configure terminal
Enter configuration commands, one per line.  End with CNTL/Z.
SW-Floor-1(config)# line console 0
SW-Floor-1(config-line)# password cisco
SW-Floor-1(config-line)# login
SW-Floor-1(config-line)# exit
SW-Floor-1(config)#
SW-Floor-1(config)# line vty 0 4
SW-Floor-1(config-line)# password cisco
SW-Floor-1(config-line)# login
SW-Floor-1(config-line)# end
SW-Floor-1#
%SYS-5-CONFIG_I: Configured from console by console

SW-Floor-1#
```

Note

While passwords provide an initial level of access security, configuring IOS devices to authenticate with user IDs and passwords is considered best practice. The configuration for user authentication is beyond the scope of this text.

Encrypting Password Display (2.2.2.4)

Another useful command prevents passwords from being displayed as plain text when viewing the configuration files. This is the **service password-encryption** command.

This command causes the encryption of passwords to occur when a password is configured. The **service password-encryption** command applies weak encryption to all unencrypted passwords. This encryption applies only to passwords in the configuration file, not to passwords as they are sent over media. The purpose of this command is to keep unauthorized individuals from viewing passwords in the configuration file.

If you execute the **show running-config** or **show startup-config** command prior to the **service password-encryption** command being executed, the unencrypted passwords are visible in the configuration output. The **service password-encryption** command can then be executed and the encryption will be applied to the passwords. After the encryption has been applied, removing the encryption service does not reverse the encryption.

Example 2-6 illustrates the protecting of passwords by encrypting them in the configuration. The Console 0 password of **cisco** was added to the configuration. With the **service password-encryption** command, the password is displayed in the output of the running configuration. When the **service password-encryption** command is added to the configuration, the password shows as an encrypted string of **0822455D0A16**.

Example 2-6   Configuration to Encrypt Passwords

```
SW-Floor-1# configure terminal
Enter configuration commands, one per line.  End with CNTL/Z.
SW-Floor-1(config)# line console 0
SW-Floor-1(config-line)# password cisco
SW-Floor-1(config-line)# end
%SYS-5-CONFIG_I: Configured from console by console

SW-Floor-1# show running-config

    <output omitted>
!
line con 0
 password cisco
!
    <output omitted>

SW-Floor-1#
SW-Floor-1# configure terminal
Enter configuration commands, one per line.  End with CNTL/Z.

SW-Floor-1(config)# service password-encryption
SW-Floor-1(config)#
```

```
SW-Floor-1#
%SYS-5-CONFIG_I: Configured from console by console

SW-Floor-1#
SW-Floor-1# show running-config

%SYS-5-CONFIG_I: Configured from console by console

    <output omitted>
!
line con 0
 password 7 0822455D0A16
!

    <output omitted>

SW-Floor-1#
```

Note

The encryption performed by the IOS password encryption service uses a weak algorithm, and there are readily available utilities to decrypt these to recover the passwords. Therefore, configuration should be protected.

Banner Messages (2.2.2.5)

Although requiring passwords is one way to keep unauthorized personnel out of a network, it is vital to provide a method for declaring that only authorized personnel should attempt to gain entry into the device. To do this, add a banner to the device output.

Banners can be an important part of the legal process in the event that someone is prosecuted for breaking into a device. Some legal systems do not allow prosecution, or even the monitoring of users, unless a notification is visible.

The exact content or wording of a banner depends on the local laws and corporate policies. Here are some examples of information to include in a banner:

- "Use of the device is specifically for authorized personnel."

- "Activity can be monitored."

- "Legal action will be pursued for any unauthorized use."

Because banners can be seen by anyone who attempts to log in, the message must be worded very carefully. Any wording that implies that a login is "welcome" or "invited" is not appropriate. If a person disrupts the network after gaining unauthorized entry, proving liability will be difficult if there is the appearance of an invitation.

The creation of banners is a simple process; however, banners should be used appropriately. When a banner is utilized, it should never welcome someone to the device. It should detail that only authorized personnel are allowed to access the device. Further, the banner can include scheduled system shutdowns and other information that affect all network users.

The IOS provides multiple types of banners. One common banner is the message of the day (MOTD). It is often used for legal notification because it is displayed to all connected terminals.

Configure MOTD using the **banner motd** command from global configuration mode.

The **banner motd** command requires the use of delimiters to identify the content of the banner message. The **banner motd** command is followed by a space and a delimiting character. Then, one or more lines of text are entered to represent the banner message. A second occurrence of the delimiting character denotes the end of the message. The delimiting character can be any character as long as it does not occur in the message. For this reason, symbols such as the "#" are often used.

The syntax to configure a MOTD from global configuration mode is

```
Switch(config)# banner motd # message #
```

After the command is executed, the banner will be displayed on all subsequent attempts to access the device until the banner is removed.

Note

Regardless of what delimiting character is used when the MOTD configuration is added, the output of the configuration will be display "^C" (Ctrl-C) as the delimiter. For example, the configuration with delimiting "#" will be viewed as "^C" in the running config.

Example 2-7 illustrates a banner configured with the delimiting "#" symbol. Notice how the banner is now displayed when accessing the switch.

Example 2-7   Configuration to Provide Message of the Day

```
SW-Floor-1(config)# banner motd #
Enter TEXT message.  End with the character '#'.


*******************************************
* This system should be accessed only by *
* Authorized Personnel. All activity may *
* be monitored and violators prosecuted. *
*******************************************
```

```
#
SW-Floor-1(config)# end
%SYS-5-CONFIG_I: Configured from console by console
SW-Floor-1#

SW-Floor-1# exit
SW-Floor-1 con0 is now available

Press RETURN to get started.

********************************************
* This system should be accessed only by *
* Authorized Personnel. All activity may *
* be monitored and violators prosecuted. *
********************************************
SW-Floor-1>
```

Saving Configurations (2.2.3)

Configuration changes to Cisco IOS–based devices occur to the running configuration. This working configuration should be backed up to support network recovery. This section will examine some the methods used to back up and restore the running configuration on Cisco IOS devices.

Configuration Files (2.2.3.1)

The running configuration file reflects the current configuration applied to a Cisco IOS device. It contains the commands used to determine how the device operates on the network. Modifying a running configuration affects the operation of a Cisco device immediately.

The running configuration file is stored in the working memory of the device, or random-access memory (RAM). This means that the running configuration file is temporarily active while the Cisco device is running (powered on). However, if power to the device is lost or if the device is restarted, all configuration changes will be lost unless they have been saved.

After making changes to a running configuration file, consider these distinct options:

- Return the device to its original configuration.
- Remove all configurations from the device.
- Make the changed configuration the new startup configuration.

The startup configuration file reflects the configuration that will be used by the device upon reboot. The startup configuration file is stored in NVRAM. When a network device has been configured and the running configuration has been modified, it is important to save those changes to the startup configuration file. Doing so prevents changes from being lost because of power failure or a deliberate restart.

Before committing to the changes, use the appropriate **show** commands to verify the device's operation. The **show running-config** command can be used to see a running configuration file. When the changes are verified to be correct, use the **copy running-config startup-config** command at the privileged EXEC mode prompt. The command to save the running configuration to startup configuration file is

```
Switch# copy running-config startup-config
```

After being executed, the running configuration file updates the startup configuration file.

However, if the changes made to the running configuration do not have the desired effect, it might become necessary to restore the device to its previous configuration. Assuming that we have not overwritten the startup configuration with the changes, we can replace the running configuration with the startup configuration. This is best done by restarting the device using the **reload** command at the privileged EXEC mode prompt.

When initiating a reload, the IOS will detect that the running config has changes that were not saved to startup configuration. A prompt will appear to ask whether to save the changes made. To discard the changes, enter **n** or **no**.

An additional prompt will appear to confirm the reload. To confirm, press Enter. Pressing any other key will abort the process.

For example:

```
Switch# reload
System configuration has been modified. Save? [yes/no]: n
Proceed with reload? [confirm]
*Apr 13 01:34:15.758: %SYS-5-RELOAD: Reload requested by console.
   Reload Reason:
Reload Command.
System Bootstrap, Version 12.3(8r)T8, RELEASE SOFTWARE (fc1)
Technical Support: http://www.cisco.com/techsupport
Copyright (c) 2004 by cisco Systems, Inc.
PLD version 0x10
GIO ASIC version 0x127
c1841 processor with 131072 Kbytes of main memory
Main memory is configured to 64 bit mode with parity disabled
```

If undesired changes are saved to the startup configuration, it might be necessary to clear all the configurations. This requires erasing the startup configuration and restarting the device.

The startup configuration is removed by using the **erase startup-config** command.

To erase the startup configuration file, use **erase NVRAM:startup-config** or **erase startup-config** at the privileged EXEC mode prompt:

```
Switch# erase startup-config
```

After the command is issued, the switch will prompt you for confirmation:

```
Erasing the nvram filesystem will remove all configuration files!
  Continue? [confirm]
```

Confirm is the default response. To confirm and erase the startup configuration file, press Enter. Pressing any other key will abort the process.

Caution

Exercise caution when using the **erase** command. This command can be used to erase any file in the device. Improper use of the command can erase the IOS itself or another critical file.

On a switch, you must also issue the **delete vlan.dat** command in addition to the **erase startup-config** command to return the device to its default "out-of-the-box" configuration (comparable to a factory reset):

```
Switch# delete vlan.dat
Delete filename [vlan.dat]?
Delete flash:vlan.dat? [confirm]
Switch# erase startup-config
Erasing the nvram filesystem will remove all configuration files!
  Continue? [confirm]
[OK]
Erase of nvram: complete
Switch#
```

After removing the startup configuration from NVRAM (and deleting the vlan.dat file in the case of a switch), reload the device to remove the current running configuration file from RAM. The device will then load the default startup configuration that was originally shipped with the device into the running configuration.

Capturing Text (2.2.3.2)

This section demonstrates how to capture and save the device configurations as a text document.

Back Up Configurations with Text Capture

In addition to saving running configurations to the startup configuration, configuration files can also be saved and archived to a text document. This sequence of steps ensures that a working copy of the configuration files is available for editing or reuse later.

Configuration files can be saved or archived to a text document using Tera Term. Follow these steps:

Step 1.   On the File menu, click **Log**.

Step 2.   Choose the location. Tera Term will begin capturing text.

Step 3.   After the capture has been started, execute the **show running-config** or **show startup-config** command at the privileged EXEC prompt. Text displayed in the terminal window will be placed into the chosen file.

Step 4.   When the capture is complete, select **Close** in the Tera Term: Log window.

Step 5.   View the output to verify that it was not corrupted.

Figure 2-4 illustrates the menu in Tera Term when setting up to capture text.

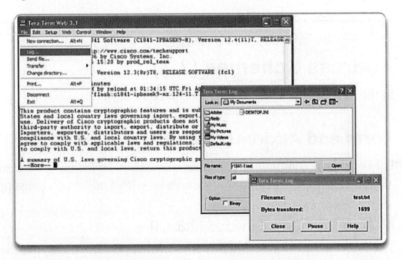

Figure 2-4   User Interface to an Operating System

Restoring Text Configurations

A configuration file can be copied from storage to a device. When copied into the terminal, the IOS executes each line of the configuration text as a command. The file will probably require editing before copying. It is advisable to change the encrypted passwords to plain text and remove the parameter, either the number 5 or 7, which specifies that the password is encrypted. Noncommand text such as "--More--" and IOS messages must be removed.

Further, at the CLI, the device must be set at the global configuration mode to receive the commands from the text file being copied. When using Tera Term, follow these steps:

Step 1.   Edit text to remove noncommands and save.

Step 2.   On the **File** menu, click **Send File**.

Step 3.   Locate the file to be copied into the device and click **Open**.

Step 4.   Tera Term will paste the file into the device.

The text in the file will be applied as commands in the CLI and become the running configuration on the device. This is a convenient method for manually configuring a device.

Packet Tracer Activity 2.2.3.3: Configuring Switch Settings

In this activity, you will perform basic switch configurations. You will secure access to the command-line interface (CLI) and console ports using encrypted and plain text passwords. You will also learn how to configure messages for users logging in to the switch. These banners are also used to warn unauthorized users that access is prohibited.

Address Schemes (2.3)

In this section IPv4 addresses are supplied to devices.

Ports and Addresses (2.3.1)

For devices to communicate on a network, each device must have addressing information applied. This section introduces how IPv4 addresses are supplied to devices.

IP Addressing of Devices (2.3.1.1)

The use of IP addresses, whether IPv4 or IPv6, is the primary means of enabling devices to locate one another and establish end-to-end communication on the Internet. In fact, in any internetwork, IP addresses are essential for devices to communicate from source to destination and back.

Each end device on a network must be configured with IP addresses. Some examples of end devices are

- Computers (workstations, laptops, file servers, web servers)
- Network printers

- *VoIP* phones
- Security cameras
- Smartphones
- Mobile handheld devices (such as wireless barcode scanners)

The structure of an *IPv4 address* is called dotted-decimal notation and is represented with four decimal numbers between 0 and 255. IPv4 addresses are numbers assigned to individual devices connected to a network.

With the IPv4 address, a *subnet mask* is also necessary. A subnet mask is a special type of IPv4 address that, coupled with the IP address, determines to which particular subnet of a larger network the device is a member.

IP addresses can be assigned to both physical ports and virtual interfaces on devices. A virtual interface means that there is no physical hardware on the device associated with it.

Interfaces and Ports (2.3.1.2)

Network communications depend on end-user device interfaces, networking device interfaces, and the cables that connect them.

Each physical interface has specifications, or standards, that define it; a cable connecting to the interface must be designed to match the physical standards of the interface. Types of network media include twisted-pair copper cables, fiber-optic cables, coaxial cables, or wireless. Different types of network media have different features and benefits. Not all network media have the same characteristics and are appropriate for the same purpose. Some of the differences between various types of media include

- Distance the media can successfully carry a signal
- Environment in which the media is to be installed
- Amount of data and the speed at which it must be transmitted
- Cost of the media and installation

Not only does each link on the Internet require a specific network media type, but each link also requires a particular network technology. Ethernet is the most common local-area network (LAN) technology used today. Ethernet ports are found on end-user devices, switch devices, and other networking devices that can physically connect to the network using a cable. For a cable to connect devices using an Ethernet port, the cable must have the correct connector, an RJ-45.

Cisco IOS switches have physical ports for devices to connect to, but also have one or more *switch virtual interfaces (SVI)*. These are virtual interfaces because there is no physical hardware on the device associated with it; an SVI is created in software. The virtual interface provides a means to remotely manage a switch over a network using IP. Each switch comes with one SVI appearing in the default configuration "out-of-the-box." The default SVI is interface VLAN1.

Addressing Devices (2.3.2)

In addition to the IPv4 address, additional addressing information must be configured for devices to communicate on a network. This section introduces how this addressing information is configured on devices.

Configuring a Switch Virtual Interface (2.3.2.1)

To access the switch remotely, an IP address and a subnet mask must be configured on the SVI:

- **IP address:** Together with the subnet mask, uniquely identifies the end device on the internetwork

- **Subnet mask:** Determines which part of a larger network is used by an IP address

For now, the focus is IPv4; later you will explore IPv6.

You will learn the meaning behind all these IP addresses soon, but for now, the point is to quickly configure the switch to support remote access.

- **interface vlan 1:** Used to navigate to the interface configuration mode from the global configuration mode

- **ip address 192.168.10.2 255.255.255.0:** Configures the IP address and subnet mask for the switch (this is just one of many possible combinations for an IP address and subnet mask)

- **no shutdown:** Administratively enables the interface to an active state

After these commands are configured, the switch has all the IP elements ready for management communication over the network.

Note

The switch will still need to have one or more physical ports configured, as well as the VTY lines, to complete the configuration, which enables remote management of the switch.

Example 2-8 illustrates the commands to enable IPv4 connectivity to S1, using IP address 192.168.10.2.

Example 2-8   Configuring a Switch Virtual Interface

```
S1# configure terminal
Enter configuration commands, one per line. End with CNTL/Z.
S1(config)# interface vlan 1
S1(config-if)# ip address 192.168.10.2 255.255.255.0
S1(config-if)# no shutdown
S1(config-if)# exit
S1(config)# ip default-gateway 192.168.10.1
S1(config)# exit
S1#
```

Manual IP Address Configuration for End Devices (2.3.2.2)

For an end device to communicate over the network, it must be configured with the correct IP address information. Much like a switch SVI, the end device must be configured with an IP address and subnet mask.

All of these settings must be configured on an end device for it to properly connect to the network. This information is configured under the PC network settings. In addition to IP address and subnet mask information, it is also possible to configure default gateway and DNS server information, as shown in Figure 2-5.

The default gateway address is the IP address of the router interface used for network traffic to exit the local network. The default gateway is an IP address that is often assigned by the network administrator and is used when traffic must be routed to another network.

The DNS server address is the IP addressof the *Domain Name System (DNS)* server, which is used to translate IP addresses to web addresses, such as www.cisco.com. All devices on the Internet are assigned and reached through an IP address. However, it is easier for people to remember names rather than numbers. Therefore, websites are given names for simplicity. The DNS server is used to maintain the mapping between the IP addresses and names of various devices.

Figure 2-5   Static Assignment of IPv4 Addressing Information

Automatic IP Address Configuration for End Devices (2.3.2.3)

IP address information can be entered into the PC manually or by using Dynamic *Host Configuration Protocol (DHCP)*. DHCP allows end devices to have IP information automatically configured.

DHCP is a technology that is used in most networks. The best way to understand why DHCP is so popular is by considering all the extra work that would have to take place without it.

DHCP enables automatic IPv4 address configuration for every end device in a network with DHCP enabled. Imagine the amount of time that would be consumed if every time you connected to the network you had to manually enter the IP address, the subnet mask, the default gateway, and the DNS server. Multiply that by every user and every one of the user's devices on the network and you see the problem.

DHCP is an example of technology at its best. One of the primary purposes of any technology is to make it easier to perform the tasks that the user wants to do or needs to do. With DHCP, the end user walks into the area served by a given network and plugs in an Ethernet cable or enables a wireless connection, and she is immediately allocated the necessary IPv4 information required to fully communicate over the network.

As shown in Figure 2-6, to configure DHCP on a Windows PC, you only need to select "Obtain an IP address automatically" and "Obtain DNS server address automatically." Your PC will be assigned information from an IP address pool and associated IP information set up on the DHCP server.

It is possible to display the IP configuration settings on a Windows PC by using the **ipconfig** command at the command prompt. The output will show the IP address, subnet mask, and gateway that the PC received from the DHCP server.

Figure 2-6   Static Assignment of IPv4 Addressing Information

IP Address Conflicts (2.3.2.4)

It is important that each host have a unique Layer 3 address. When two or more hosts have the same IP address, address conflicts exist and need to be resolved. Address conflicts create network communication issues. These issues can range from hampering the communication between the two hosts with the common address to completely shutting down network communication.

If a static (manual) IP address is defined for a network device—for example, a printer—and then a DHCP server is installed, duplicate IP address conflicts can occur between the network device and a PC obtaining automatic IP addressing information from the DHCP server. The conflict can also occur if you manually define a static IP address to a network device during a network failure involving the DHCP server; after the network failure resolves and the DHCP server becomes accessible over the network, the conflict arises.

To resolve such an IP addressing conflict, convert the network device with the static IP address to a DHCP client; or on the DHCP server, exclude the static IP address of the end device from the DHCP scope.

The second solution requires that you have administrative privileges on the DHCP server and that you are familiar with configuring DHCP on a server.

You might also encounter IP addressing conflicts when manually configuring IP on an end device in a network that only uses static IP addresses. In this case, you must determine which IP addresses are available on the particular IP subnet and configure accordingly. This case illustrates why it is so important for a network administrator to maintain detailed documentation, including IP address assignments, for end devices.

Note

Usually, static IP addresses are used with servers and printers in a small- to medium-sized business network, while employee devices use DHCP-allocated IP address information.

Packet Tracer
☐ Activity

Packet Tracer Activity 2.3.2.5: Implementing Basic Connectivity

In this activity, you will first perform basic switch configurations. Then you will implement basic connectivity by configuring IP addressing on switches and PCs. When the IP addressing configuration is complete, you will use various **show** commands to verify configurations and use the **ping** command to verify basic connectivity between devices.

Verifying Connectivity (2.3.3)

A principal troubleshooting technique is to verify the logical connectivity between two or more IPv4 devices. This section introduces some of the steps used to verify this connectivity.

Test the Loopback Address on an End Device (2.3.3.1)

As part of troubleshooting, ping verifies the logical configuration and connectivity. This section introduces the verification of local IPv4 operation using ping.

Testing the Loopback

The first step in the testing sequence is to ping the host loopback address. The **ping** command is used to verify the internal IP configuration on a local host. This test is accomplished by using the **ping** command on a reserved address called the *loopback* (127.0.0.1). The loopback address, 127.0.0.1, is defined by the TCP/IP protocol as a reserved address that routes packets back to the host.

Ping commands are entered into a command line on the local host using the syntax shown in Example 2-9. This example indicates that four test packets of 32 bytes each were sent and returned from host 127.0.0.1 in a time of less than 1 ms. This successful ping request verifies that the network interface card, the drivers, and the TCP/IP implementation are all functioning correctly.

Example 2-9   Ping Local Loopback

```
C:\> ping 127.0.0.1
Reply from 127.0.0.1: bytes=32 time<1ms TTL=128
Reply from 127.0.0.1: bytes=32 time<1ms TTL=128
Reply from 127.0.0.1: bytes=32 time<1ms TTL=128
Reply from 127.0.0.1: bytes=32 time<1ms TTL=128

Ping statistics for 127.0.0.1:
Packets: Sent = 4, Received = 4, Lost = 0 (0% loss),
Approximate round trip times in milli-seconds:
Minimum = 0ms, Maximum = 0ms, Average = 0ms
```

Testing the Interface Assignment (2.3.3.2)

In the same way that you use commands and utilities to verify a host configuration, you use commands to verify the interfaces of intermediary devices. The IOS provides commands to verify the operation of router and switch interfaces.

Verifying the Switch Interfaces

Examining S1 and S2, use the **show ip interface brief** command to verify the condition of the switch interfaces, as shown in Example 2-10. The IP address assigned to VLAN 1 interface on S1 is 192.168.10.2. The IP address assigned to VLAN 1 interface on S2 is 192.168.10.3. The physical interfaces Gi0/1 and Gi0/2 on S1 are operational, as are the physical interfaces Gi0/1 and Gi0/2 on S2.

Example 2-10   show ip interface brief Command Output

```
S1# show ip interface brief
Interface          IP-Address      OK? Method Status Protocol
GigabitEthernet0/1 unassigned      YES manual up     up
GigabitEthernet0/2 unassigned      YES manual up     up
   <output omitted>
Vlan1              192.168.10.2 YES manual up        up


S2# show ip interface brief
Interface          IP-Address      OK? Method Status Protocol
GigabitEthernet0/1 unassigned      YES manual up     up
GigabitEthernet0/2 unassigned      YES manual up     up
   <output omitted>
Vlan1              192.168.10.3 YES manual up        up
```

Testing End-to-End Connectivity (2.3.3.3)

This section demonstrates how to use ping to verify connectivity between two end devices.

Testing PC-to-Switch Connectivity

Just as on a Cisco IOS device, a ping from PC1 to the IP address of the S1 VLAN 1 interface, 192.168.10.2, should be successful.

Testing End-to-End Connectivity

The IP address of PC1 is 192.168.10.10, with subnet mask 255.255.255.0 and default gateway 192.168.10.1.

The IP address of PC2 is 192.168.10.11, with subnet mask 255.255.255.0 and default gateway 192.168.10.1.

As shown in Example 2-11, a ping from PC1 to PC2 should also be successful. A successful ping from PC1 to PC2 verifies end-to-end connectivity in the network!

Example 2-11   ping Command to Test End-to-End Connectivity

```
C:\> ping 192.168.10.11
Reply from 192.168.10.11: bytes=32 time=838ms TTL=35
Reply from 192.168.10.11: bytes=32 time=820ms TTL=35
Reply from 192.168.10.11: bytes=32 time=883ms TTL=36
Reply from 192.168.10.11: bytes=32 time-828 TTL=36
Ping statistics for 192.168.10.11:
Packets: Sent = 4, Received = 4, Lost = 0 (0% loss),
Approximate round trip times in milli-seconds:
Minimum = 820ms, Maximum = 883ms, Average = 842ms
```

Lab 2.3.3.4: Building a Simple Network

In this lab, you will complete the following objectives:

- Part 1: Set Up the Network Topology (Ethernet only)
- Part 2: Configure PC Hosts
- Part 3: Configure and Verify Basic Switch Settings

Lab 2.3.3.5: Configuring a Switch Management Address

In this lab, you will complete the following objectives:

- Part 1: Configure a Basic Network Device
- Part 2: Verify and Test Network Connectivity

Summary (2.4)

Class Activity 2.4.1.1: Tutor Me!

Students will work in pairs. Packet Tracer is required for this activity. Assume that a new colleague has asked you for an orientation to the Cisco IOS CLI. This colleague has never worked with Cisco devices before.

You explain the basic CLI commands and structure, because you want your colleague to understand that the CLI is a simple, yet powerful, command language that can be easily understood and navigated.

Use Packet Tracer and one of the activities available in this chapter as a simple network model (for example, Lab Activity 2.3.3.5, Configuring a Switch Management Address).

Focus on these areas:

- While the commands are technical, do they resemble any statements from plain English?

- How is the set of commands organized into subgroups or modes? How does an administrator know which mode he or she is currently using?

- What are the individual commands to configure the basic settings of a Cisco device? How would you explain this command in simple terms? Use parallels to real life whenever appropriate.

Suggest how to group different commands together according to their modes so that a minimum number of moves between modes will be needed.

Packet Tracer Activity 2.4.1.2: Skill Integration Challenge

As a recently hired LAN technician, your network manager has asked you to demonstrate your ability to configure a small LAN. Your tasks include configuring initial settings on two switches using the Cisco IOS and configuring IP address parameters on host devices to provide end-to-end connectivity. You are to use two switches and two hosts/PCs on a cabled and powered network.

Cisco IOS is a term that encompasses a number of different operating systems that run on various networking devices. The technician can enter commands to configure the device to perform various networking functions. Cisco IOS routers and switches perform functions that network professionals depend upon to make their networks operate as expected.

The services provided by the Cisco IOS are generally accessed using a command-line interface (CLI), which is accessed by the console port, by the AUX port, or through Telnet or SSH. After being connected to the CLI, network technicians can make configuration changes to Cisco IOS devices. The Cisco IOS is designed as a modal operating system, which means that a network technician must navigate through various hierarchical modes of the IOS. Each mode supports different IOS commands.

The Cisco IOS Command Reference is a collection of online documents that describe in detail the IOS commands used on Cisco devices, such as Cisco IOS 1routers and switches.

Cisco IOS routers and switches support a similar modal operating system, support similar command structures, and support many of the same commands. In addition, both devices have identical initial configuration steps when implementing them in a network.

This chapter introduced the Cisco IOS. It detailed the various modes of the Cisco IOS and examined the basic command structure that is used to configure it. It also walked you through the initial settings of a Cisco IOS switch device, include setting a name, limiting access to the device configuration, configuring banner messages, and saving the configuration.

The next chapter explores how packets are moved across the network infrastructure and introduces you to the rules of packet communication.

Practice

The following activities provide practice with the topics introduced in this chapter. The labs and class activities are available in the companion *The Introduction to Networking Lab Manual* (ISBN 978-1-58713-312-1). The Packet Tracer Activities PKA files are found in the online course.

Class Activities

- Class Activity 2.0.1.2: It Is Just an Operating System
- Class Activity 2.4.1.1: Tutor Me!

Labs

- Lab 2.1.4.9: Establishing a Console Session with Tera Term
- Lab 2.3.3.4: Building a Simple Network
- Lab 2.3.3.5: Configuring a Switch Management Address

Packet Tracer Activities

- Packet Tracer Activity 2.1.4.8: Navigating the IOS
- Packet Tracer Activity 2.2.3.3: Configuring Switch Settings
- Packet Tracer Activity 2.3.2.5: Implementing Basic Connectivity
- Packet Tracer Activity 2.4.1.2: Skill Integration Challenge

Check Your Understanding

Complete all the review questions listed here to test your understanding of the topics and concepts in this chapter. The appendix "Answers to the 'Check Your Understanding' Questions" lists the answers.

1. What is the Cisco IOS?

   A. The memory for the Cisco network device

   B. The configuration for the Cisco network device

   C. The operating system for the Cisco network device

   D. The CPU for the Cisco network device

2. What type of connection to a Cisco IOS switch is used to make the initial configuration?

   A. AUX port

   B. Console port

   C. SSH

   D. Telnet

   E. Web interface

3. What command will display a list of keywords available for viewing the status of an IOS switch?

   A.   Switch# **sh?**

   B.   Switch# **help**

   C.   Switch# **show ?**

   D.   Switch# **status ?**

4. How is the Cisco IOS generally accessed and navigated?

   A.   Through the CLI using a terminal emulator

   B.   Using a web browser

   C.   With a Cisco-proprietary application

   D.   By the use of a custom GUI

5. What is initially entered at the CLI of the Cisco IOS when typing a command sequence?

   A.   Argument

   B.   A space

   C.   Command

   D.   Keyword

6. When the command "Switch(config)# **hostname EaSt-2+56**" is entered in a Cisco IOS device using the CLI, what will be returned in the CLI?

   A.   Switch(config)#

   B.   % Invalid input detected

   C.   EaSt-2+56(config)#

   D.   EaSt-58(config)#

   E.   East-2+56(config)#

   F.   Switch EaSt-2+56(config)#

7. What is the primary defense against unauthorized remote access to network devices?

   A.   Configuring a default gateway

   B.   Configuring an IP address

   C.   Configuring a VTY password

   D.   Configuring a console password

8. Where is the configuration used during startup on Cisco IOS devices located?

    A. Running config

    B. NVRAM

    C. Startup config

    D. Terminal emulator

9. What is the purpose of the following switch configuration?

    ```
    S1(config)# interface vlan 1

    S1(config-if)# ip address 192.168.122.222 255.255.255.0

    S1(config-if)# no shutdown

    S1(config-if)# exit
    ```

    A. Allows communication to manage the switch

    B. Allows the switch to forward traffic

    C. Allows the switch to provide name resolution

    D. Allows dynamic host configuration

10. From the CLI of a switch with an address of 192.168.1.44, what command would be used to verify end-to-end connectivity to another host?

    A. **show ip interface brief**

    B. **ping 127.0.0.1**

    C. **ping 192.168.1.44**

    D. **ping 192.168.1.43**

CHAPTER 3

Network Protocols and Communications

Objectives

Upon completion of this chapter, you will be able to answer the following questions:

- Why are protocols necessary in communication?

- What is the purpose of adhering to a protocol suite?

- What is the role of standards organizations in establishing protocols for network interoperability?

- How are the TCP/IP model and the OSI model used to facilitate standardization in the communication process?

- Why did RFCs become the process for establishing standards?

- What is the RFC process?

- How does data encapsulation allow data to be transported across the network?

- How do local hosts access local resources on a network?

- How do local hosts access remote resources on a network?

Key Terms

This chapter uses the following key terms. You can find the definitions in the Glossary.

Introduction (3.0.1.1)

More and more, it is networks that connect us. People communicate online from everywhere. Conversations in classrooms spill into instant message chat sessions, and online debates continue at school. New services are being developed daily to take advantage of the network.

Rather than developing unique and separate systems for the delivery of each new service, the network industry as a whole has adopted a developmental framework that allows designers to understand current network platforms, and maintain them. At the same time, this framework is used to facilitate the development of new technologies to support future communications needs and technology enhancements.

Central to this developmental framework is the use of generally accepted models that describe network rules and functions.

Within this chapter, you will learn about these models, as well as the standards that make networks work, and how communication occurs over a network.

Class Activity 3.0.1.2: Designing a Communications System

Let's just talk about this . . .

You have just purchased a new automobile for your personal use. After driving the car for a week or so, you find that it is not working correctly.

After discussing the problem with several of your peers, you decide to take it to an automotive repair facility that they highly recommend. It is the only repair facility located in close proximity to you.

When you arrive at the repair facility, you find that all the mechanics speak another language. You are having difficulty explaining the automobile's performance problems, but the repairs really need to be done. You are not sure you can drive it back home to research other options.

You must find a way to work with the repair facility to ensure that your automobile is fixed correctly.

How will you communicate with the mechanics in this firm? Design a communications model to ensure that the car is properly repaired.

Rules of Communication (3.1)

For communication to occur between two people or objects, both must follow a set of predetermined rules.

The Rules (3.1.1)

A network can be as complex as devices connected across the Internet, or as simple as two computers directly connected to one another with a single cable, and anything in between. Networks can vary in size, shape, and function. However, simply having the physical connection between end devices is not enough to enable communication. For communication to occur, devices must know "how" to communicate.

What Is Communication? (3.1.1.1)

People exchange ideas using many different communication methods. However, regardless of the method chosen, all communication methods have three elements in common. The first of these elements is the message *source*, or sender. Message sources are people, or electronic devices, that need to send a message to other individuals or devices. The second element of communication is the *destination*, or receiver, of the message. The destination receives the message and interprets it. A third element, called a *channel*, consists of the media that provides the pathway over which the message travels from source to destination. This is shown in Figure 3-1.

Figure 3-1   Communications

Communication begins with a message, or information, that must be sent from a source to a destination. The sending of this message, whether by face-to-face communication or over a network, is governed by rules called protocols. These protocols are specific to the type of communication method that is occurring. In our day-to-day personal communication, the rules we use to communicate over one medium, like a telephone call, are not necessarily the same as the protocols for using another medium, such as sending a letter.

For example, consider two people communicating face to face. Prior to communicating, they must agree on how to communicate. If the communication is using voice, they must first agree on the language. Next, when they have a message to share, they must be able to format that message in a way that is understandable. For example, if someone uses the English language, but poor sentence structure, the message can easily be misunderstood. Each of these tasks describes protocols put in place to accomplish communication. This is also true of computer communication.

Think of how many different rules or protocols govern all the different methods of communication that exist in the world today.

Establishing the Rules (3.1.1.2)

Before communicating with one another, individuals must use established rules or agreements to govern the conversation. Figure 3-2 shows why *protocols* are necessary for effective communication. Without correct formatting and adherence to established rules and protocols, it is very difficult to interpret the message.

humans communication between govern rules.
Itisverydifficulttounderstandmessagesthatarenotcorrectlyformattedanddonotfollow
theestablishedrulesandprotocols. A estrutura da gramatica, da lingua, da
pontuacao e do sentance faz a configuracao humana compreensivel por muitos
individuos diferentes.

Rules govern communication between humans. It is very difficult to understand
messages that are not correctly formatted and do not follow the established rules
and protocols. The structure of the grammar, the language, the punctuation and
the sentence make the configuration humanly understandable for many different
individuals.

Figure 3-2   Importance of Protocols

The protocols used are specific to the characteristics of the communication method, including the characteristics of the source, destination, and channel. These rules, or protocols, must be followed for the message to be successfully delivered and understood. There are many protocols available that govern successful human communication. After there is an agreed-upon method of communicating (face-to-face, telephone, letter, photography), the protocols put in place must account for the following requirements:

- An identified sender and receiver
- Common language and grammar
- Speed and timing of delivery
- Confirmation or acknowledgement requirements

As shown in Figure 3-3, the protocols that are used in network communications share many of the fundamental traits as those protocols used to govern successful human conversations. In addition to identifying the source and destination, computer and network protocols define the details of how a message is transmitted across a network to answer the previous requirements. While there are many protocols that must interact, common computer protocols include

- Message encoding
- Message formatting and encapsulation
- Message size
- Message timing
- Message delivery options

Each of these will be discussed in more detail next.

Figure 3-3   Protocols

Message Encoding (3.1.1.3)

One of the first steps to sending a message is *encoding* it. Encoding is the process of converting information into another, acceptable form for transmission. Decoding reverses this process to interpret the information.

Imagine a person planning a holiday trip with a friend, and calling the friend to discuss the details of where they want to go. To communicate the message, the sender must first convert, or encode, his thoughts and perceptions about the location into words. The words are spoken into the telephone using the sounds and inflections of spoken language that convey the message. On the other end of the telephone line, the person listening to the description receives and decodes the sounds to visualize the image of the sunset described by the sender.

Encoding also occurs in computer communication. Encoding between hosts must be in an appropriate form for the medium. Messages sent across the network are first converted into bits by the sending host. Each bit is encoded into a pattern of sounds, light waves, or electrical impulses, depending on the network media over which the bits are transmitted. The destination host receives and decodes the signals to interpret the message.

Message Formatting and Encapsulation (3.1.1.4)

When a message is sent from source to destination, it must use a specific format or structure. Message formats depend on the type of message and the channel that is used to deliver the message.

Letter writing is one of the most common forms of written human communication. For centuries, the agreed-upon format for personal letters has not changed. In many cultures, a personal letter contains the following elements:

- An identifier of the recipient
- A salutation or greeting
- The message content
- A closing phrase
- An identifier of the sender

In addition to having the correct format, most personal letters must also be enclosed, or encapsulated, in an envelope for delivery, as shown in Figure 3-4. The envelope has the address of the sender and receiver on it, each located at the proper place on the envelope. If the destination address and formatting are not correct, the letter is not delivered. The process of placing one message format (the letter) inside another message format (the envelope) is called *encapsulation*. Deencapsulation occurs when the process is reversed by the recipient and the letter is removed from the envelope.

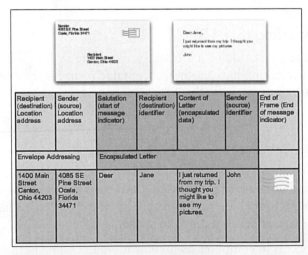

Recipient (destination) Location address	Sender (source) Location address	Salutation (start of message indicator)	Recipient (destination) identifier	Content of Letter (encapsulated data)	Sender (source) identifier	End of Frame (End of message indicator)
Envelope Addressing		Encapsulated Letter				
1400 Main Street Canton, Ohio 44203	4085 SE Pine Street Ocala, Florida 34471	Dear	Jane	I just returned from my trip. I thought you might like to see my pictures.	John	

Figure 3-4   Formatting and Encapsulation for a Postal Letter

A letter writer uses an accepted format to ensure that the letter is delivered and understood by the recipient. In the same way, a message that is sent over a computer network follows specific format rules for it to be delivered and processed. Just as a letter is encapsulated in an envelope for delivery, so too are computer messages encapsulated. Each computer message is encapsulated in a specific format, called a frame, before it is sent over the network. A frame acts like an envelope; it provides the address of the intended destination and the address of the source host, as shown in Figure 3-5.

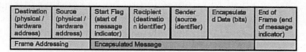

Destination (physical / hardware address)	Source (physical / hardware address)	Start Flag (start of message indicator)	Recipient (destination identifier)	Sender (source identifier)	Encapsulated Data (bits)	End of Frame (end of message indicator)
Frame Addressing		Encapsulated Message				

Figure 3-5 Frame

The format and contents of a frame are determined by the type of message being sent and the channel over which it is communicated. Messages that are not correctly formatted are not successfully delivered to or processed by the destination host.

Message Size (3.1.1.5)

Another rule of communication is size. When people communicate with each other, the messages that they send are usually broken into smaller parts or sentences. These sentences are limited in size to what the receiving person can process at one time. An individual conversation can be made up of many smaller sentences to ensure that each part of the message is received and understood. Imagine what it would be like to read this course if it all appeared as one long sentence; it would not be easy to read and comprehend.

Likewise, when a long message is sent from one host to another over a network, it is necessary to break the message into smaller pieces. The rules that govern the size of the pieces, or frames, communicated across the network are very strict. They can also be different, depending on the channel used. Frames that are too long or too short are not delivered.

The size restrictions of frames require the source host to break a long message into individual pieces that meet both the minimum and maximum size requirements. This is known as *segmenting*. Each segment is encapsulated in a separate frame with the address information, and is sent over the network. At the receiving host, the messages are deencapsulated and put back together to be processed and interpreted.

Message Timing (3.1.1.6)

Another factor that affects how well a message is received and understood is timing. People use timing to determine when to speak, how fast or slow to talk, and how long to wait for a response. These are the rules of engagement.

Access Method

The access method determines when someone is able to send a message. These timing rules are based on the environment. For example, you might be able to speak whenever you have something to say. In this environment, a person must wait until no one else is talking before speaking. If two people talk at the same time, a collision of information occurs and it is necessary for the two to back off and start again. Likewise, it is necessary for computers to define an access method. Hosts on a network need an access method to know when to begin sending messages and how to respond when errors occur.

Flow Control

Timing also affects how much information can be sent and the speed in which it can be delivered. If one person speaks too quickly, it is difficult for the other person to hear and understand the message. The receiving person must ask the sender to slow down. In network communication, a sending host can transmit messages at a faster rate than the destination host can receive and process. Source and destination hosts use flow control to negotiate correct timing for successful communication.

Response Timeout

If a person asks a question and does not hear a response within an acceptable amount of time, the person assumes that no answer is coming and reacts accordingly. The person might repeat the question or might go on with the conversation. Hosts on the network also have rules that specify how long to wait for responses and what action to take if a response timeout occurs.

Message Delivery Options (3.1.1.7)

A message might need to be best delivered in different ways. Sometimes, a person wants to communicate information to a single individual. At other times, the person might need to send information to a group of people at the same time, or even to all people in the same area. A conversation between two people is an example of a one-to-one delivery. When a group of recipients need to receive the same message simultaneously, a one-to-many or one-to-all message delivery is necessary.

There are also times when the sender of a message needs to be sure that the message is delivered successfully to the destination. In these cases, it is necessary for the recipient to return an *acknowledgement* to the sender. If no acknowledgement is required, the delivery option is referred to as unacknowledged.

Hosts on a network use similar delivery options to communicate.

A one-to-one delivery option is referred to as a *unicast*, meaning that there is only a single destination for the message.

When a host needs to send messages using a one-to-many delivery option, it is referred to as a *multicast*. Multicasting is the delivery of the same message to a group of host destinations simultaneously.

If all hosts on the network need to receive the message at the same time, a *broadcast* is used. Broadcasting represents a one-to-all message delivery option. Additionally, hosts have requirements for acknowledged versus unacknowledged messages.

Network Protocols and Standards (3.2)

A strict set of rules must be adhered to in order to allow communication to occur between humans or machines. To ensure that these rules or protocols function together and in a predictable manner, a number of organizations and processes have been developed to provide standards.

Protocols (3.2.1)

Just like in human communication, the various network and computer protocols must be able to interact and work together for network communication to be successful. A group of inter-related protocols necessary to perform a communication function is called a *protocol suite*. Protocol suites are implemented by hosts and networking devices in software, hardware, or both.

Protocols: Rules That Govern Communications (3.2.1.1)

One of the best ways to visualize how the protocols within a suite interact is to view the interaction as a stack. A protocol stack shows how the individual protocols within a suite are implemented. The protocols are viewed in terms of layers, with each higher-level service depending on the functionality defined by the protocols shown in the lower levels. The lower layers of the stack are concerned with moving data over the network and providing services to the upper layers, which are focused on the content of the message being sent. As shown in Figure 3-6, we can use layers to describe the activity occurring in our face-to-face communication example. At the bottom layer, the physical layer, we have two people, each with a voice that can say words out loud. At the second layer, the rules layer, we have an agreement to speak in a common language. At the top layer, the content layer, there are words that are actually spoken. This is the content of the communication.

Figure 3-6   Protocols—Rules That Govern Communications

Were we to witness this conversation, we would not actually see layers floating in space. The use of layers is a model that provides a way to conveniently break a complex task into parts and describe how they work.

Network Protocols (3.2.1.2)

At the human level, some communication rules are formal and others are simply understood based on custom and practice. For devices to successfully communicate, a network protocol suite must describe precise requirements and interactions. Networking protocols define a common format and set of rules for exchanging messages between devices. Some common networking protocols are IP, HTTP, and DHCP.

Figure 3-7 illustrates networking protocols that describe the following processes:

- How the message is formatted or structured, as shown in Figure 3-7a

- The process by which networking devices share information about pathways with other networks, as shown in Figure 3-7b

- How and when error and system messages are passed between devices, as shown in Figure 3-7c

- The setup and termination of data transfer sessions, as shown in Figure 3-7d

a

b

c

d

Figure 3-7   Role of Protocols

For example, IP defines how a packet of data is delivered within a network or to a remote network. The information in the IPv4 protocol is transmitted in a specific format so that the receiver can interpret it correctly. This is not much different than the protocol used to address an envelope when mailing a letter. The information must adhere to a certain format, or the letter cannot be delivered to the destination by the post office.

Interaction of Protocols (3.2.1.3)

An example of using the protocol suite in network communications is the interaction between a web server and a web client, as shown in Figure 3-8.

Figure 3-8   Interaction of Protocols

This interaction uses a number of protocols and standards in the process of exchanging information between them. The different protocols work together to ensure that the messages are received and understood by both parties. Examples of these protocols are

- **Application protocol:** Hypertext Transfer Protocol (HTTP) is a protocol that governs the way that a web server and a web client interact. HTTP defines the content and formatting of the requests and responses that are exchanged between the client and server. Both the client and the web server software implement HTTP as part of the application. HTTP relies on other protocols to govern how the messages are transported between the client and server.

- **Transport protocol:** Transmission Control Protocol (TCP) is the transport protocol that manages the individual conversations between web servers and web clients. TCP divides the HTTP messages into smaller pieces, called segments. These segments are sent between the web server and client processes running at the destination host. TCP is also responsible for controlling the size and rate at which messages are exchanged between the server and the client.

- **Internet protocol:** IP is responsible for taking the formatted segments from TCP, encapsulating them into packets, assigning them the appropriate addresses, and delivering them across the best path to the destination host.

- **Network access protocols:** Network access protocols describe two primary functions: communication over a data link and the physical transmission of data on the network media. Data-link management protocols take the packets from IP and format them to be transmitted over the media. The standards and protocols for the physical media govern how the signals are sent and how they are interpreted by the receiving clients. An example of a network access protocol is Ethernet.

Protocol Suites (3.2.2)

As stated previously, a protocol suite is a set of protocols that work together to provide comprehensive network communication services. A protocol suite can be specified by a standards organization or developed by a vendor.

Protocol Suites and Industry Standards (3.2.2.1)

The protocols IP, HTTP, and DHCP are all part of the Internet protocol suite known as Transmission Control Protocol/IP (TCP/IP). The TCP/IP protocol suite is an open standard, meaning that these protocols are freely available to the public, and any vendor is able to implement these protocols on its hardware or in its software.

A standards-based protocol is a process or protocol that has been endorsed by the networking industry and ratified, or approved, by a standards organization. The use of standards in developing and implementing protocols ensures that products from different manufacturers can interoperate successfully. If a protocol is not rigidly observed by a particular manufacturer, its equipment or software might not be able to successfully communicate with products made by other manufacturers.

In data communications, for example, if one end of a conversation is using a protocol to govern one-way communication and the other end is assuming a protocol describing two-way communication, in all probability, no data will be exchanged.

Some protocols are *proprietary*. Proprietary, in this context, means that one company or vendor controls the definition of the protocol and how it functions. Some proprietary protocols can be used by different organizations with permission from the owner. Others can only be implemented on equipment manufactured by the proprietary vendor. Examples of proprietary protocols are AppleTalk and Novell NetWare.

Several companies might even work together to create a proprietary protocol. It is not uncommon for a vendor (or a group of vendors) to develop a proprietary protocol to meet the needs of its customers and later assist in making that proprietary protocol an open standard. For example, *Ethernet* was a protocol originally developed by Bob Metcalfe at the Xerox Palo Alto Research Center (PARC) in the 1970s. In 1979, Bob Metcalfe formed his own company, 3COM, and worked with Digital Equipment Corporation (DEC), Intel, and Xerox to promote the "DIX" standard for Ethernet. In 1985, the Institute of Electrical and Electronics Engineers (IEEE) published the IEEE 802.3 standard that was almost identical to Ethernet. Today, 802.3 is the common standard used in local-area networks (LAN). As another example, most recently, Cisco opened the Enhanced Interior Gateway Routing Protocol (EIGRP) as an informational RFC to meet the needs of customers who desire to use the protocol in a multivendor network.

Figure 3-9 shows some common protocol suites and industry standards.

Protocol Suites and Industry Standards			
TCP/IP	**ISO**	**AppleTalk**	**Novell Netware**
HTTP DNS DHCP FTP	ACSE ROSE TRSE SESE	AFP	NDS
TCP UDP	TP0 TP1 TP2 TP3 TP4	ATP AEP NBP RTMP	SPX
IPv4 IPv6 ICMPv4 ICMPv6	CONP/CMNS CLNP/CLNS	AARP	IPX
Ethernet PPP Frame Relay ATM WLAN			

Figure 3-9   Protocol Suites and Industry Standards

Creation of the Internet and Development of TCP/IP (3.2.2.2)

The IP suite is a suite of protocols required for transmitting and receiving information using the Internet. It is commonly known as TCP/IP because the first two networking protocols defined for this standard were TCP and IP. The open standards–based TCP/IP has replaced other vendor-proprietary protocol suites, such as Apple's AppleTalk and Novell's Internetwork Packet Exchange/Sequenced Packet Exchange (IPX/SPX).

The first packet-switching network and predecessor to today's Internet was the Advanced Research Projects Agency Network (ARPANET), which came to life in 1969 by connecting mainframe computers at four locations. ARPANET was funded by the U.S. Department of Defense for use by universities and research laboratories. Bolt, Beranek and Newman (BBN) was the contractor that did much of the initial development of the ARPANET, including creating the first router known as an Interface Message Processor (IMP).

In 1973, Robert Kahn and Vinton Cerf began work on TCP to develop the next generation of the ARPANET. TCP was designed to replace ARPANET's current Network Control Program (NCP). In 1978, TCP was divided into two protocols: TCP and IP. Later, other protocols were added to the TCP/IP suite of protocols, including Telnet, FTP, DNS, and many others.

Some important dates in the development of network protocols and applications are

- 1969: On October 29, 1969, the first message is transmitted from an SDS Sigma 7 mainframe computer at the University of California, Los Angeles (UCLA) to an SDS 940 mainframe computer at Stanford Research Institute.

- 1970: ALOHAnet becomes operational. It is the first packet radio network, developed by Norman Abramson, University of Hawaii.

- 1972: Ray Tomlinson chooses the @ sign to signify the recipient's destination.

- 1972: Larry Roberts writes the first email management program.

- 1972: The Telnet specification is written (RFC 318).

- 1981: The TCP and IP protocols are formalized (RFC 793 and RFC 791).

- 1982: The Exterior Gateway Protocol (EGP) is developed to allow routers to exchange network information (RFC 827).

- 1984: The Domain Name Service (DNS) is introduced.

- 1985: The File Transfer Protocol (FTP) is documented (RFC 765).

- 1986: Cisco launches its first routing innovation, the AGS multiprotocol router.

- 1988: The Internet Relay Chat (IRC) is developed by Jarkko Oikarinen.

- 1991: Tim Bemers-Lee and Robert Cailliau release the specifications for WWW.

- 1993: The first web browser, MOSAIC, is developed by Marc Andreessen at the University of Illinois, Champaign-Urbana.

- 1995: The first specifications for IPv6 (the eventual successor to IPv4) are released (RFC 1883).

- 2011: The first World IPv6 Day (June 8, 2011). Many websites and Internet service providers around the world, including Google, Facebook, and Yahoo!, participate with more than 1000 other companies for a worldwide trial of IPv6.

- 2012: The launch of the permanent IPv6 Internet on June 6, 2012.

TCP/IP Protocol Suite and Communication Process (3.2.2.3)

Today, the suite includes dozens of protocols, as shown in Figure 3-10. They are organized in layers using the TCP/IP protocol model. TCP/IP protocols are included in the Internet layer to the application layer when referencing the TCP/IP model. The lower-layer protocols in the data link or network access layer are responsible for delivering the IP packet over the physical medium. These lower-layer protocols are developed by standards organizations such as IEEE. Table 3-1 describes the function of some of the protocols found in the TCP/IP suite.

Figure 3-10   TCP/IP Protocol Suite and Communication Process

Table 3-1   Common TCP/IP Protocols and Processes

Protocol or Process	Description
Domain Name System (or Service) (DNS)	Translates domain names, such as cisco.com, into IP addresses.
Bootstrap Protocol (BOOTP)	Enables a diskless workstation to discover its own IP address, the IP address of a BOOTP server on the network, and a file to be loaded into memory to boot the machine. BOOTP is being superseded by DHCP.
Dynamic Host Configuration Protocol (DHCP)	Dynamically assigns IP addresses to client stations at startup. Allows the addresses to be reused when no longer needed.
Simple Mail Transfer Protocol (SMTP)	Enables clients to send email to a mail server. Enables mail servers to send email to other servers.
Post Office Protocol version 3 (POP3)	Enables clients to retrieve email from a mail server. Downloads email from the mail server to the desktop.
Internet Message Access Protocol (IMAP)	Enables clients to access email stored on a mail server. Maintains email on the server.

Protocol or Process	Description
File Transfer Protocol (FTP)	Sets rules that enable a user on one host to access and transfer files to and from another host over a network.
	A reliable, connection-oriented, and acknowledged file-delivery protocol.
Trivial File Transfer Protocol (TFTP)	A simple, connectionless file transfer protocol.
	A best-effort, unacknowledged file delivery protocol.
	Utilizes less overhead than FTP.
Hypertext Transfer Protocol (HTTP)	A set of rules for exchanging text, graphic images, sound, video, and other multimedia files on the World Wide Web.
User Datagram Protocol (UDP)	Enables a process running on one host to send packets to a process running on another host.
	Does not confirm successful datagram transmission.
Transmission Control Protocol (TCP)	Enables reliable communication between processes running on separate hosts.
	Reliable, acknowledged transmissions that confirm successful delivery.
Internet Protocol (IP)	Receives message segments from the transport layer.
	Packages messages into packets.
	Addresses packets for end-to-end delivery over an internetwork.
Network Address Translation (NAT)	Translates IP addresses from a private network into a globally unique public IP address.
Internet Control Message Protocol (ICMP)	Provides feedback from a destination host to a source host about errors in packet delivery.
Open Shortest Path First (OSPF)	Link-state routing protocol.
	Hierarchical design based on areas.
	Open standard interior routing protocol.
Enhanced Interior Gateway Routing Protocol (EIGRP)	Cisco-proprietary routing protocol.
	Uses composite metric based on bandwidth, delay, load, and reliability.

Protocol or Process	Description
Address Resolution Protocol (ARP)	Provides dynamic address mapping between an IP address and a hardware address.
Point-to-Point Protocol (PPP)	Provides a means of encapsulating packets for transmission over a serial link.
Ethernet	Defines the rules for wiring and signaling standards of the network access layer.
Interface driver	Provides instruction to a machine for the control of a specific interface on a network device.

The TCP/IP protocol suite is implemented within the operating system and software as a TCP/IP stack on both the sending and receiving hosts to provide end-to-end delivery of applications over a network. The 802.3 or Ethernet protocols are used to transmit the IP packet over the physical medium used by the LAN.

Figure 3-11 and the following list show the complete communication process using an example of a web server transmitting data to a client.

Figure 3-11   Protocol Operation of Sending and Receiving a Message

1. The web server's Hypertext Markup Language (HTML) page is the data to be sent.

2. The application protocol HTTP header is added to the front of the HTML data. The header contains various information, including the HTTP version the server is using and a status code indicating that it has information for the web client.

3. The HTTP application layer protocol delivers the HTML-formatted web page data to the transport layer. The TCP transport layer protocol is used to manage the individual conversation between the web server and web client.

4. The IP information is added to the front of the TCP information. IP assigns the appropriate source and destination IP addresses. This information is known as an IP packet.

5. The Ethernet protocol adds information to both ends of the IP packet, known as a data-link frame. This frame is delivered to the nearest router along the path toward the web client. This router removes the Ethernet information, analyzes the IP packet, determines the best path for the packet, inserts the packet into a new frame, and sends it to the next neighboring router toward the destination. Each router removes and adds new data-link information before forwarding the packet.

6. This data is now transported through the internetwork, which consists of media and intermediary devices.

7. The client receives the data-link frames that contain the data, and each protocol header is processed and then removed in the opposite order that it was added. The Ethernet information is processed and removed, followed by the IP protocol information, then the TCP information, and finally the HTTP information.

8. The web page information is then passed on to the client's web browser software.

Interactive Graphic

Activity 3.2.2.4: Mapping the Protocols of the TCP/IP Suite

Go to the course online to perform this practice activity.

Standards Organizations (3.2.3)

Standards organizations are important in maintaining an open Internet with freely accessible specifications and protocols that can be implemented by any vendor. A standards organization might draft a set of rules entirely on its own or in other cases might select a proprietary protocol as the basis for the *standard*. If a proprietary protocol is used, it usually involves the vendor who created the protocol.

Open Standards (3.2.3.1)

Open standards encourage competition and innovation. They also guarantee that no single company's product can monopolize the market, or have an unfair advantage over its competition. A good example of this is when purchasing a wireless router for the home. There are many different choices available from a variety of vendors, all of which incorporate standard protocols such as IPv4, DHCP, 802.3 (Ethernet), and 802.11 (wireless LAN). These open standards also allow a client running Apple's OS X operating system to download a web page from a web server running the

Linux operating system. This is because both operating systems implement the open standard protocols, such as those in the TCP/IP suite.

Standards organizations are usually vendor-neutral, nonprofit organizations established to develop and promote the concept of open standards.

Standards organizations include

- The Internet Society (ISOC)
- The Internet Architecture Board (IAB)
- The Internet Engineering Task Force (IETF)
- The Institute of Electrical and Electronics Engineers (IEEE)
- The International Organization for Standardization (ISO)

ISOC, IAB, and IETF (3.2.3.2)

The Internet Society (ISOC) is responsible for promoting open development, evolution, and Internet use throughout the world. ISOC facilitates the open development of standards and protocols for the technical infrastructure of the Internet, including the oversight of the Internet Architecture Board (IAB).

The Internet Architecture Board (IAB) is responsible for the overall management and development of Internet standards. The IAB provides oversight of the architecture for protocols and procedures used by the Internet. The IAB consists of 13 members, including the chair of the Internet Engineering Task Force (IETF). IAB members serve as individuals and not representatives of any company, agency, or other organization.

The IETF's mission is to develop, update, and maintain Internet and TCP/IP technologies. One of the key responsibilities of the IETF is to produce Request for Comments (RFC) documents, which are a memorandum describing protocols, processes, and technologies for the Internet. The IETF consists of working groups (WG), the primary mechanism for developing IETF specifications and guidelines. WGs are short term, and after the objectives of the group are met, the WG is terminated. The Internet Engineering Steering Group (IESG) is responsible for the technical management of the IETF and the Internet standards process.

The Internet Research Task Force (IRTF) is focused on long-term research related to Internet and TCP/IP protocols, applications, architecture, and technologies. While the IETF focuses on shorter-term issues of creating standards, the IRTF consists of research groups for long-term development efforts. Some of the current research groups include Anti-Spam Research Group (ASRG), Crypto Forum Research Group (CFRG), Peer-to-Peer Research Group (P2PRG), and Router Research Group (RRG).

IEEE (3.2.3.3)

The Institute of Electrical and Electronics Engineers (IEEE, pronounced "I-triple-E") is a professional organization for those in the electrical engineering and electronics fields who are dedicated to advancing technological innovation and creating standards. As of 2012, IEEE consists of 38 societies, publishes 130 journals, and sponsors more than 1300 conferences each year worldwide. The IEEE has over 1300 standards and projects currently under development.

The IEEE has more than 400,000 members in more than 160 countries. More than 107,000 of those members are student members. IEEE provides educational and career enhancement opportunities to promote the skills and knowledge with the electronics industry.

The IEEE is one of the leading standards-producing organizations in the world. It creates and maintains standards affecting a wide range of industries including power and energy, healthcare, telecommunications, and networking. The IEEE 802 family of standards deals with local-area networks and metropolitan-area networks, including both wired and wireless. Each IEEE standard consists of a WG responsible for creating and improving the standards. Table 3-2 lists some of these working groups.

Table 3-2   IEEE 802 Working Groups and Study Groups

Group	Responsibility
802.1	Higher Layer LAN Protocols Working Group
802.3	Ethernet Working Group
802.11	Wireless LAN Working Group
802.15	Wireless Personal Area Network (WPAN) Working Group
802.16	Broadband Wireless Access Working Group
802.18	Radio Regulatory TAG
802.19	Wireless Coexistence Working Group
802.21	Media Independent Handover Services Working Group
802.22	Wireless Regional Area Networks
802.24	Smart Grid TAG

The IEEE 802.3 and IEEE 802.11 standards are significant IEEE standards in computer networking. The IEEE 802.3 standard defines Media Access Control (MAC) for wired Ethernet. This technology is usually for LANs, but also has wide-area network (WAN) applications. The 802.11 standard defines a set of standards for implementing wireless local-area networks (WLAN). This standard defines the Open Systems Interconnection (OSI) physical and data link MAC for wireless communications.

ISO (3.2.3.4)

ISO, the International Organization for Standardization, is the world's largest developer of international standards for a wide variety of products and services. ISO is not an acronym for the organization's name; rather the ISO term is based on the Greek word *isos*, meaning equal. The International Organization for Standardization chose the ISO term to affirm its position as being equal to all countries.

In networking, ISO is best known for its Open Systems Interconnection (OSI) reference model. ISO published the OSI reference model in 1984 to develop a layered framework for networking protocols. The original objective of this project was not only to create a reference model but also to serve as a foundation for a suite of protocols to be used for the Internet. This was known as the OSI protocol suite. However, because of the rising popularity of the TCP/IP suite, developed by Robert Kahn, Vinton Cerf, and others, the OSI protocol suite was not chosen as the protocol suite for the Internet. Instead, the TCP/IP protocol suite was selected. The OSI protocol suite was implemented on telecommunications equipment and can still be found in legacy telecommunication networks.

You might be familiar with some of the products that use ISO standards. The ISO file extension is used on many CD images to signify that it uses the ISO 9660 standard for its file system. ISO is also responsible for creating standards for routing protocols.

Other Standards Organizations (3.2.3.5)

Networking standards involve several other standards organizations. Some of the more common ones are

- **EIA:** The Electronic Industries Alliance (EIA), previously known as the Electronics Industries Association, is an international standards and trade organization for electronics organizations. The EIA is best known for its standards related to electrical wiring, connectors, and the 19-inch racks used to mount networking equipment.

- **TIA:** The Telecommunications Industry Association (TIA) is responsible for developing communication standards in a variety of areas including radio equipment, cellular towers, Voice over IP (VoIP) devices, satellite communications, and more. Many of its standards are produced in collaboration with the EIA.

- **ITU-T:** The International Telecommunications Union-Telecommunication Standardization Sector (ITU-T) is one of the largest and oldest communication standard organizations. The ITU-T defines standards for video compression, Internet Protocol Television (IPTV), and broadband communications, such as a digital subscriber line (DSL). For example, when dialing another country, ITU country codes are used to make the connection.

- **ICANN:** The Internet Corporation for Assigned Names and Numbers (ICANN) is a nonprofit organization based in the United States that coordinates IP address allocation, the management of domain names used by DNS, and the protocol identifiers or port numbers used by TCP and UDP protocols. ICANN creates policies and has overall responsibility for these assignments.

- **IANA:** The Internet Assigned Numbers Authority (IANA) is a department of ICANN responsible for overseeing and managing IP address allocation, domain name management, and protocol identifiers for ICANN.

Familiarization with the organizations that develop standards used in networking will help you have a better understanding of how these standards create an open, vendor-neutral Internet, and allow you to learn about new standards as they develop.

Lab 3.2.3.6: Researching Networking Standards

In this lab, you will complete the following objectives:

- Part 1: Research Networking Standards Organizations
- Part 2: Reflect on Internet and Computer Networking Experiences

---

Interactive Graphic

Activity 3.2.3.7: Standards Body Scavenger Hunt

Go to the course online to perform this practice activity.

Reference Models (3.2.4)

There are two basic types of networking models:

- **Protocol model:** This model closely matches the structure of a particular protocol suite. The hierarchical set of related protocols in a suite typically represents all the functionality required to interface the human network with the data network. The TCP/IP model is a protocol model, because it describes the functions that occur at each layer of protocols within the TCP/IP suite.

■ **Reference model:** This model provides consistency within all types of network protocols and services by describing what has to be done at a particular layer, but not prescribing how it should be accomplished. A reference model is not intended to be an implementation specification or to provide a sufficient level of detail to define precisely the services of the network architecture. The primary purpose of a reference model is to aid in clearer understanding of the functions and processes involved.

The Benefits of Using a Layered Model (3.2.4.1)

A layered model, such as the TCP/IP model, is often used to help visualize the interaction between various protocols. A layered model depicts the operation of the protocols occurring within each layer, as well as the interaction of protocols with the layers above and below each layer.

There are benefits to using a layered model to describe network protocols and operations. Using a layered model

■ Assists in protocol design, because protocols that operate at a specific layer have defined information that they act upon and a defined interface to the layers above and below.

■ Fosters competition because products from different vendors can work together.

■ Prevents technology or capability changes in one layer from affecting other layers above and below.

■ Provides a common language to describe networking functions and capabilities.

The OSI model is the most widely known internetwork reference model. It is used for data network design, operation specifications, and troubleshooting.

The TCP/IP and OSI models, shown in Figure 3-12, are the primary models used when discussing network functionality. Designers of network protocols, services, or devices can create their own models to represent their products. Ultimately, designers are required to communicate to the industry by relating their product or service to either the OSI model or the TCP/IP model, or to both.

Figure 3-12   OSI and TCP/IP Models

The OSI Reference Model (3.2.4.2)

Initially the OSI model was designed by the ISO to provide a framework on which to build a suite of open systems protocols. The vision was that this set of protocols would be used to develop an international network that would not be dependent on proprietary systems.

Ultimately, the speed at which the TCP/IP-based Internet was adopted, and the rate at which it expanded, caused the development and acceptance of the OSI protocol suite to lag behind. Although a few of the developed protocols using the OSI specifications are widely used today, the seven-layer OSI model has made major contributions to the development of other protocols and products for all types of new networks.

The OSI model provides an extensive list of functions and services that can occur at each layer. It also describes the interaction of each layer with the layers directly above and below it. Although the content of this course is structured around the OSI reference model, the focus of discussion is the protocols identified in the TCP/IP protocol model. Table 3-3 lists the function of each of the layers found in the OSI reference model.

Table 3-3   OSI Reference Model

Layer	Layer Name	Description
7	Application	The application layer provides the means for end-to-end connectivity between individuals in the human network using data networks.
6	Presentation	The presentation layer provides common representation of the data transferred between application layer services.
5	Session	The session layer provides services to the presentation layer to organize its dialogue and to manage data exchange.
4	Transport	The transport layer defines services to segment, transfer, and reassemble the data for individual communications between end devices.
3	Network	The network layer provides services to exchange the individual pieces of data over the network between identified end devices.
2	Data Link	The data link layer protocols describe methods for exchanging data frames between devices over a common media.
1	Physical	The physical layer protocols describe the mechanical, electrical, functional, and procedural means to activate, maintain, and deactivate physical connections for bit transmissions to and from a network device.

Note

Whereas the TCP/IP model layers are referred to only by name, the seven OSI model layers are more often referred to by number rather than by name. For example, the physical layer is referred to as Layer 1 of the OSI model.

The TCP/IP Protocol Model (3.2.4.3)

The TCP/IP protocol model for internetwork communications was created in the early 1970s and is sometimes referred to as the Internet model. As shown in Figure 3-13, it defines four categories of functions that must occur for communications to be successful. The architecture of the TCP/IP protocol suite follows the structure of this model. Because of this, the Internet model is commonly referred to as the TCP/IP model.

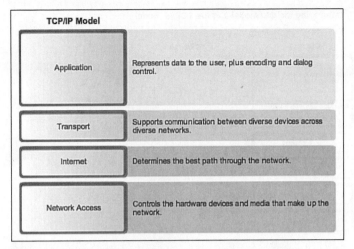

Figure 3-13 TCP/IP Model

Most protocol models describe a vendor-specific protocol stack. However, because the TCP/IP model is an open standard, one company does not control the definition of the model. The definitions of the standard and the TCP/IP protocols are discussed in a public forum and defined in a publicly available set of *RFCs*. The RFCs contain both the formal specification of data communications protocols and resources that describe the use of the protocols.

The RFCs also contain technical and organizational documents about the Internet, including the technical specifications and policy documents produced by the IETF.

Comparing the OSI Model with the TCP/IP Model (3.2.4.4)

The protocols that make up the TCP/IP protocol suite can be described in terms of the OSI reference model. In the OSI model, the network access layer and the application layer of the TCP/IP model are further divided to describe discrete functions that must occur at these layers.

At the network access layer, the TCP/IP protocol suite does not specify which protocols to use when transmitting over a physical medium; it only describes the handoff from the Internet layer to the physical network protocols. OSI Layers 1 and 2 discuss the necessary procedures to access the media and the physical means to send data over a network.

As shown in Figure 3-14, the critical parallels between the two network models occur at OSI Layers 3 and 4. OSI Layer 3, the network layer, is almost universally used to describe the range of processes that occur in all data networks to address and route messages through an internetwork. IP is the TCP/IP suite protocol that includes the functionality described at OSI Layer 3.

Figure 3-14 Comparing the OSI Model and the TCP/IP Model

Layer 4, the transport layer of the OSI model, describes general services and functions that provide ordered and reliable delivery of data between source and destination hosts. These functions include acknowledgement, error recovery, and sequencing. At this layer, the TCP/IP protocols TCP and User Datagram Protocol (UDP) provide the necessary functionality.

The TCP/IP application layer includes a number of protocols that provide specific functionality to a variety of end-user applications. The OSI model Layers 5, 6, and 7 are used as references for application software developers and vendors to produce products that operate on networks.

Interactive Graphic

Activity 3.2.4.5: Identify Layers and Functions

Go to the course online to perform this practice activity.

Packet Tracer ☐ Activity

Packet Tracer Activity 3.2.4.6: Investigating the TCP/IP and OSI Models in Action

This simulation activity is intended to provide a foundation for understanding the TCP/IP protocol suite and the relationship to the OSI model. Simulation mode allows you to view the data contents being sent across the network at each layer.

As data moves through the network, it is broken down into smaller pieces and identified so that the pieces can be put back together when they arrive at the destination. Each piece is assigned a specific name (protocol data unit [PDU]) and associated with a specific layer of the TCP/IP and OSI models. Packet Tracer simulation mode enables you to view each of the layers and the associated PDU. The following steps lead the user through the process of requesting a web page from a web server by using the web browser application available on a client PC.

Even though much of the information displayed will be discussed in more detail later, this is an opportunity to explore the functionality of Packet Tracer and be able to visualize the encapsulation process.

Lab 3.2.4.7: Researching RFCs

In this lab, you will complete the following objectives:

- Part 1: RFC Editor
- Part 2: Publishing RFCs

Moving Data in the Network (3.3)

To move through the network, data must be properly encapsulated with sufficient control and addressing information to allow it to move from the sender to the receiver. The actual information required depends on whether the data is destined for a local or remote resource.

Data Encapsulation (3.3.1)

In theory, a single communication, such as a music video or an email message, could be sent across a network from a source to a destination as one massive, uninterrupted stream of bits. If messages were actually transmitted in this manner, it would mean that no other device would be able to send or receive messages on the same network while this data transfer was in progress. These large streams of data would result in significant delays. Further, if a link in the interconnected network infrastructure failed during the transmission, the complete message would be lost and have to be retransmitted in full.

Communicating the Messages (3.3.1.1)

A better approach is to divide the data into smaller, more manageable pieces to send over the network. This division of the data stream into smaller pieces is called *segmentation*. Segmenting messages has two primary benefits:

- By sending smaller individual pieces from source to destination, many different conversations can be interleaved on the network. The process used to interleave the pieces of separate conversations together on the network is called *multiplexing*.

■ Segmentation can increase the reliability of network communications. The separate pieces of each message need not travel the same pathway across the network from source to destination. If a particular path becomes congested with data traffic or fails, individual pieces of the message can still be directed to the destination using alternate pathways. If part of the message fails to make it to the destination, only the missing parts need to be retransmitted.

The downside to using segmentation and multiplexing to transmit messages across a network is the level of complexity that is added to the process. Imagine if you had to send a 100-page letter, but each envelope would only hold one page. The process of addressing, labeling, sending, receiving, and opening the entire 100 envelopes would be time-consuming for both the sender and the recipient.

In network communications, each segment of the message must go through a similar process to ensure that it gets to the correct destination and can be reassembled into the content of the original message. This is shown in Figure 3-15.

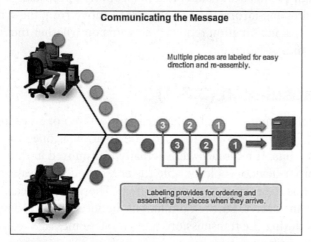

Figure 3-15   Communicating the Message

Various types of devices throughout the network participate in ensuring that the pieces of the message arrive reliably at their destination.

Protocol Data Units (PDU) (3.3.1.2)

As application data is passed down the protocol stack on its way to be transmitted across the network media, various protocols add information to it at each level. This is commonly known as the encapsulation process.

The form that a piece of data takes at any layer is called a ***protocol data unit (PDU)***. During encapsulation, each succeeding layer encapsulates the PDU that it receives from the layer above in accordance with the protocol being used. At each stage of the process, a PDU has a different name to reflect its new functions. This is shown in Figure 3-16.

Figure 3-16   Encapsulation

Although there is no universal naming convention for PDUs, in this course, the PDUs are named according to the protocols of the TCP/IP suite.

- **Data:** The general term for the PDU used at the application layer

- **Segment:** Transport layer PDU

- **Packet:** Internet layer PDU

- **Frame:** Network access layer PDU

- **Bits:** A PDU used when physically transmitting data over the medium

Encapsulation (3.3.1.3)

Data encapsulation is the process that adds additional protocol header information to the data before transmission. In most forms of data communications, the original data is encapsulated or wrapped in several protocols before being transmitted.

When sending messages on a network, the protocol stack on a host operates from top to bottom. In the web server example, we can use the TCP/IP model to illustrate the process of sending an HTML web page to a client.

The application layer protocol, HTTP, begins the process by delivering the HTML-formatted web page data to the transport layer. There the application data is broken into TCP segments. Each TCP segment is given a label, called a header, containing information about which process running on the destination computer should receive the message. It also contains the information that enables the destination process to reassemble the data to its original format.

The transport layer encapsulates the web page HTML data within the segment and sends it to the Internet layer, where the IP protocol is implemented. Here the entire TCP segment is encapsulated within an IP packet, which adds another label, called the IP header. The IP header contains source and destination host IP addresses, as well as information necessary to deliver the packet to its corresponding destination process.

Next, the IP packet is sent to the network access layer, where it is encapsulated within a frame header and trailer. Each frame header contains a source and destination physical address. The physical address uniquely identifies the devices on the local network. The trailer contains error-checking information. Finally, the bits are encoded onto the media by the server network interface card (NIC).

Deencapsulation (3.3.1.4)

This process is reversed at the receiving host and is known as deencapsulation. Deencapsulation is the process used by a receiving device to remove one or more of the protocol headers. The data is deencapsulated as it moves up the stack toward the end-user application.

Interactive Graphic

Activity 3.3.1.5: Identify the PDU Layer

Go to the course online to perform this practice activity.

Accessing Local Resources (3.3.2)

To access a network resource, the data must be encapsulated with the correct destination addresses and must also contain proper source addressing information to allow the destination device to reply. Accessing a local network resource requires two types of addresses with different roles.

Network Addresses and Data-Link Addresses (3.3.2.1)

The OSI model describes the processes of encoding, formatting, segmenting, and encapsulating data for transmission over the network. The network layer and data link layer are responsible for delivering the data from the source device or sender to the destination device or receiver. Protocols at both layers contain source and destination addresses, but their addresses have different purposes.

Network Address

The network layer, or Layer 3, logical address contains information required to deliver the IP packet from the source device to the destination device. A Layer 3 IP address has two parts, the *network prefix* and the host part. The network prefix is used by routers to forward the packet to the proper network. The host part is used by the last router in the path to deliver the packet to the destination device.

An IP packet contains two IP addresses:

- **Source IP address:** The IP address of the sending device.

- **Destination IP address:** The IP address of the receiving device. The destination IP address is used by routers to forward a packet to its destination.

Data Link Address

The data link, or Layer 2, physical address has a different role. The purpose of the data-link address is to deliver the data-link frame from one network interface to another network interface on the same network. Before an IP packet can be sent over a wired or wireless network, it must be encapsulated in a data-link frame so that it can be transmitted over the physical medium, the actual network. Ethernet LANs and wireless LANs are two examples of networks that have different physical media, each with its own type of data-link protocol.

The IP packet is encapsulated into a data-link frame to be delivered to the destination network. The source and destination data-link addresses are added, as shown in Figure 3-17:

- **Source data-link address:** The physical address of the device that is sending the packet. Initially this is the NIC that is the source of the IP packet.

- **Destination data-link address:** The physical address of the network interface of either the next-hop router or the network interface of the destination device.

Figure 3-17   Network Addresses and Data-Link Addresses

Communicating with a Device on the Same Network (3.3.2.2)

To understand how communication is successful in the network, it is important to understand the roles of both the network layer addresses and the data-link addresses when a device is communicating with another device on the same network. In this example shown in Figure 3-18, we have a client computer, PC1, communicating with a file server, FTP server, on the same IP network.

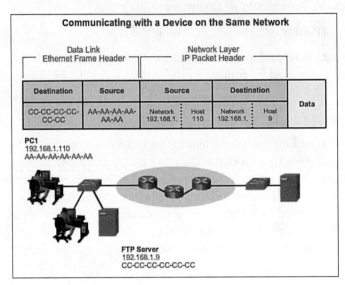

Figure 3-18   Communication with a Device on the Same Network

Network Addresses

The network layer addresses, or IP addresses, indicate the network and host address of the source and destination. The network portion of the address will be the same; only the host or device portion of the address will be different.

- **Source IP address:** The IP address of the sending device, the client computer PC1: 192.168.1.110.

- **Destination IP address:** The IP address of the receiving device, FTP server: 192.168.1.9.

Data Link Addresses

When the sender and receiver of the IP packet are on the same network, the data-link frame is sent directly to the receiving device. On an Ethernet network, the data-link addresses are known as Ethernet MAC addresses. MAC addresses are 48-bit addresses that are physically embedded on the Ethernet NIC. A MAC address is also known as the physical address or *burned-in address (BIA)*.

- **Source MAC address:** This is the data-link address, or the Ethernet MAC address, of the device that sends the IP packet, PC1. The MAC address of the Ethernet NIC of PC1 is AA-AA-AA-AA-AA-AA.

- **Destination MAC address:** When the receiving device is on the same network as the sending device, this is the data-link address of the receiving device. In this example, the destination MAC address is the MAC address of the FTP server: CC-CC-CC-CC-CC-CC.

The source and destination addresses are added to the Ethernet frame. The frame with the encapsulated IP packet can now be transmitted from PC1 directly to the FTP server.

MAC and IP Addresses (3.3.2.3)

It should now be clear that to send data to another host on the same LAN, the source host must know both the physical and logical addresses of the destination host. After this is known, it can create a frame and send it out on the network media. The source host can learn the destination IP address in a number of ways. For example, it can learn the IP address through the use of the Domain Name System (DNS), or it can know the destination IP address because the address is entered in the application manually, such as when a user specifies the IP address of a destination FTP server. But how does a host determine the Ethernet MAC address of another device?

Most network applications rely on the logical IP address of the destination to identify the location of the communicating hosts. The data-link MAC address is required to deliver the encapsulated IP packet inside the Ethernet frame across the network to the destination.

The sending host uses a protocol called *Address Resolution Protocol (ARP)* to discover the MAC address of any host on the same local network, as shown in Figure 3-19. The sending host sends an ARP Request message to the entire LAN. The ARP Request is a broadcast message. The ARP Request contains the IP address of the destination device. Every device on the LAN examines the ARP Request to see whether it contains its own IP address. Only the device with the IP address contained in the ARP Request responds with an ARP Reply. The ARP Reply includes the MAC address associated with the IP address in the ARP Request.

Figure 3-19 Address Resolution Protocol

Accessing Remote Resources (3.3.3)

The method that a host uses to send messages to a destination on a remote network differs from the way a host sends messages to a destination on the same local network. When a host needs to send a message to another host located on the same network, it will forward the message directly. A host will use ARP to discover the MAC address of the destination host. It includes the destination IP address within the packet header and encapsulates the packet into a frame containing the MAC address of the destination and forwards it.

Default Gateway (3.3.3.1)

When a host needs to send a message to a remote network, it must use the router, also known as the default gateway. The default gateway is the IP address of an interface on a router on the same network as the sending host.

It is important that the address of the default gateway be configured on each host on the local network. If no default gateway address is configured in the host TCP/IP settings, or if the wrong default gateway is specified, messages addressed to hosts on remote networks cannot be delivered.

In the example shown in Figure 3-20, the hosts on the LAN are using R1 as the default gateway with its 192.168.1.1 address configured in their TCP/IP settings. If the destination of a PDU is on a different IP network, the hosts send the PDUs to the default gateway on the router for further transmission.

Figure 3-20 Accessing Remote Resources

Communicating with a Device on a Remote Network (3.3.3.2)

But what are the roles of the network layer address and the data link layer address when a device is communicating with a device on a remote network? In this example, shown in Figure 3-21, we have a client computer, PC1, communicating with a server, named Web Server, on a different IP network.

Figure 3-21 Communicating with a Device on a Remote Network

Network Addresses

IP addresses indicate the network and device addresses of the source and destination. When the sender of the packet is on a different network from the receiver, the source and destination IP addresses will represent hosts on different networks. This will be indicated by the network portion of the IP address of the destination host.

- **Source IP address:** The IP address of the sending device, the client computer PC1: 192.168.1.110.

- **Destination IP address:** The IP address of the receiving device, the server, Web Server: 172.16.1.99.

Data Link Addresses

When the sender and receiver of the IP packet are on different networks, the Ethernet data-link frame cannot be sent directly to the destination host because the host is not directly reachable in the network of the sender. The Ethernet frame must be sent to another device known as the router or default gateway. In our example, the default gateway is R1. R1 has an interface and an IP address that is on the same network as PC1. This allows PC1 to reach the router directly.

- **Source MAC address:** The Ethernet MAC address of the sending device, PC1. The MAC address of the Ethernet interface of PC1 is AA-AA-AA-AA-AA-AA.

- **Destination MAC address:** When the receiving device is on a different network from the sending device, this is the Ethernet MAC address of the default gateway or router. In this example, the destination MAC address is the MAC address of the R1 Ethernet interface that is attached to the PC1 network, which is 11-11-11-11-11-11.

The Ethernet frame with the encapsulated IP packet can now be transmitted to R1. R1 forwards the packet to the destination, Web Server. This can mean that R1 forwards the packet to another router or directly to Web Server if the destination is on a network connected to R1.

How does the sending device determine the MAC address of the router?

Each device knows the IP address of the router through the default gateway address configured in its TCP/IP settings. The *default gateway* address is the address of the router interface connected to the same local network as the source device. All devices on the local network use the default gateway address to send messages to the router. After the host knows the default gateway IP address, it can use ARP to determine the MAC address of that default gateway. The MAC address of the default gateway is then placed in the frame.

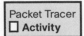

Packet Tracer Activity 3.3.3.3: Explore a Network

This simulation activity is intended to help you understand the flow of traffic and the contents of data packets as they traverse a complex network. Communications will be examined at three different locations simulating typical business and home networks.

Lab 3.3.3.4: Using Wireshark to View Network Traffic

In this lab, you will complete the following objectives:

- Part 1: Download and Install Wireshark
- Part 2: Capture and Analyze Local ICMP Data in Wireshark
- Part 3: Capture and Analyze Remote ICMP Data in Wireshark

Summary (3.4)

Class Activity 3.4.1.1: Guaranteed to Work!

You have just completed the Chapter 3 content regarding network protocols and standards.

Assuming that you resolved the beginning of this chapter's modeling activity, how would you compare the following steps taken to design a communications system to the networking models used for communications?

- Establishing a language to communicate

- Dividing the message into small steps, delivered a little at a time, to facilitate understanding of the problem

- Checking to see whether the data has been delivered fully and correctly

- Timing needed to ensure quality data communication and delivery

Data networks are systems of end devices, intermediary devices, and the media connecting the devices. For communication to occur, these devices must know how to communicate.

These devices must comply with communication rules and protocols. TCP/IP is an example of a protocol suite. Most protocols are created by a standards organization such as the IETF or IEEE. The Institute of Electrical and Electronics Engineers is a professional organization for those in the electrical engineering and electronics fields. ISO, the International Organization for Standardization, is the world's largest developer of international standards for a wide variety of products and services.

The most widely used networking models are the OSI and TCP/IP models. Associating the protocols that set the rules of data communications with the different layers of these models is useful in determining which devices and services are applied at specific points as data passes across LANs and WANs.

Data that passes down the stack of the OSI model is segmented into pieces and encapsulated with addresses and other labels. The process is reversed as the pieces are deencapsulated and passed up the destination protocol stack. The OSI model describes the processes of encoding, formatting, segmenting, and encapsulating data for transmission over the network.

The TCP/IP protocol suite is an open standard protocol that has been endorsed by the networking industry and ratified, or approved, by a standards organization. The Internet protocol suite is a suite of protocols required for transmitting and receiving information using the Internet.

Protocol data units (PDU) are named according to the protocols of the TCP/IP suite: data, segment, packet, frame, and bits.

Applying models allows individuals, companies, and trade associations to analyze current networks and plan the networks of the future.

Practice

The following activities provide practice with the topics introduced in this chapter. The labs and class activities are available in the companion *The Introduction to Networks Lab Manual* (ISBN 978-1-58713-312-1). The Packet Tracer Activities PKA files are found in the online course.

Class Activities

- Class Activity 3.0.1.2: Designing a Communications System
- Class Activity 3.4.1.1: Guaranteed to Work!

Labs

- Lab 3.2.3.6: Researching Networking Standards
- Lab 3.2.4.7: Researching RFCs
- Lab 3.3.3.4: Using Wireshark to View Network Traffic

Packet Tracer Activities

- Packet Tracer Activity 3.2.4.6: Investigating the TCP/IP and OSI Models in Action
- Packet Tracer Activity 3.3.3.3: Explore a Network

Check Your Understanding

Complete all the review questions listed here to test your understanding of the topics and concepts in this chapter. The appendix "Answers to the 'Check Your Understanding' Questions" lists the answers.

1. Which of the following elements do both human and computer communication systems have in common? (Choose three.)

   A. Source

   B. Keyboard

   C. Channel

   D. Default gateway

   E. Receiver

2. What happens to frames that are too long or too short for the channel used?

   A. They are broken up into smaller pieces.

   B. They are dropped.

   C. They clog the network and block the delivery of other frames.

   D. They are returned to the sender.

   E. They are delivered but much slower than proper-size frames.

3. Which message timing factor impacts how much information can be sent and the speed at which it can be delivered?

   A. Access method

   B. Delay speed

   C. Flow control

   D. Response timeout

4. What is the name given to a one-to-many message delivery option?

   A. Unicast

   B. Multicast

   C. Broadcast

   D. Manycast

5. What name is given to a group of interrelated protocols necessary to perform a communication function?

    A. Functional collection

    B. Functional protocol

    C. Protocol suite

    D. Protocol stack

6. What type of protocol describes communication over a data link and the physical transmission of data on the network media?

    A. Application protocol

    B. Transport protocol

    C. Internet protocol

    D. Network access protocol

7. Which of the following are examples of proprietary protocols? (Choose two.)

    A. TCP/IP

    B. ISO

    C. AppleTalk

    D. Novell NetWare

8. Which organization is responsible for the standard that defines Media Access Control for wired Ethernet?

    A. ISOC

    B. IAB

    C. IETF

    D. IEEE

    E. ISO

9. What organization is responsible for the overall management and development of Internet standards?

    A. IAB

    B. IETF

    C. IRTF

    D. IEEE

    E. ISO

10. Which organization is responsible for developing communications standards for Voice over IP (VoIP) devices?

    A. The Electronics Industry Alliance (EIA)

    B. The Telecommunications Industry Association (TIA)

    C. The International Telecommunications Union – Telecommunications Standardization Sector (ITU-T)

    D. The Internet Corporation for Assigned Names and Numbers (ICANN)

11. Which of the following TCP/IP protocols exist at the transport layer of the TCP/IP reference model? (Choose two.)

    A. HTTP

    B. FTP

    C. TCP

    D. DNS

    E. UDP

12. Which of the following OSI model layers have the same functionality as the network access layer in the TCP/IP model? (Choose two.)

    A. Application

    B. Transport

    C. Session

    D. Physical

    E. Presentation

    F. Data link

    G. Network

13. Which OSI reference model layer is responsible for common representation of the data transferred between application layer services?

    A. Application

    B. Transport

    C. Session

    D. Physical

    E. Presentation

    F. Data link

    G. Network

14. Which TCP/IP model layer is responsible for providing the best path through the network?

   A. Application

   B. Transport

   C. Internet

   D. Network access

15. Which application layer protocol allows users on one network to reliably transfer files to and from a host on another network?

   A. HTTP

   B. FTP

   C. IMAP

   D. TFTP

   E. DHCP

16. What is the transport layer PDU?

   A. Data

   B. Segment

   C. Packet

   D. Frame

   E. Bit

17. What is the correct order of data decapsulation?

   A. Data > segment > packet > frame > bit

   B. Bit > frame> segment > packet > data

   C. Bit > frame > packet > segment > data

   D. Data > frame > packet > segment > bit

   E. Bit > packet > frame > segment > data

18. What pieces of information are required for a host to access resources on the local network? (Choose three.)

   A. Physical address

   B. Network address

   C. Process number (port)

   D. Default gateway address

   E. Host name

19. What pieces of information are required for a host to access resources on a remote network? (Choose four.)

    A. Physical address

    B. Network address

    C. Process number (port)

    D. Default gateway address

    E. Host name

20. What are some of the four major responsibilities of network protocols?

CHAPTER 4

Network Access

Objectives

Upon completion of this chapter, you will be able to answer the following questions:

- What are options for connecting devices to a data network?

- What are the purpose and functions of the physical layer in data networks?

- What are the basic characteristics of physical layer standards?

- What are the basic characteristics of copper cabling?

- How are UTP cables built for use in Ethernet networks?

- What are the basic characteristics of fiber-optic cabling?

- What are advantages of using fiber-optic cabling over using other media in data networks?

- What are the basic characteristics of using wireless media in data networks?

- What are the purpose and functions of the data link layer in preparing communications for transmission on specific data network media?

- What are the fields and structure of Layer 2 frames?

- What are the standards that identify the protocols and standards of the data link layer?

- How do the functions of physical topologies compare with the functions of logical topologies?

- What are the basic characteristics of Media Access Control on WAN topologies?

- What are the basic characteristics of Media Access Control on LAN topologies?

- What are the characteristics and functions of the data link layer frame?

Key Terms

This chapter uses the following key terms. You can find the definitions in the Glossary.

Introduction (4.0.1.1)

In networks, all data has to be prepared for transmission and placed onto the media by the sending node as well as taken off the media by the receiving node. These are the functions of the TCP/IP data link layer.

To support our communication, the OSI model divides the functions of a data network into layers. Each layer works with the layers above and below to transmit data. Two layers within the OSI model are so closely tied that according to the TCP/IP model, they are in essence one layer. Those two layers are the data link layer and the physical layer.

On the sending device, it is the role of the data link layer to prepare data for transmission and control how that data accesses the physical media. However, the physical layer controls how the data is transmitted onto the *physical media* by encoding the binary digits that represent data into signals.

On the receiving end, the physical layer receives signals across the connecting media. After decoding the signal back into data, the physical layer passes the data to the data link layer for acceptance and processing.

This chapter begins with the general functions of the physical layer and the standards and protocols that manage the transmission of data across local media. It also introduces the functions of the data link layer and the protocols associated with it.

Class Activity 4.0.1.2: Managing the Medium

You and your colleague are attending a networking conference. There are many lectures and presentations held during this event, and because they overlap, each of you can only choose a limited set of sessions to attend.

Therefore, you decide to split, each of you attending a separate set of presentations, and after the event ends, you share the slides and the knowledge that each of you gained during the event.

Try to answer the following questions:

- How would you personally organize a conference where multiple sessions are held at the same time? Would you put all of them into a single conference room or would you use multiple rooms? What would be the reason?

- Assume that the conference room is properly fitted with audiovisual equipment to display large-size video and amplify voice. If a person wanted to attend a specific session, does the seating arrangement make a difference, or is it sufficient to visit the proper conference room?

- Would it be considered positive or harmful if the speech from one conference room somehow leaked into another?

- If questions or inquiries arise during a presentation, should attendees simply shout out their questions, or should there be some form of process for handling questions, such as documenting them and handing them over to a facilitator? What would happen without this process?

- If an interesting topic elicits a larger discussion where many attendees have questions or comments, can this result in the session running out of its time without going through the entire intended content? Why is that so?

- Imagine that the session is a panel, that is, a more free discussion of attendees with panelists and optionally with themselves. If a person wants to address another person within the same room, can he/she do it directly? What would be necessary to do if a panelist wanted to invite another person to join who is not presently in the room?

- What was accomplished by the isolation of multiple sessions into separate conference rooms if, after the event, people can meet and share the information?

Physical Layer Protocols (4.1)

An important element of data networks is the ability to move data across media. Depending on the media, rules are required to govern the use of media to transport data. In this section, these physical layer protocols will be explored.

Getting It Connected (4.1.1)

Data in a network will be transported across one of various types of physical media. The rules regarding the physical connections and the representation of data on the media are defined by protocols. This section will introduce the basic elements of making network connectivity.

Connecting to the Network (4.1.1.1)

Whether connecting to a local printer in the home or to a website in another country, before any network communications can occur, a physical connection to a local network must be established first. A physical connection can be a wired connection using a cable or a wireless connection using radio waves.

The type of physical connection used is totally dependent upon the setup of the network. For example, in many corporate offices, employees have desktop or laptop computers that are physically connected, through a cable, to a shared switch. This type of setup is a wired network, in which data is transmitted across a physical cable.

In addition to wired connections, some businesses might also offer wireless connections for laptops, tablets, and smartphones. With wireless devices, data is transmitted using radio waves. The use of wireless connectivity is becoming more common as individuals, and businesses alike, discover the advantages of offering wireless services. To offer wireless capability, a network must incorporate a *wireless access point (WAP)* to which to connect devices.

Switch devices and wireless access points are often two separate dedicated devices within a network implementation. However, there are also devices that offer both wired and wireless connectivity. In many homes, for example, individuals are implementing home integrated service routers (ISR). ISRs offer a switching component with multiple ports, allowing multiple devices to be connected to the local-area network (LAN) using cables. Additionally, many ISRs also include a WAP, which allows wireless devices to connect as well.

Network Interface Cards (4.1.1.2)

Network interface cards (NIC) connect a device to the network. Ethernet NICs are used for a wired connection, whereas WLAN (wireless local-area network) NICs are used for wireless. An end-user device can include one or both types of NICs. A network printer, for example, might only have an Ethernet NIC, and therefore must connect to the network using an Ethernet cable. Other devices, such as tablets and smartphones, might only contain a WLAN NIC and must use a wireless connection.

Not all physical connections are equal, in terms of the performance level, when connecting to a network.

For example, a wireless device will experience degradation in performance based on its distance to a wireless access point. The further the device is from the access point, the weaker the wireless signal it receives. This can mean less bandwidth or no wireless connection at all. A wireless range extender can be used to regenerate the wireless signal to other parts of the house that are too far from the wireless access point. Alternatively, a wired connection will not degrade in performance; however, is extremely limited in movement and generally requires static positioning.

All wireless devices must share access to the airwaves connecting to the wireless access point. This means that slower network performance might occur as more wireless devices access the network simultaneously. A wired device does not need to share its access to the network with other devices. Each wired device has a separate communications channel over its own Ethernet cable. This is important when considering some applications, like online gaming, streaming video, and videoconferencing, which require more dedicated bandwidth than other applications.

Over the next couple of topics, you will learn more about the physical layer connections that occur and how those connections affect the transportation of data.

Purpose of the Physical Layer (4.1.2)

All data being transferred over a network must be represented on a medium by the sending node and interpreted on a medium by the receiving node. The physical layer is responsible for these functions. In this section, the physical layer will be explored.

The Physical Layer (4.1.2.1)

The OSI physical layer provides the means to transport the bits that make up a data link layer frame across the network media. This layer accepts a complete frame from the data link layer and encodes it as a series of signals that are transmitted onto the local media. The encoded bits that comprise a frame are received by either an end device or an intermediate device.

Figure 4-1 demonstrates the full encapsulation process and the transmitting of encoded binary bits across the OSI Layer 1 medium to the destination. The processes that data undergoes from a source node to a destination node are

- The user data is segmented by the transport layer, placed into packets by the network layer, and further encapsulated as frames by the data link layer.

- The physical layer encodes the frames and creates the electrical, optical, or radio wave signals that represent the bits in each frame.

- These signals are then sent on the media one at a time.

Figure 4-1   Physical Layer Encoding

Physical Layer Media (4.1.2.2)

There are three basic forms of network media. The physical layer produces the representation and groupings of bits for each type of media as

- **Copper cable:** The signals are patterns of electrical pulses.

- **Fiber-optic cable:** The signals are patterns of light.

- **Wireless:** The signals are patterns of radio transmissions.

Table 4-1 displays signaling examples for copper, fiber-optic, and wireless.

Table 4-1   Signal Types for Each of the Media at the Physical Layer

Media	Signal Type
Copper cable	Patterns of electrical pulses
Fiber-optic cable	Patterns of light pulses
Wireless	Patterns of radio transmissions

To enable physical layer interoperability, all aspects of these functions are governed by standards organizations.

Physical Layer Standards (4.1.2.3)

The protocols and operations of the upper OSI layers are performed in software designed by software engineers and computer scientists. For example, the services and protocols in the TCP/IP suite are defined by the Internet Engineering Task Force (IETF) in RFCs.

The physical layer consists of electronic circuitry, media, and connectors developed by engineers. Therefore, it is appropriate that the standards governing this hardware are defined by the relevant electrical and communications engineering organizations.

There are many different international and national organizations, regulatory government organizations, and private companies involved in establishing and maintaining physical layer standards. For example, the physical layer hardware, media, encoding, and signaling standards are defined and governed by the

- *International Organization for Standardization (ISO)*
- *Telecommunications Industry Association*/Electronic Industries Association (TIA/EIA)
- International Telecommunication Union (ITU)
- American National Standards Institute (ANSI)
- *Institute of Electrical and Electronics Engineers (IEEE)*
- National telecommunications regulatory authorities including the Federal Communication Commission (FCC) in the United States and the European Telecommunications Standards Institute (ESTI)

In addition to these, there are often regional cabling standards groups such as CSA (Canadian Standards Association), CENELEC (European Committee for Electrotechnical Standardization), and JSA/JSI (Japanese Standards Association), developing local specifications.

Table 4-2 lists some of the major contributors and some of their relevant physical layer standards.

Table 4-2   Organizations and Corresponding Physical Layer Standards

Standards Organization	Networking Standards
ISO	ISO 8877: Officially adopted the RJ connections (for example, RJ-11 and RJ-45)
	ISO 11801: Network cabling standard similar to EIA/TIA 568
EIA/TIA	TIA-568-C: Telecommunications cabling standards used by most voice, video, and data networks
	TIA-569-B: Commercial Building Standards for Telecommunications Pathways and Spaces
	TIA-598-C: Fiber-optic color coding
	TIA-942: Telecommunications Infrastructure Standard for Data Centers
ANSI	568-C: RJ-45 pinouts. Codeveloped with EIA/TIA.
ITU-T	G.992: ADSL
IEEE	802.3: Ethernet
	802.11: Wireless LAN (WLAN) and Mesh (Wi-Fi)
	802.15: Bluetooth

Lab 4.1.2.4: Identifying Network Devices and Cabling

In this lab, you will complete the following objectives:

- Part 1: Identify Network Devices

- Part 2: Identify Network Media

Fundamental Principles of Layer 1 (4.1.3)

At the foundation of network communications is the physical layer, Layer 1. This section examines components that make up the physical layer.

Physical Layer Fundamental Principles (4.1.3.1)

The physical layer standards address three functional areas: physical components, encoding, and signaling.

Physical Components

The physical components are the electronic hardware devices, media, and other connectors that transmit and carry the signals to represent the bits. Hardware components such as network adapters (NICs), interfaces and connectors, cable materials, and cable designs are all specified in standards associated with the physical layer. The various ports and interfaces on a Cisco 1941 router are also examples of physical components with specific connectors and pinouts resulting from standards.

Encoding

Encoding or line encoding is a method of converting a stream of data bits into a predefined "code." Codes are groupings of bits used to provide a predictable pattern that can be recognized by both the sender and the receiver. In the case of networking, encoding is a pattern of voltage or current used to represent bits: the 0s and 1s.

In addition to creating codes for data, encoding methods at the physical layer can also provide codes for control purposes such as identifying the beginning and end of a frame.

Common network encoding methods include

- *Manchester encoding:* A 0 is represented by a high-to-low voltage transition, and a 1 is represented as a low-to-high voltage transition. This type of encoding is used in older versions of Ethernet, RFID, and Near Field Communication.

- *Nonreturn to zero (NRZ):* This is a common means of encoding data that has two states termed "zero" and "one" and no neutral or rest position. A 0 might be represented by one voltage level on the media, and a 1 might be represented by a different voltage on the media.

Note

Faster data rates require more complex encoding, such as 4B/5B; however, the explanation of these methods is beyond the scope of this course.

Signaling

The physical layer must generate the electrical, optical, or wireless signals that represent the "1" and "0" on the media. The method of representing the bits is called the signaling method. The physical layer standards must define what type of signal represents a 1 and what type of signal represents a 0. This can be as simple as a change in the level of an electrical signal or optical pulse. For example, a long pulse might represent a 1, whereas a short pulse represents a 0.

This is similar to how Morse code is used for communication. Morse code is another signaling method that uses a series of on-off tones, lights, or clicks to send text over telephone wires or between ships at sea.

Signals can be transmitted in one of two ways:

- **Asynchronous:** Data signals are transmitted without an associated clock signal. The time spacing between data characters or blocks can be of arbitrary duration, meaning that the spacing is not standardized. Therefore, frames require start and stop indicator flags.

- **Synchronous:** Data signals are sent along with a clock signal that occurs at evenly spaced time durations referred to as the bit time.

There are many ways to transmit signals. A common method to send data is using modulation techniques. Modulation is the process by which the characteristic of one wave (the signal) modifies another wave (the carrier). The following modulation techniques have been widely used in transmitting data on a medium:

- **Frequency modulation (FM):** A method of transmission in which the carrier frequency varies in accordance with the signal.

- **Amplitude modulation (AM):** A transmission technique in which the amplitude of the carrier varies in accordance with the signal.

- **Pulse-coded modulation (PCM):** A technique in which an analog signal, such as a voice, is converted into a digital signal by sampling the signal's amplitude and expressing the different amplitudes as a binary number. The sampling rate must be at least twice the highest frequency in the signal.

The nature of the actual signals representing the bits on the media will depend on the signaling method in use. Some methods might use one attribute of signaling to represent a single 0 and use another attribute of signaling to represent a single 1.

Bandwidth (4.1.3.2)

Different physical media support the transfer of bits at different speeds. Data transfer is usually discussed in terms of bandwidth and throughput.

Bandwidth is the capacity of a medium to carry data. Digital bandwidth measures the amount of data that can flow from one place to another in a given amount of time. Bandwidth is typically measured in kilobits per second (kbps) or megabits per second (Mbps).

The practical bandwidth of a network is determined by a combination of factors:

- The properties of the physical media

- The technologies chosen for signaling and detecting network signals

Physical media properties, current technologies, and the laws of physics all play a role in determining available bandwidth.

Table 4-3 shows the commonly used units of measure for bandwidth.

Table 4-3 Bandwidth Units of Measure

Units of Bandwidth	Abbreviation	Equivalence
Bits per second	bps	1 bps = Base unit
Kilobits per second	kbps	1 kbps = 1000 bps = 10^3 bps
Megabits per second	Mbps	1 Mbps = 1,000,000 bps = 10^6 bps
Gigabits per second	Gbps	1 Gbps = 1,000,000,000 bps = 10^9 bps
Terabits per second	Tbps	1 Tbps = 1,000,000,000,000 bps = 10^{12} bps

Throughput (4.1.3.3)

Throughput is the measure of the transfer of bits across the media over a given period of time.

Because of a number of factors, throughput usually does not match the specified bandwidth in physical layer implementations. Many factors influence throughput including

- The amount of traffic
- The type of traffic
- The latency created by the number of network devices encountered between source and destination

Latency refers to the amount of time, including delays, for data to travel from one given point to another.

In an internetwork or network with multiple segments, throughput cannot be faster than the slowest link of the path from source to destination. Even if all or most of the segments have high bandwidth, it will only take one segment in the path with low throughput to create a bottleneck to the throughput of the entire network.

There are many online speed tests that can reveal the throughput of an Internet connection.

Note

There is a third way to measure the transfer of usable data that is known as *goodput*. Goodput is the measure of usable data transferred over a given period of time. Goodput is throughput minus traffic overhead for establishing sessions, acknowledgements, and encapsulation.

Types of Physical Media (4.1.3.4)

The physical layer produces the representation and groupings of bits as voltages, radio frequencies, or light pulses. Various standards organizations have contributed to the definition of the physical, electrical, and mechanical properties of the media available for different data communications. These specifications guarantee that cables and connectors will function as anticipated with different data link layer implementations.

As an example, standards for copper media are defined for the

- Type of copper cabling used
- Bandwidth of the communication
- Type of connectors used
- Pinout and color codes of connections to the media
- Maximum distance of the media

Interactive Graphic

Activity 4.1.3.5: Physical Layer Terminology

Go to the course online to perform this practice activity.

Network Media (4.2)

Much of the aspects of the physical layer are dependent on the type of media used. The characteristics of media types will be explored in this section.

Copper Cabling (4.2.1)

One of the oldest and most used media for communications is copper cabling. The characteristics and use of copper media in data networks will be examined in this section.

Characteristics of Copper Media (4.2.1.1)

Networks use copper media because it is relatively inexpensive, easy to install, and has low resistance to electrical current. However, copper media is limited by distance and signal interference.

Data is transmitted on copper cables as electrical pulses. A detector in the network interface of a destination device must receive a signal that can be successfully decoded to match the signal sent. However, the longer the signal travels, the more it deteriorates in a phenomenon referred to as signal attenuation. For this reason, all copper media must follow strict distance limitations as specified by the guiding standards.

The timing and voltage values of the electrical pulses are also susceptible to interference from two sources:

- *Electromagnetic interference (EMI)* or *radio frequency interference (RFI):* EMI and RFI signals can distort and corrupt the data signals being carried by copper media. Potential sources of EMI and RFI include radio waves and electromagnetic devices such as fluorescent lights or electric motors.

- *Crosstalk:* Crosstalk is a disturbance caused by the electric or magnetic fields of a signal on one wire to the signal in an adjacent wire. In telephone circuits, crosstalk can result in hearing part of another voice conversation from an adjacent circuit. Specifically, when electrical current flows through a wire, it creates a small, circular magnetic field around the wire that can be picked up by an adjacent wire.

Figure 4-2 shows how data transmission can be affected by interference. The original pure data signal represents a specific bit pattern. Nearby electrical noise creates an interface signal on the same wire. The noise combines with the original signal and results in a corrupted or changed signal being received by the destination computer.

To counter the negative effects of EMI and RFI, some types of copper cables are wrapped in metallic shielding and require proper grounding connections.

To counter the negative effects of crosstalk, some types of copper cables have opposing circuit wire pairs twisted together, which effectively cancels the crosstalk.

The susceptibility of copper cables to electronic noise can also be limited by

- Selecting the cable type or category most suited to a given networking environment

- Designing a cable infrastructure to avoid known and potential sources of interference in the building structure

- Using cabling techniques that include the proper handling and termination of the cables

Figure 4-2   How Data Transmission Is Affected by Interference

Copper Media (4.2.1.2)

There are three main types of copper media used in networking:

- Unshielded twisted-pair (UTP)

- Shielded twisted-pair (STP)

- Coaxial

These cables are used to interconnect nodes on a LAN and infrastructure devices such as switches, routers, and wireless access points. Each type of connection and the accompanying devices have cabling requirements stipulated by physical layer standards.

Different physical layer standards specify the use of different connectors. These standards specify the mechanical dimensions of the connectors and the acceptable electrical properties of each type. Networking media use modular jacks and plugs to provide easy connection and disconnection. Also, a single type of physical connector might be used for multiple types of connections. For example, the RJ-45 connector is widely used in LANs with one type of media and in some WANs with another media type.

Unshielded Twisted-Pair Cable (4.2.1.3)

Unshielded twisted-pair (UTP) cabling is the most common networking media. UTP cabling, terminated with RJ-45 connectors, is used for interconnecting network hosts with intermediate networking devices, such as switches and routers.

In LANs, UTP cable consists of four pairs of color-coded wires that have been twisted together and then encased in a flexible plastic sheath that protects them from minor physical damage. The twisting of wires helps protect against signal interference from other wires.

As seen in the Figure 4-3, the color codes identify the individual pairs and wires in the pairs and aid in cable termination. Most UTP cables used in networking commonly have four wire pairs. The color coding for this cabling is orange-white/orange, blue-white/blue, green-white/green, and brown-white/brown.

Figure 4-3   Unshielded Twisted-Pair (UTP) Cable

Shielded Twisted-Pair (STP) Cable (4.2.1.4)

Shielded twisted-pair (STP) cabling provides better noise protection than UTP cabling. However, compared to UTP cable, STP cable is significantly more expensive and difficult to install. Like UTP cable, STP uses an RJ-45 connector.

STP cable combines the techniques of shielding to counter EMI and RFI and wire twisting to counter crosstalk. To gain the full benefit of the shielding, STP cables are terminated with special shielded STP data connectors. If the cable is improperly grounded, the shield can act like an antenna and pick up unwanted signals.

Different types of STP cables with different characteristics are available. However, there are two common variations of STP:

- STP cable shields the entire bundle of wires with foil, eliminating virtually all interference (more common).

- STP cable shields the entire bundle of wires as well as the individual wire pairs, with foil eliminating all interference.

The STP cable shown Figure 4-4 uses four pairs of wires, each wrapped in a foil shield, which are then wrapped in an overall metallic braid or foil.

For many years, STP was the cabling structure specified for use in Token Ring network installations. With the decline of Token Ring, the demand for shielded twisted-pair cabling also waned. However, the new 10-GB standard for Ethernet has a provision for the use of STP cabling that is providing a renewed interest in shielded twisted-pair cabling.

Figure 4-4   Shielded Twisted-Pair (STP) Cable

Coaxial Cable (4.2.1.5)

Coaxial cable, or *coax* for short, gets its name from the fact that there are two conductors that share the same axis. As shown in the Figure 4-5, coaxial cable consists of

- A copper conductor used to transmit the electronic signals.

- The copper conductor is surrounded by a layer of flexible plastic insulation.

- The insulating material is surrounded in a woven copper braid, or metallic foil, that acts as the second wire in the circuit and as a shield for the inner conductor. This second layer, or shield, also reduces the amount of outside electromagnetic interference.

- The entire cable is covered with a cable jacket to protect it from minor physical damage.

Figure 4-5   Coaxial Cable

Note

There are different types of connectors used with coax cable.

Coaxial cable was traditionally used in cable television capable of transmitting in one direction. It was also used extensively in early Ethernet installations.

Although UTP cable has essentially replaced coaxial cable in modern Ethernet installations, the coaxial cable design has been adapted for use in

- **Wireless installations:** Coaxial cables attach antennas to wireless devices. The coaxial cable carries radio frequency (RF) energy between the antennas and the radio equipment.

- **Cable Internet installations:** Cable service providers are currently converting their one-way systems to two-way systems to provide Internet connectivity to their customers. To provide these services, portions of the coaxial cable and supporting amplification elements are replaced with *fiber-optic cable*. However, the final connection to the customer's location and the wiring inside the customer's premises are still coax cable. This combined use of fiber and coax is referred to as hybrid fiber coax (HFC).

Copper Media Safety (4.2.1.6)

All three types of copper media are susceptible to fire and electrical hazards.

Fire hazards exist because cable insulation and sheaths can be flammable or produce toxic fumes when heated or burned. Building authorities or organizations can stipulate related safety standards for cabling and hardware installations.

Electrical hazards are a potential problem because the copper wires could conduct electricity in undesirable ways. This could subject personnel and equipment to a range of electrical hazards. For example, a defective network device could conduct currents to the chassis of other network devices. Additionally, network cabling could present undesirable voltage levels when used to connect devices that have power sources with different ground potentials. Such situations are possible when copper cabling is used to connect networks in different buildings or on different floors of buildings that use different power facilities. Finally, copper cabling can conduct voltages caused by lightning strikes to network devices.

The result of undesirable voltages and currents can include damage to network devices and connected computers, or injury to personnel. It is important that copper cabling be installed appropriately, and according to the relevant specifications and building codes, to avoid potentially dangerous and damaging situations.

Some of the proper cabling practices to avoid potential fire and electrical hazards are

- Maintain separation of data and electrical power.
- Properly connect cables.
- Inspect installations for damage.
- Properly ground equipment.

Interactive Graphic

Activity 4.2.1.7: Copper Media Characteristics

Go to the course online to perform this practice activity.

UTP Cabling (4.2.2)

Copper media has some inherent issues. Twisting the internal pairs of the copper media, as used in UTP, is a low-cost solution to improve some of the cabling performance. This section will further explore UTP cabling.

Properties of UTP Cabling (4.2.2.1)

When used as a networking medium, unshielded twisted-pair (UTP) cabling consists of four pairs of color-coded wires that have been twisted together and then encased in a flexible plastic sheath. Network UTP cable has four pairs of either 22- or 24-gauge copper wire. A UTP cable has an external diameter of approximately 0.43 cm (0.17 inches), and its small size can be advantageous during installation.

UTP cable does not use shielding to counter the effects of EMI and RFI. Instead, cable designers have discovered that they can limit the negative effect of crosstalk by:

- **Cancellation:** Designers now pair wires in a circuit. When two wires in an electrical circuit are placed close together, their magnetic fields are the exact opposite of each other. Therefore, the two magnetic fields cancel each other out and cancel out any outside EMI and RFI signals.

- **Varying the number of twists per wire pair:** To further enhance the cancellation effect of paired circuit wires, designers vary the number of twists of each wire pair in a cable. For example, the orange/orange-white pairs are twisted less than the blue/white-blue pairs. Each colored pair is twisted a different number of times. UTP cable must follow precise specifications governing how many twists or braids are permitted per meter (3.28 feet) of cable.

UTP cable relies solely on the cancellation effect produced by the twisted wire pairs to limit signal degradation and effectively provide self-shielding for wire pairs within the network media.

UTP Cabling Standards (4.2.2.2)

UTP cabling conforms to the standards established jointly by the TIA/EIA. Specifically, TIA/EIA-568A stipulates the commercial cabling standards for LAN installations and is the standard most commonly used in LAN cabling environments. Some of the elements defined are

- Cable types
- Cable lengths
- Connectors
- Cable termination
- Methods of testing cable

The electrical characteristics of copper cabling are defined by the Institute of Electrical and Electronics Engineers (IEEE). IEEE rates UTP cabling according to its performance. Cables are placed into categories according to their ability to carry higher-bandwidth rates. For example, Category 5 (Cat5) cable is used commonly in 100BASE-TX Fast Ethernet installations. Other categories include Enhanced Category 5 (Cat5e) cable, Category 6 (Cat6), and Category 6a.

Cables in higher categories are designed and constructed to support higher data rates. As new multigigabit-speed Ethernet technologies, such as 10 Gigabit, are being developed and adopted, Cat5e is now the minimally acceptable cable type, with Cat6 being the recommended type for new building installations.

Note

Some manufacturers are making cables exceeding the TIA/EIA Category 6a specifications and refer to these unofficially as Category 7.

Figure 4-6 highlights the various categories of UTP cabling. Some characteristics follow.

Figure 4-6   Categories of UTP

The following are characteristics of Category 3 cable:

- Used for voice communication.

- Most often used for phone lines.

The following are characteristics of Category 5 and 5e cable:

- Used for data transmission.

- Cat 5 supports 100 Mbps and can support 1000 Mbps (Gigabit), but it is not recommended.

- Cat 5e supports 1000 Mbps (Gigabit).

- Defined in 568 standard.

The following are characteristics of Category 6 cable:

- Used for data transmission.

- A separator is added between each pair of wires, allowing it to function at higher speeds.

- Supports 1000 Mbps (Gigabit) to 10 Gbps, although 10 Gbps is not recommended.

- Defined in 568 standard.

The following are characteristics of Category 7 cable (ScTP):

- Used for data transmission.

- Individual pairs are wrapped in a shield, and then the entire four pairs wrapped in another shield.

UTP Connectors (4.2.2.3)

UTP cable is usually terminated with an ISO 8877–specified RJ-45 connector. This connector is used for a range of physical layer specifications, one of which is Ethernet. The TIA/EIA 568 standard describes the wire color codes to pin assignments (pinouts) for Ethernet cables.

Video

Video 4.2.2.3: View the video in the online course for a demonstration of a UTP cable terminated with an RJ-45 connector.

As shown in Figure 4-7, the RJ-45 connector is the male component, crimped at the end of the cable. The socket is the female component in a network device, wall, cubicle partition outlet, or patch panel.

Figure 4-7   Categories of UTP

Each time copper cabling is terminated, there is the possibility of signal loss and the introduction of noise to the communication circuit. When terminated improperly, each cable is a potential source of physical layer performance degradation. It is essential that all copper media terminations be of high quality to ensure optimum performance with current and future network technologies.

Figure 4-8 displays an example of a badly terminated UTP cable and a well-terminated UTP cable.

Bad connector—
Wires are untwisted for
too great a length.

Good connector—
Wires are untwisted to the
extent necessary to
attach the connector.

Figure 4-8   RJ-45 Terminations

Types of UTP Cable (4.2.2.4)

Different situations might require UTP cables to be wired according to different wiring conventions. This means that the individual wires in the cable have to be connected in different orders to different sets of pins in the RJ-45 connectors.

The following are the main cable types that are obtained by using specific wiring conventions:

- **Ethernet straight-through:** The most common type of networking cable. It is commonly used to interconnect a host to a switch and a switch to a router.

- **Ethernet crossover:** An uncommon cable used to interconnect similar devices, for example, to connect a switch to a switch, a host to a host, or a router to a router.

- **Rollover:** A Cisco-proprietary cable used to connect to a router or switch console port.

Table 4-4 shows the UTP cable type, related standards, and typical application of these cables.

Table 4-4   UTP Cable Types

Cable Type	TIA/EIA Standard	Cable Use
Straight-through cable	Both ends the same, either 568A or 568B.	Connects a network host to a hub or switch.
Crossover cable	One end 568A and the other 568B. It does not matter which end goes to which device.	Directly connects like devices, such as two hosts, two switches, or two routers. Also used to directly a host to a router.
Rollover cable (also known as a "Cisco" cable)	Cisco-proprietary.	Connects a workstation serial port to a Cisco device console port.

Using a crossover or straight-through cable incorrectly between devices might not damage the devices, but connectivity and communication between the devices will not take place. This is a common error in the lab, and checking that the device connections are correct should be the first troubleshooting action if connectivity is not achieved.

Figure 4-9 identifies the individual wire pairs for the TIA-568A and TIA-568B standards.

Figure 4-9   568A and 568B Pinouts on an RJ-45 Connector

Testing UTP Cables (4.2.2.5)

After installation, a UTP cable tester should be used to test for the following parameters:

- Wire map
- Cable length
- Signal loss because of attenuation
- Crosstalk

It is recommended to thoroughly check that all UTP installation requirements are met.

Activity 4.2.2.6: Cable Pinouts

Go to the course online to perform this practice activity.

Lab 4.2.2.7: Building an Ethernet Crossover Cable

In this lab, you will complete the following objectives:

- Part 1: Analyze Ethernet Cabling Standards and Pinouts
- Part 2: Build an Ethernet Crossover Cable
- Part 3: Test an Ethernet Crossover Cable

Fiber-Optic Cabling (4.2.3)

Networking media selection is being driven by the growing needs for network bandwidth. The distance and performance of fiber-optic cable make it a good media choice to support these network needs. This section will examine the characteristics of fiber-optic cabling use in data networks.

Properties of Fiber-Optic Cabling (4.2.3.1)

Optical fiber cable has become very popular for interconnecting infrastructure network devices. It permits the transmission of data over longer distances and at higher bandwidths (data rates) than any other networking media.

Optical fiber is a flexible but extremely thin transparent strand of very pure glass (silica) not much bigger than a human hair. Bits are encoded on the fiber as light impulses. The fiber-optic cable acts as a waveguide, or "light pipe," to transmit light between the two ends with minimal loss of signal.

As an analogy, consider a flexible pipe with the inside coated as a mirror that is a thousand meters in length and a small flashlight is used to send Morse code signals at the speed of light. Essentially that is how a fiber-optic cable operates, except that it is smaller in diameter and uses sophisticated light emitting and receiving technologies.

Unlike copper wires, fiber-optic cable can transmit signals with less attenuation and is immune to EMI and RFI.

Fiber-optic cabling is now being used in four types of industry:

- **Enterprise networks:** Fiber is used for backbone cabling applications and interconnecting infrastructure devices.

- **FTTH and access networks:** Fiber-to-the-home (FTTH) is used to provide always-on broadband services to homes and small businesses. FTTH supports relatively affordable high-speed Internet access, as well as telecommuting, telemedicine, and video on demand.

- **Long-haul networks:** Service providers use long-haul terrestrial optical fiber networks to connect countries and cities. Networks typically range from a few dozen to a few thousand kilometers and use up to 10 Gbps-based systems.

- **Submarine networks:** Special fiber cables are used to provide reliable high-speed, high-capacity solutions capable of or surviving in harsh undersea environments up to transoceanic distances.

Our focus is the use of fiber within the enterprise.

Fiber Media Cable Design (4.2.3.2)

Although an optical fiber is very thin, it is comprised of two kinds of glass and a protective outer shield. Specifically, these are the

- **Core:** Consists of pure glass and is the part of the fiber where light is carried.

- **Cladding:** The glass that surrounds the core and acts as a mirror. The light pulses propagate down the core while the cladding reflects the light pulses. This keeps the light pulses contained in the fiber core in a phenomenon known as total internal reflection.

- **Jacket:** Typically a PVC jacket that protects the core and cladding. It can also include strengthening materials and a buffer (coating) whose purpose is to protect the glass from scratches and moisture.

Figure 4-10 shows the parts of a typical fiber-optic cable.

Although susceptible to sharp bends, the properties of the core and cladding have been altered at the molecular level to make it very strong. Optical fiber is proof tested through a rigorous manufacturing process for strength at a minimum of 100,000 pounds per square inch. Optical fiber is durable enough to withstand handling during installation and deployment in harsh environmental conditions in networks all around the world.

Figure 4-10   Cutout of a Fiber-Optic Cable

Types of Fiber Media (4.2.3.3)

Light pulses representing the transmitted data as bits on the media are generated by either

- Lasers

- Light-emitting diodes (LED)

Electronic semiconductor devices called photodiodes detect the light pulses and convert them to voltages that can then be reconstructed into data frames.

Note

The laser light transmitted over fiber-optic cabling can damage the human eye. Care must be taken to avoid looking into the end of an active optical fiber.

Fiber-optic cables can be broadly classified into two types:

- **Single-mode fiber (SMF):** Consists of a very small core and uses expensive laser technology to send a single ray of light. Popular in long-distance situations spanning hundreds of kilometers such as required in long-haul telephony and cable TV applications.

- **Multimode fiber (MMF):** Consists of a larger core and uses LED emitters to send light pulses. Specifically, light from an LED enters the multimode fiber at different angles. Popular in LANs because they can be powered by low-cost LEDs. It provides bandwidth up to 10 Gbps over link lengths of up to 550 meters.

Note

With reflection of the light bouncing inside the multimode fiber, there are many different paths, or modes, that the light can take from one end to the other of the fiber; therefore, the name *multimode*. In contrast, *single-mode* is so named because the fiber has a single light beam down the center.

Table 4-5 describes the differences between single-mode and multimode fiber-optic cable.

Table 4-5   Single-Mode and Multimode Fiber-Optic Cable

Single-Mode	Multimode
Small glass core: 8–10 microns	Larger core: 50+ microns, can be glass or plastic
Less dispersion of light	Greater dispersion (loss of light)
Longer distance: Typically up to about 100 km	Shorter distance: Generally up to 2 km
Uses lasers as light source	Uses LEDs as light source on shorter runs

One of the highlighted differences between multimode and single-mode fiber is the amount of dispersion. Dispersion refers to the spreading out of a light pulse over time. The use of lasers as the light source in single-mode fiber allows a focused beam of light, hence less dispersion. The more dispersion there is, the greater the loss in signal strength and the less the effective distance of the signal over the fiber.

Figure 4-11 shows the overview of single-mode and multimode fiber construction.

Figure 4-11   Dispersion in Single-Mode and Multimode Fiber

Network Fiber Connectors (4.2.3.4)

An optical fiber connector terminates the end of an optical fiber. A variety of optical fiber connectors are available. The main differences among the types of connectors are dimensions and methods of mechanical coupling. Generally, organizations standardize on one kind of connector, depending on the equipment that they commonly use, or they standardize per type of fiber (one for MMF, one for SMF). Taking into account all the generations of connectors, about 70 connector types are in use today.

As shown Figure 4-12, the three most popular network fiber-optic connectors include

- **Straight-tip (ST):** An older bayonet style connector widely used with multi-mode fiber, as well as single-mode.

- **Subscriber connector (SC):** Sometimes referred to as square connector or standard connector. It is a widely adopted LAN and WAN connector that uses a push-pull mechanism to ensure positive insertion. This connector type is used with multimode and single-mode fiber.

- **Lucent connector (LC):** Sometimes called a little or local connector, it is quickly growing in popularity because of its smaller size. It is used with single-mode fiber and also supports multimode fiber.

Note

Other fiber connectors, such as the Ferrule Connector (FC) and Sub Miniature A (SMA), are not popular in LAN and WAN deployments. Obsolete connectors include biconic (obsolete) and D4 connectors. These connectors are beyond the scope of this chapter.

Because light typically only travels in one direction over optical fiber, two fibers are usually required to support full-duplex operation. Therefore, fiber-optic patch cables bundle together two optical fiber cables and terminate them with a pair of standard single fiber connectors. Some fiber connectors accept both the transmitting and receiving fibers in a single connector known as a duplex connector, also shown in Figure 4-12.

Note

While not in common use, two-way communication up to 10km can be provided over a single strand of single-mode fiber. This bi-directional transmission is achieved by transmitting at a different wave length into the fiber from each end.

Figure 4-12 Fiber-Optic Connectors

Fiber patch cords are required for interconnecting infrastructure devices. Some of the common patch cords are

- SC-SC multimode patch cord
- LC-LC single-mode patch cord
- ST-LC multimode patch cord
- SC-ST single-mode patch cord

Fiber cables should be protected with a small plastic cap when not in use.

The color of the fiber jacket is often used to distinguish between single-mode and multimode patch cords. This is because of the TIA-598 standard, which recommends the use of a yellow jacket for single-mode fiber cables and orange (or aqua) for multimode fiber cables.

Testing Fiber Cables (4.2.3.5)

Terminating and splicing fiber-optic cabling require special training and equipment. Incorrect termination of fiber-optic media will result in diminished signaling distances or complete transmission failure.

Three common types of fiber-optic termination and splicing errors are

- **Misalignment:** The fiber-optic media are not precisely aligned to one another when joined.

- **End gap:** The media do not completely touch at the splice or connection.

- **End finish:** The media ends are not well polished or dirt is present at the termination.

A quick and easy field test can be performed by shining a bright flashlight into one end of the fiber while observing the other end of the fiber. If light is visible, the fiber is capable of passing light. Although this does not ensure the performance of the fiber, it is a quick and inexpensive way to find a broken fiber.

It is recommended that an optical tester be used to test fiber-optic cables. An Optical Time Domain Reflectometer (OTDR) can be used to test each fiber-optic cable segment. This device injects a test pulse of light into the cable and measures backscatter and reflection of light detected as a function of time. The OTDR will calculate the approximate distance at which these faults are detected along the length of the cable.

Fiber Versus Copper (4.2.3.6)

There are many advantages to using fiber-optic cable compared to copper cables.

Given that the fibers used in fiber-optic media are not electrical conductors, the media is immune to electromagnetic interference. It will also not conduct unwanted electrical currents because of grounding issues. Because optical fibers are thin and have relatively low signal loss, they can be operated at much greater lengths than copper media, without the need for signal regeneration. Some optical fiber physical layer specifications allow lengths that can reach multiple kilometers.

Optical fiber media implementation issues include

- More expensive (usually) than copper media over the same distance (but for a higher capacity)

- Different skills and equipment required to terminate and splice the cable infrastructure

- More careful handling than copper media

At present, in most enterprise environments, optical fiber is primarily used as backbone cabling for high-traffic, point-to-point connections between data distribution facilities and for the interconnection of buildings in multibuilding campuses.

Because optical fiber does not conduct electricity and has low signal loss, it is well suited for these uses.

Table 4-6 highlights some of these differences.

Table 4-6   UTP Cable Compared with Fiber-Optic Cable

Implementation Issues	UTP Cabling	Fiber-Optic Cabling
Bandwidth supported	10 Mbps – 10 Gbps	10 Mbps – 100 Gbps
Distance	Relatively short (1 – 100 meters)	Relatively high (1 to greater than 100,000 meters)
Immunity to EMI and RFI	Low	High
Immunity to electrical hazards	Low	High
Media and connector costs	Lowest	Highest
Installation skills required	Lowest	Highest
Safety precautions	Lowest	Highest

Activity 4.2.3.7: Fiber Optics Terminology

Go to the course online to perform this practice activity.

Wireless Media (4.2.4)

With more mobile devices being used, wireless networking is also growing in demand. This section explores wireless media characteristic and uses.

Properties of Wireless Media (4.2.4.1)

Wireless media carry electromagnetic signals that represent the binary digits of data communications using radio or microwave frequencies.

As a networking medium, wireless is not restricted to conductors or pathways, as are copper and fiber media. Wireless media provides the greatest mobility options of all media. As well, the number of wireless-enabled devices is continuously increasing. For these reasons, wireless has become the medium of choice for home networks. As network bandwidth options increase, wireless is quickly gaining in popularity in enterprise networks.

However, wireless does have some areas of concern including

- **Coverage area:** Wireless data communication technologies work well in open environments. However, certain construction materials used in buildings and structures, and the local terrain, will limit the effective coverage.

- **Interference:** Wireless is susceptible to interference and can be disrupted by such common devices as household cordless phones, some types of fluorescent lights, microwave ovens, and other wireless communications.

- **Security:** Wireless communication coverage requires no access to a physical strand of media. Therefore, devices and users who are not authorized for access to the network can gain access to the transmission. Consequently, network security is a major component of wireless network administration.

Although wireless is increasing in popularity for desktop connectivity, copper and fiber are the most popular physical layer media for network deployments.

Types of Wireless Media (4.2.4.2)

The IEEE and telecommunications industry standards for wireless data communications cover both the data link and physical layers.

Three common data communications standards that apply to wireless media are

- **IEEE 802.11 standard:** Wireless LAN (WLAN) technology, commonly referred to as Wi-Fi, uses a contention or nondeterministic system with a carrier sense multiple access/collision avoidance (CSMA/CA) media access process.

- **IEEE 802.15 standard:** Wireless personal-area network (WPAN) standard, commonly known as "Bluetooth," uses a device pairing process to communicate over distances from 1 to 100 meters.

- **IEEE 802.16 standard:** Commonly known as Worldwide Interoperability for Microwave Access (WiMAX), uses a point-to-multipoint topology to provide wireless broadband access.

Figure 4-13 highlights some of the differences among wireless media.

Figure 4-13   Wireless Media Types

Note

Other wireless technologies, such as cellular and satellite communications, can also provide data network connectivity. However, these wireless technologies are beyond the scope of this chapter.

In each of the examples shown, physical layer specifications are applied to areas that include

- Data-to-radio signal encoding

- Frequency and power of transmission

- Signal reception and decoding requirements

- Antenna design and construction

Note

Wi-Fi is a trademark of the Wi-Fi Alliance. Wi-Fi is used with certified products that belong to WLAN devices that are based on the IEEE 802.11 standards.

Wireless LAN (4.2.4.3)

A common wireless data implementation is enabling devices to connect wirelessly through a LAN. In general, a wireless LAN requires the following network devices:

- **Wireless access point (AP):** Concentrates the wireless signals from users and connects, usually through a copper cable, to the existing copper-based network infrastructure, such as Ethernet. Home and small-business wireless routers integrate the functions of a router, switch, and access point into one device.

- **Wireless NIC adapters:** Provide wireless communication capability to each network host.

As the technology has developed, a number of WLAN Ethernet-based standards have emerged. Care needs to be taken in purchasing wireless devices to ensure compatibility and interoperability.

The benefits of wireless data communications technologies are evident, especially the savings on costly premises wiring and the convenience of host mobility. However, network administrators need to develop and apply stringent security policies and processes to protect wireless LANs from unauthorized access and damage.

802.11 Wi-Fi Standards (4.2.4.4)

Various 802.11 standards have evolved over the years. Standards include

- **IEEE 802.11a:** Operates in the 5-GHz frequency band and offers speeds of up to 54 Mbps. Because this standard operates at higher frequencies, it has a smaller coverage area and is less effective at penetrating building structures. Devices operating under this standard are not interoperable with the 802.11b and 802.11g standards that are described as follows.

- **IEEE 802.11b:** Operates in the 2.4-GHz frequency band and offers speeds of up to 11 Mbps. Devices implementing this standard have a longer range and are better able to penetrate building structures than devices based on 802.11a.

- **IEEE 802.11g:** Operates in the 2.4-GHz frequency band and offers speeds of up to 54 Mbps. Devices implementing this standard therefore operate at the same radio frequency and range as 802.11b but with the bandwidth of 802.11a.

- **IEEE 802.11n:** Operates in the 2.4- or 5-GHz frequency bands. The typical expected data rates are 100 Mbps to 600 Mbps, with a distance range of up to 70 meters. It is backward compatible with 802.11a/b/g devices.

- **IEEE 802.11ac:** Can simultaneously operate in the 2.4- and 5-GHz frequency bands, providing data rates up to 450 Mbps and 1.3 Gbps (1300 Mbps). It is backward compatible with 802.11a/b/g/n devices.

- **IEEE 802.11ad:** Also known as "WiGig." It uses a tri-band Wi-Fi solution using 2.4 GHz, 5 GHz, and 60 GHz and offers theoretical speeds of up to 7 Gbps.

Table 4-7 highlights some of these differences.

Table 4-7   802.11 Wireless LAN Standards

Standard	Maximum Speed	Frequency	Backward Capability
802.11a	54 Mbps	5 GHz	No
802.11b	11 Mbps	2.4 GHz	No
802.11g	54 Mbps	2.4 GHz	802.11b
802.11n	600 Mbps	2.4 GHz or 5GHz	802.11a/b/g
802.11ac	1.3 Gbps	2.4 GHz and 5GHz	802.11a/b/g/n
802.11ad	7 Gbps	2.4 GHz, 5GHz, and 60GHz	802.11a/b/g/n/ac

Packet Tracer Activity 4.2.4.5: Connecting a Wired and Wireless LAN

When working in Packet Tracer (a lab environment or a corporate setting), you should know how to select the appropriate cable and how to properly connect devices. This activity will examine device configurations in Packet Tracer, selecting the proper cable based on the configuration, and connecting the devices. This activity will also explore the physical view of the network in Packet Tracer.

Lab 4.2.4.6: Viewing Wired and Wireless NIC Information

In this lab, you will complete the following objectives:

- Part 1: Identify and Work with PC NICs
- Part 2: Identify and Use the System Tray Network Icons

Data Link Layer Protocols (4.3)

This section introduces the role of the data link layer in sending and receiving data over the physical layer.

Purpose of the Data Link Layer (4.3.1)

Just above physical layer is the data link layer. This layer provides structure to the 1s and 0s that are sent over the media. By adding grouping to the seemingly arbitrary bits being placed on and extracted from the network media, the data link layer provides meaningful data between the upper layers of the sending and receiving nodes. This section will inspect the important functions of the data link layer.

The Data Link Layer (4.3.1.1)

The TCP/IP network access layer is the equivalent of the following OSI layers:

- Data link (Layer 2)
- Physical (Layer 1)

The data link layer is responsible for the exchange of frames between nodes over a physical network media. It allows the upper layers to access the media and controls how data is placed and received on the media.

Note

The Layer 2 notation for network devices connected to a common medium is called a node.

Specifically, the data link layer performs these two basic services:

- It accepts Layer 3 packets and packages them into data units called frames.
- It controls Media Access Control and performs error detection.

The data link layer effectively separates the media transitions that occur as the packet is forwarded from the communication processes of the higher layers. The data link layer receives packets from and directs packets to an upper-layer protocol, in this case IPv4 or IPv6. This upper-layer protocol does not need to be aware of which media the communication will use.

Note

In this chapter, *media* and *medium* do not refer to digital content and multimedia such as audio, animation, television, and video. Media refers to the material that actually carries the data signals, such as copper cable and optical fiber.

Data Link Sublayers (4.3.1.2)

The data link layer is divided into two sublayers:

- *Logical Link Control (LLC):* This upper sublayer defines the software processes that provide services to the network layer protocols. It places information in the frame that identifies which network layer protocol is being used for the frame. This information allows multiple Layer 3 protocols, such as IPv4 and IPv6, to utilize the same network interface and media.

- *Media Access Control (MAC):* This lower sublayer defines the media access processes performed by the hardware. It provides data link layer addressing and delimiting of data according to the physical signaling requirements of the medium and the type of data link layer protocol in use.

Separating the data link layer into sublayers allows one type of frame defined by the upper layer to access different types of media defined by the lower layer. Such is the case in many LAN technologies, including Ethernet.

Figure 4-14 illustrates how the data link layer is separated into the LLC and MAC sublayers. The LLC sublayer communicates with the network layer, while the MAC sublayer allows various network access technologies. For example, the MAC sublayer communicates with Ethernet LAN technology to send and receive frames over copper or fiber-optic cable. The MAC sublayer also communicates with wireless technologies such as Wi-Fi and Bluetooth to send and receive frames wirelessly.

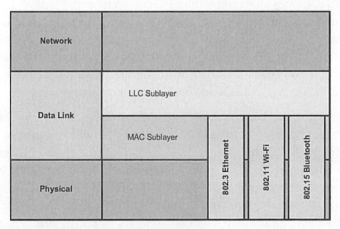

Figure 4-14   Data Link Sublayers

Media Access Control (4.3.1.3)

Layer 2 protocols specify the encapsulation of a packet into a frame and the techniques for getting the encapsulated packet on and off each medium. The technique used for getting the frame on and off media is called the Media Access Control method.

As packets travel from source host to destination host, they typically traverse different physical networks. These physical networks can consist of different types of physical media such as copper wires, optical fibers, and wireless consisting of electromagnetic signals, radio and microwave frequencies, and satellite links.

The packets do not have a way to directly access these different media. It is the role of the OSI data link layer to prepare network layer packets for transmission and to control access to the physical media. The media access control methods described by the data link layer protocols define the processes by which network devices can access the network media and transmit frames in diverse network environments.

Without the data link layer, network layer protocols such as IP would have to make provisions for connecting to every type of media that could exist along a delivery path. Moreover, IP would have to adapt every time a new network technology or medium was developed. This process would hamper protocol and network media innovation and development. This is a key reason for using a layered approach to networking.

Figure 4-15 provides an example of a PC connecting to a laptop across several network segments. Although the two hosts are communicating using IP at the network layer, at each link between the devices, a different medium is used. Each transition at a router might require a different data link layer protocol for transport on a new medium. Numerous data link layer protocols are being used to transport the IP packets over various types of LAN and WAN segments.

On the first segment, between the PC and the router, an Ethernet link exists. So, as an IP packet travels from the PC to the laptop, it will be encapsulated into an Ethernet frame (802.3) leaving the PC. At the first router, the Ethernet frame is deencapsulated, processed, and then encapsulated into a new data link frame to cross the satellite link using a WAN protocol (HDLC, PPP, and so on). For the final segment, the laptop is connected through a wireless link. The packet will use one of the wireless data link frame protocols (802.11b, 802.11g, 802.11n, and so on) from the router to the laptop.

Figure 4-15   Data Link Layer Communication

Providing Access to Media (4.3.1.4)

Different Media Access Control methods might be required during the course of a single communication. Each network environment that packets encounter as they travel from a local host to a remote host can have different characteristics. For example, an Ethernet LAN consists of many hosts contending to access the network medium on an ad hoc basis. Serial links consist of a direct connection between only two devices over which data flows sequentially as bits in an orderly way.

Router interfaces encapsulate the packet into the appropriate frame, and a suitable Media Access Control method is used to access each link. In any given exchange of network layer packets, there can be numerous data link layer and media transitions. At each hop along the path, a router

- Accepts a frame from a medium
- Deencapsulates the frame
- Reencapsulates the packet into a new frame
- Forwards the new frame appropriate to the medium of that segment of the physical network

The router in Figure 4-16 has an Ethernet interface to connect to the LAN and a serial interface to connect to the WAN. As the router processes frames, it will use data link layer services to receive the frame from one medium, deencapsulate it to the Layer 3 PDU, reencapsulate the PDU into a new frame, and place the frame on the medium of the next link of the network.

Figure 4-16   Transfer of Frames

Layer 2 Frame Structure (4.3.2)

As previously mentioned, the data link layer provides grouping to the seemingly random bits being placed on and extracted from the network media. This grouping is accomplished by providing encapsulation using a header and a trailer to create logical units of data. This section will provide an overview of the data link layer encapsulation process.

Formatting Data for Transmission (4.3.2.1)

The data link layer prepares a packet for transport across the local media by encapsulating it with a header and a trailer to create a frame. The description of a frame is a key element of each data link layer protocol.

Data link layer protocols require control information to enable the protocols to function. Control information typically answers the following questions:

- Which nodes are in communication with each other?
- When does communication between individual nodes begin and when does it end?
- Which errors occurred while the nodes communicated?
- Which nodes will communicate next?

Unlike the other PDUs that have been discussed in this course, the data link layer frame includes

- **Header:** Contains control information, such as addressing, and is located at the beginning of the PDU.

- **Data:** Contains the IP header, transport layer header, and application data.

- **Trailer:** Contains control information for error detection added to the end of the PDU.

Creating a Frame (4.3.2.2)

When data travels on the media, it is converted into a stream of bits, or 1s and 0s. If a node is receiving long streams of bits, how does it determine where a frame starts and stops or which bits represent the address?

Framing breaks the stream into decipherable groupings, with control information inserted in the header and trailer as values in different fields. This format gives the physical signals a structure that can be received by nodes and decoded into packets at the destination.

As shown in Figure 4-17, generic frame field types include

- **Frame start and stop indicator flags:** Used by the MAC sublayer to identify the beginning and end limits of the frame.

- **Addressing:** Used by the MAC sublayer to identify the source and destination nodes.

- **Type:** Used by the LLC sublayer to identify the Layer 3 protocol.

- **Control:** Identifies special flow control services.

- **Data:** Contains the frame payload (that is, packet header, segment header, and the data).

- **Error detection:** Included after the data to form the trailer, these frame fields are used for error detection.

Note

Not all protocols include all of these fields. The standards for a specific data-link protocol define the actual frame format. Examples of frame formats will be discussed at the end of this chapter.

Figure 4-17   Fields of a Generic Layer 2 Frame

Activity 4.3.2.3: Generic Frame Fields

Go to the course online to perform this practice activity.

Layer 2 Standards (4.3.3)

The encapsulation process uses very specific formats defined by data link layer protocols. This section will examine some of these protocols.

Data Link Layer Standards (4.3.3.1)

Unlike the protocols of the upper layers of the TCP/IP suite, data link layer protocols are generally not defined by *Requests for Comments (RFC)*. Although the Internet Engineering Task Force (IETF) maintains the functional protocols and services for the TCP/IP protocol suite in the upper layers, the IETF does not define the functions and operation of that model's network access layer.

Specifically the data link layer services and specifications are defined by multiple standards based on a variety of technologies and media to which the protocols are applied. Some of these standards integrate both Layer 2 and Layer 1 services.

The functional protocols and services at the data link layer are described by

- Engineering organizations, which set public and open standards and protocols

- Communications companies, which set and use proprietary protocols to take advantage of new advances in technology or market opportunities

Engineering organizations that define open standards and protocols that apply to the data link layer include

- Institute of Electrical and Electronics Engineers (IEEE)

- International Telecommunication Union (ITU)

- International Organization for Standardization (ISO)
- American National Standards Institute (ANSI)

Table 4-8 highlights various standard organizations and some of their more important data link layer protocols.

Table 4-8 Network Organizations and Standards

Standard Organizations	Networking Standards
IEEE	802.2: Logic Link Control (LLC)
	802.3: Ethernet
	802.4: Token bus
	802.5: Token Ring
	802.11: Wireless LAN (WLAN) and Mesh (Wi-Fi Certification)
	802.15: Bluetooth
	802.16: WiMax
ITU-T	G.992: ADSL
	G.8100–G.8199: MPLS over Transport aspects
	Q 921: ISDN
	Q 922: Frame Relay
ISO	HDLC: (High Level Data Link Control)
	ISO 9314: FDDI Media Access Control
ANSI	X3T9.5 and X3T12: Fiber Distributed Data Interface (FDDI)

Interactive Graphic

Activity 4.3.3.2: Data Link Layer Standards Organizations

Go to the course online to perform this practice activity.

Media Access Control (4.4)

The data entering and exiting nodes is connected; the network media requires coordination. This section will provide an overview of the data link sublayer, which provides this function: Media Access Control.

Topologies (4.4.1)

Nodes on a network can be interconnected in numerous ways. How these nodes are connected or how they communicate is described by the topology of the network. This section will provide an overview of network topologies and how data access to the media is regulated helps define the topology.

Controlling Access to the Media (4.4.1.1)

As with any resource, there need to be rules defining how it is used and shared. The same is true with network media. The rules need to specify how and when a node can place data onto the media. Regulating the placement of data frames onto the media is controlled by the Media Access Control sublayer.

Media Access Control is the equivalent of traffic rules that regulate the entrance of motor vehicles onto a roadway. The absence of any Media Access Control would be the equivalent of vehicles ignoring all other traffic and entering the road without regard to the other vehicles. However, not all roads and entrances are the same. Traffic can enter the road by merging, by waiting for its turn at a stop sign, or by obeying signal lights. A driver follows a different set of rules for each type of entrance.

In the same way, there are different ways to regulate placing frames onto the media. The protocols at the data link layer define the rules for access to different media. Some Media Access Control methods use highly controlled processes to ensure that frames are safely placed on the media. These methods are defined by sophisticated protocols, which require mechanisms that introduce overhead onto the network.

Among the different implementations of the data link layer protocols, there are different methods of controlling access to the media. These Media Access Control techniques define if and how the nodes share the media.

The actual Media Access Control method used depends on

- **Topology:** How the connection between the nodes appears to the data link layer.

- **Media sharing:** How the nodes share the media. The media sharing can be point-to-point, such as in WAN connections, or shared, such as in LAN networks.

Physical and Logical Topologies (4.4.1.2)

The topology of a network is the arrangement or relationship of the network devices and the interconnections between them. LAN and WAN topologies can be viewed in two ways:

- *Physical topology:* Refers to the physical connections and identifies how end devices and infrastructure devices such as routers, switches, and wireless access points are interconnected. Physical topologies are usually point-to-point or star. See Figure 4-18.

- *Logical topology:* Refers to the way a network transfers frames from one node to the next. This arrangement consists of virtual connections between the nodes of a network. These logical signal paths are defined by data link layer protocols. The logical topology of point-to-point links is relatively simple while shared media offers deterministic and nondeterministic Media Access Control methods. See Figure 4-19.

The data link layer "sees" the logical topology of a network when controlling data access to the media. It is the logical topology that influences the type of network framing and Media Access Control used.

Figure 4-18   Physical Topology

Figure 4-19   Logical Topology

WAN Topologies (4.4.2)

Traditional WANs technologies have some common methods of interconnection and associated Media Access Control. This section will introduce some of these physical and logical topologies.

Common Physical WAN Topologies (4.4.2.1)

WANs are commonly interconnected using the following physical topologies:

- **Point-to-point:** This is the simplest topology that consists of a permanent link between two endpoints. For this reason, this is a very popular WAN topology.

- **Hub-and-spoke:** A WAN version of the star topology in which a central site interconnects branch sites using point-to-point links.

- **Mesh:** This topology provides high availability, but requires that every end system be interconnected to every other system. Therefore, the administrative and physical costs can be significant. Each link is essentially a point-to-point link to the other node. Variations of this topology include a partial mesh, where some but not all the end devices are interconnected.

The three common physical topologies are illustrated in Figure 4-20.

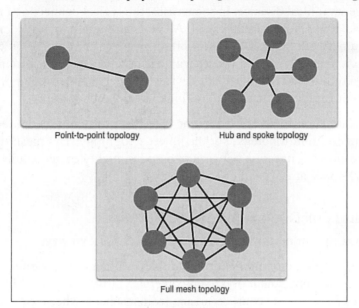

Figure 4-20   Common Physical Topologies

Physical Point-to-Point Topology (4.4.2.2)

Physical point-to-point topologies directly connect two nodes.

In this arrangement, two nodes do not have to share the media with other hosts. Additionally, a node does not have to make any determination about whether an incoming frame is destined for it or another node. Therefore, the logical data-link protocols can be very simple as all frames on the media can only travel to or from the two nodes. The frames are placed on the media by the node at one end and taken off the media by the node at the other end of the point-to-point circuit.

Data link layer protocols could provide more sophisticated Media Access Control processes for logical point-to-point topologies, but this would only add unnecessary protocol overhead.

Logical Point-to-Point Topology (4.4.2.3)

The end nodes communicating in a point-to-point network can be physically connected through a number of intermediate devices. However, the use of physical devices in the network does not affect the logical topology.

The source and destination node can be indirectly connected to each other over some geographical distance. In some cases, the logical connection between nodes forms what is called a virtual circuit. A virtual circuit is a logical connection created within a network between two network devices. The two nodes on either end of the virtual circuit exchange the frames with each other. This occurs even if the frames are directed through intermediary devices. Virtual circuits are important logical communication constructs used by some Layer 2 technologies.

The media access method used by the data-link protocol is determined by the logical point-to-point topology, not the physical topology. This means that the logical point-to-point connection between two nodes might not necessarily be between two physical nodes at each end of a single physical link.

Half and Full Duplex (4.4.2.4)

In point-to-point networks, data can flow in one of two ways:

- **Half-duplex communication:** Both devices can both transmit and receive on the media but cannot do so simultaneously. Ethernet has established arbitration rules for resolving conflicts arising from instances when more than one station attempts to transmit at the same time.

- **Full-duplex communication:** Both devices can transmit and receive on the media at the same time. The data link layer assumes that the media is available for transmission for both nodes at any time. Therefore, there is no media arbitration necessary in the data link layer.

LAN Topologies (4.4.3)

Like WANs, some physical and logical topologies are more predominately used in LANs. These topologies will be examined in this section.

Physical LAN Topologies (4.4.3.1)

Physical topology defines how the end systems are physically interconnected. In shared media LANs, end devices can be interconnected using the following physical topologies:

- **Star:** End devices are connected to a central intermediate device. Early star topologies interconnected end devices using hubs. However, star topologies now use switches. The star topology is the most common physical LAN topology primarily because it is easy to install, very scalable (easy to add and remove end devices), and easy to troubleshoot.

- **Extended star or hybrid:** This is a combination of the other topologies, such as star networks interconnected to each other using a bus topology.

- **Bus:** All end systems are chained to each other and terminated in some form on each end. Infrastructure devices such as switches are not required to interconnect the end devices. Bus topologies were used in legacy Ethernet networks because they were inexpensive to use and easy to set up.

- **Ring:** End systems are connected to their respective neighbor, forming a ring. Unlike the bus topology, the ring does not need to be terminated. Ring topologies were used in legacy Fiber Distributed Data Interface (FDDI) networks. Specifically, FDDI networks employ a second ring for fault tolerance or performance enhancements.

Figure 4-21 illustrates some common methods for interconnecting end devices on LANs.

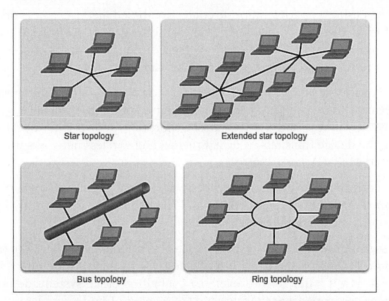

Figure 4-21   Physical Topologies Commonly Used in LANs

Logical Topology for Shared Media (4.4.3.2)

Logical topology of a network is closely related to the mechanism used to manage network access. Access methods provide the procedures to manage network access so that all stations have access. When several entities share the same media, some mechanism must be in place to control access. Access methods are applied to networks to regulate this media access.

Some network topologies share a common medium with multiple nodes. At any one time, there can be a number of devices attempting to send and receive data using the network media. There are rules that govern how these devices share the media.

There are two basic Media Access Control methods for shared media:

- **Contention-based access:** All nodes compete for the use of the medium but have a plan if there are collisions.

- **Controlled access:** Each node has its own time to use the medium.

The data link layer protocol specifies the Media Access Control method that will provide the appropriate balance between frame control, frame protection, and network overhead.

Contention-Based Access (4.4.3.3)

When using a nondeterministic contention-based method, a network device can attempt to access the medium whenever it has data to send. To prevent complete chaos on the media, these methods use a carrier sense multiple access (CSMA) process to first detect whether the media is carrying a signal.

If a carrier signal on the media from another node is detected, it means that another device is transmitting. When the device attempting to transmit sees that the media is busy, it will wait and try again after a short time period. If no carrier signal is detected, the device transmits its data. Ethernet and wireless networks use contention-based Media Access Control.

It is possible that the CSMA process will fail and two devices will transmit at the same time, creating a data collision. If this occurs, the data sent by both devices will be corrupted and will need to be resent.

Contention-based Media Access Control methods do not have the overhead of controlled access methods. A mechanism for tracking whose turn it is to access the media is not required. However, the contention-based systems do not scale well under heavy media use. As use and the number of nodes increase, the probability of successful media access without a collision decreases. Additionally, the recovery mechanisms required to correct errors due to these collisions further diminishes the throughput.

CSMA is usually implemented in conjunction with a method for resolving the media contention. The two commonly used methods are

- **Carrier sense multiple access with collision detection (CSMA/CD):** The end device monitors the media for the presence of a data signal. If a data signal is absent and therefore the media is free, the device transmits the data. If signals are then detected that show another device was transmitting at the same time, all devices stop sending and try again later. Traditional forms of Ethernet use this method.

- **Carrier sense multiple access with collision avoidance (CSMA/CA):** The end device examines the media for the presence of a data signal. If the media is free, the device sends a notification across the media of its intent to use it. After it receives a clearance to transmit, the device then sends the data. This method is used by 802.11 wireless networking technologies.

Some characteristics of contention-based access are

- Stations can transmit onto the media at any time.

- Collisions exist on the media.

- Mechanisms resolve media contention.

Multiaccess Topology (4.4.3.4)

A logical multiaccess topology enables a number of nodes to communicate by using the same shared media. Data from only one node can be placed on the medium at any one time. Every node sees all the frames that are on the medium, but only the node to which the frame is addressed processes the contents of the frame.

Having many nodes share access to the medium requires a data-link Media Access Control method to regulate the transmission of data and thereby reduce collisions between different signals.

Controlled Access (4.4.3.5)

When using the controlled access method, network devices take turns, in sequence, to access the medium. If an end device does not need to access the medium, the opportunity passes to the next end device. This process is facilitated by use of a token. An end device acquires the token and places a frame on the media. No other device can do so until the frame has arrived and been processed at the destination, releasing the token.

Note

This method is also known as scheduled access or deterministic.

Although controlled access is well-ordered and provides predictable throughput, deterministic methods can be inefficient because a device has to wait for its turn before it can use the medium.

Controlled access examples include

- Token Ring (IEEE 802.5)
- Fiber Distributed Data Interface (FDDI), which is based on the IEEE 802.4 token bus protocol.

Note

Both of these Media Access Control methods are considered obsolete.

Some characteristics of controlled access are

- Only one station can transmit at a time.
- Devices wanting to transmit must wait their turn.
- No collisions on the media.
- Can use token passing to avoid contention.

Ring Topology (4.4.3.6)

In a logical ring topology, each node in turn receives a frame. If the frame is not addressed to the node, the node passes the frame to the next node. This allows a ring to use a controlled Media Access Control technique called token passing.

Nodes in a logical ring topology remove the frame from the ring, examine the address, and send it on if it is not addressed for that node. In a ring, all nodes around the ring (between the source and destination node) examine the frame.

There are multiple Media Access Control techniques that could be used with a logical ring, depending on the level of control required. For example, only one frame at a time is usually carried by the media. If there is no data being transmitted, a signal (known as a token) can be placed on the media and a node can only place a data frame on the media when it has the token.

Remember that the data link layer "sees" a logical ring topology. The actual physical cabling topology could be another topology.

Activity 4.4.3.7: Logical and Physical Topologies

Go to the course online to perform this practice activity.

Data-Link Frame (4.4.4)

The data link layer needs to provide intelligible data between the Layer 3 of the sending host and the Layer 3 of the receiving host. To do this, the Layer 3 PDU is wrapped with a header and trailer to form the Layer 2 frame. This section will examine the common elements of within the frame structure as well as explore some of the commonly used data link layer protocols.

The Frame (4.4.4.1)

Although there are many different data link layer protocols that describe data link layer frames, each frame type has three basic parts:

- Header

- Data

- Trailer

All data link layer protocols encapsulate the Layer 3 PDU within the data field of the frame. However, the structure of the frame and the fields contained in the header and trailer vary according to the protocol.

The data link layer protocol describes the features required for the transport of packets across different media. These features of the protocol are integrated into the encapsulation of the frame. When the frame arrives at its destination and the data-link protocol takes the frame off the media, the framing information is read and discarded.

There is no one frame structure that meets the needs of all data transportation across all types of media. Depending on the environment, the amount of control information needed in the frame varies to match the Media Access Control requirements of the media and logical topology.

A fragile environment requires more control. However, a protected environment needs fewer controls.

The Header (4.4.4.2)

The frame header contains the control information specified by the data link layer protocol for the specific logical topology and media used.

Frame control information is unique to each type of protocol. It is used by the Layer 2 protocol to provide features demanded by the communication environment.

The Ethernet frame header fields are as follows:

- **Start Frame field:** Indicates the beginning of the frame. This field tells other devices on the network segment that a frame is starting to be transmitted on the medium.

- **Source and Destination Address fields:** Indicate the source and destination nodes on the media.

- **Type field:** Indicates the upper-layer service contained in the frame or the length of the frame.

Different data link layer protocols might use different fields from those mentioned. For example, other Layer 2 protocol header frame fields could include

- **Priority/Quality of Service field:** Indicates a particular type of communication service for processing.

- **Logical Connection Control field:** Used to establish a logical connection between nodes.

- **Physical Link Control field:** Used to establish the media link.

- **Flow Control field:** Used to start and stop traffic over the media.

- **Congestion Control field:** Indicates congestion in the media.

Because the purposes and functions of data link layer protocols are related to the specific topologies and media, each protocol has to be examined to gain a detailed understanding of its frame structure. As protocols are discussed in this course, more information about the frame structure will be explained.

Layer 2 Address (4.4.4.3)

The data link layer provides addressing that is used in transporting a frame across a shared local media. Device addresses at this layer are referred to as physical addresses. Data link layer addressing is contained within the frame header and specifies the frame destination node on the local network. The frame header can also contain the source address of the frame.

Unlike Layer 3 logical addresses, which are hierarchical, physical addresses do not indicate on what network the device is located. Rather, the physical address is a unique device-specific address. If the device is moved to another network or subnet, it will still function with the same Layer 2 physical address.

An address that is device specific and nonhierarchical cannot be used to locate a device across large networks or the Internet. This would be like trying to find a single house within the entire world, with nothing more than a house number and street name. The physical address, however, can be used to locate a device within a limited area. For this reason, the data link layer address is only used for local delivery. Addresses at this layer have no meaning beyond the local network. Compare this to Layer 3, where addresses in the packet header are carried from source host to destination host regardless of the number of network hops along the route.

If the data must pass onto another network segment, an intermediate device, such as a router, is necessary. The router must accept the frame based on the physical address and deencapsulate the frame to examine the hierarchical address, or IP address. Using the IP address, the router is able to determine the network location of the destination device and the best path to reach it. After it knows where to forward the packet, the router then creates a new frame for the packet, and the new frame is sent onto the next segment toward its final destination.

The Trailer (4.4.4.4)

Data link layer protocols add a trailer to the end of each frame. The trailer is used to determine whether the frame arrived without error. This process is called error detection and is accomplished by placing a logical or mathematical summary of the bits that comprise the frame in the trailer. Error detection is added at the data link layer because the signals on the media could be subject to interference, distortion, or loss that would substantially change the bit values that those signals represent.

The FCS is used for error checking. A transmitting node creates a logical summary of the contents of the frame. This summary is a calculated number based on the frame's data. This is known as the cyclic redundancy check (CRC) value. This value is placed in the Frame Check Sequence (FCS) field of the frame to represent the contents of the frame's data.

When the frame arrives at the destination node, the receiving node calculates its own logical summary, or CRC, of the frame. The receiving node compares the two CRC values. If the two values are the same, the frame is considered to have arrived intact. If the CRC value in the FCS differs from the CRC calculated at the receiving node, the frame is discarded.

Note

In unreliable Layer 2 protocols such as Ethernet, bad frames are quietly discarded. There is no feedback by Layer 2 services to the transmitting node that the frame has been discarded.

Therefore, the FCS field is used to determine whether errors occurred in the transmission and reception of the frame. The error-detection mechanism provided by the use of the FCS field discovers most errors caused on the media.

There is always the small possibility that a frame with a good CRC result is actually corrupt. Errors in bits can cancel each other out when the CRC is calculated. Upper-layer protocols would then be required to detect and correct this data loss.

The Stop Frame field is a delimiter that indicates the end of the frame. The transmitting node adds this after the FCS to indicate that the entire frame has been sent. The receiving node examines the bits as received, looking for the specific Stop Frame pattern. When this pattern is recognized, the receiving node knows that the entire frame has been captured off the media.

Note

Error detections should not be confused with reliability or error correction. Reliability is the process of using error detection to determine whether there are errors in the data and to retransmit the data if necessary. Error correction is the ability to determine whether a frame contains an error and the ability to repair the error from the information sent with the frame communication.

Both error detection and error correction involve the additional bits. With error checking, these bits are only used to determine the error. With error correction, the bits are used to restore the flawed data to the original bits of data as they were transmitted. Therefore, error correction is more complex and requires more overhead than error detection.

LAN and WAN Frames (4.4.4.5)

In a TCP/IP network, all OSI Layer 2 protocols work with the IP at OSI Layer 3. However, the actual Layer 2 protocol used depends on the logical topology of the network and the implementation of the physical layer. Given the wide range of physical media used across the range of topologies in networking, there are a correspondingly high number of Layer 2 protocols in use.

Each protocol performs Media Access Control for specified Layer 2 logical topologies. This means that a number of different network devices can act as nodes that operate at the data link layer when implementing these protocols. These devices include the network adapter or network interface cards (NIC) on computers as well as the interfaces on routers and Layer 2 switches.

The Layer 2 protocol used for a particular network topology is determined by the technology used to implement that topology. The technology is, in turn, determined by the size of the network—in terms of the number of hosts and the geographic scope—and the services to be provided over the network.

A LAN typically uses a high-bandwidth technology that is capable of supporting large numbers of hosts. A LAN's relatively small geographic area (a single building or a multibuilding campus) and its high density of users make this technology cost effective.

However, using a high-bandwidth technology is usually not cost effective for WANs that cover large geographic areas (cities or multiple cities, for example). The cost of the long-distance physical links and the technology used to carry the signals over those distances typically results in lower bandwidth capacity.

Difference in bandwidth normally results in the use of different protocols for LANs and WANs.

Common data link layer protocols include

- Ethernet

- Point-to-Point Protocol (PPP)

- 802.11 Wireless

Other protocols covered in the CCNA curriculum are High-Level Data Link Control (HDLC) and Frame Relay. In Figure 4-22, the data is in transit from the wireless laptop to the Ethernet host. At each hop, the Layer 2 framing of the receiving media is removed and the framing of the new media is added before sending on the media. Initially, the data link layer framing is an 802.11 for wireless. Then along the three WAN segments, there is a different WAN framing used on each segment: PPP, HDLC, and Frame Relay. The last segment is an Ethernet LAN segment using Ethernet framing. Even though multiple Layer 2 encapsulations are used, the packet with the Layer 3 encapsulation inside remains relatively unchanged.

Figure 4-22   Examples of Layer 2 Protocols

Ethernet Frame (4.4.4.6)

This section introduces the Ethernet frame structure.

Ethernet

Ethernet is the dominant LAN technology. It is a family of networking technologies that are defined in the IEEE 802.2 and 802.3 standards.

Ethernet standards define both the Layer 2 protocols and the Layer 1 technologies. Ethernet is the most widely used LAN technology and supports data bandwidths of 10 Mbps, 100 Mbps, 1 Gbps (1000 Mbps), or 10 Gbps (10,000 Mbps).

The basic frame format and the IEEE sublayers of OSI Layers 1 and 2 remain consistent across all forms of Ethernet. However, the methods for detecting and placing data on the media vary with different implementations.

Traditionally, Ethernet provides unacknowledged connectionless service over a shared media using CSMA/CD as the media access methods. Shared media requires that the Ethernet frame header use a data link layer address to identify the source and destination nodes. As with most LAN protocols, this address is referred to as the MAC address of the node. An Ethernet MAC address is 48 bits and is generally represented in hexadecimal format.

Figure 4-23 shows the many fields of the Ethernet frame. Some of these fields are

- **Preamble:** Used to time synchronization; this also contains a delimiter to mark the end of the timing information.

- **Destination Address:** 48-bit MAC address for the destination node.

- **Source Address:** 48-bit MAC address for the source node.

- **Type:** Value to indicate which upper-layer protocol will receive the data after the Ethernet process is complete.

- **Data or Payload:** This is the PDU, typically an IPv4 packet, that is to be transported over the media.

- **Frame Check Sequence (FCS):** A CRC value used to check for damaged frames.

At the data link layer, the frame structure is nearly identical for all speeds of Ethernet. However, at the physical layer, different versions of Ethernet place the bits onto the media differently. Ethernet is discussed in more detail in the next chapter.

Figure 4-23   Ethernet Frame Fields

PPP Frame (4.4.4.7)

This section introduces the PPP WAN protocol.

Point-to-Point Protocol

Another data link layer protocol is the Point-to-Point Protocol (PPP). PPP is a protocol used to deliver frames between two nodes. Unlike many data link layer protocols that are defined by electrical engineering organizations, the PPP standard is defined by RFCs. PPP was developed as a WAN protocol and remains the protocol of choice to implement many serial WANs. PPP can be used on various physical media, including twisted-pair, fiber-optic lines, and satellite transmission, as well as for virtual connections.

PPP uses a layered architecture. To accommodate the different types of media, PPP establishes logical connections, called sessions, between two nodes. The PPP session hides the underlying physical media from the upper layers of PPP. These sessions also provide PPP with a method for encapsulating multiple protocols over a point-to-point link. Each protocol encapsulated over the link establishes its own PPP session.

PPP also allows the two nodes to negotiate options within the PPP session. This includes authentication, compression, and multilink (the use of multiple physical connections).

Figure 4-24 shows some of these basic fields in a PPP frame:

- **Flag:** A single byte that indicates the beginning or end of a frame. The flag field consists of the binary sequence 01111110.

- **Address:** A single byte that contains the standard PPP broadcast address. PPP does not assign individual station addresses.

- **Control:** A single byte that contains the binary sequence 00000011, which calls for transmission of user data in an unsequenced frame.

- **Protocol:** Two bytes that identify the protocol encapsulated in the data field of the frame. The most up-to-date values of the protocol field are specified in the most recent Assigned Numbers RFC.

- **Data:** Zero or more bytes that contain the datagram for the protocol specified in the protocol field.

- **Frame Check Sequence (FCS):** Normally 16 bits (2 bytes). By prior agreement, consenting PPP implementations can use a 32-bit (4-byte) FCS for improved error detection.

	Flag	Address	Control	Protocol	Data	Frame Check Sequence
Field Name						
Size (Bytes)	1 Byte	1 Byte	1 Byte	2 Bytes	Variable	2 or 4 Bytes

Figure 4-24   PPP Frame Fields

802.11 Wireless Frame (4.4.4.8)

An overview of the 802.11 wireless protocol family is presented in this section.

802.11 Wireless

The IEEE 802.11 standard uses the same 802.2 LLC and 48-bit addressing scheme as other 802 LANs. However, there are many differences at the MAC sublayer and physical layer. In a wireless environment, the environment requires special considerations. There is no definable physical connectivity; therefore, external factors can interfere with data transfer and it is difficult to control access. To meet these challenges, wireless standards have additional controls.

The IEEE 802.11 standard is commonly referred to as Wi-Fi. It is a contention-based system using a CSMA/CA media access process. CSMA/CA specifies a random backoff procedure for all nodes that are waiting to transmit. The most likely opportunity for medium contention is just after the medium becomes available. Making the nodes back off for a random period greatly reduces the likelihood of a collision.

802.11 networks also use data-link acknowledgements to confirm that a frame is received successfully. If the sending station does not detect the acknowledgement frame, either because the original data frame or the acknowledgement was not received intact, the frame is retransmitted. This explicit acknowledgement overcomes interference and other radio-related problems.

Other services supported by 802.11 are authentication, association (connectivity to a wireless device), and privacy (encryption).

As shown in Figure 4-25, an 802.11 frame contains these fields:

- **Protocol Version field:** Version of 802.11 frame in use

- **Type and Subtype fields:** Identify one of three functions and subfunctions of the frame: control, data, and management

- **To DS field:** Set to 1 in data frames destined for the distribution system (devices in the wireless structure)

- **From DS field:** Set to 1 in data frames exiting the distribution system

- **More Fragments field:** Set to 1 for frames that have another fragment

- **Retry field:** Set to 1 if the frame is a retransmission of an earlier frame

- **Power Management field:** Set to 1 to indicate that a node will be in power-save mode

- **More Data field:** Set to 1 to indicate to a node in power-save mode that more frames are buffered for that node

- **Wired Equivalent Privacy (WEP) field:** Set to 1 if the frame contains WEP-encrypted information for security

- **Order field:** Set to 1 in a data type frame that uses Strictly Ordered service class (does not need reordering)

- **Duration/ID field:** Depending on the type of frame, represents either the time, in microseconds, required to transmit the frame or an association identity (AID) for the station that transmitted the frame

- **Destination Address (DA) field:** MAC address of the final destination node in the network

- **Source Address (SA) field:** MAC address of the node that initiated the frame

- **Receiver Address (RA) field:** MAC address that identifies the wireless device that is the immediate recipient of the frame

- **Fragment Number field:** Indicates the number for each fragment of a frame

- **Sequence Number field:** Indicates the sequence number assigned to the frame; retransmitted frames are identified by duplicate sequence numbers

- **Transmitter Address (TA) field:** MAC address that identifies the wireless device that transmitted the frame

- **Frame Body field:** Contains the information being transported; for data frames, typically an IP packet

- **FCS field:** Contains a 32-bit cyclic redundancy check (CRC) of the frame

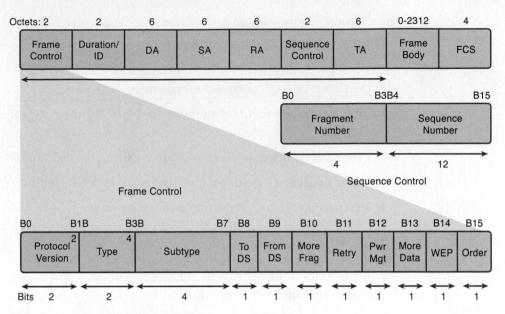

Figure 4-25   802.11 Frame Fields

Activity 4.4.4.9: Frame Fields

Go to the course online to perform this practice activity.

Summary (4.5)

Class Activity 4.5.1.1: Linked In!

Note

This activity is best completed in groups of 2–3 students.

Your small business is moving to a new location! Your building is brand new, and you have been tasked to come up with a physical model so that network port installation can begin.

Use the blueprint provided for this activity (your instructor will provide you with a copy from the Instructor Planning Guide). The area indicated by Number 1 is the reception area; the area numbered RR is the restroom area.

All rooms are within Category 6, UTP specifications (100 meters), so you have no worries about hard-wiring the building to code. Each room in the diagram must have at least one network connection available for users/intermediary devices.

With your teammate(s), indicate the following on the drawing:

- The location of your network main distribution facility, while keeping security in mind

- The number of intermediary devices that you would use and where you would place them

- The type of cabling that would be used (UTP, STP, wireless, fiber-optic, and so on) and where would the ports be placed

- The types of end devices that would be used (wired, wireless, laptops, desktops, tablets, and so on)

Do not go "overboard" on your design; just use the content from the chapter to be able to justify your decisions to the class.

The TCP/IP network access layer is the equivalent of the OSI data link layer (Layer 2) and the physical layer (Layer 1).

The OSI physical layer provides the means to transport the bits that make up a data link layer frame across the network media. The physical components are the electronic hardware devices, media, and other connectors that transmit and carry the signals to represent the bits. Hardware components such as network adapters (NICs), interfaces and connectors, cable materials, and cable designs are all specified in standards associated with the physical layer. The physical layer standards address three functional areas: physical components, frame encoding technique, and signaling method.

Using the proper media is an important part of network communications. Without the proper physical connection, either wired or wireless, communications between any two devices will not occur.

Wired communication consists of copper media and fiber cable, as follows

- There are three main types of copper media used in networking: unshielded twisted-pair (UTP), shielded twisted-pair (STP), and coaxial cable. UTP cabling is the most common copper networking media.

- Optical fiber cable has become very popular for interconnecting infrastructure network devices. It permits the transmission of data over longer distances and at higher bandwidths (data rates) than any other networking media. Unlike copper wires, fiber-optic cable can transmit signals with less attenuation and is immune to EMI and RFI.

Wireless media carry electromagnetic signals that represent the binary digits of data communications using radio or microwave frequencies.

The number of wireless-enabled devices continues to increase. For these reasons, wireless has become the medium of choice for home networks and is quickly gaining in popularity in enterprise networks.

The data link layer is responsible for the exchange of frames between nodes over a physical network media. It allows the upper layers to access the media and controls how data is placed and received on the media.

Among the different implementations of the data link layer protocols, there are different methods of controlling access to the media. These Media Access Control techniques define if and how the nodes share the media. The actual Media Access Control method used depends on the topology and media sharing. LAN and WAN topologies can be physical or logical. It is the logical topology that influences the type of network framing and Media Access Control used. WANs are commonly interconnected using the point-to-point, hub-and-spoke, or mesh physical topologies. In shared media LANs, end devices can be interconnected using the star, bus, ring, or extended star (hybrid) physical topologies.

All data link layer protocols encapsulate the Layer 3 PDU within the data field of the frame. However, the structure of the frame and the fields contained in the header and trailer vary according to the protocol.

Practice

The following activities provide practice with the topics introduced in this chapter. The labs and class activities are available in the companion *Introduction to Networking Lab Manual* (ISBN 978-1-58713-312-1). The Packet Tracer Activities PKA files are found in the online course.

Class Activities

- Class Activity 4.0.1.2: Managing the Medium
- Class Activity 4.5.1.1: Linked In!

Labs

- Lab 4.1.2.4: Identifying Network Devices and Cabling
- Lab 4.2.2.7: Building an Ethernet Crossover Cable
- Lab 4.2.4.6: Viewing Wired and Wireless NIC Information

Packet Tracer Activities

- Packet Tracer Activity 4.2.4.5: Connecting a Wired and Wireless LAN

Check Your Understanding

Complete all the review questions listed here to test your understanding of the topics and concepts in this chapter. The appendix, "Answers to the 'Check Your Understanding' Questions" lists the answers.

1. What are the purpose and functions of the physical layer in data networks? (Choose two.)

   A. Controls how the data is transmitted onto the physical media

   B. Encodes the data into signals

   C. Provides logical addressing

   D. Packages bits into data units

   E. Controls media access

2. Which of these statements regarding UTP network cabling are true? (Choose two.)

   A. Uses light to transmit data

   B. Susceptible to EMI and RFI

   C. Commonly used between buildings

   D. Most difficult type of networking cable to install

   E. Most commonly used type of networking cable

3. What is the purpose of cladding in fiber-optic cables?

   A. Cable grounding

   B. Noise cancellation

   C. Prevention of light loss

   D. EMI protection

4. Identify the wire colors associated with the pins when building a 568B network cable.

   A. Pin 1 _____

   B. Pin 2 _____

   C. Pin 3 _____

   D. Pin 4 _____

   E. Pin 5 _____

   F. Pin 6 _____

   G. Pin 7 _____

   H. Pin 8 _____

5. What are the advantages of using fiber-optic cable over copper cable? (Choose three.)

   A. Copper is more expensive.

   B. Immunity to electromagnetic interference.

   C. Careful cable handling.

   D. Longer maximum cable length.

   E. Efficient electrical current transfer.

   F. Greater bandwidth potential.

6. What occurs when another wireless device connects to a wireless access point (WAP)?

    A. The WAP adds an additional channel to support the new client.

    B. The WAP throughput for all the connected clients decreases.

    C. The WAP decreases the radio coverage area.

    D. The WAP will change frequencies to reduce interference caused by the new client.

7. If a node receives a frame and the calculated CRC does not match the CRC in the FCS, what action will the node take?

    A. Drop the frame

    B. Reconstruct the frame from the CRC

    C. Forward the frame as it is to the next host

    D. Disable the interface on which the frame arrives

8. What are the contents of the data field in a frame?

    A. A CRC

    B. The network layer PDU

    C. The Layer 2 source address

    D. The length of the frame

9. Which of the following is true about the logical topology of a network?

    A. Is always multiaccess

    B. Provides the physical addressing

    C. Is determined by how the nodes in the network are connected

    D. Defines how frames are transferred from one node to the next

10. Which of the following is a characteristic of contention-based MAC?

    A. Used in point-to-point topologies.

    B. Nodes compete for the use of the medium.

    C. Leaves MAC to the upper layer.

    D. Each node has a specific time to use the medium.

Objectives

Upon completion of this chapter, you will be able to answer the following questions:

- What is the function of each of the Ethernet sublayers?

- What are the major fields in an Ethernet frame?

- What are the characteristics and purpose of the Ethernet MAC address?

- What is the role of ARP in an Ethernet network?

- How do ARP requests impact network and host performance?

- How is traffic switched in a Layer 2 switched network?

- How do fixed configuration and modular switches compare?

- How does a Layer 3 switch function?

- What steps are required to configure a Layer 3 switch?

Key Terms

This chapter uses the following key terms. You can find the definitions in the Glossary.

protocol data units (PDU)   page 233

carrier sense multiple access (CSMA) page 236

contention-based   page 237

CSMA/collision detection (CSMA/CD) page 237

CSMA/collision avoidance (CSMA/ CA)   page 237

overhead   page 238

Organizationally Unique Identifier (OUI)   page 238

collision fragment   page 242

runt frame   page 242

virtual local-area network (VLAN) page 242

cyclic redundancy check (CRC)   page 244

hexadecimal   page 244

ARP table   page 254

gateway   page 256

next hop   page 256

spoofing   page 260

switch fabric   page 261

MAC address table   page 261

content addressable memory (CAM) table   page 263

Introduction (5.0.1.1)

The OSI physical layer provides the means to transport the bits that make up a data link layer frame across the network media.

Ethernet is now the predominant LAN technology in the world. Ethernet operates in the data link layer and the physical layer. The Ethernet protocol standards define many aspects of network communication including frame format, frame size, timing, and encoding. When messages are sent between hosts on an Ethernet network, the hosts format the messages into the frame layout that is specified by the standards. Frames are also referred to as *protocol data units (PDU)*.

Because Ethernet is comprised of standards at these lower layers, it can best be understood in reference to the OSI model. The OSI model separates the data link layer functionalities of addressing, framing, and accessing the media from the physical layer standards of the media. Ethernet standards define both the Layer 2 protocols and the Layer 1 technologies. Although Ethernet specifications support different media, bandwidths, and other Layer 1 and 2 variations, the basic frame format and address scheme are the same for all varieties of Ethernet.

This chapter examines the characteristics and operation of Ethernet as it has evolved from a shared media, contention-based data communications technology to today's high-bandwidth, full-duplex technology.

Class Activity 5.0.1.2: Join My Social Circle!

Much of our network communication takes the form of messaging (text or instant), video contact, social media postings, and so on.

For this activity, choose one of the communication networks that you use most:

- Text (or instant) messaging
- Audio/videoconferencing
- Emailing
- Gaming

Now that you have selected a network communication type, record your answers to the following questions:

- Is there a procedure you must follow to register others and yourself so that you form a communications group?
- How do you initiate contact with the person/people with whom you want to communicate?
- How do you limit your conversations so that they are received by only those with whom you want to communicate?

Be prepared to discuss your recorded answers in class.

Ethernet Protocol (5.1)

As previously stated, Ethernet is the most widely used LAN technology today. It provides high-speed communications between end devices in most local-area networks. For this reason, a good understanding of Ethernet technology is a requirement for anyone working with LAN technology.

Ethernet Operation (5.1.1)

Ethernet operates in the data link layer and the physical layer. It is a family of networking technologies that are defined in the IEEE 802.2 and 802.3 standards. Ethernet supports data bandwidths of

- 10 Mbps
- 100 Mbps
- 1000 Mbps (1 Gbps)
- 10,000 Mbps (10 Gbps)
- 40,000 Mbps (40 Gbps)
- 100,000 Mbps (100 Gbps)

As shown in Figure 5-1, Ethernet standards define both the Layer 2 protocols and the Layer 1 technologies. For the Layer 2 protocols, as with all 802 IEEE standards, Ethernet relies on the two separate sublayers of the data link layer to operate: the Logical Link Control (LLC) and the MAC sublayers.

Figure 5-1   Ethernet

LLC and MAC Sublayers (5.1.1.1)

Each of the two sublayers of the data link layer has specific functions.

LLC Sublayer

The Ethernet LLC sublayer handles the communication between the upper layers and the lower layers. This is typically between the networking software and the device hardware. The LLC sublayer takes the network protocol data, which is typically an IPv4 packet, and adds control information to help deliver the packet to the destination node. The LLC is used to communicate with the upper layers of the application and transition the packet to the lower layers for delivery.

LLC is implemented in software, and its implementation is independent of the hardware. In a computer, the LLC can be considered the driver software for the network interface card (NIC). The NIC driver is a program that interacts directly with the hardware on the NIC to pass the data between the MAC sublayer and the physical media.

MAC Sublayer

The MAC sublayer is the lower portion of the data link layer. MAC is implemented by hardware, typically in the computer NIC. The specifics are specified in the IEEE 802.3 standards. Figure 5-2 shows some common IEEE Ethernet standards.

Figure 5-2   Common IEEE Ethernet Standards

MAC Sublayer (5.1.1.2)

The Ethernet MAC sublayer has two primary responsibilities:

- Data encapsulation
- Media access control

Data Encapsulation

The data encapsulation process includes frame assembly before transmission and frame disassembly upon reception of a frame. In forming the frame, the MAC layer adds a header and trailer to the network layer PDU.

Data encapsulation provides three primary functions:

- **Frame delimiting:** The framing process provides important delimiters that are used to identify a group of bits that make up a frame. This process provides synchronization between the transmitting and receiving nodes.

- **Addressing:** The encapsulation process also provides for data link layer addressing. Each Ethernet header added in the frame contains the physical address (MAC address) that enables a frame to be delivered to a destination node.

- **Error detection:** Each Ethernet frame contains a trailer with a cyclic redundancy check (CRC) of the frame contents. After reception of a frame, the receiving node creates a CRC to compare to the one in the frame. If these two CRC calculations match, the frame can be trusted to have been received without error.

The use of frames aids in the transmission of bits as they are placed on the media and in the grouping of bits at the receiving node.

Media Access Control

The second responsibility of the MAC sublayer is media access control. Media access control is responsible for the placement of frames on the media and the removal of frames from the media. As its name implies, it controls access to the media. This sublayer communicates directly with the physical layer.

The underlying logical topology of Ethernet is a multiaccess bus; therefore, all nodes (devices) on a single network segment share the medium. Ethernet is a contention-based method of networking. Recall that a contention-based method, or nondeterministic method, means that any device can try to transmit data across the shared medium whenever it has data to send. However, much like if two people try to talk simultaneously, if multiple devices on a single medium attempt to forward data simultaneously, the data will collide, resulting in corrupted, unusable data. For this reason, Ethernet provides a method for controlling how the nodes share access through the use of *carrier sense multiple access (CSMA)* technology.

Media Access Control (5.1.1.3)

The CSMA process is used to first detect whether the media is carrying a signal. If a carrier signal on the media from another node is detected, it means that another device is transmitting. When the device attempting to transmit sees that the media is busy, it will wait and try again after a short time period. If no carrier signal is detected, the device transmits its data. It is possible that, because of signal delay on the media, the CSMA process will fail to detect a carrier signal and two devices will transmit at the same time. When this happens a data collision occurs and the data sent by both devices will be corrupted and will need to be resent.

Contention-based media access control methods do not require mechanisms for tracking whose turn it is to access the media; therefore, they do not have the overhead of controlled access methods. However, the contention-based systems do not scale well under heavy media use. As use and the number of nodes increase, the probability of successful media access without a collision decreases. Additionally, the recovery mechanisms required to correct errors because of these collisions further diminishes the throughput.

CSMA is usually implemented in conjunction with a method for resolving media contention. The two commonly used methods are CSMA/CD and CSMA/CA.

CSMA/Collision Detection

In *CSMA/collision detection (CSMA/CD)*, the device monitors the media for the presence of a data signal. If a data signal is absent, indicating that the media is free, the device transmits the data. If signals are then detected that show another device was transmitting at the same time, all devices stop sending and try again later. Traditional forms of Ethernet were developed to use this method.

The widespread incorporation of switched technologies in modern networks has largely displaced the original need for CSMA/CD in local-area networks. Almost all wired connections between devices in a LAN today are full-duplex connections—a device is able to send and receive simultaneously. This means that, while Ethernet networks are designed with CSMA/CD technology, with today's intermediate devices, collisions do not occur and the processes utilized by CSMA/CD are really unnecessary.

However, wireless connections in a LAN environment still have to take collisions into account. Wireless LAN devices utilize the *CSMA/collision avoidance (CSMA/ CA)* media access method.

CSMA/Collision Avoidance

In CSMA/CA, the device examines the media for the presence of a data signal. If the media is free, the device sends a notification across the media of its intent to use it. The device then sends the data. This method is used by 802.11 wireless networking technologies.

MAC Address: Ethernet Identity (5.1.1.4)

As previously stated, the underlying logical topology of Ethernet is a multiaccess bus. Every network device is connected to the same, shared media, and all the nodes receive all frames transmitted. The issue is if all devices are receiving every frame, how can each individual device identify whether it is the intended receiver without the *overhead* of having to process and deencapsulate the frame to get to the IP address? The issue becomes even more problematic in large, high-traffic volume networks, where lots of frames are forwarded.

To prevent the excessive overhead involved in the processing of every frame, a unique identifier called a MAC address was created to identify the actual source and destination nodes within an Ethernet network. Regardless of which variety of Ethernet was used, MAC addressing provided a method for device identification at the lower level of the OSI model. As you might recall, MAC addressing is added as part of a Layer 2 PDU. An Ethernet MAC address is a 48-bit binary value normally expressed as 12 hexadecimal digits (4 bits per hexadecimal digit).

MAC Address Structure

MAC addresses must be globally unique. The MAC address value is a direct result of IEEE-enforced rules for vendors to ensure globally unique addresses for each Ethernet device. The rules established by IEEE require any vendor that sells Ethernet devices to register with IEEE. The IEEE assigns the vendor a 3-byte (24-bit) code, called the *Organizationally Unique Identifier (OUI)*.

IEEE requires a vendor to follow two simple rules, as shown in Figure 5-3:

- All MAC addresses assigned to a NIC or other Ethernet device must use that vendor's assigned OUI as the first 3 bytes.

- All MAC addresses with the same OUI must be assigned a unique value (vendor code or serial number) in the last 3 bytes.

Figure 5-3   Ethernet MAC Address Structure

Frame Processing (5.1.1.5)

The MAC address is often referred to as a burned-in address (BIA) because, historically, this address was burned into ROM (read-only memory) on the NIC. This means that the address was encoded into the ROM chip permanently; it could not be changed by software.

Note

On modern PC operating systems and NICs, it is possible to change the MAC address in software. This is useful when attempting to gain access to a network that filters based on BIA. Consequently, filtering, or controlling, traffic based on the MAC address is no longer secure.

MAC addresses are assigned to workstations, servers, printers, switches, and routers—any device that must originate and/or receive data on the Ethernet network. All devices connected to an Ethernet LAN have MAC-addressed interfaces. Different hardware and software manufacturers might represent the MAC address in different hexadecimal formats. The address formats might be similar to

- 00-05-9A-3C-78-00

- 00:05:9A:3C:78:00

- 0005.9A3C.7800

When the computer starts up, the first thing the NIC does is to copy the MAC address from ROM into RAM. When a device is forwarding a message to an Ethernet network, it attaches header information to the packet. The header information contains the source and destination MAC address. The source device sends the data through the network. This is shown in Figure 5-4.

Figure 5-4 Ethernet Frame Delivery

Each NIC in the network views the information, at the MAC sublayer, to see whether the destination MAC address in the frame matches the device's physical MAC address stored in RAM. If there is no match, the device discards the frame. When the frame reaches the destination where the MAC of the NIC matches the destination MAC of the frame, the NIC passes the frame up the OSI layers, where the deencapsulation process takes place.

Interactive Graphic

Activity 5.1.1.6: MAC and LLC Sublayers

Go to the course online to perform this practice activity.

Ethernet Frame Attributes (5.1.2)

Since the creation of Ethernet in 1973, standards have evolved for specifying faster and more flexible versions of the technology. This ability for Ethernet to improve over time is one of the main reasons that it has become so popular. Early versions of Ethernet were relatively slow at 10 Mbps. The latest versions of Ethernet operate at 10 gigabits per second and faster. Table 5-1 highlights changes in the various versions of Ethernet.

Table 5-1   Ethernet Versions

Year	Standard	Description
1973	Ethernet	Ethernet invented by Dr. Robert Metcalfe of Xerox Corp.
1980	DIX standard Ethernet II	Digital Equipment Corp., Intel, and Xerox (DIX) release a standard for 10-Mbps Ethernet over coaxial cable.
1983	IEEE 802.3 10BASE5	10-Mbps Ethernet over thick coaxial cable.
1985	IEEE 802.3a 10BASE2	10-Mbps Ethernet over thin coaxial cable.
1990	IEEE 802.3i 10BASE-T	10-Mbps Ethernet over twisted pair (TP).
1993	IEEE 802.3j 10BASE-F	10-Mbps Ethernet over fiber-optic.
1995	IEEE 802.3u 100BASE-xx	Fast Ethernet: 100-Mbps Ethernet over twisted pair (TP) and fiber (various standards).
1998	IEEE 802.3z 1000BASE-X	Gigabit Ethernet over fiber-optic.
1999	IEEE 802.3ab 1000BASE-T	Gigabit Ethernet over twisted pair (TP).
2002	IEEE 802.3ae 10G BASE-xx	10 Gigabit Ethernet over fiber-optic (various standards).
2006	IEEE 802.3an 10G BASE-T	10 Gigabit Ethernet over twisted pair (TP).

Ethernet Encapsulation (5.1.2.1)

At the data link layer, the frame structure is nearly identical for all speeds of Ethernet. The Ethernet frame structure adds headers and trailers around the Layer 3 PDU to encapsulate the message being sent.

Both the Ethernet header and trailer have several sections of information that are used by the Ethernet protocol. Each section of the frame is called a field. As shown in Figure 5-5, there are two styles of Ethernet framing:

- The IEEE 802.3 Ethernet standard, which has been updated several times to include new technologies

- The DIX Ethernet standard, which is now referred to as Ethernet II

Figure 5-5   Comparison of 802.3 and Ethernet II Frame Structures and Field Size

The differences between framing styles are minimal. The most significant difference between the two standards is the addition of a Start Frame Delimiter (SFD) and the change of the Type field to a Length field in the 802.3 standard.

Ethernet II is the Ethernet frame format used in TCP/IP networks.

Ethernet Frame Size (5.1.2.2)

Both the Ethernet II and IEEE 802.3 standards define the minimum frame size as 64 bytes and the maximum as 1518 bytes. This includes all bytes from the Destination MAC Address field through the Frame Check Sequence (FCS) field. The Preamble and Start Frame Delimiter fields are not included when describing the size of a frame.

Any frame less than 64 bytes in length is considered a "*collision fragment*" or "*runt frame*" and is automatically discarded by receiving stations.

The IEEE 802.3ac standard, released in 1998, extended the maximum allowable frame size to 1522 bytes. The frame size was increased to accommodate a technology called *virtual local-area network (VLAN)*. VLANs are created within a switched network and will be presented in a later course. Also, many quality of service (QoS) technologies leverage the User Priority field to implement various levels of service, such as priority service for voice traffic. Figure 5-6 displays the additional fields (known collectively as a tag), specified by the IEEE 802.1Q standard, that are inserted into an Ethernet frame to enable VLAN and other information to be included.

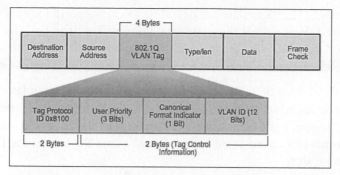

Figure 5-6   Extra 4 Bytes Allows QoS and VLAN Technologies

If the size of a transmitted frame is less than the minimum or greater than the maximum, the receiving device drops the frame. Dropped frames are likely to be the result of collisions or other unwanted signals and are therefore considered invalid.

At the data link layer, the frame structure is nearly identical. At the physical layer, different versions of Ethernet vary in their method for detecting and placing data on the media.

Introduction to the Ethernet Frame (5.1.2.3)

The primary fields in the Ethernet frame are shown in Figure 5-7. These are

- **Preamble and Start of Frame Delimiter fields:** The Preamble (7 bytes) and Start of Frame Delimiter (SFD), also called the Start of Frame (1 byte), fields are used for synchronization between the sending and receiving devices. These first 8 bytes of the frame are used to get the attention of the receiving nodes. Essentially, the first few bytes tell the receivers to get ready to receive a new frame.

- **Destination MAC Address field:** This 6-byte field is the identifier for the intended recipient. As you will recall, this address is used by Layer 2 to assist devices in determining whether a frame is addressed to them. The address in the frame is compared to the MAC address in the device. If there is a match, the device accepts the frame.

- **Source MAC Address field:** This 6-byte field identifies the frame's originating NIC or interface.

- **Length field:** For any IEEE 802.3 standard earlier than 1997, the Length field defines the exact length of the frame's Data field. This is used later as part of the FCS to ensure that the message was received properly. Otherwise, the purpose of the field is to describe which higher-layer protocol is present. If the two-octet value is equal to or greater than 0x0600 hexadecimal or 1536 decimal, the contents of the Data field are decoded according to the EtherType protocol indicated. However, if the value is equal to or less than 0x05DC hexadecimal or 1500 decimal, the Length field is being used to indicate the use of the IEEE 802.3 frame format. This is how Ethernet II and 802.3 frames are differentiated.

- **Data field:** This field (46–1500 bytes) contains the encapsulated data from a higher layer, which is a generic Layer 3 PDU, or more commonly, an IPv4 packet. All frames must be at least 64 bytes long. If a small packet is encapsulated, additional bits called a pad are used to increase the size of the frame to this minimum size.

- **Frame Check Sequence field:** The Frame Check Sequence (FCS) field (4 bytes) is used to detect errors in a frame. It uses a *cyclic redundancy check (CRC)*. The sending device includes the results of a CRC in the FCS field of the frame. The receiving device receives the frame and generates a CRC to look for errors. If the calculations match, no error occurred. Calculations that do not match are an indication that the data has changed; therefore, the frame is dropped. A change in the data could be the result of a disruption of the electrical signals that represent the bits.

Figure 5-7   Ethernet Frame Fields

Activity 5.1.2.4: Ethernet Frame Fields

Go to the course online to perform this practice activity.

Ethernet MAC (5.1.3)

Ethernet technology relies on MAC addresses to function. MAC addresses are used to identify the frame source and destination.

MAC Addresses and Hexadecimal (5.1.3.1)

The use of the MAC address is one of the most important aspects of the Ethernet LAN technology. MAC addresses use hexadecimal numbering.

Hexadecimal is a word that is used both as a noun and as an adjective. When used by itself (as a noun), it means the hexadecimal number system. Hexadecimal provides a convenient way to represent binary values. Just as decimal is a base 10 number system and binary is a base 2 number system, hexadecimal is a base 16 system.

The base 16 number system uses the numbers 0 to 9 and the letters A to F. Figure 5-8 shows the equivalent decimal and hexadecimal values for binary 0000 to 1111. It is easier for us to express a value as a single hexadecimal digit than as 4 binary bits.

Decimal and Binary equivalents of 0 to F Hexadecimal		
Decimal	Binary	Hexadecimal
0	0000	0
1	0001	1
2	0010	2
3	0011	3
4	0100	4
5	0101	5
6	0110	6
7	0111	7
8	1000	8
9	1001	9
10	1010	A
11	1011	B
12	1100	C
13	1101	D
14	1110	E
15	1111	F

Figure 5-8   Hexadecimal Numbering

Given that 8 bits (a byte) is a common binary grouping, binary 00000000 to 11111111 can be represented in hexadecimal as the range 00 to FF. Leading 0s are always displayed to complete the 8-bit representation. For example, the binary value 0000 1010 is shown in hexadecimal as 0A.

Note

It is important to distinguish hexadecimal values from decimal values regarding the characters 0 to 9.

Representing Hexadecimal Values

Hexadecimal is usually represented in text by the value preceded by 0x (for example 0x73) or a subscript 16. Less commonly, it can be followed by an H, for example, 73H. However, because subscript text is not recognized in command-line or programming environments, the technical representation of hexadecimal is preceded with "0x" (zero X). Therefore, the previous examples would be shown as 0x0A and 0x73, respectively.

Hexadecimal is used to represent Ethernet MAC addresses and IP version 6 addresses.

Hexadecimal Conversions

Number conversions between decimal and hexadecimal values are straightforward, but quickly dividing or multiplying by 16 is not always convenient. If such conversions are required, it is usually easier to convert the decimal or hexadecimal value to binary, and then to convert the binary value to either decimal or hexadecimal as appropriate.

With practice, it is possible to recognize the binary bit patterns that match the decimal and hexadecimal values. Figure 5-9 shows these patterns for selected 8-bit values.

Selected Decimal, Binary, and Hexadecimal equivalents

Decimal	Binary	Hexadecimal
0	0000 0000	00
1	0000 0001	01
2	0000 0010	02
3	0000 0011	03
4	0000 0100	04
5	0000 0101	05
6	0000 0110	06
7	0000 0111	07
8	0000 1000	08
10	0000 1010	0A
15	0000 1111	0F
16	0001 0000	10
32	0010 0000	20
64	0100 0000	40
128	1000 0000	80
192	1100 0000	C0
202	1100 1010	CA
240	1111 0000	F0
255	1111 1111	FF

Figure 5-9   Selected Decimal, Binary, and Hexadecimal Equivalents

MAC Address Representations (5.1.3.2)

On a Windows host, the **ipconfig /all** command can be used to identify the MAC address of an Ethernet adapter. In Figure 5-10, notice that the display indicates the physical address (MAC) of the computer to be 00-18-DE-C7-F3-FB. If you have access, you might want to try this on your own computer.

```
C:\>ipconfig/all

Ethernet adapter Local Area Connection:

   Connection-specific DNS Suffix  . : example.com
   Description . . . . . . . . . . . : Intel(R) Gigabit Network Connection
   Physical Address. . . . . . . . . : 00-18-DE-C7-F3-FB
   DHCP Enabled. . . . . . . . . . . : Yes
   Autoconfiguration Enabled . . . . : Yes
   IPv4 Address. . . . . . . . . . . : 192.168.1.67(Preferred)
   Subnet Mask . . . . . . . . . . . : 255.255.255.0
   Lease Obtained. . . . . . . . . . : Monday, November 26, 2012 12:14:48 PM
   Lease Expires . . . . . . . . . . : Saturday, December 01, 2012 12:15:02 AM
   Default Gateway . . . . . . . . . : 192.168.1.254
   DHCP Server . . . . . . . . . . . : 192.168.1.254
   DNS Servers . . . . . . . . . . . : 192.168.1.254
```

Figure 5-10   Physical Address of a Host

Depending on the device and the operating system, you will see various representations of MAC addresses, as displayed in Figure 5-11. Cisco routers and switches use the form XXXX.XXXX.XXXX, where X is a hexadecimal character.

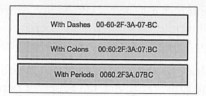

With Dashes   00-60-2F-3A-07-BC

With Colons   00:60:2F:3A:07:BC

With Periods   0060.2F3A.07BC

Figure 5-11   Different Representations of MAC Addresses

Unicast MAC Address (5.1.3.3)

In Ethernet, different MAC addresses are used for Layer 2 unicast, broadcast, and multicast communications.

A unicast MAC address is the unique address used when a frame is sent from a single transmitting device to a single destination device.

In the example shown in Figure 5-12, a host with IP address 192.168.1.5 (source) requests a web page from the server at IP address 192.168.1.200. For a unicast packet to be sent and received, a destination IP address must be in the IP packet header. A corresponding destination MAC address must also be present in the Ethernet frame header. The IP address and MAC address combine to deliver data to one specific destination host.

Figure 5-12   Unicast Communication

Broadcast MAC Address (5.1.3.4)

A broadcast packet contains a destination IP address that has all ones (1s) in the host portion. This numbering in the address means that all hosts on that local network (broadcast domain) will receive and process the packet. Many network protocols, such as DHCP and Address Resolution Protocol (ARP), use broadcasts. How ARP uses broadcasts to map Layer 2 to Layer 3 addresses is discussed later in this chapter.

As shown in Figure 5-13, a broadcast IP address for a network needs a corresponding broadcast MAC address in the Ethernet frame. On Ethernet networks, the broadcast MAC address is 48 1s displayed as hexadecimal FF-FF-FF-FF-FF-FF.

Figure 5-13   Broadcast Communication

Multicast MAC Address (5.1.3.5)

Multicast addresses allow a source device to send a packet to a group of devices. Devices that belong to a multicast group are assigned a multicast group IP address. The range of IPv4 multicast addresses is 224.0.0.0 to 239.255.255.255. Because multicast addresses represent a group of addresses (sometimes called a host group), they can only be used as the destination of a packet. The source will always have a unicast address.

Multicast addresses would be used in remote gaming, where many players are connected remotely but playing the same game. Another use of multicast addresses is in distance learning through videoconferencing, where many students are connected to the same class.

As with the unicast and broadcast addresses, the multicast IP address requires a corresponding multicast MAC address to actually deliver frames on a local network.

The multicast MAC address is a special value that begins with 01-00-5E in hexadecimal. The remaining portion of the multicast MAC address is created by converting the lower 23 bits of the IP multicast group address into six hexadecimal characters.

An example, as shown in Figure 5-14, is the multicast hexadecimal address 01-00-5E-00-00-C8.

Figure 5-14   Multicast Communication

 Lab 5.1.3.6: Viewing Network Device MAC Addresses

In this lab, you will complete the following objectives:

- Part 1: Set Up the Topology and Initialize Devices

- Part 2: Configure Devices and Verify Connectivity

- Part 3: Display, Describe, and Analyze Ethernet MAC Addresses

MAC and IP (5.1.4, 5.1.4.1)

There are two primary addresses assigned to a host device:

- Physical address (the MAC address)

- Logical address (the IP address)

Both the MAC address and IP address work together to identify a device on the network. The process of using the MAC address and the IP address to find a computer is similar to the process of using a name and address of an individual to send a letter.

A person's name usually does not change. A person's address on the other hand, relates to where they live and can change.

Similar to the name of a person, the MAC address on a host does not change; it is physically assigned to the host NIC and is known as the physical address. The physical address remains the same regardless of where the host is placed.

The IP address is similar to the address of a person. This address is based on where the host is actually located. Using this address, it is possible for a frame to determine the location of where a frame should be sent. The IP address, which is a network layer address, is known as a logical address because it is nonpermanent and configured within the device software. It is assigned to each host by a network administrator based on the local network that the host is connected to. Figure 5-15 demonstrates the hierarchical nature of locating an individual based on a "logical" address.

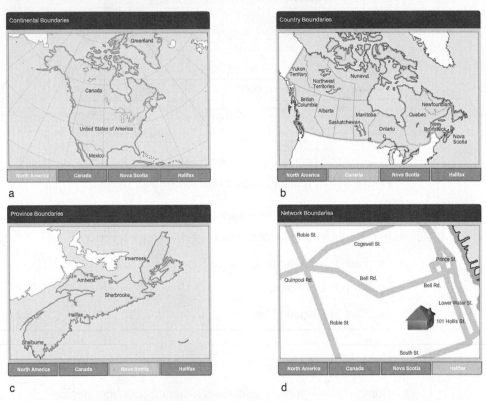

Figure 5-15   Logical Postal Address

Both the physical MAC and logical IP addresses are required for a computer to communicate on a hierarchical network, just like both the name and address of a person are required to send a letter.

End-to-End Connectivity, MAC, and IP (5.1.4.2)

A source device will send a packet based on an IP address. One of the most common ways that a source device determines the IP address of a destination device is through the Domain Name System (DNS), in which an IP address is associated to a domain name. For example, www.cisco.com is equal to 209.165.200.225. This IP address will get the packet to the network location of the destination device. It is this IP address that routers will use to determine the best path to reach a destination. So, in short, IP addressing determines the end-to-end behavior of an IP packet.

However, along each link in a path, an IP packet is encapsulated in a frame specific to the particular data-link technology associated with that link, such as Ethernet. End devices on an Ethernet network do not accept and process frames based on IP addresses. Rather, a frame is accepted and processed based on MAC addresses.

On Ethernet networks, MAC addresses are used to identify, at a lower level, the source and destination hosts. When a host on an Ethernet network communicates, it sends frames containing its own MAC address as the source and the MAC address of the intended recipient as the destination. All hosts that receive the frame will read the destination MAC address. If the destination MAC address matches the MAC address configured on the host NIC, only then will the host process the message.

Figure 5-16 shows how a data packet, containing IP address information, is encapsulated with data link layer framing containing the MAC address information.

Destination MAC Address BB:BB:BB:BB:BB:BB	Source MAC Address AA:AA:AA:AA:AA:AA	Source IP Address 10.0.0.1	Destination IP Address 192.168.1.5	Data	Trailer

Figure 5-16   IP Packet Encapsulated in an Ethernet Frame

Figure 5-17 shows how frames are encapsulated based on the technology of the actual link.

Figure 5-17   Frame Encapsulation Based on Technology

How are the IP addresses of the IP packets in a data flow associated with the MAC addresses on each link along the path to the destination? This is done through a process called Address Resolution Protocol (ARP).

Lab 5.1.4.3: Using Wireshark to Examine Ethernet Frames

In this lab, you will complete the following objectives:

- Part 1: Examine the Header Fields in an Ethernet II Frame

- Part 2: Use Wireshark to Capture and Analyze Ethernet Frames

Packet Tracer Activity 5.1.4.4: Identify MAC and IP Addresses

This activity is optimized for viewing PDUs. The devices are already configured. You will gather PDU information in simulation mode and answer a series of questions about the data you collect.

Address Resolution Protocol (5.2, 5.2.1, 5.2.1.1)

Recall that each node on an IP network has both a MAC address and an IP address. To send data, the node must use both of these addresses. The node must use its own MAC and IP addresses in the source fields and must provide both a MAC address and an IP address for the destination. While the IP address of the destination will be provided by a higher OSI layer, the sending node needs a way to find the MAC address of the destination for a given Ethernet link. This is the purpose of ARP.

ARP relies on certain types of Ethernet broadcast messages and Ethernet unicast messages, called ARP requests and ARP replies.

The ARP protocol provides two basic functions:

- Resolving IPv4 addresses to MAC addresses

- Maintaining a table of mappings

ARP Functions (5.2.1.2)

As previously mentioned, both an IP address and a MAC address are required to send data on an Ethernet network. ARP is responsible for discovering and maintaining the relationship between these addresses.

Resolving IPv4 Addresses to MAC Addresses

For a frame to be placed on the LAN media, it must have a destination MAC address. When a packet is sent to the data link layer to be encapsulated into a frame, the node refers to a table in its memory to find the data link layer address that is mapped to the destination IPv4 address. This table is called the ARP table or the ARP cache. The ARP table is stored in the RAM of the device.

Each entry, or row, of the ARP table binds an IP address with a MAC address. We call the relationship between the two values a map; it simply means that you can locate an IP address in the table and discover the corresponding MAC address. The ARP table temporarily saves (caches) the mapping for the devices on the local LAN.

To begin the process, a transmitting node attempts to locate the MAC address mapped to an IPv4 destination. If this map is found in the table, the node uses the MAC address as the destination MAC in the frame that encapsulates the IPv4 packet. The frame is then encoded onto the networking media.

Maintaining the ARP Table

The ARP table is maintained dynamically. There are two ways that a device can gather MAC addresses. One way is to monitor the traffic that occurs on the local network segment. As a node receives frames from the media, it can record the source IP and MAC address as a mapping in the ARP table. As frames are transmitted on the network, the device populates the ARP table with address pairs.

Another way a device can get an address pair is to send an ARP request. An ARP request is a Layer 2 broadcast to all devices on the Ethernet LAN. The ARP request contains the IP address of the destination host and the broadcast MAC address, FFFF.FFFF.FFFF. Because this is a broadcast, all nodes on the Ethernet LAN will receive it and look at the contents. The node with the IP address that matches the IP address in the ARP request will reply. The reply will be a unicast frame that includes the MAC address that corresponds to the IP address in the request. This response is then used to make a new entry in the ARP table of the sending node.

Entries in the ARP table are time stamped. If a device does not receive a frame from a particular device by the time the time stamp expires, the entry for this device is removed from the ARP table.

Additionally, static map entries can be entered in an ARP table, but this is rarely done. Static ARP table entries do not expire over time and must be manually removed.

ARP Operation (5.2.1.3)

To maintain the relationship between IP and MAC address, ARP uses two different packet types: an ARP Request and an ARP Reply.

Creating the Frame

What does a node do when it needs to create a frame and the ARP cache does not contain a map of an IP address to a destination MAC address? It generates an ARP request!

The ARP process is illustrated in Figure 5-18a–e. When ARP receives a request to map an IPv4 address to a MAC address, it looks for the cached map in its *ARP table*. If an entry is not found, the encapsulation of the IPv4 packet fails and the Layer 2 processes notify ARP that it needs a map (Figure 5-18a). The ARP processes then send out an ARP request packet to discover the MAC address of the destination device on the local network (Figure 5-18b). If a device receiving the request has the destination IP address, it responds with an ARP reply (Figure 5-18c). A map is created in the ARP table (Figure 5-18d). Packets for that IPv4 address can now be encapsulated in frames (Figure 5-18e).

If no device responds to the ARP request, the packet is dropped because a frame cannot be created. This encapsulation failure is reported to the upper layers of the device. If the device is an intermediary device, like a router, the upper layers might choose to respond to the source host with an error in an ICMPv4 packet.

Figure 5-18   ARP Process

ARP Role in Remote Communication (5.2.1.4)

All frames must be delivered to a node on the local network segment. If the destination IPv4 host is on the local network, the frame will use the MAC address of this device as the destination MAC address.

If the destination IPv4 host is not on the local network, the source node needs to deliver the frame to the router interface that is the *gateway* or *next hop* used to reach that destination. The source node will use the MAC address of the gateway as the destination address for frames containing an IPv4 packet addressed to hosts on other networks.

The gateway address of the router interface is stored in the IPv4 configuration of the hosts. When a host creates a packet for a destination, it compares the destination IP address and its own IP address to determine whether the two IP addresses are located on the same Layer 3 network. If the receiving host is not on the same network, the source uses the ARP process to determine a MAC address for the router interface serving as the gateway.

In the event that the gateway entry is not in the table, the normal ARP process will send an ARP request to retrieve the MAC address associated with the IP address of the router interface. This is shown in Figure 5-19a–e.

Figure 5-19   ARP Process—Communicating Remotely

Removing Entries from an ARP Table (5.2.1.5)

For each device, an ARP cache timer removes ARP entries that have not been used for a specified period of time. The times differ depending on the device and its operating system. For example, some Windows operating systems store ARP cache entries for 2 minutes. If the entry is used again during that time, the ARP timer for that entry is extended to 10 minutes.

Commands can also be used to manually remove all or some of the entries in the ARP table. After an entry has been removed, the process for sending an ARP request and receiving an ARP reply must occur again to enter the map in the ARP table.

Each device has an operating system–specific command to delete the contents of the ARP cache. These commands do not invoke the execution of ARP in any way. They merely remove the entries of the ARP table. ARP service is integrated within the IPv4 protocol and implemented by the device. Its operation is transparent to both upper-layer applications and users.

ARP Tables on Networking Devices (5.2.1.6)

On a Cisco router, the **show ip arp** command is used to display the ARP table, as shown in Figure 5-20.

```
Router#show ip arp

                         Age
Protocol  Address        (min)  Hardware Addr   Type  Interface
Internet  172.16.233.229   -    0000.0c59.f892  ARPA  Ethernet0/0
Internet  172.16.233.218   -    0000.0c07.ac00  ARPA  Ethernet0/0
Internet  172.16.168.11    -    0000.0c63.1300  ARPA  Ethernet0/0
Internet  172.16.168.254   9    0000.0c36.6965  ARPA  Ethernet0/0
```

Figure 5-20   Displaying the ARP Table on a Cisco Router

On a Windows 7 PC, the **arp –a** command is used to display the ARP table, as shown in Figure 5-21.

```
C:\>arp -a

Interface: 192.168.1.67 --- 0xa
  Internet Address      Physical Address      Type
  192.168.1.254         64-0f-29-0d-36-91     dynamic
  192.168.1.255         ff-ff-ff-ff-ff-ff     static
  224.0.0.22            01-00-5e-00-00-16     static
  224.0.0.251           01-00-5e-00-00-fb     static
  224.0.0.252           01-00-5e-00-00-fc     static
  255.255.255.255       ff-ff-ff-ff-ff-ff     static

Interface: 10.82.253.91 --- 0x10
  Internet Address      Physical Address      Type
  10.82.253.92          64-0f-29-0d-36-91     dynamic
  224.0.0.22            01-00-5e-00-00-16     static
  224.0.0.251           01-00-5e-00-00-fb     static
  224.0.0.252           01-00-5e-00-00-fc     static
  255.255.255.255       ff-ff-ff-ff-ff-ff     static
```

Figure 5-21   Displaying the ARP Table on a Windows 7 Host

Packet Tracer Activity 5.2.1.7: Examine the ARP Table

This activity is optimized for viewing PDUs. The devices are already configured. You will gather PDU information in simulation mode and answer a series of questions about the data you collect.

Lab 5.2.1.8: Observing ARP with the Windows CLI, IOS CLI, and Wireshark

In this lab, you will complete the following objectives:

- Part 1: Build and Configure the Network
- Part 2: Use the Windows ARP Command
- Part 3: Use the IOS Show ARP Command
- Part 4: Use Wireshark to Examine ARP Exchanges

ARP Issues (5.2.2)

Although required for communication on Ethernet-based networks, ARP can cause several issues.

How ARP Can Create Problems (5.2.2.1)

An increase in network overhead and a decrease in network security are two of the potential issues with ARP.

Overhead on the Media

As a broadcast frame, an ARP request is received and processed by every device on the local network. On a typical business network, these broadcasts would probably have minimal impact on network performance. However, if a large number of devices were to be powered up and all start accessing network services at the same time, there could be some reduction in performance for a short period of time. For example, if all students in a lab logged in to classroom computers and attempted to access the Internet at the same time, there could be delays. However, after the devices send out the initial ARP broadcasts and have learned the necessary MAC addresses, any impact on the network will be minimized.

Security

In some cases, the use of ARP can lead to a potential security risk. ARP spoofing, or ARP poisoning, is a technique used by an attacker to inject the wrong MAC address association into a network by issuing fake ARP requests. An attacker forges the MAC address of a device, and then frames can be sent to the wrong destination.

Manually configuring static ARP associations is one way to prevent ARP *spoofing*. Authorized MAC addresses can be configured on some network devices to restrict network access to only those devices listed.

Mitigating ARP Problems (5.2.2.2)

Broadcast and security issues related to ARP can be mitigated with modern switches. Cisco switches support several security technologies specifically designed to mitigate Ethernet issues related to broadcasts, in general, and ARP, in particular.

Switches provide segmentation of a LAN, dividing the LAN into independent collision domains. Each port on a switch represents a separate collision domain and provides the full media bandwidth to the node or nodes connected on that port. While switches do not by default prevent broadcasts from propagating to connected devices, they do isolate unicast Ethernet communications so that they are only "heard" by the source and destination devices. So if there are a large number of ARP requests, each ARP reply will only be between two devices.

With regard to mitigating various types of broadcast attacks, to which Ethernet networks are prone, network engineers implement Cisco switch security technologies such as specialized access lists and port security.

LAN Switches (5.3)

Switches are used in Ethernet networks to improve both security and efficiency. Although traditionally most LAN switches operate at Layer 2 of the OSI model, an increasing number of Layer 3 switches are now being implemented.

Switching (5.3.1)

Switching makes use of either the physical or logical address in a PDU to control the flow of information between network segments. By controlling what information moves between segments, it is possible to keep unnecessary traffic off of segments, thus maximizing the available bandwidth.

Switch Port Fundamentals (5.3.1.1)

Recall that the logical topology of an Ethernet network is a multiaccess bus in which devices all share access to the same medium. This logical topology determines how hosts on the network view and process frames sent and received on the network. However, the physical topology of most Ethernet networks today is that of a star or extended star. This means that on most Ethernet networks, end devices are typically connected, in a point-to-point basis, to a Layer 2 LAN switch.

A Layer 2 LAN switch typically performs switching and filtering based only on the OSI data link layer (Layer 2) MAC address. A switch is completely transparent to network protocols and user applications. A Layer 2 switch builds a MAC address table that it uses to make forwarding decisions. Layer 2 switches depend on routers to pass data between independent IP subnetworks.

Switch MAC Address Table (5.3.1.2)

Switches use MAC addresses to direct network communications through their switch fabric toward the destination node. The *switch fabric* is the integrated circuits and the accompanying machine programming that allows the data paths through the switch to be controlled. For a switch to know which port to use to transmit a unicast frame, it must first learn which nodes exist on each of its ports.

A switch determines how to handle incoming data frames by using its MAC address table. A switch builds its *MAC address table* by recording the MAC addresses of the nodes connected to each of its ports. After a MAC address for a specific node on a specific port is recorded in the address table, the switch then knows to send traffic destined for that specific node out the port mapped to that node for subsequent transmissions.

When an incoming data frame is received by a switch and the destination MAC address is not in the table, the switch forwards the frame out all ports, except for the port on which it was received. When the destination node responds, the switch records the node's MAC address in the address table from the frame's source address field. In networks with multiple interconnected switches, the MAC address tables record multiple MAC addresses for the ports connecting the switches, which reflect the nodes beyond.

This is shown in Figure 5-22a–d.

a

b

c   d

Figure 5-22   MAC Addressing and Switch MAC Tables

The following describes this process:

Step 1.   The switch receives a broadcast frame from PC1 on Port 1.

Step 2.   The switch enters the source MAC address and the switch port that
received the frame into the address table. (See Figure 5-22a.)

Step 3.   Because the destination address is a broadcast, the switch floods the frame
to all ports, except the port on which it received the frame. (See Figure
5-22b.)

Step 4.   The destination device replies to the broadcast with a unicast frame
addressed to PC1.

Step 5.   The switch enters the source MAC address of PC2 and the port number
of the switch port that received the frame into the address table. The
destination address of the frame and its associated port are found in the
MAC address table. (See Figure 5-22c.)

Step 6. The switch can now forward frames between source and destination devices without flooding, because it has entries in the address table that identify the associated ports. (See Figure 5-22d.)

Typically, switch ports used to interconnect two switches have multiple MAC addresses recorded in the MAC address table.

Note

The MAC address table is sometimes referred to as a *content addressable memory (CAM) table.* While the term *CAM table* is fairly common, for the purposes of this course, we will refer to it as a MAC address table.

Duplex Settings (5.3.1.3)

Though transparent to network protocols and user applications, switches can operate in different modes that can have both positive and negative effects when forwarding Ethernet frames on a network. One of the most basic settings of a switch is the duplex setting of each individual port connected to each host device. A port on a switch must be configured to match the duplex settings of the media type. There are two types of *duplex* settings used for communications on an Ethernet network: half duplex and full duplex.

Half Duplex

Half-duplex communication relies on unidirectional data flow, where sending and receiving data are not performed at the same time. This is similar to how walkie-talkies or two-way radios function in that only one person can talk at any one time. If someone talks while someone else is already speaking, a collision occurs. As a result, half-duplex communication implements CSMA/CD to help reduce the potential for collisions and detect them when they do happen. Half-duplex communications have performance issues because of the constant waiting, because data can only flow in one direction at a time. Half-duplex connections are typically seen in older hardware, such as hubs. Nodes that are attached to hubs that share their connection to a switch port must operate in half-duplex mode because the end computers must be able to detect collisions. Nodes can operate in a half-duplex mode if the NIC cannot be configured for full-duplex operations. In this case, the port on the switch defaults to a half-duplex mode as well. Because of these limitations, full-duplex communication has replaced half-duplex in more current hardware.

Full Duplex

In full-duplex communication, data flow is bidirectional, so data can be sent and received at the same time. The bidirectional support enhances performance by reducing the wait time between transmissions. Most Ethernet, Fast Ethernet, and Gigabit Ethernet NICs sold today offer full-duplex capability. In full-duplex mode, the collision detect circuit is disabled. Frames sent by the two connected end nodes cannot collide because the end nodes use two separate circuits in the network cable. Each full-duplex connection uses only one port. Full-duplex connections require a switch that supports full duplex or a direct connection between two nodes that each support full duplex. Nodes that are directly attached to a dedicated switch port with NICs that support full duplex should be connected to switch ports that are configured to operate in full-duplex mode.

Figure 5-23 shows the two duplex settings available on modern network equipment.

Figure 5-23 Duplex Settings

A Cisco Catalyst switch supports three duplex settings:

- The full option sets full-duplex mode.

- The half option sets half-duplex mode.

- The auto option sets autonegotiation of duplex mode. With autonegotiation enabled, the two ports communicate to decide the best mode of operation.

For Fast Ethernet and 10/100/1000 ports, the default is auto. For 100BASE-FX ports, the default is full. The 10/100/1000 ports operate in either half- or full-duplex mode when they are set to 10 or 100 Mbps, but when set to 1000 Mbps, they operate only in full-duplex mode.

Auto-MDIX (5.3.1.4)

In addition to having the correct duplex setting, it is also necessary to have the correct cable type defined for each port. Connections between specific devices, such as switch to switch, switch to router, switch to host, and router to host device, once required the use of a specific cable type (crossover or straight-through). Instead, most switch devices now support the **mdix auto** interface configuration command in the CLI to enable the *automatic medium-dependent interface crossover (auto-MDIX)* feature.

When the auto-MDIX feature is enabled, the switch detects the required cable type for copper Ethernet connections and configures the interfaces accordingly. Therefore, you can use either a crossover or a straight-through cable for connections to a copper 10/100/1000 port on the switch, regardless of the type of device on the other end of the connection.

The auto-MDIX feature is enabled by default on switches running Cisco IOS Release 12.2(18)SE or later. For releases between Cisco IOS Release 12.1(14)EA1 and 12.2(18)SE, the auto-MDIX feature is disabled by default.

Frame-Forwarding Methods on Cisco Switches (5.3.1.5)

In the past, switches used one of the following forwarding methods for switching data between network ports:

- Store-and-forward switching

- Cut-through switching

Figure 5-24 highlights differences between these two methods.

Figure 5-24   Switch Forwarding Methods

In store-and-forward switching, when the switch receives the frame, it stores the data in buffers until the complete frame has been received. During the storage process, the switch analyzes the frame for information about its destination. In this process, the switch also performs an error check using the cyclic redundancy check (CRC) trailer portion of the Ethernet frame.

CRC uses a mathematical formula, based on the number of bits (1s) in the frame, to determine whether the received frame has an error. After confirming the integrity of the frame, the frame is forwarded out the appropriate port toward its destination. When an error is detected in a frame, the switch discards the frame. Discarding frames with errors reduces the amount of bandwidth consumed by corrupt data. Store-and-forward switching is required for quality of service (QoS) analysis on converged networks where frame classification for *traffic prioritization* is necessary. For example, Voice over IP data streams need to have priority over web-browsing traffic.

Store-and-forward is the sole forwarding method used on current models of Cisco Catalyst switches.

Cut-Through Switching (5.3.1.6)

In cut-through switching, the switch acts upon the data as soon as it is received, even if the transmission is not complete. The switch buffers just enough of the frame to read the destination MAC address so that it can determine to which port to forward the data. The destination MAC address is located in the first 6 bytes of the frame following the preamble. The switch looks up the destination MAC address in its switching table, determines the outgoing interface port, and forwards the frame onto its destination through the designated switch port. The switch does not perform any error checking on the frame. Because the switch does not have to wait for the entire frame to be completely buffered, and because the switch does not perform any error checking, cut-through switching is faster than store-and-forward switching. However, because the switch does not perform any error checking, it forwards corrupt frames throughout the network. The corrupt frames consume bandwidth while they are being forwarded. The destination NIC eventually discards the corrupt frames.

There are two variants of cut-through switching:

- **Fast-forward switching:** Fast-forward switching offers the lowest level of latency. Fast-forward switching immediately forwards a packet after reading the destination address. Because fast-forward switching starts forwarding before the entire packet has been received, there might be times when packets are relayed with errors. This occurs infrequently, and the destination network adapter discards the faulty packet upon receipt. In fast-forward mode, latency is measured from the first bit received to the first bit transmitted. Fast-forward switching is the typical cut-through method of switching.

- **Fragment-free switching:** In fragment-free switching, the switch stores the first 64 bytes of the frame before forwarding. Fragment-free switching can be viewed as a compromise between store-and-forward switching and fast-forward switching. The reason fragment-free switching stores only the first 64 bytes of the frame is that most network errors and collisions occur during the first 64 bytes. Fragment-free switching tries to enhance fast-forward switching by performing a small error check on the first 64 bytes of the frame to ensure that a collision has not occurred before forwarding the frame. Fragment-free switching is a compromise between the high latency and high integrity of store-and-forward switching, and the low latency and reduced integrity of fast-forward switching.

Some switches are configured to perform cut-through switching on a per-port basis until a user-defined error threshold is reached and then they automatically change to store-and-forward. When the error rate falls below the threshold, the port automatically changes back to cut-through switching.

Interactive Graphic

Activity 5.3.1.7: Frame-Forwarding Methods

Go to the course online to perform this practice activity.

Memory Buffering on Switches (5.3.1.8)

As discussed, a switch analyzes some or all of a packet before it forwards it to the destination host. An Ethernet switch can use a buffering technique to store frames before forwarding them. Buffering can also be used when the destination port is busy because of congestion and the switch stores the frame until it can be transmitted.

There are two methods of memory buffering: port-based and shared memory.

Port-Based Memory Buffering

In port-based memory buffering, frames are stored in queues that are linked to specific incoming and outgoing ports. A frame is transmitted to the outgoing port only when all the frames ahead of it in the queue have been successfully transmitted. It is possible for a single frame to delay the transmission of all the frames in memory because of a busy destination port. This delay occurs even if the other frames could be transmitted to open destination ports.

Shared Memory Buffering

Shared memory buffering deposits all frames into a common memory buffer that all the ports on the switch share. The amount of buffer memory required by a port is dynamically allocated. The frames in the buffer are linked dynamically to the destination port. This allows the packet to be received on one port and then transmitted on another port, without moving it to a different queue.

The switch keeps a map of frame-to-port links showing where a packet needs to be transmitted. The map link is cleared after the frame has been successfully transmitted. The number of frames stored in the buffer is restricted by the size of the entire memory buffer and not limited to a single port buffer. This permits larger frames to be transmitted with fewer dropped frames. This is especially important to asymmetric switching. *Asymmetric switching* allows different data rates on different ports. This allows more bandwidth to be dedicated to certain ports, such as a port connected to a server.

Activity 5.3.1.9: Switch It!

Go to the course online to perform this practice activity.

Lab 5.3.1.10: Viewing the Switch MAC Address Table

In this lab, you will complete the following objectives:

- Part 1: Build and Configure the Network
- Part 2: Examine the Switch MAC Address Table

Fixed or Modular (5.3.2)

Switch selection should be done only after fully understanding the role of the switch in the network and how that network could change in the future.

Fixed Versus Modular Configuration (5.3.2.1)

When selecting a switch, it is important to understand the key features of the switch options available. This means that it is necessary to decide on features such as whether *Power over Ethernet (PoE)* is necessary, and the preferred "forwarding rate."

As shown in Figure 5-25, PoE allows a switch to deliver power to a device, such as IP phones and some wireless access points, over the existing Ethernet cabling. This allows more flexibility for installation.

Figure 5-25   Power over Ethernet (PoE)

The forwarding rate defines the processing capabilities of a switch by rating how much data the switch can process per second. Switch product lines are classified by forwarding rates. Entry-layer switches have lower forwarding rates than enterprise-layer switches. Other considerations include whether the device is stackable or non-stackable as well as the thickness of the switch (expressed in number of rack units) and port density, or the number of ports available on a single switch. The port density of a device can vary depending on whether the device is a fixed configuration device or a modular device.

These options are sometimes referred to as switch form factors.

Fixed-Configuration Switches

Fixed-configuration switches are, just as you might expect, fixed in their configuration. What that means is that you cannot add features or options to the switch beyond those that originally came with the switch. The particular model you purchase determines the features and options available. For example, if you purchase a 24-port gigabit fixed switch, you cannot add additional ports when you need them. There are typically different configuration choices that vary in how many and what types of ports are included.

Modular Switches

Modular switches offer more flexibility in their configuration. Modular switches typically come with different-sized chassis that allow the installation of different numbers of modular line cards. The line cards actually contain the ports. The line card fits into the switch chassis like expansion cards fit into a PC. The larger the chassis, the more modules it can support. As you can see in the figure, there can be many different chassis sizes to choose from. If you bought a modular switch with a 24-port line card, you could easily add an additional 24-port line card, to bring the total number of ports up to 48.

Figure 5-26 displays examples of fixed-configuration, modular, and stackable configuration switches.

Figure 5-26   Switch Form Factors

Module Options for Cisco Switch Slots (5.3.2.2)

The Cisco switch product lines are widely deployed globally, in large part because of the flexibility they provide for add-on options. Not only does the Cisco IOS have the richest set of features available relative to any other network operating system, but the IOS is also tailor fit to each Cisco networking device, switches in particular.

To illustrate the options available, which are literally too voluminous to list here, we focus on the Catalyst 3560 switches. The Catalyst 3560 switches have *Switch Form-Factor Pluggable (SFP)* ports that support a number of SFP transceiver modules. Figure 5-27 shows some of the available SFP modules.

Figure 5-27   Switch Form-Factor Pluggable (SFP) Modules

Here is a list of the SFP modules supported on one or more types of 3560 switches:

Fast Ethernet SFP modules:

- 100BASE-FX (multimode fiber-optic [MMF]) for 2 kilometers (km)
- 100BASE-LX10 (single-mode fiber-optic [SMF]) for 2km
- 100BASE-BX10 (SMF) for 10 km
- 100BASE-EX (SMF) for 40 km
- 100BASE-ZX (SMF) for 80 km

Gigabit Ethernet SFP modules:

- 1000BASE-SX 50/62.5 μm (MMF) up to 550/220 m
- 1000BASE-LX/LH (SMF/MMF) up to 10/0.550 km
- 1000BASE-ZX (SMF) up to 70 km
- 1000BASE-BX10-D and 1000BASE-BX10-U (SMF) up to 10 km
- 1000BASE-T (copper wire transceiver)

10 Gigabit Ethernet SFP modules:

- 10G-SR (MMF) up 400 m
- 10G-SR-X (MMF) up to 400 m (supporting extended temperature range)
- 10G-LRM (MMF) up to 220 m
- FET-10G (MMF) up to 100 m (for Nexus fabric uplinks)

- 10G-LR (SMF) up to 10 km

- 10G-LR-X (SMF) up to 10 km (supporting extended temperature range)

- 10G-ER (SMF) up to 40 km

- 10G-ZR (SMF) up to 80 km

- Twinax (copper wire transceiver) up to 10 m

- Active Optical up to 10 m (for intra-/inter-rack connections)

40 Gigabit Ethernet and 100 Gigabit Ethernet modules are supported on high-end Cisco devices, such as the Catalyst 6500, the CRS router, the ASR 9000 Series router, and the Nexus 7000 Series switch.

Layer 3 Switching (5.3.3)

In addition to determining the switch form factor and features, it might also be necessary to choose between a Layer 2 LAN switch and a Layer 3 switch.

Layer 2 Versus Layer 3 Switching (5.3.3.1)

Recall that a Layer 2 LAN switch performs switching and filtering based only on the OSI data link layer (Layer 2) MAC address and depends upon routers to pass data between independent IP subnetworks.

A Layer 3 switch, such as the Catalyst 3560, functions similarly to a Layer 2 switch, such as the Catalyst 2960, but instead of using only the Layer 2 MAC address information for forwarding decisions, a Layer 3 switch can also use IP address information. Instead of only learning which MAC addresses are associated with each of its ports, a Layer 3 switch can also learn which IP addresses are associated with its interfaces. This allows the Layer 3 switch to direct traffic throughout the network based on IP address information as well.

Layer 3 switches are also capable of performing Layer 3 routing functions, reducing the need for dedicated routers on a LAN. Because Layer 3 switches have specialized switching hardware, they can typically route data as quickly as they can switch.

Cisco Express Forwarding (5.3.3.2)

Cisco devices that support Layer 3 switching utilize *Cisco Express Forwarding (CEF)*. This forwarding method is quite complex, but fortunately, like any good technology, is carried out in large part "behind the scenes." Normally very little CEF configuration is required on a Cisco device.

Basically, CEF decouples the usual strict interdependence between Layer 2 and Layer 3 decision making. What makes forwarding IP packets slow is the constant referencing back and forth between Layer 2 and Layer 3 constructs within a networking device. So, to the extent that Layer 2 and Layer 3 data structures can be decoupled, forwarding is accelerated.

The two main components of CEF operation are the

- *Forwarding Information Base (FIB)*

- *Adjacency tables*

The FIB is conceptually similar to a routing table. A router uses the routing table to determine the best path to a destination network based on the network portion of the destination IP address. With CEF, information previously stored in the route cache is, instead, stored in several data structures for CEF switching. The data structures provide optimized lookup for efficient packet forwarding. A networking device uses the FIB lookup table to make destination-based switching decisions without having to access the route cache.

The FIB is updated when changes occur in the network and contains all routes known at the time.

Adjacency tables maintain Layer 2 next-hop addresses for all FIB entries.

The separation of the reachability information (in the FIB table) and the forwarding information (in the adjacency table), provides a number of benefits:

- The adjacency table can be built separately from the FIB table, allowing both to be built without any packets being process switched.

- The MAC header rewrite used to forward a packet is not stored in cache entries, so changes in a MAC header rewrite string do not require invalidation of cache entries.

This is illustrated in Figure 5-28. CEF is enabled by default on most Cisco devices that perform Layer 3 switching.

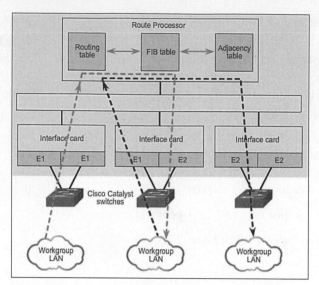

Figure 5-28   Cisco Express Forwarding (CEF)

Types of Layer 3 Interfaces (5.3.3.3)

Cisco networking devices support a number of distinct types of Layer 3 interfaces. A Layer 3 interface is one that supports forwarding IP packets toward a final destination based on the IP address.

The major types of Layer 3 interfaces are

- **Switch virtual interface (SVI):** Logical interface on a switch associated with a virtual local-area network (VLAN).

- **Routed port:** Physical port on a Layer 3 switch configured to act as a router port.

- **Layer 3** *EtherChannel*: Logical interface on a Cisco device associated with a bundle of routed ports.

As shown previously, an SVI for the default VLAN (VLAN1) must be enabled to provide IP host connectivity to the switch and permit remote switch administration. SVIs must also be configured to allow routing between VLANs. As stated, SVIs are logical interfaces configured for specific VLANs; to route between two or more VLANs, each VLAN must have a separate SVI enabled. This is shown in Figure 5-29.

Figure 5-29   Switch Virtual Interfaces (SVIs)

Routed ports enable (Layer 3) Cisco switches to effectively serve as routers. Each port on such a switch can be configured as a port on an independent IP network.

Layer 3 EtherChannels are used to bundle Layer 3 Ethernet links between Cisco devices to aggregate bandwidth, typically on uplinks.

> **Note**
>
> In addition to SVIs and L3 EtherChannels, other logical interfaces on Cisco devices include loopback interfaces and tunnel interfaces.

Configuring a Routed Port on a Layer 3 Switch (5.3.3.4)

A switch port can be configured to be a Layer 3 routed port and behave like a regular router interface.

Specifically, a routed port

- Is not associated with a particular VLAN

- Can be configured with a Layer 3 routing protocol

- Is a Layer 3 interface only and does not support Layer 2 switching

Configure routed ports by putting the interface into Layer 3 mode with the **no switchport** interface configuration command. Then assign an IP address to the port. That's it! Figure 5-30 shows a switch port configured as a routed port.

Additional configuration is necessary before the Layer 3 switch can perform routing.

```
S1(config)#interface f0/6
S1(config-if)#no switchport
S1(config-if)#ip address 192.168.200.1 255.255.255.0
S1(config-if)#no shutdown
S1(config-if)#end
S1#
*Mar  1 00:15:40.115: %SYS-5-CONFIG_I: Configured from console by console
S1#show ip interface brief
Interface          IP-Address      OK? Method Status                Protocol
Vlan1              unassigned      YES unset  administratively down  down
FastEthernet0/1    unassigned      YES unset  down                   down
FastEthernet0/2    unassigned      YES unset  down                   down
FastEthernet0/3    unassigned      YES unset  down                   down
FastEthernet0/4    unassigned      YES unset  down                   down
FastEthernet0/5    unassigned      YES unset  down                   down
FastEthernet0/6    192.168.200.1   YES manual up                     up
FastEthernet0/7    unassigned      YES unset  up                     up
FastEthernet0/8    unassigned      YES unset  up                     up
<output omitted>
```

Figure 5-30   Routed Port Configuration

You will learn more about the functions of routing in the next chapter.

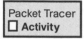

Packet Tracer Activity 5.3.3.5: Configure Layer 3 Switches

The network administrator is replacing the current router and switch with a new Layer 3 switch. As the network technician, it is your job to configure the switch and place it into service. You will be working after hours to minimize disruption to the business.

Summary (5.4)

Class Activity 5.4.1.1: MAC and Choose . . .

Note: This activity can be completed individually, in small groups, or in a full-classroom learning environment.

View the video located at the following link: www.netevents.tv/video/bob-metcalfe-the-history-of-ethernet.

Topics discussed include not only where we have come from in Ethernet development but also where we are going with Ethernet technology (a futuristic approach).

After viewing the video and comparing its contents to this chapter, go to the web and search for information about Ethernet. Use a constructivist approach:

- What did Ethernet look like when it was first developed?

- How has Ethernet stayed the same over the past 25 years or so, and what changes are being made to make it more useful/applicable to today's data transmission methods?

Collect three pictures of old, current, and future Ethernet physical media and devices (focus on switches). Share these pictures with the class and discuss

- How have Ethernet physical media and intermediary devices changed?

- How have Ethernet physical media and intermediary devices stayed the same?

- How will Ethernet change in the future?

Ethernet is the most widely used LAN technology today. It is a family of networking technologies that are defined in the IEEE 802.2 and 802.3 standards. Ethernet standards define both the Layer 2 protocols and the Layer 1 technologies. For the Layer 2 protocols, as with all 802 IEEE standards, Ethernet relies on the two separate sublayers of the data link layer to operate: the Logical Link Control (LLC) and the MAC sublayers.

At the data link layer, the frame structure is nearly identical for all speeds of Ethernet. The Ethernet frame structure adds headers and trailers around the Layer 3 PDU to encapsulate the message being sent.

There are two styles of Ethernet framing: the IEEE 802.3 Ethernet standard and the DIX Ethernet standard, which is now referred to as Ethernet II. The most significant difference between the two standards is the addition of a Start Frame Delimiter (SFD) and the change of the Type field to a Length field in the 802.3. Ethernet II is the Ethernet frame format used in TCP/IP networks. As an implementation of the

IEEE 802.2/3 standards, the Ethernet frame provides MAC addressing and error checking.

The Layer 2 addressing provided by Ethernet supports unicast, multicast, and broadcast communications. Ethernet uses the Address Resolution Protocol to determine the MAC addresses of destinations and map them against known network layer addresses.

Each node on an IP network has both a MAC address and an IP address. The node must use its own MAC and IP addresses in the source fields and must provide both a MAC address and an IP address for the destination. While the IP address of the destination will be provided by a higher OSI layer, the sending node must find the MAC address of the destination for a given Ethernet link. This is the purpose of ARP.

ARP relies on certain types of Ethernet broadcast messages and Ethernet unicast messages, called ARP requests and ARP replies. The ARP protocol resolves IPv4 addresses to MAC addresses and maintains a table of mappings.

On most Ethernet networks, end devices are typically connected, in a point-to-point basis, to a Layer 2 LAN switch. A Layer 2 LAN switch performs switching and filtering based only on the OSI data link layer (Layer 2) MAC address. A Layer 2 switch builds a MAC address table that it uses to make forwarding decisions. Layer 2 switches depend on routers to pass data between independent IP subnetworks.

Layer 3 switches are also capable of performing Layer 3 routing functions, reducing the need for dedicated routers on a LAN. Because Layer 3 switches have specialized switching hardware, they can typically route data as quickly as they can switch.

Practice

The following activities provide practice with the topics introduced in this chapter. The labs and class activities are available in the companion *Introduction to Networking Lab Manual* (ISBN 978-1-58713-312-1). The Packet Tracer Activities PKA files are found in the online course.

Class Activities

- Class Activity 5.0.1.2: Join My Social Circle!
- Class Activity 5.4.1.1: MAC and Choose . . .

Labs

- Lab 5.1.3.6: Viewing Network Device MAC Addresses
- Lab 5.1.4.3: Using Wireshark to Examine Ethernet Frames
- Lab 5.2.1.8: Observing ARP with the Windows CLI, IOS CLI, and Wireshark
- Lab 5.3.1.10: Viewing the Switch MAC Address Table

Packet Tracer Activities

- Packet Tracer Activity 5.1.4.4: Identify MAC and IP Addresses
- Packet Tracer Activity 5.2.1.7: Examine the ARP Table
- Packet Tracer Activity 5.3.3.5: Configure Layer 3 Switches

Check Your Understanding

Complete all the review questions listed here to test your understanding of the topics and concepts in this chapter. The appendix, "Answers to the 'Check Your Understanding' Questions," lists the answers.

1. At which layers of the OSI model does Ethernet function? (Choose two.)

   A. Application
   B. Presentation
   C. Session
   D. Transport
   E. Network
   F. Data link
   G. Physical

2. Which standard specifies the Ethernet MAC sublayer functionality in a computer NIC?

   A. IEEE 802.2
   B. IEEE 802.3
   C. IEEE 802.5
   D. IEEE 802.11
   E. IEEE 802.15

3. What is the name given to the Ethernet MAC sublayer PDU?

   A. Segment

   B. Packet

   C. Frame

   D. Bit

4. What are the primary functions associated with data encapsulation at the Ethernet MAC sublayer? (Choose three.)

   A. Media recovery

   B. Frame deliminating

   C. Addressing

   D. Frame placement on the media

   E. Error detection

5. What happens when a data collision occurs on an Ethernet bus?

   A. The CRC value is used to repair the data frames.

   B. All devices stop transmitting and try again later.

   C. The device with the lower MAC address stops transmitting to give the device with the higher MAC address priority.

   D. The MAC sublayer prioritizes the frame with the lower MAC address.

6. What is true about the Ethernet MAC address? (Choose three.)

   A. A MAC address is 32 bits in length.

   B. The first 6 hexadecimal digits of a MAC address represent the OUI.

   C. The IEEE is responsible for assigning vendors a unique 6-byte code.

   D. The vendor is responsible for assigning the last 24 bits of the MAC address.

   E. The MAC address is also known as a burned-in address.

7. What is the minimum and maximum Ethernet frame size as defined by IEEE 802.3?

   A. 64 bytes – 1518 bytes

   B. 64 bytes – 1522 byres

   C. 32 bytes – 1518 bytes

   D. 32 bytes – 1522 bytes

8. Which field in an Ethernet frame is used for error detection?

   A. Preamble

   B. Type

   C. Destination MAC Address

   D. Frame Check Sequence

9. Which address is used as a destination address on a broadcast Ethernet frame?

   A. 0.0.0.0

   B. 255.255.255.255

   C. FF-FF-FF-FF-FF-FF

   D. 0C-FA-94-24-EF-00

10. Which address is a multicast MAC address?

    A. 0-07-E9-00-00-D4

    B. 01-00-5E-00-00-C8

    C. FF-FF-FF-FF-FF-FF

    D. FF-FF-FF-01-00-5E

11. What functions are provided by the ARP process? (Choose two.)

    A. Resolving IPv4 addresses to MAC addresses

    B. Resolving host names to MAC addresses

    C. Maintaining a table of mappings

    D. Resolving host names to IP addresses

    E. Maintaining a table of active IP addresses

12. Which devices on a network will hear an ARP request?

    A. Only the device that has the IPv4 address that the request is looking for

    B. All devices in the L2 broadcast domain

    C. Only devices in the same collision domain

13. **Fill in the blanks.** When ARP receives a request to map an IPv4 address to a MAC address, it first looks in its ____. If no entry is found, ARP will send out an ARP__.

14. **Fill in the blanks.** When a device receives an ARP request for a device with a different IP address, it will use the ____ information to update its ARP table and then it will ____ the packet.

15. **Fill in the blanks.** ARP ____ are sent to a broadcast MAC address, and ARP replies are sent to a ____ MAC address.

16. **Fill in the blanks.** When a switch receives a broadcast frame, it enters the source information in its ____ and then it ____ the frame to all ports except the one the frame was ____ on.

17. **Fill in the blanks.** The MAC address table is sometimes referred to as a ____ table because it is stored in ____ memory.

18. What type of switching is used on current L2 switches to allow QoS?

    A. Store-and-forward

    B. Cut-through

    C. Fragment-free

    D. Fast-forward

19. What name is given to a physical port on a Layer 3 switch configured to act as a router port?

    A. Switch virtual interface

    B. Routed port

    C. Layer 3 EtherChannel

20. **Fill in the blanks.** To configure a routed port, the interface must be put into Layer 3 mode by using the ____ interface configuration command. After this, the interface must be assigned an ____ address.

CHAPTER 6

Network Layer

Objectives

Upon completion of this chapter, you will be able to answer the following questions:

- What is the purpose of the network layer in data communications?

- Why does the IPv4 protocol require services of other layers to provide reliability?

- What is the role of the major header fields in the IPv4 and IPv6 packets?

- How does a host device use routing tables to direct packets to itself, a local destination, or a default gateway?

- What are the similarities and differences between host routing tables and routing tables of a router?

- What are the common components and interfaces of a router?

- What are the steps in the bootup process of a Cisco IOS router?

- How do you configure active interfaces on a Cisco IOS router?

- How do you configure the default gateway on network devices?

Key Terms

This chapter uses the following key terms. You can find the definitions in the Glossary.

Introduction (6.0.1.1)

Network applications and services on one end device can communicate with applications and services running on another end device. How is this data communicated across the network in an efficient way?

The protocols of the OSI model network layer specify addressing and processes that enable transport layer data to be packaged and transported. The network layer encapsulation enables data to be passed to a destination within a network (or on another network) with minimum overhead.

This chapter focuses on the role of the network layer. It examines how it divides networks into groups of hosts to manage the flow of data packets within a network. It also covers how communication between networks is facilitated. This communication between networks is called *routing*.

Class Activity 6.0.1.2: The Road Less Traveled . . . or Is It?

During the upcoming weekend, you decide to visit a schoolmate who is currently at home sick. You know his street address but you have never been to his town before. Instead of looking up the address on the map, you decide to take it easy and to simply ask town residents for directions after you arrive by train. The citizens you ask for directions are very helpful. However, they all have an interesting habit. Instead of explaining the entire route to your destination, they all tell you, "Take this road, and as soon as you arrive at the nearest crossroad, ask somebody there again."

Somewhat bemused at this apparent oddity, you follow these instructions and finally arrive, crossroad by crossroad, and road by road, at your friend's house.

Answer the following questions:

- Would it have made a significant difference if you were told about the entire route or a larger part of the route instead of just being directed to the nearest crossroad?

- Would it have been more helpful to ask about the specific street address or just about the street name? What would happen if the person you asked for directions did not know where the destination street was or directed you through an incorrect road?

- Assume that on your way back home, you again choose to ask residents for directions. Would it be guaranteed that you would be directed through the same route you took to get to your friend's home? Explain your answer.

Is it necessary to explain where you depart from when asking directions to an intended destination?

Network Layer Protocols (6.1)

This section will introduce the protocols and functions of the network layer.

Network Layer in Communication (6.1.1)

Without network layer services, there would be no Internet. The function of the network layer is to facilitate the transport of data from one network to another. This section will introduce elementary functions of the network layer.

The Network Layer (6.1.1.1)

The network layer, or OSI Layer 3, provides services to allow end devices to exchange data across the network. To accomplish this end-to-end transport, the network layer uses four basic processes:

- **Addressing end devices:** In the same way that a phone has a unique telephone number, end devices must be configured with a unique IP address for identification on the network. An end device with a configured IP address is referred to as a host.

- **Encapsulation:** The network layer receives a protocol data unit (PDU) from the transport layer. In a process called encapsulation, the network layer adds IP header information, such as the IP address of the source (sending) and destination (receiving) hosts. After header information is added to the PDU, the PDU is called a packet.

- **Routing:** The network layer provides services to direct packets to a destination host on another network. To travel to other networks, the packet must be processed by a router. The role of the router is to select paths for and direct packets toward the destination host in a process known as routing. A packet can cross many intermediary devices before reaching the destination host. Each route the packet takes to reach the destination host is called a hop.

- *Deencapsulation* (also called *decapsulation*)**:** When the packet arrives at the network layer of the destination host, the host checks the IP header of the packet. If the destination IP address within the header matches its own IP address, the IP header is removed from the packet. This process of removing headers from lower layers is known as deencapsulation. After the packet is deencapsulated by the network layer, the resulting Layer 4 PDU is passed up to the appropriate service at the transport layer.

Unlike the transport layer (OSI Layer 4), which manages the data transport between the processes running on each host, network layer protocols specify the packet structure and processing used to carry the data from one host to another host.

Operating without regard to the data carried in each packet allows the network layer to carry packets for multiple types of communications between multiple hosts.

Figure 6-1 demonstrates the exchange of data. In this figure, segments are encapsulated at the network layer and become IP packets. The process is then reversed at the destination.

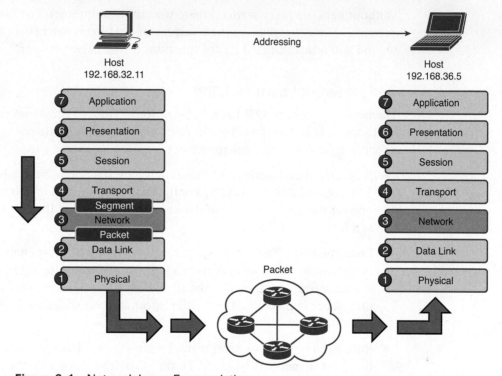

Figure 6-1   Network Layer Encapsulation

Network Layer Protocols (6.1.1.2)

There are several network layer protocols in existence; however, only the following two are commonly implemented:

- Internet Protocol version 4 (IPv4)

- Internet Protocol version 6 (IPv6)

Other legacy network layer protocols that are not widely used include

- Novell Internetwork Packet Exchange (IPX)

- AppleTalk

- Connectionless Network Service (CLNS/DECNet)

Discussion of these legacy protocols will be minimal.

Table 6-1 lists some of the common and some legacy network layer protocols.

Table 6-1   Network Layer Protocols

Protocol	Description
Internet Protocol version 4 (IPv4)	Most widely used network protocol. Basic protocol of the Internet.
Internet Protocol version 6 (IPv6)	Currently becoming rapidly deployed. Will likely replace IPv4.
Novell IPX	A legacy protocol as a part of Novell NetWare and popular in the 1980s and 1990s.
AppleTalk	Legacy protocol that was Apple Computer's proprietary networking protocol.
Connectionless Network Service (CLNS)	A protocol used in telecommunication networks that does not require established circuits.

Characteristics of the IP Protocol (6.1.2)

IPv4 is the premier network layer protocol. This section will introduce the characteristics of IPv4.

Characteristics of IP (6.1.2.1)

IP is the network layer service implemented by the TCP/IP protocol suite.

IP was designed as a protocol with low overhead. It provides only the functions that are necessary to deliver a packet from a source to a destination over an interconnected system of networks. The protocol was not designed to track and manage the flow of packets. These functions, if required, are performed by other protocols in other layers.

The basic characteristics of IP are

- **Connectionless:** No connection with the destination is established before sending data packets.

- **Best effort (unreliable):** Packet delivery is not guaranteed.

- *Media independent*: Operation is independent of the medium carrying the data.

IP—Connectionless (6.1.2.2)

The role of the network layer is to transport packets between hosts while placing as little burden on the network as possible. The network layer is not concerned with, or even aware of, the type of communication contained inside of a packet. IP is *connectionless*, meaning that no dedicated end-to-end connection is created before data is sent. Connectionless communication is conceptually similar to sending a letter to someone without notifying the recipient in advance.

The postal service uses the information on a letter to deliver the letter to a recipient. The address on the envelope does not provide information as to whether the receiver is present, whether the letter arrives, or whether the receiver can read the letter. In fact, the postal service is unaware of the information contained within the contents of the packet that it is delivering and therefore cannot provide any error-correction mechanisms.

Connectionless data communications work on the same principle.

IP is connectionless and, therefore, requires no initial exchange of control information to establish an end-to-end connection before packets are forwarded. IP also does not require additional fields in the protocol data unit (PDU) header to maintain an established connection. This process greatly reduces the overhead of IP. However, with no preestablished end-to-end connection, senders are unaware whether destination devices are present and functional when sending packets, nor are they aware whether the destination receives the packet, or if it is able to access and read the packet.

IP—Best-Effort Delivery (6.1.2.3)

IP is often referred to as an unreliable or best-effort delivery protocol. This does not mean that IP works properly sometimes and does not function well at other times, nor does it mean that it is a poor data communications protocol. Unreliable simply means that IP does not have the capability to manage and recover from undelivered or corrupt packets. This is because while IP packets are sent with information about the location of delivery, it contains no information that can be processed to inform the sender whether delivery was successful. There is no synchronization data included in the packet header for tracking the order of packet delivery. There are also no acknowledgements of packet delivery with IP, and there is no error control data to track whether packets were delivered without corruption. Packets can arrive at the destination corrupted, out of sequence, or not at all. Based on the information provided in the IP header, there is no capability for packet retransmissions if errors such as these occur.

If out-of-order or missing packets create problems for the application using the data, upper-layer services, such as TCP, must resolve these issues. This allows IP to function very efficiently. If reliability overhead were included in IP, communications that do not require connections or reliability would be burdened with the bandwidth consumption and delay produced by this overhead. In the TCP/IP suite, the transport layer can use either TCP or UDP based on the need for reliability in communication. Leaving the reliability decision to the transport layer makes IP more adaptable and accommodating for different types of communication.

Connection-oriented protocols, such as TCP, require that control data be exchanged to establish the connection. To maintain information about the connection, TCP also requires additional fields in the PDU header.

IP—Media Independent (6.1.2.4)

The network layer is also not burdened with the characteristics of the media on which packets are transported. IP operates independently of the media that carry the data at lower layers of the protocol stack. As shown in the Figure 6-2, any individual IP packet can be communicated electrically over cable, as optical signals over fiber, or wirelessly as radio signals. This figure demonstrates that there can be several different physical layer media between the source host and destination host, but the IP packet is transported end to end. That is, the same IP packet leaving the source host arrives at the destination host.

Figure 6-2 IP Packets Are Media Independent

It is the responsibility of the OSI data link layer to take an IP packet and prepare it for transmission over the communications medium. This means that the transport of IP packets is not limited to any particular medium.

There is, however, one major characteristic of the media that the network layer considers: the maximum size of the PDU that each medium can transport. This characteristic is referred to as the *maximum transmission unit (MTU)*. Part of the control communication between the data link layer and the network layer is the establishment of a maximum size for the packet. The data link layer passes the MTU value up to the network layer. The network layer then determines how large packets should be.

In some cases, an intermediate device, usually a router, must split up a packet when forwarding it from one medium to a medium with a smaller MTU. This process is called fragmenting the packet or *fragmentation*.

Encapsulating IP (6.1.2.5)

IP encapsulates, or packages, the transport layer segment by adding an IP header. This header is used to deliver the packet to the destination host. The IP header remains in place from the time the packet leaves the network layer of the source host until it arrives at the network layer of the destination host.

Figure 6-3 shows the process for creating the transport layer PDU and the subsequent process for creating the network layer PDU. The network layer adds a header so that packets can be routed through complex networks to reach the destination host. In TCP/IP-based network, the network layer PDU is the IP packet.

Figure 6-3   Generating IP Packets

The process of encapsulating data layer by layer enables the services at the different layers to develop and scale without affecting other layers. This means that transport layer segments can be readily packaged by IPv4 or IPv6 or by any new protocol that might be developed in the future.

Routers can implement these different network layer protocols to operate concurrently over a network to and from the same or different hosts. The routing performed by these intermediate devices only considers the contents of the packet header that encapsulates the segment. In all cases, the data portion of the packet, that is, the encapsulated transport layer PDU, remains unchanged during the network layer processes.

Activity 6.1.2.6: IP Characteristics

Go to the course online to perform this practice activity.

IPv4 Packet (6.1.3)

The ability to provide the end-to-end transfer of data by the network layer is based on the content and interpretation of the Layer 3 header. This section will examine the structure and contents of the IPv4 header.

IPv4 Packet Header (6.1.3.1)

IPv4 has been in use since 1983, when it was deployed on the Advanced Research Projects Agency Network (ARPANET), which was the precursor to the Internet. The Internet is largely based on IPv4, which is still the most widely used network layer protocol.

An IPv4 packet has two parts:

- **IP header:** Identifies the packet characteristics.

- **Payload:** Contains the Layer 4 segment information and the actual data.

As shown in Figure 6-4, an IPv4 packet header consists of fields containing important information about the packet. These fields contain binary numbers that are examined by the Layer 3 process. The binary values of each field identify various settings of the IP packet.

Significant fields in the IPv4 header include

- **Version:** Contains a 4-bit binary value identifying the IP packet version. For IPv4 packets, this field is always set to 0100.

- **Differentiated Services (DS):** Formerly called the Type of Service (ToS) field, the DS field is an 8-bit field used to determine the priority of each packet. The first 6 bits identify the Differentiated Services Code Point (DSCP) value that is used by a quality of service (QoS) mechanism. The last 2 bits identify the explicit congestion notification (ECN) value that can be used to prevent dropped packets during times of network congestion.

- *Time-to-Live (TTL)*: Contains an 8-bit binary value that is used to limit the life-time of a packet. It is specified in seconds but is commonly referred to as hop count. The packet sender sets the initial time-to-live (TTL) value and is decreased by 1 each time the packet is processed by a router, or hop. If the TTL field decrements to 0, the router discards the packet and sends an *Internet Control Message Protocol (ICMP)* Time Exceeded message to the *source IP address*. The **traceroute** command uses this field to identify the routers used between the source and destination.

- **Protocol:** This 8-bit binary value indicates the data payload type that the packet is carrying, which enables the network layer to pass the data to the appropriate upper-layer protocol. Common values include ICMP (0x01), TCP (0x06), and UDP (0x11).

- **Source IP Address:** Contains a 32-bit binary value that represents the source IP address of the packet.

- *Destination IP Address*: Contains a 32-bit binary value that represents the destination IP address of the packet.

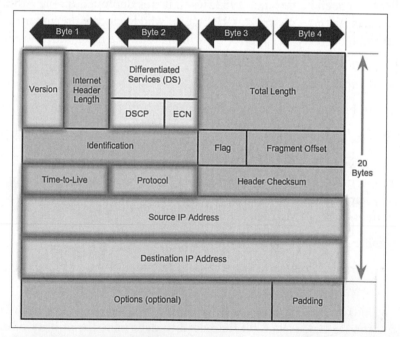

Figure 6-4   IPv4 Packet Structure

The two most commonly referenced fields are the source and destination IP address-es. These fields identify where the packet is from and where it is going. Typically, these addresses do not change while traveling from the source to the destination.

IPv4 Header Fields (6.1.3.2)

The remaining fields are used to identify and validate the packet, or to reorder a fragmented packet.

The fields used to identify and validate the packet include

- **Internet Header Length (IHL):** Contains a 4-bit binary value identifying the number of 32-bit words in the header. The IHL value varies because of the Options and Padding fields. The minimum value for this field is 5 (that is, $5 \times 32 = 160$ bits = 20 bytes) and the maximum value is 15 (that is, $15 \times 32 = 480$ bits = 60 bytes).

- **Total Length:** Sometimes referred to as the Packet Length, this 16-bit field defines the entire packet (fragment) size, including header and data, in bytes. The minimum-length packet is 20 bytes (20-byte header + 0 bytes data), and the maximum is 65,535 bytes.

- **Header Checksum:** The 16-bit field is used for error checking of the IP header. The checksum of the header is recalculated and compared to the value in the checksum field. If the values do not match, the packet is discarded.

A router might have to fragment a packet when forwarding it from one medium to another medium that has a smaller MTU. When this happens, fragmentation occurs and the IPv4 packet uses the following fields to keep track of the fragments:

- **Identification:** This 16-bit field uniquely identifies the fragment of an original IP packet.

- **Flags:** This 3-bit field identifies how the packet is fragmented. It is used with the Fragment Offset and Identification fields to help reconstruct the fragment into the original packet.

- **Fragment Offset:** This 13-bit field identifies the order in which to place the packet fragment in the reconstruction of the original unfragmented packet.

Note

The Options and Padding fields are rarely used and beyond the scope of this chapter.

Sample IPv4 Headers (6.1.3.3)

Wireshark is a useful network monitoring tool for anyone working with networks and can be used with most labs in the Cisco Certified Network Associate (CCNA) courses for data analysis and troubleshooting. It can be used to view sample values contained in various header fields within a communication. For any captured frame, each Layer, 1 through 4, can be expanded for a detailed analysis of the communication.

Figure 6-5 displays the contents of captured packet number 3 in this sample capture. Note that the Source is listed as 192.168.254.7, the Destination is listed as 192.168.254.250, and the Layer 4 protocol is TCP. The middle window has the IP portion expanded to show the information about the IPv4 header. Details of the fields such as the header length, total length, and any flags can be seen.

Figure 6-6 shows the expanded contents of the TCP header of the same captured packet number 3. This packet contains a request for HTTP. In subsequent chapters, more information about TCP fields will be presented.

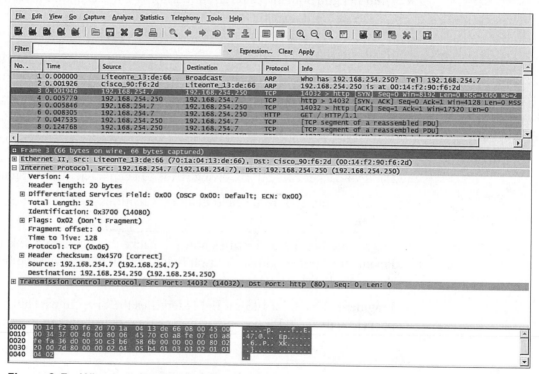

Figure 6-5   Wireshark IPv4 Packet Structure

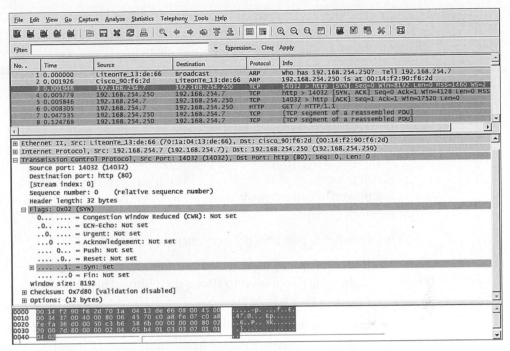

Figure 6-6 Wireshark TCP Segment Structure

Activity 6.1.3.4: IPv4 Header Fields

Go to the course online to perform this practice activity.

IPv6 Packet (6.1.4)

This section introduces the up-and-coming replacement for IPv4: IPv6.

Limitations of IPv4 (6.1.4.1)

Through the years, IPv4 has been updated to address new challenges. However, even with changes, IPv4 still has three major issues:

- **IP address depletion:** IPv4 has a limited number of unique public IP addresses available. Although there are approximately 4 billion IPv4 addresses, the increasing number of new IP-enabled devices, always-on connections, and the potential growth of less-developed regions have increased the need for more addresses.

- **Internet routing table expansion:** A routing table is used by routers to make best-path determinations. As the number of networks and entities connected to the Internet increases, so too does the number of network routes. These IPv4 routes consume a great deal of memory and processor resources on Internet routers.

- **Lack of end-to-end connectivity:** *Network Address Translation (NAT)* is a technology commonly implemented within IPv4 networks. NAT provides a way for multiple devices to share a single public IP address. However, because the public IP address is shared, the IP address of an internal network host is hidden. This can be problematic for technologies that require end-to-end connectivity.

Introducing IPv6 (6.1.4.2)

In the early 1990s, the Internet Engineering Task Force (IETF) grew concerned about the issues with IPv4 and began to look for a replacement. This activity led to the development of IP version 6 (IPv6). IPv6 overcomes the limitations of IPv4 and is a powerful enhancement with features that better suit current and foreseeable network demands.

Improvements that IPv6 provides include

- **Increased address space:** IPv6 addresses are based on 128-bit hierarchical addressing as opposed to IPv4 with 32 bits. This dramatically increases the number of available IP addresses.

- **Improved packet handling:** The IPv6 header has been simplified with fewer fields. This improves packet handling by intermediate routers and also provides support for extensions and options for increased scalability/longevity.

- **Eliminates the need for NAT:** With such a large number of public IPv6 addresses, Network Address Translation (NAT) is not needed. Customer sites, from the largest enterprises to single households, can get a public IPv6 network address. This avoids some of the NAT-induced application problems experienced by applications requiring end-to-end connectivity.

- **Integrated security:** IPv6 natively supports authentication and privacy capabilities. With IPv4, additional features had to be implemented to do this.

The 32-bit IPv4 address space provides approximately 4,294,967,296 unique addresses. Of these, only 3.7 billion addresses are assignable, because the IPv4 addressing system traditionally separates the addresses into classes, and reserves addresses for multicasting, testing, and other specific uses.

IP version 6 address space provides 340,282,366,920,938,463,463,374,607,431,768, 211,456, or 340 undecillion, addresses, which is roughly equivalent to every grain of sand on Earth.

Encapsulating IPv6 (6.1.4.3)

One of the major design improvements of IPv6 over IPv4 is the simplified IPv6 header.

The IPv4 header consists of 20 octets (up to 60 bytes if the Options field is used) and 12 basic header fields, not including the Options field and Padding field.

The IPv6 header consists of 40 octets (largely because of the length of the source and destination IPv6 addresses) and eight header fields (three IPv4 basic header fields and five additional header fields).

The IPv6 simplified header is shown in Figure 6-7. As shown in this figure, some of IPv6 fields have remained the same, some fields from the IPv4 header are not used, and some fields have changed names and position. In addition, a new field has been added to IPv6 that is not used in IPv4.

The IPv6 simplified header offers several advantages over IPv4:

- Better routing efficiency for performance and forwarding-rate scalability

- No requirement for processing checksums

- Simplified and more efficient extension header mechanisms (as opposed to the IPv4 Options field)

- A Flow Label field for per-flow processing with no need to open the transport inner packet to identify the various traffic flows

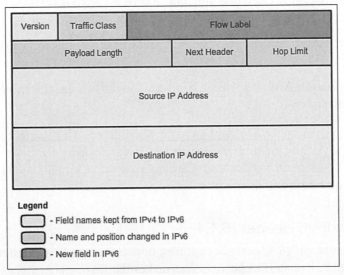

Figure 6-7   Simplified IPv6 Packet Header

IPv6 Packet Header (6.1.4.4)

The fields in the IPv6 packet header include

- **Version:** This field contains a 4-bit binary value identifying the IP packet version. For IPv6 packets, this field is always set to 0110.

- **Traffic Class:** This 8-bit field is equivalent to the IPv4 Differentiated Services (DS) field. It also contains a 6-bit Differentiated Services Code Point (DSCP) value used to classify packets and a 2-bit Explicit Congestion Notification (ECN) used for traffic congestion control.

- **Flow Label:** This 20-bit field provides a special service for real-time applications. It can be used to inform routers and switches to maintain the same path for the packet flow so that packets are not reordered.

- **Payload Length:** This 16-bit field is equivalent to the Total Length field in the IPv4 header. It defines the entire packet (fragment) size, including header and optional extensions.

- **Next Header:** This 8-bit field is equivalent to the IPv4 Protocol field. It indicates the data payload type that the packet is carrying, enabling the network layer to pass the data to the appropriate upper-layer protocol. This field is also used if there are optional extension headers added to the IPv6 packet.

- **Hop Limit:** This 8-bit field replaces the IPv4 TTL field. This value is decremented by 1 by each router that forwards the packet. When the counter reaches 0, the packet is discarded and an ICMPv6 message is forwarded to the sending host, indicating that the packet did not reach its destination.

- **Source Address:** This 128-bit field identifies the IPv6 address of the receiving host.

- **Destination Address:** This 128-bit field identifies the IPv6 address of the receiving host.

An IPv6 packet might also contain extension headers (EH), which provide optional network layer information. Extension headers are optional and are placed between the IPv6 header and the payload. EHs are used for fragmentation, for security, to support mobility, and more.

Sample IPv6 Header (6.1.4.5)

When viewing IPv6 Wireshark captures, notice that the IPv6 header has markedly fewer fields than an IPv4 header. This makes the IPv6 header easier and quicker for the router to process.

The IPv6 address itself looks very different. Because of the larger 128-bit IPv6 addresses, the hexadecimal numbering system is used to simplify the address representation. IPv6 addresses use colons to separate entries into a series of 16-bit hexadecimal blocks.

Figure 6-8 displays the contents of packet number 46 in this sample capture. The packet contains the initial message of the TCP three-way handshake between an IPv6 host and an IPv6 server. Notice the values in the expanded IPv6 header section. Also notice how this is a TCP packet and that it does not contain any other information beyond the TCP section.

Figure 6-8   Fields in IPv6 Header

Interactive Graphic

Activity 6.1.4.6: IPv6 Header Fields

Go to the course online to perform this practice activity.

Routing (6.2)

The basic principle of internetworks is routing. This section introduces the routing between networks.

How a Host Routes (6.2.1)

Hosts need to communicate with hosts that might be on networks other than the local network. This section examines how communication from hosts is able to reach hosts on remote networks.

Host Forwarding Decision (6.2.1.1)

Another role of the network layer is to direct packets between hosts. A host can send a packet to

- **Itself:** This is a special IPv4 address of 127.0.0.1, which is referred to as the loopback interface. This loopback address is automatically assigned to a host when TCP/IP is running. The ability for a host to send a packet to itself using network functionality is useful for testing purposes. Any IP within the network 127.0.0.0/8 refers to this host.

- **Local host:** This is a host on the same network as the sending host. The hosts share the same network address.

- **Remote host:** This is a host on a remote network. The hosts do not share the same network address.

Whether a packet is destined for a local host or a remote host is determined by the IP address and subnet mask combination of the source (or sending) device compared to the IP address of the destination device.

In a home or business network, you might have several wired and wireless devices interconnected using an intermediate device such as a LAN switch and/or a wireless access point (WAP). This intermediate device provides interconnections between local hosts on the local network. Local hosts can reach each other and share information without the need of any additional devices. If a host is sending a packet to a device that is configured with the same IP network as the host device, the packet is simply forwarded out of the host interface, through the intermediate device, to the destination device directly.

Of course, in most situations, we want our devices to be able to connect beyond the local network segment: out to other homes, businesses, and the Internet. Devices that are beyond the local network segment are known as remote hosts. When a source device sends a packet to a remote destination device, the help of routers and routing is needed. Routing is the process of identifying the best path to a destination. The router connected to the local network segment is referred to as the default gateway.

Default Gateway (6.2.1.2)

The default gateway is the device that routes traffic from the local network to devices on remote networks. In a home or small-business environment, the default gateway is often used to connect the local network to the Internet.

If the host is sending a packet to a device on a different IP network, the host must forward the packet through the intermediate device to the default gateway. This is because a host device does not maintain routing information, beyond the local network, to reach remote destinations. The default gateway does. The default gateway, which is most often a router, maintains a routing table. A routing table is a data file in RAM that is used to store route information about directly connected networks, as well as entries of remote networks that the device has learned. A router uses the information in the routing table to determine the best path to reach those destinations.

So how does a host keep track of whether to forward packets to the default gateway? Hosts must maintain their own, local, routing table to ensure that network layer packets are directed to the correct destination network. The local table of the host typically contains

- **Direct connection:** This is a route to the loopback interface (127.0.0.1).

- **Local network route:** The network that the host is connected to is automatically populated in the host routing table.

- **Local default route:** The default route represents the route that packets must take to reach all remote network addresses. The default route is created when a default gateway address is present on the host. The default gateway address is the IP address of the network interface of the router that is connected to the local network. The default gateway address can be configured on the host manually or learned dynamically.

It is important to note that the default route, and therefore the default gateway, is only used when a host must forward packets to a remote network. It is not required, nor even needs to be configured, if only sending packets to devices on the local network.

For example, consider a network printer/scanner. If the network printer has an IP address and subnet mask configured, local hosts can send documents to the printer to be printed. Additionally, the printer can forward documents that have been scanned to any local hosts. As long as the printer is only used locally, a default gateway address is not required. In fact, by not configuring a default gateway address on the printer, you are effectively denying Internet access, which can be a wise security choice. No Internet access means low security risk. While devices, such as printers, can offer the capability to perform automatic updates through the Internet, it is usually easier and more secure to achieve those same updates through a local upload from a secured local host, such as a PC.

IPv4 Host Routing Table (6.2.1.3)

On a Windows host, the **route print** or **netstat -r** command can be used to display the host routing table. Both commands generate the same output. The output might seem overwhelming at first, but is fairly simple to understand.

Entering the **netstat -r** command or the equivalent **route print** command displays three sections related to the current TCP/IP network connections:

- **Interface List:** Lists the Media Access Control (MAC) address and assigned interface number of every network-capable interface on the host, including Ethernet, Wi-Fi, and Bluetooth adapters.

- **IPv4 Route Table:** Lists all known IPv4 routes, including direct connections, local network, and local default routes.

- **IPv6 Route Table:** Lists all known IPv6 routes, including direct connections, local network, and local default routes.

Note

Command output varies, depending on how the host is configured and the interface types it has.

In Figure 6-9, the output of the **netstat -r** command displays the IPv4 Route Table section of the output. Notice that the output is divided into five columns that identify

- **Network Destination:** Lists the reachable networks.

- **Netmask:** Lists a subnet mask that informs the host how to determine the network and the host portions of the IP address.

- **Gateway:** Lists the address used by the local computer to get to a remote network destination. If a destination is directly reachable, it will show as "on-link" in this column.

- **Interface:** Lists the address of the physical interface used to send the packet to the gateway that is used to reach the network destination.

- **Metric:** Lists the cost of each route and is used to determine the best route to a destination.

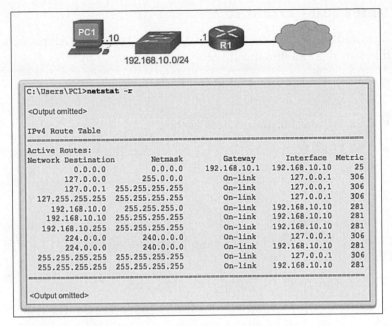

Figure 6-9   Output of **netstat -r** with IPv4 Routes

IPv4 Host Routing Entries (6.2.1.4)

To help simplify the output of the **netstat -r** command, the destination networks can be grouped into five sections. These sections are shown in Figure 6-10.

0.0.0.0

The local default route; that is, all packets with destinations that do not match other specified addresses in the routing table are forwarded to the gateway. Therefore, all nonmatching destination routes are sent to the gateway with IP address 192.168.10.1 (R1) exiting from the interface with IP address 192.168.10.10. Note that the final destination address specified in the packet does not change; rather, the host simply knows to forward the packet to the gateway for further processing.

127.0.0.0 – 127.255.255.255

These loopback addresses all relate to the direct connection and provide services to the local host.

192.168.10.0 – 192.168.10.255

These addresses all relate to the host and local network. All packets with destination addresses that fall into this category will exit out of the 192.168.10.10 interface.

- **192.168.10.0:** The local network route address; represents all computers on the 192.168.10.x network.

- **192.168.10.10:** The address of the local host.

- **192.168.10.255:** The network broadcast address; sends messages to all hosts on the local network route.

224.0.0.0

These are special multicast addresses (also known as class D addresses) reserved for use through either the loopback interface (127.0.0.1) or the host IP address (192.168.10.10).

255.255.255.255

The last two address entries (255.255.255.255) represent the limited broadcast IP address values. This broadcast can either use the loopback interface (127.0.0.1) or the host IP address (192.168.10.10). These addresses can be used to find a DHCP server before the local IP address is determined.

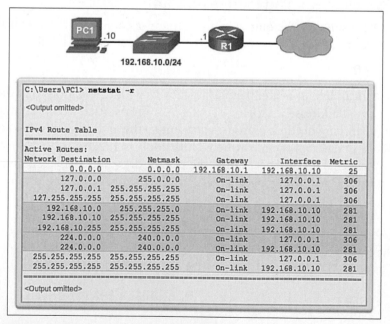

Figure 6-10   Sections of the **netstat -r** Output

Sample IPv4 Host Routing Table (6.2.1.5)

For example, if PC1 wanted to send a packet to 192.168.10.20, it would

1. Consult the IPv4 Route Table.

2. Examining the line in Figure 6-11 with the destination IP address of 192.168.10.0, the Network Destination reveals that the host is on the same network (On-link).

3. PC1 would then send the packet toward the final destination using its local interface (192.168.10.10).

If PC1 wanted to send a packet to a remote host located at 10.10.10.10, it would

1. Consult the IPv4 Route Table.

2. Find that there is no exact match for the destination IP address.

3. Examining the line in Figure 6-11 with the destination IP address of the local default route (0.0.0.0) will reveal that it should forward the packet to the 192.168.10.1 gateway address.

4. PC1 then forwards the packet to the gateway through the local interface (192.168.10.10). The gateway device then determines the next path for the packet to reach the final destination address of 10.10.10.10.

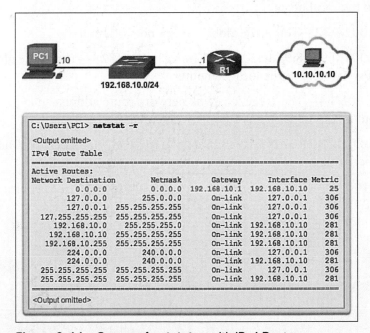

Figure 6-11   Output of **netstat -r** with IPv4 Routes

Sample IPv6 Host Routing Table (6.2.1.6)

The output of the IPv6 Route Table differs in column headings and format because of the longer IPv6 addresses.

The IPv6 Route Table section displays four columns that identify

- **If:** Lists the interface numbers from the Interface List section of the **netstat –r** command. The interface numbers correspond to the network-capable interface on the host, including Ethernet, Wi-Fi, and Bluetooth adapters.

- **Metric:** Lists the cost of each route to a destination. Lower numbers indicate preferred routes.

- **Network Destination:** Lists the reachable networks.

- **Gateway:** Lists the address used by the local host to forward packets to a remote network destination. On-link indicates that the host is currently connected to it.

For example, Figure 6-12 displays the IPv6 Route Table section generated by the **netstat –r** command to reveal the following network destinations:

- **::/0**—This is the IPv6 equivalent of the local default route.

- **::1/128**—This is equivalent to the IPv4 loopback address and provides services to the local host.

- **2001::/32**—This is the global unicast network prefix.

- **2001:0:9d38:953c:2c30:3071:e718:a926/128**—This is the global unicast IPv6 address of the local computer.

- **fe80::/64**—This is the local link network route address and represents all computers on the local link IPv6 network.

- **fe80::2c30:3071:e718:a926/128**—This is the link local IPv6 address of the local computer.

- **ff00::/8**—These are special reserved multicast addresses equivalent to the IPv4 224.x.x.x addresses.

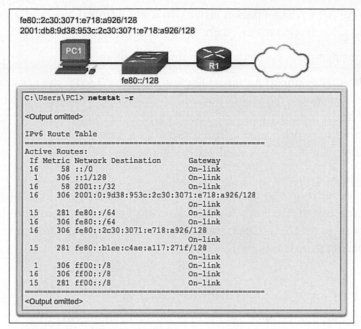

Figure 6-12   Output of **netstat -r** with IPv6 Routes

Note

Interfaces in IPv6 commonly have two IPv6 addresses: a link local address and a global unicast address. Also, notice that there are no broadcast addresses in IPv6. IPv6 addresses will be discussed further in the next chapter.

Activity 6.2.1.7: Identify Elements of a Host Routing Table Entry

Go to the course online to perform this practice activity.

Router Routing Tables (6.2.2)

This section will introduce the role of the routing table in routing.

Router Packet-Forwarding Decision (6.2.2.1)

When a host sends a packet to another host, it will use its routing table to determine where to send the packet. If the destination host is on a remote network, the packet is forwarded to the address of a gateway device.

What happens when a packet arrives on a router interface? The router looks at its routing table to determine where to forward packets.

The routing table of a router stores information about

- **Directly connected routes:** These routes come from the active router interfaces. Routers add a directly connected route when an interface is configured with an IP address and is activated. Each of the router's interfaces is connected to a different network segment. Routers maintain information about the network segments that they are connected to within the routing table.

- **Remote routes:** These routes come from remote networks connected to other routers. Routes to these networks can be either manually configured on the local router by the network administrator or dynamically configured by enabling the local router to exchange routing information with other routers using dynamic routing protocols.

IPv4 Router Routing Table (6.2.2.2)

A host routing table includes only information about directly connected networks. A host requires a default gateway to send packets to a remote destination. The routing table of a router contains similar information but can also identify specific remote networks.

The routing table of a router is similar to the routing table of a host. They both identify the

- Destination network

- Metric associated with the destination network

- Gateway to get to the destination network

On a Cisco IOS router, the **show ip route** command can be used to display the routing table of a router. A router also provides additional route information, including how the route was learned, when it was last updated, and which specific interface to use to get to a predefined destination.

When a packet arrives at the router interface, the router examines the packet header to determine the destination network. If the destination network matches a route in the routing table, the router forwards the packet using the information specified in the routing table. If there are two or more possible routes to the same destination, the metric is used to decide which route appears on the routing table.

The routing table of R1, shown in Example 6-1 from Figure 6-13, shows the typical output of a router. Unlike the host routing table, there are no column headings identifying the information contained in a routing table entry. Therefore, it is important to learn the meaning of the different types of information included in each entry.

This routing table and the associated Figure 6-13 will be used a reference in this section.

Example 6-1   Routing Table of R1 in Figure 6-13

```
R1# show ip route
Codes:
L - local, C - connected, S - static, R - RIP, M - mobile, B - BGP
D - EIGRP, EX - EIGRP external, O - OSPF, IA - OSPF inter area
N1 - OSPF NSSA external type 1, N2 - OSPF NSSA external type 2
E1 - OSPF external type 1, E2 - OSPF external type 2, E - EGP
i - IS-IS, L1 - IS-IS level-1, L2 - IS-IS level-2, ia - IS-IS inter area
* - candidate default, U - per-user static route, o - ODR
P - periodic downloaded static route

Gateway of last resort is not set

      10.0.0.0/24 is subnetted, 2 subnets
D        10.1.1.0/24 [90/2170112] via 209.165.200.226, 00:00:18, Serial0/0/0
D        10.1.2.0/24 [90/2170112] via 209.165.200.226, 00:00:18, Serial0/0/0
      192.168.10.0/24 is variably subnetted, 2 subnets, 2 masks
C        192.168.10.0/24 is directly connected, GigabitEthernet0/0
L        192.168.10.1/32 is directly connected, GigabitEthernet0/0
      192.168.11.0/24 is variably subnetted, 2 subnets, 2 masks
C        192.168.11.0/24 is directly connected, GigabitEthernet0/1
L        192.168.11.1/32 is directly connected, GigabitEthernet0/1
      209.165.200.0/24 is variably subnetted, 2 subnets, 2 masks
C        209.165.200.224/30 is directly connected, Serial0/0/0
L        209.165.200.225/32 is directly connected, Serial0/0/0
R1#
```

Figure 6-13   Network with Remote Routes

Directly Connected Routing Table Entries (6.2.2.3)

In the current versions of the IOS, two routing table entries are automatically created when an active router interface is configured with an IP address and subnet mask. The automatically added routes for interface Gigabit Ethernet 0/0 are shown in Table 6-2. These entries were automatically added to the routing table when the Gigabit Ethernet 0/0 interface was configured and activated. The entries contain the following information:

- **Route source:** The "How Route Was Learned" column in Table 6-2 shows the two route source codes for directly connected networks:

    - **C:** Identifies a directly connected network. Directly connected networks are automatically created when an interface is configured with an IP address and activated.

    - **L:** Identifies that this is a local route. Local routes are automatically created when an interface is configured with an IP address and activated.

- **Destination network:** The "Destination and How Reached" column in Table 6-2 identifies the address of the network and how a packet can reach the destination network.

- **Outgoing interface:** The "Interface to Reach Network" column of Table 6-2 identifies the outgoing interface that forwarded packets exit to reach the destination network.

Table 6-2   Automatically Added Routes

How Route was Learned	Destination and How Reached	Interface to Reach Network
C	192.168.10.0/24 is directly connected,	GigabitEthernet0/0
L	192.168.10.1/32 is directly connected,	GigabitEthernet0/0

Note

Local routing table entries did not appear in routing tables prior to IOS Release 15.

A router typically has multiple interfaces configured. The routing table stores information about both directly connected and remote routes. As with directly connected networks, the route source identifies how the route was learned. For example, common codes for remote networks include

- **S:** Identifies that the route was manually created by an administrator to reach a specific network. This is known as a static route.

- **D:** Identifies that the route was learned dynamically from another router using the Enhanced Interior Gateway Routing Protocol (EIGRP).

- **O:** Identifies that the route was learned dynamically from another router using the Open Shortest Path First (OSPF) routing protocol.

Note

Other codes are beyond the scope of this chapter.

Remote Network Routing Table Entries (6.2.2.4)

Table 6-3 details a routing table entry on R1 for the route to remote network 10.1.1.0 and 10.1.2.9. The entry identifies the following information:

- **Route source:** Identifies how the route was learned.

- **Destination network:** Identifies the address of the remote network.

- **Administrative distance:** Identifies the trustworthiness of the route source.

- **Metric:** Identifies the value assigned to reach the remote network. Lower values indicate preferred routes.

- **Next hop:** Identifies the IP address of the next router to forward the packet.

- **Route timestamp:** Identifies when the route was last heard from.

- **Outgoing interface:** Identifies the exit interface to use to forward a packet toward the final destination.

Table 6-3   Remotely Learned Routes

Route Source	Destination Network	Administrative Distance	Metric	Next Hop	Route Timestamp	Outgoing Interface
D	10.1.1.0/24	[90	/2170112] via	209.165.200.226	00:00:18	Serial0/0/0
D	10.1.2.0/24	[90	/2170112] via	209.165.200.226	00:00:18	Serial0/0/0

Next-Hop Address (6.2.2.5)

A next hop is the address of the device that will process the packet next. For a host on a network, the address of the default gateway (router interface) is the next hop for all packets that must be sent to another network. In the routing table of a router, each route to a remote network lists a next hop.

When a packet destined for a remote network arrives at the router, the router matches the destination network to a route in the routing table. If a match is found, the router forwards the packet to the IP address of the next-hop router using the interface identified by the route entry.

A next-hop router is the gateway to remote networks.

Referencing back to Table 6-3, a packet arriving at R1 destined for either the 10.1.1.0 or 10.1.2.0 network is forwarded to the next-hop address 209.165.200.226 using the Serial 0/0/0 interface.

Networks directly connected to a router have no next-hop address, because a router can forward packets directly to hosts on these networks using the designated interface.

Packets cannot be forwarded by the router without a route for the destination network in the routing table. If a route representing the destination network is not in the routing table, the packet is dropped (that is, not forwarded).

However, just as a host can use a default gateway to forward a packet to an unknown destination, a router can also be configured to use a default static route to create a Gateway of Last Resort. The Gateway of Last Resort will be covered in more detail in the Routing and Switching Essentials course.

Sample Router IPv4 Routing Table (6.2.2.6)

Assume that PC1 with IP address 192.168.10.10 in Figure 6-13 wants to send a packet to another host on the same network. PC1 would check the IPv4 route table based on the destination IP address. Then, PC1 would discover that the host is on the same network and simply send it out of its interface (On-link).

Note

R1 is not involved in the transfer of the packet. If PC1 forwards a packet to any network other than its local network, it must use the services of Router R1 and forward the packet to its local default route (192.168.10.1).

The following examples are based on previously shown R1 router output in Example 6-1. These illustrate how a host and a router make packet-routing decisions by consulting their respective routing tables.

Example 1: PC1 wants to verify connectivity to its local default gateway at 192.168.10.1 (the router interface):

1. PC1 consults the IPv4 route table based on the destination IP address.

2. PC1 discovers that the host is on the same network and simply sends a ping packet out of its interface (On-link).

3. R1 receives the packet on its Gigabit Ethernet 0/0 (G0/0) interface and looks at the destination IP address.

4. R1 consults its routing table.

5. R1 matches the destination IP address to the L 192.168.10.1/32 routing table entry and discovers that this route points to its own local interface, as shown:

```
L       192.168.10.1/32 is directly connected, GigabitEthernet0/0
```

6. R1 opens the remainder of the IP packet and responds accordingly.

Example 2: PC1 wants to send a packet to PC2 (192.168.11.10):

1. PC1 consults the IPv4 route table and discovers that there is no exact match.

2. PC1 therefore uses the all-route network (0.0.0.0) and sends the packet using the local default route (192.168.10.1).

3. R1 receives the packet on its Gigabit Ethernet 0/0 (G0/0) interface and looks at the destination IP address (192.168.11.10).

4. R1 consults its routing table and matches the destination IP address to the C 192.168.11.0/24 routing table entry, as shown:

```
C       192.168.11.0/24 is directly connected, GigabitEthernet0/1
```

5. R1 forwards the packet out of its directly connected Gigabit Ethernet 0/1 interface (G0/1).

6. PC2 receives the packet and consults its host IPv4 routing table.

7. PC2 discovers that the packet is addressed to it, opens the remainder of the packet, and responds accordingly.

Example 3: PC1 wants to send a packet to 209.165.200.226:

1. PC1 consults the IPv4 route table and discovers that there is no exact match.

2. PC1 therefore uses the default route (0.0.0.0/0) and sends the packet using the default gateway (192.168.10.1).

3. R1 receives the packet on its Gigabit Ethernet 0/0 (G0/0) interface and looks at the destination IP address (209.165.200.226).

4. R1 consults its routing table and matches the destination IP address to the C 209.165.200.224/30 routing table entry, as shown:

```
C        209.165.200.224/30 is directly connected, Serial0/0/0
```

5. R1 forwards the packet out of its directly connected Serial 0/0/0 interface (S0/0/0).

Example 4: PC1 wants to send a packet to the host with IP address 10.1.1.10:

1. PC1 consults the IPv4 route table and discovers that there is no exact match.

2. PC1 therefore uses the all-route network (0.0.0.0) and sends it to its local default route (192.168.10.1).

3. R1 receives the packet on its Gigabit Ethernet 0/0 (G0/0) interface and looks at the destination IP address (10.1.1.10).

4. R1 consults its routing table and matches the destination IP address to the D 10.1.1.0/24 routing table entry, as shown:

```
D        10.1.1.0/24 [90/2170112] via 209.165.200.226, 00:00:18, Serial0/0/0
```

5. R1 discovers it has to send the packet to the next-hop address 209.165.200.226.

6. R1 again consults its routing table and matches the destination IP address to the C 209.165.200.224/30 routing table entry, as shown previously in the R1 router output for Figure 6-13.

7. R1 forwards the packet out of its directly connected Serial 0/0/0 interface (S0/0/0).

Activity 6.2.2.7: Identify Elements of a Router Routing Table Entry

Go to the course online to perform this practice activity.

Lab 6.2.2.8: View Host Routing Tables

In this lab, you will complete the following objectives:

- Part 1: Access the Host Routing Table
- Part 2: Examine IPv4 Host Routing Table Entries
- Part 3: Examine IPv6 Host Routing Table Entries

Routers (6.3)

This section will introduce routers.

Anatomy of a Router (6.3.1)

The router is the fundamental network infrastructure device. This section will introduce the structure and operation of routers.

A Router Is a Computer (6.3.1.1)

There are many types of infrastructure routers available. In fact, Cisco routers are designed to address the needs of

- **Branch:** Teleworkers, small business, and medium-size branch sites. Includes Cisco 800, 1900, 2900, and 3900 Integrated Series Routers (ISR) G2 (2nd generation).

- **WAN:** Large businesses, organizations, and enterprises. Includes the Cisco Catalyst 6500 Series switches and the Cisco Aggregation Service Router (ASR) 1000.

- **Service provider:** Large service providers. Includes Cisco ASR 1000, Cisco ASR 9000, Cisco XR 12000, Cisco CRS-3 Carrier Routing System, and 7600 Series routers.

The focus of CCNA Routing and Switching certification is on the branch family of routers. These include the Cisco 1900, 2900, and 3900 ISR G2 family of routers.

Regardless of their function, size, or complexity, all router models are essentially computers. Just like computers, tablets, and smart devices, routers also require

- Operating systems (OS)

- Central processing units (CPU)

- Random-access memory (RAM)

- Read-only memory (ROM)

A router also has special memory that includes flash and nonvolatile random-access memory (NVRAM).

Router CPU and OS (6.3.1.2)

Like all computers, tablets, and smart devices, Cisco devices require a CPU to execute OS instructions, such as system initialization, routing functions, and switching functions.

The CPU requires an OS to provide routing and switching functions. The Cisco Internetwork Operating System (IOS) is the system software used for most Cisco devices regardless of the size and type of the device. The IOS is used for routers, LAN switches, small wireless access points, large routers with dozens of interfaces, and many other devices.

Router Memory (6.3.1.3)

A router has access to four types of memory: RAM, ROM, NVRAM, and flash.

RAM

RAM is used to store various applications and processes including

- **Cisco IOS:** The IOS is copied into RAM during bootup.

- **Running configuration file:** This is the configuration file that stores the configuration commands that the router IOS is currently using. It is also known as the running config.

- **IP routing table:** This table stores information about directly connected and remote networks. It is used to determine the best path to use to forward packets.

- *ARP cache*: This cache contains the IPv4 address–to–MAC address mappings, similar to the Address Resolution Protocol (ARP) cache on a PC. The ARP cache is used on routers that have LAN interfaces, such as Ethernet interfaces.

- **Packet buffer:** Packets are temporarily stored in a buffer when received on an interface or before they exit an interface.

Like computers, Cisco routers actually use dynamic random-access memory (DRAM). DRAM is a very common kind of RAM that stores the instructions and data needed to be executed by the CPU. Unlike ROM, RAM is volatile memory and requires continual power to maintain its information. It loses all its content when the router is powered down or restarted.

By default, 1941 routers come with 512 MB of DRAM soldered on the main system board (onboard) and one dual in-line memory module (DIMM) slot for memory upgrades of up to an additional 2.0 GB. Cisco 2901, 2911, and 2921 models come with 512 MB of onboard DRAM. Note that first-generation ISRs and older Cisco routers do not have onboard RAM.

ROM

Cisco routers use ROM to store

- **Bootup instructions:** Provides the startup instructions.

- **Basic diagnostic software:** Performs the power-on self-test (POST) of all components.

- **Limited IOS:** Provides a limited backup version of the OS, in case the router cannot load the full-featured IOS.

ROM is firmware embedded on an integrated circuit inside the router and does not lose its contents when the router loses power or is restarted.

NVRAM

NVRAM is used by the Cisco IOS as permanent storage for the startup configuration file (startup config). Like ROM, NVRAM does not lose its contents when power is turned off.

Flash Memory

Flash memory is nonvolatile computer memory used as permanent storage for the IOS and other system-related files. The IOS is copied from flash into RAM during the bootup process.

Cisco 1941 routers come with two external Compact Flash slots. Each slot can support high-speed storage densities upgradeable to 4 GB in density.

Table 6-4 summarizes the four types of memory.

Table 6-4   Four Types of Router Memory

Memory	Volatile/Nonvolatile	Stores
RAM	Volatile	■ Running IOS
		■ Running configuration
		■ IP routing and ARP tables
		■ Packet buffer
ROM	Nonvolatile	■ Bootup instructions
		■ Basic diagnostic software
		■ Limited IOS
NVRAM	Nonvolatile	■ Startup configuration file
Flash	Nonvolatile	■ IOS
		■ Other system files

Inside a Router (6.3.1.4)

Although there are several different types and models of routers, every router has the same general hardware components.

Figure 6-14 shows the inside of a Cisco 1841 first-generation ISR. Table 6-5 provides a brief description of these components.

Many of the components found in a router, such as the power supply, cooling fan, heat shields, and an advanced integration module (AIM), shown in Figure 6-14 and Table 6-5, are beyond the scope of this chapter.

Figure 6-14 Internal Components of a Cisco 1841 Router

Table 6-5 Internal Router Components

Component	Function
Power supply	Provides various voltages to internal router components
WIC slot	Supports HWICs (high-speed WAN interface cards)
RAM	Holds running configuration, running IOS, routing tables, and buffers. Also, called SRAM (synchronous RAM)
ROM	Nonvolatile
NVRAM	Startup configuration file
Flash	Basic diagnostic, IOS file, ROMMON
CPU	Microprocessor supporting router operations

Component	Function
AIC	Advanced Integration Module option that offloads from the CPU processor-intensive functions such as encryption
Fan	Provides cooling for internal components

A networking professional should be familiar with and understand the function of the main internal components of a router, rather than the exact location of those components inside a specific router. Depending on the model, those components are located in different places inside the router.

Router Backplane (6.3.1.5)

A Cisco 1941 router includes the following connections:

- **Console ports:** Two console ports for the initial configuration and command-line interface (CLI) management access using a regular RJ-45 port and a new USB Type-B (mini-B USB) connector.

- **AUX port:** An RJ-45 port for remote management access; this is similar to the Console port.

- **Two LAN interfaces:** Two Gigabit Ethernet interfaces for LAN access.

- **Enhanced high-speed WAN interface card (EHWIC) slots:** Two slots that provide modularity and flexibility by enabling the router to support different types of interface modules, including serial, digital subscriber line (DSL), switch port, and wireless.

Figure 6-15 identifies the location of these connections and slots on a Cisco 1941 router. The Cisco 1941 ISR also has storage slots to support expanded capabilities. Dual-compact flash memory slots are capable of supporting a 4-GB Compact Flash card each for increased storage space. Two USB host ports are included for additional storage space and secure token capability.

Compact Flash can store the Cisco IOS software image, log files, voice configuration files, HTML files, backup configurations, or any other file needed for the system. By default, only slot 0 is populated with a Compact Flash card from the factory, and it is the default boot location.

Figure 6-15   Connections on a Cisco 1941 Router

Connecting to a Router (6.3.1.6)

Cisco devices, routers, and switches typically interconnect many devices. For this reason, these devices have several types of ports and interfaces. These ports and interfaces are used to connect cables to the device.

The connections on a Cisco router can be grouped into two categories:

- **Management ports:** These are the console and auxiliary ports used to configure, manage, and troubleshoot the router. Unlike LAN and WAN interfaces, management ports are not used for packet forwarding.

- **In-band router interfaces:** These are the LAN and WAN interfaces configured with IP addressing to carry user traffic. Ethernet interfaces are the most common LAN connections, while common WAN connections include serial and DSL interfaces.

Like many networking devices, Cisco devices use light-emitting diode (LED) indicators to provide status information. An interface LED indicates the activity of the corresponding interface. If an LED is off when the interface is active and the interface is correctly connected, this can be an indication of a problem with that interface. If an interface is extremely busy, its LED is always on.

LAN and WAN Interfaces (6.3.1.7)

Similar to a Cisco switch, there are several ways to access the CLI environment on a Cisco router. The most common methods are

- **Console:** Uses a low-speed serial or USB connection to provide direct connect, out-of-band management access to a Cisco device.

- **Telnet or SSH:** Two methods for remotely accessing a CLI session across an active network interface.

- **AUX port:** Used for remote management of the router using a dialup telephone line and modem.

The console and AUX port are located on the router.

In addition to these ports, routers also have network interfaces to receive and forward IP packets. Routers have multiple interfaces that are used to connect to multiple networks. Typically, the interfaces connect to various types of networks, which means that different types of media and connectors are required.

Every interface on the router is a member or host on a different IP network. Each interface must be configured with an IP address and subnet mask of a different network. The Cisco IOS does not allow two active interfaces on the same router to belong to the same network.

Router interfaces can usually be grouped into two broad categories:

- **Ethernet LAN interfaces:** Used for connecting cables that terminate with LAN devices, such as computers and switches. This interface can also be used to connect routers to each other. Several conventions for naming Ethernet interfaces are popular: the older Ethernet, Fast Ethernet, and Gigabit Ethernet. The name used depends on the device type and model.

- **Serial WAN interfaces:** Used for connecting routers to external networks, usually over a larger geographical distance. Similar to LAN interfaces, each serial WAN interface has its own IP address and subnet mask, which identifies it as a member of a specific network.

Interactive Graphic

Activity 6.3.1.8: Identify Router Components

Go to the course online to perform this practice activity.

Lab 6.3.1.9: Exploring Router Physical Characteristics

In this lab, you will complete the following objectives:

- Part 1: Examine Router External Characteristics
- Part 2: Examine Router Internal Characteristics Using show Commands

Packet Tracer 6.3.1.10: Exploring Internetworking Devices

In this activity, you will explore the different options available on internetworking devices. You will also be required to determine which options provide the necessary connectivity when connecting multiple devices. Finally, you will add the correct modules and connect the devices.

Router Bootup (6.3.2)

Understanding the bootup process of Cisco IOS and the associated messages is important when diagnosing a nonoperational device. This section will provide an overview of the IOS boot process.

Cisco IOS (6.3.2.1)

The Cisco IOS operational details vary on different internetworking devices, depending on the device's purpose and feature set. However, Cisco IOS for routers provides the following:

- Addressing
- Interfaces
- Routing
- Security
- QoS
- Resources Management

The IOS file itself is several megabytes in size and, similar to Cisco IOS switches, is stored in flash memory. Using flash allows the IOS to be upgraded to newer versions or to have new features added. During bootup, the IOS is copied from flash memory into RAM. DRAM is much faster than flash; therefore, copying the IOS into RAM increases the performance of the device.

Bootset Files (6.3.2.2)

A router loads the following two files into RAM when it is booted:

- **IOS image file:** The Cisco IOS facilitates the basic operation of the device's hardware components. The IOS image file is stored in flash memory. This image is loaded into the device's RAM to provide the operating system for the router.

- **Startup configuration file:** The startup configuration file contains commands that are used to initially configure a router and create the running configuration file stored in RAM. The startup configuration file is stored in NVRAM and is copied to RAM to provide the "program" to the device that tells the device how to operate. All configuration changes are stored in the running configuration file and are implemented immediately by the IOS.

The running configuration is modified when the network administrator performs device configuration. When changes are made to the running config file, it should be saved to NVRAM as the startup configuration file, in case the router is restarted or loses power.

Router Bootup Process (6.3.2.3)

There are three major phases to the bootup process that is shown in Figure 6-16:

1. Perform the POST and load the bootstrap program.

2. Locate and load the Cisco IOS Software.

3. Locate and load the startup configuration file or enter setup mode.

Performing POST and Load Bootstrap Program (Phase 1)

The power-on self-test (POST) is a common process that occurs on almost every computer during bootup. The POST process is used to test the router hardware. When the router is powered on, software on the ROM chip conducts the POST. During this self-test, the router executes diagnostics from ROM on several hardware components, including the CPU, RAM, and NVRAM. After the POST has been completed, the router executes the bootstrap program.

After the POST, the bootstrap program is copied from ROM into RAM. After the program is in RAM, the CPU executes the instructions in the bootstrap program. The main task of the bootstrap program is to locate the Cisco IOS and load it into RAM.

Note

At this point in the boot process, if you have a console connection to the router, you begin to see output on the screen.

Locating and Loading Cisco IOS (Phase 2)

The IOS is typically stored in flash memory and is copied into RAM for execution by the CPU. During self-decompression of the IOS image file, a string of hash (pound) signs (#) will be displayed. This output looks similar to this:

```
Digitally Signed Release Software
program load complete, entry point: 0x81000000, size: 0x2bb1c58
Self decompressing the image :
############################################################################## [OK]
```

If the IOS image is not located in flash, the router can look for it on a TFTP server. If a full IOS image cannot be located, a scaled-down version of the IOS is copied from ROM into RAM. This version of IOS is used to help diagnose any problems and can be used to load a complete version of the IOS into RAM.

Locating and Loading the Configuration File (Phase 3)

The bootstrap program then searches for the startup configuration file (also known as startup config) in NVRAM. This file has the previously saved configuration commands and parameters. If it exists, it is copied into RAM as the running configuration file, running config. The running config file contains interface addresses, starts routing processes, configures router passwords, and defines other characteristics of the router.

If the startup config file does not exist in NVRAM, the router can search for a Trivial File Transfer Protocol (TFTP) server. If the router detects that it has an active link to another configured router, it sends a broadcast searching for a configuration file across the active link.

If a TFTP server is not found, the router displays the setup mode prompt. Setup mode is a series of questions prompting the user for basic configuration information. Setup mode is not intended to be used to enter complex router configurations, and it is not commonly used by network administrators.

Figure 6-16   IOS Bootup Process

Note

Setup mode is not used in this course to configure the router. When prompted to enter setup mode, always answer no. If you answer yes and enter setup mode, press **Ctrl+C** at any time to terminate the setup process.

Show Version Output (6.3.2.4)

You can use the **show version** command to verify and troubleshoot some of the basic hardware and software components of the router. The command displays information about the version of the Cisco IOS Software currently running on the router, the version of the bootstrap program, and information about the hardware configuration, including the amount of system memory.

The output from the **show version** command includes

- **IOS version:** Version of the Cisco IOS Software in RAM and that is being used by the router. The output is similar to

  ```
  Cisco IOS Software, C1900 Software (C1900-UNIVERSALK9-M), Version 15.1(4)M4,
  RELEASE SOFTWARE (fc2)
  ```

- **ROM bootstrap program:** Displays the version of the system bootstrap software, stored in ROM that was initially used to boot up the router. The output is similar to

  ```
  ROM: System Bootstrap, Version 15.1(4)M4, RELEASE SOFTWARE (fc1)
  ```

- **Location of IOS:** Displays where the bootstrap program is located and loaded in the Cisco IOS, and the complete filename of the IOS image. The output is similar to

  ```
  System image file is "flash0:c1900-universalk9-mz.SPA.151-1.M4.bin"
  ```

- **CPU and amount of RAM:** The first part of this line displays the type of CPU on this router. The last part of this line displays the amount of DRAM. Some series of routers, like the Cisco 1941 ISR, use a fraction of DRAM as packet memory. Packet memory is used for buffering packets. To determine the total amount of DRAM on the router, add both numbers. The output is similar to

  ```
  Cisco CISCO1941/K9 (revision 1.0) with 491520K/32768K bytes of memory.
  ```

- **Interfaces:** Displays the physical interfaces on the router. For example, the Cisco 1941 ISR has two Gigabit Ethernet interfaces as well as two WIC slots. These slots support various WIC cards such as low-speed serial interfaces, VoIP modules, or additional Ethernet interfaces. The output is similar to

  ```
  2 Gigabit Ethernet interfaces
  4 Low-speed serial(sync/async) network interface(s)
  ```

- **Amount of NVRAM and flash:** This is the amount of NVRAM and the amount of flash memory on the router. NVRAM is used to store the startup config file, and flash is used to permanently store the Cisco IOS. The output is similar to

```
255K bytes of non-volatile configuration memory.
249856K bytes of ATA System CompactFlash 0 (Read/Write)
```

- The last line of the **show version** command displays the current, configured value of the software configuration register in hexadecimal. If there is a second value displayed in parentheses, it denotes the configuration register value that is used during the next reload. The output is similar to

```
Configuration register is 0x2102
```

- The configuration register has several uses, including password recovery. The factory default setting for the configuration register is 0x2102. This value indicates that the router attempts to load a Cisco IOS Software image from flash memory and load the startup configuration file from NVRAM.

Video

Video Demonstration 6.3.2.5: The Router Boot Process

Video 6.3.2.5: View the video in the online course to examine the router boot process.

Interactive Graphic

Activity 6.3.2.6: The Router Boot Process

Go to the course online to perform this practice activity.

Configuring a Cisco Router (6.4)

This section will present the basic configuration needed for all IOS routers.

Configure Initial Settings (6.4.1)

Cisco routers require configuration before they are operational. This section will introduce the basic CLI configuration of routers.

Router Configuration Steps (6.4.1.1)

Cisco routers and Cisco switches have many similarities. They support a similar modal operating system, support similar command structures, and support many of the same commands. In addition, both devices have identical initial configuration steps when implementing them in a network.

How To 🔍   Similar to configuring a switch, the following steps should be completed when configuring initial settings on a router:

Step 1.   Enter the global configuration mode:

```
Router> enable
Router# configure terminal
Enter configuration commands, one per line. End with CNTL/Z.
Router(config)#
```

Step 2.   Assign a device name using the **hostname** global configuration command:

```
Router(config)# hostname R1
```

Step 3.   Set passwords.

Secure privileged EXEC mode access using the **enable secret** command:

```
R1(config)# enable secret class
```

Secure EXEC mode access using the **login** command on the console port, and the **password** command to set the password:

```
R1(config)# line console 0
R1(config-line)# password cisco
R1(config-line)# login
R1(config-line)# exit
```

Secure virtual access similar to securing EXEC access mode, except on the Virtual Teletype (VTY) port:

```
R1(config)# line vty 0 4
R1(config-line)# password cisco
R1(config-line)# login
R1(config-line)# exit
```

Use the **service password-encryption** global configuration command to prevent passwords from displaying as plain text in the configuration file:

```
R1(config)# service password-encryption
```

Step 4.   Provide legal notification using the **banner motd** (message of the day [MOTD]) global configuration command:

```
R1(config)# banner motd #Authorized Access Only!#
```

Step 5.   Exit configuration mode:

```
R1(config)# exit
R1#
%SYS-5-CONFIG_I: Configured from console by console
```

Step 6.   Save the configuration using the **copy run start** command:

```
R1# copy running-config startup-config
Destination filename [startup-config]?
Building configuration...
[OK]
R1#
```

Step 7.   Verify the configuration using the **show run** command.

> **Note**
>
> Remember to save the configuration using the **copy running-config startup-config** command.

Packet Tracer Activity 6.4.1.2: Configure Initial Router Settings

In this activity, you will perform basic router configurations. You will secure access to the CLI and console port using encrypted and plain-text passwords. You will also configure messages for users logging in to the router. These banners also warn unauthorized users that access is prohibited. Finally, you will verify and save your running configuration.

Configure Interfaces (6.4.2)

This section introduces the basic router interface configuration.

Configure LAN Interfaces (6.4.2.1)

For routers to be reachable, router interfaces must be configured. Therefore, to enable a specific interface, enter interface configuration mode using the **interface** *type-and-number* global configuration mode command.

There are many different types of interfaces available on Cisco routers. A Cisco 1941 router is equipped with two Gigabit Ethernet interfaces. With an additional WIC two-port serial WAN interface card (WIC), the interfaces would be named as follows:

- GigabitEthernet 0/0 (G0/0)

- GigabitEthernet 0/1 (G0/1)

- Serial 0/0/0 (S0/0/0)

- Serial 0/0/1 (S0/0/1)

The minimum configuration required on a router interface is to configure the following:

- **IPv4 address and subnet mask:** Configures the IP address and subnet mask using the **ip address** *subnet-mask* interface configuration command.

- **Activate the interface:** By default, LAN and WAN interfaces are not activated. The interface must be activated using the **no shutdown** command. This is similar to powering on the interface. The interface must also be connected to another device (a hub, a switch, or another router) for the physical layer to be active.

Although not required, it is good practice to configure a description on each interface to help document the network information. The description text is limited to 240 characters. On production networks, a description can be helpful in troubleshooting by providing information about the type of network that the interface is connected to and if there are any other routers on that network. If the interface connects to an ISP or service carrier, it is helpful to enter the third-party connection and contact information.

To enable a router interface, configure the following:

Step 1. Enter the global configuration mode:

```
R1# configure terminal
Enter configuration commands, one per line. End with
CNTL/Z.
Router(config)#
```

Step 2. Enter the interface configuration mode for the interface:

```
R1(config)# interface gigabitethernet 0/0
```

Step 3. Add IP addressing information to the interface:

```
R1(config-if)# ip address 192.168.10.1 255.255.255.0
```

Step 4. Add a description to the interface:

```
R1(config-if)# description LAN-10
```

Step 5. Enable the interface:

```
R1(config-if)# no shutdown
R1(config-if)#
%LINK-5-CHANGED: Interface GigabitEthernet0/0, changed
state to up
```

Step 6. Exit configuration modes:

```
R1(config-if)# exit
R1(config)# exit
R1#
%SYS-5-CONFIG_I: Configured from console by console
```

Step 7. Save the configuration using the **copy run start** command:

```
R1# copy running-config startup-config
Destination filename [startup-config]?
Building configuration...
[OK]
R1#
```

Step 8. Verify the configuration using the **show run** command.

Note

Command abbreviations, such as **inter g0/0**, could be used for the configuration of GigabitEthernet 0/0.

Verify Interface Configuration (6.4.2.2)

There are several commands that can be used to verify interface configuration. The most useful of these is the **show ip interface brief** command. The output generated displays all interfaces, their IP address, and their current status. The configured and connected interfaces should display a status of "up" and protocol of "up." Anything else would indicate a problem with either the configuration or the cabling.

The output of the **show ip interface brief** command shows the device's interfaces and the status of each interface. In the following example, the LAN interfaces and the Serial 0/0/0 WAN link for R1 are all activated and operational. The Serial 0/0/1 interface has not been configured and is disabled.

```
R1# show ip interface brief
Interface          IP-Address      OK? Method Status Protocol
GigabitEthernet0/0 192.168.10.1    YES manual up     up
GigabitEthernet0/1 192.168.11.1    YES manual up     up
Serial0/0/0        209.165.200.225 YES manual up     up
Serial0/0/1        unassigned      YES unset  admin  down
                                                     down
Vlan1              unassigned      YES unset  admin  down
                                                     down
R1#
```

You can verify connectivity from the interface using the **ping** command. Cisco routers send five consecutive pings and measure minimal, average, and maximum round-trip times. Exclamation marks verify connectivity. In the following example, the **ping** command generated five exclamation marks, verifying connectivity to a device with an IPv4 address of 209.165.200.226 that directly connected to R1.

```
R1# ping 209.165.200.226

Type escape sequence to abort.
Sending 5, 100-byte ICMP Echos to 209.165.200.226, timeout is 2 seconds:
!!!!!
Success rate is 100 percent (5/5), round-trip min/avg/max = 1/3/11 ms

R1#
```

Other interface verification commands include

- **show ip route:** Displays the contents of the IPv4 routing table stored in RAM.

- **show interfaces:** Displays statistics for all interfaces on the device.

- **show ip interface:** Displays the IPv4 statistics for all interfaces on a router.

The output of the **show ip route** command is shown in the following example. Notice that R1 has three directly connected network entries and the local link interface entries.

```
R1# show ip route
Codes:
L - local, C - connected, S - static, R - RIP, M - mobile,
B - BGP, D - EIGRP, EX - EIGRP external, O - OSPF,
IA - OSPF inter area, N1 - OSPF NSSA external type 1,
N2 - OSPF NSSA external type 2, E1 - OSPF external type 1,
E2 - OSPF external type 2, E - EGP, i - IS-IS,
L1 - IS-IS level-1, L2 - IS-IS level-2, ia - IS-IS inter area
* - candidate default, U - per-user static route, o - ODR
P - periodic downloaded static route

Gateway of last resort is not set

      192.168.10.0/24 is variably subnetted, 2 subnets, 2 masks
C        192.168.10.0/24 is directly connected, GigabitEthernet0/0
L        192.168.10.1/32 is directly connected, GigabitEthernet0/0
      192.168.11.0/24 is variably subnetted, 2 subnets, 2 masks
C        192.168.11.0/24 is directly connected, GigabitEthernet0/1
L        192.168.11.1/32 is directly connected, GigabitEthernet0/1
      209.165.200.0/24 is variably subnetted, 2 subnets, 2 masks
C        209.165.200.224/30 is directly connected, Serial0/0/0
L        209.165.200.225/32 is directly connected, Serial0/0/0
R1#
```

Configuring the Default Gateway (6.4.3)

To send a packet outside of the local network, a device needs to know where to forward the packet. For an end device, this generally called the default gateway. This section will introduce the concept and use of the default gateway.

Default Gateway on a Host (6.4.3.1)

Most routers have, at a minimum, two interfaces. Each interface is configured with a separate IP address in a separate network.

For an end device to communicate over the network, it must be configured with the correct IP address information, including the default gateway address. The default gateway is only used when the host wants to send a packet to a device on another network. The default gateway address is generally the router interface address attached to the local network of the host. While it does not matter what address is actually configured on the router interface, the IP address of the host device and the router interface address must be in the same network.

Figure 6-17 displays a topology of a router with two separate interfaces. Each interface is connected to a separate network. G0/0 is connected to network 192.168.10.0, while G0/1 is connected to network 192.168.11.0. Each host device is configured with the appropriate default gateway address.

In Figure 6-17, when PC1 sends a packet to PC2, the default gateway is not used. With PC1 and PC2 in the some network, no gateway is required. Therefore, PC1 addresses the packet with the IP address of PC2 and forwards the packet directly to PC2 through the switch.

In Figure 6-17, when PC1 sends a packet to PC3, the packets must be routed between the two networks: the network where PC1 is connected and the network where PC3 is connected. PC1 addresses the packet with the IP address of PC3 but then forwards the packet to its default gateway, the router interface in its network. The router accepts the packet, accesses its route table to determine the appropriate exit interface based on the destination address, and then forwards the packet out the appropriate interface to reach PC3.

Figure 6-17   Host Communication

Default Gateway on a Switch (6.4.3.2)

A default gateway is used by all devices that require the use of a router to determine a path to a remote destination. End devices require default gateway addresses, but so do intermediate devices, such as the Cisco IOS switch.

The IP address information on a switch is only necessary to manage the switch remotely. In other words, to be able to SSH to the switch, the switch must have an IP address with which to SSH. If the switch is only accessed from devices within the local network, only an IP address and subnet mask are required.

Configuring the IP address on a switch is done on the switch virtual interface (SVI). For example:

```
S1(config)# interface vlan1
S1(config-vlan)# ip address 192.168.10.50 255.255.255.0
S1(config-vlan)# no shut
```

However, if the switch must be accessible by devices in a different network, the switch must be configured with a default gateway address, because packets that originate from the switch are handled just like packets that originate from a host device. Therefore, packets that originate from the switch and are destined for a device on the same network are forwarded directly to the appropriate device. Packets that originate from the switch and are destined for a device on a remote network must be forwarded to the default gateway for path determination.

To configure a default gateway on a switch use the following **ip default-gateway** global configuration command. For example:

```
S1(config)# ip default-gateway 192.168.10.1
```

A common misconception is that the switch uses its configured default gateway address to determine where to forward packets originating from hosts connected to the switch and destined for hosts on a remote network. Actually, the IP address and default gateway information is only used for packets that originate from the switch. Packets originating from hosts connected to the switch must already have default gateway information configured to communicate on remote networks.

Packet Tracer
☐ Activity

Packet Tracer Activity 6.4.3.3: Connect a Router to a LAN

In this activity, you will use various **show** commands to display the current state of the router. You will then use the addressing table to configure router Ethernet interfaces. Finally, you will use commands to verify and test your configurations.

Packet Tracer
☐ Activity

Packet Tracer Activity 6.4.3.4: Troubleshooting Default Gateway Issues

For a device to communicate across multiple networks, it must be configured with an IP address, a subnet mask, and a default gateway. The default gateway is used when the host wants to send a packet to a device on another network. The default gateway address is generally the router interface address attached to the local network to which the host is connected. In this activity, you will finish documenting the network. You will then verify the network documentation by testing end-to-end connectivity and troubleshooting issues. The troubleshooting method you will use consists of the following steps:

- Verify the network documentation and use tests to isolate problems.

- Determine an appropriate solution for a given problem.

- Implement the solution.

- Test to verify that the problem is resolved.

- Document the solution.

Lab 6.4.3.5: Initializing and Reloading a Router and Switch

In this lab, you will complete the following objectives:

- Part 1: Set Up the Topology and Initialize Devices

- Part 2: Configure Devices and Verify Connectivity

- Part 3: Display Device Information

Summary (6.5)

Class Activity 6.5.1.1: Can You Read This Map?

Note

It is suggested that students work in pairs; however,
activity individually.

Your instructor will provide you with output ge
command. Use Packet Tracer to build a topolog
information.

At a minimum, the following should be used in your topology model:

- One Catalyst 2960 switch

- One Cisco Series 1941 router with one HWIC-4ESW switching port modular
  card and IOS version 15.1 or higher

- Three PCs (can be servers, generic PCs, laptops, and so on)

Use the note tool in Packet Tracer to indicate the addresses of the router interfaces
and possible addresses for the end devices you chose for your model. Label all end
devices, ports, and addresses ascertained from the **show ip route** output/routing
table information in your Packet Tracer file. Save your work in hard or soft copy to
share with the class.

Packet Tracer Activity 6.5.1.2: Skills Integration Challenge

Your network manager is impressed with your performance in your job as a LAN
technician. She would like you to now demonstrate your ability to configure a
router connecting two LANs. Your tasks include configuring basic settings on a
router and a switch using the Cisco IOS. You will then verify your configurations, as
well as configurations on existing devices by testing end-to-end connectivity.

The network layer, or OSI Layer 3, provides services to allow end devices to
exchange data across the network. To accomplish this end-to-end transport,
the network layer uses four basic processes: IP addressing for end devices,
encapsulation, routing, and deencapsulation.

The Internet is largely based on IPv4, which is still the most widely used network layer protocol. An IPv4 packet contains the IP header and the payload. However, IPv4 has a limited number of unique public IP addresses available. This led to the development of IP version 6 (IPv6). The IPv6 simplified header offers several advantages over IPv4, including better routing efficiency, simplified extension headers, and capability for per-flow processing. Plus, IPv6 addresses are based on 128-bit hierarchical addressing as opposed to IPv4 with 32 bits. This dramatically increases the number of available IP addresses.

In addition to hierarchical addressing, the network layer is also responsible for routing.

Hosts require a local routing table to ensure that packets are directed to the correct destination network. The local table of a host typically contains the direct connection, the local network route, and the local default route. The local default route is the route to the default gateway.

The default gateway is the IP address of a router interface connected to the local network. When a host needs to forward a packet to a destination address that is not on the same network as the host, the packet is sent to the default gateway for further processing.

When a router, such as the default gateway, receives a packet, it examines the destination IP address to determine the destination network. The routing table of a router stores information about directly connected routes and remote routes to IP networks. If the router has an entry in its routing table for the destination network, the router forwards the packet. If no routing entry exists, the router can forward the packet to its own default route, if one is configured, or it will drop the packet.

Routing table entries can be configured manually on each router to provide static routing, or the routers can communicate route information dynamically between each other using a routing protocol.

For routers to be reachable, the router interface must be configured. To enable a specific interface, enter interface configuration mode using the **interface** *type-and-number* global configuration mode command.

Practice

The following activities provide practice with the topics introduced in this chapter. The labs and class activities are available in the companion *Introduction to Networking Lab Manual* (ISBN 978-1-58713-312-1). The Packet Tracer Activities PKA files are found in the online course.

Class Activities

- Class Activity 6.0.1.2: The Road Less Traveled . . . or Is It?

- Class Activity 6.5.1.1: Can You Read This Map?

Labs

- Lab 6.2.2.8: View Host Routing Tables

- Lab 6.3.1.9: Exploring Router Physical Characteristics

- Lab 6.4.3.5: Initializing and Reloading a Router and Switch

Packet Tracer
☐ Activity

Packet Tracer Activities

- Packet Tracer Activity 6.3.1.10: Exploring Internetworking Devices

- Packet Tracer Activity 6.4.1.2: Configure Initial Router Settings

- Packet Tracer Activity 6.4.3.3: Connect a Router to a LAN

- Packet Tracer Activity 6.4.3.4: Troubleshooting Default Gateway Issues

- Packet Tracer Activity 6.5.1.2: Skills Integration Challenge

Check Your Understanding

Complete all the review questions listed here to test your understanding of the topics and concepts in this chapter. The appendix, "Answers to the 'Check Your Understanding' Questions", lists the answers.

1. Which layer of the OSI model is concerned with end-to-end communication over the network?

   A. Network

   B. Transport

   C. Data link

   D. Application

2. Which of the following is associated with the network layer?

   A. IP address

   B. Frames

   C. MAC address

   D. Physical addressing

3. Why was IPv4 designed as a connectionless protocol? _____

_____

_____

_____

_____

_____

4. On a router, what field in an IPv4 header should be examined to determine that the maximum number of hops have been reached by the packet on its way from the source to this destination?

   A. Version

   B. DS

   C. TTL

   D. Protocol

   E. Source IP address

   F. Destination IP address

5. When configuring a host, the gateway was not configured. How will this affect communication to and from this device?

   A. Host communication will not be affected.

   B. The host will not be able to communicate with devices by name.

   C. Communication will be limited to hosts in the local network.

   D. No communication will be successful to or from the host.

6. In what part of a router is the current configuration being used located?

   A. ROM

   B. NVRAM

   C. Flash

   D. RAM

7. During the boot process of a Cisco router, you notice a series of hash symbols (#) appearing on the terminal emulator screen from the console session. In what phase is the boot process?

   A. Loading the startup configuration

   B. Loading the IOS

   C. POST

   D. Loading the bootstrap

8. What are the required steps for configuring an interface on a router? (Choose two.)

   A. Provide Layer 3 addressing information

   B. Add a description to the interface

   C. Turn on routing on the interface

   D. Activate the interface

9. The **ip default-gateway** command was not used when configuring a switch. How will this affect network communication? (Choose two.)

   A. Host communication through the switch will not be affected.

   B. The hosts communicating through the switch will not be able to communicate with devices by name.

   C. The host communication through the switch will be limited to hosts in the local network.

   D. No communication through the switch will be successful.

   E. Communication to and from the switch will be limited to hosts in the local network.

10. When using the **netstat -r** command on a host, you see a route 0.0.0.0 0.0.0.0.0. What does this route represent?

    A. The host has no routes available for forwarding packets.

    B. This is a route for testing local communication.

    C. Destinations without a specified route are forwarded to the gateway.

    D. The host does not have an IP address configured.

CHAPTER 7

Transport Layer

Objectives

Upon completion of this chapter, you will be able to answer the following questions:

- What is the purpose of the transport layer in managing the transportation of data in end-to-end communications?

- What are the characteristics of TCP and UDP?

- What is a port number and what is it used for?

- How do the TCP session establishment and termination processes facilitate reliable communication?

- How are TCP protocol data units transmitted and acknowledged to guarantee delivery?

- How does UDP establish communications with a server?

- What factors determine whether high-reliability TCP transmissions, or non-guaranteed UDP transmissions, are best suited for common applications?

Key Terms

This chapter uses the following key terms. You can find the definitions in the Glossary.

Introduction (7.0.1.1)

Data networks and the Internet support the human network by supplying reliable communication between people. On a single device, people can use multiple applications and services such as email, the web, and instant messaging to send messages or retrieve information. Applications such as email clients, web browsers, and instant messaging clients allow people to use computers and networks to send messages and find information.

Data from each of these applications is packaged, transported, and delivered to the appropriate application on the destination device. The processes described in the OSI transport layer accept data from the application layer and prepare it for addressing at the network layer. The transport layer prepares data for transmission across the network. A source computer communicates with a receiving computer to decide how to break up data into segments, how to make sure that none of the segments get lost, and how to verify that all the segments arrived. When thinking about the transport layer, think of a shipping department preparing a single order of multiple packages for delivery.

In this chapter, we examine the role of the transport layer in encapsulating application data for use by the network layer. The transport layer also encompasses these functions:

- Enables multiple applications such as emailing and social networking to communicate over the network at the same time on a single device
- Ensures that, if required, all the data is received reliably and in order by the correct application
- Employs error-handling mechanisms

Learning Objectives

Upon completion of this chapter, you will be able to

- Explain the need for the transport layer
- Identify the role of the transport layer as it provides the end-to-end transfer of data between applications
- Describe the role of two TCP/IP transport layer protocols: TCP and UDP
- Explain the key functions of the transport layer, including reliability, port addressing, and segmentation
- Explain how TCP and UDP each handle key functions
- Identify when it is appropriate to use TCP or UDP and provide examples of applications that use each protocol

Class Activity 7.0.1.2: We Need to Talk Game

Note

This activity works best with medium-sized groups of six to eight students per group.

The instructor will whisper a complex message to the first student in a group. An example of the message might be "Our final exam will be given next Tuesday, February 5, at 2 p.m. in Room 1151."

That student whispers the message to the next student in the group. Each group follows this process until all members of each group have heard the whispered message. Here are the rules you are to follow:

- You can whisper the message only once to your neighbor.

- The message must keep moving from one person to the other with no skipping of participants.

- The instructor should ask a student to keep time of the full message activity from first participant to last participant stating the messages. The first or last person would mostly likely be the best one to keep this time.

- The last student will say aloud exactly what he or she heard.

The instructor will then restate the original message so that the group can compare it to the message that was delivered by the last student in the group.

Transport Layer Protocols (7.1)

As previously discussed, for communication to occur between source and destination, a set of rules or protocols must be followed.

Transportation of Data (7.1.1)

In the TCP/IP model, data that originates from application programs is passed to the application layer, which in turn passes the data to the transport layer.

Role of the Transport Layer (7.1.1.1, 7.1.1.2)

The transport layer is responsible for establishing a temporary communication session between two applications and delivering data between them. An application generates data that is sent from an application on a source host to an application on a destination host, without regard to the destination host type, the type of media over which the data must travel, the path taken by the data, the congestion on a link, or the size of the network. As shown in Figure 7-1, the transport layer is the link between the application layer and the lower layers that are responsible for network transmission.

Figure 7-1   Enabling Applications on Devices to Communicate

The transport layer provides a method of delivering data across the network in a way that ensures that the data can be properly put back together on the receiving end. The transport layer provides the segmentation of data and the controls necessary to reassemble these segments into the various communication streams. In TCP/IP, these segmentation and reassembly processes can be achieved using two very different transport layer protocols: *Transmission Control Protocol (TCP)* and *User Datagram Protocol (UDP)*.

The primary responsibilities of transport layer protocols are

- Tracking the individual communication between applications on the source and destination hosts

- Segmenting data for manageability and reassembling segmented data into streams of application data at the destination

- Identifying the proper application for each communication stream

Tracking Individual Conversations

At the transport layer, each particular set of data flowing between a source application and a destination application is known as a conversation. A host can have multiple applications that are communicating across the network simultaneously. Each of these applications communicates with one or more applications on one or more remote hosts. It is the responsibility of the transport layer to maintain and track these multiple conversations. This is shown in Figure 7-2.

Figure 7-2   Tracking the Conversations

Segmenting Data and Reassembling Segments

Data must be prepared to be sent across the media in manageable pieces. Most networks have a limitation on the amount of data that can be included in a single packet. Transport layer protocols have services that segment the application data into blocks of data that are an appropriate size, as shown in Figure 7-3. This service includes the encapsulation required on each piece of data. A *header*, used for reassembly, is added to each block of data. This header is used to track the data stream.

At the destination, the transport layer must be able to reconstruct the pieces of data into a complete data stream that is useful to the application layer. The protocols at the transport layer describe how the transport layer header information is used to reassemble the data pieces into streams to be passed to the application layer.

The transport layer divides the data into segments that are easier to manage and transport.

Figure 7-3   Segmenting the Data

Identifying the Applications

There can be many applications or services running on each host in the network. To pass data streams to the proper applications, the transport layer must identify the target application, as shown in Figure 7-4. To accomplish this, the transport layer assigns each application an identifier. This identifier is called a port number. Each software process that needs to access the network is assigned a *port* number unique in that host. The transport layer uses ports to identify the application or service.

The transport layer ensures that even with multiple applications running on a device, all applications receive the correct data.

Figure 7-4   Identifying the Application

Conversation *Multiplexing* (7.1.1.3)

Sending some types of data (for example, a streaming video) across a network as one complete communication stream could use all the available bandwidth and prevent other communications from occurring at the same time. It also makes error recovery and retransmission of damaged data difficult.

Figure 7-5 shows that segmenting the data into smaller chunks enables many different communications, from many different users, to be interleaved (multiplexed) on the same network. Segmentation of the data by transport layer protocols also provides the means to both send and receive data when running multiple applications concurrently on a computer.

Figure 7-5   Conversation Multiplexing

Without segmentation, only one application would be able to receive data. For example, in a streaming video, the media would be completely consumed by the one communication stream instead of being shared. You could not receive emails, chat on instant messenger, or view web pages while also viewing the video.

To identify each segment of data, the transport layer adds a header to the segment. This header contains fields of bits. It is the values in these fields that enable different transport layer protocols to perform different functions in managing data communication.

Transport Layer Reliability (7.1.1.4)

The transport layer is also responsible for managing reliability requirements of a conversation. Different applications have different transport reliability requirements.

IP is concerned only with the structure, addressing, and routing of packets. IP does not specify how the delivery or transportation of the packets takes place. Transport protocols specify how to transfer messages between hosts. TCP/IP provides two transport layer protocols, Transmission Control Protocol (TCP) and User Datagram Protocol (UDP), as shown in Figure 7-6. IP uses these transport protocols to enable hosts to communicate and transfer data.

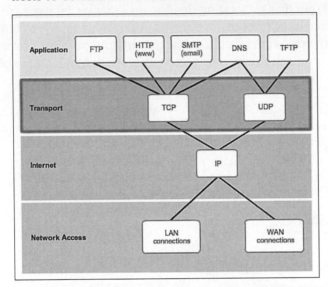

Figure 7-6   Transport Layer Protocols in the TCP/IP Model

TCP is considered a *reliable*, full-featured transport layer protocol, which ensures that all the data arrives at the destination. In contrast, UDP is a very simple transport layer protocol that does not provide any reliability.

TCP (7.1.1.5)

As previously stated, TCP is considered a reliable transport protocol, which means that TCP includes processes to ensure reliable delivery between applications through the use of acknowledged delivery. TCP transport is analogous to sending packages that are tracked from source to destination. If a parcel delivery service order is broken up into several shipments, a customer can check online to see the order of the delivery.

With TCP, the three basic operations of reliability are

- Tracking transmitted data segments

- Acknowledging received data

- Retransmitting any unacknowledged data

TCP breaks up a message into small pieces known as segments. The segments are numbered in sequence and passed to the IP process for assembly into packets. TCP keeps track of the number of segments that have been sent to a specific host from a specific application. If the sender does not receive an acknowledgement within a certain period of time, it assumes that the segments were lost and retransmits them. Only the portion of the message that is lost is resent, not the entire message. On the receiving host, TCP is responsible for reassembling the message segments and passing them to the application. The File Transfer Protocol (FTP) and the Hypertext Transfer Protocol (HTTP) are examples of applications that use TCP to ensure data delivery.

Video 7.1.1.5: TCP

Go to the online course to view an animation of TCP segments being transmitted from source to destination.

These reliability processes place additional overhead on network resources because of the processes of acknowledgement, tracking, and retransmission. To support these reliability processes, more control data is exchanged between the sending and receiving hosts. This control information is contained in a TCP header.

UDP (7.1.1.6)

While the TCP reliability functions provide more robust communication between applications, they also incur additional overhead and possible delays in transmission. There is a trade-off between the value of reliability and the burden it places on network resources. Imposing overhead to ensure reliability for some applications could reduce the usefulness of the application and can even be detrimental to the application. In such cases, UDP is a better transport protocol.

UDP provides just the basic functions for delivering data segments between the appropriate applications, with very little overhead and data checking. UDP is known as a *best-effort delivery* protocol. In the context of networking, best-effort delivery is referred to as unreliable, because there is no acknowledgement that the data is received at the destination. With UDP, there are no transport layer processes that inform the sender whether successful delivery has occurred.

UDP is similar to placing a regular, nonregistered letter in the mail. The sender of the letter is not aware of whether a receiver is available to receive the letter, nor is the post office responsible for tracking the letter or informing the sender if the letter does not arrive at the final destination.

Figure 7-7 illustrates how UDP segments are transmitted from sender to receiver.

Figure 7-7   Sending a Message Using UDP

The Right Transport Layer Protocol for the Right Application (7.1.1.7)

Both TCP and UDP are valid transport protocols. Depending upon the application requirements, either one, or sometimes both, of these transport protocols can be used. Application developers must choose which transport protocol type is appropriate based on the requirements of the applications, as shown in Figure 7-8.

Figure 7-8   Selecting the Right Transport Layer Protocol

For some applications, segments must arrive in a very specific sequence to be processed successfully. With other applications, all data must be fully received before any of it is considered useful. In both of these instances, TCP is used as the transport protocol. For example, applications such as databases, web browsers, and email clients require that all data that is sent arrives at the destination in its original condition. Any missing data could cause a corrupt communication that is either incomplete or unreadable. Therefore, these applications are designed to use TCP. The additional network overhead is considered to be required for these applications.

In other cases, an application can tolerate some data loss during transmission over the network, but delays in transmission are unacceptable. UDP is the better choice for these applications because less network overhead is required. UDP is preferable with applications such as streaming audio, video, and Voice over IP (VoIP). Acknowledgements would slow delivery and retransmissions are undesirable.

For example, if one or two segments of a video stream fail to arrive, it creates a momentary disruption in the stream. This can appear as distortion in the image, but might not even be noticeable to the user. On the other hand, the image in a streaming video would be greatly degraded if the destination device had to account for lost data and delay the stream while waiting for retransmissions. In this case, it is better to render the best video possible with the segments received, and forego reliability.

Internet radio is another example of an application that uses UDP. If some of the message is lost during its journey over the network, it is not retransmitted. If a few packets are missed, the listener might hear a slight break in the sound. If TCP were used and the lost packets were resent, the transmission would pause to receive them and the disruption would be more noticeable.

Introducing TCP and UDP (7.1.2)

As previously mentioned, both TCP and UDP are valid transport layer protocols. It is up to the developer to determine which of these protocols best match the requirements of the application being developed. Regardless of the choice, a good understanding of both protocols is required by any networker.

Introducing TCP (7.1.2.1)

To really understand the differences between TCP and UDP, it is important to understand how each protocol implements specific reliability functions and how they track communications.

Transmission Control Protocol (TCP)

TCP was initially described in RFC 793. In addition to supporting the basic functions of data segmentation and reassembly, TCP, as shown in Figure 7-9, also provides

- *Connection-oriented* conversations by establishing sessions
- Reliable delivery
- Ordered data reconstruction
- Flow control

Figure 7-9   TCP Services

Establishing a Session

TCP is a connection-oriented protocol. A connection-oriented protocol is one that negotiates and establishes a permanent connection (or *session*) between source and destination devices prior to forwarding any traffic. Session establishment prepares the devices to communicate with one another. Through session establishment, the devices negotiate the amount of traffic that can be forwarded at a given time, and the communication data between the two can be closely managed. The session is terminated only after all communication is completed.

Reliable Delivery

TCP can implement a method to ensure reliable delivery of the data. In networking terms, reliability means ensuring that each piece of data that the source sends arrives at the destination. For many reasons, it is possible for a piece of data to become corrupted, or lost completely, as it is transmitted over the network. TCP can ensure that all pieces reach their destination by having the source device retransmit lost or corrupted data.

Same-Order Delivery

Because networks can provide multiple routes that can have different transmission rates, data can arrive in the wrong order. By numbering and sequencing the segments, TCP can ensure that these segments are reassembled into the proper order.

Flow Control

Network hosts have limited resources, such as memory or bandwidth. When TCP is aware that these resources are overtaxed, it can request that the sending application reduce the rate of data flow. This is done by TCP regulating the amount of data the source transmits. Flow control can prevent the loss of segments on the network and avoid the need for retransmission.

Role of TCP (7.1.2.2)

After TCP establishes a session, it is then able to keep track of the conversation within that session. Because of the ability of TCP to track actual conversations, it is considered a *stateful* protocol. A stateful protocol is a protocol that keeps track of the state of the communication session. For example, when data is transmitted using TCP, the sender expects the destination to acknowledge that it has received the data. TCP tracks which information it has sent and which information has been acknowledged. If the data is not acknowledged, the sender assumes that the data did not arrive and resends it. The stateful session begins with the session establishment and ends when the session is closed with session termination.

Note

Maintaining this state information requires resources that are not necessary for a stateless protocol, such as UDP.

TCP incurs additional overhead to gain these functions. As shown in Figure 7-10, each TCP segment has 20 bytes of overhead in the header encapsulating the application layer data. This is considerably more than a UDP segment, which only has 8 bytes of overhead. Extra overhead includes

- **Sequence number (32 bits):** Used for data reassembly purposes.

- **Acknowledgement number (32 bits):** Indicates that the data that has been received.

- **Header length (4 bits):** Known as "data offset." Indicates the length of the TCP segment header.

- **Reserved (6 bits):** This field is reserved for the future.

- **Control bits (6 bits):** Includes bit codes, or flags, that indicate the purpose and function of the TCP segment.

- **Window size (16 bits):** Indicates the number of segments that can be accepted at one time.

- **Checksum (16 bits):** Used for error checking of the segment header and data.

- **Urgent (16 bits):** Indicates whether data is urgent.

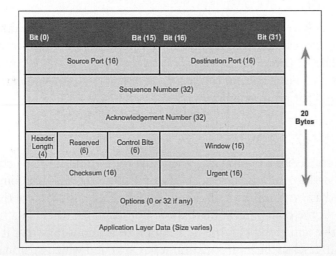

Figure 7-10   TCP Segment

Examples of applications that use TCP are web browsers, email, and file transfers.

Introducing UDP (7.1.2.3)

User Datagram Protocol (UDP) is considered a best-effort transport protocol, described in RFC 768. UDP is a lightweight transport protocol that offers the same data segmentation and reassembly as TCP, but without TCP reliability and flow control. UDP is such a simple protocol that it is usually described in terms of what it does not do compared to TCP.

As shown Figure 7-11, the following features describe UDP:

- **Connectionless:** UDP does not establish a connection between the hosts before data can be sent and received.

- **Unreliable delivery:** UDP does not provide services to ensure that the data will be delivered reliably. There are no processes within UDP to have the sender retransmit any data that is lost or is corrupted.

- **No ordered data reconstruction:** Occasionally data is received in a different order than it was sent. UDP does not provide any mechanism for reassembling the data in its original sequence. The data is simply delivered to the application in the order that it arrives.

- **No flow control:** There are no mechanisms within UDP to control the amount of data transmitted by the source to avoid overwhelming the destination device. The source sends the data. If resources on the destination host become over-taxed, the destination host mostly likely drops data sent until resources become available. Unlike TCP, with UDP, there is no mechanism for automatic retransmission of dropped data.

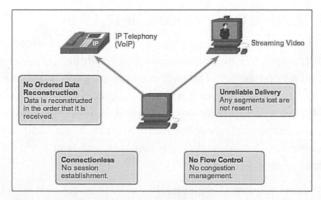

Figure 7-11   UDP Characteristics

Role of UDP (7.1.2.4)

Although UDP does not include the reliability and flow control mechanisms of TCP, as shown in Figure 7-12, UDP's low overhead data delivery makes it an ideal transport protocol for applications that can tolerate some data loss. The pieces of communication in UDP are called datagrams. These datagrams are sent as best effort by the transport layer protocol. Some applications that use UDP are Domain Name System (DNS), video streaming, and Voice over IP (VoIP).

Figure 7-12   UDP Datagram

One of the most important requirements for delivering live video and voice over the network is that the data continues to flow quickly. Video and voice applications can tolerate some data loss with minimal or no noticeable effect, and are perfectly suited to UDP.

UDP is a stateless protocol, meaning that neither the client nor the server is obligated to keep track of the state of the communication session. As shown in the figure, UDP is not concerned with reliability or flow control. Data can be lost or received out of sequence without any UDP mechanisms to recover or reorder the data. If reliability is required when using UDP as the transport protocol, it must be handled by the application.

Separating Multiple Communications (7.1.2.5)

The transport layer must be able to separate and manage multiple communications with different transport requirement needs. For example, consider a user connected to a network on an end device. The user is simultaneously receiving and sending email and instant messages, viewing websites, and conducting a Voice over IP (VoIP) phone call. Each of these applications is sending and receiving data over the network at the same time, despite different reliability requirements. Additionally, data from the phone call is not directed to the web browser, and text from an instant message does not appear in an email.

For reliability, users require that an email or web page be completely received and presented in full, for the information to be considered useful. Slight delays in loading the email or web page are generally acceptable, as long as the final product is shown in its entirety and correctly. In this example, the network manages the resending or replacement of missing information, and does not display the final product until everything is received and correctly assembled.

In contrast, occasionally missing small parts of a telephone conversation might be considered acceptable. Even if some small parts of a few words are dropped, one can either infer the missing audio from the context of the conversation or ask the other person to repeat what was said. This is considered preferable to the incurred delays if the network were to manage and resend missing segments. In this example, the user, not the network, manages the resending or replacement of missing information.

For TCP and UDP to manage these simultaneous conversations with varying requirements, the TCP- and UDP-based services must keep track of the various applications communicating. To differentiate the segments and datagrams for each application, both TCP and UDP have header fields that can uniquely identify these applications. These unique identifiers are the port numbers.

TCP and UDP Port Addressing (7.1.2.6 – 7.1.2.9)

In the header of each segment or datagram, there is a source and destination port. The source port number is the number for this communication associated with the originating application on the local host. As shown in Figure 7-13, the destination port number is the number for this communication associated with the destination application on the remote host.

Figure 7-13   Port Addressing

When a message is delivered using either TCP or UDP, the protocols and services requested are identified by a port number. A port is a numeric identifier within each segment that is used to keep track of specific conversations and destination services requested. Every message that a host sends contains both a source and destination port.

Destination Port

The client places a destination port number in the segment to tell the destination server what service is being requested. For example, port 80 refers to HTTP or web service. When a client specifies port 80 in the destination port, the server that receives the message knows that web services are being requested. A server can offer more than one service simultaneously. For example, a server can offer web services on port 80 at the same time that it offers FTP connection establishment on port 21.

Source Port

The source port number is randomly generated by the sending device to identify a conversation between two devices. This allows multiple conversations to occur simultaneously. In other words, a device can send multiple HTTP service requests to a web server at the same time. The separate conversations are tracked based on the source ports.

The source and destination ports are placed within the segment. The segments are then encapsulated within an IP packet. The IP packet contains the IP address of the source and destination. The combination of the source and destination IP addresses and the source and destination port numbers is known as a *socket*. The socket is used to identify the server and service being requested by the client. Every day, thousands of hosts communicate with millions of different servers. Those communications are identified by the sockets.

It is the combination of the transport layer port number, and the network layer IP address of the host, that uniquely identifies a particular application process running on an individual host device. A socket pair, consisting of the source and destination IP addresses and port numbers, uniquely identifies the specific conversation between the two hosts.

A client socket might look like this, with 1099 representing the source port number: 192.168.1.5:1099.

The socket on a web server might be 192.168.1.7:80.

Together, these two sockets combine to form a socket pair: 192.168.1.5:1099, 192.168.1.7:80.

With the creation of sockets, communication endpoints are known so that data can move from an application on one host to an application on another. Sockets enable multiple processes running on a client to distinguish themselves from each other, and multiple connections to a server process to be distinguished from each other.

The source port of a client request is randomly generated. This port number acts like a return address for the requesting application. The transport layer keeps track of this port and the application that initiated the request so that when a response is returned, it can be forwarded to the correct application. The requesting application port number is used as the destination port number in the response coming back from the server.

The Internet Assigned Numbers Authority (IANA) assigns port numbers. IANA is a standards body that is responsible for assigning various addressing standards.

There are different types of port numbers:

- **Well-known ports (Numbers 0 to 1023):** These numbers are reserved for services and applications. They are commonly used for applications such as HTTP (web server), Internet Message Access Protocol (IMAP)/Simple Mail Transfer Protocol (SMTP) (email server), and Telnet. By defining these well-known ports for server applications, client applications can be programmed to request a connection to that specific port and its associated service.

- **Registered ports (Numbers 1024 to 49151):** These port numbers are assigned to user processes or applications. These processes are primarily individual applications that a user has chosen to install, rather than common applications that would receive a well-known port number. When not used for a server resource, these ports can also be dynamically selected by a client as its source port.

- **Dynamic or private ports (Numbers 49152 to 65535):** Also known as ephemeral ports, these are usually assigned dynamically to client applications when the client initiates a connection to a service. The dynamic port is most often used to identify the client application during communication, whereas the client uses the well-known port to identify and connect to the service being requested on the server. It is uncommon for a client to connect to a service using a dynamic or private port (although some peer-to-peer file sharing programs do use these ports).

Figure 7-14 displays some common well-known and registered ports within TCP. Figure 7-15 displays common well-known and registered ports within UDP.

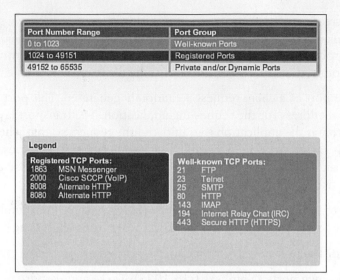

Figure 7-14 Well-Known and Registered TCP Ports

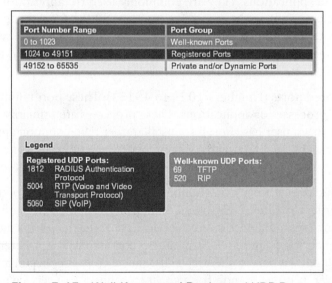

Figure 7-15 Well-Known and Registered UDP Ports

Using Both TCP and UDP

Some applications can use both TCP and UDP. For example, the low overhead of UDP enables DNS to serve many client requests very quickly. Sometimes, however, sending the requested information might require the reliability of TCP. In this case, the well-known port number, 53, is used by both TCP and UDP with this service. Figure 7-16 shows applications that use common TCP/UDP ports.

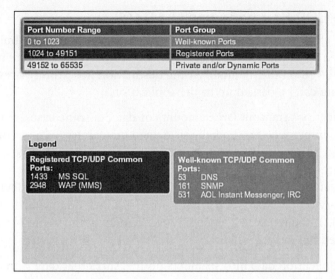

Port Number Range	Port Group
0 to 1023	Well-known Ports
1024 to 49151	Registered Ports
49152 to 65535	Private and/or Dynamic Ports

Legend

Registered TCP/UDP Common Ports:
1433   MS SQL
2948   WAP (MMS)

Well-known TCP/UDP Common Ports:
53   DNS
161   SNMP
531   AOL Instant Messenger, IRC

Figure 7-16   Well-Known and Registered Common TCP/UDP Ports

A current list of port numbers and the associated applications can be found on the IANA organizational website (www.iana.org).

Sometimes it is necessary to know which active TCP connections are open and running on a networked host. Netstat is an important network utility that can be used to verify those connections. Netstat lists the protocol in use, the local address and port number, the foreign address and port number, and the connection state.

Unexplained TCP connections can pose a major security threat, because they can indicate that something or someone is connected to the local host. Additionally, unnecessary TCP connections can consume valuable system resources, thus slowing the host's performance. Netstat should be used to examine the open connections on a host when performance appears to be compromised.

Many useful options are available for the **netstat** command. Figure 7-17 shows the information output from the **netstat** command.

A – Protocol used
B – Source Port
C – Address of name of remote host
D – Destination Port
E – Connection State

```
C:\> netstat

Active Connections

Proto   Local Address   Foreign Address         State
TCP     kenpc:3126      192.168.0.2:netbios-asn ESTABLISHED
TCP     kenpc:3158      207.138.126.152:http    ESTABLISHED
TCP     kenpc:3159      207.138.126.169:http    ESTABLISHED
TCP     kenpc:3160      207.138.126.169:http    ESTABLISHED
TCP     kenpc:3161      sc.msn.com:http         ESTABLISHED
TCP     kenpc:3166      www.cisco.com:http      ESTABLISHED

C:\>
```

A   B   C   D   E

Figure 7-17   netstat Output

TCP and UDP Segmentation (7.1.2.10)

A previous chapter explained how protocol data units (PDU) are built by passing data from an application down through the various layers to create a PDU that is then transmitted on the medium. At the destination host, this process is reversed until the data can be passed up to the application.

Some applications transmit large amounts of data, in some cases, many gigabytes. It would be impractical to send all this data in one large piece. No other network traffic could be transmitted while this data was being sent. A large piece of data could take minutes or even hours to send. In addition, if there were any errors, the entire data file would be lost or have to be resent. Network devices would not have memory buffers large enough to store this much data while it is transmitted or received. The limit varies depending on the networking technology and specific physical medium in use.

Dividing application data into segments both ensures that data is transmitted within the limits of the media and that data from different applications can be multiplexed on to the media.

TCP and UDP Handle Segmentation Differently

As shown in Figure 7-18, each TCP segment header contains a sequence number that allows the transport layer functions on the destination host to reassemble segments in the order in which they were transmitted. This ensures that the destination application has the data in the exact form that the sender intended.

Although services using UDP also track the conversations between applications, they are not concerned with the order in which the information was transmitted or concerned with maintaining a connection. There is no sequence number in the UDP header. UDP is a simpler design and generates less overhead than TCP, resulting in a faster transfer of data.

Information might arrive in a different order than it was transmitted, because different packets can take different paths through the network. An application that uses UDP must tolerate the fact that data might not arrive in the order in which it was sent.

a

b

Figure 7-18   Transport Layer Functions

Activity 7.1.2.11: Compare TCP and UDP Characteristics

Go to the course online to perform this practice activity.

TCP and UDP (7.2)

We have seen that two different protocols exist at the transport layer, each with distinct characteristics. Both of these protocols support communication between source and destination, but the way this communication occurs is different between the two protocols.

TCP Communication (7.2.1)

Recall that TCP is considered a stateful protocol because it establishes a session between source and destination and keeps track of the data within that session. UDP is a stateless protocol and does not keep track of the data. So how does TCP establish this connection and track the data?

TCP Reliable Delivery (7.2.1.1)

The key distinction between TCP and UDP is reliability. The reliability of TCP communication is obtained through the use of connection-oriented sessions. Before a host using TCP sends data to another host, TCP initiates a process to create a connection with the destination. This stateful connection enables the tracking of a session, or communication stream, between the hosts. This process ensures that each host is aware of and prepared for the communication stream. A TCP conversation requires the establishment of a session between the hosts in both directions.

After a session has been established and data transfer begins, the destination sends acknowledgements to the source for the segments that it receives. These acknowledgements form the basis of reliability within the TCP session. When the source receives an acknowledgement, it knows that the data has been successfully delivered and can quit tracking that data. If the source does not receive an acknowledgement within a predetermined amount of time, it retransmits that data to the destination.

Part of the additional overhead of using TCP is the network traffic generated by acknowledgements and retransmissions. The establishment of sessions creates overhead in the form of additional segments being exchanged. There is also additional overhead on the individual hosts created by the necessity to keep track of which segments are awaiting acknowledgement and by the retransmission process.

TCP Server Processes (7.2.1.2)

Application processes run on servers. A single server can run multiple application processes at the same time. These processes wait until a client initiates communication with a request for information or other services.

Each application process running on the server is configured to use a port number, either by default or manually by a system administrator. An individual server cannot have two services assigned to the same port number within the same transport layer services. A host running a web server application and a file transfer application cannot have both configured to use the same port (for example, TCP port 8080). An active server application assigned to a specific port is considered to be open, which means that the transport layer accepts and processes segments addressed to that port. Any incoming client request addressed to the correct socket is accepted, and the data is passed to the server application. There can be many simultaneous ports open on a server, one for each active server application. It is common for a server to provide more than one service at the same time, such as a web server and an FTP server.

One way to improve security on a server is to restrict server access to only those ports associated with the services and applications that should be accessible by authorized requestors.

Figure 7-19 shows a typical allocation of source and destination ports in TCP client/server operations.

Figure 7-19   Source and Destination Ports in a TCP Conversation

TCP Connection Establishment and Termination (7.2.1.3)

In some cultures, when two persons meet, they often greet each other by shaking hands. The act of shaking hands is understood by both parties as a signal for a friendly greeting. Connections on the network are similar. The first handshake requests synchronization. The second handshake acknowledges the initial synchronization request and synchronizes the connection parameters in the opposite direction. The third handshake segment is an acknowledgement used to inform the destination that both sides agree that a connection has been established.

When two hosts communicate using TCP, a connection is established before data can be exchanged. After the communication is completed, the sessions are closed and the connection is terminated. The connection and session mechanisms enable TCP's reliability function.

Hosts track each data segment within a session and exchange information about what data is received using the information in the TCP header. TCP is a full-duplex protocol, where each connection represents two one-way communication streams, or sessions. To establish the connection, the hosts perform a three-way handshake. Control bits in the TCP header indicate the progress and status of the connection.

The *three-way handshake*

- Establishes that the destination device is present on the network

- Verifies that the destination device has an active service and is accepting requests on the destination port number that the initiating client intends to use for the session

- Informs the destination device that the source client intends to establish a communication session on that port number

In TCP connections, the host client establishes the connection with the server. The three steps in TCP connection establishment, shown in Figure 7-20, are

Step 1.   The initiating client requests a client-to-server communication session with the server.

Step 2.   The server acknowledges the client-to-server communication session and requests a server-to-client communication session.

Step 3.   The initiating client acknowledges the server-to-client communication session.

Figure 7-20   TCP Connection Establishment

To understand the three-way handshake process, look at the various values that the two hosts exchange. Within the TCP segment header, there are six 1-bit fields that contain control information used to manage the TCP processes. Those fields are

- **URG:** Urgent pointer field significant

- **ACK:** Acknowledgement field significant

- **PSH:** Push function

- **RST:** Reset the connection

- **SYN:** Synchronize sequence numbers

- **FIN:** No more data from sender

The ACK and SYN fields are relevant to our analysis of the three-way handshake.

TCP Three-Way Handshake Analysis—Step 1 (7.2.1.4)

Using the output of protocol analysis software, such as Wireshark, you can examine the operation of the TCP 3-way handshake.

Step 1: The initiating client requests a client-to-server communication session with the server.

A TCP client begins the three-way handshake by sending a segment with the synchronize sequence number (SYN) control flag set, indicating an initial value in the sequence number field in the header. This initial value for the sequence number, known as the *initial sequence number (ISN)*, is randomly chosen and is used to begin tracking the flow of data from the client to the server for this session. The ISN in the header of each segment is increased by 1 for each byte of data sent from the client to the server as the data conversation continues.

Figure 7-21 is the output from a protocol analyzer and shows the SYN control flag and the relative sequence number.

Figure 7-21   TCP Three-Way Handshake (SYN)

The SYN control flag is set and the relative sequence number is at 0. Although the protocol analyzer in the graphic indicates the relative values for the sequence and acknowledgement numbers, the true values are 32-bit binary numbers. The figure shows the 4 bytes represented in hexadecimal.

TCP Three-Way Handshake Analysis—Step 2 (7.2.1.5)

After the SYN is received, the TCP server responds to the connection request.

Step 2: The server acknowledges the client-to-server communication session and requests a server-to-client communication session.

The TCP server must acknowledge the receipt of the SYN segment from the client to establish the session from the client to the server. To do so, the server sends a segment back to the client with the acknowledgement (ACK) flag set, indicating that the acknowledgement number is significant. With this flag set in the segment, the client recognizes this as an acknowledgement that the server received the SYN from the TCP client.

The value of the acknowledgement number field is equal to the ISN plus 1. This establishes a session from the client to the server. The ACK flag remains set for the balance of the session. Recall that the conversation between the client and the server is actually two one-way sessions: one from the client to the server and the other from the server to the client. In this second step of the three-way handshake, the server must initiate the response to the client. To start this session, the server uses the SYN flag in the same way that the client did. It sets the SYN control flag in the header to establish a session from the server to the client. The SYN flag indicates that the initial value of the sequence number field is in the header. This value is used to track the flow of data in this session from the server back to the client.

The protocol analyzer output displayed in Figure 7-22 shows that the ACK and SYN control flags are set and the relative sequence and acknowledgement numbers are displayed.

No.	Time	Source	Destination	Protocol	Info
10	16.303490	10.1.1.1	192.168.254.254	TCP	kiosk > http [SYN] Seq=0 W
11	16.304896	192.168.254.254	10.1.1.1	TCP	http > kiosk [SYN, ACK] Se
12	16.304925	10.1.1.1	192.168.254.254	TCP	kiosk > http [ACK] Seq=1 A
13	16.305153	10.1.1.1	192.168.254.254	HTTP	GET / HTTP/1.1
14	16.307875	192.168.254.254	10.1.1.1	TCP	http > kiosk [ACK] Seq=1 A

```
⊞ Frame 11: 62 bytes on wire (496 bits), 62 bytes captured (496 bits)
⊞ Ethernet II, Src: Cisco_63:74:a0 (00:0f:24:63:74:a0), Dst: Vmware_be:62:88 (00:50:56:be
⊞ Internet Protocol Version 4, Src: 192.168.254.254 (192.168.254.254), Dst: 10.1.1.1 (10.1
⊟ Transmission Control Protocol, Src Port: http (80), Dst Port: kiosk (1061), Seq: 0, Ack
     Source port: http (80)
     Destination port: kiosk (1061)
     [Stream index: 0]
     Sequence number: 0    (relative sequence number)
     Acknowledgement number: 1    (relative ack number)
     Header length: 28 bytes
  ⊟ Flags: 0x12 (SYN, ACK)
     000. .... .... = Reserved: Not set
     ...0 .... .... = Nonce: Not set
     .... 0... .... = Congestion Window Reduced (CWR): Not set
     .... .0.. .... = ECN-Echo: Not set
     .... ..0. .... = Urgent: Not set
     .... ...1 .... = Acknowledgement: Set
     .... .... 0... = Push: Not set
     .... .... .0.. = Reset: Not set
  ⊞ .... .... ..1. = Syn: Set
     .... .... ...0 = Fin: Not set
     Window size value: 5840
     [Calculated window size: 5840]
  ⊞ Checksum: 0x4159 [validation disabled]
  ⊞ Options: (8 bytes)
  ⊟ [SEQ/ACK analysis]
     [This is an ACK to the segment in frame: 10]
     [The RTT to ACK the segment was: 0.001406000 seconds]
```

Figure 7-22   TCP Three-Way Handshake (SYN, ACK)

TCP Three-Way Handshake Analysis—Step 3 (7.2.1.6)

The final step in the three-way handshake is taken by the initiating client.

Step 3: The initiating client acknowledges the server-to-client communication session.

Finally, the TCP client responds with a segment containing an ACK that is the response to the TCP SYN sent by the server. There is no user data in this segment. The value in the acknowledgement number field contains one more than the ISN received from the server. After both sessions are established between client and server, all additional segments exchanged in this communication will have the ACK flag set. This is shown in Figure 7-23, which shows the ACK control flag set and the relative sequence and acknowledgement numbers.

Figure 7-23 TCP Three-Way Handshake (ACK)

Security can be added to the data network by

- Denying the establishment of TCP sessions

- Only allowing sessions to be established for specific services

- Only allowing traffic as a part of already established sessions

These security measures can be implemented for all TCP sessions or only for selected sessions.

TCP Session Termination Analysis (7.2.1.7)

To close a connection, the Finish (FIN) control flag must be set in the segment header. To end each one-way TCP session, a two-way handshake is used, consisting of a FIN segment and an ACK segment. Therefore, to terminate a single conversation supported by TCP, four exchanges are needed to end both sessions, as shown in Figure 7-24.

Note

In this explanation, the terms *client* and *server* are used as a reference for simplicity, but the termination process can be initiated by any two hosts that have an open session:

Step 1.   When the client has no more data to send in the stream, it sends a segment with the FIN flag set.

Step 2.   The server sends an ACK to acknowledge the receipt of the FIN to terminate the session from client to server.

Step 3.   The server sends a FIN to the client to terminate the server-to-client session.

Step 4.   The client responds with an ACK to acknowledge the FIN from the server.

Figure 7-24   TCP Session Termination

When the client has no more data to transfer, it sets the FIN flag in the header of a segment. Next, the server end of the connection sends a normal segment containing data with the ACK flag set using the acknowledgement number, confirming that all the bytes of data have been received. When all segments have been acknowledged, the session is closed.

The session in the other direction is closed using the same process. The receiver indicates that there is no more data to send by setting the FIN flag in the header of a segment sent to the source. A return acknowledgement confirms that all bytes of data have been received and that session is, in turn, closed.

Figure 7-25 shows the FIN and ACK control flags set in the segment header, thereby closing an HTTP session.

```
No.    Time        Source           Destination       Protocol  Info
15 16.308976  192.168.254.254   10.1.1.1          HTTP      HTTP/1.1 304 Not Modified
16 16.309088  192.168.254.254   10.1.1.1          TCP       http > kiosk [FIN, ACK] Se
17 16.309140  10.1.1.1          192.168.254.254   TCP       kiosk > http [ACK] Seq=374
18 16.309268  10.1.1.1          192.168.254.254   TCP       kiosk > http [FIN, ACK] Se
19 16.310327  192.168.254.254   10.1.1.1          TCP       http > kiosk [ACK] Seq=146
```

```
⊞ Frame 16: 60 bytes on wire (480 bits), 60 bytes captured (480 bits)
⊞ Ethernet II, Src: Cisco_63:74:a0 (00:0f:24:63:74:a0), Dst: Vmware_be:62:88 (00:50:56:be
⊞ Internet Protocol Version 4, Src: 192.168.254.254 (192.168.254.254), Dst: 10.1.1.1 (10.
⊟ Transmission Control Protocol, Src Port: http (80), Dst Port: kiosk (1061), Seq: 145, A
     Source port: http (80)
     Destination port: kiosk (1061)
     [Stream index: 0]
     Sequence number: 145    (relative sequence number)
     Acknowledgement number: 374    (relative ack number)
     Header length: 20 bytes
  ⊟ Flags: 0x11 (FIN, ACK)
     000. .... .... = Reserved: Not set
     ...0 .... .... = Nonce: Not set
     .... 0... .... = Congestion Window Reduced (CWR): Not set
     .... .0.. .... = ECN-Echo: Not set
     .... ..0. .... = Urgent: Not set
     .... ...1 .... = Acknowledgement: Set
     .... .... 0... = Push: Not set
     .... .... .0.. = Reset: Not set
     .... .... ..0. = Syn: Not set
  ⊞ .... .... ...1 = Fin: Set
     Window size value: 6432
     [Calculated window size: 6432]
     [Window size scaling factor: -2 (no window scaling used)]
  ⊞ Checksum: 0x69c7 [validation disabled]
```

a

```
No.    Time        Source           Destination       Protocol  Info
15 16.308976  192.168.254.254   10.1.1.1          HTTP      HTTP/1.1 304 Not Modified
16 16.309088  192.168.254.254   10.1.1.1          TCP       http > kiosk [FIN, ACK] Se
17 16.309140  10.1.1.1          192.168.254.254   TCP       kiosk > http [ACK] Seq=374
18 16.309268  10.1.1.1          192.168.254.254   TCP       kiosk > http [FIN, ACK] Se
19 16.310327  192.168.254.254   10.1.1.1          TCP       http > kiosk [ACK] Seq=146
```

```
⊞ Frame 17: 54 bytes on wire (432 bits), 54 bytes captured (432 bits)
⊞ Ethernet II, Src: Vmware_be:62:88 (00:50:56:be:62:88), Dst: Cisco_63:74:a0 (00:0f:24:63
⊞ Internet Protocol Version 4, Src: 10.1.1.1 (10.1.1.1), Dst: 192.168.254.254 (192.168.25
⊟ Transmission Control Protocol, Src Port: kiosk (1061), Dst Port: http (80), Seq: 374, A
     Source port: kiosk (1061)
     Destination port: http (80)
     [Stream index: 0]
     Sequence number: 374    (relative sequence number)
     Acknowledgement number: 146    (relative ack number)
     Header length: 20 bytes
  ⊟ Flags: 0x10 (ACK)
     000. .... .... = Reserved: Not set
     ...0 .... .... = Nonce: Not set
     .... 0... .... = Congestion Window Reduced (CWR): Not set
     .... .0.. .... = ECN-Echo: Not set
     .... ..0. .... = Urgent: Not set
     .... ...1 .... = Acknowledgement: Set
     .... .... 0... = Push: Not set
     .... .... .0.. = Reset: Not set
     .... .... ..0. = Syn: Not set
     .... .... ...0 = Fin: Not set
     Window size value: 64096
     [Calculated window size: 64096]
     [Window size scaling factor: -2 (no window scaling used)]
  ⊞ Checksum: 0x8886 [validation disabled]
  ⊟ [SEQ/ACK analysis]
     [This is an ACK to the segment in frame: 16]
     [The RTT to ACK the segment was: 0.000052000 seconds]
```

b

Figure 7-25 TCP Session Termination

It is also possible to terminate the connection by a three-way handshake. When the client has no more data to send, it sends a FIN to the server. If the server also has no more data to send, it can reply with both the FIN and ACK flags set, combining two steps into one. The client then replies with an ACK.

Lab 7.2.1.8: Using Wireshark to Observe the TCP Three-Way Handshake

In this lab, you will complete the following objectives:

- Part 1: Prepare Wireshark to Capture Packets
- Part 2: Capture, Locate, and Examine Packets

Activity 7.2.1.9: TCP Connection and Termination Process

Go to the course online to perform this practice activity.

Reliability and Flow Control (7.2.2)

Reliability and flow control are the two main advantages that TCP exhibits over UDP.

TCP Reliability—Ordered Delivery (7.2.2.1)

As segments travel through the network, they can encounter delays. Different segments can experience different delays, resulting in varying lengths of delivery time between segments.

Resequencing Segments

When services send data using TCP, segments may arrive at their destination out of order. For the original message to be understood by the recipient, the data in these segments is reassembled into the original order. *Sequence numbers* are assigned in the header of each packet to achieve this goal.

During session setup, an initial sequence number (ISN) is set. This ISN represents the starting value for the bytes for this session that is transmitted to the receiving application. As data is transmitted during the session, the sequence number is incremented by the number of bytes that have been transmitted. This data byte tracking enables each segment to be uniquely identified and acknowledged. Missing segments can be identified.

Segment sequence numbers enable the reliability by indicating how to reassemble and reorder received segments, as shown in Figure 7-26.

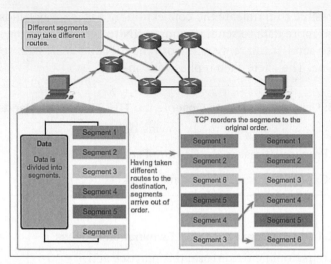

Figure 7-26   Reordering of TCP Segments

The receiving TCP process places the data from a segment into a receiving buffer. Segments are placed in the proper sequence number order and passed to the application layer when reassembled. Any segments that arrive with noncontiguous sequence numbers are held for later processing. Then, when the segments with the missing bytes arrive, these segments are processed in order.

TCP Reliability—Acknowledgement and Window Size (7.2.2.2)

Along with the ability to reorder segments, a mechanism is required to ensure that all segments are delivered.

Confirming Receipt of Segments

One of the functions of TCP is ensuring that each segment reaches its destination. When the TCP services on the destination host receives data, it sends an acknowledgement back to the host where the data originated. When the host that sourced the data receives this acknowledgement, this confirms that the data has been received.

The sequence (SEQ) number and acknowledgement (ACK) number are used together to confirm receipt of the bytes of data contained in the transmitted segments. The SEQ number indicates the relative number of bytes that have been transmitted in this session, including the bytes in the current segment. TCP uses the ACK number sent back to the source to indicate the next byte that the receiver expects to receive. This is called *expectational acknowledgement.*

The source is informed that the destination has received all bytes in this data stream up to, but not including, the byte indicated by the ACK number. The sending host is expected to send a segment that uses a sequence number that is equal to the ACK number.

Remember, each connection is actually two one-way sessions. SEQ and ACK numbers are being exchanged in both directions.

In the example in Figure 7-27, the host on the left is sending data to the host on the right. It sends a segment containing 10 bytes of data for this session and a sequence number equal to 1 in the header.

The receiving host receives the segment at Layer 4 and determines that the sequence number is 1 and that it has 10 bytes of data. The host then sends a segment back to the host on the left to acknowledge the receipt of this data. In this segment, the host sets the ACK number to 11 to indicate that the next byte of data it expects to receive in this session is byte number 11. When the sending host receives this acknowledgement, it can now send the next segment containing data for this session starting with byte number 11.

Looking at this example, if the sending host had to wait for acknowledgement of receiving each 10 bytes, the network would have a lot of overhead. To reduce the overhead of these acknowledgements, multiple segments of data can be sent and acknowledged with a single TCP message in the opposite direction. This acknowledgement contains an ACK number based on the total number of bytes received in the session. For example, starting with a sequence number of 2000, if 10 segments of 1000 bytes each were received, an ACK number of 12001 would be returned to the source.

The amount of data that a source can transmit before an acknowledgement must be received is called the *window size*, which is a field in the TCP header that enables the management of lost data and flow control.

Figure 7-27   Acknowledgement of TCP Segments

TCP Reliability—Data Loss and Retransmission (7.2.2.3)

But what happens if a segment never reaches the destination? How is the loss of a segment handled by TCP?

Handling Segment Loss

No matter how well designed a network is, data loss occasionally occurs; therefore, TCP provides methods of managing these segment losses. Among these is a mechanism to retransmit segments with unacknowledged data.

A destination host service using TCP usually only acknowledges data for contiguous sequence bytes. If one or more segments are missing, only the data in the first contiguous sequence of bytes is acknowledged. For example, if segments with sequence numbers 1500 to 3000 and 3400 to 3500 were received, the ACK number would be 3001. This is because there are segments with the SEQ numbers 3001 to 3399 that have not been received.

When TCP at the source host has not received an acknowledgement after a predetermined amount of time, it returns to the last ACK number received and retransmits the data from that point forward. The retransmission process is not specified by the Request for Comments (RFC), but is left up to the particular implementation of TCP.

For a typical TCP implementation, a host can transmit a segment, put a copy of the segment in a retransmission queue, and start a timer. When the data acknowledgement is received, the segment is deleted from the queue. If the acknowledgement is not received before the timer expires, the segment is retransmitted.

Video

Video 7.2.2.3: TCP

Go to the online course to view an animation of how TCP handles segment loss.

Hosts today can also employ an optional feature called *selective acknowledgements (SACK)*. If both hosts support SACKs, it is possible for the destination to acknowledge bytes in discontinuous segments and the host would only need to retransmit the missing data.

TCP Flow Control—Window Size and Acknowledgements (7.2.2.4)

TCP also provides mechanisms for flow control. Flow control helps maintain the reliability of TCP transmission by adjusting the rate of data flow between source and destination for a given session. Flow control is accomplished by limiting the amount of data segments forwarded at one time and by requiring acknowledgements of receipt prior to sending more.

To accomplish flow control, the first thing that TCP determines is the amount of data segments that the destination device can accept. The TCP header includes a 16-bit field called the window size. This is the number of bytes that the destination device of a TCP session is able to accept and process at one time. The initial window size is agreed upon during the session startup through the three-way handshake between source and destination. After this is agreed upon, the source device must limit the amount of data segments sent to the destination device based on the window size. Only after the source device receives an acknowledgement that the data segments have been received, can it continue sending more data for the session.

During the delay in receiving the acknowledgement, the sender does not send any additional segments. In periods when the network is congested or the resources of the receiving host are strained, the delay can increase. As this delay grows longer, the effective transmission rate of the data for this session decreases. The slowdown in data transmission from each session helps reduce resource conflict on the network and destination device when multiple sessions are running.

Figure 7-28 presents a simplified representation of window size and acknowledgements. In this example, the initial window size for a TCP session represented is set to 3000 bytes. When the sender has transmitted 3000 bytes, it waits for an acknowledgement of these bytes before transmitting more segments in this session. After the sender has received an acknowledgement from the receiver, the sender can transmit an additional 3000 bytes.

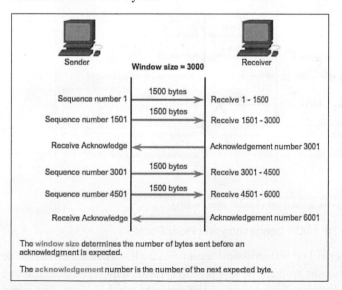

Figure 7-28   TCP Segment Acknowledgement and Window Size

TCP uses window sizes to attempt to manage the rate of transmission to the maximum flow that the network and destination device can support, while minimizing loss and retransmissions.

TCP Flow Control—Congestion Avoidance (7.2.2.5)

Another way to control the data flow is to use dynamic window sizes. When network resources are constrained, TCP can reduce the window size to require that received segments be acknowledged more frequently. This effectively slows the rate of transmission because the source waits for data to be acknowledged more frequently.

The receiving host sends the window size value to the sending host to indicate the number of bytes that it is prepared to receive. If the destination needs to slow the rate of communication because of limited buffer memory, for example, it can send a smaller window size value to the source as part of an acknowledgement.

As shown in Figure 7-29, if a receiving host has congestion, it can respond to the sending host with a segment that specifies a reduced window size. In this figure, there was a loss of one of the segments. The receiver changed the window field in the TCP header of the returning segments in this conversation from 3000 down to 1500, which caused the sender to reduce the window size to 1500.

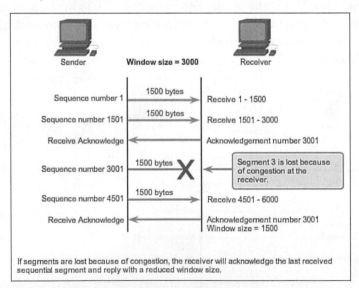

Figure 7-29 TCP Congestion and Flow Control

After a period of transmission with no data losses or constrained resources, the receiver begins to increase the window field, which reduces the overhead on the network, because fewer acknowledgements must be sent. The window size continues to increase until there is data loss, which causes the window size to decrease.

This dynamic increasing and decreasing of window size is a continuous process in TCP. In highly efficient networks, window sizes can become very large because data is not lost. In networks where the underlying infrastructure is under stress, the window size likely remains small.

UDP Communication (7.2.3)

Sometimes the reliability associated with TCP is not required or the overhead associated with providing this reliability is not suitable for the application. This is where UDP is used.

UDP Low Overhead Versus Reliability (7.2.3.1)

UDP is a simple protocol that provides the basic transport layer functions. It has much lower overhead than TCP, because it is not connection oriented and does not offer the sophisticated retransmission, sequencing, and flow control mechanisms that provide reliability.

This does not mean that applications that use UDP are always unreliable, nor does it mean that UDP is an inferior protocol. It simply means that these functions are not provided by the transport layer protocol and must be implemented elsewhere, if required. Figure 7-30 illustrates the behavior of UDP.

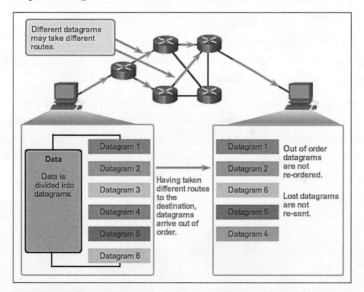

Figure 7-30   UDP: Connectionless and Unreliable

Although the total amount of UDP traffic found on a typical network is often relatively low, key application layer protocols that use UDP include

- Domain Name System (DNS)

- Simple Network Management Protocol (SNMP)

- Dynamic Host Configuration Protocol (DHCP)

- Routing Information Protocol (RIP)

- Trivial File Transfer Protocol (TFTP)

- IP telephony or Voice over IP (VoIP)

- Online games

Some applications, such as online games or VoIP, can tolerate some data loss. If these applications used TCP, they could experience large delays while TCP detects data loss and retransmits data. These delays would be more detrimental to the performance of the application than small data losses. Some applications, such as DNS, simply retry the request if no response is received; therefore, they do not need TCP to guarantee message delivery.

The low overhead of UDP makes it very desirable for such applications.

UDP Datagram Reassembly (7.2.3.2)

Because UDP is connectionless, sessions are not established before communication takes place as they are with TCP. UDP is said to be transaction-based; that is, when an application has data to send, it simply sends the data.

Many applications that use UDP send small amounts of data that can fit in one segment. However, some applications send larger amounts of data that must be split into multiple segments. The UDP PDU is referred to as a *datagram*, although the terms *segment* and *datagram* are sometimes used interchangeably to describe a transport layer PDU.

When multiple datagrams are sent to a destination, they can take different paths and arrive in the wrong order. UDP does not track sequence numbers the way TCP does. UDP has no way to reorder the datagrams into their transmission order, as shown in the figure.

Therefore, UDP simply reassembles the data in the order that it was received and forwards it to the application. If the data sequence is important to the application, the application must identify the proper sequence and determine how the data should be processed.

UDP Server Processes and Requests (7.2.3.3)

Like TCP-based applications, UDP-based server applications are assigned well-known or registered port numbers. When these applications or processes are running on a server, they accept the data matched with the assigned port number. When UDP receives a datagram destined for one of these ports, it forwards the application data to the appropriate application based on its port number.

UDP Client Processes (7.2.3.4)

As with TCP, client/server communication is initiated by a client application that requests data from a server process. The UDP client process randomly selects a port number from the range of dynamic port numbers and uses this as the source port for the conversation. The destination port is usually the well-known or registered port number assigned to the server process.

Randomized source port numbers also help with security. If there is a predictable pattern for destination port selection, an intruder can more easily simulate access to a client by attempting to connect to the port number most likely to be open.

Because there is no session to be created with UDP, as soon as the data is ready to be sent and the ports identified, UDP can form the datagrams and pass them to the network layer to be addressed and sent on the network.

After a client has selected the source and destination ports, the same pair of ports is used in the header of all datagrams used in the transaction. For the data returning to the client from the server, the source and destination port numbers in the datagram header are reversed.

Figure 7-31 shows the details of UDP client processes.

Figure 7-31   UDP Client Processes

Lab 7.2.3.5: Using Wireshark to Examine a UDP DNS Capture

In this lab, you will complete the following objectives:

- Part 1: Record a PC's IP Configuration Information
- Part 2: Use Wireshark to Capture DNS Queries and Responses
- Part 3: Analyze Captured DNS or UDP Packets

TCP or UDP, That Is the Question (7.2.4)

As previously stated, the decision to use TCP or UDP as a transport layer protocol rests with the application developer. Each protocol has unique characteristics that must be matched to the specific application.

Applications That Use TCP (7.2.4.1)

Many applications require reliability and other services provided by TCP. These are applications that can tolerate some delay or performance loss because of the overhead imposed by TCP.

This makes TCP best suited for applications that need reliable transport and can tolerate some delay. TCP is a great example of how the different layers of the TCP/IP protocol suite have specific roles. Because the transport layer protocol TCP handles all tasks associated with segmenting the data stream into segments, reliability, flow control, and reordering of segments, it frees the application from having to manage any of this. The application can simply send the data stream to the transport layer and use the services of TCP.

Some examples of well-known applications that use TCP include

- Hypertext Transfer Protocol (HTTP)
- File Transfer Protocol (FTP)
- Simple Mail Transfer Protocol (SMTP)
- Telnet

Applications That Use UDP (7.2.4.2)

There are three types of applications that are best suited for UDP:

- Applications that can tolerate some data loss, but require little or no delay
- Applications with simple request and reply transactions
- Unidirectional communications, where reliability is not required or can be handled by the application

Many video and multimedia applications, such as VoIP and Internet Protocol Television (IPTV), use UDP. These applications can tolerate some data loss with little or no noticeable effect. The reliability mechanisms of TCP introduce some delay that can be noticeable in the quality of the sound or video being received.

Other types of applications that are well suited for UDP are those that use simple request and reply transactions. This is where a host sends a request and might or might not receive a reply. These types of applications include

- DHCP
- DNS; can also use TCP
- SNMP
- TFTP

Some applications handle reliability themselves. These applications do not need the services of TCP and can better utilize UDP as the transport layer protocol. TFTP is one example of this type of protocol. TFTP has its own mechanisms for flow control, error detection, acknowledgements, and error recovery. It does not need to rely on TCP for those services.

Lab 7.2.4.3: Using Wireshark to Examine FTP and TFTP Captures

In this lab, you will complete the following objectives:

- Part 1: Identify TCP Header Fields and Operation Using a Wireshark FTP Session Capture
- Part 2: Identify UDP Header Fields and Operation Using a Wireshark TFTP Session Capture

Summary (7.3)

Class Activity 7.3.1.1: We Need to Talk, Again: Game

Note: It is important that the students have completed the Introductory Modeling Activity for this chapter. This activity works best in medium-sized groups of six to eight students.

The instructor will whisper a complex message to the first student in a group. An example of the message might be "We are expecting a blizzard tomorrow. It should be arriving in the morning and school will be delayed two hours so bring your homework."

That student whispers the message to the next student in the group. Each group follows this process until all members of each group have heard the whispered message.

Here are the rules you are to follow:

- You can whisper the message in short parts to your neighbor *and* you can repeat the message parts after verifying that your neighbor heard the correct message.

- Small parts of the message can be checked and repeated again (clockwise *or* counterclockwise to ensure the accuracy of the message parts) by whispering. A student will be assigned to time the entire activity.

- When the message has reached the end of the group, the last student will say aloud what she or he heard. Small parts of the message can be repeated (that is, resent), and the process can be restarted to ensure that *all* parts of the message are fully delivered and correct.

- The instructor will restate the original message to check for quality delivery.

Packet Tracer
☐ Activity

Packet Tracer Activity 7.3.1.2: TCP and UDP Communications

This simulation activity is intended to provide a foundation for understanding the TCP and UDP in detail. Simulation mode provides the ability to view the functionality of the different protocols.

As data moves through the network, it is broken down into smaller pieces and identified in some fashion so that the pieces can be put back together. Each of these pieces is assigned a specific name (protocol data unit [PDU]) and associated with a specific layer. Packet Tracer Simulation mode enables the user to view each of the protocols and the associated PDU. The following steps lead the user through the process of requesting services using various applications available on a client PC.

This activity provides an opportunity to explore the functionality of TCP and UDP, multiplexing, and the function of port numbers in determining which local application requested the data or is sending the data.

The transport layer provides transport-related services by

- Dividing data received from an application into segments
- Adding a header to identify and manage each segment
- Using the header information to reassemble the segments into application data
- Passing the assembled data to the correct application

UDP and TCP are common transport layer protocols.

UDP datagrams and TCP segments have headers added in front of the data that include a source port number and destination port number. These port numbers enable data to be directed to the correct application running on the destination computer.

TCP does not pass any data to the network until it knows that the destination is ready to receive it. TCP then manages the flow of the data and resends any data segments that are not acknowledged as being received at the destination. TCP uses mechanisms of handshaking, timers, acknowledgement messages, and dynamic windowing to achieve reliability. The reliability process, however, imposes overhead on the network in terms of much larger segment headers and more network traffic between the source and destination.

If the application data needs to be delivered across the network quickly, or if network bandwidth cannot support the overhead of control messages being exchanged between the source and the destination systems, UDP would be the developer's preferred transport layer protocol. This is because UDP does not track or acknowledge the receipt of datagrams at the destination—it just passes received datagrams to the application layer as they arrive. However, this does not necessarily mean that the communication itself is unreliable; there can be mechanisms in the application layer protocols and services that process lost or delayed datagrams if the application has these requirements.

The application developer decides the transport layer protocol that best meets the requirements for the application. It is important to remember that the other layers all play a part in data network communications and influence its performance.

Practice

The following activities provide practice with the topics introduced in this chapter. The labs and class activities are available in the companion *Introduction to Networks Lab Manual, (ISBN: 978-1-58713-312-1)*. The Packet Tracer Activities PKA files are found in the online course.

Class Activities

- Class Activity 7.0.1.2: We Need to Talk Game

- Class Activity 7.3.1.1: We Need to Talk, Again: Game

Labs

- Lab 7.2.1.8: Using Wireshark to Observe the TCP Three-Way Handshake

- Lab 7.2.3.5: Using Wireshark to Examine a UDP DNS Capture

- Lab 7.2.4.3: Using Wireshark to Examine FTP and TFTP Captures

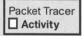
Packet Tracer
☐ Activity

Packet Tracer Activities

- Packet Tracer Activity 7.3.1.2: TCP and UDP Communications

Check Your Understanding

Complete all the review questions listed here to test your understanding of the topics and concepts in this chapter. The appendix, "Check Your Understanding Answer Key," lists the answers.

1. What are the primary purposes of the transport layer? (Choose three.)

   A. Determining the best route between source and destination

   B. Adding the source and destination MAC address to frames

   C. Tracking the individual communication between applications on the source and destination hosts

   D. Adding the source and destination IP address

   E. Segmenting data for and reassembling segmented data into streams of application data at the destination

   F. Identifying the proper application for each communication stream

2. What is assigned by the transport layer to identify an application or service?

    A. Segment

    B. Packet

    C. Port

    D. MAC address

    E. IP address

3. Fill in the blank. _____ is the term used to describe the interleaving of data from multiple users on the same network.

4. What is a characteristic of UDP?

    A. Reliable delivery

    B. Connectionless

    C. Windowing

    D. Expectational acknowledgements

    E. Flow control

5. Which of the following types of applications would use UDP? (Choose three.)

    A. Telnet

    B. VoIP

    C. FTP

    D. HTTP

    E. DHCP

    F. TFTP

6. Which TCP header field specifies the number of segments that can be accepted before an acknowledgement is required?

    A. Acknowledgement number

    B. Header length

    C. Window size

    D. Checksum

7. Fill in the blank. Both TCP and UDP use _____ to separate multiple communications on the same channel.

8. What is an advantage that UDP has over TCP?

   A. Advanced flow control

   B. Low overhead

   C. Reordering of segments

   D. Reliable delivery

9. What range of ports can either be used by TCP to identify the requested service on the destination device or as a client source port?

   A. 0 to 1023

   B. 0 to 49151

   C. 1024 to 49151

   D. 49152 to 65535

10. Fill in the blank. A dynamic port in the range of 49152 to 65535 is also known as a(n) _____ port.

11. What does UDP do when receiving messages that are more than one datagram in length?

   A. UDP place the datagrams into the correct order before passing them to the application.

   B. UDP reassembles that data in the order it was received and passes it to the application.

   C. UDP requests retransmission of the datagrams in the correct order before passing to the application.

   D. UDP transmissions are limited to a single datagram.

12. Which TCP header control bit is set on to terminate a TCP conversation?

   A. URG

   B. ACK

   C. PSH

   D. RST

   E. SYN

   F. FIN

13. If a client sends an ISN of 2 to a server and a server responds with an ISN of 1 to the client, what is the final stage of the TCP three-way handshake?

A.   Client sends an acknowledgement of 2.

B.   Server sends an acknowledgement of 2.

C.   Client sends an acknowledgement of 3.

D.   Server sends an acknowledgement of 3.

E.   Client sends a new ISN of 3.

F.   Server sends a new ISN of 2.

14. A client is downloading a large file from a server using FTP. One of the segments is lost during transit. What will happen?

A.   The FTP session is immediately terminated.

B.   The FTP client responds to the server with a smaller window size in the TCP header.

C.   The FTP client responds to the client with an increased window size in the TCP header.

D.   The FTP server responds to the client with a smaller window size in the TCP header.

E.   The FTP server responds to the client with an increased window size in the TCP header.

F.   The FTP session continues, but the result is a corrupt file that must be downloaded again.

G.   The FTP session continues with no alteration in window size, and the missing segment is requested again after the rest of the file is downloaded.

15. Fill in the blank. TCP will normally retransmit lost data from the last successful acknowledgement. To allow the destination to acknowledge bytes in discontinuous segments and request retransmission of only the missing data, both hosts must be able to support an optional feature called _____.

CHAPTER 8

IP Addressing

Objectives

Upon completion of this chapter, you will be able to answer the following questions:

- What are the parts of an IPv4 address?

- What is the purpose of the subnet address?

- What are the similarities and differences among unicast, broadcast, and multicast IPv4 addresses?

- What are the uses of public and private address space?

- What are the reasons for the development of IPv6 addressing?

- How are IPv6 addresses represented?

- What are the different types of IPv6 addresses?

- How are global unicast addresses configured?

- What are the purpose and uses of multicast addresses?

- How is ICMP used in IPv4 and IPv6 addresses?

- How are the ping and traceroute utilities used to test network connectivity?

Key Terms

This chapter uses the following key terms. You can find the definitions in the Glossary.

subnetwork   page 393

American Standard Code for Information Interchange (ASCII)   page 394

octet   page 394

network address   page 402

prefix length   page 402

slash notation   page 402

host address   page 405

broadcast address   page 405

logical AND   page 406

directed broadcast   page 412

limited broadcast   page 412

multicast client   page 414

public address   page 416

private address   page 416

link-local address   page 418

TEST-NET address   page 418

classful addressing   page 419

classless addressing   page 421

Internet Assigned Numbers Authority (IANA)   page 422

Internet service provider (ISP)   page 422

Introduction (8.0.1.1)

This chapter examines in detail the structure of IP addresses and their application to the construction and testing of IP networks and *subnetworks*.

Addressing as a key function of network layer protocols enables data communication between hosts, regardless of whether the hosts are on the same network or on different networks. Both Internet Protocol version 4 (IPv4) and Internet Protocol version 6 (IPv6) provide hierarchical addressing for packets that carry data.

Designing, implementing, and managing an effective IP addressing plan ensures that networks can operate efficiently.

Class Activity 8.0.1.2: The Internet of Everything (IoE)

If nature, traffic, transportation, networking, and space exploration depend on digital information sharing, how will that information be identified from source to destination?

In this activity, you will begin to think about not only what will be identified in the IoE world but also how everything will be addressed in the same world!

- Read the blog/news source provided by John Chambers regarding the Internet of Everything (IoE): http://blogs.cisco.com/news/internet-of-everything-2. View the video halfway down the page.

- Next, venture to the IoE main page: www.cisco.com/web/tomorrow-starts-here/index.html. Click a category that interests you.

- View the video, blog, or .pdf file that belongs to your IoE category of interest.

- Write five comments or questions about what you saw or read, and share with the class.

IPv4 Network Addresses (8.1)

For communication to take place between hosts, the appropriate addresses must be applied to these devices. Managing the addressing of the devices and understanding the IPv4 address structure and its representation are essential.

IPv4 Address Structure (8.1.1)

This section will present the IPv4 address structure.

Binary Notation (8.1.1.1)

To understand the operation of devices on a network, we need to look at addresses and other data the way devices do—in binary notation. Binary notation is a representation of information using only 1s and 0s. Computers communicate using binary data. Binary data can be used to represent many different forms of data. For example, when typing letters on a keyboard, those letters appear on screen in a form that you can read and understand; however, the computer translates each letter to a series of binary digits for storage and transport. To translate those letters, the computer uses *American Standard Code for Information Interchange (ASCII)*.

With ASCII, each character is represented by a string of 7 bits. This allows a total of 128 different characters to be represented. Extended ASCII uses 8 bits per character, allowing the representation of 256 different characters. Each byte is used to represent a single character using extended ASCII. For example, the uppercase letter *A* is represented by the bit pattern 0100 0001 while the lowercase letter *a* is represented in bit form as 01100001, the character for the number 9 is represented by the pattern 0011 1001, and the # symbol is represented by 0010 0011.

While it is not generally necessary for people to concern themselves with binary conversion of letters, it is necessary to understand the use of binary for IP addressing. Each device on a network must be uniquely identified using a binary address. In IPv4 networks, this address is represented using a string of 32 bits (1s and 0s). At the network layer, the packets then include this unique identification information for both the source and destination systems. Therefore, in an IPv4 network, each packet includes a 32-bit source address and a 32-bit destination address in the Layer 3 header.

For most individuals, a string of 32 bits is difficult to interpret and even more difficult to remember. Therefore, we represent IPv4 addresses using dotted-decimal format instead of binary. This means that we look at each byte (*octet*) as a decimal number in the range of 0 to 255. To understand how this works, we need to have some skill in binary-to-decimal conversion.

Positional Notation

Learning to convert binary to decimal requires an understanding of the mathematical basis of a numbering system called positional notation. Positional notation means that a digit represents different values depending on the position the digit occupies. In a positional notation system, the number base is called the radix. In the base 10 system, the radix is 10. In the binary system, we use a radix of 2. The terms radix and base can be used interchangeably. More specifically, the value that a digit represents is that value multiplied by the power of the base, or radix, represented by the position the digit occupies. Some examples will help to clarify how this system works.

For the decimal number 192, the value that the 1 represents is $1*10^2$ (1 times 10 to the power of 2). The 1 is in what we commonly refer to as the "100s" position. Positional notation refers to this position as the base 2 position because the base, or radix, is 10 and the power is 2. The 9 represents $9*10^1$ (9 times 10 to the power of 1). The 2 represents $2*10^0$ (2 times 10 to the power of 0)

Using positional notation in the base 10 number system, 192 represents:

$$192 = (1 * 10^2) + (9 * 10^1) + (2 * 10^0)$$

or

$$192 = (1 * 100) + (9 * 10) + (2 * 1)$$

Binary Number System (8.1.1.2)

In IPv4, addresses are 32-bit binary numbers. However, for ease of use by people, binary patterns representing IPv4 addresses are expressed as dotted decimals. This representation is first accomplished by separating each byte (8 bits) of the 32-bit binary pattern, called an octet, with a dot. It is called an octet because each decimal number represents 1 byte, or 8 bits.

The binary address

11000000 10101000 00001010 00001010

is expressed in dotted decimal as

192.168.10.10

Table 8-1 shows different representations of the IPv4 address of 192.168.10.10. This includes dotted-decimal, binary octets, and the full 32 bit address.

Table 8-1   IPv4 Address Representation

Dotted Decimal	192	168	10	10
Octets	11000000	10101000	00001010	00001010
32-Bit Address	11000000101010000000101000001010			

To understand the dotted-decimal representation, you need to understand how actual decimal equivalents are determined.

Binary Numbering System

In the binary numbering system, the radix is 2. Therefore, each position represents increasing powers of 2. In 8-bit binary numbers, the positions represent these quantities:

2^7 2^6 2^5 2^4 2^3 2^2 2^1 2^0

128   64   32   16   8   4   2   1

The base 2 numbering system only has two digits: 0 and 1.

When we interpret a byte as a decimal number, we have the quantity that position represents if the digit is a 1 and we do not have that quantity if the digit is a 0.

Table 8-2 illustrates the representation of the decimal number 192 in binary. A 1 in a certain position means that we add that value to the total. A 0 means we do not add that value. The binary number 11000000 has a 1 in the 2^7 position (decimal value 128) and a 1 in the 2^6 position (decimal value 64). The remaining bits are all 0. So, no further corresponding decimal values are added. The result of adding 128+64 is 192, the decimal equivalent of 11000000.

Table 8-2   Representation of Decimal Number 192

Radix Exponent	2^7	2^6	2^5	2^4	2^3	2^2	2^1	2^0	
Positional Value	128	64	32	16	8	4	2	1	
Binary Address bit	1	1	0	0	0	0	0	0	= 1100000
Binary Value	128	64	0	0	0	0	0	0	= 192

Examples 8-1 and 8-2 show the extreme values of an octet. A 1 in each position means that we add the value for that position to the total. In Example 8-1, all 1s means that the values of every position are included in the total; therefore, the value of all 1s in an octet is 255.

Example 8-1   Octet Containing All 1s: 11111111

128		64		32		16		8		4		2		1	
1		1		1		1		1		1		1		1	**= 1111111**
128	+	64	+	32	+	16	+	8	+	4	+	2	+	1	**= 255**

A 0 in each position indicates that the value for that position is not included in the total. In Example 8-2, a 0 in every position yields a total of 0.

Example 8-2   Octet Containing All 0s: 00000000

128	64	32	16	8	4	2	1	
0	0	0	0	0	0	0	0	= 00000000
0 +	0 +	0 +	0 +	0 +	0 +	0 +	0	= 0

Each different combination of 1s and 0s will yield a different decimal value.

Converting a Binary Address to Decimal (8.1.1.3)

Each octet is made up of 8 bits and each bit has a value, either 0 or 1. The four groups of 8 bits have the same set of valid values in the range of 0 to 255 inclusive. The value of each bit placement, from right to left is 1, 2, 4, 8, 16, 32, 64, and 128.

Determine the value of the octet by adding the values of positions wherever there is a binary 1 present:

- If there is a 0 in a position, do not add the value.

- If all 8 bits are 0s, 00000000, the value of the octet is 0.

- If all 8 bits are 1s, 11111111, the value of the octet is 255 (128+64+32+16+8+4+2+1).

- If the 8 bits are mixed, the values are added together. For example, the octet 00100111 has a value of 39 (32+4+2+1).

So the value of each of the four octets can range from 0 to a maximum of 255.

Table 8-3, shows how a binary address is converted to dotted decimal. Using the 32-bit IPv4 address 11000000101010000000101000001010, convert the binary representation to dotted decimal using the following steps:

How To

Step 1.   Divide the 32 bits into 4 octets.

Step 2.   Convert each octet to decimal.

Step 3.   Add a "dot" between each decimal.

Table 8-3 Representation of Dotted-Decimal Address

32-Bit IPv4 Address

	Octet 1	Octet 2	Octet 3	Octet 4
Octet Bit Value	128 64 32 16 8 4 2 1	128 64 32 16 8 4 2 1	128 64 32 16 8 4 2 1	128 64 32 16 8 4 2 1
Binary Address	1 1 0 0 0 0 0 0	1 0 1 0 1 0 0 0	0 0 0 0 1 0 1 0	0 0 0 0 1 0 1 0
Binary Value	128 64 0 0 0 0 0 0	128 0 32 0 8 0 0 0	0 0 0 0 8 0 2 0	0 0 0 0 8 0 2 0
Add Binary Value	128+64 = 192	128+32+8 = 168	8+2 = 10	8+2 = 10
Dotted-Decimal Address	192.168.10.10			

Interactive Graphic	**Activity 8.1.1.4: Binary-to-Decimal Conversions**
	Go to the course online to perform this practice activity.

Converting from Decimal to Binary (8.1.1.5, 8.1.1.6)

In addition to being able to convert from binary to decimal, it is also necessary to understand how to convert from decimal to binary.

Because we represent IPv4 addresses using dotted-decimal format, it is only necessary that we examine the process of converting 8-bit binary to the decimal values of 0 to 255 for each octet in an IPv4 address.

To begin the conversion process, we start by determining whether the decimal number is equal to or greater than our largest decimal value represented by the most significant bit. In the highest position, we determine whether the octet number is equal to or greater than 128. If the octet number is smaller than 128, we place a 0 in the bit position for decimal value 128 and move to the bit position for decimal value 64.

If the octet number in the bit position for decimal value 128 is larger than or equal to 128, we place a 1 in the bit position for decimal value 128 and subtract 128 from the octet number being converted. We then compare the remainder of this operation to the next smaller value, 64. We continue this process for all the remaining bit positions.

Figure 8-1 shows the process of converting 168 to the binary equivalent of 10101000.

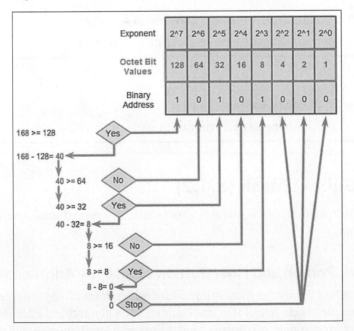

Figure 8-1   Decimal-to-Binary Conversion

The conversion steps shown in Figure 8-2 outline the process to convert an IP address to binary. Each octet is converted to binary and then combined. The steps for this example are

How To

Step 1.   Convert 192 to binary.

Step 2.   Convert 168 to binary.

Step 3.   Convert 10 to binary.

Step 4.   Convert 10 to binary.

Step 5.   Combine the converted octets beginning with the first octet.

Figure 8-2   Decimal-to-Binary Conversion of IPv4 Address

Interactive Graphic

Activity 8.1.1.7: Decimal-to-Binary Conversion Activity

Go to the course online to perform this practice activity.

Interactive Graphic

Activity 8.1.1.8: Binary Game

Go to the course online to perform this practice activity.

IPv4 Subnet Mask (8.1.2)

This section introduces the use and structure of the subnet mask used in IPv4 addressing.

Network Portion and Host Portion of an IPv4 Address (8.1.2.1)

Understanding binary notation is important when determining whether two hosts are in the same network. Recall that an IP address is a hierarchical address that is made up of two parts: a network portion and a host portion. However, when determining the network portion versus the host portion, it is necessary to look, not at the decimal value, but at the 32-bit stream. Within the 32-bit stream, a portion of the bits makes up the IPv4 network and a portion of the bits makes up the host.

The bits within the network portion of the address must be identical for all devices that reside in the same network. The bits within the host portion of the address must be unique to identify a specific host within a network. If two hosts have the same bit pattern in the specified network portion of the 32-bit stream, those two hosts will reside in the same network.

However, how do hosts know which portion of the 32 bits is network and which is host? That is the job of the subnet mask.

When an IP host is configured, a subnet mask is assigned along with an IPv4 address. Like the IP address, the subnet mask is 32 bits long. The subnet mask signifies which part of the IP address is network and which part is host.

The subnet mask is compared to the IP address from left to right, bit for bit. The 1s in the subnet mask represent the network portion; the 0s represent the host portion. As shown in Figure 8-3, the subnet mask is created by placing a binary 1 in each bit position that represents the network portion and placing a binary 0 in each bit position that represents the host portion.

Note

The subnet mask does not actually contain the network or host portion of an IPv4 address; it just tells the computer where to look for these portions in a given IPv4 address.

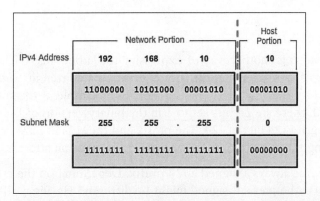

Figure 8-3 Decimal-to-Binary Conversion of IPv4 Address

Similar to IPv4 addresses, the subnet mask is represented in dotted-decimal format for ease of use. The subnet mask is configured on a host device, in conjunction with the IPv4 address, and is required so that the host can determine to which network it belongs. Table 8-4 displays the valid subnet masks for an IPv4 octet as well as the number of bits used to identify both the **network address** and host address within a single octet.

Table 8-4   Subnet Mask Values Within an Octet

Mask (Decimal)	Mask (Binary)	Network Bits	Host Bits
0	00000000	0	8
128	10000000	1	7
192	11000000	2	6
224	11100000	3	5
240	11110000	4	4
248	11111000	5	3
252	11111100	6	2
254	11111110	7	1
255	11111111	8	0

Examining the Prefix Length (8.1.2.2)

Subnet masks are often a cumbersome way of indicating the network and host portion of an IPv4 address. This section will present the use of an alternative representation.

Network Prefixes

The **prefix length** is another way of expressing the subnet mask. The prefix length is the number of bits set to 1 in the subnet mask. It is written in "**slash notation**," a "/" followed by the number of bits set to 1. For example, if the subnet mask is 255.255.255.0, there are 24 bits set to 1 in the binary version of the subnet mask, so the prefix length is 24 bits or /24. The prefix and the subnet mask are different ways of representing the same thing—the network portion of an address.

Networks are not always assigned a /24 prefix. Depending on the number of hosts on the network, the prefix assigned might be different. Having a different prefix number changes the host range and broadcast address for each network.

Table 8-5 illustrates different prefixes using the same 10.1.1.0 address.

Table 8-5   Subnet Addresses in Slash Notation

Network Address in Slash Notation	Network Address with Subnet Mask
10.1.1.0 /24	10.1.1.0 mask 255.255.255.0
10.1.1.0 /25	10.1.1.0 mask 255.255.255.128
10.1.1.0 /26	10.1.1.0 mask 255.255.255.192
10.1.1.0 /27	10.1.1.0 mask 255.255.255.224
10.1.1.0 /28	10.1.1.0 mask 255.255.255.240
10.1.1.0 /29	10.1.1.0 mask 255.255.255.248
10.1.1.0 /30	10.1.1.0 mask 255.255.255.252
10.1.1.0 /31	10.1.1.0 mask 255.255.255.254
10.1.1.0 /32	10.1.1.0 mask 255.255.255.255

Note

Generally, the /31 subnet mask is not used. It is only used in special configurations that are beyond the scope of this book. Additionally, 10.1.1.0 would not be a valid address with /31 or with /24 but is shown here to illustrate the slash notation.

IPv4 Network, Host, and Broadcast Addresses (8.1.2.3)

There are three types of addresses within the address range of each IPv4 network:

- Network address
- Host address
- Broadcast address

Network Address

The network address is a standard way to refer to a network. The subnet mask or the prefix length might also be used when referring to a network address. For example, the network shown in Figure 8-4 could be referred to as the 10.1.1.0 network, the 10.1.1.0 255.255.255.0 network, or the 10.1.1.0/24 network. All hosts in the 10.1.1.0/24 network will have the same network portion bits.

Within the IPv4 address range of a network, the first address (lowest address) is reserved for the network address. This address has a 0 for each host bit in the host portion of the address. All hosts within the network share the same network address. The network is only a reference to the network. This address is not used for communication.

Host Address

Every end device requires a unique address to communicate on the network. In IPv4 addresses, the values between the network address and the broadcast address can be assigned to end devices in a network. A host address has any combination of 0 and 1 bits in the host portion of the address but cannot contain all 0 bits or all 1 bits. In Figure 8-4, each network portion of all the hosts is 10.1.1. Each of the hosts has a unique host portion of the address of 10, 11, 12, 254, and the router interface is 1.

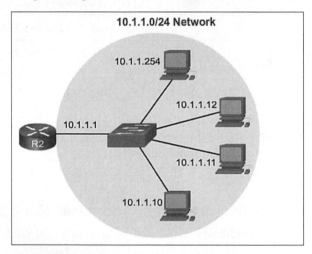

Figure 8-4 Example Network 10.1.1.0 /24

Broadcast Address

The IPv4 broadcast address is a special address for each network that allows communication to all the hosts in that network. To send data to all hosts in a network at once, a host can send a single packet that is addressed to the broadcast address of the network, and each host in the network that receives this packet will process its contents.

The broadcast address uses the last (highest) address in the network range. This is the address in which the bits in the host portion are all 1s. All 1s in an octet in binary form is equal to the number 255 in decimal form. For the network 10.1.1.0/24, in which the last octet is used for the host portion, the broadcast address would be 10.1.1.255.

Note

The host portion might not always be an entire octet. This address is also referred to as the directed broadcast address.

Table 8-6 shows that the network address could remain the same with different subnets. However, the host range and the broadcast address are different for the different prefix lengths. Also, the number of hosts that can be addressed on the network also changes.

Table 8-6   Subnet with Different Masks

Network Address	10.1.1.0 /24	10.1.1.0 /25	10.1.1.0 /26	10.1.1.0 /27
First Host Address	10.1.1.1	10.1.1.1	10.1.1.1	10.1.1.1
Last Host Address	10.1.1.254	10.1.1.126	10.1.1.62	10.1.1.30
Broadcast Address	10.1.1.255	10.1.1.127	10.1.1.63	10.1.1.31
Number of Hosts	254	126	62	30

First Host and Last Host Addresses (8.1.2.4)

To ensure that all hosts within a network are assigned a unique IP address within that network range, it is important to identify the first *host address* and the last host address. Hosts within a network can be assigned IP addresses within this range.

First Host Address

Also seen in Table 8-6, the host portion of the first host address will contain all 0 bits with a 1 bit for the lowest-order or rightmost bit. This address is always 1 greater than the network address. The first host address on the 10.1.1.0/24 network is 10.1.1.1. It is common in many addressing schemes to use the first host address for the router or default gateway address.

Last Host Address

The host portion of the last host address will contain all 1 bits with a 0 bit for the lowest-order or rightmost bit. This address is always 1 less than the *broadcast address.* As seen in Table 8-6, the last host address on the 10.1.1.0/24 network is 10.1.1.254.

Note

Because the lowest host address in any network has a 1 in the least significant bit, all first host addresses will be odd numbers. In contrast, the last host address will a 0 in the least significant bit, So, last host addresses will be even. Similarly, network addresses are always even numbers and broadcast addresses will be odd.

Bitwise AND Operation (8.1.2.5)

When an IPv4 address is assigned to a device, that device uses the subnet mask to determine to what network address the device belongs. The network address is the address that represents all the devices on the same network.

When sending network data, the device uses this information to determine whether it can send packets locally, or whether it must send the packets to a default gateway for remote delivery. When a host sends a packet, it compares the network portion of its own IP address to the destination IP address, based on the host's subnet mask. The network portion of the addresses of the source and destination IPv4 addresses are determined based on a logical AND of the subnet mask with each of these addresses. If the network bits of the source and destination match, both the source and destination host are on the same network and the packet can be delivered locally. If they do not match, the sending host forwards the packet to the default gateway to be sent on to the other network.

The AND Operation

ANDing is one of three basic binary operations used in digital logic. The other two are OR and NOT. While all three are used in data networks, AND is used in determining the network address. Therefore, our discussion here will be limited to *logical AND*. Logical AND is the comparison of two bits that yields the following results:

1 AND 1 = 1

0 AND 1 = 0

0 AND 0 = 0

1 AND 0 = 0

The IPv4 host address is logically ANDed, bit by bit, with its subnet mask to determine the network address to which the host is associated. When this bitwise ANDing between the address and the subnet mask is performed, the result yields the network address.

Importance of ANDing (8.1.2.6)

Any address bit ANDed with a 1 bit value from the subnet mask will yield the original bit value from the address. So, a 0 (from the IPv4 address) AND 1 (from the subnet mask) is 0. 1 (from the IPv4 address) AND 1 (from the subnet mask) is 1. Consequently, anything ANDed with a 0 yields a 0. These properties of ANDing are used with the subnet mask to "mask" the host bits of an IPv4 address. Each bit of the address is ANDed with the corresponding bit of the subnet mask.

Because all the bits of the subnet mask that represent host bits are 0s, the host portion of the resulting network address becomes all 0s. Recall that an IPv4 address with all 0s in the host portion represents the network address.

Likewise, all the bits of the subnet mask that indicate the network portion are 1s. When each of these 1s is ANDed with the corresponding bit of the address, the resulting bits are identical to the original address bits.

As shown in Table 8-7, the 1 bits in the subnet mask will result in the network portion of the network address having the same bits as the network portion of the host. The host portion of the network address will result in all 0s.

For a given IP address and its subnet mask, ANDing can be used to determine what subnetwork the address belongs to, as well as what other addresses belong to the same subnet. Remember that if two addresses are in the same network or subnetwork, they are considered to be local to each other and can therefore communicate directly with each other. Addresses that are not in the same network or subnetwork are considered to be remote to each other and must therefore have a Layer 3 device (like a router or Layer 3 switch) between them to communicate.

In network verification/troubleshooting, we often need to determine whether two hosts are on the same local network. We need to make this determination from the perspective of the network devices. Because of improper configuration, a host might see itself on a network that was not the intended one. This can create an operation that seems erratic unless diagnosed by examining the ANDing processes used by the host.

Table 8-7 Logical AND to Determine Subnet

	Dotted Decimal				Binary Octets			
Host	192	168	10	10	11000000	10101000	00001010	00001010
Mask	255	255	255	0	11111111	11111111	11111111	00000000
AND								
Network	192	168	10	0	11000000	10101000	00001010	00000000

Lab 8.1.2.7: Using the Windows Calculator with Network Addresses

In this lab, you will complete the following objectives:

- Part 1: Access the Windows Calculator
- Part 2: Convert Between Numbering Systems
- Part 3: Convert Host IPv4 Addresses and Subnet Masks into Binary
- Part 4: Determine the Number of Hosts in a Network Using Powers of 2
- Part 5: Convert MAC Addresses and IPv6 Addresses to Binary

Lab 8.1.2.8: Converting IPv4 Addresses to Binary

In this lab, you will complete the following objectives:

- Part 1: Convert IPv4 Addresses from Dotted Decimal to Binary
- Part 2: Use Bitwise ANDing Operation to Determine Network Addresses
- Part 3: Apply Network Address Calculations

Activity 8.1.2.9: ANDing to Determine the Network Address

Go to the course online to perform this practice activity.

IPv4 Unicast, Broadcast, and Multicast (8.1.3)

In data networks, communication can take place as either unicast, broadcast, or multicast. This section will discuss these three methods of communication in IPv4.

Assigning a Static IPv4 Address to a Host (8.1.3.1)

For a host to participate in IPv4 unicast, multicast, or broadcast, the host must first have IPv4 addressing configured. This section will introduce static IPv4 host configuration.

Addresses for User Devices

In most data networks, the largest population of hosts includes the end devices such as PCs, tablets, smartphones, printers, and IP phones. Because this represents the largest number of devices within a network, the largest number of addresses should be allocated to these hosts. These hosts are assigned IP addresses from the range of available addresses in the network. These IP addresses can be assigned either statically or dynamically.

Static Assignment

With a static assignment, the network administrator must manually configure the network information for a host. To configure a static IPv4 address, choose IPv4 on the network adapter screen and then key in the static address, subnet mask, and default gateway. Figure 8-5 shows the minimum static configuration: the host IP address, subnet mask, and default gateway.

There are several advantages to static addressing. For example, it is useful for printers, servers, and other networking devices that do not change location often and need to be accessible to clients on the network based on a fixed IP address. If hosts normally access a server at a particular IP address, it would cause problems if that address changed. Additionally, static assignment of addressing information can provide increased control of network resources. For example, it is possible to create access filters based on traffic to and from a specific IP address. However, static addressing can be time-consuming to enter on each host.

When using static IP addressing, it is necessary to maintain an accurate list of the IP address assigned to each device. Assigning duplicate addresses within a network can create communication problems.

Figure 8-5   Configuring IPv4 Addressing on Windows Host

Assigning a Dynamic IPv4 Address to a Host (8.1.3.2)

This section will introduce dynamic IPv4 host configuration.

Dynamic Assignment

On local networks, it is often the case that the user population changes frequently. New users arrive with laptops and need a connection. Others have new workstations or other network devices, such as smartphones, that need to be connected. Rather than have the network administrator assign IP addresses for each workstation, it is easier to have IP addresses assigned automatically. This is done using a protocol known as Dynamic Host Configuration Protocol (DHCP).

DHCP enables the automatic assignment of addressing information such as IP address, subnet mask, default gateway, and other configuration information. The configuration of the DHCP server requires that a block of addresses, called an address pool, is used for assigning to the DHCP clients on a network. Addresses assigned to this pool should be planned so that they exclude any static addresses used by other devices.

DHCP is generally the preferred method of assigning IPv4 addresses to hosts on large networks because it reduces the burden on network support staff and virtually eliminates entry errors.

Another benefit of DHCP is that an address is not permanently assigned to a host but is only "leased" for a period of time. If the host is powered down or taken off the network, the address is returned to the pool for reuse. This feature is especially helpful for mobile users that come and go on a network.

If DCHP is enabled on a host device, the **ipconfig** command can be used to view the IP address information assigned by the DHCP server, as shown in Example 8-3.

Example 8-3   Confirming the IP Address and Gateway Route

```
C:\> ipconfig

Windows IP Configuration

Ethernet adapter Local Area Connection:

   Connection-specific DNS Suffix  . :
   IPv4 Address. . . . . . . . . . . .: 192.168.254.11
   Subnet Mask . . . . . . . . . . . : 255.255.255.0
     Default Gateway . . . . . . . . . : 192.168.254.1
```

Unicast Transmission (8.1.3.3)

In an IPv4 network, the hosts can communicate one of three ways:

- **Unicast:** The process of sending a packet from one host to an individual host

- **Broadcast:** The process of sending a packet from one host to all hosts in the network

- **Multicast:** The process of sending a packet from one host to a selected group of hosts, possibly in different networks

These three types of communication are used for different purposes in data networks. In all three cases, the IPv4 address of the originating host is placed in the packet header as the source address.

Unicast Traffic

Unicast communication is used for normal host-to-host communication in both a client/server and a peer-to-peer network. Unicast packets use the address of the destination device as the destination address and can be routed through an internetwork. In Figure 8-6, host 172.16.4.1 is communicating with the host (printer) at 172.16.4.253 as a unicast communication.

In an IPv4 network, the unicast address applied to an end device is referred to as the host address. For unicast communication, the addresses assigned to the two end devices are used as the source and destination IPv4 addresses. During the encapsulation process, the source host places its IPv4 address in the unicast packet header as the source address and the IPv4 address of the destination host in the packet header as the destination address. The source address of any packet is always the unicast address of the originating host.

Figure 8-6   Unicast Communication

Note

In this course, all communication between devices is unicast communication unless otherwise noted.

IPv4 addresses are unicast addresses and are in the address range of 0.0.0.0 to 223.255.255.255. However, within this range are many addresses that are reserved for special purposes. These special purpose addresses will be discussed later in this chapter.

Broadcast Transmission (8.1.3.4)

This section will introduce different types of IPv4 broadcast.

Broadcast Transmission

Broadcast traffic is used to send packets to all hosts in the network using the broadcast address for the network. With a broadcast, the packet contains a destination IP address with all 1s in the host portion. This means that all hosts on that local network (broadcast domain) will receive and look at the packet. Many network protocols, such as DHCP, use broadcasts. When a host receives a packet sent to the network broadcast address, the host processes the packet as it would a packet addressed to its unicast address.

Some examples for using broadcast transmission are

- Mapping upper-layer addresses to lower-layer addresses.

- Requesting an address.

- Unlike unicast, where the packets can be routed throughout the internetwork, broadcast packets are usually restricted to the local network. This restriction is dependent on the configuration of the gateway router and the type of broadcast. There are two types of broadcasts: *directed broadcast* and *limited broadcast*.

Directed Broadcast

A directed broadcast is sent to all hosts on a specific network. This type of broadcast is useful for sending a broadcast to all hosts on a nonlocal network. For example, for a host outside of the 172.16.4.0/24 network to communicate with all the hosts within that network, the destination address of the packet would be 172.16.4.255. With a default configuration, Cisco routers do not forward directed broadcasts. However, they can be configured to do so.

Limited Broadcast

These packets always use a destination IPv4 address 255.255.255.255. Routers do not forward a limited broadcast. For this reason, an IPv4 network is also referred to as a broadcast domain. Routers form the boundary for a broadcast domain.

As an example, a host within the 172.16.4.0/24 network would broadcast to all hosts in its network using a packet with a destination address of 255.255.255.255. This type of communication is shown in Figure 8-7, where host 172.16.4.1 is communicating to all the hosts in the network using broadcast.

Figure 8-7   Broadcast Communication

When a packet is broadcast, it uses resources on the network and causes every receiving host on the network to process the packet. Therefore, broadcast traffic should be limited so that it does not adversely affect performance of the network or devices. Because routers separate broadcast domains, subdividing networks with excessive broadcast traffic can improve network performance.

Multicast Transmission (8.1.3.5)

This section presents IPv4 multicast addressing and communication.

Multicast Transmission

Multicast transmission is designed to conserve the bandwidth of an IPv4 network. It reduces traffic by allowing a host to send a single packet to a selected set of hosts that are part of a subscribing multicast group. To reach multiple destination hosts using unicast communication, a source host would need to send an individual packet addressed to each host. With multicast, the source host can send a single packet that can reach thousands of destination hosts. The internetwork's responsibility is to replicate the multicast flows in an efficient manner so that they reach only their intended recipients.

Some examples of multicast transmission are

- Video and audio broadcasts
- Routing information exchange by routing protocols
- Distribution of software
- Remote gaming

Multicast Addresses

IPv4 has a block of addresses reserved for addressing multicast groups. This address range is 224.0.0.0 to 239.255.255.255. The multicast address range is subdivided into different types of addresses: reserved link-local addresses and globally scoped addresses. One additional type of multicast address is the administratively scoped address, also called the limited scope address.

The IPv4 multicast addresses 224.0.0.0 to 224.0.0.255 are reserved link-local addresses. These addresses are to be used for multicast groups on a local network. A router connected to the local network recognizes that these packets are addressed to a link-local multicast group and never forwards them farther. A typical use of reserved link-local addresses is in routing protocols using multicast transmission to exchange routing information.

The globally scoped addresses are 224.0.1.0 to 238.255.255.255. They can be used to multicast data across the Internet. For example, 224.0.1.1 has been reserved for the Network Time Protocol (NTP) to synchronize the time-of-day clocks of network devices.

Multicast Clients

Hosts that receive particular multicast data are called **multicast clients**. The multicast clients use services requested by a client program to subscribe to the multicast group.

Each multicast group is represented by a single IPv4 multicast destination address. When an IPv4 host subscribes to a multicast group, the host processes packets addressed to this multicast address, as well as packets addressed to its uniquely allocated unicast address.

In the multicast communication shown in Figure 8-8, the source host A, with the address 172.16.4.1, creates a single packet addressed to the multicast address 224.10.10.5. In this example, host C and host D have an application or service running that subscribes to this multicast group. When a copy of this packet arrives, these devices will process the packet.

Figure 8-8   Multicast Communication

Interactive Graphic

Activity 8.1.3.6: Unicast, Broadcast, or Multicast

Go to the course online to perform this practice activity.

Interactive Graphic

Activity 8.1.3.7: Calculate the Network, Broadcast, and Host Addresses

Go to the course online to perform this practice activity.

Packet Tracer ☐ Activity

Packet Tracer Activity 8.1.3.8: Investigate Unicast, Broadcast, and Multicast Traffic

This activity will examine unicast, broadcast, and multicast behavior. Most traffic in a network is unicast. When a PC sends an ICMP echo request to a remote router, the source address in the IP packet header is the IP address of the sending PC. The destination address in the IP packet header is the IP address of the interface on the remote router. The packet is sent only to the intended destination.

Using the **ping** command or the Add Complex PDU feature of Packet Tracer, you can directly ping broadcast addresses to view broadcast traffic.

For multicast traffic, you will view Enhanced Interior Gateway Routing Protocol (EIGRP) traffic. EIGRP is used by Cisco routers to exchange routing information between routers. Routers using EIGRP send packets to multicast address 224.0.0.10, which represents the group of EIGRP routers. Although these packets are received by other devices, they are dropped at Layer 3 by all devices except EIGRP routers, with no other processing required.

Types of IPv4 Addresses (8.1.4)

This section will introduce the different types and uses of IPv4 addresses.

Public and Private IPv4 Addresses (8.1.4.1)

Although most IPv4 host addresses are *public addresses* designated for use in networks that are accessible on the Internet, there are blocks of addresses that are used in networks that require limited or no Internet access. These addresses are called *private addresses*.

Private Addresses

The private address blocks are

> 10.0.0.0 to 10.255.255.255 (10.0.0.0/8)
>
> 172.16.0.0 to 172.31.255.255 (172.16.0.0/12)
>
> 192.168.0.0 to 192.168.255.255 (192.168.0.0/16)

Private addresses are defined in RFC 1918, Address Allocation for Private Internets, and are sometimes referred to as RFC 1918 addresses. Private space address blocks are used in private networks. Hosts that do not require access to the Internet can use private addresses. However, within the private network, hosts still require unique IP addresses within the private space.

Hosts in different networks can use the same private space addresses. Packets using these addresses as the source or destination should not appear on the public Internet. The router or firewall device at the perimeter of these private networks must block or translate these addresses. Even if these packets were to make their way to the Internet, the routers would not have routes to forward them to the appropriate private network.

In RFC 6598, the Internet Assigned Numbers Authority (IANA) reserved another group of addresses known as shared address space. Similar to RFC 1918 private address space, shared address space addresses are not globally routable. However, these addresses are intended only for use in service provider networks. The shared address block is 100.64.0.0/10.

Public Addresses

The vast majority of the addresses in the IPv4 unicast host range are public addresses. These addresses are designed to be used in the hosts that are publicly accessible from the Internet. Even within these IPv4 address blocks, there are many addresses that are designated for other special purposes.

Interactive Graphic

Activity 8.1.4.2: Pass or Block IPv4 Addresses

Go to the course online to perform this practice activity.

Special-Use IPv4 Addresses (8.1.4.3)

There are certain addresses that cannot be assigned to hosts. There are also special addresses that can be assigned to hosts, but with restrictions on how those hosts can interact within the network.

Network and Broadcast Addresses

As explained earlier, within each network, the first and last addresses cannot be assigned to hosts. These are the network address and the broadcast address, respectively.

Loopback

One such reserved address is the IPv4 loopback address 127.0.0.1. The loopback is a special address that hosts use to direct traffic to themselves. The loopback address creates a shortcut method for TCP/IP applications and services that run on the same device to communicate with one another. By using the loopback address instead of the assigned IPv4 host address, two services on the same host can bypass the lower layers of the TCP/IP stack. You can also ping the loopback address to test the configuration of TCP/IP on the local host.

Although only the single 127.0.0.1 address is used, addresses 127.0.0.0 to 127.255.255.255 are reserved. Any address within this block will loop back to the local host. No address within this block should ever appear on any network.

Link-Local Addresses

IPv4 addresses in the address block 169.254.0.0 to 169.254.255.255 (169.254.0.0/16) are designated as *link-local addresses*. These addresses can be automatically assigned to the local host by the operating system in environments where no IP configuration is available. These might be used in a small peer-to-peer network or for a host that could not automatically obtain an address from a DHCP server.

Communication using IPv4 link-local addresses is only suitable for communication with other devices connected to the same network. A host must not send a packet with an IPv4 link-local destination address to any router for forwarding and should set the IPv4 time to live (TTL) for these packets to 1.

Link-local addresses do not provide services outside of the local network. However, many client/server and peer-to-peer applications will work properly with IPv4 link-local addresses.

TEST-NET Addresses

The address block 192.0.2.0 to 192.0.2.255 (192.0.2.0/24) is set aside for teaching and learning purposes. These *TEST-NET addresses* can be used in documentation and network examples. Unlike the experimental addresses, network devices will accept these addresses in their configurations. You can often find these addresses used with the domain names example.com or example.net in RFCs and vendor and protocol documentation. Addresses within this block should not appear on the Internet.

Experimental Addresses

The addresses in the block 240.0.0.0 to 255.255.255.254 are listed as reserved for future use (RFC 3330). Currently, these addresses can only be used for research or experimentation purposes, but cannot be used in an IPv4 network. Though, according to RFC 3330, they could, technically, be converted to usable addresses in the future.

Table 8-8 is a summary of the reserved and special-purpose IPv4 addresses presented in this section. These do not represent all the special address blocks used in IPv4 networks. Additionally, the status of these blocks can be changed. You should consult the RFCs for any changes.

Table 8-8   Major Reserved and Special-Purpose IPv4 Addresses

Type	Block	Range	Reference
Multicast	224.0.0.0 /4	224.0.0.0 – 239.255.255.255	RFC 1700
Network address	—	—	One per network
Broadcast	—	—	One per network plus 255.255.255.255
Experimental addresses	240.0.0.0 /4	240.0.0.0 – 255.255.255.254	RFC 3330
Private space addresses	10.0.0.0 /8	10.0.0.0 – 10.255.255.255	RFC 1918
	172.16.0.0 /12	172.16.0.0 – 172.31.255.255	
	192.168.0.0 /16	192.168.0.0 – 192.168.255.255	
Default route	0.0.0.0 /0*	0.0.0.0	RFC 1700
Loopback	127.0.0.0 /8	127.0.0.0 – 127.255.255.255	RFC 1700
Link-local addresses	169.254.0.0. /16	169.254.0.0 – 169.254.255.255	RFC 3927
TEST-NET addresses	192.0.2.0 /24	192.0.2.0 – 192.0.2.255	—

*The default address is represented by 0.0.0.0 0.0.0.0. While this would normally cover the entire IPv4 address range, only the specific address 0.0.0.0 is used.

Legacy Classful Addressing (8.1.4.4)

Historically, RFC 1700, Assigned Numbers, grouped the unicast ranges into specific sizes called class A, class B, and class C addresses. It also defined class D (multicast) and class E (experimental) addresses, as previously presented. The unicast address classes A, B, and C defined specifically sized networks and specific address blocks for these networks. A company or organization was assigned an entire network from a class A, class B, or class C address block. This use of address space is referred to as *classful addressing*.

Class A Blocks

A class A address block was designed to support extremely large networks with more than 16 million host addresses. Class A IPv4 addresses used a fixed /8 prefix with the first octet to indicate the network address. The remaining three octets were used for host addresses. All class A addresses required that the most significant bit of the high-order octet be a 0. This meant that there were only 128 possible class A networks, 0.0.0.0/8 to 127.0.0.0/8. Even though the class A addresses reserved one-half of the address space, because of their limit of 128 networks, they could only be allocated to approximately 120 companies or organizations.

Class B Blocks

Class B address space was designed to support the needs of moderate- to large-size networks with up to approximately 65,000 hosts. A class B IP address used the two high-order octets to indicate the network address. The other two octets specified host addresses. As with class A, address space for the remaining address classes needed to be reserved. For class B addresses, the most significant 2 bits of the high-order octet were 10. This restricted the address block for class B to 128.0.0.0/16 to 191.255.0.0/16. Class B had slightly more efficient allocation of addresses than class A because it equally divided 25 percent of the total IPv4 address space among approximately 16,000 networks.

Class C Blocks

The class C address space was the most commonly available of the historic address classes. This address space was intended to provide addresses for small networks with a maximum of 254 hosts. Class C address blocks used a /24 prefix. This meant that a class C network used only the last octet as host addresses with the three high-order octets used to indicate the network address. Class C address blocks set aside address space by using a fixed value of 110 for the 3 most significant bits of the high-order octet. This restricted the address block for class C from 192.0.0.0/24 to 223.255.255.0/24. Although it occupied only 12.5 percent of the total IPv4 address space, it could provide addresses to 2 million networks.

Limits to the Class-Based System

Not all organizations' requirements fit well into one of these three classes. Classful allocation of address space often wasted many addresses, which exhausted the availability of IPv4 addresses. For example, a company that had a network with 260 hosts would need to be given a class B address with more than 65,000 addresses.

Even though this classful system was all but abandoned in the late 1990s, you will see remnants of it in networks today. For example, when you assign an IPv4 address to a computer, the operating system examines the address being assigned to determine whether this address is a class A, class B, or class C. The operating system then assumes the prefix used by that class and makes the default subnet mask assignment.

Classless Addressing

The system in use today is referred to as *classless addressing*. The formal name is Classless Inter-Domain Routing (CIDR, pronounced "cider"). The classful allocation of IPv4 addresses was very inefficient, allowing only /8, /16, or /24 prefix lengths, each from a separate address space. In 1993, the Internet Engineering Task Force (IETF) created a new set of standards that allowed service providers to allocate IPv4 addresses on any address bit boundary (prefix length) instead of only by a class A, B, or C address.

The IETF knew that CIDR was only a temporary solution and that a new IP protocol would have to be developed to accommodate the rapid growth in the number of Internet users. In 1994, the IETF began its work to find a successor to IPv4, which eventually became IPv6.

Table 8-9 illustrates the classful address ranges.

Table 8-9   Legacy IPv4 Address Classes

Address Class	First Octet Range (Decimal)	First Octet Bits (Bold Bits Do Not Change)	Network (N) and Host (H) Parts of Address	Default Subnet Mask (Decimal)	Number of Possible Network and Hosts per Network
A	1–127	00000000-01111111	N.H.H.H	255.0.0.0	128 networks (2^7) 16,777,214 hosts ($2^{24}-2$)
B	128–191	10000000-10111111	N. N.H.H	255.255.0.0	16,384 networks (2^{14}) 65,534 hosts ($2^{16}-2$)
C	192–223	11000000-11011111	N. N. N.H	255.255.255.0	2,097,150 networks (2^{21}) 254 hosts (2^8-2)
D	224–239	11100000-11101111	—	—	—
E	240–255	11110000-11111111	—	—	—

Note: All 0s and all 1s are invalid host addresses.

Assignment of IP Addresses (8.1.4.5, 8.1.4.6)

For a company or organization to have network hosts, such as web servers, accessible from the Internet, that organization must have a block of public addresses assigned. Remember that public addresses must be unique, and use of these public addresses is regulated and allocated to each organization separately. This is true for IPv4 and IPv6 addresses.

IANA and RIRs

The *Internet Assigned Numbers Authority (IANA)* (www.iana.org) manages the allocation of IPv4 and IPv6 addresses. Until the mid-1990s, all IPv4 address space was managed directly by the IANA. At that time, the remaining IPv4 address space was allocated to various other registries to manage for particular purposes or for regional areas. These registration companies are called Regional Internet Registries (RIR).

The major registries are

- AfriNIC (African Network Information Centre) - Africa Region, www.afrinic.net

- APNIC (Asia Pacific Network Information Centre) - Asia/Pacific Region, www.apnic.net

- ARIN (American Registry for Internet Numbers) - North America Region, www.arin.net

- LACNIC (Regional Latin-American and Caribbean IP Address Registry) - Latin America and some Caribbean Islands, www.lacnic.net

- RIPE NCC (Réseaux IP Européens) - Europe, the Middle East, and Central Asia, www.ripe.net

ISPs

RIRs are responsible for allocating IP addresses to the *Internet service providers (ISP)*. Most companies or organizations obtain their IPv4 address blocks from an ISP. An ISP will generally supply a small number of usable IPv4 addresses (for example, 6 or 14) to their customers as a part of their services. Larger blocks of addresses can be obtained based on justification of needs and for additional service costs.

In a sense, the ISP loans or rents these addresses to the organization. If we choose to move our Internet connectivity to another ISP, the new ISP will provide us with addresses from the address blocks that have been provided to it, and our previous ISP returns the blocks loaned to us to its allocation to be loaned to another customer.

IPv6 addresses can be obtained from the ISP or in some cases directly from the RIR. IPv6 addresses and typical address block sizes will be discussed later in this chapter.

ISP Services

To get access to the services of the Internet, we have to connect our data network to the Internet using an Internet service provider (ISP).

ISPs have their own set of internal data networks to manage Internet connectivity and to provide related services. Among the other services that an ISP generally provides to its customers are Domain Name System (DNS) services, email services, and a website. Depending on the level of service required and available, customers use different tiers of an ISP.

ISP Tiers

ISPs are designated by a hierarchy based on their level of connectivity to the Internet backbone. Each lower tier obtains connectivity to the backbone through a connection to a higher-tier ISP.

Tier 1

At the top of the ISP hierarchy are Tier 1 ISPs. These ISPs are large national or international ISPs that are directly connected to the Internet backbone. The customers of Tier 1 ISPs are either lower-tiered ISPs or large companies and organizations. Because they are at the top of Internet connectivity, they engineer highly reliable connections and services. Among the technologies used to support this reliability are multiple connections to the Internet backbone.

The primary advantages for customers of Tier 1 ISPs are reliability and speed. Because these customers are only one connection away from the Internet, there are fewer opportunities for failures or traffic bottlenecks. The drawback for Tier 1 ISP customers is its high cost.

Tier 2

Tier 2 ISPs acquire their Internet service from Tier 1 ISPs. Tier 2 ISPs generally focus on business customers. Tier 2 ISPs usually offer more services than the other two tiers of ISPs. These Tier 2 ISPs tend to have the IT resources to operate their own services such as DNS, email servers, and web servers. Other services that Tier 2 ISPs might offer include website development and maintenance, e-commerce/e-business, and VoIP.

The primary disadvantage of Tier 2 ISPs, as compared to Tier 1 ISPs, is slower Internet access. Because Tier 2 ISPs are at least one more connection away from the Internet backbone, they also tend to have lower reliability than Tier 1 ISPs.

Tier 3

Tier 3 ISPs purchase their Internet service from Tier 2 ISPs. The focus of these ISPs is the retail and home markets in a specific locale. Tier 3 customers typically do not need many of the services required by Tier 2 customers. Their primary need is connectivity and support.

These customers often have little or no computer or network expertise. Tier 3 ISPs often bundle Internet connectivity as a part of network and computer service contracts for their customers. While they might have reduced bandwidth and less reliability than Tier 1 and Tier 2 providers, they are often good choices for small- to medium-size companies.

Activity 8.1.4.7: Public or Private IPv4 Addresses

Go to the course online to perform this practice activity.

Lab 8.1.4.8: Identifying IPv4 Addresses

In this lab, you will complete the following objectives:

- Part 1: Identify IPv4 Addresses
- Part 2: Classify IPv4 Addresses

IPv6 Network Addresses (8.2)

This section will introduce IPv6.

IPv4 Issues (8.2.1)

The useful life of IPv4 has almost been reached. This section will examine the reasons for the migration to IPv6.

The Need for IPv6 (8.2.1.1)

IPv6 is designed to be the successor to IPv4. IPv6 has a larger 128-bit address space, providing for 340 undecillion addresses (that is the number 340, followed by 36 zeroes). However, IPv6 is much more than just larger addresses. When the IETF began its development of a successor to IPv4, it used this opportunity to fix the limitations of IPv4 and include additional enhancements. One example is Internet Control Message Protocol version 6 (ICMPv6), which includes address resolution and address autoconfiguration not found in ICMP for IPv4 (ICMPv4). ICMPv4 and ICMPv6 will be discussed later in this chapter.

Need for IPv6

The depletion of IPv4 address space has been the motivating factor for moving to IPv6. As Africa, Asia, and other areas of the world become more connected to the Internet, there are not enough IPv4 addresses to accommodate this growth. On Monday, January 31, 2011, the IANA allocated the last two /8 IPv4 address blocks to the Regional Internet Registries (RIR). Various projections show that all five RIRs will have run out of IPv4 addresses between 2013 and 2020. At that point, the remaining IPv4 addresses will have been allocated to ISPs.

IPv4 has a theoretical maximum of 4.3 billion addresses. RFC 1918 private addresses in combination with Network Address Translation (NAT) have been instrumental in slowing the depletion of IPv4 address space. NAT has limitations that severely impede peer-to-peer communications.

Internet of Things

The Internet of today is significantly different than the Internet of past decades. The Internet of today is more than email, web pages, and file transfer between computers. The evolving Internet is becoming an Internet of things. No longer will the only devices accessing the Internet be computers, tablets and smartphones. The sensor-equipped, Internet-ready devices of tomorrow will include everything from automobiles and biomedical devices to household appliances and natural ecosystems. Imagine a meeting at a customer site that is automatically scheduled on your calendar application to begin an hour before you normally start work. This could be a significant problem, especially if you forget to check the calendar or adjust the alarm clock accordingly. Now imagine that the calendar application communicates this information directly to your alarm clock for you and to your automobile. Your car automatically warms up to melt the ice on the windshield before you enter the car and reroutes you to your meeting.

With an increasing Internet population, a limited IPv4 address space, issues with NAT and an Internet of things, the time has come to begin the transition to IPv6.

IPv4 and IPv6 Coexistence (8.2.1.2)

There is not a single date to move to IPv6. For the foreseeable future, both IPv4 and IPv6 will coexist. The transition is expected to take years. The IETF has created various protocols and tools to help network administrators migrate their networks to IPv6. The migration techniques can be divided into three categories:

- **Dual-stack:** As shown in Figure 8-9a, dual-stack allows IPv4 and IPv6 to coexist on the same network. Dual-stack devices run both IPv4 and IPv6 protocol stacks simultaneously.

- **Tunneling:** As shown in Figure 8-9b, tunneling is a method of transporting an IPv6 packet over an IPv4 network. The IPv6 packet is encapsulated inside an IPv4 packet, similar to other types of data.

- **Translation:** As shown in Figure 8-9c, Network Address Translation 64 (NAT64) allows IPv6-enabled devices to communicate with IPv4-enabled devices using a translation technique similar to NAT for IPv4. An IPv6 packet is translated to an IPv4 packet and vice versa.

Figure 8-9   IPv4 and IPv6 Coexistence Methods

Interactive
Graphic

Activity 8.2.1.3: IPv4 Issues and Solutions

Go to the course online to perform this practice activity.

IPv6 Addressing (8.2.2)

At their core, both IPv4 and IPv6 are binary. However, to make it easier to work with the expanded address range of IPv6, these addresses are represented differently. This section will present the representation of IPv6 addresses.

Hexadecimal Number System (8.2.2.1)

Unlike IPv4 addresses that are expressed in dotted-decimal notation, IPv6 addresses are represented using hexadecimal values. You have seen hexadecimal used in the Packets Byte pane of Wireshark. In Wireshark, hexadecimal is used to represent the binary values within frames and packets. Hexadecimal is also used to represent Ethernet Media Access Control (MAC) addresses.

Hexadecimal Numbering

Hexadecimal ("hex") is a convenient way to represent binary values. Just as decimal is a base 10 numbering system and binary is base 2, hexadecimal is a base 16 system.

The base 16 numbering system uses the numbers 0 to 9 and the letters A to F. Table 8-10 shows the equivalent decimal, binary, and hexadecimal values. There are 16 unique combinations of 4 bits, from 0000 to 1111. The 16-digit hexadecimal is the perfect number system to use, because any 4 bits can be represented with a single hexadecimal value.

Table 8-10   Hexadecimal Numbers

Hexadecimal	Decimal	Binary
0	0	0000
1	1	0001
2	2	0010
3	3	0011
4	4	0100
5	5	0101
6	6	0110
7	7	0111

Hexadecimal	Decimal	Binary
8	8	1000
9	9	1001
A	10	1010
B	11	1011
C	12	1100
D	13	1101
E	14	1110
F	15	1111

Understanding Bytes

Given that 8 bits (a byte) is a common binary grouping, binary 00000000 to 11111111 can be represented in hexadecimal as the range from 00 to FF. Leading 0s can be displayed to complete the 8-bit representation. For example, the binary value 0000 1010 is shown in hexadecimal as 0A.

Representing Hexadecimal Values

Note

It is important to distinguish hexadecimal values from decimal values regarding the characters 0 to 9.

Hexadecimal is usually represented in text by the value preceded by 0x (for example 0x73) or a subscript 16. Less commonly, it can be followed by an H, for example 73H. However, because subscript text is not recognized in command-line or programming environments, the technical representation of hexadecimal is preceded with "0x" (zero X). Therefore, the previous examples would be shown as 0x0A and 0x73, respectively.

Hexadecimal Conversions

Number conversions between decimal and hexadecimal values are straightforward, but quickly dividing or multiplying by 16 is not always convenient. With practice, it is possible to recognize the binary bit patterns that match the decimal and hexadecimal values.

IPv6 Address Representation (8.2.2.2)

IPv6 addresses are 128 bits in length and written as a string of hexadecimal values. Every 4 bits is represented by a single hexadecimal digit, for a total of 32 hexadecimal values. IPv6 addresses are not case sensitive and can be written in either lowercase or uppercase.

Preferred Format

As shown in Figure 8-10, the preferred format for writing an IPv6 address is x:x:x:x:x:x:x:x, with each "x" consisting of four hexadecimal values. When referring to 8 bits of an IPv4 address, we use the term *octet*. In IPv6, a *hextet* is the unofficial term used to refer to a segment of 16 bits or four hexadecimal values. Each "x" is a single hextet, 16 bits, or four hexadecimal digits.

Preferred format means that the IPv6 address is written using all 32 hexadecimal digits. It does not necessarily mean that it is the ideal method for representing the IPv6 address. In the following pages, we will see two rules to help reduce the number of digits needed to represent an IPv6 address.

Figure 8-10   IPv6 Preferred Format

Some examples of IPv6 addresses in the preferred format are

```
2001:0DB8:0000:1111:0000:0000:0000:0200
FE80:0000:0000:0000:0123:4567:89AB:CDEF
FF02:0000:0000:0000:0000:0000:0001:FF00:0200
0000:0000:0000:0000:0000:0000:0000:0001
```

Rule 1: Omit Leading 0s (8.2.2.3)

The first rule to help reduce the notation of IPv6 addresses is that any leading 0s in any 16-bit section or hextet can be omitted. For example:

- 01AB can be represented as 1AB.

- 09F0 can be represented as 9F0.

- 0A00 can be represented as A00.

- 00AB can be represented as AB.

This rule only applies to leading 0s, *not* to trailing 0s; otherwise, the address would be ambiguous. For example, the hextet "ABC" could be either "0ABC" or "ABC0."

Table 8-11 shows several examples of how omitting leading 0s can be used to reduce the size of an IPv6 address. For each example, the preferred format is shown. Notice how omitting the leading 0s in most examples results in a smaller address representation.

Table 8-11   IPv6 Addresses Omitting Leading 0s

Preferred	No Leading 0s
2001:0DB8:0000:1111:0000:0000:0000:0200	2001: DB8: 0:1111: 0: 0: 0:200
FE80:0000:0000:0000:0123:4567:89AB:CDEF	FE80: 0: 0: 0: 123:4567:89AB:CDEF
FF02:0000:0000:0000:0000:0001:FF00:0200	FF02: 0: 0: 0: 0: 1:FF00: 200
0000:0000:0000:0000:0000:0000:0000:0001	0: 0: 0: 0: 0: 0: 0: 1

Rule 2: Omit All 0 Segments (8.2.2.4)

The second rule to help reduce the notation of IPv6 addresses is that a double colon (::) can replace any single, contiguous string of one or more 16-bit segments (hextets) consisting of all 0s.

The double colon (::) can only be used once within an address; otherwise, there would be more than one possible resulting address. When used with the omitting leading 0s technique, the notation of IPv6 address can often be greatly reduced. This is commonly known as the compressed format.

Here is an incorrect address:

- 2001:0DB8::ABCD::1234

Possible expansions of the ambiguous compressed address are

- 2001:0DB8::ABCD:0000:0000:1234

- 2001:0DB8::ABCD:0000:0000:0000:1234

- 2001:0DB8:0000:ABCD::1234

- 2001:0DB8:0000:0000:ABCD::1234

Table 8-12 shows several examples of how using the double colon (::) and omitting leading 0s can reduce the size of an IPv6 address.

Table 8-12   IPv6 Addresses Using Double Colons

Preferred	No Leading 0s
2001:0DB8:0000:1111:0000:0000:0000:0200	2001:DB8:0:1111::200
FE80:0000:0000:0000:0123:4567:89AB:CDEF	FE80::123:4567:89AB:CDEF
FF02:0000:0000:0000:0000:0001:FF00:0200	FF02::1:FF00:200
0000:0000:0000:0000:0000:0000:0000:0001	::1

Interactive Graphic

Activity 8.2.2.5: Practicing IPv6 Address Representations

Go to the course online to perform this practice activity.

Types of IPv6 Addresses (8.2.3)

This section will introduce the different types and uses of IPv6 addresses.

IPv6 Address Types (8.2.3.1)

There are three types of IPv6 addresses:

- **Unicast:** An IPv6 unicast address uniquely identifies an interface on an IPv6-enabled device. A source IPv6 address must be a unicast address.

- **Multicast:** An IPv6 multicast address is used to send a single IPv6 packet to multiple destinations.

- **Anycast:** An IPv6 anycast address is any IPv6 unicast address that can be assigned to multiple devices. A packet sent to an anycast address is routed to the nearest device having that address. Anycast addresses are beyond the scope of this course.

Unlike IPv4, IPv6 does not have a broadcast address. However, there is an IPv6 all-nodes multicast address that essentially gives the same result.

IPv6 Prefix Length (8.2.3.2)

Recall that the prefix, or network, portion of an IPv4 address can be identified by a dotted-decimal subnet mask or prefix length (slash notation). For example, an IP address of 192.168.1.10 with dotted-decimal subnet mask 255.255.255.0 is equivalent to 192.168.1.10/24.

IPv6 uses the prefix length to represent the prefix portion of the address. IPv6 does not use the dotted-decimal subnet mask notation. The prefix length is used to indicate the network portion of an IPv6 address using the IPv6 address/prefix length.

The prefix length can range from 0 to 128. A typical IPv6 prefix length for LANs and most other types of networks is /64. This means that the prefix or network portion of the address is 64 bits in length, leaving another 64 bits for the interface ID (host portion) of the address.

IPv6 Unicast Addresses (8.2.3.3)

An IPv6 unicast address uniquely identifies an interface on an IPv6-enabled device. A packet sent to a unicast address is received by the interface that is assigned that address. Similar to IPv4, a source IPv6 address must be a unicast address. The destination IPv6 address can be either a unicast or a multicast address.

There are six types of IPv6 unicast addresses, described in the following sections.

Global Unicast

A global unicast address is similar to a public IPv4 address. These are globally unique, Internet routable addresses. Global unicast addresses can be configured statically or assigned dynamically. There are some important differences in how a device receives its IPv6 address dynamically compared to DHCP for IPv4.

Link-Local

Link-local addresses are used to communicate with other devices on the same local link. With IPv6, the term *link* refers to a subnet. Link-local addresses are confined to a single link. Their uniqueness must only be confirmed on that link because they are not routable beyond the link. In other words, routers will not forward packets with a link-local source or destination address.

Loopback

The loopback address is used by a host to send a packet to itself and cannot be assigned to a physical interface. Similar to an IPv4 loopback address, you can ping an IPv6 loopback address to test the configuration of TCP/IP on the local host. The IPv6 loopback address is all-0s except for the last bit, represented as ::1/128, or just ::1 in the compressed format.

Unspecified Address

An *unspecified address* is an all-0s address represented in the compressed format as ::/128, or just :: in the compressed format. It cannot be assigned to an interface and is only to be used as a source address in an IPv6 packet. An unspecified address is used as a source address when the device does not yet have a permanent IPv6 address or when the source of the packet is irrelevant to the destination.

Unique Local

IPv6 unique local addresses have some similarity to RFC 1918 private addresses for IPv4, but there are significant differences as well. *Unique local addresses* are used for local addressing within a site or between a limited number of sites. These addresses should not be routable in the global IPv6. Unique local addresses are in the range of FC00::/7 to FDFF::/7.

With IPv4, private addresses are combined with NAT/PAT to provide a many-to-one translation of private to public addresses. This is done because of the limited availability of IPv4 address space. Many sites also use the private nature of RFC 1918 addresses to help secure or hide their network from potential security risks. However, this was never the intended use of these technologies, and the IETF has always recommended that sites take the proper security precautions on their Internet-facing router. Although IPv6 does provide site-specific addressing, it is not intended to be used to help hide internal IPv6-enabled devices from the IPv6 Internet. IETF recommends that limiting access to devices should be accomplished using proper, best-practice security measures.

Note

The original IPv6 specification defined site-local addresses for a similar purpose, using the prefix range FEC0::/10. There were several ambiguities in the specification, and site-local addresses were deprecated by the IETF in favor of unique local addresses.

IPv4 embedded

The last type of unicast address type is the IPv4 embedded address. These addresses are used to help transition from IPv4 to IPv6. IPv4 embedded addresses are beyond the scope of this course.

IPv6 Link-Local Unicast Addresses (8.2.3.4)

An IPv6 link-local address enables a device to communicate with other IPv6-enabled devices on the same link and only on that link (subnet). Packets with a source or destination link-local address cannot be routed beyond the link from where the packet originated.

Unlike IPv4 link-local addresses, IPv6 link-local addresses have a significant role in various aspects of the network. The global unicast address is not a requirement; however, every IPv6-enabled network interface is required to have a link-local address.

If a link-local address is not configured manually on an interface, the device will automatically create its own without communicating with a DHCP server. IPv6-enabled hosts create an IPv6 link-local address even if the device has not been assigned a global unicast IPv6 address. This allows IPv6-enabled devices to communicate with other IPv6-enabled devices on the same subnet. This includes communication with the default gateway (router).

IPv6 link-local addresses are in the FE80::/10 range. The /10 indicates that the first 10 bits are 1111 1110 10xx xxxx. The first hextet has a range of 1111 1110 10**00 0000** (FE80) to 1111 1110 10**11 1111** (FEBF).

Figure 8-11 shows the format of an IPv6 link-local address.

Figure 8-11   IPv6 Link-Local Address

IPv6 link-local addresses are also used by IPv6 routing protocols to exchange messages and as the next-hop address in the IPv6 routing table. Link-local addresses are discussed in more detail in a later course.

Note

Typically, it is the link-local address of the router and not the global unicast address that is used as the default gateway for other devices on the link.

Activity 8.2.3.5: Identify Types of IPv6 Addresses

Go to the course online to perform this practice activity.

IPv6 Unicast Addresses (8.2.4)

This section will introduce IPv6 unicast addressing.

Structure of an IPv6 Global Unicast Address (8.2.4.1)

IPv6 global unicast addresses are globally unique and routable on the IPv6 Internet. These addresses are equivalent to public IPv4 addresses. The Internet Committee for Assigned Names and Numbers (ICANN), the operator for the Internet Assigned Numbers Authority (IANA), allocates IPv6 address blocks to the five RIRs. Currently, only global unicast addresses with the first three bits of 001 or 2000::/3 are being assigned. This is only 1/8th of the total available IPv6 address space, excluding only a very small portion for other types of unicast and multicast addresses.

Note

The 2001:0DB8::/32 address has been reserved for documentation purposes, including use in examples.

Figure 8-12 shows the structure and range of a global unicast address.

A global unicast address has three parts:

- Global routing prefix
- Subnet ID
- Interface ID

Figure 8-12   Parts of a IPv6 Global Unicast Address

Global Routing Prefix

The global routing prefix is the prefix, or network, portion of the address that is assigned by the provider, such as an ISP, to a customer or site. Currently, RIRs assign a /48 global routing prefix to customers. This includes everyone from enterprise business networks to individual households. This is more than enough address space for most customers.

Figure 8-13 shows the structure of a global unicast address using a /48 global routing prefix. /48 prefixes are the most common global routing prefixes assigned and will be used in most of the examples throughout this course.

Figure 8-13   Division of an IPv6 Global Unicast Address

For example, the IPv6 address 2001:0DB8:ACAD::/48 has a prefix that indicates that the first 48 bits (3 hextets) (2001:0DB8:ACAD) is the prefix or network portion of the address. The double colon (::) prior to the /48 prefix length means that the rest of the address contains all 0s.

Subnet ID

The subnet ID is used by an organization to identify subnets within its site.

Interface ID

The IPv6 interface ID is equivalent to the host portion of an IPv4 address. The term *interface ID* is used because a single host can have multiple interfaces, each having one or more IPv6 addresses.

Note

Unlike IPv4, in IPv6, the all-0s address can be assigned to a device. However, the all-0s address is reserved as a Subnet-Router anycast address, and should be assigned only to routers.

An easy way to read most IPv6 addresses is to count the number of hextets. As shown in Figure 8-14, in a /64 global unicast address, the first four hextets are for the network portion of the address, with the fourth hextet indicating the subnet ID. The remaining four hextets are for the interface ID.

Figure 8-14   Interpreting an IPv6 Global Unicast Address

Static Configuration of a Global Unicast Address (8.2.4.2)

This section will introduce the configuration of IPv6 global unicast addresses.

Router Configuration

Most IPv6 configuration and verification commands in the Cisco IOS are similar to their IPv4 counterparts. In many cases, the only difference is the use of **ipv6** in place of **ip** within the commands.

The **interface** command to configure an IPv6 global unicast address on an interface is **ipv6 address** *ipv6-address/prefix-length*.

Notice that there is not a space between *ipv6-address* and *prefix-length*.

The example configuration will use the topology shown in Figure 8-15 and these IPv6 subnets:

- 2001:0DB8:ACAD:0001:/64 (*or* 2001:DB8:ACAD:1::/64)
- 2001:0DB8:ACAD:0002:/64 (*or* 2001:DB8:ACAD:2::/64)
- 2001:0DB8:ACAD:0003:/64 (*or* 2001:DB8:ACAD:3::/64)

Figure 8-15   Example IPv6 Topology

Manually configuring the IPv6 address on a host is similar to configuring an IPv4 address. Example 8-4 shows the IPv6 configuration of the router in Figure 8-15.

Example 8-4   Configuration of IPv6 on a Router

```
Router> enable
Router# configure terminal
Enter configuration commands, one per line.  End with CNTL/Z.
Router(config)# interface gigabitethernet 0/0
Router(config-if)# ipv6 address 2001:db8:acad:1::1/64
Router(config-if)# no shutdown

%LINK-5-CHANGED: Interface GigabitEthernet0/0, changed state to up
%LINKPROTO-5-UPDOWN: Line protocol on Interface GigabitEthernet0/0,
  changed state to up


Router(config-if)#
Router(config-if)# interface gigabitethernet 0/1
Router(config-if)# ipv6 address 2001:db8:acad:2::2/64
Router(config-if)# no shutdown

%LINK-5-CHANGED: Interface GigabitEthernet0/1, changed state to up
%LINKPROTO-5-UPDOWN: Line protocol on Interface GigabitEthernet0/1,
  changed state to up

Router(config-if)#
Router(config-if)# interface serial 0/0/0
Router(config-if)# ipv6 address 2001:db8:acad:3::1/64
Router(config-if)# no shutdown

%LINK-5-CHANGED: Interface Serial0/0/0, changed state to up
%LINKPROTO-5-UPDOWN: Line protocol on Interface Serial0/0/0, changed state to up

Router(config-if)# exit

Router(config)# ipv6 unicast-routing
Router(config)# end
Router#
%SYS-5-CONFIG_I: Configured from console by console

Router# copy running-config startup-config
Destination filename [startup-config]?
Building configuration...
[OK]
Router#
```

IPv6 routing is not enabled by default. To enable a router as an IPv6 router, the **ipv6 unicast-routing** global configuration command must be used.

Note

Cisco routers are enabled as IPv4 routers by default.

Figure 8-16 shows the IPv6 configuration of PC1 shown in Figure 8-15. In this configuration, the default gateway address configured for PC1 is 2001:DB8:ACAD:1::1, the global unicast address of the R1 Gigabit Ethernet interface on the same network.

Figure 8-16   IPv6 Configuration of PC1

Just as with IPv4, configuring static addresses on clients does not scale to larger environments. For this reason, most network administrators in an IPv6 network will enable dynamic assignment of IPv6 addresses.

A device can obtain an IPv6 global unicast address automatically in two ways:

- *Stateless Address Autoconfiguration (SLAAC)*
- DHCPv6

Dynamic Configuration of a Global Unicast Address Using SLAAC (8.2.4.3)

This section will introduce the dynamic assignment of IPv6 addresses with Stateless Address Autoconfiguration.

Stateless Address Autoconfiguration

Stateless Address Autoconfiguration (SLAAC) is a method that allows a device to obtain its prefix, prefix length, and default gateway address information from an

IPv6 router without the use of a DHCPv6 server. Using SLAAC, devices rely on the local router's ICMPv6 Router Advertisement (RA) messages to obtain the necessary information.

IPv6 routers periodically send out ICMPv6 RA messages to all IPv6-enabled devices on the network. By default, Cisco routers send out RA messages every 200 seconds to the IPv6 all-nodes multicast group address. An IPv6 device on the network does not have to wait for these periodic RA messages. A device can send a Router Solicitation (RS) message to the router, using the IPv6 all-routers multicast group address. When an IPv6 router receives an RS message, it will immediately respond with a Router Advertisement.

As previously mentioned, even though an interface on a Cisco router can be configured with an IPv6 address, this does not make it an "IPv6 router." When the **ipv6 unicast-routing** global configuration command is used, the router becomes an IPv6 router and can

- Forward IPv6 packets between networks

- Be configured with static IPv6 routes or a dynamic IPv6 routing protocol

- Send ICMPv6 RA messages

The ICMPv6 RA message contains the prefix, prefix length, and other information for the IPv6 device. The RA message also informs the IPv6 device how to obtain its addressing information. The RA message can contain one of the following three options:

- **Option 1 – SLAAC only:** The device should use the prefix, prefix length, and default gateway address information contained in the RA message. No other information is available from a DHCPv6 server.

- **Option 2 – SLAAC and DHCPv6:** The device should use the prefix, prefix length, and default gateway address information in the RA message. There is other information available from a DHCPv6 server, such as the DNS server address. The device will, through the normal process of discovering and querying a DHCPv6 server, obtain this additional information. This is known as stateless DHCPv6 because the DHCPv6 server does not need to allocate or keep track of any IPv6 address assignments, but only provide additional information such as the DNS server address.

- **Option 3 – DHCPv6 only:** The device should not use the information in this RA message for its addressing information. Instead, the device will use the normal process of discovering and querying a DHCPv6 server to obtain all its addressing information. This includes an IPv6 global unicast address, a prefix length, a default gateway address, and the addresses of DNS servers. In this case, the DHCPv6 server is acting as a stateful DHCP server similar to DHCP for IPv4. The DHCPv6 server allocates and keeps track of IPv6 addresses so that it does not assign the same IPv6 address to multiple devices.

Routers send ICMPv6 RA messages using the link-local address as the source IPv6 address. Devices using SLAAC use the router's link-local address as their default gateway address.

Dynamic Configuration of a Global Unicast Address Using DHCPv6 (8.2.4.4)

This section will introduce the dynamic assignment of IPv6 addresses with Dynamic Host Configuration Protocol for IPv6.

DHCPv6

Dynamic Host Configuration Protocol for IPv6 (DHCPv6) is similar to DHCP for IPv4. A device can automatically receive its addressing information, including a global unicast address, prefix length, default gateway address, and the addresses of DNS servers using the services of a DHCPv6 server.

A device can receive all or some of its IPv6 addressing information from a DHCPv6 server depending upon whether Option 2 (SLAAC and DHCPv6) or Option 3 (DHCPv6 only) is specified in the ICMPv6 RA message. Additionally, the host OS can choose to ignore whatever is in the router's RA message and obtain its IPv6 address and other information directly from a DHCPv6 server.

For Option 2 (SLAAC and DHCPv6), the steps are

Step 1. The client sends a Router Solicitation (RS) message to all IPv6 routers requesting addressing information.

Step 2. One or more IPv6 routers send a Router Advertisement (RA) to all IPv6 nodes containing prefix, prefix length, and gateway information.

Step 3. The node requires more IPv6 configuration. Therefore, the node contacts a DHCPv6 server for the remaining configuration.

Before deploying IPv6 devices in a network, it is a good idea to first verify whether the host observes the options within the router's ICMPv6 RA message.

A device can obtain its IPv6 global unicast address dynamically and can also be configured with multiple static IPv6 addresses on the same interface. IPv6 allows multiple IPv6 addresses, belonging to the same IPv6 network, to be configured on the same interface.

A device can also be configured with more than one default gateway IPv6 address. For further information about how the decision is made regarding which address is used as a source IPv6 address or which default gateway address is used, refer to RFC 6724, Default Address Selection for IPv6.

The Interface ID

If the client does not use the information contained within the RA message and relies solely on DHCPv6, the DHCPv6 server will provide the entire IPv6 global unicast address, including the prefix and the interface ID.

However, if Option 1 (SLAAC only) or Option 2 (SLAAC with DHCPv6) is used, the client does not obtain the actual interface ID portion of the address from this process. The client device must determine its own 64-bit interface ID, either by using the EUI-64 process or by generating a random 64-bit number.

EUI-64 Process or Randomly Generated (8.2.4.5)

This section shows how the EUI-64 process uses the MAC address to generate an IPv6 interface ID.

EUI-64 Process

IEEE defined the Extended Unique Identifier (EUI) or modified EUI-64 process. This process uses a client's 48-bit Ethernet MAC address and inserts another 16 bits in the middle of the 48-bit MAC address to create a 64-bit interface ID.

Ethernet MAC addresses are usually represented in hexadecimal and are made up of two parts:

- **Organizationally Unique Identifier (OUI):** The OUI is a 24-bit (6 hexadecimal digits) vendor code assigned by the IEEE.

- **Device identifier:** The device identifier is a unique 24-bit (6 hexadecimal digits) value within a common OUI.

An EUI-64 interface ID is represented in binary and is made up of three parts:

- 24-bit OUI from the client MAC address, but the seventh bit (the Universally/ Locally [U/L] bit) is reversed. This means that if the seventh bit is a 0, it becomes a 1 and vice versa.

- The inserted 16-bit value FFFE (in hexadecimal).

- 24-bit device identifier from the client MAC address.

The EUI-64 process is illustrated in Figure 8-17, using R1's Gigabit Ethernet MAC address of FC99:4775:CEE0.

Step 1.   Divide the MAC address between the OUI and device identifier.

Step 2.   Insert the hexadecimal value FFFE, which in binary is 1111 1111 1111 1110.

Step 3.   Convert the first two hexadecimal values of the OUI to binary and flip the U/L bit (bit 7). In this example, the 0 in bit 7 is changed to a 1.

The result is an EUI-64 generated interface ID of FE99:47FF:FE75:CEE0.

Figure 8-17   EUI-64 Process

Note

The use of the U/L bit and the reasons for reversing its value are discussed in RFC 5342.

The advantage of EUI-64 is that the Ethernet MAC address can be used to determine the interface ID. It also allows network administrators to easily track an IPv6 address to an end device using the unique MAC address. However, this has caused privacy concerns among many users. They are concerned that their packets can be traced to the actual physical computer. Because of these concerns, a randomly generated interface ID can be used instead.

Randomly Generated Interface IDs

Depending upon the operating system, a device might use a randomly generated interface ID instead of using the MAC address and the EUI-64 process. For example, beginning with Windows Vista, Windows uses a randomly generated interface ID instead of one created with EUI-64. Windows XP and previous Windows operating systems used EUI-64.

An easy way to identify that an address was more than likely created using EUI-64 is the FFFE located in the middle of the interface ID, as shown in Example 8-5.

Example 8-5 Configuration of IPv6 on a Router

```
Router# show ipv6 interface brief
GigabitEthernet0/0         [up/up]
    FE80::2D0:58FF:FE75:C3E0
    2001:DB8:1::1
GigabitEthernet0/1         [up/up]
    FE80::2D0:58FF:FE75:C3E1
    2001:DB8:ACAD:2::2
Serial0/0/0                [up/up]
    FE80::240:BFF:FE75:C3E0
    2001:DB8:ACAD:3::1
Serial0/0/1                [administratively down/down]
Vlan1                      [administratively down/down]
  Router#
```

Note

With EUI-64 for interfaces that do not have MAC addresses, such as serial and loopback, the router uses the first MAC address in the device. In Example 8-5, interface Serial 0/0/0 is using the MAC identifier of interface Gigabit Ethernet 0/0.

After the interface ID is established, either through the EUI-64 process or through random generation, it can be combined with an IPv6 prefix to create a global unicast address or a link-local address:

- **Global unicast address:** When using SLAAC, the device receives its prefix from the ICMPv6 RA and combines it with the interface ID.

- **Link-local address:** A link-local prefix begins with FE80::/10. A device typically uses FE80::/64 as the prefix/prefix length, followed by the interface ID.

Dynamic Link-Local Addresses (8.2.4.6)

When using SLAAC (SLAAC only or SLAAC with DHCPV6), a device receives its prefix and prefix length from the ICMPv6 RA. Because the prefix of the address has been designated by the RA message, the device must provide only the interface ID portion of its address. As stated previously, the interface ID can be automatically generated using the EUI-64 process or, depending on the OS, be randomly generated. Using the information from the RA message and the interface ID, the device can establish its global unicast address.

After a global unicast address is assigned to an interface, the IPv6-enabled device will automatically generate its link-local address. IPv6-enabled devices must have, at a minimum, the link-local address. Recall that an IPv6 link-local address enables a device to communicate with other IPv6-enabled devices on the same subnet.

IPv6 link-local addresses are used for a variety of purposes including

- A host uses the link-local address of the local router for its default gateway IPv6 address.

- Routers exchange dynamic routing protocol messages using link-local addresses.

- Routers' routing tables use the link-local address to identify the next-hop router when forwarding IPv6 packets.

A link-local address can be established dynamically or configured manually as a static link-local address.

Dynamically Assigned Link-Local Address

The link-local address is dynamically created using the FE80::/10 prefix and the interface ID.

By default, Cisco IOS routers use EUI-64 to generate the interface ID for all link-local addresses on IPv6 interfaces. For serial interfaces, the router will use the MAC address of an Ethernet interface. Recall that a link-local address must be unique only on that link or network. However, a drawback to using the dynamically assigned link-local address is its length, which makes it challenging to identify and remember assigned addresses.

Static Link-Local Addresses (8.2.4.7)

This section introduces manually configuring the IPv6 link-local addressing.

Static Link-Local Address

Configuring the link-local address manually provides the ability to create an address that is recognizable and easier to remember.

Link-local addresses can be configured manually using the same interface command used to create IPv6 global unicast addresses but with an additional parameter:

```
Router(config-if)# ipv6 address link-local-address link-local
```

Example 8-6 shows that a link-local address has a prefix within the range of FE80 to FEBF. When an address begins with this hextet (16-bit segment), the link-local parameter must follow the address. Also, shown in Example 8-6 is the configuration of a link-local address using the **ipv6 address interface** command. The link-local address FE80::1 is used to make it easily recognizable as belonging to Router R1. The same IPv6 link-local address is configured on all of R1's interfaces. FE80::1 can be configured on each link because it only has to be unique on that link.

Example 8-6   Configuration and Verification of IPv6 Link-Local Address

```
Router# configure terminal
Enter configuration commands, one per line.  End with CNTL/Z.
R1(config)# interface gigabitethernet 0/0
R1(config-if)# ipv6 address FE80::1 ?
  link-local  Use link-local address
R1(config-if)# ipv6 address FE80::1 link-local
R1(config-if)# no shutdown

%LINK-5-CHANGED: Interface GigabitEthernet0/0, changed state to up
R1(config-if)# exit

R1(config)# interface gigabitethernet 0/1
R1(config-if)# ipv6 address FE80::1 link-local
R1(config-if)# no shutdown

%LINK-5-CHANGED: Interface GigabitEthernet0/1, changed state to up
R1(config-if)# exit

R1(config)# interface serial 0/0/0
R1(config-if)# ipv6 address FE80::1 link-local
R1(config-if)# no shutdown

%LINK-5-CHANGED: Interface Serial0/0/0, changed state to down
R1(config-if)# end

R1(config-if)# exit

R1(config)# ipv6 unicast-routing
R1(config)# end
R1#

R1# show ipv6 interface brief
GigabitEthernet0/0          [up/up]
    FE80::1
GigabitEthernet0/1          [up/up]
    FE80::1
```

```
Serial0/0/0                [up/up]
    FE80::1
Serial0/0/1                [administratively down/down]
Vlan1                      [administratively down/down]
  R1#
```

Verifying IPv6 Address Configuration (8.2.4.8)

As shown in Example 8-6, the commands to verify the IPv6 interface configuration, IPv6 routes, and IPv6 connectivity are similar to the commands used for IPv4.

The **show ipv6 interface brief** command displays abbreviated output for each of the interfaces. The [up/up] output on the same line as the interface indicates the Layer 1/ Layer 2 interface state. This is the same as the Status and Protocol columns in the equivalent IPv4 command.

Notice that each interface has two IPv6 addresses. The second address for each interface is the global unicast address that was configured. The first address, the one that begins with FE80, is the link-local unicast address for the interface. Recall that the link-local address is automatically added to the interface when a global unicast address is assigned.

Also, notice that R1's Serial 0/0/0 link-local address is the same as its Gigabit Ethernet 0/0 interface. Serial interfaces do not have an Ethernet MAC address, so Cisco IOS uses the MAC address of the first available Ethernet interface. This is possible because link-local interfaces only have to be unique on that link.

The link-local address of the router interface is typically the default gateway address for devices on that link or network.

As shown in Example 8-7, the **show ipv6 route** command can be used to verify that IPv6 networks and specific IPv6 interface addresses have been installed in the IPv6 routing table. The **show ipv6 route** command will only display IPv6 networks, not IPv4 networks.

Within the route table, a C next to a route indicates that this is a directly connected network. When the router interface is configured with a global unicast address and is in the "up/up" state, the IPv6 prefix and prefix length are added to the IPv6 routing table as a connected route.

The IPv6 global unicast address configured on the interface is also installed in the routing table as a local route. The local route has a /128 prefix. Local routes are used by the routing table to efficiently process packets with a destination address of the router's interface address.

The **ping** command for IPv6 is identical to the command used with IPv4, except that an IPv6 address is used. Also shown in Example 8-7, the command is used to verify Layer 3 connectivity between R1 and a host. When pinging a link-local address from a router, Cisco IOS will prompt the user for the exit interface. Because the destination link-local address can be on one or more of its links or networks, the router needs to know on which interface to send the ping.

Example 8-7   Configuration and Verification of IPv6 Link-Local Address

```
R1#
R1# show ipv6 interface brief
GigabitEthernet0/0          [up/up]
    FE80::1
    2001:DB8:ACAD:1::
GigabitEthernet0/1          [up/up]
    FE80::1
    2001:DB8:ACAD:2::
Serial0/0/0                 [up/up]
    FE80::1
    2001:DB8:ACAD:3::
Serial0/0/1                 [administratively down/down]
Vlan1                       [administratively down/down]


R1# show ipv6 route
IPv6 Routing Table - 7 entries
Codes: C - Connected, L - Local, S - Static, R - RIP, B - BGP
       U - Per-user Static route, M - MIPv6
       I1 - ISIS L1, I2 - ISIS L2, IA - ISIS interarea, IS - ISIS summary
       O - OSPF intra, OI - OSPF inter, OE1 - OSPF ext 1, OE2 - OSPF ext 2
       ON1 - OSPF NSSA ext 1, ON2 - OSPF NSSA ext 2
       D - EIGRP, EX - EIGRP external
C   2001:DB8:ACAD:1::/64 [0/0]
    via ::, GigabitEthernet0/0
L   2001:DB8:ACAD:1::/128 [0/0]
    via ::, GigabitEthernet0/0
C   2001:DB8:ACAD:2::/64 [0/0]
    via ::, GigabitEthernet0/1
L   2001:DB8:ACAD:2::/128 [0/0]
    via ::, GigabitEthernet0/1
C   2001:DB8:ACAD:3::/64 [0/0]
    via ::, Serial0/0/0
L   2001:DB8:ACAD:3::/128 [0/0]
    via ::, Serial0/0/0
L   FF00::/8 [0/0]
    via ::, Null0
R1#


R1# ping ipv6 2001:gb8:acad:1::10
Type escape sequence to abort.
Sending 5, 100-byte ICMP Echos to 2001:gb8:acad:1::10 timeout is 2 seconds.
!!!!!
Success rate is 100 percent (5/5)
R1#
```

IPv6 Multicast Addresses (8.2.5)

This section will present IPv6 multicast addressing.

Assigned IPv6 Multicast Addresses (8.2.5.1)

IPv6 multicast addresses are similar to IPv4 multicast addresses. Recall that a multicast address is used to send a single packet to one or more destinations (multicast group). IPv6 multicast addresses have the prefix FF00::/8.

Note

Multicast addresses can only be destination addresses and not source addresses.

There are two types of IPv6 multicast addresses:

- Assigned multicast
- Solicited-node multicast

Assigned Multicast

Assigned multicast addresses are reserved multicast addresses for predefined groups of devices. An assigned multicast address is a single address used to reach a group of devices running a common protocol or service. Assigned multicast addresses are used in context with specific protocols such as DHCPv6.

Two common IPv6 assigned multicast groups include

- **FF02::1 All-nodes multicast group:** This is a multicast group that all IPv6-enabled devices join. A packet sent to this group is received and processed by all IPv6 interfaces on the link or network. This has the same effect as a broadcast address in IPv4. An IPv6 router sends Internet Control Message Protocol version 6 (ICMPv6) RA messages to the all-node multicast group. The RA message informs all IPv6-enabled devices on the network about addressing information, such as the prefix, prefix length, and default gateway.

- **FF02::2 All-routers multicast group:** This is a multicast group that all IPv6 routers join. A router becomes a member of this group when it is enabled as an IPv6 router with the **ipv6 unicast-routing** global configuration command. A packet sent to this group is received and processed by all IPv6 routers on the link or network.

IPv6-enabled devices send ICMPv6 Router Solicitation (RS) messages to the all-routers multicast address. The RS message requests an RA message from the IPv6 router to assist the device in its address configuration.

Solicited-Node IPv6 Multicast Addresses (8.2.5.2)

A solicited-node multicast is similar to the all-nodes multicast address. Recall that the all-nodes multicast address is essentially the same thing as an IPv4 broadcast. All devices on the network must process traffic sent to the all-nodes address. To reduce the number of devices that must process traffic, use a solicited-node multicast address.

A solicited-node multicast address is an address that matches only the last 24 bits of the IPv6 global unicast address of a device. The only devices that need to process these packets are those devices that have these same 24 bits in the least significant, far right portion of their interface ID.

An IPv6 solicited-node multicast address is automatically created when the global unicast or link-local unicast addresses are assigned. The IPv6 solicited-node multicast address is created by combining a special FF02:0:0:0:0:FF00::/104 prefix with the far right 24 bits of its unicast address.

The solicited-node multicast address consists of two parts:

- **FF02:0:0:0:0:FF00::/104 multicast prefix:** This is the first 104 bits of the solicited-node multicast address.

- **Least significant 24 bits:** These are the last or far right 24 bits of the solicited-node multicast address. These bits are copied from the far right 24 bits of the global unicast or link-local unicast address of the device.

It is possible that multiple devices will have the same solicited-node multicast address. Although rare, this can occur when devices have the same far right 24 bits in their interface IDs. This does not create any problems because the device will still process the encapsulated message, which will include the complete IPv6 address of the device in question.

Packet Tracer Activity 8.2.5.3: Configuring IPv6 Addressing

In this activity, you will practice configuring IPv6 addresses on a router, servers, and clients. You will also practice verifying your IPv6 addressing implementation.

Lab 8.2.5.4: Identifying IPv6 Addresses

In this lab, you will complete the following objectives:

- Part 1: Identify the Different Types of IPv6 Addresses
- Part 2: Examine a Host IPv6 Network Interface and Address

- Part 3: Practice IPv6 Address Abbreviation

- Part 4: Identify the Hierarchy of the IPv6 Global Unicast Address Network Prefix

---

Lab 8.2.5.5: Configuring IPv6 Addresses on Network Devices

In this lab, you will complete the following objectives:

- Part 1: Set Up Topology and Configure Basic Router and Switch Settings

- Part 2: Configure IPv6 Addresses Manually

- Part 3: Verify End-to-End Connectivity

Connectivity Verification (8.3)

This section will introduce verifying IPv6 connectivity.

ICMP (8.3.1)

Both IPv4 and IPv6 use an ICMP protocol as the principal means to verify connectivity. This section will introduce the use of ICMP in IPv4 and IPv6.

ICMPv4 and ICMPv6 Messages (8.3.1.1)

Although IP is not a reliable protocol, the TCP/IP suite does provide for messages to be sent in the event of certain errors. These messages are sent using the services of ICMP. The purpose of these messages is to provide feedback about issues related to the processing of IP packets under certain conditions, not to make IP reliable. ICMP messages are not required and are often not allowed within a network for security reasons.

ICMP is available for both IPv4 and IPv6. ICMPv4 is the messaging protocol for IPv4. ICMPv6 provides these same services for IPv6 but includes additional functionality. In this course, the term ICMP will be used when referring to both ICMPv4 and ICMPv6.

The types of ICMP messages, and the reasons why they are sent, are extensive. We will discuss some of the more common messages.

ICMP messages common to both ICMPv4 and ICMPv6 include

- Host confirmation

- Destination or Service Unreachable

- Time Exceeded

- Route redirection

Host Confirmation

An ICMP Echo message can be used to determine whether a host is operational. The local host sends an ICMP Echo Request to a host. If the host is available, the destination host responds with an Echo Reply. In Figure 8-18, an ICMP Echo Request is sent from H1 to H2. When H2 receives the ICMP packet, it responds with an ICMP Echo Reply. This use of the ICMP Echo messages is the basis of the ping utility.

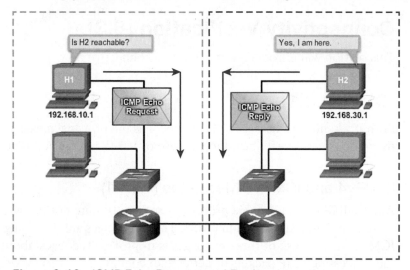

Figure 8-18 ICMP Echo Request and Reply

Destination or Service Unreachable

When a host or gateway receives a packet that it cannot deliver, it can use an ICMP Destination Unreachable message to notify the source that the destination or service is unreachable. The message will include a code that indicates why the packet could not be delivered.

Some of the Destination Unreachable codes for ICMPv4 are

- 0: Net unreachable

- 1: Host unreachable

- 2: Protocol unreachable
- 3: Port unreachable

Note

ICMPv6 has similar but slightly different codes for Destination Unreachable messages.

Time Exceeded

An ICMPv4 Time Exceeded message is used by a router to indicate that a packet cannot be forwarded because the Time to Live (TTL) field of the packet was decremented to 0. If a router receives a packet and decrements the TTL field in the IPv4 packet to 0, it discards the packet and sends a Time Exceeded message to the source host.

ICMPv6 also sends a Time Exceeded message if the router cannot forward an IPv6 packet because the packet has expired. IPv6 does not have a TTL field; it uses the hop limit field to determine whether the packet has expired.

Route Redirection

A router can use the ICMP Redirect message to notify the hosts on a network that a better route is available for a particular destination. This message can only be used when the source host is on the same physical network as both gateways.

Both ICMPv4 and ICMPv6 use route redirection messages.

ICMPv6 Router Solicitation and Router Advertisement Messages (8.3.1.2)

The informational and error messages found in ICMPv6 are very similar to the control and error messages implemented by ICMPv4. However, ICMPv6 has new features and improved functionality not found in ICMPv4.

ICMPv6 includes four new protocols as part of the Neighbor Discovery Protocol (ND or NDP):

- Router Solicitation message
- Router Advertisement message
- Neighbor Solicitation message
- Neighbor Advertisement message

Router Solicitation and Router Advertisement Messages

IPv6-enabled devices can be divided into two categories: routers and hosts. Router Solicitation and Router Advertisement messages are sent between hosts and routers:

- **Router Solicitation (RS) message:** When a host is configured to obtain its addressing information automatically using Stateless Address Autoconfiguration (SLAAC), the host will send an RS message to the router. The RS message is sent as an IPv6 all-routers multicast message.

- **Router Advertisement (RA) message:** RA messages are sent by routers to provide addressing information to hosts using SLAAC. The RA message can include addressing information for the host such as the prefix and prefix length. A router will send an RA message periodically or in response to an RS message. By default, Cisco routers send RA messages every 200 seconds. RA messages are sent to the IPv6 all-nodes multicast address. A host using SLAAC will set its default gateway to the link-local address of the router that sent the RA.

ICMPv6 Neighbor Solicitation and Neighbor Advertisement Messages (8.3.1.3)

ICMPv6 Neighbor Discovery Protocol includes two additional message types, Neighbor Solicitation (NS) and Neighbor Advertisement (NA) messages.

Neighbor Solicitation and Neighbor Advertisement messages are used for

- Address resolution
- Duplicate Address Detection (DAD)

Address Resolution

Address resolution is used when a device on the LAN knows the IPv6 unicast address of a destination but does not know its Ethernet MAC address. To determine the MAC address for the destination, the device will send an NS message to the solicited-node address. The message will include the known (targeted) IPv6 address. The device that has the targeted IPv6 address will respond with an NA message containing its Ethernet MAC address.

Duplicate Address Detection

When a device is assigned a global unicast or link-local unicast address, it is recommended that DAD is performed on the address to ensure that it is unique. To check the uniqueness of an address, the device will send an NS message with its own IPv6 address as the targeted IPv6 address. If another device on the network has this address, it will respond with an NA message. This NA message will notify the sending device that the address is in use. If a corresponding NA message is not returned within a certain period of time, the unicast address is unique and acceptable for use.

Note

DAD is not required, but RFC 4861 recommends that DAD be performed on unicast addresses.

Testing and Verification (8.3.2)

This section will introduce the use of the ping and traceroute utilities for testing networks.

Ping: Testing the Local Stack (8.3.2.1)

Ping is a testing utility that uses ICMP Echo Request and Echo Reply messages to test connectivity between hosts. Ping works with both IPv4 and IPv6 hosts.

To test connectivity to another host on a network, an Echo Request is sent to the host address using the **ping** command. If the host at the specified address receives the Echo Request, it responds with an Echo Reply. As each Echo Reply is received, ping provides feedback on the time between when the request was sent and when the reply was received. This can be a measure of network performance.

Ping has a timeout value for the reply. If a reply is not received within the timeout, ping provides a message indicating that a response was not received. This usually indicates that there is a problem, but could also indicate that security features blocking ping messages have been enabled on the network.

After all the requests are sent, the ping utility provides a summary that includes the success rate and average round-trip time to the destination.

Pinging the Local Loopback

There are some special testing and verification cases for which we can use ping. One case is for testing the internal configuration of IPv4 or IPv6 on the local host. To perform this test, we ping the local loopback address of 127.0.0.1 for IPv4 (::1 for IPv6).

A response from 127.0.0.1 for IPv4, or ::1 for IPv6, indicates that IP is properly installed on the host. This response comes from the network layer. This response is not, however, an indication that the addresses, masks, or gateways are properly configured. Nor does it indicate anything about the status of the lower layer of the network stack. This simply tests IP down through the network layer of IP. If we get an error message, it is an indication that TCP/IP is not operational on the host.

Ping: Testing Connectivity to the Local LAN (8.3.2.2)

You can also use ping to test the ability of a host to communicate on the local network. This is generally done by pinging the IP address of the gateway of the host. A ping to the gateway indicates that the host and the router interface serving as the gateway are both operational on the local network.

For this test, the gateway address is most often used, because the router is normally always operational. If the gateway address does not respond, a ping can be sent to the IP address of another host on the local network that is known to be operational.

If either the gateway or another host responds, the local host can successfully communicate over the local network. If the gateway does not respond but another host does, this could indicate a problem with the router interface serving as the gateway.

One possibility is that the wrong gateway address has been configured on the host. Another possibility is that the router interface might be fully operational but has security applied to it that prevents it from processing or responding to ping requests.

Ping: Testing Connectivity to Remote (8.3.2.3)

Ping can also be used to test the ability of a local host to communicate across an internetwork. The local host can ping an operational IPv4 host of a remote network.

If this ping is successful, the operation of a large piece of the internetwork can be verified. A successful ping across the internetwork confirms communication on the local network, the operation of the router serving as our gateway, and the operation of all other routers that might be in the path between the local network and the network of the remote host.

Additionally, functionality of the remote host can be verified. If the remote host could not communicate outside of its local network, it would not have responded.

Note

Many network administrators limit or prohibit the entry of ICMP messages into the corporate network; therefore, the lack of a ping response could be due to security restrictions.

Traceroute: Testing the Path (8.3.2.4)

Ping is used to test connectivity between two hosts, but does not provide information about the details of devices between the hosts. Traceroute (tracert) is a utility that generates a list of hops that were successfully reached along the path. This list can provide important verification and troubleshooting information. If the data reaches the destination, the trace lists the interface of every router in the path between the hosts. If the data fails at some hop along the way, the address of the last router that responded to the trace can provide an indication of where the problem or security restrictions are found.

Round-Trip Time (RTT)

Using traceroute provides *round-trip time (RTT)* for each hop along the path and indicates whether a hop fails to respond. The round-trip time is the time a packet takes to reach the remote host and for the response from the host to return. An asterisk (*) is used to indicate a lost or unreplied packet.

This information can be used to locate a problematic router in the path. If the display shows high response times or data losses from a particular hop, this is an indication that the resources of the router or its connections might be stressed.

IPv4 Time-to-Live (TTL) and IPv6 Hop Limit

Traceroute makes use of a function of the TTL field in IPv4 and the Hop Limit field in IPv6 in the Layer 3 headers, along with the ICMP Time Exceeded message.

Figure 8-19 and Example 8-8 show how traceroute takes advantage of TTL.

The first sequence of three messages sent from traceroute on H1 to H2 will have a TTL field value of 1. When this packet reaches R1, the TTL is decremented to 0. This causes the TTL to time-out the IPv4 packet at this first router. This router then responds with an ICMPv4 Time Exceeded message. The ICMPv4 message contains the address of the inbound interface of the first router. Traceroute now has the address of the first hop, 192.168.254.1, as well as the amount of time for the round trips (2 msec, 2 msec, 2 msec).

Traceroute then increments the TTL field to 2 and sends another sequence of three messages. As the message passes through R1, it will be decremented to 1. This allows the message to be forwarded by R1 to reach the next router, R2, before expiring. This provides the trace with the address of the next hop, R2, as well at the round-trip time (99 msec, 95 msec, 94 msec).

Traceroute on H1 then increments the TTL field to 3 to allow the packet to get one hop farther down the path toward H2. This sequence of messages reaches R3 before the timeout of the TTL. The ICMP Time Exceeded reply from R3 provides information about R3.

With the TTL now incremented to 4, the traceroute packets reach the destination of 192.168.0.110 (H2). H2 then responds with either an ICMP Port Unreachable message or an ICMP Echo Reply message instead of the ICMP Time Exceeded message.

Figure 8-19   Example Network for Traceroute

Example 8-8   Traceroute Example Output

```
C:\H1\Users> tracert 192.168.0.110

Tracing route to 192.168.0.110 over a maximum of 30 hops

 1     2 ms     2 ms     2 ms   192.168.254.1
 2    99 ms    95 ms    94 ms   192.168.100.1
 3    98 ms    93 ms    94 ms   172.16.2.1
 4    98 ms    93 ms    94 ms   192.168.0.110

Trace complete.
```

Packet Tracer
☐ Activity

Packet Tracer Activity 8.3.2.5: Verifying IPv4 and IPv6 Addressing

IPv4 and IPv6 can coexist on the same network. From the command prompt of a PC, there are some differences in the way that commands are issued and in the way that output is displayed.

Packet Tracer
☐ Activity

Packet Tracer Activity 8.3.2.6: Pinging and Tracing to Test the Path

There are connectivity issues in this activity. In addition to gathering and documenting information about the network, you will locate the problems and implement acceptable solutions to restore connectivity.

Lab 8.3.2.7: Testing Network Connectivity with Ping and Traceroute

In this lab, you will complete the following objectives:

- Part 1: Build and Configure the Network
- Part 2: Use the Ping Command for Basic Network Testing
- Part 3: Use the Tracert and Traceroute Commands for Basic Network Testing
- Part 4: Troubleshoot the Topology

Packet Tracer Activity 8.3.2.8: Troubleshooting IPv4 and IPv6 Addressing

You are a network technician working for a company that has decided to migrate from IPv4 to IPv6. In the interim, the company must support both protocols (dual-stack). Three coworkers have called the help desk with problems and have received limited assistance. The help desk has escalated the matter to you, a Level 2 support technician.

Summary (8.4)

Class Activity 8.4.1.1: The Internet of Everything . . . Naturally!

In this chapter, you learned about how small- to medium-sized businesses are connected to networks in groups. The Internet of Everything was also introduced in the beginning modeling activity.

For this activity, choose one of the following:

- Online banking
- World news
- Weather forecasting/climate
- Traffic conditions

Devise an IPv6 addressing scheme for the area you chose. Include in your addressing scheme how you would plan for

- Subnetting
- Unicasts
- Multicasts
- Broadcasts

Keep a copy of your scheme to share with the class or learning community. Be prepared to explain

- How subnetting, unicasts, multicasts and broadcasts would be incorporated
- Where your addressing scheme could be used
- How small- to medium-sized businesses would be impacted by using your plan

Packet Tracer
□ Activity

Packet Tracer Activity 8.4.1.2: Skills Integration Challenge

Your company has won a contract to set up a small network for a restaurant owner. There are two restaurants near each other, and they all share one connection. The equipment and cabling are installed, and the network administrator has designed the implementation plan. You job is to implement the rest of the addressing scheme according to the abbreviated addressing table and verify connectivity.

IP addresses are hierarchical, with network, subnetwork, and ho... address can represent a complete network, a specific host, or the b... of the network.

Understanding binary notation is important when determining whether tv... are in the same network. The bits within the network portion of the IP addi... be identical for all devices that reside in the same network. The subnet mask o... -fix is used to determine the network portion of an IP address. IP addresses can be assigned either statically or dynamically. DHCP enables the automatic assignment of addressing information such as IP address, subnet mask, default gateway, and other configuration information.

IPv4 hosts can communicate in one of three different ways: unicast, broadcast, and multicast. Also, blocks of addresses that are used in networks that require limited or no Internet access are called private addresses. The private IPv4 address blocks are 10.0.0.0/8, 172.16.0.0/12, and 192.168.0.0/16.

The depletion of IPv4 address space is the motivating factor for moving to IPv6. Each IPv6 address has 128 bits versus the 32 bits in an IPv4 address. IPv6 does not use the dotted-decimal subnet mask notation. The prefix length is used to indicate the network portion of an IPv6 address using the following format: IPv6 address/ prefix length.

There are three types of IPv6 addresses: unicast, multicast, and anycast. An IPv6 link-local address enables a device to communicate with other IPv6-enabled devices on the same link and only on that link (subnet). Packets with a source or destination link-local address cannot be routed beyond the link from where the packet originated. IPv6 link-local addresses are in the FE80::/10 range.

ICMP is available for both IPv4 and IPv6. ICMPv4 is the messaging protocol for IPv4. ICMPv6 provides the same services for IPv6 but includes additional functionality.

After it is implemented, an IP network needs to be tested to verify its connectivity and operational performance.

Practice

The following activities provide practice with the topics introduced in this chapter. The labs and class activities are available in the companion *Introduction to Networks Lab Manual* (ISBN 978-1-58713-312-1). The Packet Tracer Activities PKA files are found in the online course.

Class Activities

- Class Activity 8.0.1.2: The Internet of Everything (IoE)
- Class Activity 8.4.1.2: The Internet of Everything . . . Naturally!

Labs

- Lab 8.1.2.7: Using the Windows Calculator with Network Addresses
- Lab 8.1.2.8: Converting IPv4 Addresses to Binary
- Lab 8.1.4.8: Identifying IPv4 Addresses
- Lab 8.2.5.4: Identifying IPv6 Addresses
- Lab 8.2.5.5: Configuring IPv6 Addresses on Network Devices
- Lab 8.3.2.7: Testing Network Connectivity with Ping and Traceroute

Packet Tracer
☐ **Activity**

Packet Tracer Activities

- Packet Tracer Activity 8.1.3.8: Investigate Unicast, Broadcast, and Multicast Traffic
- Packet Tracer Activity 8.2.5.3: Configuring IPv6 Addressing
- Packet Tracer Activity 8.3.2.5: Verifying IPv4 and IPv6 Addressing
- Packet Tracer Activity 8.3.2.6: Pinging and Tracing to Test the Path
- Packet Tracer Activity 8.3.2.8: Troubleshooting IPv4 and IPv6 Addressing
- Packet Tracer Activity 8.4.1.2: Skills Integration Challenge

Check Your Understanding

Complete all the review questions listed here to test your understanding of the topics and concepts in this chapter. The appendix, "Check Your Understanding Answer Key," lists the answers.

1. What are the parts of an IPv4 address? (Choose two.)

   A. Host

   B. Network

   C. Next hop

   D. Broadcast

   E. Subnet mask

2. What is the purpose of the network address?

    A. To support communication to all hosts within a subnet

    B. To refer to a network

    C. To provide a gate for hosts in the network

    D. To allow multicast

3. What are characteristics in common among unicast, broadcast, and multicast IPv4 communication? (Choose two.)

    A. The source address is always a unicast address.

    B. There is only one host that receives the packet.

    C. There are never multiple destination addresses in the header.

    D. There are equal numbers of addresses used for each.

    E. All are used for the same purpose.

4. Which of the following addresses IPv4 would be used in a private network?

    A. 240.23.56.12

    B. 192.0.1.12

    C. 127.27.20.10

    D. 192.168.1.1

    E. 169.254.72.6

5. What is the principal reason for the development of IPv6?

_____

6. How are IPv6 addresses represented?

    A. 4 octets separated by periods

    B. 64 binary bits with no division

    C. 8 hextets separated by colons

    D. As an octal number

7. What type of IPv6 address should be used for communication that is limited to a single network segment?

    A. Global unicast

    B. Link-local

    C. Unspecified

    D. Unique local

8. What methods automatically provide global unicast addresses? (Choose two.)

    A. SLAAC

    B. DHCPv6

    C. ICMP

    D. DAD

    E. ANDing

9. Which type of IPv4 address allows a host to send a message to a group of hosts?

    A. Unicast

    B. Multicast

    C. Broadcast

10. What protocol is used in IP networks to verify connectivity?

    _____

11. What utility is used to identify network path between hosts?

    A. DHCP

    B. Ping

    C. Multicast

    D. Traceroute

CHAPTER 9

Subnetting IP Networks

Objectives

Upon completion of this chapter, you will be able to answer the following questions:

- Why is routing necessary for hosts on different subnets to be able to communicate?

- How does IP function as a communication protocol to identify a single device on a network?

- How would you calculate the number of host addresses available given a network and subnet mask?

- How would you calculate the required subnet mask to accommodate a given number of hosts?

- What are the benefits of variable-length subnet masking (VLSM)?

- How would you design and implement a hierarchical addressing scheme?

- How are IPv6 address assignments implemented in a business environment?

Key Terms

This chapter uses the following key terms. You can find the definitions in the Glossary.

variable-length subnet masking (VLSM)   page 492

nibble boundary   page 505

Introduction (9.0.1.1)

Designing, implementing, and managing an effective IP addressing plan ensures that networks can operate effectively and efficiently. This is especially true as the number of host connections to a network increases. Understanding the hierarchical structure of the IP address and how to modify that hierarchy to more efficiently meet routing requirements is an important part of planning an IP addressing scheme.

In the original IPv4 address, there are two levels of hierarchy: a network and a host. These two levels of addressing allow basic network groupings that facilitate in routing packets to a destination network. A router forwards packets based on the network portion of an IP address; after the network is located, the host portion of the address allows identification of the destination device.

However, as networks grow, with many organizations adding hundreds and even thousands of hosts to their networks, the two-level hierarchy is insufficient.

Subdividing a network adds a level to the network hierarchy, creating, in essence, three levels: a network, a subnetwork, and a host. Introducing an additional level to the hierarchy creates additional subgroups within an IP network that facilities faster packet delivery and added filtration, by helping to minimize "local" traffic.

This chapter examines, in detail, the creation and assignment of IP network and subnetwork addresses through the use of the subnet mask.

Class Activity 9.0.1.2: Activity: Call Me!

In this chapter, you will be learning how devices can be grouped into subnets, or smaller network groups, from a large network.

In this modeling activity, you are asked to think about a number you probably use every day, a number such as your telephone number. As you complete the activity, think about how your telephone number compares to strategies that network administrators might use to identify hosts for efficient data communication.

Answer the following two questions and record your answers. Save the two sections in either hard- or soft-copy format to use later for class discussion purposes.

- Explain how your smartphone or landline telephone number is divided into identifying groups of numbers. Does your telephone number use an area code? An ISP identifier? A city, state, or country code?

- In what ways does separating your telephone number into managed parts assist in contacting or communicating with others?

Subnetting an IPv4 Network (9.1)

Without subnetting an IPv4-based network, performance would quickly decrease as the number of hosts increased. Proper subnetting allows better control of network traffic and greatly improves network efficiency.

Network Segmentation (9.1.1)

Subnetting allows network segmentation, thus breaking a larger network into multiple smaller networks.

Reasons for Subnetting (9.1.1.1)

In early network implementations, it was common for organizations to have all computers and other networked devices connected to a single IP network. All devices in the organization were assigned an IP address with a matching network ID. This type of configuration is known as a flat network design. In a small network, with a limited number of devices, a flat network design is not problematic. However, as the network grows, this type of configuration can create major issues.

Consider how on an Ethernet LAN, devices use broadcasts to locate needed services and devices. Recall that a broadcast is sent to all hosts on an IP network. The Dynamic Host Configuration Protocol (DHCP) is an example of a network service that depends on broadcasts. Devices send broadcasts across the network to locate the DHCP server. On a large network, this could create a significant amount of traffic, slowing network operations. Additionally, because a broadcast is addressed to all devices, all devices must accept and process the traffic, resulting in increased device processing requirements. If a device must process a significant amount of broadcasts, it could even slow device operations. For reasons such as these, larger networks must be segmented into smaller subnetworks, keeping them localized to smaller groups of devices and services.

The process of segmenting a network, by dividing it into multiple smaller network spaces, is called *subnetting*. These subnetworks are called subnets. Network administrators can group devices and services into subnets that are determined by geographic location (perhaps the third floor of a building), by organizational unit (perhaps the Sales department), by device type (printers, servers, WAN), or by any other division that makes sense for the network. Subnetting can reduce overall network traffic and improve network performance.

Note

A subnet is equivalent to a network, and these terms can be used interchangeably. Most networks are a subnet of some larger address block.

Communication Between Subnets (9.1.1.2)

A router is necessary for devices on different networks to communicate. Devices on a network use the router interface attached to their LAN as their default gateway. Traffic that is destined for a device on a remote network will be processed by the router and forwarded toward the destination. To determine whether traffic is local or remote, the router uses the subnet mask.

In a subnetted network space, this works exactly the same way. As shown in Figure 9-1, subnetting creates multiple logical networks from a single address block or network address. Each subnet is treated as a separate network space. Devices on the same subnet must use an address, subnet mask, and default gateway that correlate to the subnet that they are a part of.

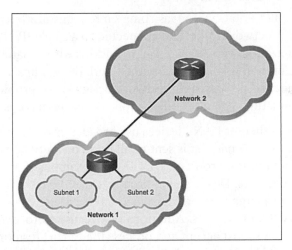

Figure 9-1   Communicating Between Networks

Traffic cannot be forwarded between subnets without the use of a router. Every interface on the router must have an IPv4 host address that belongs to the network or subnet to which the router interface is connected.

IP Subnetting Is FUNdamental (9.1.2)

Before any subnetting is carried out, it is important to understand the requirements of the network and to formulate a plan.

The Plan (9.1.2.1)

As shown in Figure 9-2, planning network subnets requires examination of both the needs of an organization's network usage and how the subnets will be structured.

Doing a network requirement study is the starting point. This means looking at the entire network and determining the main sections of the network and how they will be segmented. The address plan includes deciding the needs for each subnet in terms of size, how many hosts per subnet, how host addresses will be assigned, which hosts will require static IP addresses, and which hosts can use DHCP for obtaining their addressing information.

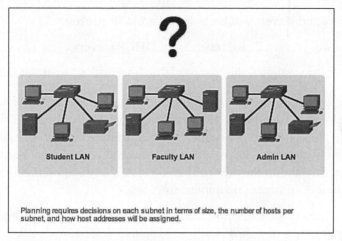

Figure 9-2   Planning the Addressing Scheme

The size of the subnet involves planning the number of hosts that will require IP host addresses in each subnet of the subdivided private network. For example, in a campus network design, you might consider how many hosts are needed in the Administrative LAN, how many in the Faculty LAN, and how many in the Student LAN. In a home network, a consideration might be done by the number of hosts in the Main House LAN and the number of hosts in the Home Office LAN.

As discussed earlier, the private IP address range used on a LAN is the choice of the network administrator and needs careful consideration to be sure that enough host addresses will be available for the currently known hosts and for future expansion. Remember that the private IP address ranges are

- 10.0.0.0 with a subnet mask of 255.0.0.0

- 172.16.0.0 with a subnet mask of 255.240.0.0

- 192.168.0.0 with a subnet mask of 255.255.0.0

Knowing your IP address requirements will determine the range or ranges of host addresses you implement. Subnetting the selected private IP address space will provide the host addresses to cover your network needs.

Public addresses used to connect to the Internet are typically allocated from a service provider. So while the same principles for subnetting would apply, this is not generally the responsibility of the organization's network administrator.

The Plan: Address Assignment (9.1.2.2)

Create standards for IP address assignments within each subnet range. For example:

- Printers and servers will be assigned static IP addresses.

- Users will receive IP addresses from DHCP servers using /24 subnets.

- Routers are assigned the first available host addresses in the range.

Two very important factors that will lead to the determination of which private address block is required are the number of subnets required and the maximum number of hosts needed per subnet. Each of these address blocks will allow you to appropriately allocate hosts based on the given size of a network and its required hosts currently and in the near future. Your IP space requirements will determine the range or ranges of hosts you implement.

In the upcoming examples, you will see subnetting based on address blocks that have subnet masks of 255.0.0.0, 255.255.0.0, and 255.255.255.0.

Subnetting an IPv4 Network (9.1.3)

Subnetting consists of borrowing host network bits to create a new subnet field in the IP address. The subnet mask is used to indicate how a network has been subnetted.

Basic Subnetting (9.1.3.1)

Every network address has a valid range of host addresses. All devices attached to the same network will have an IPv4 host address for that network and a common subnet mask or network prefix.

The prefix and the subnet mask are different ways of representing the same thing: the network portion of an address.

IPv4 subnets are created by using one or more of the host bits as network bits. This is done by extending the mask to borrow some of the bits from the host portion of the address to create additional network bits. The more host bits borrowed, the more subnets that can be defined. For each bit borrowed, the number of subnetworks available is doubled. For example, if 1 bit is borrowed, 2 subnets can be created. If 2 bits are borrowed, 4 subnets are created. If 3 bits are borrowed, 8 subnets are created, and so on. However, with each bit borrowed, fewer host addresses are available per subnet.

Bits can only be borrowed from the host portion of the address. The network portion of the address is allocated by the service provider and cannot be changed.

Note

In the examples in the figures, only the last octet is shown in binary because only bits from the host portion can be borrowed.

As shown in Figure 9-3, the 192.168.1.0/24 network has 24 bits in the network portion and 8 bits in the host portion, which is indicated with the subnet mask 255.255.255.0 or /24 notation. With no subnetting, this network supports a single LAN interface. If an additional LAN is needed, the network would need to be subnetted.

Figure 9-3   IPv4 Address

In Figure 9-4, 1 bit is borrowed from the most significant bit position (leftmost) of the host portion of the IP address, thus extending the network portion to 25 bits. This creates two subnets identified by using a 0 in the borrowed bit for the first network and a 1 in the borrowed bit for the second network. The subnet mask for both networks uses a 1 in the borrowed bit position to indicate that this bit is now part of the network portion.

Figure 9-4   Borrowing Bits to Create Subnets

As shown in Figure 9-5, when we convert the binary octet to decimal, we see that the first subnet address is 192.168.1.0 and the second subnet address is 192.168.1.128. Because a bit has been borrowed, the subnet mask for each subnet is 255.255.255.128 or /25.

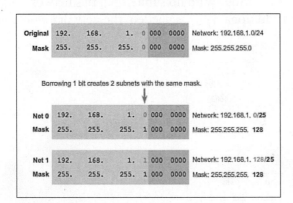

Figure 9-5   Decimal Representation of a Subnetted Network

Subnets in Use (9.1.3.2)

In the previous example, the 192.168.1.0/24 network was subnetted to create two subnets:

> 192.168.1.0/25
>
> 192.168.1.128/25

In Figure 9-6, notice that Router R1 has two LAN segments attached to its Gigabit Ethernet interfaces. The subnets will be used for the segments attached to these interfaces. To serve as the gateway for devices on the LAN, each of the router interfaces must be assigned an IP address within the range of valid addresses for the assigned subnet. It is common practice to use the first or last available address in a network range for the router interface address.

Figure 9-6   Simple Routed Network

The first subnet, 192.168.1.0/25, is used for the network attached to Gigabit Ethernet 0/0, and the second subnet, 192.168.1.128/25, is used for the network attached to Gigabit Ethernet 0/1. To assign an IP address for each of these interfaces, it is necessary to determine the range of valid IP addresses for each subnet.

The following are guidelines for each of the subnets:

- **Network address:** All 0 bits in the host portion of the address.

- **First host address:** All 0 bits plus a rightmost 1 bit in the host portion of the address.

- **Last host address:** All 1 bits plus a rightmost 0 bit in the host portion of the address.

- **Broadcast address:** All 1 bits in the host portion of the address.

As shown in Figure 9-7, the first host address for the 192.168.1.0/25 network is 192.168.1.1, and the last host address is 192.168.1.126. Figure 9-8 shows that the first host address for the 192.168.1.128/25 network is 192.168.1.129, and the last host address is 192.168.1.254.

```
Network Address
  192.    168.    1.    0   000 0000   = 192.168.1.0

First Host Address
  192.    168.    1.    0   000 0001   = 192.168.1.1

Last Host Address
  192.    168.    1.    0   111 1110   = 192.168.1.126

Broadcast Address
  192.    168.    1.    0   111 1111   = 192.168.1.127
```

Figure 9-7   Address Range for the 192.168.1.0/25 Subnet

Network Address

| 192. | 168. | 1. | 1 | 000 0000 | = 192.168.1.128 |

First Host Address

| 192. | 168. | 1. | 1 | 000 0001 | = 192.168.1.129 |

Last Host Address

| 192. | 168. | 1. | 1 | 111 1110 | = 192.168.1.254 |

Broadcast Address

| 192. | 168. | 1. | 1 | 111 1111 | = 192.168.1.255 |

Figure 9-8   Address Range for the 192.168.1.128/25 Subnet

To assign the first host address in each subnet to the router interface for that subnet, use the **ip address** command in interface configuration mode as shown in Figure 9-9a. Notice that each subnet uses the subnet mask of 255.255.255.128 to indicate that the network portion of the address is 25 bits.

A host configuration for the 192.168.1.128/25 network is shown in Figure 9-9b. Notice that the gateway IP address is the address configured on the G0/1 interface of R1, 192.168.1.129, and the subnet mask is 255.255.255.128.

a

b

Figure 9-9   Assigning Addresses to Devices

Subnetting Formulas (9.1.3.3)

Because each bit can only have one of two values (0 or 1), it is possible to mathematically determine the number of subnets created and also the number of hosts per subnet based on the number of bits borrowed to create subnets.

Calculating Subnets

Use this formula to calculate the number of subnets:

2^n (where n = the number of bits borrowed)

As shown in Figure 9-10a, for the 192.168.1.0/25 example, the calculation looks like this:

$2^1 = 2$ subnets

Calculating Hosts

Use this formula to calculate the number of hosts per subnetwork:

2^n (where n = the number of bits remaining in the host field)

As shown in Figure 9-10b, for the 192.168.1.0/25 example, the calculation looks like this:

$2^7 = 128$

a   b

Figure 9-10   Calculating Subnets and Hosts per Subnet When Borrowing 1 Bit

Because hosts cannot use the network address or broadcast address from a subnet, two of these addresses are not valid for host assignment. This means that each of the subnets has 126 (128–2) valid host addresses.

So in this example, borrowing 1 host bit toward the network results in creating two subnets, and each subnet can have a total of 126 hosts assigned.

Creating Four Subnets (9.1.3.4)

Consider an internetwork that requires three subnets.

Using the same 192.168.1.0/24 address block, host bits must be borrowed to create at least three subnets. Borrowing a single bit would only provide two subnets. To provide more networks, more host bits must be borrowed. Calculate the number of subnets created if 2 bits are borrowed using the formula $2^{\text{number of bits borrowed}}$:

$2^2 = 4$ subnets

Borrowing 2 bits creates four subnets, as shown in Figure 9-11a.

Recall that the subnet mask must change to reflect the borrowed bits. In this example, when 2 bits are borrowed, the mask is extended 2 bits into the last octet. In decimal, the mask is represented as 255.255.255.192, because the last octet is 1100 0000 in binary.

Host Calculation

To calculate the number of hosts, examine the last octet. After borrowing 2 bits for the subnet, there are 6 host bits remaining.

Apply the host calculation formula as shown in Figure 9-11b:

$$2^6 = 64$$

But remember that all 0 bits in the host portion of the address is the network address, and all 1s in the host portion is a broadcast address. Therefore, there are only 62 host addresses that are actually available for each subnet.

a   b

Figure 9-11   Calculating Subnets and Hosts per Subnet When Borrowing 2 Bits

As shown in Figure 9-12, the first host address for the first subnet is 192.168.1.1, and the last host address is 192.168.1.62. Figure 9-13 shows the ranges for subnets 0–2. Remember that each host must have a valid IP address within the range defined for that network segment. The subnet assigned to the router interface will determine which segment a host belongs to.

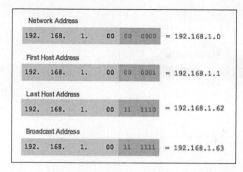

Figure 9-12   Address Range for the 192.168.1.0/26 Subnet

		192.	168.	1.	00	00	0000	192.168.1.0
	Network	192.	168.	1.	00	00	0000	192.168.1.0
Net 0	First	192.	168.	1.	00	00	0001	192.168.1.1
	Last	192.	168.	1.	00	11	1110	192.168.1.62
	Broadcast	192.	168.	1.	00	11	1111	192.168.1.63
	Network	192.	168.	1.	01	00	0000	192.168.1.64
Net 1	First	192.	168.	1.	01	00	0001	192.168.1.65
	Last	192.	168.	1.	01	11	1110	192.168.1.126
	Broadcast	192.	168.	1.	01	11	1111	192.168.1.127
	Network	192.	168.	1.	10	00	0000	192.168.1.128
Net 2	First	192.	168.	1.	10	00	0001	192.168.1.129
	Last	192.	168.	1.	10	11	1110	192.168.1.190
	Broadcast	192.	168.	1.	10	11	1111	192.168.1.191

Figure 9-13   Address Ranges for Subnets 0–2

In Figure 9-14, a sample configuration is shown. In this configuration, the first network is assigned to the Gigabit Ethernet 0/0 interface, the second network is assigned to the Gigabit Ethernet 0/1 interface, and the third network is assigned to the Serial 0/0/0 network.

Figure 9-14   Example Routed Network Using Three Subnets

Using a common addressing plan, the first host address in the subnet is assigned to the router interface. Hosts on each subnet will use the address of the router interface as the default gateway address:

- PC1 (192.168.1.2/26) will use 192.168.1.1 (G0/0 interface address of R1) as its default gateway address.

- PC2 (192.168.1.66/26) will use 192.168.1.65 (G0/1 interface address of R1) as its default gateway address.

Note

All devices on the same subnet will have a host IPv4 address from the range of host addresses and will use the same subnet mask.

Creating Eight Subnets (9.1.3.5)

Next, consider an internetwork that requires five subnets, as shown in Figure 9-15.

Figure 9-15   Network Requiring Five Subnets

Using the same 192.168.1.0/24 address block, host bits must be borrowed to create at least five subnets. Borrowing 2 bits would only provide four subnets, as seen in the previous example. To provide more networks, more host bits must be borrowed. Calculate the number of subnets created if 3 bits are borrowed using this formula:

$$2^3 = 8 \text{ subnets}$$

As shown in Figure 9-16, borrowing 3 bits creates eight subnets. When 3 bits are borrowed, the subnet mask is extended 3 bits into the last octet, resulting in a subnet mask of 255.255.255.224. All devices on these subnets will use the subnet mask 255.255.255.224 (/27).

Net 0	Network	192.	168.	1.	000	0	0000	192.168.1.0
	First	192.	168.	1.	000	0	0001	192.168.1.1
	Last	192.	168.	1.	000	1	1110	192.168.1.30
	Broadcast	192.	168.	1.	000	1	1111	192.168.1.31
Net 1	Network	192.	168.	1.	001	0	0000	192.168.1.32
	First	192.	168.	1.	001	0	0001	192.168.1.33
	Last	192.	168.	1.	001	1	1110	192.168.1.62
	Broadcast	192.	168.	1.	001	1	1111	192.168.1.63
Net 2	Network	192.	168.	1.	010	0	0000	192.168.1.64
	First	192.	168.	1.	010	0	0001	192.168.1.65
	Last	192.	168.	1.	010	1	1110	192.168.1.94
	Broadcast	192.	168.	1.	010	1	1111	192.168.1.95
Net 3	Network	192.	168.	1.	011	0	0000	192.168.1.96
	First	192.	168.	1.	011	0	0001	192.168.1.97
	Last	192.	168.	1.	011	1	1110	192.168.1.126
	Broadcast	192.	168.	1.	011	1	1111	192.168.1.127

Net 4	Network	192.	168.	1.	100	0	0000	192.168.1.128
	First	192.	168.	1.	100	0	0001	192.168.1.129
	Last	192.	168.	1.	100	1	1110	192.168.1.158
	Broadcast	192.	168.	1.	100	1	1111	192.168.1.159
Net 5	Network	192.	168.	1.	101	0	0000	192.168.1.160
	First	192.	168.	1.	101	0	0001	192.168.1.161
	Last	192.	168.	1.	101	1	1110	192.168.1.190
	Broadcast	192.	168.	1.	101	1	1111	192.168.1.191
Net 6	Network	192.	168.	1.	110	0	0000	192.168.1.192
	First	192.	168.	1.	110	0	0001	192.168.1.193
	Last	192.	168.	1.	110	1	1110	192.168.1.222
	Broadcast	192.	168.	1.	110	1	1111	192.168.1.223
Net 7	Network	192.	168.	1.	111	0	0000	192.168.1.224
	First	192.	168.	1.	111	0	0001	192.168.1.225
	Last	192.	168.	1.	111	1	1110	192.168.1.254
	Broadcast	192.	168.	1.	111	1	1111	192.168.1.255

Figure 9-16   Subnet Address Ranges

Host Calculation

To calculate the number of hosts, examine the last octet. After borrowing 3 bits for the subnet, there are 5 host bits remaining.

Apply the host calculation formula:

$$2^5 = 32$$

but subtract 2 for the all 0s in the host portion (network address) and all 1s in the host portion (broadcast address).

The subnets are assigned to the network segments required for the topology, as shown in Figure 9-17a.

Again, using a common addressing plan, the first host address in the subnet is assigned to the router interface, as shown in Figure 9-17b. Hosts on each subnet will use the address of the router interface as the default gateway address:

- PC1 (192.168.1.2/27) will use the 192.168.1.1 address as its default gateway address.

- PC2 (192.168.1.34/27) will use the 192.168.1.33 address as its default gateway address.

- PC3 (192.168.1.98/27) will use the 192.168.1.97 address as its default gateway address.

- PC4 (192.168.1.130/27) will use the 192.168.1.129 address as its default gateway address.

a

b

Figure 9-17   Assigning Addresses to Devices

Interactive Graphic	**Activity 9.1.3.6: Determining the Network Address: Basic** Go to the course online to perform this practice activity.

Interactive Graphic	**Activity 9.1.3.7: Calculate the Number of Hosts: Basic** Go to the course online to perform this practice activity.

Interactive Graphic	**Activity 9.1.3.8: Determining the Valid Addresses for Hosts: Basic** Go to the course online to perform this practice activity.

Interactive Graphic	**Activity 9.1.3.9: Calculate the Subnet Mask** Go to the course online to perform this practice activity.

Creating 100 Subnets with a /16 prefix (9.1.3.10)

In the previous examples, we considered an internetwork that required three subnets and one that required five subnets. To achieve the goal of creating four subnets, we borrowed 2 bits from the 8 hosts bits available with an IP address that has a default mask of 255.255.255.0, or a /24 prefix. The resulting subnet mask was 255.255.255.192, and a total of four possible subnets were created. Applying the host calculation formula of 2^6-2, we determined that on each one of those four subnets, we could have 62 host addresses to assign to nodes.

To acquire five subnets, we borrowed 3 bits from the 8 hosts bits available with an IP address that has a default mask of 255.255.255.0, or a /24 prefix. In borrowing those 3 bits from the host portion of the address, we left 5 hosts bits remaining. The resulting subnet mask was 255.255.255.224, with a total of eight subnets created, and 30 host addresses per subnet.

Consider large organizations or campuses with an internetwork that requires 100 subnets. Just as in the previous examples, to achieve the goal of creating 100 subnets, we must borrow bits from the host portion of the IP address of the existing internetwork. As before, to calculate the number of subnets, we must look at the number of available host bits and use the subnet calculation formula $2^{\text{number of bits borrowed}} - 2$. Using the IP address of the last example, 192.168.10.0/24, we have 8 host bits; to create 100 subnets, we must borrow 7 bits.

Calculate the number of subnets if 7 bits are borrowed: $2^7 = 128$ subnets.

However, borrowing 7 bits will leave just 1 remaining host bit, and if we apply the host calculation formula, the result would be no hosts on these subnets. Calculate the number of hosts if 1 bit is remaining: $2^1=2$, and then subtract 2 for the network address and the network broadcast; the result is 0 hosts ($2^1-2=0$).

In a situation requiring a larger number of subnets, an IP network is required that has more hosts bits to borrow from, such as an IP address with a default subnet mask of /16, or 255.255.0.0. Addresses that have a range of 128–191 in the first octet have a default mask of 255.255.0.0, or /16. Addresses in this range have 16 bits in the network portion and 16 bits in the host portion. These 16 bits are the bits that are available to borrow for creating subnets.

Using a new IP address of 172.16.0.0/16 address block, host bits must be borrowed to create at least 100 subnets. Starting from left to right with the first available host bit, we will borrow a single bit at a time until we reach the number of bits necessary to create 100 subnets. Borrowing 1 bit, we would create two subnets; borrowing 2 bits, we would create four subnets; 3 bits, eight subnets, and so on. Calculate the number of subnets created if 7 bits are borrowed using the formula $2^{\text{number of bits borrowed}}$:

$$2^7 = 128 \text{ subnets}$$

Borrowing 7 bits creates 128 subnets, as shown in Figure 9-18.

Figure 9-18   Borrowing 7 Bits to Create 128 Subnets

Recall that the subnet mask must change to reflect the borrowed bits. In this example, when 7 bits are borrowed, the mask is extended 7 bits into the third octet. In decimal, the mask is represented as 255.255.254.0, or a /23 prefix, because the third octet is 11111110 in binary and the fourth octet is 00000000 in binary.

Subnetting will be done in the third octet, with the host bits in the third and fourth octets.

Calculating the Hosts (9.1.3.11)

To calculate the number of hosts, examine the third and fourth octet. After borrowing 7 bits for the subnet, there is 1 host bit remaining in the third octet and there are 8 host bits remaining in the fourth octet.

Apply the host calculation formula as shown in Figure 9-19.

$$2^9 = 512$$

Figure 9-19   Calculating the Number of Hosts in a Subnet

But remember that all 0 bits in the host portion of the address is the network address, and all 1s in the host portion is a broadcast address. Therefore, there are only 510 host addresses that are actually available for each subnet.

As shown in Figure 9-20, the first host address for the first subnet is 172.16.0.1 and the last host address is 172.16.1.254. Remember that each host must have a valid IP address within the range defined for that network segment. The subnet assigned to the router interface will determine which segment a host belongs to.

Note

Bits can only be borrowed from the host portion of the address. The network portion of the address is allocated by the service provider and cannot be changed. So organizations that required a significant number of subnets were required to communicate this need to their ISP so that the ISP would allocate an IP address with a default mask with enough bits to create the needed subnets.

Address Range for 172.16.0.0/23 Subnet

Network Address

172.   16.   0000 000 0.0000 0000 = 172.16.0.0

First Host Address

172.   16.   0000 000 0.0000 0001 = 172.16.0.1

Last Host Address

172.   16.   0000 000 1.1111 1110 = 172.16.1.254

Broadcast Address

172.   16.   0000 000 1.1111 1111 = 172.16.1.255

Figure 9-20   Address Range for the 172.16.0.0/23 Subnet

Calculating the Hosts (9.1.3.12)

There are some organizations, such as small service providers, that might need even more subnets than 100. Take for example, an organization that requires 1000 subnets. As always, to create subnets, we must borrow bits from the host portion of the IP address of the existing internetwork. As before, to calculate the number of subnets, it is necessary to look at the number of available hosts bits. A situation such as this requires that the IP address assigned by the ISP have enough host bits available to calculate 1000 subnets. IP addresses that have the range of 1–126 in the first octet have a default mask of 255.0.0.0, or /8. This means there are 8 bits in the network portion and 24 host bits available to borrow toward subnetting.

Using the 10.0.0.0/8 address block, host bits must be borrowed to create at least 1000 subnets. Starting from left to right with the first available host bit, we will borrow a single bit at a time until we reach the number of bits necessary to create 1000 subnets. Calculate the number of subnets created if 10 bits are borrowed using the formula $2^{\text{number of bits borrowed}}$:

$2^{10} = 1024$ subnets

Borrowing 10 bits creates 1024 subnets, as shown in Figure 9-21.

Figure 9-21   Borrowing 10 Bits to Create 1024 Subnets

Recall that the subnet mask must change to reflect the borrowed bits. In this example, when 10 bits are borrowed, the mask is extended 10 bits into the third octet. In decimal, the mask is represented as 255.255.192.0 or a /18 prefix, because the third octet of the subnet mask is 11000000 in binary and the fourth octet is 00000000 in binary. Subnetting will be done in the third octet, but don't forget about the host bits in the third and fourth octets.

Host Calculation

To calculate the number of hosts, examine the third and fourth octet. After borrowing 10 bits for the subnet, there are 6 host bits remaining in the third octet and 8 host bits remaining in the fourth octet. A total of 14 host bits remain.

Apply the host calculation formula as shown in Figure 9-22.

$$2^{14} - 2 = 16,382$$

Figure 9-22   Calculating the Number of Hosts per Subnet

The first host address for the first subnet is 10.0.0.1, and the last host address is 10.0.63.254. Remember that each host must have a valid IP address within the range defined for that network segment. The subnet assigned to the router interface will determine which segment a host belongs to. Figure 9-23 shows the resultant address range for the 10.0.0.0/18 subnet.

Note:

All devices on the same subnet will have a host IPv4 address from the range of host addresses and will use the same subnet mask.

Figure 9-23   Address Range for the 10.0.0.0/18 Subnet

Interactive
Graphic

Activity 9.1.3.13: Determining the Network Address: Advanced

Go to the course online to perform this practice activity.

Interactive
Graphic

Activity 9.1.3.14: Calculating the Number of Hosts: Advanced

Go to the course online to perform this practice activity.

Interactive
Graphic

Activity 9.1.3.15: Determining the Valid Addresses for Hosts: Advanced

Go to the course online to perform this practice activity.

Determining the Subnet Mask (9.1.4)

After an IPv4 network address has been subnetted, we must alter the subnet mask to indicate how many bits have been borrowed to create the subnets.

Subnetting Based on Host Requirements (9.1.4.1)

The decision about how many host bits to borrow to create subnets is an important planning decision. There are two considerations when planning subnets: the number of host addresses required for each network and the number of individual subnets needed. The selection of a number of bits for the subnet ID affects both the number of possible subnets and the number of host addresses in each subnet.

Notice that there is an inverse relationship between the number of subnets and the number of hosts. The more bits borrowed to create subnets, the fewer host bits are available; therefore, fewer hosts per subnet. If more host addresses are needed, more host bits are required, resulting in fewer subnets. This is shown in Figure 9-24.

Subnet ID Bits	Host ID Bits	Number of Subnets	Number of Hosts per Subnets	Bit Pattern
0	8	1	254	hhhhhhhh
1	7	2	126	shhhhhhh
2	6	4	62	sshhhhhh
3	5	8	30	ssshhhhh
4	4	16	14	sssshhhh
5	3	32	6	ssssshhh
6	2	64	2	sssssshh

Figure 9-24 Inverse Relationship Between the Number of Subnets and the Number of Hosts per Subnet

Number of Hosts

When borrowing bits to create multiple subnets, you leave enough host bits for the largest subnet. The number of host addresses required in the largest subnet will determine how many bits must be left in the host portion. The formula 2^n (where n is the number of host bits remaining) is used to calculate how many addresses will be available on each subnet. Recall that two of the addresses cannot be used, so the usable number of addresses can be calculated as 2^n-2.

Subnetting Network-Based Requirements (9.1.4.2)

Sometimes a certain number of subnets are required, with less emphasis on the number of host addresses per subnet. This can be the case if an organization chooses to separate its network traffic based on internal structure or department setup. For example, an organization might choose to put all host devices used by employees in the Engineering department in one network and all host devices used by management in a separate network. In this case, the number of subnets is most important in determining how many bits to borrow.

Recall that the number of subnets created when bits are borrowed can be calculated using the formula 2^n (where n is the number of bits borrowed). There is no need to subtract any of the resulting subnets, as they are all usable.

The key is to balance the number of subnets needed and the number of hosts required for the largest subnet. The more bits borrowed to create additional subnets means fewer hosts available per subnet.

Subnetting to Meet Network Requirements (9.1.4.3, 9.1.4.4)

Every network within an organization is designed to accommodate a finite number of hosts. Basic subnetting requires enough subnets to accommodate the networks while also providing enough host addresses per subnet.

Some networks, such as point-to-point WAN links, require only two hosts. Other networks, such as a user LAN in a large building or department, might need to accommodate hundreds of hosts. Network administrators must devise the internetwork addressing scheme to accommodate the maximum number of hosts for each network. The number of hosts in each division should allow for growth in the number of hosts.

Determine the Total Number of Hosts

First, consider the total number of hosts required by the entire corporate internetwork. A block of addresses large enough to accommodate all devices in all the corporate networks must be used. These devices include end-user devices, servers, intermediate devices, and router interfaces.

Consider the example of a corporate internetwork that must accommodate a total of 800 hosts in its five locations (see Figure 9-25). In this example, the service provider has allocated a network address of 172.16.0.0/22 (10 host bits). This will provide 1022 host addresses, which will more than accommodate the addressing needs for this internetwork.

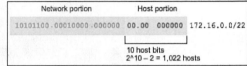

a   b

Figure 9-25   Example Corporate Network and IPv4 Address

Determine the Number and Size of the Networks

Next, consider the number of subnets required and the number of host addresses needed on each subnet. Based on the network topology consisting of five LAN segments and four internetwork connections between routers, nine subnets are required. The largest subnet requires 40 hosts. When designing an addressing scheme, you should anticipate growth in both the number of subnets and the hosts per subnet.

The 172.16.0.0/22 network address has 10 host bits. Because the largest subnet requires 40 hosts, a minimum of 6 host bits should be retained. This is determined by using this formula: $2^6 - 2 = 62$ hosts. The 4 remaining host bits can be used to allocate subnets. Using the formula for determining subnets, this results in 16 subnets: $2^4 = 16$. Because the example internetwork requires nine subnets, this will meet the requirement and allow some additional growth.

When 4 bits are borrowed, the new prefix length is /26 with a subnet mask of 255.255.255.192.

As shown in Figure 9-26, using the /26 prefix length, the 16 subnet addresses can be determined. Only the subnet portion of the address is incremented. The original 22 bits of the network address cannot change and the host portion will contain all 0 bits.

Note

Because the subnet portion is in both the third and fourth octets, one or both of these values will vary in the subnet addresses.

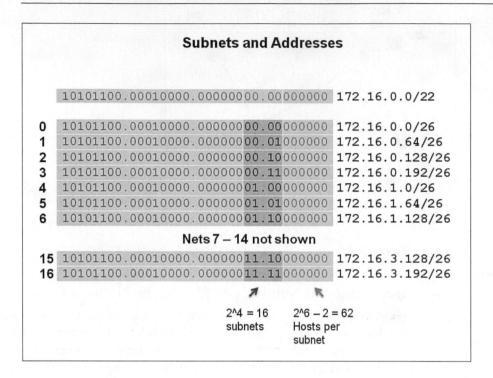

Figure 9-26   Subnets and Addresses for Example Corporate Network

The original 172.16.0.0/22 network was a single network with 10 host bits, providing 1022 usable addresses to assign to hosts. By borrowing 4 host bits, 16 subnets (0000 through 1111) can be created. Each subnet has 6 host bits or 62 usable host addresses per subnet.

As shown in Figure 9-27, the subnets can be assigned to the LAN segments and router-to-router connections.

Figure 9-27 Addressing Scheme Applied to Example Network

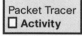

Activity 9.1.4.5: Determining the Number of Bits to Borrow

Go to the course online to perform this practice activity.

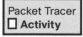

Packet Tracer Activity 9.1.4.6: Subnetting Scenario 1

In this activity, you are given the network address of 192.168.100.0/24 to subnet and provide the IP addressing for the network shown in the topology. Each LAN in the network requires enough space for at least 25 addresses for end devices, the switch, and the router. The connection between R1 to R2 will require an IP address for each end of the link.

Packet Tracer Activity 9.1.4.7: Subnetting Scenario 2

In this activity, you are given the network address of 172.31.1.0/24 to subnet and provide the IP addressing for the network shown in the topology. The required host addresses for each WAN and LAN link are labeled in the topology.

Lab 9.1.4.8: Calculating IPv4 Subnets

In this lab, you will complete the following objectives:

- Part 1: Determine IPv4 Address Subnetting
- Part 2: Calculate IPv4 Address Subnetting

Lab 9.1.4.9: Subnetting Network Topologies

In this lab, you will complete the following objectives:

Parts 1 to 5, for each network topology:

- Determine the number of subnets.

- Design an appropriate addressing scheme.

- Assign addresses and subnet mask pairs to device interfaces.

- Examine the use of the available network address space and future growth potential.

Lab 9.1.4.10: Researching Subnet Calculators

In this lab, you will complete the following objectives:

- Part 1: Review Available Subnet Calculators
- Part 2: Perform Network Calculations Using a Subnet Calculator

Benefits of Variable-Length Subnet Masking (9.1.5)

By using *variable-length subnet masking (VLSM)*, we are able to exercise more control over the way we divide up the hosts in an IPv4 network, allocating addresses in a manner that more closely matches the requirements of the network.

Traditional Subnetting Wastes Addresses (9.1.5.1)

Using traditional subnetting, the same number of addresses is allocated for each subnet. If all the subnets have the same requirements for the number of hosts, these fixed-size address blocks would be efficient. However, most often that is not the case.

For example, the topology shown in Figure 9-28 requires seven subnets, one for each of the four LANs and one for each of the three WAN connections between routers. Using traditional subnetting with the given address of 192.168.20.0/24, 3 bits can be borrowed from the host portion in the last octet to meet the requirement of seven subnets. As shown in Figure 9-29, borrowing 3 bits creates eight subnets and leaves 5 host bits with 30 usable hosts per subnet. This scheme creates the needed subnets and meets the host requirement of the largest LAN.

Figure 9-28 Sample Network Topology

```
        Network portion          Host portion
      ┌──────────────────────┐ ┌──────────┐
      │ 11000000.10101000.00010100 │ .000 │ 00000 │ 192.168.20.0/24

   0  11000000.10101000.00010100 .000  00000  192.168.20.0/27    ┐ Building
   1  11000000.10101000.00010100 .001  00000  192.168.20.32/27   │ LANs A,
   2  11000000.10101000.00010100 .010  00000  192.168.20.64/27   │ B, C, and
   3  11000000.10101000.00010100 .011  00000  192.168.20.96/27   ┘ D
   4  11000000.10101000.00010100 .100  00000  192.168.20.128/27  ┐ Site to
   5  11000000.10101000.00010100 .101  00000  192.168.20.160/27  │ Site WANs
   6  11000000.10101000.00010100 .110  00000  192.168.20.192/27  ┘
   7  11000000.10101000.00010100 .111  00000  192.168.20.224/27  ] Unused /
                                                                   Available

   Subnet portion              Host portion
   2^3 = 8 subnets             2^5 – 2 = 30 hosts per subnet
```

Figure 9-29 Basic Subnet Scheme for Sample Network

Although this traditional subnetting meets the needs of the largest LAN and divides the address space into an adequate number of subnets, it results in significant waste of unused addresses.

For example, only two addresses are needed in each subnet for the three WAN links. Because each subnet has 30 usable addresses, there are 28 unused addresses in each of these subnets. This results in 84 unused addresses (28 x 3).

Further, this limits future growth by reducing the total number of subnets available. This inefficient use of addresses is characteristic of traditional subnetting of classful networks.

Applying a traditional subnetting scheme to this scenario is not very efficient and is wasteful. In fact, this example is a good model for showing how subnetting a subnet can be used to maximize address utilization.

Subnetting a subnet, or using variable-length subnet masks (VLSM), was designed to avoid wasting addresses.

Variable-Length Subnet Masks (VLSM) (9.1.5.2)

In all the previous examples of subnetting, notice that the same subnet mask was applied for all the subnets. This means that each subnet has the same number of available host addresses.

As illustrated in Figure 9-30a, traditional subnetting creates subnets of equal size. Each subnet in a traditional scheme uses the same subnet mask. As shown in Figure 9-30b, VLSM allows a network space to be divided in unequal parts. With VLSM, the subnet mask will vary depending on how many bits have been borrowed for a particular subnet, thus the "variable" part of the VLSM.

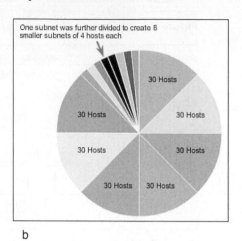

a

b

Figure 9-30   Subnet Size in Traditional Subnetting and Using Variable-Length Subnet Masks

VLSM subnetting is similar to traditional subnetting in that bits are borrowed to create subnets. The formulas to calculate the number of hosts per subnet and the number of subnets created still apply. The difference is that subnetting is not a single-pass activity. With VLSM, the network is first subnetted, and then the subnets are subnetted again. This process can be repeated multiple times to create subnets of various sizes.

Basic VLSM (9.1.5.3)

To better understand the VLSM process, go back to the previous example.

In the previous example, shown in Figure 9-31, the network 192.168.20.0/24 was subnetted into eight equal-sized subnets; seven of the eight subnets were allocated. Four subnets were used for the LANs, and three subnets were used for the WAN connections between the routers. Recall that the wasted address space was in the subnets used for the WAN connections, because those subnets required only two usable addresses: one for each router interface. To avoid this waste, VLSM can be used to create smaller subnets for the WAN connections.

Figure 9-31   Subnetting Scheme for Sample Network

To create smaller subnets for the WAN links, one of the subnets will be divided. In Figure 9-32, the last subnet, 192.168.20.224/27, will be further subnetted.

Recall that when the number of needed host addresses is known, the formula $2^n - 2$ (where n equals the number of host bits remaining) can be used. To provide two usable addresses, 2 host bits must be left in the host portion:

$$2^2 - 2 = 2$$

Because there are 5 host bits in the 192.168.20.224/27 address space, 3 bits can be borrowed, leaving 2 bits in the host portion.

The calculations at this point are exactly the same as those used for traditional subnetting. The bits are borrowed and the subnet ranges are determined.

This VLSM subnetting scheme reduces the number of addresses per subnet to a size appropriate for the WANs. Subnetting subnet 7 for WANs allows subnets 4, 5, and 6 to be available for future networks, as well as several other subnets available for WANs.

```
7  11000000.10101000.00010100.11100000  192.168.20.224/27

     3 more bits borrowed from subnet
     7:

7:0  11000000.10101000.00010100.11100000  192.168.20.224/30 ⎤
7:1  11000000.10101000.00010100.11100100  192.168.20.228/30 ⎥ WANs
7:2  11000000.10101000.00010100.11101000  192.168.20.232/30 ⎥
7:3  11000000.10101000.00010100.11101100  192.168.20.236/30 ⎦
7:4  11000000.10101000.00010100.11110000  192.168.20.240/30 ⎤ Unused /
7:5  11000000.10101000.00010100.11110100  192.168.20.244/30 ⎥ Available
7:6  11000000.10101000.00010100.11111000  192.168.20.248/30 ⎥
7:7  11000000.10101000.00010100.11111100  192.168.20.252/30 ⎦

                Subnetting a subnet
```

Figure 9-32   VLSM Subnetting Scheme

VLSM in Practice (9.1.5.4)

Using the VLSM subnets, the LAN and WAN segments can be addressed without unnecessary waste.

The hosts in each of the LANs will be assigned a valid host address with the range for that subnet and /27 mask. Each of the four routers will have a LAN interface with a /27 subnet and one or more serial interfaces with a /30 subnet.

Using a common addressing scheme, the first host IPv4 address for each subnet is assigned to the LAN interface of the router. The WAN interfaces of the routers are assigned the IP addresses and mask for the /30 subnets.

Hosts on each subnet will have a host IPv4 address from the range of host addresses for that subnet and an appropriate mask. Hosts will use the address of the attached router LAN interface as the default gateway address:

- Building A hosts (192.168.20.0/27) will use the router 192.168.20.1 address as the default gateway address.

- Building B hosts (192.168.20.32/27) will use the router 192.168.20.33 address as the default gateway address.

- Building C hosts (192.168.20.64/27) will use the router 192.168.20.65 address as the default gateway address.

- Building D hosts (192.168.20.96/27) will use the router 192.168.20.97 address as the default gateway address.

VLSM Chart (9.1.5.5)

Address planning can also be accomplished using a variety of tools. One method is to use a VLSM chart to identify which blocks of addresses are available for use and which ones are already assigned. This method helps to prevent assigning addresses that have already been allocated. Using the network from the previous example, the VLSM chart can be used to plan address assignment.

Examining the /27 Subnets

As shown in Figure 9-33a, when using traditional subnetting, the first seven address blocks were allocated for LANs and WANs. Recall that this scheme resulted in eight subnets with 30 usable addresses each (/27). While this scheme worked for the LAN segments, there were many wasted addresses in the WAN segments.

When designing the addressing scheme on a new network, the address blocks can be assigned in a way that minimizes waste and keeps unused blocks of addresses contiguous.

Assigning VLSM Address Blocks

As shown in Figure 9-33b, to use the address space more efficiently, /30 subnets are created for WAN links. To keep the unused blocks of addresses together, the last

/27 subnet was further subnetted to create the /30 subnets. The first three subnets were assigned to WAN links:

- 224 /30 host address range 225 to 226: WAN link between R1 and R2

- 228 /30 host address range 229 to 230: WAN link between R2 and R3

- 232 /30 host address range 233 to 234: WAN link between R3 and R4

- 236 /30 host address range 237 to 238: Available to be used

- 240 /30 host address range 241 to 242: Available to be used

- 244 /30 host address range 245 to 246: Available to be used

- 248 /30 host address range 249 to 250: Available to be used

- 252 /30 host address range 253 to 254: Available to be used

Designing the addressing scheme in this way leaves three unused /27 subnets and five unused /30 subnets.

	/27 Network	Hosts
Building A	.0	.1 - .30
Building B	.32	.33 - .62
Building C	.64	.65 - .94
Building D	.96	.97 - .126
WAN R1 – R2	.128	.129 - .158
WAN R2 – R3	.160	.161 - .190
WAN R3 – R4	.192	.193 - .222
Unused	.224	.225 - .254

a

	/27 Network	Hosts
Bldg A	.0	.1 - .30
Bldg B	.32	.33 - .62
Bldg C	.64	.65 - .94
Bldg D	.96	.97 - .126
Unused	.128	.129 - .158
Unused	.160	.161 - .190
Unused	.192	.193 - .222
	.224	.225 - .254

	/30 Network	Hosts
WAN R1–R2	.224	.225 - .226
WAN R2–R3	.228	.229 - .230
WAN R3–R4	.232	.233 - .234
Unused	.236	.237 - .238
Unused	.240	.241 - .242
Unused	.244	.245 - .246
Unused	.248	.249 - .250
Unused	.252	.253 - .254

b

Figure 9-33 Basic and VLSM Subnetting Tables for 192.168.20.0/24

| Interactive Graphic | **Activity 9.1.5.6: Practicing VLSM** |

Go to the course online to perform this practice activity.

Addressing Schemes (9.2)

Many different network devices require IP addresses. To accommodate all of these devices with the minimum amount of problems, it is necessary to develop a proper addressing scheme.

Structured Design (9.2.1)

The best addressing scheme is one based on the structure and function of the network devices that must be addressed.

Planning to Address the Network (9.2.1.1)

The allocation of network layer address space within the corporate network needs to be well designed. Address assignment should not be random. There are three primary considerations when planning address allocation:

- **Preventing duplication of addresses:** Each host in an internetwork must have a unique address. Without the proper planning and documentation, an address could be assigned to more than one host, resulting in access issues for both hosts.

- **Providing and controlling access:** Some hosts, such as servers, provide resources to internal hosts as well as to external hosts. The Layer 3 address assigned to a server can be used to control access to that server. If, however, the address is randomly assigned and not well documented, controlling access is more difficult.

- **Monitoring security and performance:** Similarly, the security and performance of network hosts and the network as a whole must be monitored. As part of the monitoring process, network traffic is examined for addresses that are generating or receiving excessive packets. If there is proper planning and documentation of the network addressing, problematic network devices can be easily found.

Assigning Addresses Within a Network

Within a network, there are different types of devices, including

- End-user clients
- Servers and peripherals

- Hosts that are accessible from the Internet
- Intermediary devices
- Gateways

When developing an IP addressing scheme, it is generally recommended to have a set pattern of how addresses are allocated to each type of device. This benefits administrators when adding and removing devices and filtering traffic based on IP, as well as simplifies documentation.

Assigning Addresses to Devices (9.2.1.2)

A network addressing plan might include using a different range of addresses within each subnet, for each type of device.

Addresses for Clients

Because of the challenges associated with static address management, end-user devices often have addresses dynamically assigned using Dynamic Host Configuration Protocol (DHCP). DHCP is generally the preferred method of assigning IP addresses to hosts on large networks because it reduces the burden on network support staff and virtually eliminates entry errors.

Another benefit of DHCP is that an address is not permanently assigned to a host but is only leased for a period of time. If we need to change the subnetting scheme of our network, we do not have to statically reassign individual host addresses. With DHCP, we only need to reconfigure the DHCP server with the new subnet information. After this has been done, the hosts only need to renew their IP addresses.

Addresses for Servers and Peripherals

Any network resource, such as a server or a printer, should have a static IP address. The client hosts access these resources using the IP addresses of these devices. Therefore, predictable addresses for each of these servers and peripherals are necessary.

Servers and peripherals are a concentration point for network traffic. There are many packets sent to and from the IPv4 addresses of these devices. When monitoring network traffic with a tool like Wireshark, a network administrator should be able to rapidly identify these devices. Using a consistent numbering system for these devices makes the identification easier.

Addresses for Hosts That Are Accessible from the Internet

In most internetworks, only a few devices are accessible by hosts outside of the corporation. For the most part, these devices are usually servers of some type. As with all devices in a network that provide network resources, the IP addresses for these devices should be static.

In the case of servers accessible from the Internet, each of these must have a public space address associated with it. Additionally, variations in the address of one of these devices will make this device inaccessible from the Internet. In many cases, these devices are on a network that is numbered using private addresses. This means that the router or firewall at the perimeter of the network must be configured to translate the internal private address of the server into an outside public address. Because of this additional configuration on the perimeter intermediary device, it is even more important that these devices have a predictable address.

Addresses for Intermediary Devices

Intermediary devices are also a concentration point for network traffic. Almost all traffic within or between networks passes through some form of intermediary device. Therefore, these network devices provide an opportune location for network management, monitoring, and security.

Most intermediary devices are assigned Layer 3 addresses, either for device management or for their operation. Devices such as hubs, switches, and wireless access points do not require IPv4 addresses to operate as intermediary devices. However, if we must access these devices as hosts to configure, monitor, or troubleshoot network operation, they must have addresses assigned.

Because we must know how to communicate with intermediary devices, they should have predictable addresses. Therefore, their addresses are typically assigned manually. Additionally, the addresses of these devices should be in a different range within the network block than user device addresses.

Address for the Gateway (Routers and Firewalls)

Unlike the other intermediary devices mentioned, routers and firewall devices have an IP address assigned to each interface. Each interface is in a different network and serves as the gateway for the hosts in that network. Typically, the router interface uses either the lowest or highest address in the network. This assignment should be uniform across all networks in the corporation so that network personnel will always know the gateway of the network no matter which network they are working on.

Router and firewall interfaces are the concentration point for traffic entering and leaving the network. Because the hosts in each network use a router or firewall device interface as the gateway out of the network, many packets flow through these interfaces. Therefore, these devices can play a major role in network security by filtering packets based on source and/or destination IP addresses. Grouping the different types of devices into logical addressing groups makes the assignment and operation of this packet filtering more efficient.

Lab 9.2.1.3: Designing and Implementing a Subnetted IPv4 Addressing Scheme

In this lab, you will complete the following objectives:

- Part 1: Design a Network Subnetting Scheme
- Part 2: Configure the Devices
- Part 3: Test and Troubleshoot the Network

Lab 9.2.1.4: Designing and Implementing a VLSM Addressing Scheme

In this lab, you will complete the following objectives:

- Part 1: Examine Network Requirements
- Part 2: Design the VLSM Addressing Scheme
- Part 3: Cable and Configure the IPv4 Network

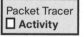
Packet Tracer
☐ Activity

Packet Tracer Activity 9.2.1.5: Designing and Implementing a VLSM Addressing Scheme

In this activity, you are given a network address to develop a VLSM addressing scheme for the network shown in the included topology.

Design Considerations for IPv6 (9.3)

The current IPv4 address space is exhausted. Many network administrators are now incorporating IPv6 into their addressing plans.

Subnetting an IPv6 Network (9.3.1)

Subnetting an IPv6 address is very similar to the way we subnet IPv4 address space with some minor differences.

Subnetting Using the Subnet ID (9.3.1.1)

IPv6 subnetting requires a different approach than IPv4 subnetting. The primary reason is that with IPv6, there are so many addresses, and the reason for subnetting is completely different. An IPv6 address space is not subnetted to conserve addresses; rather, it is subnetted to support hierarchical, logical design of the network. While IPv4 subnetting is about managing address scarcity, IPv6 subnetting is about building an addressing hierarchy based on the number of routers and the networks they support.

Recall that an IPv6 address block with a /48 prefix has 16 bits for the subnet ID, as shown in Figure 9-34. Subnetting using the 16-bit subnet ID yields a possible 65,536 /64 subnets and does not require borrowing any bits from the interface ID, or host portion of the address. Each IPv6 /64 subnet contains roughly 18 quintillion addresses, obviously more than will ever be needed in one IP network segment.

Figure 9-34   IPv6 /48 Address Block

Subnets created from the subnet ID are easy to represent because there is no conversion to binary required. To determine the next available subnet, just count up in hexadecimal. As shown in Figure 9-35, this means counting by hexadecimal in the subnet ID portion.

Figure 9-35   IPv6 Address Block 2001:0DB8:ACAD::/48

The global routing prefix is the same for all subnets. Only the subnet ID quartet is incremented for each subnet.

IPv6 Subnet Allocation (9.3.1.2)

With over 65,000 subnets to choose from, the task of the network administrator becomes one of designing a logical scheme to address the network.

As shown in Figure 9-36a, the example topology will require subnets for each LAN as well as for the WAN link between R1 and R2. Unlike the example for IPv4, with IPv6, the WAN link subnet will not be subnetted further. Although this can "waste" addresses, that is not a concern when using IPv6.

Figure 9-36b shows the allocation of five IPv6 subnets, with the subnet ID field 0001 through 0005, that will be used for this example. Each /64 subnet will provide more addresses than will ever be needed.

Figure 9-36c shows a /64 subnet assigned to each of the LAN and WAN links.

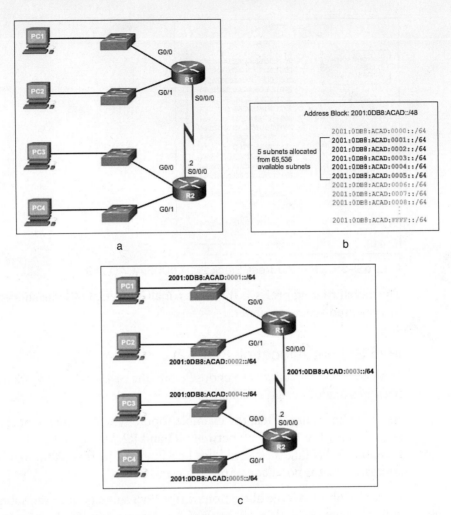

Figure 9-36   IPv6 Subnetting of a Sample Network

Similar to configuring IPv4, Figure 9-37 shows that each of the router interfaces has been configured to be on a different IPv6 subnet.

```
R1(config)#interface gigabitethernet 0/0
R1(config-if)#ipv6 address 2001:db8:acad:1::1/64
R1(config-if)#exit
R1(config)#interface gigabitethernet 0/1
R1(config-if)#ipv6 address 2001:db8:acad:2::1/64
R1(config-if)#exit
R1(config)#interface serial 0/0/0
R1(config-if)#ipv6 address 2001:db8:acad:3::1/64
R1(config-if)#end
R1#
```

Figure 9-37   IPv6 Address Configuration

Subnetting into the Interface ID (9.3.1.3)

Similar to borrowing bits from the host portion of an IPv4 address, with IPv6, bits can be borrowed from the interface ID to create additional IPv6 subnets. This is typically done for security reasons to create fewer hosts per subnet and not necessarily to create additional subnets.

When extending the subnet ID by borrowing bits from the interface ID, the best practice is to subnet on a *nibble boundary*. A nibble is 4 bits or one hexadecimal digit. As shown in Figure 9-38, the /64 subnet prefix is extended 4 bits or 1 nibble to /68. Doing this reduces the size of the interface ID by 4 bits, from 64 to 60 bits.

Figure 9-38   Subnetting on a Nibble Boundary

Subnetting on nibble boundaries means only using nibble-aligned subnet masks. Starting at /64, the nibble-aligned subnet masks are /68, /72, /76, /80, and so on.

Subnetting on a nibble boundary creates subnets by using the additional hexadecimal value. In the example, the new subnet ID consists of the five hexadecimal values, ranging from 00000 through FFFFF.

It is possible to subnet within a nibble boundary, within a hexadecimal digit, but it is not recommended or even necessary. Subnetting within a nibble takes away the advantage of easily determining the prefix from the interface ID. For example, if a /66 prefix length is used, the first 2 bits would be part of the subnet ID and the second 2 bits would be part of the interface ID.

Packet Tracer Activity 9.3.1.4: Implementing a Subnetted IPv6 Addressing Scheme

Your network administrator wants you to assign five /64 IPv6 subnets to the network shown in the topology. Your job is to determine the IPv6 subnets, assign IPv6 addresses to the routers, and set the PCs to automatically receive IPv6 addressing. Your final step is to verify connectivity between IPv6 hosts.

Summary (9.4)

Class Activity 9.4.1.1: Can You Call Me Now?

Note

This activity can be completed individually or in small/large groups using Packet Tracer software.

You are setting up a dedicated, computer addressing scheme for patient rooms in a hospital. The switch will be centrally located in the nurses' station, as each of the five rooms will be wired so that patients can just connect to an RJ-45 port built into the wall of their room. Devise a physical and logical topology for only one of the six floors using the following addressing scheme requirements:

- There are six floors with five patient rooms on each floor for a total of 30 connections. Each room needs a network connection.

- Subnetting must be incorporated into your scheme.

- Use one router, one switch, and five host stations for addressing purposes.

- Validate that all PCs can connect to the hospital's in-house services.

Keep a copy of your scheme to share later with the class or learning community. Be prepared to explain how subnetting, unicasts, multicasts, and broadcasts would be incorporated, and where your addressing scheme could be used.

Packet Tracer
☐ **Activity**

Packet Tracer Activity 9.4.1.2: Skills Integration Challenge

As a network technician familiar with IPv4 and IPv6 addressing implementations, you are now ready to take an existing network infrastructure and apply your knowledge and skills to finalize the configuration. The network administrator has already configured some commands on the routers. Do not erase or modify those configurations. Your task is to complete the IPv4 and IPv6 addressing scheme, implement IPv4 and IPv6 addressing, and verify connectivity.

The process of segmenting a network, by dividing it into to multiple smaller network spaces, is called subnetting.

Every network address has a valid range of host addresses. All devices attached to the same network will have an IPv4 host address for that network and a common subnet mask or network prefix. Traffic can be forwarded between hosts directly if they are on the same subnet. Traffic cannot be forwarded between subnets without the use of a router. To determine whether traffic is local or remote, the router uses the subnet mask. The prefix and the subnet mask are different ways of representing the same thing: the network portion of an address.

IPv4 subnets are created by using one or more of the host bits as network bits. Two very important factors that will lead to the determination of the IP address block with the subnet mask are the number of subnets required and the maximum number of hosts needed per subnet. There is an inverse relationship between the number of subnets and the number of hosts. The more bits borrowed to create subnets, the fewer host bits are available; therefore fewer hosts per subnet.

The formula 2^n (where n is the number of host bits remaining) is used to calculate how many addresses will be available on each subnet. However, the network address and broadcast address within a range are not usable; therefore, to calculate the usable number of addresses, the calculation 2^n-2 is required.

Subnetting a subnet, or using variable-length subnet masks (VLSM), was designed to avoid wasting addresses.

IPv6 subnetting requires a different approach than IPv4 subnetting. An IPv6 address space is not subnetted to conserve addresses; rather it is subnetted to support hierarchical, logical design of the network. So, while IPv4 subnetting is about managing address scarcity, IPv6 subnetting is about building an addressing hierarchy based on the number of routers and the networks they support.

Careful planning is required to make best use of the available address space. Size, location, use, and access requirements are all considerations in the address-planning process.

After it is implemented, an IP network needs to be tested to verify its connectivity and operational performance.

Practice

The following activities provide practice with the topics introduced in this chapter. The labs and class activities are available in the companion *The Introduction to Networks Lab Manual* (ISBN 978-1-58713-312-1). The Packet Tracer Activities PKA files are found in the online course.

Class Activities

- Class Activity 9.0.1.2: Activity: Call Me!
- Class Activity 9.4.1.1: Can You Call Me Now?

Labs

- Lab 9.1.4.8: Calculating IPv4 Subnets

- Lab 9.1.4.9: Subnetting Network Topologies

- Lab 9.1.4.10: Researching Subnet Calculators

- Lab 9.2.1.3: Designing and Implementing a Subnetted IPv4 Addressing Scheme

- Lab 9.2.1.4: Designing and Implementing a VLSM Addressing Scheme

Packet Tracer Activities

- Packet Tracer Activity 9.1.4.6: Subnetting Scenario 1

- Packet Tracer Activity 9.1.4.7: Subnetting Scenario 2

- Packet Tracer Activity 9.2.1.5: Designing and Implementing a VLSM Addressing Scheme

- Packet Tracer Activity 9.3.1.4: Implementing a Subnetted IPv6 Addressing Scheme

- Packet Tracer Activity 9.4.1.2: Skills Integration Challenge

Check Your Understanding

Complete all the review questions listed here to test your understanding of the topics and concepts in this chapter. The appendix, "Check Your Understanding Answer Key," lists the answers.

1. What are advantages of subnetting a large network? (Choose two.)

    A. More address space is created.

    B. Overall network traffic is reduced.

    C. IP addresses can be reused on the same subnetwork.

    D. Network performance is improved.

    E. Layer 3 devices are not required when a network is subnetted.

2. What would allow devices on different subnets to be able to communicate?

    A. Hub

    B. Layer 2 switch

    C. Router

3. Fill in the blank. To create subnets, bits are borrowed from the ____ portion of an IP address.

4. How many subnets can be created if 4 bits are borrowed to specify subnets?

A. 4

B. 8

C. 14

D. 16

5. What best describes a network broadcast address?

A. All 0 bits in the host portion of the address

B. All 0 bits plus a rightmost 1 bit in the host portion of the address

C. All 1 bits plus a rightmost 0 bit in the host portion of the address

D. All 1 bits in the host portion of the address

6. How many valid host addresses are created when 4 host bits are borrowed from the 10.20.20.0/24 network?

A. 2

B. 4

C. 14

D. 16

E. 126

F. 128

G. 254

H. 256

7. A junior network technician has subnetted the 10.20.30.0/24 address space by borrowing 3 bits. The technician decides to use the second subnet for the Accounting department computers. Which of the following addresses could the network technician assign to hosts? (Choose three.)

A. 10.20.30.29/27

B. 10.20.30.31/27

C. 10.20.30.32/27

D. 10.20.30.33/27

E. 10.20.30.34/27

F. 10.20.30.35/27

8. A junior network technician is assigning host addresses to devices in the
   192.168.1.0/25 subnet. The departmental printer is assigned the address
   192.168.1.131/25 with a 192.168.1.1/25 default gateway. No one in the department is able to print. What is the cause of the problem?

   A. The default gateway is not correct for the departmental subnet.

   B. The printer has been assigned a broadcast IP address.

   C. The printer has been assigned an address on another subnet.

   D. The printer has been assigned a network IP address.

9. A new department has been established with 511 hosts that require addresses.
   Currently the company uses the 10.20.0.0/16 address space. How many bits
   must the network administrator borrow to provide addresses for this subnet
   without wasting addresses?

   A. 5

   B. 6

   C. 7

   D. 8

   E. 9

10. A network technician borrows 5 bits from the 10.0.0.0/16 network to create
    subnets. What is the subnet mask that should be associated with each of the
    newly created subnets?

    A. 255.248.0.0

    B. 255.255.0.0

    C. 255.255.248.0

    D. 255.255.255.0

    E. 255.255.255.248

11. Fill in the blank. _____ provides a more efficient IP address allocation by allowing
    the use of different-size subnets in the same network.

12. A network administrator has borrowed 3 bits from the 10.20.0.0/25 network to create subnets. The administrator then decided to use the first subnet for point-to-point serial WAN connections each requiring two addresses. How many WAN connections can the administrator address using only the first subnet if he is using VLSM?

    A. 1

    B. 2

    C. 4

    D. 16

    E. 32

    F. 64

    G. 128

13. A network administrator has decided to use VLSM to subnet the 10.11.0.0/20 network to provide addresses for two new departments and the point-to-point link that separates the two departments. The first department has 796 users and the second department has 31 users. The WAN link requires only two addresses. Which of the following subnets will provide the required contiguous space and waste the fewest addresses? (Choose three.)

    A. 10.11.0.0/21

    B. 10.11.0.0/22

    C. 10.11.253.0/25

    D. 10.11.253.0/26

    E. 10.11.253.128/29

    F. 10.11.253.64/30

14. What is the primary purpose of subnetting IPv6 address space?

    A. Conservation of addresses

    B. Support hierarchical network design

    C. Minimize network broadcast traffic

    D. Improve network performance

15. When subnetting IPv6 address space, why is it wise to subnet on a nibble boundary?

    A. IPv6 is expressed in hexadecimal, and each nibble is one hexadecimal character.

    B. You can only subnet IPv6 address space on nibble boundaries.

    C. Subnetting on a nibble boundary is the most efficient use of IPv6 address space.

    D. Subnetting on a nibble boundary is mandated by the Internet Numbering Authority.

16. What is the third subnet address of the 2001:0DB8:ACAD::/48 network when borrowing 8 bits (2 nibbles)?

    A. 2001:0DB8:ACAD:0002::/56

    B. 2001.0DB8:ACAD:0020::/56

    C. 2001:0DB8:ACAD:0200::/56

    D. 2001:0DB8:ACAD:2000::/56

CHAPTER 10

Application Layer

Objectives

Upon completion of this chapter, you will be able to answer the following questions:

- How do the functions of the application layer, session layer, and presentation layer work together to provide network services to end-user applications?

- How do common application layer protocols interact with end-user applications?

- How do common application layer protocols provide Internet services to end users, including WWW services and email?

- What application layer protocols provide IP addressing services, including DNS and DHCP?

- What are the features and operation of well-known application layer protocols that allow file-sharing services, including FTP, File Sharing Services, and SMB protocol?

- How is data moved across the network, from opening an application to receiving data?

Key Terms

This chapter uses the following key terms. You can find the definitions in the Glossary.

Telnet   page 519

Simple Mail Transfer Protocol (SMTP) page 519

File Transfer Protocol (FTP)   page 519

Trivial File Transfer Protocol (TFTP) page 519

Bootstrap Protocol (BOOTP)   page 519

Post Office Protocol (POP)   page 520

Internet Message Access Protocol (IMAP)   page 520

peer-to-peer (P2P)   page 520

client-server   page 523

daemon   page 524

nslookup   page 533

Server Message Block (SMB)   page 539

Introduction (10.0.1.1)

In this chapter, we will explore the role of the application layer and how the applications, services, and protocols within the application layer make robust communication across data networks possible.

We experience the Internet through the World Wide Web when streaming videos, playing online games, chatting with and emailing friends, and shopping for deals on websites. Applications, such as the ones used to provide the services mentioned, provide the human interface to the underlying network. They enable us to send and receive data with relative ease. Typically, we can access and use these applications without knowing how they work. However, for network professionals, it is important to understand how an application is able to format, transmit, and interpret messages that are sent and received across the network.

Visualizing the mechanisms that enable communication across the network is made easier if we use the layered framework of the OSI model.

Class Activity 10.0.1.2: Application Investigation

What would happen if your employer decided to have IP telephones installed in your workplace, resulting in the network being inoperable until next week?

Your work however, must continue. You have emails to send and quotes to write for your manager's approval. Because of possible security issues, you are not allowed to use personal or external computer systems, equipment, or off-site equipment and systems to complete your corporate workload.

Your instructor might ask you to complete the questions from both of the following scenarios, or to choose one scenario (A. Emails or B. Quote for Manager's Approval). Answer the questions fully for the scenario(s). Be prepared to discuss your answers in class.

A. Emails

- What method(s) can you use to send email communication?

- How could you send the same email to multiple recipients?

- How would you get a large attachment to multiple recipients, if necessary?

- Are these methods cost-effective to your corporation?

- Do they violate any security policies of your corporation?

B. Quote for Manager's Approval

- You have a desktop application software package installed on your computer. Will it be relatively easy to produce the quote that your manager needs for the new contract due by the end of the week? What limitations will be experienced while trying to complete the quote?

- How will you present the quote to your manager for approval? How do you think he or she will send the quote to the client for his approval?

- Are these methods cost-effective to your corporation? Justify your answer.

Application Layer Protocols (10.1)

This section will describe the protocols, applications, and services of the TCP/IP model.

Application, Session, and Presentation (10.1.1)

This section will introduce some protocols of the TCP/IP application layer, which also relates to the top three layers of the OSI model.

OSI and TCP/IP Models Revisited (10.1.1.1)

Networking professionals use the OSI and TCP/IP models to communicate both verbally and in written technical documentation. As such, networking professionals can use these models to describe the behavior of protocols and applications.

In the OSI model, data is passed from one layer to the next. The data starts at the application layer on the transmitting host, proceeding down the hierarchy to the physical layer and then passing over the communications channel. At the destination host, the data proceeds back up the hierarchy, ending at the application layer.

The application layer is the top layer of both the OSI and TCP/IP models. The TCP/IP application layer includes a number of protocols that provide specific functionality to a variety of end-user applications. The functionality of the TCP/IP application layer protocols fit roughly into the framework of the top three layers of the OSI model: application, presentation, and session layers. The OSI model Layers 5, 6, and 7 are used as references for application software developers and vendors to produce products, such as web browsers that need to access networks.

Application Layer (10.1.1.2)

This section provides a brief overview of the application layer.

The Application Layer

The application layer is closest to the end user. It is the layer that provides the interface between the applications used to communicate and the underlying network over which our messages are transmitted. Application layer protocols are used to exchange data between programs running on the source and destination hosts. There are many application layer protocols, and new protocols are always being developed. Some of the most widely known application layer protocols include Hypertext Transfer Protocol (HTTP), File Transfer Protocol (FTP), Trivial File Transfer Protocol (TFTP), Internet Message Access Protocol (IMAP), and Domain Name System (DNS) protocol.

Presentation and Session Layers (10.1.1.3)

This section provides a brief overview of the presentation and session layers.

The Presentation Layer

The presentation layer has three primary functions:

- Formats, or presents, data from the source device into a compatible form for receipt by the destination device

- Compression of the data in a way that can be decompressed by the destination device

- Encryption of the data for transmission and the decryption of data upon receipt by the destination

The presentation layer formats data for the application layer and it sets standards for file formats. Some well-known standards for video include QuickTime and Motion Picture Experts Group (MPEG). QuickTime is an Apple computer specification for video and audio, and MPEG is a standard for video and audio compression and coding.

Among the well-known graphic image formats that are used on networks are Graphics Interchange Format (GIF), Joint Photographic Experts Group (JPEG), and Portable Network Graphics (PNG) format. GIF and JPEG are compression and coding standards for graphic images. PNG was designed to address some of the limitations of the GIF format and to eventually replace it.

The Session Layer

As the name implies, functions at the session layer create and maintain dialogs between source and destination applications. The session layer handles the exchange of information to initiate dialogs, to keep them active, and to restart sessions that are disrupted or idle for a long period of time.

TCP/IP Application Layer Protocols (10.1.1.4)

While the OSI model separates the individual application, presentation, and session functions, most widely known and implemented TCP/IP applications incorporate the functionality of all three layers.

The TCP/IP application protocols specify the format and control information necessary for many common Internet communication functions. Among these TCP/IP protocols are

- **Domain Name System (DNS):** This protocol resolves Internet names to IP addresses. It translates domain names into IP addresses. *TCP/UDP port 53*

- *Telnet*: This is used to provide remote access to servers and networking devices. *TCP port 23*

- **Secure Shell (SSH):** This is a secure protocol used to provide encrypted remote access to servers and networking devices. *TCP port 22*

- *Simple Mail Transfer Protocol (SMTP):* This protocol transfers mail messages and attachments. It enables clients to send email to a mail server and supports the transfer of email between mail servers. *TCP port 25*

- **Dynamic Host Configuration Protocol (DHCP):** A protocol used to assign an IP address, subnet mask, default gateway, and DNS server addresses to a host. *UDP 67 and UDP 68 (DHCPv6 UDP 546 and UDP 547)*

- **Hypertext Transfer Protocol (HTTP):** This protocol transfers files that make up the web pages of the World Wide Web, including text, graphic images, audio, and video. *TCP port 80*

- *File Transfer Protocol (FTP):* A reliable, connection-oriented protocol used for interactive file transfer between systems. *TCP ports 20 and 21*

- *Trivial File Transfer Protocol (TFTP):* This simple protocol is used for connectionless active file transfer. As a best-effort file delivery protocol, it has low overhead. *UDP port 69*

- *Bootstrap Protocol (BOOTP):* This protocol is a precursor to the DHCP protocol. It enables a diskless workstation to discover a BOOTP server, accept its IP address, and initiate a download of a file into memory to boot the machine. *UDP 67 and UDP 68*

- *Post Office Protocol (POP)*: A protocol used by email clients to retrieve email from a remote server. *TCP port 110*

- *Internet Message Access Protocol (IMAP)*: This is another protocol for email retrieval. *TCP port 143*

Application layer protocols are used by both the source and destination devices during a communication session. For the communications to be successful, the application layer protocols implemented on the source and destination host must be compatible.

Interactive Graphic

Activity 10.1.1.5: Application Protocols and Standards

Go to the course online to perform this practice activity.

How Application Protocols Interact with End-User Applications (10.1.2)

This section introduces peer-to-peer and client-server environments.

Peer-to-Peer Networks (10.1.2.1)

When accessing information on a networking device, whether it is a PC, laptop, tablet, smartphone, or some other device connected to a network, the data might not be physically stored on the device. In this case, a request to access that information must be made to the device where the data resides. In the *peer-to-peer (P2P)* networking model, the data is accessed from a peer device without the use of a dedicated server.

The P2P network model involves two parts: P2P networks and P2P applications. Both parts have similar features, but in practice work quite differently.

P2P Networks

In a P2P network, two or more computers are connected through a network and can share resources (such as printers and files) without having a dedicated server. Every connected end device (known as a peer) can function as both a server and a client. One computer might assume the role of server for one transaction while simultaneously serving as a client for another. The roles of client and server are set on a per-request basis.

An example is a simple home network with two computers, as shown in Figure 10-1. In this example, Peer2 has a printer attached to it directly by USB, and is set up to share the printer on the network so that Peer1 can print to it. Peer1 is set up to share a drive or folder on the network. This allows Peer2 to access and save files to the shared folder. In addition to sharing files, a network such as this one would allow users to enable networked games or share an Internet connection.

P2P networks decentralize the resources on a network. Instead of locating data to be shared on dedicated servers, data can be located anywhere and on any connected device. Most of the current operating systems support file and print sharing without requiring additional server software. However, P2P networks do not use centralized user accounts or access servers to maintain permissions. Therefore, it is difficult to enforce security and access policies in networks containing more than just a few computers. User accounts and access rights must be set individually on each peer device.

Figure 10-1   Peer-to-Peer Network

Peer-to-Peer Applications (10.1.2.2)

A peer-to-peer (P2P) application allows a device to act as both a client and a server within the same communication. In this model, every client is a server and every server a client. Both can initiate a communication and are considered equal in the communication process. However, P2P applications require that each end device provide a user interface and run a background service. When you launch a specific P2P application, it loads the required user interface and background services; afterward, the devices can communicate directly.

Some P2P applications use a hybrid system where resource sharing is decentralized, but the indexes that point to resource locations are stored in a centralized directory. In a hybrid system, each peer accesses an index server to get the location of a resource stored on another peer. The index server can also help connect two peers, but after after they are connected, the communication takes place between the two peers without additional communication to the index server.

P2P applications can be used on P2P networks, on client/server networks, and across the Internet.

Common P2P Applications (10.1.2.3)

With P2P applications, each computer in the network running the application can act as a client or a server for the other computers in the network running the application. Common P2P applications include

- eDonkey
- eMule
- Shareaza
- BitTorrent
- Bitcoin
- LionShare

Some P2P applications are based on the Gnutella protocol. They enable people to share files on their hard disks with others. As shown in Figure 10-2, Gnutella-compatible client software allows users to connect to Gnutella services over the Internet and to locate and access resources shared by other Gnutella peers. Many client applications are available for accessing the Gnutella network, including BearShare, Gnucleus, LimeWire, Morpheus, WinMX, and XoloX.

While the Gnutella Developer Forum maintains the basic protocol, application vendors often develop extensions to make the protocol work better with their applications.

Many P2P applications do not use a central database to record all the files available on the peers. Instead, the devices on the network each tell the others what files are available when queried, and use the file-sharing protocol and services to support locating resources.

In a client/server netw...
server *daemon*. I...
not under an ...
request fr...
receiv...

Figure 10-2 Gnutella Protocol

Lab 10.1.2.4: Researching Peer-to-Peer ...ng

In this lab, you will complete the following objectives:

- Part 1: Identify P2P Networks, File-Sharing Protocols, and Applications
- Part 2: Research P2P File-Sharing Issues
- Part 3: Research P2P Copyright Litigations

Client-Server Model (10.1.2.5)

In the *client-server* model, the device requesting the information is called a client and the device responding to the request is called a server. Client and server processes are considered to be in the application layer. The client begins the exchange by requesting data from the server, which responds by sending one or more streams of data to the client. Application layer protocols describe the format of the requests and responses between clients and servers. In addition to the actual data transfer, this exchange might also require user authentication and the identification of a data file to be transferred.

...ork, the server runs a service, or process, sometimes called a ...ke most services, daemons typically run in the background and are ...nd user's direct control. Daemons are described as "listening" for a ...m a client, because they are programmed to respond whenever the server ...s a request for the service provided by the daemon. Each server service is ...pped to a specific transport layer port number. When a daemon "hears" a request from a client, it exchanges appropriate messages with the client, as required by its protocol, and proceeds to send the requested data to the client in the proper format. To make a request, the client constructs a segment with a destination port number of the well-known port number of the service on the server.

One example of a client-server network is using an ISP's email service to send, receive, and store email. The email client on a home computer issues a request to the ISP's email server for any unread mail. The server responds by sending the requested email to the client.

Although data is typically described as flowing from the server to the client, this is not always the case, depending on the request to the server. Some data always flows from the client to the server, even if it is only the request to start the exchange. Data flow can be equal in both directions, or can even be greater in the direction going from the client to the server. For example, a client might transfer a file to the server for storage purposes. As shown in Figure 10-3, data transfer from a client to a server is referred to as an upload and data from a server to a client as a download.

Figure 10-3   Client-Server Model

Well-Known Application Layer Protocols and Services (10.2)

The next sections describe the OSI presentation and session layers in more detail.

Common Application Layer Protocols (10.2.1)

This section focuses on three common application layer protocols that support users' everyday Internet services.

Application Layer Protocols Revisited (10.2.1.1)

There are dozens of application layer protocols, but on a typical day, you probably use only five or six. Three application layer protocols that are involved in everyday work or play are

- Hypertext Transfer Protocol (HTTP)

- Simple Mail Transfer Protocol (SMTP)

- Post Office Protocol (POP)

These application layer protocols make it possible to browse the web and send and receive email. HTTP is used to enable users to connect to websites across the Internet. SMTP is used to enable users to send email. POP is used to enable users to receive email.

Hypertext Transfer Protocol and Hypertext Markup Language (10.2.1.2)

When a web address or Uniform Resource Locator (URL) is typed into a web browser, the web browser establishes a connection to the web service running on the server using the HTTP protocol. URLs and Uniform Resource Identifiers (URI) are the names most people associate with web addresses.

The http://www.cisco.com/index.html URL is an example of a URL that refers to a specific resource: a web page named **index.html** on a server identified as **cisco.com**.

Web browsers are the type of client applications a computer uses to connect to the World Wide Web and access resources stored on a web server. As with most server processes, the web server runs as a background service and makes different types of files available.

To access the content, web clients make connections to the server and request the desired resources. The server replies with the resources, and upon receipt, the browser interprets the data and presents it to the user.

Browsers can interpret and present many data types (such as plain text or Hypertext Markup Language, the language in which web pages are constructed). Other types of data, however, might require another service or program, typically referred to as plug-ins or add-ons. To help the browser determine what type of file it is receiving, the server specifies what kind of data the file contains.

To better understand how the web browser and web client interact, we can examine how a web page is opened in a browser. For this example, use the http://www.cisco.com/index.html URL.

First, the browser interprets the three parts of the URL:

> **http** (the protocol or scheme)
>
> **www.cisco.com** (the server name)
>
> **index.html** (the specific filename requested)

Second, the browser then checks with a name server to convert www.cisco.com into a numeric address, which it uses to connect to the server. Using HTTP requirements, the browser sends a GET request to the server and asks for the **index.html** file.

Third, the server sends the HTML code for this web page to the browser.

Finally, the browser deciphers the HTML code and formats the page for the browser window.

HTTP and HTTPS (10.2.1.3)

HTTP is used across the World Wide Web for data transfer and is one of the most used application protocols today. It was originally developed to simply publish and retrieve HTML pages; however, the flexibility of HTTP has made it a vital application within distributed, collaborative information systems.

HTTP is a request/response protocol. When a client, typically a web browser, sends a request to a web server, HTTP specifies the message types used for that communication. The three common message types are

- GET
- POST
- PUT

GET is a client request for data. A client (web browser) sends the GET message to the web server to request HTML pages. When the server receives the GET request, it responds with a status line, such as HTTP/1.1 200 OK, and a message of its own. The message from the server can include the requested HTML file, if available, or it might contain an error or information message, such as "The location of the requested file has changed."

POST and PUT are used to upload data files to the web server. For example, when the user enters data into a form that is embedded within a web page (such as when completing an order request), the POST message is sent to the web server. Included within the POST message is the data that the user submitted in the form.

PUT uploads resources or content to the web server. For example, if a user attempts to upload a file or image to a website, a PUT message is sent from the client to the server with the attached file or image.

Although HTTP is remarkably flexible, it is not a secure protocol. The request messages send information to the server in plain text that can be intercepted and read. Similarly, the server responses, typically HTML pages, are also unencrypted.

For secure communication across the Internet, the HTTP Secure (HTTPS) protocol is used for accessing or posting web server information. HTTPS can use authentication and encryption to secure data as it travels between the client and server. HTTPS specifies additional rules for passing data between the application layer and the transport layer. HTTPS uses the same client request–server response process as HTTP, but the data stream is encrypted with Secure Socket Layer (SSL) or with Transport Layer Security before being transported across the network. HTTPS creates additional load and processing time on the server because of the encryption and decryption of traffic.

SMTP, POP, and IMAP (10.2.1.4-10.2.1.7)

One of the primary services offered by an ISP is email hosting. Email has revolutionized how people communicate through its simplicity and speed. Yet to run on a computer or other end device, email requires several applications and services.

Email is a store-and-forward method of sending, storing, and retrieving electronic messages across a network. Email messages are stored in databases on mail servers. ISPs often maintain mail servers that support many different customer accounts.

Email clients communicate with mail servers to send and receive email. Mail servers communicate with other mail servers to transport messages from one domain to another. An email client does not communicate directly with another email client when sending email. Instead, both clients rely on the mail server to transport messages. This is true even when both users are in the same domain.

Email clients send messages to the email server configured in the application settings. When the server receives the message, it checks to see whether the recipient domain is located in its local database. If it is not, it sends a DNS request to determine the IP address of the mail server for the destination domain. The email is then forwarded to the appropriate server.

Email supports three separate protocols for operation:

- Simple Mail Transfer Protocol (SMTP)
- Post Office Protocol (POP)
- Internet Message Access Protocol (IMAP)

The application layer process that sends mail uses SMTP. This is the case if sending from a client to a server, as well as when sending from one server to another.

A client retrieves email, however, using one of two application layer protocols:

- POP
- IMAP

Simple Mail Transfer Protocol (SMTP) transfers mail reliably and efficiently. For SMTP applications to work properly, the mail message must be formatted properly and SMTP processes must be running on both the client and server.

SMTP message formats require a message header and a message body. While the message body can contain any amount of text, the message header must have a properly formatted recipient email address and a sender address. Any other header information is optional.

When a client sends email, the client SMTP process connects with a server SMTP process on well-known port 25 or port 587. After the connection is made, the client attempts to send the email to the server across the connection. When the server receives the message, it either places the message in a local account, if the recipient is local, or forwards the message using the same SMTP connection process to another mail server for delivery.

The destination email server might not be online or might be busy when email messages are sent. Therefore, SMTP spools messages to be sent at a later time. Periodically, the server checks the queue for messages and attempts to send them again. If the message is still not delivered after a predetermined expiration time, it is returned to the sender as undeliverable.

Post Office Protocol (POP) enables a workstation to retrieve mail from a mail server. With POP, mail is downloaded from the server to the client and then deleted from the server.

The server starts the POP service by passively listening on TCP port 110 for client connection requests. When a client wants to make use of the service, it sends a request to establish a TCP connection with the server. When the connection is established, the POP server sends a greeting. The client and POP server then exchange commands and responses until the connection is closed or aborted.

Because email messages are downloaded to the client and removed from the server, there is not a centralized location where email messages are kept. Because POP does not store messages, it is undesirable for a small business that needs a centralized backup solution.

POP3 is desirable for an ISP, because it alleviates its responsibility for managing large amounts of storage for its email servers.

Figure 10-4 shows the uses of the SMTP and POP protocols supporting email.

SMTP is used to send emails from clients to server, and to forward emails between email servers.
POP is used to deliver email.

Figure 10-4   Mail Protocols

Internet Message Access Protocol (IMAP) is another protocol that describes a method to retrieve email messages. However, unlike POP, when the user connects to an IMAP-capable server, copies of the messages are downloaded to the client application. The original messages are kept on the server until manually deleted. Users view copies of the messages in their email client software.

Users can create a file hierarchy on the server to organize and store mail. That file structure is duplicated on the email client as well. When a user decides to delete a message, the server synchronizes that action and deletes the message from the server.

For small- to medium-sized businesses, there are many advantages to using IMAP. IMAP can provide long-term storage of email messages on mail servers and allows centralized backup. It also enables employees to access email messages from multiple locations, using different devices or client software. The mailbox folder structure that a user expects to see is available for viewing regardless of how the user accesses the mailbox.

For an ISP, IMAP might not be the protocol of choice. It can be expensive to purchase and maintain the disk space to support the large number of stored emails. Additionally, if customers expect their mailboxes to be backed up routinely, that can further increase the costs to the ISP.

Packet Tracer Activity 10.2.1.8: Web and Email

In this activity, you will configure HTTP and email services using the simulated server in Packet Tracer. You will then configure clients to access the HTTP and email services.

Providing IP Addressing Services (10.2.2)

This section presents addressing services including DNS and DHCP.

Domain Name System (10.2.2.1)

In data networks, devices are labeled with numeric IP addresses to send and receive data over networks. Most people cannot remember this numeric address. Domain names were created to convert the numeric address into a simple, recognizable name.

On the Internet, these domain names, such as http://www.cisco.com, are much easier for people to remember than 198.133.219.25, which is the actual numeric address for this server. If Cisco decides to change the numeric address of www.cisco.com, it is transparent to the user, because the domain name remains the same. The new address is simply linked to the existing domain name and connectivity is maintained. When networks were small, it was a simple task to maintain the mapping between domain names and the addresses they represented. As networks have grown and the number of devices increased, this manual system became unworkable.

The Domain Name System (DNS) was created for domain name to address resolution for these networks. DNS uses a distributed set of servers to resolve the names associated with these numbered addresses.

The DNS protocol defines an automated service that matches resource names with the required numeric network address. It includes the format for queries, responses, and data. The DNS protocol communications use a single format called a message. This message format is used for all types of client queries and server responses, error messages, and the transfer of resource record information between servers.

DNS Message Format (10.2.2.2)

A DNS server provides the name resolution using the Berkeley Internet Name Domain (BIND), or the name daemon, which is often called named (pronounced "name-dee"). BIND was originally developed by four students at the University of California Berkley in the early 1980s.

The DNS message format used by BIND is the most widely used DNS format on the Internet. The same message format is used for all types of client queries and server responses, error messages, and the transfer of records between servers. The parts of messages are

- **Header:** Identifies the query and type of message

- **Question:** Question for the name server

- **Answer:** Resource records answering the question

- **Authority:** Resource records pointing toward an authority

- **Additional:** Resources records holding additional information

The DNS server stores different types of resource records used to resolve names. These records contain the name, address, and type of record.

Some of these record types are

- **A:** An end device address

- **NS:** An authoritative name server

- **CNAME:** The canonical name (or Fully Qualified Domain Name) for an alias; used when multiple services have the single network address, but each service has its own entry in DNS

- **MX:** Mail exchange record; maps a domain name to a list of mail exchange servers for that domain

- **AAAA:** 128-bit IPv6 address that stores a single IPv6 node address

When a client makes a query, the server's BIND process first looks at its own records to resolve the name. If it is unable to resolve the name using its stored records, it contacts other servers to resolve the name.

The request might be passed along to a number of servers, which can take extra time and consume bandwidth. After a match is found and returned to the original requesting server, the server temporarily stores the numbered address that matches the name in cache memory.

If that same name is requested again, the first server can return the address by using the value stored in its name cache. Caching reduces both the DNS query data network traffic and the workloads of servers higher up the hierarchy. The DNS Client service on Windows PCs optimizes the performance of DNS name resolution by also storing previously resolved names in memory. The **ipconfig /displaydns** command displays all the cached DNS entries on a Windows computer system.

DNS Hierarchy (10.2.2.3)

The DNS protocol uses a hierarchical system to create a database to provide name resolution. The hierarchy looks like an inverted tree with the root at the top and branches below (see Figure 10-5). DNS uses domain names to form the hierarchy.

The naming structure is broken down into small, manageable zones. Each DNS server maintains a specific database file and is only responsible for managing name-to-IP mappings for that small portion of the entire DNS structure. When a DNS server receives a request for a name translation that is not within its DNS zone, the DNS server forwards the request to another DNS server within the proper zone for translation.

> **Note**
>
> DNS is scalable because host name resolution is spread across multiple servers.

The different top-level domains represent either the type of organization or the country of origin. Examples of top-level domains are

- **.au:** Australia
- **.co:** Colombia
- **.com:** A business or industry
- **.jp:** Japan
- **.org:** A nonprofit organization

After top-level domains are second-level domain names, and below them are other lower-level domains. Each domain name is a path down this inverted tree starting from the root. For example, as shown in the Figure 10-5, the root DNS server might not know exactly where the record for the email server, mail.cisco.com, is located, but it maintains a record for the .com domain within the top-level domain. Likewise, the servers within the .com domain might not have a record for mail.cisco.com, but they do have a record for the domain. The servers within the cisco.com domain have a record (an MX record to be precise) for mail.cisco.com.

DNS relies on this hierarchy of decentralized servers to store and maintain these resource records. The resource records list domain names that the server can resolve and alternative servers that can also process requests. If a given server has resource records that correspond to its level in the domain hierarchy, it is said to be authoritative for those records. For example, a name server in the cisco.netacad.net domain would not be authoritative for the mail.cisco.com record, because that record is held at a higher domain level server, specifically the name server in the cisco.com domain.

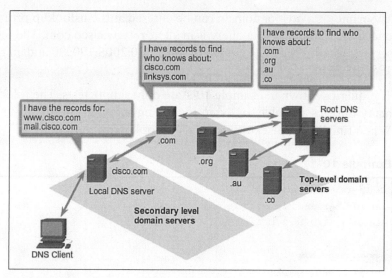

Figure 10-5   DNS Server Hierarchy

Nslookup (10.2.2.4)

DNS is a client-server service; however, it differs from the other client-server services. While other services use a client that is an application (such as web browser or email client), the DNS client runs as a service itself. The DNS client, sometimes called the DNS resolver, supports name resolution for other network applications and other services that need it.

When configuring a network device, we generally provide one or more DNS server addresses that the DNS client can use for name resolution. Usually the Internet service provider (ISP) provides the addresses to use for the DNS servers. When a user's application requests to connect to a remote device by name, the requesting DNS client queries one of these name servers to resolve the name to a numeric address.

Computer operating systems also have a utility called *nslookup* that allows the user to manually query the name servers to resolve a given host name. This utility can also be used to troubleshoot name resolution issues and to verify the current status of the name servers.

In Example 10-1, when the **nslookup** command is issued, the default DNS server configured for your host is displayed. In this example, the DNS server is dns.example.com, which has an address of 172.16.2.10.

The name of a host or domain can be entered at the **nslookup** prompt. In the first query in Example 10-1, a query is made for www.cisco.com. The responding name server provides the IPv6 address of 2001:590:2005:190::90 and an IPv4 address of 198.133.219.25.

The queries shown in Example 10-1 are only simple tests. The nslookup utility has many options available for extensive testing and verification of the DNS process. When finished, type **exit** to leave the nslookup utility.

Example 10-1   nslookup

```
C:\Users\mark> nslookup
Default Server:  dns.example.com.2.16.172.in-addr.arpa
Address:  172.16.2.10


> www.cisco.com
Server:  dns.example.com.2.16.172.in-addr.arpa
Address:  172.16.2.10

Non-authoritative answer:
Name:    e144.dscb.akamaiedge.net
Addresses:  2001:590:2005:190::90
            184.24.32.170
Aliases:  www.cisco.com
          www.cisco.com.akadns.net

> cisco.netacad.net
Server:  dns.example.com.2.16.172.in-addr.arpa
Address:  172.16.2.10

Non-authoritative answer:
  Name:    cisco.netacad.net
  Address:  72.163.6.223
```

Activity 10.2.2.5: DNS CLI Commands in Windows and UNIX

Go to the course online to perform this practice activity.

Dynamic Host Configuration Protocol (10.2.2.6)

The Dynamic Host Configuration Protocol (DHCP) service enables devices on a network to obtain IP addresses and other information from a DHCP server. This service automates the assignment of IP addresses, subnet masks, gateways, and other IP networking parameters. This is referred to as dynamic addressing. The alternative to dynamic addressing is static addressing. When using static addressing, the network administrator manually enters IP address information on network hosts.

DHCP allows a host to obtain an IP address dynamically when it connects to the network. The DHCP server is contacted and an address requested. The DHCP server chooses an address from a configured range of addresses called a pool and assigns (leases) it to the host for a set period.

On larger local networks, or where the user population changes frequently, DHCP is preferred for address assignment. New users might arrive with laptops and need a connection; others might have new workstations that must be connected. Rather than have the network administrator assign IP addresses for each workstation, it is more efficient to have IP addresses assigned automatically using DHCP.

DHCP-distributed addresses are not permanently assigned to hosts, but are only leased for a period of time. If the host is powered down or taken off the network, the address is returned to the pool for reuse. This is especially helpful with mobile users that come and go on a network. Users can freely move from location to location and reestablish network connections. The host can obtain an IP address after the hardware connection is made, either through a wired or wireless LAN.

DHCP makes it possible to access the Internet using wireless hotspots at airports or coffee shops. When a wireless device enters a hotspot, the device DHCP client contacts the local DHCP server through a wireless connection, and the DHCP server assigns an IP address to the device.

Various types of devices can be DHCP servers when running DHCP service software. The DHCP server in most medium to large networks is usually a local dedicated PC-based server. With home networks, the DHCP server is often located on the local router that connects the home network to the ISP. Local hosts receive IP address information directly from the local router. The local router receives an IP address from the DHCP server at the ISP.

DHCP can pose a security risk because any device connected to the network can receive an address. This risk makes physical security a determining factor of whether to use dynamic or manual addressing. Both dynamic and static addressing have a place in network design. Many networks use both DHCP and static addressing. DHCP is used for general-purpose hosts, such as end-user devices; static addressing is used for network devices, such as gateways, switches, servers, and printers.

DHCPv4 Operation (10.2.2.7)

Without DHCP, users have to manually input the IP address, subnet mask, and other network settings to join the network. The DHCP server maintains a pool of IP addresses and leases an address to any DHCP-enabled client when the client is powered on. Because the IP addresses are dynamic (leased), rather than static (permanently assigned), addresses no longer in use are automatically returned to the pool for reallocation. As shown in Figure 10-6, the DHCPv4 process consisted of four exchanges:

- DHCPDISCOVER

- DHCPOFFER

- DHCPREQUEST

- DHCPACK

When a DHCPv4-configured device boots up or connects to the network, the client broadcasts (255.255.255.255) a DHCP discover (DHCPDISCOVER) message to identify any available DHCPv4 servers on the network. Because the host has no IP address, it uses 0.0.0.0 as the source address.

A DHCPv4 server replies with a DHCP offer (DHCPOFFER) message, which offers a lease to the client. The offer message contains the IP address and subnet mask to be assigned, the IP address of the DNS server, and the IP address of the default gateway. The lease offer also includes the duration of the lease. In Figure 10-6, the DHCP server is offering 192.168.1.222, which is also used as the destination address in the IP packet containing the DHCPOFFER.

The client can receive multiple DHCPOFFER messages if there is more than one DHCPv4 server on the local network; therefore, it must choose between them and sends a DHCP request (DHCPREQUEST) message that identifies the explicit server and lease offer that the client is accepting. A client might also choose to request an address that it had previously been allocated by the server. Like the DHCPDISCOVER, the DHCPREQUEST is broadcast (255.255.255.255) with a source address of 0.0.0.0.

Assuming that the IP address requested by the client, or offered by the server, is still available, the server returns a DHCP acknowledgement (DHCPACK) message that acknowledges to the client that the lease is finalized. The DHCPACK is sent unicast with the DHCPv4 server as the source address and the acknowledged address as the destination address. In Figure 10-6, the source address is the 192.168.1.10 address of the DHCPv4 server and the destination address is the offered address of 192.168.1.222.

If the offer is no longer valid, perhaps because of a timeout or another client taking the lease, the selected server responds with a DHCP negative acknowledgement (DHCPNAK) message. If a DHCPNAK message is returned, the selection process must begin again with a new DHCPDISCOVER message being transmitted. After the client has the lease, it must be renewed prior to the lease expiration through another DHCPREQUEST message.

The DHCPv4 server ensures that all IP addresses are unique (the same IP address cannot be assigned to two different network devices simultaneously). Using DHCP enables network administrators to easily reconfigure client IP addresses without having to manually make changes to the clients. Most Internet providers use DHCP to allocate addresses to their customers that do not require a static address.

Figure 10-6   DHCP Process

As presented in Chapter 8, "IP Addressing," the DHCP process for IPv6 is similar except DHCPv6 multicast addresses are used. While the messages used in the DHCP processes are not identical, Table 10-1 shows the approximate equivalent DHCPv4 messages for DHCPv6.

Table 10-1   DHCPv4 and DHCPv6 Message Type Equivalencies

DHCPv4 Messages	DHCPv6 Messages
DHCPDISCOVER	SOLICIT
DHCPOFFER	ADVERTISE
DHCPREQUEST	REQUEST
DHCPACK	REPLY

Packet Tracer Activity 10.2.2.8: DNS and DHCP

In this activity, you will configure and verify static IP addressing and DHCP addressing. You will then configure a DNS server to map IP addresses to the website names.

Lab 10.2.2.9: Observing DNS Resolution

In this lab, you will complete the following objectives:

■ Part 1: Observe the DNS Conversion of a URL to an IP Address

- Part 2: Observe DNS Lookup Using the **nslookup** Command on a Website
- Part 3: Observe DNS Lookup Using the **nslookup** Command on Mail Servers

Providing File-Sharing Services (10.2.3)

Transferring files from one computer to another is a common process. This section will introduce protocols that support file transfers.

File Transfer Protocol (10.2.3.1)

The File Transfer Protocol (FTP) is another commonly used application layer protocol. FTP was developed to allow data transfers between a client and a server. An FTP client is an application that runs on a computer that is used to push and pull data from a server running an FTP daemon (FTPd).

As Figure 10-7 illustrates, to successfully transfer data, FTP requires two connections between the client and the server: one for commands and replies and the other for the actual file transfer:

- The client establishes the first connection to the server for control traffic, consisting of client commands and server replies.

- The client establishes the second connection to the server for the actual data transfer. This connection is created every time there is data to be transferred.

The data transfer can happen in either direction. The client can download (pull) data from the server or the client can upload (push) data to the server.

Figure 10-7   FTP Process

Packet Tracer
☐ Activity

Packet Tracer Activity 10.2.3.2: FTP

In this activity, you will configure FTP services. You will then use the FTP services to transfer files between clients and the server.

Lab 10.2.3.3: Exploring FTP

In this lab, you will complete the following objectives:

- Part 1: Use FTP from a Command Prompt
- Part 2: Download an FTP File Using WS_FTP LE
- Part 3: Use FTP in a Browser

Server Message Block (10.2.3.4)

The *Server Message Block (SMB)* is a client-server file-sharing protocol, developed by IBM in the late 1980s, to describe the structure of shared network resources, such as directories, files, printers, and serial ports. It is a request-response protocol.

The SMB protocol describes file system access and how clients can make requests for files. It also describes the SMB protocol interprocess communication. All SMB messages share a common format. This format uses a fixed-sized header, followed by a variable-sized parameter and data component.

SMB messages can

- Start, authenticate, and terminate sessions
- Control file and printer access
- Allow an application to send or receive messages to or from another device

SMB file-sharing and print services have become the mainstay of Microsoft networking. With the introduction of the Windows 2000 software series, Microsoft changed the underlying structure for using SMB. In previous versions of Microsoft products, the SMB services used a non-TCP/IP protocol to implement name resolution. Beginning with Windows 2000, all subsequent Microsoft products use DNS naming, which allows TCP/IP protocols to directly support SMB resource sharing. Unlike the file sharing supported by File Transfer Protocol (FTP), clients establish a long-term connection to servers. After the connection is established, the user of the client can access the resources on the server as if the resource is local to the client host.

The Linux and UNIX operating systems also provide a method of sharing resources with Microsoft networks using a version of SMB called SAMBA. The Apple Macintosh operating systems also support resource sharing using the SMB protocol.

The Message Heard Around the World (10.3)

This section will summarize the process of moving data from one host to another.

Move It! (10.3.1)

This section will examine some of the current and developing trends in data network usage.

The Internet of Things (10.3.1.1)

The application layer is responsible for directly accessing the underlying processes that manage and deliver communication through the network. This layer serves as the source and destination of communications across data networks, regardless of the type of data network being used. In fact, advances in how we network are having a direct effect on the type of applications that are being developed.

Trends like Bring Your Own Device (BYOD), access anywhere, virtualization, and machine-to-machine (M2M) connections have made way for a new breed of applications. It is estimated that approximately 50 billion devices will be connected by 2020. In 2010 alone, more than 350,000 applications were developed with more than 3 million downloads. All of this leads to a world of intuitive connections among people, processes, data, and things on the network.

Using smart-tagging and advanced connectivity to digitize unintelligent products—from bikes and bottles to refrigerators and cars—and connect them to the Internet, will allow people and companies to interact in new and almost unimaginable ways. Objects will be able to collect, receive, and send information to users and other connected objects. This new wave in Internet development is known as the Internet of Things!

Over 100 million vending machines, vehicles, smoke alarms, and other devices are already sharing information automatically today, a figure that market analysts at Berg Insight expect to rise to 360 million by 2016. Today, photocopiers with an M2M module can order fresh toner and paper automatically or alert technicians to a fault—even telling them which parts to bring.

Message Travels Through a Network (10.3.1.2)

The massive explosion of applications is due in large part to the genius of the layered approach for processing data through a network. Specifically, keeping the functionality of the application layer separate from the functionality of transporting the data allows the application layer protocols to be changed and new applications to be developed, without the developer having to worry about the mechanics of getting the data across the network. That is the functionality of other layers and, therefore, other developers.

As shown in Figure 10-8, when an application sends a request to a server application, the message is built by the application layer, but is then passed down through all the various layer functionalities on the client for delivery. As it moves through the stack, each lower layer encapsulates the data with a header that contains the protocols of communication for that layer. These protocols, which are implemented on both the sending and receiving hosts, interact to provide end-to-end delivery of applications over the network.

Figure 10-8   TCP/IP Model Communication

Protocols like HTTP, for example, support the delivery of web pages to end devices. Now that we have learned all the various layers and their functionalities, we can follow a client request of a web page from the web server to see how each of these independent functionalities work fully, together.

Using the TCP/IP model, a complete communication process includes six steps:

1. Creation of the data

2. Segmentation and initial encapsulation

3. Addressing

4. Preparing for transportation

5. Transporting the data

6. Delivering the data to the correct destination application

Creation of the Data

The first step is the creation of data at the application layer of the originating source end device. In this case, after building the web client's request, known as an HTTP GET, that data will then be encoded, compressed, and encrypted if necessary. This is the job of the application layer protocol within the TCP/IP model, but this includes the functionality described by the application, presentation, and session layers of the OSI model. The application layer sends this data as a stream to the transport layer.

Segmentation and Initial Encapsulation

The next step is segmentation and encapsulation of the data as it passes down the protocol stack. At the transport layer, the HTTP GET message will be broken down into smaller, more manageable pieces, and each part of the message will have a transport layer header added to it. Inside the transport layer header are indicators on how to rebuild the message. Also included is an identifier, port number 80. This is used to tell the destination server that the message is destined for its web server application. A randomly generated source port is added as well, to ensure that the client can track return communication and forward it up to the correct client application.

Getting the Data to the End Device (10.3.1.3)

This section examines how identifiers are used to select the end device to which data should be delivered across a network.

Addressing

Next, address identifiers are added to the segments, as shown in Figure 10-8. Just as there are multiple layers of protocols that prepare the data for transmission to its destination, there are multiple layers of addressing to ensure its delivery. The role of the network layer is to add addressing that allows transfer of the data from the host that originates the data to the host that uses it. The network layer accomplishes this by encapsulating each segment within an IP packet header. The IP packet header contains the IP addresses of the source and destination devices. (The IP address of the destination device is usually determined through an earlier application process known as Domain Name Service.) The combination of the source and destination IP address, with the source and destination port number, is known as a socket. The socket is used to identify the server and service being requested by the client.

Getting the Data Through the Internetwork (10.3.1.4)

This section provides an overview of sending data across the network media.

Preparing for Transportation

After IP addressing is added, the packet is passed to the network access layer for generation of the data onto the media, as shown in Figure 10-8. For this to occur, the network access layer must first prepare the packet for transmission by placing it into a frame with a header and trailer. This frame includes the host physical address of the source, as well as the physical address of the next hop on the path to the final destination. This is equivalent to the Layer 2, or data link layer, functionality of the OSI model. Layer 2 is concerned with the delivery of messages on a single local network. The Layer 2 address is unique on the local network and represents the address of the end device on the physical media. In a LAN using Ethernet, this address is called the Media Access Control (MAC) address. After the network access layer has prepared the frame with source and destination addresses, it then encodes the frame into bits and then into electrical pulses or flashes of light that are sent across the network media.

Transporting the Data

The data is transported through the internetwork, which consists of media and any intermediate devices. As the encapsulated message is transmitted across the network, it can travel across several different media and network types. The network access layer specifies the techniques for getting the frame on and off each medium, otherwise known as the media access control method.

If the destination host is in the same network as the source host, the packet is delivered between the two hosts on the local media without the need for a router. However, if the destination host and source host are not in the same network, the packet might be carried across many networks, on many different media types, and through many routers. As it passes along the network, the information contained within the frame is not altered.

At the boundary of each local network, an intermediate network device, usually a router, deencapsulates the frame to read the destination host address contained in the header of the packet. Routers use the network identifier portion of this address to determine which path to use to reach the destination host. After the path is determined, the router encapsulates the packet in a new frame and sends it to the next hop on its way toward the destination end device.

Getting the Data to the Right Application (10.3.1.5)

This section reviews the role of the transport layer in delivering data to the appropriate application on the destination host.

Delivering the Data to the Correct Destination Application

Finally, at the destination end device, the frame is received. Deencapsulation and reassembly of the data occur, as the data is passed up the stack in the destination device. The data is continually passed up the layers, from the network access layer to the network layer to the transport layer, until it finally reaches the application layer and can then be processed. But how can the device be sure that the correct application process is identified?

As shown in Figure 10-9, recall that at the transport layer, information contained in the protocol data unit (PDU) header identifies the specific process or service running on the destination host device that will act on the data. Hosts, whether they are clients or servers on the Internet, can run multiple network applications simultaneously. People using PCs often have an email client running at the same time as a web browser, an instant messaging program, some streaming media, and perhaps even a game. All these separately running programs are examples of individual processes.

Viewing a web page invokes at least one network process. Clicking a hyperlink causes a web browser to communicate with a web server. At the same time, in the background, an email client might be sending and receiving email, and a colleague or friend might be sending an instant message.

Think about a computer that has only one network interface on it. All the data streams created by the applications that are running on the PC enter and leave through that one interface, yet instant messages do not suddenly appear in the middle of word processor documents, nor do emails show up in the interface of a game.

This is because the individual processes running on the source and destination hosts communicate with each other. Each application or service is represented at Layer 4 by a port number. A unique dialogue between devices is identified with a pair of Layer 4 source and destination port numbers that are representative of the two communicating applications. When the data is received at the host, the port number is examined to determine which application or process is the correct destination for the data.

Figure 10-9   Multiple Service Ports on a Server

Warriors of the Net (10.3.1.6)

An entertaining resource to help you visualize networking concepts is the animated movie "Warriors of the Net" by TNG Media Lab. Before viewing the video, there are a few things to consider. First, in terms of concepts you have learned in this chapter, think about when in the video you are on the LAN, on the WAN, on the intranet, and on the Internet; what are end devices versus intermediate devices; how do the OSI and TCP/IP models apply; and what protocols are involved.

Second, while port numbers 21, 23, 25, 53, and 80 are referred to explicitly in the video, IP addresses are referred to only implicitly. Can you see where? Where in the video might MAC addresses have been involved?

Finally, though all animations often have simplifications in them, there is one outright error in the video. About 5 minutes in, the statement is made "What happens when Mr. IP doesn't receive an acknowledgement? He simply sends a replacement packet." This is not a function of the Layer 3 Internet Protocol, which is an "unreliable," best-effort delivery protocol, but rather a function of the transport layer TCP protocol.

Interactive Graphic

Download the movie from www.warriorsofthe.net.

Summary (10.4)

Class Activity 10.4.1.1: Make It Happen!

Refer to the modeling activity from the beginning of this chapter as the basis for this activity. Your IP telephones were installed in a half day versus the full week originally anticipated. Your network has been restored to full capacity and network applications are available for your use. You have the same emails to answer and quotes to write for your manager's approval.

Use the same scenario you completed in the introduction modeling activity to answer the following questions.

A. Emails

- What method(s) can you use to send email correspondence now that the network is working?

- In what format will your emails be sent over the network?

- How can you now send the same message to multiple recipients?

- How can you send the large attachments to multiple recipients using network applications?

- Would using network applications prove to be a cost-effective communication method for your corporation?

B. Quote for Manager's Approval

- Because you have desktop application programs installed on your computer, will it be relatively easy to produce the quote your manager needs for the new contract due by the end of the week? Explain your answer.

- When you finish writing the quote, how will you present it to your manager for approval? How will he or she send the quote to the client for his approval?

- Is using network applications a cost-effective way to complete business transactions? Justify your answer.

Save a hard copy or an electronic copy of your answers. Be prepared to discuss your answers in class.

Packet Tracer Activity 10.4.1.2: Multiuser Tutorial

The multiuser feature in Packet Tracer allows multiple point-to-point connections between multiple instances of Packet Tracer. This first Packet Tracer Multiuser (PTMU) activity is a quick tutorial demonstrating the steps to establish and verify a multiuser connection to another instance of Packet Tracer within the same LAN. Ideally, this activity is meant for two students. However, it can also be completed as a solo activity simply by opening the two separate files to create two separate instances of Packet Tracer on your local machine.

Packet Tracer Activity 10.4.1.3: Multiuser Implement Services

In this multiuser activity, two students (players) cooperate to implement and verify services including DHCP, HTTP, Email, DNS, and FTP. The server-side player will implement and verify services on one server. The client-side player will configure two clients and verify access to services.

The application layer is responsible for directly accessing the underlying processes that manage and deliver communication to the human network. This layer serves as the source and destination of communications across data networks. The application layer applications, services, and protocols enable users to interact with the data network in a way that is meaningful and effective.

- Applications are computer programs with which the user interacts and that initiate the data transfer process at the user's request.

- Services are background programs that provide the connection between the application layer and the lower layers of the networking model.

- Protocols provide a structure of agreed-upon rules and processes that ensure that services running on one particular device can send and receive data from a range of different network devices.

Delivery of data over the network can be requested from a server by a client, or between devices that operate in a P2P arrangement, where the client-server relationship is established, according to which device is the source and destination at that time. Messages are exchanged between the application layer services at each end device in accordance with the protocol specifications to establish and use these relationships.

Protocols like HTTP, for example, support the delivery of web pages to end devices. SMTP and POP support sending and receiving email. SMB and FTP enable users to share files. P2P applications make it easier for consumers to seamlessly share media in a distributed fashion. DNS resolves the human-legible names used to refer to network resources into numeric addresses usable by the network. Clouds are remote upstream locations that store data and host applications so that users do not require as many local resources, and so that users can seamlessly access content on different devices from any location.

All of these elements work together at the application layer. The application layer enables users to work and play over the Internet.

Practice

The following activities provide practice with the topics introduced in this chapter. The labs and class activities are available in the companion *Introduction to Networks Lab Manual* (ISBN 978-1-58713-312-1). The Packet Tracer Activities PKA files are found in the online course.

Class Activities

- Class Activity 10.0.1.2: Application Investigation
- Class Activity 10.4.1.1: Make It happen!

Labs

- Lab 10.1.2.4: Researching Peer-to-Peer File Sharing
- Lab 10.2.2.9: Observing DNS Resolution
- Lab 10.2.3.3: Exploring FTP

Packet Tracer Activities

- Packet Tracer Activity 10.2.1.8: Web and Email
- Packet Tracer Activity 10.2.2.8: DNS and DHCP
- Packet Tracer Activity 10.2.3.2: FTP
- Packet Tracer Activity 10.4.1.2: Tutorial
- Packet Tracer Activity 10.4.1.3: Implement Services

Check Your Understanding

Complete all the review questions listed here to test your understanding of the topics and concepts in this chapter. The appendix, "Check Your Understanding Answer Key," lists the answers.

1. The TCP/IP application layer effectively consists of which three OSI layers?

   A. Application, session, transport

   B. Application, presentation, session

   C. Application, transport, network

   D. Application, network, data link

2. What main protocols do email users and servers normally use to process email? (Choose three.)

   A. DHCP

   B. SMTP

   C. IMAP4

   D. DNS

   E. POP3

3. DHCP enables clients on a network to do which of the following?

   A. Have unlimited telephone conversations

   B. Play back video streams

   C. Obtain IP addresses

   D. Track intermittent denial of service attacks

4. What TCP/IP layer supports the exchange of data between programs running on the source and destination hosts?

   A. Application

   B. Transport

   C. Internetwork

   D. Network

5. What is the purpose of DNS? _____

   _____

CHAPTER 11

It's a Network

Objectives

Upon completion of this chapter, you will be able to answer the following questions:

- What devices and protocols are used in a small network?

- How does a small network serve as the basis for a larger network?

- Why are basic security measures required on network devices?

- What security vulnerabilities and common mitigation techniques exist to protect against these vulnerabilities?

- How are network devices configured with hardening features to mitigate security threats?

- How can the **ping** and **tracert** commands be used to establish relative network performance?

- How can **show** commands be used to verify the configuration and status of device interfaces?

- How can basic host and IOS commands be used to acquire information about devices in the network?

- What file systems are used on routers and switches?

- What commands are required to back up and restore IOS configuration files?

Key Terms

This chapter uses the following key terms. You can find the definitions in the Glossary.

redundancy   *page 556*

real-time traffic   *page 558*

protocol analyzer   *page 563*

ping of death   *page 572*

winuke   *page 572*

teardrop   *page 572*

Introduction (11.0.1.1)

Up to this point in the course, we have considered the services that a data network can provide to the human network, examined the features of each layer of the OSI model and the operations of TCP/IP protocols, and looked in detail at Ethernet, a universal LAN technology. The next step is to learn how to assemble these elements together in a functioning network that can be maintained.

Class Activity 11.0.1.2: Did You Notice . . .?

Note: Students can work singularly or in pairs, or the full classroom can complete this activity together.

Take a look at the two networks shown in Figure 11-1. Visually compare and contrast the two networks. Make note of the devices used in each network design. Because the devices are labeled, you already know what types of end devices and intermediate devices are on each network.

But how are the two networks different? Is it just that there are more devices present on Network B than on Network A?

Figure 11-1 Sample Network Topologies

Select the network you would use if you owned a small- to medium-sized business. Be able to justify your selected network based on cost, speed, ports, expandability, and manageability.

Create and Grow (11.1)

Small networks become the building blocks of larger networks. To ensure that networks can grow without problems, they must be properly designed and understood.

Devices in a Small Network (11.1.1)

The number and type of network devices in a small network often differ from those found in larger networks, but they must still provide many of the same services.

Small-Network Topologies (11.1.1.1)

The majority of businesses are small businesses. It is not surprising then that the majority of networks are small networks.

With small networks, the design of the network is usually simple. The number and type of devices on the network are significantly reduced compared to that of a larger network. The network topologies for small networks typically involve a single router and one or more switches. Small networks can also have wireless access points (possibly built into the router) and IP phones. As for connection to the Internet, normally a small network has a single WAN connection provided by DSL, cable, or an Ethernet connection.

Managing a small network requires many of the same skills as those required for managing a larger one. The majority of work is focused on maintenance and troubleshooting of existing equipment, as well as securing devices and information on the network. The management of a small network is either done by an employee of the company or a person contracted by the company, depending on the size of the business and the type of business.

A typical small-business network is shown in Figure 11-2.

Figure 11-2   Typical Small-Business Network

Device Selection for a Small Network (11.1.1.2)

To meet user requirements, even small networks require planning and design. Planning ensures that all requirements, cost factors, and deployment options are given due consideration.

One of the first design considerations when implementing a small network is the type of intermediate devices to use to support the network. When selecting the type of intermediate devices, there are a number of factors that need to be considered, as shown in Figure 11-3.

Figure 11-3 Factors to Consider in Choosing a Device

Cost

Cost is typically one of the most important factors when selecting equipment for a small-business network. The cost of a switch or router is determined by its capacity and features. The device capacity includes the number and types of ports available and the backplane speed. Other factors that impact the cost are network management capabilities, embedded security technologies, and optional advanced switching technologies. The expense of cable runs required to connect every device on the network must also be considered. Another key element affecting cost consideration is how much redundancy to incorporate into the network. This includes devices, ports per device, and copper or fiber-optic cabling.

Speed and Types of Ports/Interfaces

Choosing the number and type of ports on a router or switch is a critical decision. Questions to be asked include

- Do we order just enough ports for today's needs, or do we consider growth requirements?

- Do we require a mixture of UTP speeds?

- Do we require both UTP and fiber ports?

Newer computers have built-in 1-Gbps network interface cards (NIC). 10-Gbps ports are already included with some workstations and servers. While it is more expensive, choosing Layer 2 devices that can accommodate increased speeds allows the network to evolve without replacing central devices.

Expandability

Networking devices come in both fixed and modular physical configurations. Fixed configurations have a specific number and type of ports or interfaces. Modular devices have expansion slots that provide the flexibility to add new modules as requirements evolve. Most modular devices come with a basic number of fixed ports as well as expansion slots. Switches are available with special additional ports for optional high-speed uplinks. Also, because routers can be used for connecting different numbers and types of networks, care must be taken to select the appropriate modules and interfaces for the specific media. Questions to be considered include "Do we order devices with upgradeable modules?" and "What type of WAN interfaces, if any, are required on the router(s)?"

Operating System Features and Services

Depending on the version of the operating system, a network device can support certain features and services, such as

- Security

- QoS

- VoIP

- Layer 3 switching

- NAT

- DHCP

Routers can be expensive based on interfaces and features needed. Additional modules, such as fiber-optics, increase the cost of the network devices.

IP Addressing for a Small Network (11.1.1.3)

When implementing a small network, it is necessary to plan the IP addressing space. All hosts within an internetwork must have a unique address. Even on a small network, address assignment within the network should not be random. Rather the

IP addressing scheme should be planned, documented, and maintained based on the type of device receiving the address.

Examples of different types of devices that will factor into the IP design are

- End devices for users
- Servers and peripherals
- Hosts that are accessible from the Internet
- Intermediary devices

Planning and documenting the IP addressing scheme help the administrator to track device types. For example, if all servers are assigned a host address in the range of 50–100, it is easy to identify server traffic by IP address. This can be very useful when troubleshooting network traffic issues using a protocol analyzer.

Additionally, administrators are better able to control access to resources on the network based on IP address when a deterministic IP addressing scheme is used. This can be especially important for hosts that provide resources to the internal network as well as to the external network. Web servers or e-commerce servers play such a role. If the addresses for these resources are not planned and documented, the security and accessibility of the devices are not easily controlled. If a server has a random address assigned, blocking access to this address is difficult and clients might not be able to locate this resource.

Each of these different device types should be allocated to a logical block of addresses within the address range of the network.

Redundancy in a Small Network (11.1.1.4)

Another important part of network design is reliability. Even small businesses often rely on their network heavily for business operation. A failure of the network can be very costly. To maintain a high degree of reliability, *redundancy* is required in the network design. Redundancy helps to eliminate single points of failure. There are many ways to accomplish redundancy in a network. Redundancy can be accomplished by installing duplicate equipment, but it can also be accomplished by supplying duplicate network links for critical areas, as shown in Figure 11-4.

Figure 11-4   Redundancy to a Server Farm

The smaller the network, the less the chance that redundancy of equipment will be affordable. Therefore, a common way to introduce redundancy is through the use of redundant switch connections between multiple switches on the network and between switches and routers.

Also, servers often have multiple NIC ports that enable redundant connections to one or more switches. In a small network, servers typically are deployed as web servers, file servers, or email servers.

Small networks typically provide a single exit point toward the Internet through one or more default gateways. With one router in the topology, the only redundancy in terms of Layer 3 paths is enabled by utilizing more than one inside Ethernet interface on the router. However, if the router fails, the entire network loses connectivity to the Internet. For this reason, it might be advisable for a small business to pay for a least-cost option account with a second service provider for backup.

Design Considerations for a Small Network (11.1.1.5)

Users expect immediate access to their emails and to the files that they are sharing or updating.

To help ensure this availability, the network designer should take the following steps:

Step 1.   Secure file and mail servers in a centralized location.

Step 2.   Protect the location from unauthorized access by implementing physical and logical security measures.

Step 3.   Create redundancy in the server farm that ensures if one device fails, files are not lost.

Step 4.   Configure redundant paths to the servers.

In addition, modern networks often use some form of voice or video over IP for communication with customers and business partners. This type of converged network is implemented as an integrated solution or as an additional form of raw data overlaid onto the IP network. The network administrator should consider the various types of traffic and their treatment in the network design. The router(s) and switch(es) in a small network should be configured to support *real-time traffic*, such as voice and video, in a distinct manner relative to other data traffic. In fact, a good network design will classify traffic carefully according to priority, as shown in Figure 11-5. Traffic classes could be as specific as

- File transfer
- Email
- Voice
- Video
- Messaging
- Transactional

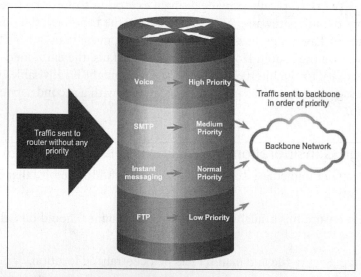

Figure 11-5   Prioritizing Traffic

In the end, the goal for a good network design, even for a small network, is to enhance the productivity of the employees and minimize network downtime.

Interactive Graphic

Activity 11.1.1.6: Identifying Devices in a Small Network

Go to the course online to perform this practice activity.

Protocols in a Small Network (11.1.2)

Along with the network devices found in a small network, it is important to examine the applications and services that it must support.

Common Applications in a Small Network (11.1.2.1)

The network is only as useful as the applications that are on it. Within the application layer, there are two forms of software programs or processes that provide access to the network: network applications and application layer services.

Network Applications

Applications are the software programs used to communicate over the network. Some end-user applications are network aware, meaning that they implement application layer protocols and are able to communicate directly with the lower layers of the protocol stack. Email clients and web browsers are examples of this type of application.

Application Layer Services

Other programs might need the assistance of application layer services to use network resources, like file transfer or network print spooling. Though transparent to an employee, these services are the programs that interface with the network and prepare the data for transfer. Different types of data, whether text, graphics, or video, require different network services to ensure that they are properly prepared for processing by the functions occurring at the lower layers of the OSI model.

Each application or network service uses protocols, which define the standards and data formats to be used. Without protocols, the data network would not have a common way to format and direct data. To understand the function of various network services, it is necessary to become familiar with the underlying protocols that govern their operation.

Common Protocols in a Small Network (11.1.2.2)

Most of a technician's work, in either a small or a large network, will in some way be involved with network protocols. Network protocols support the applications and services used by employees in a small network. Common network protocols include

- DNS
- Telnet
- IMAP, SMTP, POP (email)
- DHCP
- HTTP
- FTP

Table 11-1 provides a brief description of each of these services.

Table 11-1 Network Services

Network Service	Description
Domain Name System (DNS)	Service that provides the IP address of a site based on host or domain name.
Telnet	Service that allows the remote login to a host.
Email	Uses Simple Mail Transfer Protocol (SMTP), Post Office Protocol (POP), or Internet Message Access Protocol (IMAP) to transfer email messages between clients and servers.
Dynamic Host Configuration Protocol (DHCP)	Service that assigns the IP address, subnet mask, default gateway, and other information to clients.
Web	Most web pages are accessed using Hypertext Transfer Protocol (HTTP). Used to transfer information between clients and web servers.
File Transfer Protocol (FTP)	Services that allow the download and upload of files between a client and server.

These network protocols comprise the fundamental tool set of a network professional. Each of these network protocols defines

- Processes on either end of a communication session
- Types of messages
- Syntax of the messages

- Meaning of informational fields
- How messages are sent and the expected response
- Interaction with the next lower layer

Many companies have established a policy of using secure versions of these protocols whenever possible. These protocols are HTTPS, SFTP, and SSH.

Real-Time Applications for a Small Network (11.1.2.3)

In addition to the common network protocols described previously, modern businesses, even small ones, typically utilize real-time applications for communicating with customers and business partners. While a small company might not be able to justify the cost of an enterprise Cisco TelePresence solution, there are other real-time applications that are affordable and justifiable for small business organizations. Real-time applications require more planning and dedicated services (relative to other types of data) to ensure priority delivery of voice and video traffic. This means that the network administrator must ensure that the proper equipment is installed in the network and that the network devices are configured to ensure priority delivery.

Infrastructure

To support the existing and proposed real-time applications, the infrastructure must accommodate the characteristics of each type of traffic. The network designer must determine whether the existing switches and cabling can support the traffic that will be added to the network. Cabling that can support gigabit transmissions should be able to carry the traffic generated and not require any changes to the infrastructure. Older switches might not support Power over Ethernet (PoE). Obsolete cabling might not support the bandwidth requirements. The switches and cabling would need to be upgraded to support these applications.

VoIP

Voice over IP (VoIP) is implemented in an organization that still uses traditional telephones. VoIP uses voice-enabled routers. These routers convert analog voice from traditional telephone signals into IP packets. After the signals are converted into IP packets, the router sends those packets between corresponding locations. VoIP is much less expensive than an integrated IP telephony solution, but the quality of communications does not meet the same standards. Voice and video over IP solutions for small businesses can be realized, for example, with Skype and nonenterprise versions of Cisco WebEx.

IP Telephony

In IP telephony, the IP phone itself performs voice-to-IP conversion. Voice-enabled routers are not required within a network with an integrated IP telephony solution. IP phones use a dedicated server for call control and signaling. There are now many vendors with dedicated IP telephony solutions for small networks.

Real-Time Applications

To transport streaming media effectively, the network must be able to support applications that require delay-sensitive delivery. Real-Time Transport Protocol (RTP) and Real-Time Transport Control Protocol (RTCP) are two protocols that support this requirement. RTP and RTCP enable control and scalability of the network resources by allowing quality of service (QoS) mechanisms to be incorporated. These QoS mechanisms provide valuable tools for minimizing latency issues for real-time streaming applications.

Growing to Larger Networks (11.1.3)

Networks support the business and must be able to grow as the business grows.

Scaling a Small Network (11.1.3.1)

Growth is a natural process for many small businesses, and their networks must grow accordingly. A network administrator for a small network will either work reactively or proactively, depending on the leaders of the company, which often include the network administrator. Ideally, the network administrator has enough lead time to make intelligent decisions about growing the network in line with the growth of the company.

To scale a network, several elements are required:

- **Network documentation:** Physical and logical topology

- **Device inventory:** List of devices that use or comprise the network

- **Budget:** Itemized IT budget, including fiscal year equipment purchasing budget

- **Traffic analysis:** Protocols, applications, and services and their respective traffic requirements should be documented

These elements are used to inform the decision making that accompanies the scaling of a small network.

Protocol Analysis of a Small Network (11.1.3.2)

Supporting and growing a small network require being familiar with the protocols and network applications running over the network. While the network administrator will have more time in a small network environment to individually analyze network utilization for each network-enabled device, a more holistic approach with some type of software- or hardware-based *protocol analyzer* is recommended.

As shown in Figure 11-6, protocol analyzers enable a network professional to quickly compile statistical information about traffic flows on a network.

Figure 11-6   Protocol Analyzer

When trying to determine how to manage network traffic, especially as the network grows, it is important to understand the type of traffic that is crossing the network as well as the current traffic flow. If the types of traffic are unknown, the protocol analyzer will help identify the traffic and its source.

To determine traffic flow patterns, it is important to

- Capture traffic during peak utilization times to get a good representation of the different traffic types

- Perform the capture on different network segments, because some traffic will be local to a particular segment

Information gathered by the protocol analyzer is analyzed based on the source and destination of the traffic as well as the type of traffic being sent. This analysis can be used to make decisions on how to manage the traffic more efficiently. This can be done by reducing unnecessary traffic flows or changing flow patterns altogether by moving a server, for example.

Sometimes, simply relocating a server or service to another network segment improves network performance and accommodates the growing traffic needs. At other times, optimizing the network performance requires major network redesign and intervention.

Evolving Protocol Requirements (11.1.3.3)

In addition to understanding changing traffic trends, a network administrator must also be aware of how network use is changing. A network administrator in a small network has the ability to obtain in-person IT "snapshots" of employee application utilization for a significant portion of the employee workforce over time. These snapshots typically include information such as

- OS + OS version
- Non-network applications
- Network applications
- CPU utilization
- Drive utilization
- RAM utilization

Documenting snapshots for employees in a small network over a period of time will go a long way toward informing the network administrator of evolving protocol requirements and associated traffic flows. For example, it might be that some employees are using off-site resources such as social media to better position a company with respect to marketing. When they began working for the company, these employees might have focused less on Internet-based advertising. This shift in resource utilization might require the network administrator to shift network resource allocations accordingly.

It is the responsibility of the network administrator to track network utilization and traffic flow requirements, and implement network modifications to optimize employee productivity as the network and business grow.

Keeping the Network Safe (11.2)

We have come to expect that the information we move on a network is safe from tampering and unauthorized access. Without this assumption, such routine events as e-business and online banking would not occur. As networks grow and offer new services, the threats to their continued integrity increase and measures must be taken to ensure the security of network devices and information.

Network Device Security Measures (11.2.1)

Before we can properly secure the network, it is important to understand the threats that we must secure against.

Categories of Threats to Network Security (11.2.1.1)

Whether wired or wireless, computer networks are essential to everyday activities. Individuals and organizations alike depend on their computers and networks. Intrusion by an unauthorized person can result in costly network outages and loss of work. Attacks to a network can be devastating and can result in a loss of time and money because of damage or theft of important information or assets.

Intruders can gain access to a network through software vulnerabilities, through hardware attacks, or through guessing someone's username and password. Intruders who gain access by modifying software or exploiting software vulnerabilities are often called hackers.

After the hacker gains access to the network, four types of threats can arise. These are explained in Table 11-2.

Table 11-2   Security Threats

Threat	Description
Information theft	Breaking into a computer to obtain confidential information. Information can be used or sold for various purposes. Example: stealing an organization's proprietary information such as research and development information.
Identity theft	A form of information theft where personal information is stolen for the purpose of taking over someone's identity. Using the information, an individual can obtain legal documents, apply for credit, and make unauthorized online purchases. Identity theft is a growing problem costing billions of dollars per year.
Data loss/manipulation	Breaking into a computer to destroy or alter data records. Example of data loss: sending a virus that reformats a computer's hard drive. Example of data manipulation: breaking into a records system to change information, such as the price of an item.
Disruption of service	Preventing legitimate users from accessing services to which they should be entitled. Examples: denial of service (DoS) attacks on servers, network devices, or network communication links.

Even in small networks, it is necessary to consider security threats and vulnerabilities when planning a network implementation.

Physical Security (11.2.1.2)

When you think of network security, or even computer security, you might imagine attackers exploiting software vulnerabilities. An equally important vulnerability is the physical security of devices, as shown in Figure 11-7. An attacker can deny the use of network resources if those resources can be physically compromised.

Figure 11-7 Physical Security Plan

The four classes of physical threats are

- **Hardware threats:** Physical damage to servers, routers, switches, cabling plant, and workstations

- **Environmental threats:** Temperature extremes (too hot or too cold) or humidity extremes (too wet or too dry)

- **Electrical threats:** Voltage spikes, insufficient supply voltage (brownouts), unconditioned power (noise), and total power loss

- **Maintenance threats:** Poor handling of key electrical components (electrostatic discharge), lack of critical spare parts, poor cabling, and poor labeling

Some of these issues must be dealt with in an organizational policy. Some of them are subject to good leadership and management in the organization.

Types of Security Vulnerabilities (11.2.1.3)

Three network security factors are vulnerability, threat, and attack.

Vulnerability is the degree of weakness that is inherent in every network and device. This includes routers, switches, desktops, servers, and even security devices.

Threats include the people interested and qualified in taking advantage of each security weakness. Such individuals can be expected to continually search for new exploits and weaknesses.

Threats are realized by a variety of tools, scripts, and programs to launch attacks against networks and network devices. Typically, the network devices under attack are the endpoints, such as servers and desktop computers.

There are three primary vulnerabilities or weaknesses as shown in Tables 11-3, 11-4, and 11-5.

- Technological (Table 11-3)

- Configuration (Table 11-4)

- Security policy (Table 11-5)

Table 11-3   Vulnerabilities—Technology

Network Security Weakness
TCP/IP protocol weakness
Hypertext Transfer Protocol (HTTP), File Transfer Protocol (FTP), and Internet Control Message Protocol (ICMP) are inherently insecure. Simple Network Management Protocol (SNMP) and Simple Mail Transfer Protocol (SMTP) are related to the inherently insecure structure upon which TCP was designed.
Operating system weakness
Each operating system (UNIX, Linux, Mac OS, and Windows) has security problems that must be addressed. These are documented in the Computer Emergency Response Team (CERT) archives at www.cert.org.
Network equipment weakness
Various types of network equipment such as routers, firewalls, and switches have security weaknesses that must be recognized and protected against. Their weaknesses include password protection, lack of authentication, routing protocols, and firewall holes.

Table 11-4   Vulnerabilities—Configuration

Configuration Weakness	How the Weakness Is Exploited
Unsecure user accounts	User account information can be transmitted insecurely across the network, exposing usernames and passwords to snoopers.
System accounts with easily guessed passwords	This common problem is the result of poorly selected and easily guessed user passwords.

Configuration Weakness	How the Weakness Is Exploited
Misconfigured Internet services	A common problem is to turn on JavaScript in web browsers, enabling attacks by way of hostile JavaScript when accessing untrusted sites. IIS, FTP, and Terminal Services also pose problems.
Unsecured default settings within products	Many products have default settings that enable security holes.
Misconfigured network equipment	Misconfigurations of the equipment itself can cause significant security problems. For example, misconfigured access lists, routing tables, or SNMP community strings can open up large security holes.

Table 11-5   Vulnerabilities—Policy

Policy Weakness	How the Weakness Is Exploited
Lack of written security policy	An unwritten policy cannot be consistently applied or enforced.
Politics	Political battles and turf wars can make it difficult to implement a consistent security policy.
Lack of authentication continuity	Poorly chosen, easily cracked, or default passwords can allow unauthorized access to the network.
Logical access controls not applied	Inadequate monitoring and auditing allow attacks and unauthorized use to continue, wasting company resources. This could result in legal action against or termination of IT technicians, IT management, or even company leadership that allows these unsafe conditions to persist.
Software and hardware installation and changes do not follow policy	Unauthorized changes to the network topology or installation of unapproved applications create security holes.
Disaster recovery plan is nonexistent	The lack of a disaster recovery plan allows chaos, panic, and confusion to occur when someone attacks the enterprise.

All three of these vulnerabilities or weaknesses can lead to various attacks, including malicious code attacks and network attacks.

Interactive Graphic

Activity 11.2.1.4: Security Threats and Vulnerabilities

Go to the course online to perform this practice activity.

Vulnerabilities and Network Attacks (11.2.2)

There are many different types of attacks against networks. To secure the network, these attacks must be understood and countermeasures taken.

Viruses, Worms, and Trojan Horses (11.2.2.1)

Malicious code attacks include a number of types of computer programs that were created with the intention of causing data loss or damage. The three main types of malicious code attacks are viruses, Trojan horses, and worms.

A virus is malicious software that is attached to another program to execute a particular unwanted function on a workstation. An example is a program that is attached to command.com (the primary interpreter for Windows systems) and deletes certain files and infects any other versions of command.com that it can find.

A Trojan horse is different only in that the entire application was written to look like something else, when in fact it is an attack tool. An example of a Trojan horse is a software application that runs a simple game on a workstation. While the user is occupied with the game, the Trojan horse mails a copy of itself to every address in the user's address book. The other users receive the game and play it, thereby spreading the Trojan horse to the addresses in each address book.

Viruses normally require a delivery mechanism, a vector such as a ZIP file, or some other executable file attached to an email to carry the virus code from one system to another. The key element that distinguishes a computer worm from a computer virus is that human interaction is required to facilitate the spread of a virus.

Worms are self-contained programs that attack a system and try to exploit a specific vulnerability in the target. Upon successful exploitation of the vulnerability, the worm copies its program from the attacking host to the newly exploited system to begin the cycle again. The anatomy of a worm attack is as follows:

- **The enabling vulnerability:** A worm installs itself by exploiting known vulnerabilities in systems, such as naive end users who open unverified executable attachments in emails.

- **Propagation mechanism:** After gaining access to a host, a worm copies itself to that host and then selects new targets.

- **Payload:** After a host is infected with a worm, the attacker has access to the host, often as a privileged user. Attackers could use a local exploit to escalate their privilege level to administrator.

Reconnaissance Attacks (11.2.2.2)

In addition to malicious code attacks, it is also possible for networks to fall prey to various network attacks. Network attacks can be classified into three major categories:

- **Reconnaissance attacks:** The unauthorized discovery and mapping of systems, services, or vulnerabilities

- **Access attacks:** The unauthorized manipulation of data, system access, or user privileges

- **Denial of service attacks:** The disabling or corruption of networks, systems, or services

Reconnaissance Attacks

External attackers can use Internet tools, such as the nslookup and whois utilities, to easily determine the IP address space assigned to a given corporation or entity. After the IP address space is determined, an attacker can then ping the publicly available IP addresses to identify the addresses that are active. To help automate this step, an attacker might use a ping sweep tool, such as fping or gping, which systematically pings all network addresses in a given range or subnet. This is similar to going through a section of a telephone book and calling each number to see who answers.

Access Attacks (11.2.2.3)

Access attacks exploit known vulnerabilities in authentication services, FTP services, and web services to gain entry to web accounts, confidential databases, and other sensitive information. An access attack allows an individual to gain unauthorized access to information that he has no right to view. Access attacks can be classified into four types. One of the most common types of access attacks is the password attack. Password attacks can be implemented using a packet sniffer to yield user accounts and passwords that are transmitted as clear text. Password attacks can also refer to repeated attempts to log in to a shared resource, such as a server or router, to identify a user account, password, or both. These repeated attempts are called dictionary attacks or brute-force attacks.

An example of a trust exploitation is shown in Figure 11-8. In this example, the attacker wants to gain access to system A. This is accomplished by first compromising system B and then using the trust relationship between system A and system B to launch an attack against system A. This type of attack is common with Windows Active Directory (AD) and Network File System (NFS) and Network Information Service Plus (NIS+) forum in Linux and UNIX.

Network OS	Trust Models
Windows	Domains Active Directory (AD)
Linux and UNIX	Network File System (NFS) Network Information Service Plus (NIS+)

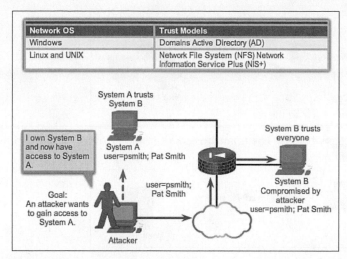

Figure 11-8 Trust Exploitation

Port redirection is a type of trust-exploitation attack that uses a compromised host to pass traffic through a firewall that would otherwise be dropped. This is shown in Figure 11-9. It is mitigated primarily through the use of proper trust models. Antivirus software and host-based intrusion detection systems (IDS) can help detect and prevent an attacker from installing port-redirecting utilities on the host.

Figure 11-9 Port Redirection

A man-in-the-middle attack places the attacker between the source and destination machine, as shown in Figure 11-10. All traffic from the victim is intercepted and compromised before being sent to the server. The victim is often unaware that anything unusual is happening.

Figure 11-10   Man-in-the-Middle Attack

DoS Attacks (11.2.2.4)

Denial of service (DoS) attacks are the most publicized form of attack and also among the most difficult to eliminate. Even within the attacker community, DoS attacks are regarded as trivial and considered bad form, because they require so little effort to execute. But because of their ease of implementation and potentially significant damage, DoS attacks deserve special attention from security administrators.

DoS attacks take many forms, some of which are listed in Table 11-6. Ultimately, they prevent authorized people from using a service by consuming system resources.

Table 11-6   DoS Attacks

Resource Overloads	Malformed Data
Disk space, bandwidth, buffers	Oversized packets such as the *ping of death*
Ping floods such as smurf	Overlapping data such as *winuke*
Packet storms such as UDP bombs and fraggle	Unhandled data such as *teardrop*

A SYN flood attack, shown in Figure 11-11, is a common DoS attack. In this attack, multiple SYN packets are sent to a server by an attacker. The server ties up its resources attempting to complete the TCP three-way handshake, preventing it from answering the SYN requests from valid clients.

Figure 11-11   SYN Flood Attack

A distributed DoS (DDoS) attack is shown in Figure 11-12. A DDoS attack differs from a regular DoS attack in that the victim is attacked in a coordinated manner from several compromised systems know as zombies. These zombie machines are under the control of the attacker. Owners of zombies are often unaware that their machine has been compromised.

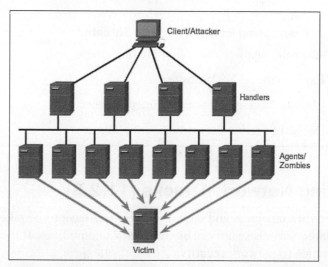

Figure 11-12   DDoS Attack

Figure 11-13 shows a smurf attack. The attacker sends a false Echo Request message, appearing to be from the victim machine, to a number of zombies. These zombies send back an Echo Reply message overloading the WAN link to the victim's machine and preventing valid clients from gaining access.

Figure 11-13   Smurf Attack

Interactive
Graphic

Activity 11.2.2.5: Types of Attack

Go to the course online to perform this practice activity.

Lab 11.2.2.6: Researching Network Security Threats

In this lab, you will complete the following objectives:

- Part 1: Explore the SANS Website

- Part 2: Identify Recent Network Security Threats

- Part 3: Detail a Specific Network Security Threat

Mitigating Network Attacks (11.2.3)

To keep network resources and data safe, measures have to be taken to mitigate the risks associated with these attacks on network vulnerabilities. It is necessary to take a proactive stance to network security.

Backup, Upgrade, Update, and Patch (11.2.3.1)

Antivirus software can detect most viruses and many Trojan horse applications and prevent them from spreading in the network. Antivirus software can be deployed at the user level and at the network level.

Keeping up to date with the latest developments in these sorts of attacks can also lead to a more effective defense against these attacks. As new virus or Trojan applications are released, enterprises need to keep current with the latest versions of antivirus software as well.

Worm attack mitigation requires diligence on the part of system and network administration staff. The following are the recommended steps for worm attack mitigation:

- **Containment:** Contain the spread of the worm within the network. Compartmentalize uninfected parts of the network.

- **Inoculation:** Start patching all systems and, if possible, scanning for vulnerable systems.

- **Quarantine:** Track down each infected machine inside the network. Disconnect, remove, or block infected machines from the network.

- **Treatment:** Clean and patch each infected system. Some worms might require complete core system reinstallations to clean the system.

The most effective way to mitigate a worm attack is to download security updates from the operating system vendor and patch all vulnerable systems. This is difficult with uncontrolled user systems in the local network. Administering numerous systems involves the creation of a standard software image (operating system and accredited applications that are authorized for use on client systems) that is deployed on new or upgraded systems. However, security requirements change and already-deployed systems might need to have updated security patches installed.

One solution to the management of critical security patches is to create a central patch server that all systems must communicate with after a set period of time. Any patches that are not applied to a host are automatically downloaded from the patch server and installed without user intervention.

Authentication, Authorization, and Accounting (11.2.3.2)

Authentication, authorization, and accounting (AAA, or "triple A") network security services provide the primary framework to set up access control on a network device. AAA is a way to control who is permitted to access a network (authenticate), what they can do while they are there (authorize), and to watch the actions they perform while accessing the network (accounting). AAA provides a higher degree of scalability than the console, AUX, VTY, and privileged EXEC authentication commands alone.

Authentication

Users and administrators must prove that they are who they say they are. Authentication can be established using username and password combinations, challenge and response questions, token cards, and other methods. For example: "I am user 'student.' I know the password to prove that I am user 'student.'"

In a small network, local authentication is often used. With local authentication, each device maintains its own database of username/password combinations. However, when there are more than a few user accounts in a local device database, managing those user accounts becomes complex. Additionally, as the network grows and more devices are added to the network, local authentication becomes difficult to maintain and does not scale. For example, if there are 100 network devices, all user accounts must be added to all 100 devices.

For larger networks, a more scalable solution is external authentication. External authentication allows all users to be authenticated through an external network server. The two most popular options for external authentication of users are RADIUS and TACACS+:

- RADIUS is an open standard with low use of CPU resources and memory. It is used by a range of network devices, such as switches, routers, and wireless devices.

- TACACS+ is a security mechanism that enables modular authentication, authorization, and accounting services. It uses a TACACS+ daemon running on a security server.

Authorization

After the user is authenticated, authorization services determine which resources the user can access and which operations the user is allowed to perform. An example is "User 'student' can access host server XYZ using Telnet only."

Accounting

Accounting records what the user does, including what is accessed, the amount of time the resource is accessed, and any changes that were made. Accounting keeps track of how network resources are used. An example is "User 'student' accessed host server XYZ using Telnet for 15 minutes."

The concept of AAA is similar to the use of a credit card. The credit card identifies who can use it and how much that user can spend, and keeps account of what items the user spent money on.

Firewalls (11.2.3.3)

In addition to protecting individual computers and servers attached to the network, it is important to control traffic traveling to and from the network.

A firewall is one of the most effective security tools available for protecting internal network users from external threats. A firewall resides between two or more networks, controls the traffic between them, and also helps prevent unauthorized access. Firewall products use various techniques for determining what is permitted or denied access to a network. These techniques are

- **Packet filtering:** Prevents or allows access based on IP or MAC addresses.

- **Application filtering:** Prevents or allows access by specific application types based on port numbers.

- **URL filtering:** Prevents or allows access to websites based on specific URLs or keywords.

- **Stateful packet inspection (SPI):** Incoming packets must be legitimate responses to requests from internal hosts. Unsolicited packets are blocked unless permitted specifically. SPI can also include the capability to recognize and filter out specific types of attacks such as denial of service (DoS).

Firewall products can support one or more of these filtering capabilities. Additionally, firewalls often perform Network Address Translation (NAT). NAT translates an internal IP address or group of IP addresses into an outside, public IP address that is sent across the network. This allows internal IP addresses to be concealed from outside users.

Firewall products come packaged in various forms:

- **Appliance-based firewalls:** An appliance-based firewall is a firewall that is built into a dedicated hardware device known as a security appliance. These devices are specialized computers that do not have peripherals or hard drives and are less prone to failure.

- **Server-based firewalls:** A server-based firewall consists of a firewall application that runs on a network operating system (NOS) such as UNIX or Windows. These are normally access-control applications that run on a general-purpose OS. Because the underlying OS has inherent weaknesses, this type of firewall is generally less secure then an appliance-based device.

- **Integrated firewalls:** An integrated firewall is implemented by adding firewall functionality to an existing device, such as a router. These are found on most home integrated routers but are also found on higher-end routers that run special operating systems like Cisco Internetwork Operating System (IOS).

■ **Personal firewalls:** Personal firewalls reside on host computers and are not designed for LAN implementations. They can be available by default from the OS or can come from an outside vendor. Personal firewalls are often used when a host device is directly connected to an ISP and provides protection only for the single host.

Endpoint Security (11.2.3.4)

A secure network is only as strong as its weakest link. The high-profile threats most often discussed in the media are external threats, such as Internet worms and DoS attacks. But securing the internal network is just as important as securing the perimeter of a network. The internal network is made up of network endpoints. An endpoint, or host, is an individual computer system or device that acts as a network client. Common endpoints are laptops, desktops, servers, smartphones, and tablets. If users are not practicing security with their endpoint devices, no amount of security precautions will guarantee a secure network.

Securing endpoint devices is one of the most challenging jobs of a network administrator, because it involves human nature. A company must have well-documented policies in place, and employees must be aware of these rules. Employees need to be trained on the proper use of the network. Policies often include the use of antivirus software and host intrusion prevention. More comprehensive endpoint security solutions rely on network access control.

Endpoint security also requires securing Layer 2 devices in the network infrastructure to prevent against Layer 2 attacks such as MAC address spoofing, MAC address table overflow attacks, and LAN storm attacks. This is known as attack mitigation.

Securing Devices (11.2.4)

Part of network security is securing actual devices, including end devices and intermediate devices such as network devices.

Introduction to Securing Devices (11.2.4.1)

When a new operating system is installed on a device, the security settings are set to the default values. In most cases, this level of security is inadequate. For Cisco routers, the Cisco AutoSecure feature can be used to assist in securing the system. There are some simple steps that should be taken that apply to most operating systems:

- Default usernames and passwords should be changed immediately.

- Access to system resources should be restricted to only the individuals that are authorized to use those resources.

- Any unnecessary services and applications should be turned off and uninstalled, when possible.

All devices should be updated with security patches as they become available. Often, devices shipped from the manufacturer have been sitting in a warehouse for a period of time and do not have the most up-to-date patches installed. It is important, prior to implementation, to update any software and install any security patches.

Passwords (11.2.4.2)

To protect network devices, it is important to use strong passwords. Here are standard guidelines to follow:

- Use a password length of at least 8 characters, preferably 10 or more characters. A longer password is a better password.

- Make passwords complex. Include a mix of uppercase and lowercase letters, numbers, symbols, and spaces, if allowed.

- Avoid passwords based on repetition, common dictionary words, letter or number sequences, usernames, relative or pet names, or biographical information, such as birth dates, ID numbers, ancestor names, or other easily identifiable pieces of information.

- Deliberately misspell a password. For example, Smith = Smyth = 5mYth or Security = 5ecur1ty.

- Change passwords often. If a password is unknowingly compromised, the window of opportunity for the attacker to use the password is limited.

- Do not write passwords down and leave them in obvious places such as on the desk or monitor.

Table 11-7 provides examples of strong and weak passwords.

Table 11-7   Passwords

Password	Weak or Strong?	Explanation
Secret	Weak	Simple dictionary password
Smith	Weak	Mother's maiden name
Toyota	Weak	Make of car
bob1967	Weak	Name and birthday of user
Blueleaf23	Weak	Simple words and numbers
B87n42d39c	Strong	Combines alphanumeric characters
12^h u4@1p7	Strong	Combines alphanumeric characters, symbols, and also a space

On Cisco routers, leading spaces are ignored for passwords, but spaces after the first character are not ignored. Therefore, one method to create a strong password is to use the spacebar in the password and create a phrase made of many words. This is called a pass phrase. A pass phrase is often easier to remember than a simple password. It is also longer and harder to guess.

Administrators should ensure that strong passwords are used across the network. One way to accomplish this is to use the same "brute force" attack tools that attackers use as a way to verify password strength.

Basic Security Practices (11.2.4.3)

When implementing devices, it is important to follow all security guidelines set by the organization. This includes naming devices in a fashion that allows easy documentation and tracking, but also maintains some form of security. It is not wise to provide too much information about the use of the device in the host name. There are many other basic security measures that should be taken.

Additional Password Security

Strong passwords are only as useful as they are secret. There are several steps that can be taken to help ensure that passwords remain secret. Using the global configuration command **service password-encryption** prevents unauthorized individuals from viewing passwords in plain text in the configuration file. This command causes the encryption of all passwords that are unencrypted.

Additionally, to ensure that all configured passwords are a minimum of a specified length, use the **security passwords min-length** command in global configuration mode.

Another way that hackers learn passwords is simply by brute-force attacks, trying multiple passwords until one works. It is possible to prevent this type of attack by blocking login attempts to the device if a set number of failures occur within a specific amount of time:

```
Router(config)# login block-for 120 attempts 3 within 60
```

This command will block login attempts for 120 seconds, if there are three failed login attempts within 60 seconds.

Banners

A banner message is similar to a No Trespassing sign. They are important to be able to prosecute, in a court of law, anyone who accesses the system inappropriately. Be sure that banner messages comply with security policies for the organization.

```
Router(config)# banner motd #message#
```

Exec Timeout

Another recommendation is setting executive timeouts. By setting the exec timeout, you are telling the Cisco device to automatically disconnect users on a line after they have been idle for the duration of the exec timeout value. Exec timeouts can be configured on console, vty, and aux ports.

```
Router(config)# line vty 0 4
Router(config-vty)# exec-timeout 10
```

This command will disconnect users after 10 minutes.

Enable SSH (11.2.4.4)

The legacy protocol to manage devices remotely is Telnet. Telnet is not secure. Data contained within a Telnet packet is transmitted unencrypted. Using a tool like Wireshark, it is possible for someone to "sniff" a Telnet session and obtain password information. For this reason, it is highly recommended to enable SSH on devices for secure remote access. It is possible to configure a Cisco device to support SSH using four steps, as shown in Figure 11-14.

```
R1#conf t
R1(config)#ip domain-name span.com
R1(config)#crypto key generate rsa general-keys modulus 1024
The name for the keys will be: R1.span.com
% The key modulus size is 1024 bits
% Generating 1024 bit RSA keys, keys will be non-exportable...[OK]
R1(config)#
*Dec 13 16:19:12.079: %SSH-5-ENABLED: SSH 1.99 has been enabled
R1(config)#username Bob secret cisco
R1(config)#line vty 0 4
R1(config-line)#login local
R1(config-line)#transport input ssh
R1(config-line)#exit
```

Figure 11-14   SSH Configuration

Step 1.   Ensure that the router has a unique host name, and then configure the IP domain name of the network using the **ip domain-name** *domain-name* command in global configuration mode.

Step 2.   One-way secret keys must be generated for a router to encrypt SSH traffic. The key is what is actually used to encrypt and decrypt data. To create an encryption key, use the **crypto key generate rsa general-keys modulus** *modulus-size* command in global configuration mode. The specific meaning of the various parts of this command are complex and out of scope for this course, but for now, just note that the modulus determines the size of the key and can be configured from 360 bits to 2048 bits. The larger the modulus, the more secure the key, but the longer it takes to encrypt and decrypt information. The minimum recommended modulus length is 1024 bits.

```
Router(config)# crypto key generate rsa general-keys modulus 1024
```

Step 3.   Create a local database username entry using the **username** *name* **secret** *secret* global configuration command.

Step 4.   Enable vty inbound SSH sessions using the line vty commands **login local** and **transport input ssh**.

The router SSH service can now be accessed using an SSH client software.

Lab 11.2.4.5: Accessing Network Devices with SSH

In this lab, you will complete the following objectives:

- Part 1: Configure Basic Device Settings

- Part 2: Configure the Router for SSH Access

- Part 3: Examine a Telnet Session with Wireshark

- Part 4: Examine an SSH Session with Wireshark

- Part 5: Configure the Switch for SSH Access

- Part 6: SSH from the CLI on the Switch

Lab 11.2.4.6: Securing Network Devices

In this lab, you will complete the following objectives:

- Part 1: Configure Basic Device Settings

- Part 2: Configure Basic Security Measures on the Router

- Part 3: Configure Basic Security Measures on the Switch

Basic Network Performance (11.3)

After the network has been implemented, a network administrator must be able to test the network connectivity to ensure that it is operating appropriately. Additionally, it is a good idea for the network administrator to document the network.

Ping (11.3.1)

Using the **ping** command is an effective way to test connectivity. The test is often referred to as testing the protocol stack, because the **ping** command moves from Layer 3 of the OSI model to Layer 2 and then Layer 1. Ping uses the ICMP protocol to check for connectivity.

Interpreting Ping Results (11.3.1.1)

The **ping** command will not always pinpoint the nature of a problem, but it can help to identify the source of the problem, an important first step in troubleshooting a network failure.

The **ping** command provides a method for checking the protocol stack and IPv4 address configuration on a host as well as testing connectivity to local or remote destination hosts, as shown in Figure 11-15. There are additional tools that can provide more information than ping, such as Telnet or Trace, which will be discussed in more detail later.

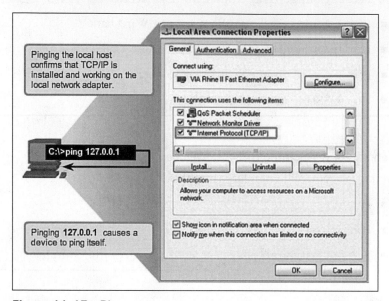

Figure 11-15   Ping

IOS Ping Indicators

A ping issued from the IOS will yield one of several indications for each ICMP echo that was sent. The most common indicators are

- !—Indicates receipt of an ICMP Echo Reply message.

- .—Indicates that a time expired while waiting for an ICMP Echo Reply message.

- U—An ICMP unreachable message was received.

The "!" (exclamation mark) indicates that the ping completed successfully and verifies Layer 3 connectivity.

The "." (period) can indicate problems in the communication. It can indicate that a connectivity problem occurred somewhere along the path. It can also indicate that a router along the path did not have a route to the destination and did not send an ICMP destination unreachable message. It also can indicate that ping was blocked by device security.

The "U" indicates that a router along the path did not have a route to the destination address or that the ping request was blocked and responded with an ICMP unreachable message.

Testing the Loopback

The **ping** command is used to verify the internal IP configuration on the local host. Recall that this test is accomplished by using the **ping** command on a reserved address called the loopback (127.0.0.1). This verifies the proper operation of the protocol stack from the network layer to the physical layer—and back—without actually putting a signal on the media.

Ping commands are entered at a command line. Example 11-1 shows the output of the command to ping the loopback interface.

Example 11-1 Pinging the Loopback Interface

```
C:\> ping 127.0.0.1
Reply from 127.0.0.1: bytes=32 time<1ms TTL=128
Reply from 127.0.0.1: bytes=32 time<1ms TTL=128
Reply from 127.0.0.1: bytes=32 time<1ms TTL=128
Reply from 127.0.0.1: bytes=32 time<1ms TTL=128
Ping statistics for 127.0.0.1:
Packets: Sent = 4, Received = 4, Lost = 0 (0% loss),
Approximate round trip times in milli-seconds:
Minimum = 0ms, Maximum = 0ms, Average = 0ms
```

The result indicates that four 32-byte test packets were sent and were returned from host 127.0.0.1 in a time of less than 1 ms. TTL stands for Time-to-Live and defines the number of hops that the ping packet has remaining before it will be dropped.

Extended Ping (11.3.1.2)

The Cisco IOS offers an "extended" mode of the **ping** command. This mode is entered by typing **ping** in privileged EXEC mode, without a destination IP address. A series of prompts are then presented, as shown in the following example. Pressing Enter accepts the indicated default values. The following example illustrates how to force the source address for a ping to be 10.1.1.1 (see R2 in Figure 11-16); the source address for a standard ping would be 209.165.200.226. By doing this, the network administrator can verify remotely (from R2) that R1 has the route 10.1.1.0/24 in its routing table. This is shown in Example 11-2.

Figure 11-16 Sample Network

Example 11-2   Extended **ping**

```
R2# ping
Protocol [ip]:
Target IP address: 192.168.10.1
Repeat count [5]:
Datagram size [100]:
Timeout in seconds [2]:
Extended commands [n]: y
Source address or interface: 10.1.1.1
Type of service [0]:
Set DF bit in IP header? [no]:
Validate reply data? [no]:
Data pattern [0xABCD]:
Loose, Strict, Record, Timestamp, Verbose[none]:
Sweep range of sizes [n]:
Type escape sequence to abort.
Sending 5, 100-byte ICMP Echos to 192.168.10.1, timeout is 2 seconds:
!!!!!
Success rate is 100 percent (5/5), round-trip min/avg/max = 36/97/132 ms
```

Entering a longer timeout period than the default allows possible latency issues to be detected. If the ping test is successful with a longer value, a connection exists between the hosts, but latency might be an issue on the network.

Note that entering **y** at the **Extended commands** prompt provides more options that are useful in troubleshooting.

Network Baseline (11.3.1.3)

One of the most effective tools for monitoring and troubleshooting network performance is to establish a network baseline. A baseline is a process for studying the network at regular intervals to ensure that the network is working as designed. A network baseline is more than a single report detailing the health of the network at a certain point in time. Creating an effective network performance baseline is accomplished over a period of time. Measuring performance at varying times and loads will assist in creating a better picture of overall network performance.

The output derived from network commands can contribute data to the network baseline.

One method for starting a baseline is to copy and paste the results from an executed **ping, trace,** or other relevant command into a text file. These text files can be time-stamped with the date and saved into an archive for later retrieval.

An effective use of the stored information is to compare the results over time. Among items to consider are error messages and the response times from host to host. If there is a considerable increase in response times, there might be a latency issue to address.

The importance of creating documentation cannot be emphasized enough. Verification of host-to-host connectivity, latency issues, and resolutions of identified problems can assist a network administrator in keeping a network running as efficiently as possible.

Corporate networks should have extensive baselines, more extensive than we can describe in this course. Professional-grade software tools are available for storing and maintaining baseline information. In this course, we only cover some basic techniques and discuss the purpose of baselines.

Tracert (11.3.2)

Sometimes more information is required then a simple end-to-end connectivity test can provide. Running a packet trace from source to destination can alert the user to where problems actually exist.

Interpreting Tracert Messages (11.3.2.1)

A trace returns a list of hops as a packet is routed through a network. The form of the command depends on where the command is issued. When performing the trace from a Windows computer, use **tracert**. When performing the trace from a router CLI, use **traceroute**, as shown in Figure 11-17.

Figure 11-17 Tracing the Route

Like **ping** commands, **trace** commands are entered at the command line and take an IP address as the argument.

Example 11-3 shows the command issued from a Windows computer.

Example 11-3   tracert Command Issued from a Windows Machine

```
C:\> tracert 10.1.0.2
Tracing route to 10.1.0.2 over a maximum of 30 hops
1 2 ms 2 ms 2 ms 10.0.0.254
2 * * * Request timed out.
3 * * * Request timed out.
4 ^C
```

The only successful response was from the gateway on Router A. Trace requests to the next hop timed out, meaning that the next-hop router did not respond. The trace results indicate that the failure is therefore in the internetwork beyond the LAN.

Capturing the traceroute output can also be done from the router prompt.

Packet Tracer Activity 11.3.2.2: Test Connectivity with Traceroute

This activity is designed to help you troubleshoot network connectivity issues using commands to trace the route from source to destination. You are required to examine the output of **tracert** (the Windows command) and **traceroute** (the IOS command) as packets traverse the network and determine the cause of a network issue. After the issue is corrected, use the **tracert** and **traceroute** commands to verify the completion.

Lab 11.3.2.3: Testing Network Latency with Ping and Traceroute

In this lab, you will complete the following objectives:

- Part 1: Use Ping to Document Network Latency
- Part 2: Use Traceroute to Document Network Latency

Show Commands (11.3.3)

Show commands allow the network technician to look at a static snapshot of a configuration or process.

Common Show Commands Revisited (11.3.3.1)

The Cisco IOS CLI **show** commands display relevant information about the configuration and operation of the device.

Network technicians use **show** commands extensively for viewing configuration files, checking the status of device interfaces and processes, and verifying the device operational status. The **show** commands are available whether the device was configured using the CLI or Cisco Configuration Professional.

The status of nearly every process or function of the router can be displayed using a **show** command. Some of the more popular show commands are

- **show running-config**
- **show interfaces**
- **show arp**
- **show ip route**
- **show protocols**
- **show version**

Example 11-4 shows sample output from the **show running-config** command. This can be used to check the active configuration.

Example 11-4 Sample Output from the **show running-config** Command

```
R1# show running-config
< Some output omitted >
Building configuration...
Current configuration : 1063 bytes
!
version 12.4
service timestamps debug datetime msec
service timestamps log datetime msec
no service password-encryption
hostname R1
enable secret 5 $1$i6w9$dvdpVM6zV10E6tSyLdkR5/
no ip domain lookup
!
interface FastEthernet0/0
 description LAN 192.168.1.0 default gateway
 ip address 192.168.1.1 255.255.255.0
 duplex auto
 speed auto
!
interface FastEthernet0/1
 no ip address
 shutdown
 duplex auto
 speed auto
```

```
!
interface Serial0/0/0
 description WAN link to R2
 ip address 192.168.2.1 255.255.255.0
 encapsulation ppp
 clock rate 64000
 no fair-queue
!
interface Serial0/0/1
 no ip address
 shutdown
!
interface Vlan1
 no ip address
!
router rip
 version 2
 network 192.168.1.0
 network 192.168.2.0
!
banner motd ^CUnauthorized Access Prohibited^C
!
ip http server
!
line con 0
 password cisco
 login
line aux 0
line vty 0 4
 password cisco
 login
```

The **show interfaces** command output, as shown in Example 11-5, can be used to see the status of each interface.

Example 11-5   Sample Output from the **show interfaces** Command

```
R1# show interfaces
< Some output omitted >
FastEthernet0/0 is up, line protocol is up
  Hardware is Gt96k FE, address is 001b.5325.256e (bia 001b.5325.256e)
  Internet address is 192.168.1.1/24
  MTU 1500 bytes, BW 100000 Kbit, DLY 100 usec,
     reliability 255/255, txload 1/255, rxload 1/255
  Encapsulation ARPA, loopback not set
  Keepalive set (10 sec)
```

```
      Full-duplex, 100Mb/s, 100BaseTX/FX
      ARP type: ARPA, ARP Timeout 04:00:00
      Last input 00:00:17, output 00:00:01, output hang never
      Last clearing of "show interface" counters never
      Input queue: 0/75/0/0 (size/max/drops/flushes); Total output drops: 0
      Queueing strategy: fifo
      Output queue: 0/40 (size/max)
      5 minute input rate 0 bits/sec, 0 packets/sec
      5 minute output rate 0 bits/sec, 0 packets/sec
         196 packets input, 31850 bytes
         Received 181 broadcasts, 0 runts, 0 giants, 0 throttles
         0 input errors, 0 CRC, 0 frame, 0 overrun, 0 ignored
         0 watchdog
         0 input packets with dribble condition detected
         392 packets output, 35239 bytes, 0 underruns
         0 output errors, 0 collisions, 3 interface resets
         0 babbles, 0 late collision, 0 deferred
         0 lost carrier, 0 no carrier
         0 output buffer failures, 0 output buffers swapped out

FastEthernet0/1 is administratively down, line protocol is down

Serial0/0/0 is up, line protocol is up
   Hardware is GT96K Serial
   Internet address is 192.168.2.1/24
   MTU 1500 bytes, BW 1544 Kbit, DLY 20000 usec,
      reliability 255/255, txload 1/255, rxload 1/255
   Encapsulation PPP, LCP Listen, loopback not set
   Keepalive set (10 sec)
   Last input 00:00:02, output 00:00:03, output hang never
   Last clearing of "show interface" counters 00:51:52
   Input queue: 0/75/0/0 (size/max/drops/flushes); Total output drops: 0
   Queueing strategy: fifo
   Output queue: 0/40 (size/max)
   5 minute input rate 0 bits/sec, 0 packets/sec
   5 minute output rate 0 bits/sec, 0 packets/sec
      401 packets input, 27437 bytes, 0 no buffer
      Received 293 broadcasts, 0 runts, 0 giants, 0 throttles
      0 input errors, 0 CRC, 0 frame, 0 overrun, 0 ignored, 0 abort
      389 packets output, 26940 bytes, 0 underruns
      0 output errors, 0 collisions, 2 interface resets
      0 output buffer failures, 0 output buffers swapped out
      6 carrier transitions
      DCD=up  DSR=up  DTR=up  RTS=up  CTS=up

Serial0/0/1 is administratively down, line protocol is down
```

Example 11-6 shows the output of the **show arp** command. This command displays the contents of the router's ARP table.

Example 11-6   Sample Output from the **show arp** Command

```
R1# show arp
Protocol  Address         Age (min)  Hardware Addr   Type   Interface
Internet  172.17.0.1            -    001b.5325.256e  ARPA   FastEthernet0/0
Internet  172.17.0.2           12    000b.db04.a5cd  ARPA   FastEthernet0/0
```

The **show ip route** command displays the contents of the router's IP routing table. Sample output is shown in Example 11-7.

Example 11-7   Sample Output from the **show ip route** Command

```
R1# show ip route
Codes: C - connected, S - static, R - RIP, M - mobile, B - BGP
       D - EIGRP, EX - EIGRP external, O - OSPF, IA - OSPF inter area
       N1 - OSPF NSSA external type 1, N2 - OSPF NSSA external type 2
       E1 - OSPF external type 1, E2 - OSPF external type 2
       i - IS-IS, su - IS-IS summary, L1 - IS-IS level-1, L2 - IS-IS level-2
       ia - IS-IS inter area, * - candidate default, U - per-user static route
       o - ODR, P - periodic downloaded static route

Gateway of last resort is not set
C    192.168.1.0/24 is directly connected, FastEthernet0/0
C    192.168.2.0/24 is directly connected, Serial0/0/0
R    192.168.3.0/24 [120/1] via 192.168.2.2, 00:00:24, Serial0/0/0
```

Example 11-8 shows sample output from the **show protocols** command. This command displays information about any configured protocols running on the router.

Example 11-8   Sample Output from the **show protocols** Command

```
R1# show protocols
Global values:
  Internet Protocol routing is enabled
FastEthernet0/0 is up, line protocol is up
  Internet address is 192.168.1.1/24
FastEthernet0/1 is administratively down, line protocol is down
FastEthernet0/1/0 is up, line protocol is down
FastEthernet0/1/1 is up, line protocol is down
FastEthernet0/1/2 is up, line protocol is down
FastEthernet0/1/3 is up, line protocol is down
```

```
Serial0/0/0 is up, line protocol is up
  Internet address is 192.168.2.1/24
Serial0/0/1 is administratively down, line protocol is down
Vlan1 is up, line protocol is down
```

The **show version** command displays system hardware and software information, including the value of the configuration register. Sample output is shown in Example 11-9.

Example 11-9   Sample Output from the **show version** Command

```
R1# show version
< Some output omitted >
Cisco IOS Software, 1841 Software (C1841-ADVIPSERVICESK9-M), Version 12.4(10b),
RELEASE SOFTWARE (fc3)
Technical Support: http://www.cisco.com/techsupport
Copyright (c) 1986-2007 by Cisco Systems, Inc.
Compiled Fri 19-Jan-07 15:15 by prod_rel_team

ROM: System Bootstrap, Version 12.4(13r)T, RELEASE SOFTWARE (fc1)
R1 uptime is 43 minutes
System returned to ROM by reload at 22:05:12 UTC Sat Jan 5 2008
System image file is "flash:c1841-advipservicesk9-mz.124-10b.bin"

Cisco 1841 (revision 6.0) with 174080K/22528K bytes of memory.
Processor board ID FTX1111W0QF
6 FastEthernet interfaces
2 Serial(sync/async) interfaces
1 Virtual Private Network (VPN) Module
DRAM configuration is 64 bits wide with parity disabled.
191K bytes of NVRAM.
62720K bytes of ATA CompactFlash (Read/Write)

Configuration register is 0x2102
```

Viewing Router Settings with the show version Command (11.3.3.2)

After the startup configuration file is loaded and the router boots successfully, the **show version** command can be used to verify and troubleshoot some of the basic hardware and software components used during the bootup process. The output from the **show version** command is shown in Figure 11-18 and includes

- The Cisco IOS Software version being used.

- The version of the system bootstrap software, stored in ROM, that was initially used to boot the router.

- The complete filename of the Cisco IOS image and where the bootstrap program located it.

- The type of CPU on the router and the amount of RAM. It might be necessary to upgrade the amount of RAM when upgrading the Cisco IOS Software.

- The number and type of physical interfaces on the router.

- The amount of NVRAM. NVRAM is used to store the startup config file.

- The amount of flash memory on the router. It might be necessary to upgrade the amount of flash when upgrading the Cisco IOS Software.

- The currently configured value of the software configuration register in hexadecimal.

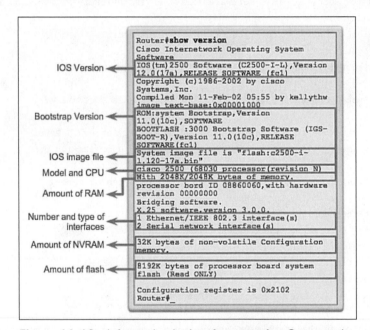

Figure 11-18   Information in the **show version** Command

The configuration register tells the router how to boot up. For example, the factory default setting for the configuration register is 0x2102. This value indicates that the router attempts to load a Cisco IOS Software image from flash and loads the startup configuration file from NVRAM. It is possible to change the configuration register and, therefore, change where the router looks for the Cisco IOS image and the startup configuration file during the bootup process. If there is a second value in parentheses, it denotes the configuration register value to be used during the next reload of the router.

Viewing Switch Settings with the show version Command (11.3.3.3)

The **show version** command on a switch displays information about the currently loaded software version, along with hardware and device information. Some of the information displayed by this command is

- **Software version:** IOS Software version

- **Bootstrap version:** Bootstrap version

- **System uptime:** Time since last reboot

- **System restart info:** Method of restart (for example, power cycle or crash)

- **Software image name:** IOS filename

- **Switch platform and processor type:** Model number and processor type

- **Memory type (shared/main):** Main processor RAM and shared packet I/O buffering

- **Hardware interfaces:** Interfaces available on the switch

- **Configuration register:** Sets bootup specifications, console speed setting, and related parameters

Packet Tracer Activity 11.3.3.4: Using show Commands

This activity is designed to reinforce the use of router **show** commands. You are not required to configure them, but rather examine the output of several **show** commands.

Host and IOS Commands (11.3.4)

In addition to the **show** commands, a number of additional commands are available on hosts and network devices.

ipconfig Command Options (11.3.4.1)

As shown in Figure 11-19, the IP address of the default gateway of a host can be viewed by issuing the **ipconfig** command at the command line of a Windows computer.

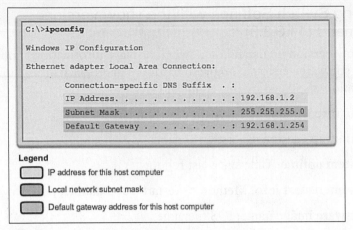

```
C:\>ipconfig

Windows IP Configuration

Ethernet adapter Local Area Connection:

        Connection-specific DNS Suffix  . :
        IP Address. . . . . . . . . . . : 192.168.1.2
        Subnet Mask . . . . . . . . . . : 255.255.255.0
        Default Gateway . . . . . . . . : 192.168.1.254
```

Legend
 IP address for this host computer
 Local network subnet mask
 Default gateway address for this host computer

Figure 11-19   Windows **ipconfig** Command Output

The **ipconfig /all** command can be used to view the MAC address of a computer. Note that in Figure 11-20, the MAC address of the computer is now displayed along with a number of details regarding the Layer 3 addressing of the device.

```
C:\>ipconfig /all
Ethernet adapter Network Connection:
        Connection-specific DNS Suffix: example.com
        Description . . . . . . . . . . : Intel(R)
        PRO/Wireless 3945ABG Network Connection
        Physical Address. . . . . . . . : 00-18-DE-C7-F3-FB
        Dhcp Enabled. . . . . . . . . . : Yes
        Autoconfiguration Enabled . . . : Yes
        IP Address. . . . . . . . . . . : 10.2.3.4
        Subnet Mask . . . . . . . . . . : 255.255.255.0
        Default Gateway . . . . . . . . : 10.2.3.254
        DHCP Server . . . . . . . . . . : 10.2.3.69
        DNS Servers . . . . . . . . . . : 192.168.226.120
        Lease Obtained. . . . . . . . . : Thursday, May 03,
                                          2007 3:47:51 PM
        Lease Expires . . . . . . . . . : Friday, May 04,
                                          2007 6:57:11 AM
C:\>
```

Figure 11-20   Windows **ipconfig /all** Command Output

In addition, the manufacturer of the network interface in the computer can be identified through the Organizationally Unique Identifier (OUI) portion of the MAC address. This can be researched on the Internet.

The DNS Client service on Windows PCs optimizes the performance of DNS name resolution by storing previously resolved names in memory, as well. The **ipconfig / displaydns** command displays all the cached DNS entries on a Windows computer system.

arp Command Options (11.3.4.2)

The **arp** command enables the creation, editing, and display of mappings of physical addresses to known IPv4 addresses. The **arp** command is executed from the Windows command prompt.

To execute an **arp** command, at the command prompt of a host, enter

```
C:\host1> arp -a
```

As shown in Figure 11-21, the **arp –a** command lists all devices currently in the ARP cache of the host, which includes the IPv4 address, physical address, and the type of addressing (static/dynamic), for each device.

The cache can be cleared by using the **arp -d** command in the event that the network administrator wants to repopulate the cache with updated information.

Figure 11-21   Windows **arp** Command

show cdp neighbors Command Options (11.3.4.3)

Cisco Discovery Protocol (CDP) is a Cisco-proprietary protocol that runs at the data link layer. Because CDP operates at the data link layer, two or more Cisco network devices, such as routers that support different network layer protocols, can learn about each other, even if Layer 3 connectivity does not exist.

Examine the output from the **show cdp neighbors** commands in Example 11-10. This corresponds to the topology shown in Figure 11-22. Notice that R3 has gathered some detailed information about R2 and the switch connected to the Fast Ethernet interface on R3.

Figure 11-22   Cisco IOS **show cdp neighbors** Command

Example 11-10   Sample Output from the **show cdp neighbors** Command

```
R3# show cdp neighbors

Capability Codes: R - Router, T - Trans Bridge, B - Source Route Bridge
                  S - Switch, H - Host, I - IGMP, r - Repeater, P - Phone


Device ID        Local Intrfce      Holdtme     Capability  Platform  Port ID
S3       Fas 0/0            151          S I       WS-C2950  Fas 0/6
R2       Ser 0/0/1          125          R         1841      Ser 0/0/1


R3# show cdp neighbors detail

-------------------------
Device ID: R2
Entry address(es):
IP address: 192.168.1.2
Platform: Cisco 1841,  Capabilities: Router Switch IGMP
Interface: Serial0/0/1,  Port ID (outgoing port): Serial0/0/1
Holdtime : 161 sec

Version :
Cisco IOS Software, 1841 Software (C1841-ADVIPSERVICESK9-M), Version 12.4(10b),
  RELEASE SOFTWARE (fc3)
Technical Support: http://www.cisco.com/techsupport
```

```
Copyright (c) 1986-2007 by Cisco Systems, Inc.
Compiled Fri 19-Jan-07 15:15 by prod_rel_team

advertisement version: 2
VTP Management Domain: ''

------------------------
Device ID: S3
Entry address(es):
Platform: cisco WS-C2950-24,  Capabilities: Switch IGMP
Interface: FastEthernet0/0,  Port ID (outgoing port): FastEthernet0/11
Holdtime : 148 sec

Version :
Cisco Internetwork Operating System Software
IOS (tm) C2950 Software (C2950-I6Q4L2-M), Version 12.1(9)EA1, RELEASE SOFTWARE (fc1)
Copyright (c) 1986-2002 by cisco Systems, Inc.
Compiled Wed 24-Apr-02 06:57 by antonino

advertisement version: 2
Protocol Hello:  OUI=0x00000C, Protocol ID=0x0112; payload len=27,
  value=00000000FFFFFFFF0
10231FF000000000000000AB769F6C0FF0000
VTP Management Domain: 'CCNA3'
Duplex: full

R3#
```

When a Cisco device boots up, CDP starts up by default. CDP automatically discovers neighboring Cisco devices running CDP, regardless of which Layer 3 protocol or suites are running. CDP exchanges hardware and software device information with its directly connected CDP neighbors.

CDP provides the following information about each CDP neighbor device:

- **Device identifiers:** For example, the configured host name of a switch
- **Address list:** Up to one network layer address for each protocol supported
- **Port identifier:** The name of the local and remote port in the form of an ASCII character string, such as ethernet0
- **Capabilities list:** For example, whether this device is a router or a switch
- **Platform:** The hardware platform of the device, for example, a Cisco 1841 Series router

The **show cdp neighbors detail** command reveals the IP address of a neighboring device. CDP will reveal the neighbor's IP address regardless of whether you can ping the neighbor. This command is very helpful when two Cisco routers cannot route across their shared data link. The **show cdp neighbors detail** command will help determine whether one of the CDP neighbors has an IP configuration error.

For network discovery situations, knowing the IP address of the CDP neighbor is often all the information needed to telnet into that device.

For obvious reasons, CDP can be a security risk. Because some IOS versions send out CDP advertisements by default, it is important to know how to disable CDP.

To disable CDP globally, use the global configuration command **no cdp run**. To disable CDP on an interface, use the interface command **no cdp enable**.

Using the show ip interface brief Command (11.3.4.4)

In the same way that commands and utilities are used to verify a host configuration, commands can be used to verify the interfaces of intermediate devices. The Cisco IOS provides commands to verify the operation of router and switch interfaces.

Verifying Router Interfaces

One of the most frequently used commands is the **show ip interface brief** command. This command provides a more abbreviated output than the **show ip interface** command. It provides a summary of the key information for all the network interfaces on a router.

Figure 11-23 shows a sample topology and Examples 11-11 and 11-12 show the output of the **show ip interface brief** command on R1 and S1. The output displays all interfaces on the device, the IP address assigned to each interface, if any, and the operational status of the interface.

Figure 11-23   Output of the **show ip interface brief** Command

Example 11-11   Verifying Router Interfaces

```
Router1# show ip interface brief

Interface        IP-Address     OK? Method Status                 Protocol
FastEthernet0/0   192.168.254.254 YES NVRAM  up                     up
FastEthernet0/1/  0unassigned    YES unset  down                   down
Serial0/0/0       172.16.0.254   YES NVRAM  up                     up
Serial0/0/1       unassigned     YES unset  administratively down  down
------------------------
Router1# ping 192.168.254.1

Type escape sequence to abort.
Sending 5, 100-byte ICMP Echos to 192.168.254.1, timeout is 2 seconds:
!!!!!
Success rate is 100 percent {5/5}, round-trip min/avg/max = 1/2/4 ms
------------------------
Router1# traceroute 192.168.0.1

Type escape sequence to abort.
Tracing the route to 192.168.0.1
1 172.16.0.253 8 msec 4 msec 8 msec
2 10.0.0.254 16 msec 16 msec 8 msec
3 192.168.0.1 16 msec * 20 msec
```

According to the output for R1, the Fast Ethernet 0/0 interface has an IP address of 192.168.254.254. The last two columns in this line show the Layer 1 and Layer 2 status of this interface. The **up** in the Status column shows that this interface is operational at Layer 1. The **up** in the Protocol column indicates that the Layer 2 protocol is operational.

Also notice that the Serial 0/0/1 interface has not been enabled. This is indicated by **administratively down** in the Status column.

As with any end device, we can verify Layer 3 connectivity with the **ping** and **traceroute** commands. In this example, both the **ping** and **trace** commands show successful connectivity.

Verifying the Switch Interfaces

The **show ip interface brief** command on S1 verifies the status of the switch interfaces. The IP address for the switch is applied to a VLAN interface. In this case, the Vlan1 interface is assigned an IP address of 192.168.254.250 and has been enabled and is operational.

The output also shows that the FastEthernet0/1 interface is down. This indicates that either no device is connected to the interface or that the device that is connected to this interface has a network interface that is not operational.

In contrast, the output shows that the FastEthernet0/2 and FastEthernet0/3 interfaces are operational. This is indicated by both the Status and Protocol being shown as **up**.

The switch can also test its Layer 3 connectivity with the **show ip interface brief** and **traceroute** commands. In this example, both the **ping** and **trace** commands show successful connectivity. This is shown in Example 11-12.

Example 11-12   Verifying Switch Interfaces

```
Switch1# show ip interface brief

Interface          IP-Address      OK? Method Status   Protocol
Vlan1              192.168.254.250 YES manual up       up
FastEthernet0/1    unassigned      YES unset  down     down
FastEthernet0/2    unassigned      YES unset  up       up
FastEthernet0/3    unassigned      YES unset  up       up
<output omitted>
----------
Switch1# ping 192.168.254.1

Type escape sequence to abort.
Sending 5, 100-byte ICMP Echos to 192.168.254.1, timeout is 2 seconds:
!!!!!
Success rate is 100 percent {5/5}, round-trip min/avg/max = 1/2/4 ms
    ---------
Switch1# traceroute 192.168.0.1
Type escape sequence to abort.
Tracing the route to 192.168.0.1
1 192.168.254.254 4 msec 2 msec 3 msec
2 172.16.0.253 8 msec 4 msec 8 msec
3 10.0.0.254 16 msec 16 msec 8 msec
4 192.168.0.1 16 msec * 20 msec
```

It is important to keep in mind that an IP address is not required for a switch to perform its job of frame forwarding at Layer 2. An IP address is only necessary if the switch will be managed over the network using Telnet or SSH. If the network administrator plans to remotely connect to the switch from a location outside of the local LAN, a default gateway must also be configured.

Interactive Graphic

Activity 11.3.4.5: Show Commands

Go to the course online to perform this practice activity.

Lab 11.3.4.6: Using the CLI to Gather Network Device Information

In this lab, you will complete the following objectives:

- Part 1: Set Up Topology and Initialize Devices
- Part 2: Configure Devices and Verify Connectivity
- Part 3: Gather Network Device Information

Managing IOS Configuration Files (11.4)

In addition to implementing and securing a small network, it is also the job of the network administrator to manage configuration files. Managing the configuration files is important for purposes of backup and retrieval in the event of a device failure.

Router and Switch File Systems (11.4.1)

Cisco routers and switches run the Cisco Internetwork Operating System (IOS), which offers both a command-line and graphical user interface.

Router File Systems (11.4.1.1)

The Cisco IOS File System (IFS) provides a single interface to all the file systems a router uses, including

- Flash memory file systems
- Network file systems (TFTP and FTP)
- Any other endpoint for reading or writing data such as NVRAM, the running configuration, ROM, and others

With Cisco IFS, all files can be viewed and classified (image, text file, and so on), including files on remote servers. For example, it is possible to view a configuration file on a remote server to verify that it is the correct configuration file before loading the file on the router.

Cisco IFS allows the administrator to move around to different directories and list the files in a directory, and to create subdirectories in flash memory or on a disk. The directories available depend on the device.

Example 11-13 displays the output of the **show file systems** command, which lists all the available file systems on a Cisco 1941 router, in this example. This command provides useful information such as the amount of available and free memory, the type of file system, and its permissions. Permissions include read only (ro), write only (wo), and read and write (rw), shown in the Flags column of the command output.

Example 11-13 Output of the **show file systems** Command

```
Router# show file systems
File Systems:

        Size(b)       Free(b)       Type   Flags   Prefixes
              -             -       opaque   rw     archive:
              -             -       opaque   rw     system:
              -             -       opaque   rw     tmpsys:
              -             -       opaque   rw     null:
              -             -       network  rw     tftp:
*     256487424     183234560      disk     rw     flash0: flash:#
              -             -       disk     rw     flash1:
         262136        254779      nvram    rw     nvram:
              -             -       opaque   wo     syslog:
              -             -       opaque   rw     xmodem:
              -             -       opaque   rw     ymodem:
              -             -       network  rw     rcp:
              -             -       network  rw     http:
              -             -       network  rw     ftp:
              -             -       network  rw     scp:
              -             -       opaque   ro     tar:
              -             -       network  rw     https:
              -             -       opaque   ro     cns:
```

Although there are several file systems listed, of interest to us will be the tftp, flash, and nvram file systems.

Notice that the flash file system also has an asterisk preceding it. This indicates that flash is the current default file system. The bootable IOS is located in flash; therefore, the pound symbol (#) is appended to the flash listing, indicating that it is a bootable disk.

The Flash File System

Example 11-14 shows the contents of the current default file system, which in this case is flash, as was indicated by the asterisks preceding the listing in the previous figure. There are several files located in flash, but of specific interest is the last listing. This is the name of the current Cisco IOS file image that is running in RAM.

Example 11-14   Flash File System

```
Router# dir
Directory of flash0:/

    1  -rw-        2903     Sep 7 2012 06:58:26 +00:00  cpconfig-19xx.cfg
    2  -rw-     3000320     Sep 7 2012 06:58:40 +00:00  cpexpress.tar
    3  -rw-        1038     Sep 7 2012 06:58:52 +00:00  home.shtml
    4  -rw-      122880     Sep 7 2012 06:59:02 +00:00  home.tar
    5  -rw-     1697952     Sep 7 2012 06:59:20 +00:00  securedesktop-
ios-3.1.1.45-k9.pkg
    6  -rw-      415956     Sep 7 2012 06:59:34 +00:00  sslclient-win-1.1.4.176.pkg
    7  -rw-    67998028     Sep 26 2012 17:32:14 +00:00  c1900-
universalk9-mz.SPA.152-4.M1.bin

256487424 bytes total (183234560 bytes free)
```

The NVRAM File System

To view the contents of NVRAM, you must change the current default file system using the **cd** (change directory) command, as shown in Example 11-15. The **pwd** (present working directory) command verifies that we are viewing the NVRAM directory. Finally, the **dir** (directory) command lists the contents of NVRAM. Although there are several configuration files listed, of specific interest is the startup configuration file.

Example 11-15   Contents of NVRAM

```
Router# cd nvram:
Router# pwd
nvram:/
Router# dir
Directory of nvram:/

  253  -rw-        1156                     <no date>  startup-config
  254  ----           5                     <no date>  private-config
  255  -rw-        1156                     <no date>  underlying-config
    1  -rw-        2945                     <no date>  cwmp_inventory
```

```
    4   ----        58             <no date>  persistent-data
    5   -rw-        17             <no date>  ecfm_ieee_mib
    6   -rw-       559             <no date>  IOS-Self-Sig#1.cer


262136 bytes total (254779 bytes free)
```

Switch File Systems (11.4.1.2)

With the Cisco 2960 switch flash file system, you can copy configuration files and archive (upload and download) software images.

The command to view the file systems on a Catalyst switch is the same as on a Cisco router: **show file systems**, as shown in Example 11-16.

Example 11-16   Cisco 2960 Switch File System

```
Switch# show file systems
File Systems:

     Size(b)     Free(b)      Type  Flags  Prefixes
*    32514048    20887552     flash    rw    flash:
        -           -         opaque   rw    vb:
        -           -         opaque   ro    bs:
        -           -         opaque   rw    system:
        -           -         opaque   rw    tmpsys:
      65536       48897       nvram    rw    nvram:
        -           -         opaque   ro    xmodem:
        -           -         opaque   ro    ymodem:
        -           -         opaque   rw    null:
        -           -         opaque   ro    tar:
        -           -         network  rw    tftp:
        -           -         network  rw    rcp:
        -           -         network  rw    http:
        -           -         network  rw    ftp:
        -           -         network  rw    scp:
        -           -         network  rw    https:
        -           -         opaque   ro    cns:.
```

Many basic UNIX commands are supported on Cisco switches and routers: **cd** for changing to a file system or directory, **dir** to display directories on a file system, and **pwd** to display the working directory.

Back Up and Restore Configuration Files (11.4.2)

It is important to have a valid copy of any configuration files required by a switch or router. This allows a rapid recovery should the file become corrupted. Whenever the configuration is altered, a new copy of the configuration should be saved.

Backing Up and Restoring Using Text Files (11.4.2.1)

Because the configuration files on routers and switches are text files, it is possible to back up and restore them using a terminal emulation program such as Tera Term.

Backup Configurations with Text Capture (Tera Term)

Configuration files can be saved/archived to a text file using Tera Term.

The steps required are

Step 1.   On the File menu, click **Log**.

Step 2.   Choose the location to save the file. Tera Term will begin capturing text.

Step 3.   After capture has been started, execute the **show running-config** or **show startup-config** command at the privileged EXEC prompt. Text displayed in the terminal window will be directed into the chosen file.

Step 4.   When the capture is complete, select **Close** in the Tera Term: Log window.

Step 5.   View the file to verify that it was not corrupted.

Restoring Text Configurations

A configuration can be copied from a file to a device. When copied from a text file and pasted into a terminal window, the IOS executes each line of the configuration text as a command. This means that the file will require editing to ensure that encrypted passwords are in plain text and that noncommand text such as "--More--" and IOS messages are removed. This process is discussed in the lab.

Further, at the CLI, the device must be set at the global configuration mode to receive the commands from the text file being pasted into the terminal window.

When using Tera Term, the steps are

Step 1.   On the File menu, click **Send**.

Step 2.   Locate the file to be copied into the device and click **Open**.

Step 3.   Tera Term will paste the file into the device.

The text in the file will be applied as commands in the CLI and become the running configuration on the device. This is a convenient method for manually configuring a router.

Backing Up and Restoring Using TFTP (11.4.2.2)

The use of a Trivial File Transfer Protocol (TFTP) server to store and retrieve configuration files allows the configuration files to be quickly reloaded on any device connected to the network.

Backing Up Configurations with TFTP

Copies of configuration files should be stored as backup files in the event of a problem. Configuration files can be stored on a TFTP server or a USB drive. A configuration file should also be included in the network documentation.

To save the running configuration or the startup configuration to a TFTP server, use either the **copy running-config tftp** or **copy startup-config tftp** command.

Follow these steps to back up the running configuration to a TFTP server:

Step 1.   Enter the **copy running-config tftp** command.

Step 2.   Enter the IP address of the host where the configuration file will be stored.

Step 3.   Enter the name to assign to the configuration file.

Step 4.   Press Enter to confirm each choice.

Restoring Configurations with TFTP

To restore the running configuration or the startup configuration from a TFTP server, use either the **copy tftp running-config** or **copy tftp startup-config** command.

Use these steps to restore the running configuration from a TFTP server:

Step 1.   Enter the **copy tftp running-config** command.

Step 2.   Enter the IP address of the host where the configuration file is stored.

Step 3.   Enter the name to assign to the configuration file.

Step 4.   Press Enter to confirm each choice.

Using USB Ports on a Cisco Router (11.4.2.3)

The Universal Serial Bus (USB) storage feature enables certain models of Cisco routers to support USB flash drives. The USB flash feature provides an optional secondary storage capability and an additional boot device. Images, configurations, and other files can be copied to or from the Cisco USB flash memory with the same reliability as storing and retrieving files using the Compact Flash card. In addition, modular integrated services routers can boot any Cisco IOS Software image saved on USB flash memory.

Cisco USB flash modules are available in 64-MB, 128-MB, and 256-MB versions.

To be compatible with a Cisco router, a USB flash drive must be formatted in a FAT16 format. If that is not the case, the **show file systems** command will display an error, indicating an incompatible file system.

Example 11-17 shows the use of the **dir** command on a USB file system.

Example 11-17   dir Command Use on a USB File System

```
Router# dir usbflash0:
Directory of usbflash0:/
1 -rw- 30125020 Dec 22 2032 05:31:32 +00:00 c3825-entservicesk9-mz.123-14.T
63158272 bytes total (33033216 bytes free)
```

Ideally, USB flash can hold multiple copies of the Cisco IOS and multiple router configurations. The USB flash allows an administrator to easily move and copy those IOS files and configurations from router to router, and many times, the copying process can take place several times faster than it would over a LAN or WAN. Note that the IOS might not recognize the proper size of the USB flash, but that does not necessarily mean that the flash is unsupported. Additionally, the USB ports on a router are usually USB 2.0, as shown in Figure 11-24.

Figure 11-24   USB Ports on a Cisco 1941 Router

Backing Up and Restoring Using a USB Flash Drive (11.4.2.4)

The availability of USB ports on many of the network devices greatly simplifies the backing up and restoring of configuration files.

Backup Configurations with a USB Flash Drive

When backing up to a USB port, it is a good idea to issue the **show file systems** command to verify that the USB drive is there and to confirm the name.

Next, use the **copy run usbflash0:/** command to copy the configuration file to the USB flash drive. Be sure to use the name of the flash drive, as indicated in the file system. The slash is optional but indicates the root directory of the USB flash drive.

The IOS will prompt for the filename. If the file already exists on the USB flash drive, the router will prompt for overwrite.

Use the **dir** command to see the file on the USB drive, and use the **more** command to see the contents.

Restore Configurations with a USB Flash Drive

To copy the file back, it will be necessary to edit the USB R1-Config file with a text editor to make it a valid config file; otherwise, there are a lot of entries that are invalid commands and no interfaces will be brought up.

Packet Tracer Activity 11.4.2.5: Backing Up Configuration Files

This activity is designed to show how to restore a configuration from a backup and then perform a new backup. Because of an equipment failure, a new router has been put in place. Fortunately, backup configuration files have been saved to a Trivial File Transfer Protocol (TFTP) server. You are required to restore the files from the TFTP server to get the router back online with as little downtime as possible.

Lab 11.4.2.6: Managing Router Configuration Files with Tera Term

In this lab, you will complete the following objectives:

- Part 1: Configure Basic Device Settings
- Part 2: Use Terminal Emulation Software to Create a Backup Configuration File
- Part 3: Use a Backup Configuration File to Restore a Router

Lab 11.4.2.7: Managing Device Configuration Files Using TFTP, Flash, and USB

In this lab, you will complete the following objectives:

- Part 1: Build the Network and Configure Basic Device Settings

- Part 2: (Optional) Download TFTP Server Software

- Part 3: Use TFTP to Back Up and Restore the Switch Running Configuration

- Part 4: Use TFTP to Back Up and Restore the Router Running Configuration

- Part 5: Back Up and Restore Running Configurations Using Router Flash Memory

- Part 6: (Optional) Use a USB Drive to Back Up and Restore the Running Configuration

Lab 11.4.2.8: Researching Password Recovery Procedures

In this lab, you will complete the following objectives:

- Part 1: Research the Configuration Register

- Part 2: Document the Password Recovery Procedure for a Specific Cisco Router

Integrated Routing Services (11.5)

As we have seen, many different devices and services are required for network functionality. Routers are used to connect networks, switches are used to connect individual hosts, and firewalls help to secure networks. We have also seen a movement to wireless devices in the network.

Integrated Router (11.5.1)

Managing networks with all of these different services and devices can be complex. One environment that is increasingly taking advantage of networking technology is the home.

Multifunction Device (11.5.1.1)

Home networks are being used to provide connectivity and Internet sharing among multiple personal computer systems and laptops throughout the house. They also allow individuals to take advantage of various services such as print sharing to a network printer; allow centralized storage of photos, music, and movies on a network attached storage (NAS) appliance; as well as allowing other end-user devices, such as tablet computers, cell phones, and even home appliances, such as a television, to have access to Internet services.

A home network is very similar to a small-business network. However, most home networks, and many small business networks, do not require high-volume devices, such as dedicated routers and switches. Smaller-scale devices, as long as they provide the same functionality of routing and switching, are all that are required. For this reason, many home and small-business networks utilize the service of a multifunction device.

For the purpose of this course, multifunction devices will be referred to as integrated routers.

An integrated router is like having several different devices connected together. For example, the connection between the switch and the router still occurs, but it occurs internally. When a packet is forwarded from one device to another on the same local network, the integrated switch will automatically forward the packet to the destination device. If a packet is forwarded to a device on a remote network, however, the integrated switch will then forward the packet to the internal router connection. The internal router will then determine the best path and forward the packet out accordingly.

Most integrated routers offer both wired switching capabilities and wireless connectivity, and serve as the access point (AP) in the wireless network, as shown in Figure 11-25. Wireless connectivity is a popular, flexible, and cost-effective way for homes and businesses alike to provide network services to end devices.

Figure 11-25   Integrated Router

Some of the benefits of using wireless technology include

- **Mobility:** Wireless allows easy connection of both stationary and mobile clients.

- **Scalability:** Wireless allows networks to be easily expanded to allow more users to connect and to increase the coverage area.

- **Flexibility:** Wireless facilitates anytime, anywhere connectivity.

- **Cost savings:** The cost of wireless equipment continues to fall as the technology matures.

- **Reduced installation time:** The installation of a single piece of equipment can provide connectivity for a large number of people.

- **Reliability in harsh environments:** Wireless is easy to install in emergency and hostile environments.

Wireless technology does have limitations including

- **Interference:** Wireless technology is susceptible to interference from other devices that produce electromagnetic energies. This includes cordless phones, microwaves, televisions, and other wireless LAN implementations.

- **Network and data security:** Wireless LAN technology is designed to provide access to the data being transmitted, not security of the data. Additionally, if not properly installed in the network, it can provide an unprotected entrance into the wired network.

In addition to supporting routing, switching and wireless connectivity, many additional features can be available on an integrated router, including DHCP service, a firewall, and even network attached storage services.

Types of Integrated Routers (11.5.1.2)

Integrated routers can range from small devices designed for home office and small-business applications to more powerful devices that can support enterprise branch offices.

An example of this type of integrated router is a Linksys wireless router, as shown in Figure 11-26. This type of integrated router is simple in design and does not typically have separate components. This reduces the cost of the device. However, in the event of a failure, it is not possible to replace any single failed component. As such, these integrated routers create a single point of failure and are not optimized for any one function.

Figure 11-26 Linksys Model WRT300N2 Router

Another example of an integrated router is the Cisco Integrated Services Router, or ISR. The Cisco ISR product family offers a wide range of products, including those designed for small-office and home office environments as well as those designed for larger networks. Many of the ISRs offer modularity and have separate components for each function, such as a switch component and a router component. This enables individual components to be added, replaced, and upgraded as necessary.

All integrated routers allow basic configuration settings such as passwords, IP addresses, and DHCP settings, which are the same whether the device is being used to connect wired or wireless hosts. However, if using the wireless functionality, additional configuration parameters are required, such as setting the wireless mode, SSID, and the wireless channel.

Wireless Capability (11.5.1.3)

When installing wireless LAN technologies, there are a number of basic settings to consider including the wireless mode, SSID, and channel.

Wireless Mode

The wireless mode refers to setting the IEEE 802.11 wireless standard that the network will use. There are four common amendments to the IEEE 802.11 standard that describe different characteristics for wireless communications; they are 802.11a, 802.11b, 802.11g, and 802.11n. Newer standards, such as 802.11ac and 802.11ad, offer increased throughput and are now becoming available.

Most integrated wireless routers support 802.11b, 802.11g, and 802.11n. The three technologies are compatible, but all devices on the network must operate at the same standard common to all devices. For example, if an 802.11n router is connected to a laptop with 802.11n, the network would function as an 802.11n standard. However, add an 802.11b wireless printer to the network and both the router and the laptop will revert to using the slower 802.11b standard for all communications. Therefore, keeping older wireless devices on the network will make the entire network slow down. It is important to keep that in mind when deciding whether to keep older wireless devices.

Service Set Identifier (SSID)

There can be many other wireless networks in your area. It is important that the wireless devices connect to the correct WLAN. This is done using a Service Set Identifier (SSID).

The SSID is a case-sensitive, alphanumeric name for your wireless network. The name can be up to 32-characters in length. The SSID is used to tell wireless devices which WLAN they belong to and with which other devices they can communicate. Regardless of the type of WLAN installation, all wireless devices in a WLAN must be configured with the same SSID to communicate.

Wireless Channel

Channels are created by dividing up the available RF spectrum. Each channel is capable of carrying a different conversation. This is similar to the way that multiple television channels are transmitted across a single medium. Multiple APs can function in close proximity to one another as long as they use different, nonoverlapping channels for communication.

Basic Security of Wireless (11.5.1.4)

Security measures should also be planned and configured before connecting the AP to the network or ISP.

Some of the more basic security measures include

- Change default values for the SSID, usernames, and passwords
- Disable broadcast SSID
- Configure encryption using WEP or WPA

Encryption is the process of transforming data so that even if it is intercepted, it is unusable.

Wired Equivalency Protocol (WEP)

WEP is an advanced security feature that encrypts network traffic as it travels through the air. WEP uses preconfigured keys to encrypt and decrypt data.

A WEP key is entered as a string of numbers and letters and is generally 64 bits or 128 bits long. In some cases, WEP supports 256-bit keys as well. To simplify creating and entering these keys, many devices include a passphrase option. The passphrase is an easy way to remember the word or phrase used to automatically generate a key.

For WEP to function, the AP, as well as every wireless device allowed to access the network, must have the same WEP key entered. Without this key, devices will not be able to understand the wireless transmissions.

There are weaknesses within WEP, including the use of a static key on all WEP-enabled devices. There are applications available to attackers that can be used to discover the WEP key. These applications are readily available on the Internet. After an attacker has extracted the key, he has complete access to all transmitted information.

One way to overcome this vulnerability is to change the key frequently. Another way is to use a more advanced and secure form of encryption known as Wi-Fi Protected Access (WPA).

Wi-Fi Protected Access (WPA)

WPA also uses encryption keys from 64 bits up to 256 bits. However, WPA, unlike WEP, generates new, dynamic keys each time a client establishes a connection with the AP. For this reason, WPA is considered more secure than WEP because it is significantly more difficult to crack.

There are several other security implementations that can be configured on a wireless AP, including MAC address filtering, authentication, and traffic filtering. However, those security implementations are beyond the scope of this course.

Configuring the Integrated Router (11.5.2)

The integrated router must be properly configured to provide the many features and services that it is designed to support.

Configuring the Integrated Router (11.5.2.1)

A Linksys wireless router is a common device used in home and small-business networks, and will be used in this course to demonstrate basic configurations of an integrated router. A typical Linksys device offers five to eight Ethernet ports for wired connectivity, in addition to acting as a wireless access point. The Linksys device also acts as both a DHCP server and a mini–web server that supports a web-based graphical user interface (GUI).

Accessing and Configuring a Linksys Router

Initially, access the router by cabling a computer to one of the router's LAN Ethernet ports. After it is cabled, the connecting device will automatically obtain IP addressing information, including a default gateway address, from the integrated router. The default gateway address is the IP address of the Linksys device. Check the computer network settings using the **ipconfig /all** command to obtain this address. You can now type that IP address into a web browser on the computer to access the web-based configuration GUI.

The Linksys device has a default configuration that allows switching and basic routing services. It is also configured, by default, as a DCHP server. Basic configuration tasks, such as changing the default username and password, changing the default Linksys IP address, and even changing the default DHCP IP address ranges, should be conducted before the AP is connected to a live network.

Enabling Wireless (11.5.2.2)

To enable wireless connectivity, the wireless mode, SSID, RF channel, and any desired security encryption mechanism must be configured.

First, select the correct wireless mode, as shown in Figure 11-27. When selecting the mode, or wireless standard, each mode includes a certain amount of overhead. If all devices on the network use the same standard, selecting the mode associated with that standard limits the amount of overhead incurred. It also increases security by not allowing devices with different standards to connect. However, if devices using different standards need access to the network, mixed mode must be selected. Network performance will decrease because of the additional overhead of supporting all modes.

Figure 11-27   Selecting the Wireless Mode on a Linksys Integrated Router

Next, set the SSID. All devices that want to participate in the WLAN must use the same SSID. For security purposes, the default SSID should be changed. To allow easy detection of the WLAN by clients, the SSID is broadcast by default. It is possible to disable the broadcast feature of the SSID. If the SSID is not broadcast, wireless clients will need to have this value manually configured.

The choice of RF channel used for the integrated router must be made relative to the other wireless networks around it.

Adjacent wireless networks must use nonoverlapping channels to optimize throughput. Most access points now offer a choice to allow the router to automatically locate the least congested channel.

Finally, select the encryption mechanism that you prefer and enter a key or passphrase.

Configure a Wireless Client (11.5.2.3)

A wireless host, or client, is defined as any device that contains wireless NIC and wireless client software. This client software allows the hardware to participate in the WLAN. Devices include some smartphones, laptops, desktop PCs, printers, televisions, game systems, and tablet computers.

For a wireless client to connect to the WLAN, the client configuration settings must match those of the wireless router. This includes the SSID, security settings, and channel information (if the channel was manually set). These settings are specified in the client software.

The wireless client software used can be software integrated into the device operating system, or can be a standalone, downloadable, wireless utility software specifically designed to interact with the wireless NIC. Figure 11-28 shows the Linksys client software.

Figure 11-28   Linksys Client Utility

After the client software is configured, verify the link between the client and the AP.

Open the wireless link information screen to display information such as the connection data rate, connection status, and wireless channel used. The Link Information feature, if available, displays the current signal strength and quality of the wireless signal.

In addition to verifying the wireless connection status, verify that data can actually be transmitted. One of the most common tests for verifying successful data transmission is the ping test. If the ping is successful, data transmission is possible.

Packet Tracer Activity 11.5.2.4: Configuring a Linksys Router

In this activity, you will configure a Linksys wireless router, allowing remote access to wireless clients as well as connectivity with WPA security.

Summary (11.6)

Class Activity 11.6.1.1 (Capstone Project): Design and Build a Small-Business Network

Use Packet Tracer and a word processing application to complete this activity: two to three students per group.

Design and build a network from scratch:

- Your design must include a minimum of one router, one switch, and one PC.

- Fully configure the network. Use IPv4 or IPv6 (subnetting must be included as a part of your addressing scheme).

- Verify the network using at least five **show** commands.

- Secure the network using SSH, secure passwords, and console passwords (minimum).

Create a rubric to use for peer grading, or your instructor can choose to use the rubric provided with this activity.

Present your Capstone Project to the class; be able to answer questions from your peers and instructor!

Packet Tracer Activity 11.6.1.2: Skills Integration Challenge

The network administrator has asked you to prepare an integrated services router for deployment. Before it can be connected to the network, security measures must be enabled.

To meet user requirements, even small networks require planning and design. Planning ensures that all requirements, cost factors, and deployment options are given due consideration. An important part of network design is reliability, scalability, and availability.

Supporting and growing a small network requires being familiar with the protocols and network applications running over the network. Protocol analyzers enable a network professional to quickly compile statistical information about traffic flows on a network. Information gathered by the protocol analyzer is analyzed based on the source and destination of the traffic as well as the type of traffic being sent. This analysis can be used by a network technician to make decisions on how to manage the traffic more efficiently. Common network protocols include DNS, Telnet, SMTP, POP, DHCP, HTTP, and FTP.

You must consider security threats and vulnerabilities when planning a network implementation. All network devices must be secured. This includes routers, switches, end-user devices, and even security devices. Networks need to be protected from malicious software such as viruses, Trojan horses, and worms. Antivirus software can detect most viruses and many Trojan horse applications and prevent them from spreading in the network. The most effective way to mitigate a worm attack is to download security updates from the operating system vendor and patch all vulnerable systems.

Networks must also be protected from network attacks. Network attacks can be classified into three major categories: reconnaissance, access attacks, and denial of service. There are several ways to protect a network from network attacks:

- Authentication, authorization, and accounting (AAA, or "triple A") network security services provide the primary framework to set up access control on a network device. AAA is a way to control who is permitted to access a network (authenticate), to control what they can do while they are there (authorize), and to watch the actions they perform while accessing the network (accounting).

- A firewall is one of the most effective security tools available for protecting internal network users from external threats. A firewall resides between two or more networks and controls the traffic between them and also helps prevent unauthorized access.

- To protect network devices, it is important to use strong passwords. Also, when accessing network devices remotely, it is highly recommended to enable SSH instead of the unsecured Telnet.

After the network has been implemented, a network administrator must be able to monitor and maintain network connectivity. There are several commands available toward this end. For testing network connectivity to local and remote destinations, commands such as **ping**, **telnet**, and **traceroute** are commonly used.

On Cisco IOS devices, the **show version** command can be used to verify and troubleshoot some of the basic hardware and software components used during the bootup process. To view information for all network interfaces on a router, the **show ip interface** command is used. The **show ip interface brief** can also be used to view a more abbreviated output than the **show ip interface** command. Cisco Discovery Protocol (CDP) is a Cisco-proprietary protocol that runs at the data link layer. Because CDP operates at the data link layer, two or more Cisco network devices, such as routers that support different network layer protocols, can learn about each other even if Layer 3 connectivity does not exist.

Cisco IOS configuration files such as startup config or running config should be archived. These files can be saved to a text file or stored on a TFTP server. Some models of routers also have a USB port, and a file can be backed up to a USB drive.

If needed, these files can be copied to the router and/or switch from the TFTP server or USB drive.

The use of networking is not limited to small businesses and large organizations. Another environment that is increasingly taking advantage of networking technology is the home. A home network is very similar to a small-business network. However, most home networks (and many small-business networks) do not require high-volume devices, such as dedicated routers and switches. Instead, most home networks use a single multifunction device. For the purpose of this course, multifunction devices will be referred to as integrated routers. Most integrated routers offer both wired switching capabilities and wireless connectivity, and serve as the access point (AP) in the wireless network. To enable wireless connectivity, the wireless mode, SSID, RF channel, and any desired security encryption mechanism must be configured.

Practice

The following activities provide practice with the topics introduced in this chapter. The labs and class activities are available in the companion *"Introduction to Networking Lab Manual (978-1-58713-312-1)*. The Packet Tracer Activities PKA files are found in the online course.

Class Activities

- Class Activity 11.0.1.2: Did You Notice . . .?
- Class Activity 11.6.1.1 (Capstone Project): Design and Build a Small-Business Network

Labs

- Lab 11.2.2.6: Researching Network Security Threats
- Lab 11.2.4.5: Accessing Network Devices with SSH
- Lab 11.2.4.6: Securing Network Devices
- Lab 11.3.2.3: Testing Network Latency with Ping and Traceroute
- Lab 11.3.4.6: Using the CLI to Gather Network Device Information
- Lab 11.4.2.6: Managing Router Configuration Files with Tera Term
- Lab 11.4.2.7: Managing Device Configuration Files Using TFTP, Flash, and USB
- Lab 11.4.2.8: Researching Password Recovery Procedures

Packet Tracer
☐ Activity

Packet Tracer Activities

- Packet Tracer Activity 11.3.2.2: Test Connectivity with Traceroute

- Packet Tracer Activity 11.3.3.4: Using show Commands

- Packet Tracer Activity 11.4.2.5: Backing Up Configuration Files

- Packet Tracer Activity 11.5.2.4: Configuring a Linksys Router

- Packet Tracer Activity 11.6.1.2: Skills Integration Challenge

Check Your Understanding Questions

Complete all the review questions listed here to test your understanding of the topics and concepts in this chapter. The appendix, "Answers to the 'Check Your Understanding' Questions," lists the answers.

1. Why should the IP addressing scheme be carefully planned and documented? (Choose two.)

   A. Improved network performance

   B. Easier control of security

   C. Easier troubleshooting

   D. Reduction in network traffic

   E. Elimination of requirement for subnetting

2. What would be considered an example of redundancy in network design? (Choose three.)

   A. Installation of a switch that functions at both Layer 2 and Layer 3.

   B. Installation of duplicate Layer 3 switches in a company network.

   C. Installation of a switch with two separate power supplies.

   D. Keeping a spare router that has already been properly configured.

   E. Installation of multiple high-speed links to the company server farm.

3. Which type of traffic should be given the highest priority on a network?

   A. Voice

   B. SMTP

   C. Instant messaging

   D. FTP

4. Which planning and design factors would be considered as part of manageability focus when implementing a small network? (Choose two.)

   A. Types of cable runs

   B. Prioritization of data traffic

   C. Upgrades to network devices

   D. Number of interfaces required

   E. IP addressing scheme

   F. Bandwidth requirement

5. What is true of an application layer service?

   A. Application layer services provide the human interface.

   B. Application layer services interface with the network and prepare the data for transfer.

   C. Application layer services include such things as email and web clients.

   D. Application layer services are dependent on the OS vendor.

6. Which network protocol should a network administrator use to remotely configure a network device?

   A. FTP

   B. FTPS

   C. HTTP

   D. HTTPS

   E. Telnet

   F. SSH

7. Fill in the blank. _____ allows users of analog phones to take advantage of the IP network.

8. What factors should be taken into account when using a protocol analyzer to determine traffic flow on a network? (Choose two.)

   A. Always capture the traffic on the same network segment.

   B. Capture traffic during peak utilization times.

   C. Capture traffic on different network segments.

   D. Capture traffic only during off-peak times.

   E. Capture traffic during both peak and off-peak times.

9. A key network switch has failed because of excessive humidity. What type of physical threat caused the problem?

   A. Hardware threat

   B. Environmental threat

   C. Electrical threat

   D. Maintenance threat

10. What is a network vulnerability?

    A. The degree of weakness inherent in a network

    B. Tools used to launch attacks against a network

    C. Individuals interested and qualified in taking advantage of security weaknesses

    D. Ping of death

11. The network administrator set the admin password on a new router to pa55w0rd. The security of the router was later compromised. What type of vulnerability allowed the attack?

    A. Technology

    B. Configuration

    C. Policy

12. Making illegal online purchases is what type of security threat?

    A. Information theft

    B. Identity theft

    C. Data loss/manipulation

    D. Disruption of service

13. What name is given to a program that is disguised as another program to attack a system?

    A. Virus

    B. Trojan horse

    C. Worm

14. An attacker runs a ping sweep against a network. What type of attack is this?

    A. Reconnaissance

    B. Access

    C. Denial of service

15. What type of attack is a smurf attack?

    A. Reconnaissance

    B. Access

    C. Denial of service

16. What is the order of steps recommended to mitigate a worm attack?

    A. Containment > Inoculation > Quarantine > Treatment

    B. Containment > Quarantine > Inoculation > Treatment

    C. Containment > Quarantine > Treatment > Inoculation

    D. Containment > Treatment > Quarantine > Inoculation

17. With regard to firewall technology, what is stateful packet inspection?

    A. Incoming packets must be legitimate responses from internal requests.

    B. The incoming packet must have been initiated from a trusted source.

    C. The incoming packet must be in an active state before being admitted to the network.

    D. Only secure traffic (SSH, HTTPS, and FTPS) is permitted through the firewall.

18. Which of the following is an example of a strong password?

    A. Champion

    B. Cisco123

    C. 2#4@Tpg%

    D. Eruces

    E. Pa55w0rd

19. How is "extended ping" entered on a Cisco router?

    A. Type **ping/e** and press Enter

    B. Type **ping** followed by a destination IP address

    C. Type **ping** followed by a source IP address

    D. Type **ping** and press Enter

20. What **show** command can be issued on a Cisco router to view the configuration register value?

    A. **show ip route**

    B. **show running-config**

    C. **show protocols**

    D. **show version**

    E. **show cdp neighbors detail**

Answers to the "Check Your Understanding" Questions

Chapter 1

1. B. Podcasting and blogs allow the one-way dissemination of information. Instant messaging allows the synchronous communication between individuals. A wiki allows groups of individuals to view and edit web pages collaboratively.

2. B, D. Peer-to-peer networks are inexpensive and easy to configure but lack any centralized management and do not scale well.

3. B, C, D, E. End devices form the interface between users and the underlying communication network.

4. C. Logical topology diagrams identify devices, ports, and IP addressing schemes. Physical topology diagrams identify the physical location of intermediate devices, configured ports, and cable installations.

5. D. A wide-area network (WAN) provides access to other networks over a wide geographic area. A metropolitan-area network (MAN) spans an area larger than a local-area network (LAN) and is typically operated by a single entity. A wireless LAN (WLAN) is similar to a LAN, and a storage-area network (SAN) is designed to provide data storage, retrieval, and replication.

6. A, C. Leased lines and Metro Ethernet are considered business-class Internet connection technologies. Mobile services and broadband cable are considered technologies to connect remote users.

7. B. DSL is an always-on technology that offers good bandwidth at reasonable cost. Dialup and cellular connections are not always-on technology and do not offer the same bandwidth capabilities as DSL. Satellite and cellular connections are also relatively expensive.

8. B. A converged network is where voice, video, and data move over the same infrastructure. The underlying infrastructure can be wired or wireless.

9. C. A fault-tolerant network is one that can continue to function if an intermediate device or path fails. A fault-tolerant network can fail if a sufficient number of intermediate devices and/or paths fail.

10. A. Tier 3 ISP are the local providers of service to end users. They normally connect to Tier 2 providers for Internet access.

11. C. Quality of service (QoS) prioritizes data based on many factors including the traffic's sensitivity to network delay. Voice over IP (VoIP) is very sensitive to network delay and must be given priority treatment.

12. A, B, C. Information security includes ensuring that only the intended recipient can access the data (confidentiality), ensuring that the data has not been altered in transmission (integrity), and that the information is available in a timely manner (availability). Quality of service is not a primary requirement of information security.

13. The ready availability of network resources continues to change the way we work, play, and learn. Some of the current trends include the increased use of video, the use of client end-user-supplied devices on corporate networks (BYOD), the increased use of collaborative technologies, and a migration to cloud computing.

14. Networks have changed the way we live our everyday lives. Some examples of ways that networks are used include

- Checking the weather forecast
- Watching movies
- Sharing photographs and movies
- Playing games
- Checking your bank balance
- Taking an online class

15. Networks extend the learning environment into the virtual world by providing tools for collaboration and mobility, thus creating a global classroom. Some of the ways that the learning environment has been transformed by networks include

- Creates virtual classrooms
- Enables mobile learning
- Creates collaborative learning spaces
- Provides enhanced tracking of student performance
- Provides a global learning environment

Chapter 2

1. C. The Cisco IOS (Internetwork Operating System) is the operating system used in most Cisco network devices.

2. B. The initial configuration of Cisco IOS devices is accomplished through the CLI on the console connection.

3. C. Entering a question mark (?) after a command will show all additional commands and keywords to be used in the command sequence.

4. A. While there are some GUI interfaces available on Cisco IOS–based devices, the current practice is to use the CLI for device configuration and troubleshooting.

5. C. The IOS command parser inspects the first entries of a command sequence, expecting to identify a known command.

6. C. When the device's host name is configured, this name is used verbatim in the CLI prompt.

7. C. Forcing authentication for remote access by requiring a password to remotely connect to a network is a basic security measure. Option C provides the configuration to require authentication of users for remote access. In practice, stronger authentication should be required.

8. C. The startup config provides the configuration for the operation of the IOS device during startup.

9. A. This configuration provides connectivity to the switch. Option B is incorrect as a switch will forward traffic without any configuration. The other two options, C and D, have no relation to this configuration.

10. D. This provides a ping to a remote host. Option A is does *not* verify connectivity. Option B verifies that the logical IP stack has been configured. Option C verifies the configuration of the local host.

Chapter 3

1. A, C, E. All communication, human or machine, requires three elements: a source or sender, a receiver, and a channel to carry the message.

2. B. The format and contents of a frame are determined by the type of message being sent and the channel being used. Frames that are not correctly formatted are not delivered. Also frames that are too long or too short are dropped.

3. C. The access method determines when a message can be sent, flow control affects how much information can be sent and at what speed, and response timeout is how long the device will wait for a response before taking action.

4. B. A unicast message is one-to-one, multicast is one-to-many, and broadcast is one-to-all.

5. C. A protocol suite is a group of interrelated protocols designed to carry out the communication function. A protocol stack is the implementation of the protocol suite.

6. D. Network access protocols control the hardware devices and the media that make up the network.

7. C, D. A proprietary protocol is one in which a single vendor controls the definition of a protocol and how it functions. Both AppleTalk and Novell NetWare fall into this category.

8. D. The Institute of Electrical and Electronics Engineers (IEEE) 802 family of standards deals with LAN and MAN networks, both wired and wireless. The 802.3 working group deals specifically with Media Access Control for wired Ethernet.

9. A. The Internet Society (ISOC) oversees the Internet Architecture Board (IAB), which is responsible for the overall management and development of Internet standards.

10. B. The Telecommunications Industry Association (TIA) is responsible for developing communication standards in a variety of areas, including radio equipment, cellular towers, VoIP devices, and satellite communications.

11. C, E. User Datagram Protocol (UDP) and Transmission Control Protocol (TCP) exist at the transport layer. Hypertext Transfer Protocol (HTTP), File Transfer Protocol (FTP), and Domain Name System (DNS) are all application layer protocols.

12. D, F. The TCP/IP model consists of four layers but has all the functionality of the seven layers found in the OSI model. The TCP/IP network access layer has the functionality of both the physical and data link layers in the OSI model. The TCP/IP application layer has the functionality of the OSI application, presentation, and session layers.

13. E. Data representation is the responsibility of the OSI presentation layer. In the TCP/IP model, the application layer has this functionality as it combines the functionality of the OSI application, presentation, and session layers.

14. C. Address in best path is the responsibility of the TCP/IP Internet layer. In the OSI model, this equates to the OSI network layer.

15. B. TFTP uses UDP but FTP makes use of TCP, providing reliability in file transfer.

16. B. A PDU is a protocol data unit in the form that the data takes at that specific layer. Data is segmented at the transport layer; thus the PDU is named a segment.

17. C. Decapsulation is the process used by the receiving device to remove control information and reassemble the bit stream into a data message. The bits arrive at the physical layer and are passed to the data link layer (PDU = frame), then the network layer (PDU = packet, then the transport layer (PDU = segment), and then up to the upper layer in the form of data.

18. A, B, C. To access local resources, a device must know the source and destination physical addresses, the source and destination logical addresses, and the source and destination port numbers. The default gateway address is only required to access resources on a remote network. Names are not used on a network. Host names are resolved into addresses by DNS.

19. A, B, C, D. To access remote resources, a device must know the source and destination physical addresses, the source and destination logical addresses, and the source and destination port numbers. The default gateway address is also required to access resources on a remote network as it specifies the way out of the local network. Names are not used on a network. Host names are resolved into addresses by DNS.

20. Protocols are responsible for many different aspects of communication. This includes such things as encoding, formatting, encapsulation, and timing.

Chapter 4

1. A, B. The physical layer controls data transmitted onto the media and provides encoding of the bits. Logical addressing is provided by Layer 3. The packaging of bits and Media Access Control is provided by the data link layer.

2. B, E. Even though the twists provide some measure of rejection of stray electrical/magnetic signals, it is still subject to EMI and RFI. Because of its relatively low cost and good performance, UDP is still the most common networking media in use.

3. C. Cladding is the glass that surrounds the core and acts as a mirror. The light pulses propagate down the core, while the cladding reflects the light pulses. This keeps the light pulses contained in the fiber core in a phenomenon known as total internal reflection.

4. Pin 1   Orange-white

   Pin 2   Orange

   Pin 3   Green-white

   Pin 4   Blue

   Pin 5   Blue-white

   Pin 6   Green

   Pin 7   Brown-white

   Pin 8   Brown

   The colors for a 568B pinout from pin 1 to pin 8 are a) orange-white, b) orange
   c) green-white, d) blue, e) blue-white, f) green, g) brown-white, and h) brown.

5. B, D, F. Unlike copper wires, fiber-optic cable can transmit signals with less
   attenuation and is immune to EMI and RFI. Fiber-optic cables can also be operated at much greater lengths than copper media and with higher bandwidth.

6. B. All wireless devices must share access to the airwaves connecting to the wireless access point. This means that slower network performance might occur as
   more wireless devices access the network simultaneously.

7. A. When the frame arrives at the destination node, the receiving node calculates
   its own logical summary, or CRC, of the frame. The receiving node compares
   the two CRC values. If the two values are the same, the frame is considered to
   have arrived intact. If the CRC value in the FCS differs from the CRC calculated
   at the receiving node, the frame is discarded.

8. B. The Layer 3 PDU is wrapped with a header and trailer to form the Layer 2
   frame.

9. D. Logical topology refers to the way a network transfers frames from one node
   to the next.

10. B. In contention-based access, all nodes compete for the use of the medium but
    have a plan if there are collisions.

Chapter 5

1. F, G. Ethernet standards define both the data link layer protocols and the physical layer technologies.

2. B. IEEE 802.3 specifies the Ethernet MAC sublayer functionality.

3. C. The MAC sublayer is part of the OSI data link layer. The frame is the data link layer PDU. Segments are associated with the transport layer, packets with the network layer, and bits with the physical layer.

4. B, C, E. The Ethernet MAC layer has two primary responsibilities: data encapsulation and media access control. Frame delimination, addressing, and error detection are part of data encapsulation. Media recovery and media access are part of CSMA/CD.

5. B. Ethernet uses CSMA/CD. When a collision is detected on the media, all devices stop transmitting to allow the collision to clear. After the collision has cleared, devices will again attempt to transmit.

6. B, D, E. The Ethernet MAC address is 48 bits in length with the first 3 bytes (6 hexadecimal digits) assigned by the IEEE. The vendor is responsible for assigning the last 24 bits in the address. Because this address was permanently configured on a device, it is also known as a burned-in address, or BIA.

7. A. The IEEE 802.3 standard defines a minimum frame size of 64 bytes and a maximum frame size of 1518 bytes. The IEEE 802.3ac standard released in 1998 extended the maximum size to 1522 bytes to allow the inclusion of an 802.1q VLAN tag in the Ethernet frame.

8. D. The Frame Check Sequence field is used to detect frames that might have been damaged in transit.

9. C. The broadcast MAC address is when all 48 bits are turned on and is represented by FF-FF-FF-FF-FF-FF.

10. B. All multicast MAC addresses start with 01-00-5E.

11. A, C. The ARP process resolves IPv4 address to MAC addresses and maintains a table of these mappings.

12. B. RP requests are sent out with a broadcast MAC address. All devices in the L2 broadcast domain will hear the request and use the information it contains to update their ARP tables with information for the source device.

13. ARP table or ARP cache, request

14. source, drop

15. requests, unicast

16. MAC address table, floods, received

17. CAM, content addressable

18. A. The sole forwarding method used on Cisco switches is store-and-forward. This is required where frame classification for traffic prioritization (QoS) is necessary.

19. B. Both an SVI and a Layer 3 EtherChannel port are logical interfaces. A routed port is a physical interface that has had Layer 2 functionality shut down in favor of Layer 3 functionality.

20. no switchport, IP

Chapter 6

1. A. The network layer, or OSI Layer 3, provides services to allow end-to-end communication across a network.

2. A. The network layer uses Layer 3 addressing such as IPv4 and IPv6 to identify end hosts.

3. IP is connectionless, which greatly reduces the overhead of IP. Therefore, there is no initial exchange of control information before packets are forwarded, and no additional fields exist in the header to maintain an established connection.

4. C. Time-to-Live (TTL) contains an 8-bit binary value that is used to limit the lifetime of a packet. It is specified in seconds but is commonly referred to as hop count.

5. C. Without a proper default gateway, a host will not know where to send packets for communication to remote networks. Therefore, the host cannot communicate outside its local network.

6. D. The running configuration file is located in RAM and is the configuration file that stores the configuration commands that the router IOS is currently using. It is also known as the running config.

7. B. During self-decompression of the IOS image file, a string of hash (pound) signs will be displayed.

8. A, D. The requirement for router interface configuration is to provide Layer 3 (IPv4, IPv6, and so on) addressing information and to enable the interface.

9. A, E. A common misconception is that the switch uses its configured default gateway address to determine where to forward packets originating from hosts connected to the switch and destined for hosts on a remote network. Actually, the IP address and default gateway information is only used for packets that originate from the switch.

10. C. The local default route (0.0.0.0)—that is, all packets with destinations that do not match other specified addresses in the routing table—are forwarded to the gateway.

Chapter 7

1. C, E, F. The transport layer is responsible for segmenting data, adding the port number to identify the proper application, and keeping track of individual conversations. MAC addresses are added by the data link layer, and IP addresses and routing are handled by the network layer.

2. C. Source port addresses are assigned by the transport layer to identify the individual conversation and destination port addresses to identify the service being looked for.

3. Multiplexing

4. B. TCP uses acknowledgements and windowing to offer flow control and reliable delivery. UDP is connectionless and does not resend lost datagrams.

5. B, E, F. Applications that are simple request and reply transactions, those sensitive to delay, and those that are unidirectional in nature make use of UDP. Applications requiring reliable delivery and that can tolerate delay associated with protocol overhead make use of TCP. In this question, Telnet, FTP, and HTTP use TCP, and VoIP, DHCP, and TFTP use UDP.

6. C. The acknowledgement number indicates that the data that has been received, the header length indicates the length of the TCP segment header, the window size specifies the number of segments that can be received before an acknowledgement is required, and the checksum is used for error-checking the segment header and data.

7. port numbers

8. B. UDP does not track conversations and has the advantage of low overhead relative to TCP.

9. C. Well-known ports (numbers 0 to 1023) are commonly used to request a connection to that specific port, and its associated service. Registered ports (numbers 1024 to 49151) are assigned to user processes or applications. These processes are primarily individual applications that a user has chosen to install, rather than common applications that would receive a well-known port number. When not used for a server resource, these ports can also be dynamically selected by a client as its source port. Dynamic or private ports (numbers 49152 to 65535) are most often used to identify the client application during communication.

10. ephemeral or private

11. B. UDP reassembles the data in the order received and passes it to the application. It is up to the application to sort out the data. UDP has no mechanism for reordering of datagrams or requesting retransmission.

12. F. The FIN control bit indicates that there is no more data from the sender.

13. A. The three-way handshake starts when a client device sends an ISN to the server. The server responds with an acknowledgement of the client ISN+1 and its own ISN. The last step in the process is when the client acknowledges the server ISN by responding with a value of the server ISN+1.

14. B. FTP makes use of TCP, so as soon as segments are lost in transit, the receiving device will send a decreased window size in returning segments.

15. selective acknowledgements (SACK)

Chapter 8

1. A, B. An IPv4 address is a hierarchical address that is made up of two parts: a network portion and a host portion.

2. B. The network address is a standard way to refer to a network.

3. A, C. For all three types of communication, the IPv4 address of the originating host is placed in the packet header as the source address, and there is *only* one IP source and destination address.

4. D. The private address blocks are 10.0.0.0 to 10.255.255.255 (10.0.0.0/8); 172.16.0.0 to 172.31.255.255 (172.16.0.0/12); and 192.168.0.0 to 192.168.255.255 (192.168.0.0/16).

5. The need for more address space is because of the exhaustion of the IPv4 addresses.

6. C. Hextet is the unofficial term used to refer to a segment of 16 bits or four hexadecimal values. An IPv6 address requires 8 hextets to represent the 128 bits.

7. B. An IPv6 link-local address enables a device to communicate with other IPv6-enabled devices on the same link and only on that link (subnet).

8. A, B. Two ways in which a device can obtain an IPv6 global unicast address automatically are Stateless Address Autoconfiguration (SLAAC) and DHCPv6.

9. B. Multicast is used to send a single IPv6 packet to multiple destinations.

10. ICMP Both IPv4 and IPv6 use an ICMP protocol as the principal means to verify connectivity.

11. D. Traceroute (tracert) is a utility that generates a list of hops that were successfully reached along the path.

Chapter 9

1. B, D. Subnetting a large address space into smaller subnetworks helps to contain network traffic and thus improve network performance.

2. C. A router or Layer 3 switch is required for devices on different networks or subnets to be able to communicate.

3. host. Subnets are created by borrowing bits from the host portion of an IP address to create additional network bits. The more bits borrowed, the more subnets created.

4. D. Every bit borrowed can have one of two values, 0 or 1. The number of subnets created is 2^n, where n is the number of bits borrowed. In this case, we have borrowed 4 bits, so 2^4, or 16, subnets are created, all of which can be used.

5. D. A network broadcast address has all host bits turned on.

6. C. The number of valid host addresses created by borrowing 4 bits is 2^4-2, or 14. It is necessary to subtract 2 because the network address and the broadcast address for each subnet cannot be used as host addresses.

7. D, E, F. By borrowing 3 bits, the technician created nine subnets, each with 30 usable hosts. The second subnet is 10.20.30.32/27 and consists of addresses from 10.20.30.32 to 10.20.30.63. The first and last addresses in this range are not usable, but all others are.

8. C. The assigned subnet has the address range from 192.168.1.0/25 to 192.168.1.127/25. The departmental printer has been placed in another subnet and will be unreachable without a router.

9. B. The new department requires 511 hosts, but in any subnet, two addresses (network and broadcast) are unusable, so a subnet must be created that can accommodate 513 addresses. The closest matching number would be a network with 1024 hosts. To create 1024 hosts requires 10 host bits ($2^{10}-1024$). Currently there are 16 host bits available, so the administrator must borrow 6 bits to create 64 subnets, each with 1022 available hosts.

10. C. Currently 16 bits are assigned to the network. If the network administrator borrows an additional 5 bits from the host field, 21 bits are now assigned to the network field. For the subnet mask, the first 21 bits (network) would be turned on and the last 11 (host) bits would be turned off. This creates a mask of 11111111.11111111.11111000.00000000 (255.255.248.0).

11. VLSM. With traditional subnetting, all subnets must be of the same size, wasting a lot of addresses. With VLSM, different subnet masks can be used on different portions of the network, thus providing a more efficient allocation of available address space.

12. C. By borrowing 3 bits from the network portion of the original network, the administrator has now assigned 28 bits to the network, leaving only 4 host bits. Each WAN link requires two addresses, but each subnet has two unusable addresses, meaning that each created subnet must have four available hosts. To create subnets with four hosts means that 2 host bits must be available, allowing the administrator to borrow 2 additional bits, creating four subnets each with four hosts.

13. B, D, F. To produce a subnet that could accommodate 796 users would require 10 bits (1024 hosts). To accommodate 31 users would require 6 bits (64 hosts). The WAN links require 2 bits (four hosts). Starting with the largest subnet would require borrowing 2 bits, leaving the 10 bits for hosts. This creates a 10.11.0.0/22 network, which includes the range 10.11.0.0/22 – 10.11.251.255/22. The second network requires 6 bits, can start at 10.11.253.0/26, and would run to 10.11.253.63/24. The third network would start at the next available address (10.11.253.64/30) and run until 10.11.253.67/30.

14. B. Unlike IPv4 addresses, subnetting IPv6 address space supports the hierarchical, logical design of networks. IPv6 address space in not in short supply.

15. A. Subnetting on nibble boundaries increases the subnets in increments equal to a hexadecimal digit, making the process easier. There is no rule stating that you must subnet at a nibble boundary, nor is it the most efficient use of address space, but this is not a primary concern with the vast amount of addresses that IPv6 supplies.

16. C. With IPv6, each hexadecimal character represents 4 bits. By borrowing 2 nibbles (8 bits), we would increase the second digit in the hextet one hexadecimal digit at a time for each subnet. The third subnet would have the hexadecimal number 2 in the second spot of the subnet hextet.

Chapter 10

1. B. The functionality of the TCP/IP application layer protocols fit roughly into the framework of the top three layers of the OSI model: application, presentation, and session.

2. B, C, E. Email supports three separate protocols for operation: Simple Mail Transfer Protocol (SMTP), Post Office Protocol (POP), and Internet Message Access Protocol (IMAP).

3. C. DHCP allows a host to obtain an IP address dynamically when it connects to the network.

4. A. Application layer protocols are used to exchange data between programs running on the source and destination hosts.

5. The Domain Name System (DNS) provides domain name to address resolution for networks allowing end users to access resources with names rather than more difficult to remember IP addresses. This automated service matches resource names with the required numeric network addresses.

Chapter 11

1. B, C. By carefully planning and documenting the address space, troubleshooting, access control, and security are greatly simplified.

2. B, C, E. Redundancy is eliminating any single point of failure. This could include equipment or links. Keeping a configured device as a spare will assist in the troubleshooting process but is not considered redundancy. Additionally having a switch that functions at both Layer 2 and Layer 3 is still a single point of failure and is not considered redundancy.

3. A. Voice traffic is very sensitive to delay and should be given the highest priority on the network.

4. B, E. The five focus areas when implementing a small network are cost, expandability, manageability, speed, and ports. Type of cable run would fall under cost, upgrades to network devices are part of expandability, prioritization of data traffic and IP addressing schemes are part of manageability, bandwidth requirement is part of speed, and number of interfaces required would be ports.

5. B. Application layer services prepare the data for transfer over the network; they are based on standards and do not provide any sort of human interface. Application programs interface with the user.

6. F. FTP and FTPS allow files to be moved on the network. HTTP and HTTPS allow communication between a host and a web server. Telnet and SSH both allow remote login to a device. FTPS, HTTPS, and SSH are the secure versions of FTP, HTTP, and Telnet, respectively, and should be used whenever possible.

7. VoIP

8. B, C. Traffic should be captured on different network segments during peak utilization times to ensure that all traffic types are collected.

9. B. The key cause of the failure was high humidity, which is an environmental threat.

10. A. Vulnerabilities are inherent weaknesses in the network that can be exploited by people and tools.

11. B. Configuring easily guessed passwords creates a vulnerability that can easily be exploited.

12. B. Making illegal online purchases by posing as another person is identity theft.

13. B. A virus is malicious software that is attached to another program to execute some unknown function. A Trojan horse is a program that is disguised as another program to trick the user into executing it. Worms are self-contained programs that attack a system to exploit a vulnerability.

14. A. The attacker is using the ping sweep to gather information on the network, making this a reconnaissance attack.

15. C. A smurf attack overloads a network link by causing multiple Echo Replies to be directed against a target, making it a denial of service attack.

16. A. The correct order is Containment > Inoculation > Quarantine > Treatment.

17. A. With stateful packet inspection (SPI), only legitimate responses from internal requests are permitted through the firewall.

18. C. Strong passwords should mix uppercase and lowercase text, numbers, and symbols into a random pattern that cannot be easily guessed.

19. D. To enter extended ping mode, type **ping** and then press Enter.

20. E. The **show version** command will display the configuration register.

A

access method A set of rules used by LAN hardware to direct traffic on the network. It determines which host or device uses the LAN next.

acknowledgement Notification sent from one network device to another to acknowledge that some event (for example, receipt of a message) has occurred.

address resolution protocol (ARP) Internet protocol used to map an IP address to a MAC address. Defined in RFC 826.

adjacency table A table in a router that contains a list of the relationship formed between selected neighboring routers and end nodes for the purpose of exchanging routing information. Adjacency is based upon the use of a common media segment.

American Standard Code for Information Interchange (ASCII) An 8-bit code for character representation (7 bits plus parity).

AND (logical) One of three basic binary logic operations. ANDing yields the following results: 1 AND 1 = 1, 1 AND 0 = 0, 0 AND 1 = 0, 1 AND 0 = 0.

ARP cache Logical storage in a host's RAM to store ARP entries. *See also* ARP table.

ARP table Logical storage in a host's RAM to store ARP entries. *See also* ARP cache.

asymmetric switching A switching technique used to allow for different data rates on different ports.

automatic medium-dependent interface crossover (auto-MDIX) A detection on a switch port or hub port to detect the type of cable used between switches or hubs. Once the cable type is detected, the port is connected and configured accordingly. With auto-MDIX, a crossover or a straight-through cable can be used for connections to a copper 10/100/1000 port on the switch, regardless of the type of device on the other end of the connection.

availability The assurance of timely and reliable access to data services for authorized users. Network firewall devices, along with desktop and server antivirus software, can ensure system reliability and the robustness to detect, repel, and cope with breaches of network security. Building fully redundant network infrastructures, with few single points of failure, can reduce the impact of these threats.

B

bandwidth The rated throughput capacity of a given network medium or protocol. Bandwidth is listed as available or consumed data communication resources expressed in bits/second.

best-effort delivery Describes a network system that does not use a sophisticated acknowledgement system to guarantee reliable delivery of information.

Bootstrap Protocol (BOOTP) Protocol used by a network node to determine the IP address of its Ethernet interfaces, in order to facilitate network booting.

Bring Your Own Device (BYOD) The concept of any device, to any content, in any way is a major global trend that requires significant changes to the way devices are used. This trend is about end users having the freedom to use personal tools to access information and communicate across a business or campus network.

broadcast A form of transmission where one device transmits to all devices within the network or on another network.

broadcast address Special address reserved for sending a message to all stations. Generally, a broadcast address is a MAC destination address of all ones. Compare with multicast address and unicast address.

burned-in address (BIA) The MAC address that is permanently assigned to a LAN interface or NIC. It is called burned-in because the address is burned into a chip on the card, and the address cannot be changed. Also called universally administered address (UAA).

C

Carrier Sense Multiple Access (CSMA) Media-access mechanism wherein devices ready to transmit data first check the channel for a carrier. If no carrier is sensed for a specific period of time, a device can transmit. *See also* CSMA/CA and CSMA/CD.

channel A communication path over a medium used to transport information from a sender to a receiver. Multiple channels can be multiplexed over a single cable.

circuit switched Switching system in which a dedicated physical circuit path must exist between sender and receiver for the duration of the call. Used heavily in the telephone company network.

Cisco Express Forwarding (CEF) A Layer 3 switching method. This technique speeds up packet forwarding by decoupling the usual strict interdependence between Layer 2 and Layer 3 decision making. The forwarding decision information is stored in several data structures for CEF switching. This forwarding information can be rapidly referenced to expedite packet forwarding decisions.

classful addressing A unicast IP address that is considered to have three parts: a network part, a subnet part, and a host part. The term classful refers to the fact that the classful network rules are first applied to the address, and then the rest of the address can be separated into a subnet and host part to perform subnetting. Originally, IPv4 addresses were divided into five classes, namely, Class A, Class B, Class C, Class D, and Class E. Classful addressing is not generally practiced in current network implementations.

classless addressing An IPv4 addressing scheme that uses a subnet mask that does not follow classful addressing limitations. It provides increased flexibility when dividing ranges of IP addresses into separate networks. Classless addressing is considered the best in current network implementations. *See also* VLSM.

client A network device that accesses a service on another computer remotely through a network.

client-server A computer system setup in which tasks are distributed between a service provider (server) and a service user, such as a workstation (client). The server is used to store the applications and data and the majority of the computer processing is done on the server.

cloud computing The use of computing resources (hardware and software) that are delivered as a service over a network. A company uses the hardware and software in the cloud and a service fee is charged.

coaxial cable/coax Cable consisting of a hollow outer cylindrical conductor that surrounds a single inner wire conductor. Two types of coaxial cable are currently used in LANs: 50-ohm cable, which is used for digital signaling, and 75-ohm cable, which is used for analog signaling.

collaboration The creation of a document or documents that can be edited by more than one person in real time across a network.

collision fragment Any frame less than 64 bytes in length. These frames are automatically discarded by receiving stations. Also called runt frame.

command-line interface (CLI) User interface to a computer operating system or application that depends on textual commands being entered by the user.

communication Transmission and receipt of information.

communities Communities consist of people who share common experiences and hobbies who exchange ideas and information. Communities allow for social interaction that is independent of location or time zone.

confidentiality Insures that only the intended and authorized recipients—individuals, processes, or devices—can access and read data. Confidentiality is accomplished by having a strong system for user authentication, enforcing passwords that are difficult to guess, and requiring users to change them frequently. Encrypting data, so that only the intended recipient can read it, is also part of confidentiality.

congested A condition where a network has more bits to transmit than what the bandwidth of the communication channel can deliver.

congestion Traffic in excess of network capacity.

connectionless Term used to describe data transfer without the existence of a virtual circuit.

connection-oriented Term used to describe data transfer that requires the establishment of a virtual circuit.

content addressable memory (CAM) table Memory that is accessed based on its contents, not on its memory address. Also known as associative memory.

contention-based A method of networking that is a non-deterministic method. That is, any device can try to transmit data across the shared medium whenever it has data to send.

converged network A network that aggregates various forms of traffic such as voice, video, and data on the same network infrastructure.

crosstalk Source of interference that occurs when cables are bundled together for long lengths. The signal from one cable can leak out and enter adjacent cables. *See also* electromagnetic interference (EMI).

CSMA/Collision Avoidance (CSMA/CA) A mechanism that regulates the transmission of data onto a network medium. CSMA/CA is similar to CSMA/CD except the devices first request the right to send, which hopefully avoids collisions. CSMA/CA is used in 802.11 WLANs.

CSMA/Collision Detection (CSMA/CD)
Media-access mechanism that requires a node wishing to transmit to listen for a carrier signal before trying to send. If a carrier is sensed, the node waits for the transmission in progress to finish before initiating its own transmission. If a collision occurs and is detected, the sending node uses the backoff algorithm before retransmitting.

cyclic redundancy check (CRC) A type of hash function (one-way encryption) that is used to produce a small, fixed-size checksum of a block of data, such as a packet or a computer file. A CRC is computed and appended before transmission or storage, and verified afterward by the recipient to confirm that no changes have happened in transit. Error-checking technique in which the frame recipient calculates a remainder by dividing frame contents by a prime binary divisor and compares the calculated remainder to a value stored in the frame by the sending node.

D

daemon A computer program that runs in the background and is usually initiated as a process. Daemons often support server processes.

data center A data center is a facility used to house computer systems and associated components, including redundant data communications connections, high-speed virtual servers, redundant storage systems, and security devices.

data networks Infrastructure historically used by businesses to record and manage the business systems. Data networks have evolved to enable the transmission of many different types of information services, including email, video, messaging, and telephony.

datagram Logical grouping of information sent as a network layer unit over a transmission medium without prior establishment of a virtual circuit. IP datagrams are the primary information units in the Internet. The terms frame, message, packet, and segment are also called datagrams. *See also* Protocol Data Unit PDU.

decapsulation (de-encapsulation) A process by which an end device, after it receives data over some transmission medium, examines the headers and trailers at each successive higher layer, eventually handing the data to the correct application. Sometimes called de-encapsulation.

default gateway A device on a network that serves as an access point to other networks. A default gateway is used by a host to forward IP packets that have destination addresses outside the local subnet. A router interface typically is used as the default gateway. When the computer needs to send a packet to another subnet, it sends the packet to its default gateway. Also known as default router.

destination The target host for a message. Ethernet/IP frames contain a destination MAC and IP address.

destination IP address The Layer 3 address to which the data is going.

directed broadcast A term that describes IPv4 packets sent to all hosts in a particular network. In a directed broadcast, a single copy of the packet is routed to the specified network, where it is broadcast to all hosts on that network.

Domain Name System (DNS) An Internet-wide system by which a hierarchical set of DNS servers collectively hold all the name-IP address mappings, with DNS servers referring users to the correct DNS server to successfully resolve a DNS name.

duplex Two types of settings used for communications on networks: half duplex and full duplex. Half-duplex communication relies on unidirectional data flow where sending and receiving data are not performed at the same time. In full-duplex communication, data flow is bidirectional, so data can be sent and received at the same time.

Dynamic Host Configuration Protocol (DHCP) A protocol used to dynamically assign IP configurations to hosts. The services defined by the protocol are used to request and assign an IP address, default gateway, and DNS server address to a network host.

E

electromagnetic interference (EMI) Interference by magnetic signals caused by the flow of electricity. EMI can cause reduced data integrity and increased error rates on transmission channels. The physics of this process are that electrical current creates magnetic fields, which in turn cause other electrical currents in nearby wires. The induced electrical currents can interfere with proper operation of the other wire.

enable password Unencrypted password used to limit access to privileged EXEC mode from IOS user EXEC mode.

enable secret Encrypted password used to limit access to privileged EXEC mode from IOS user EXEC mode.

encapsulation The process by which a device adds networking headers and trailers to data from an application for the eventual transmission of the data onto a transmission medium.

encoding Process by which bits are represented on a media.

EtherChannel Logical interface on a Cisco device associated with a bundle of routed ports in order to aggregate bandwidth.

Ethernet Baseband LAN specification invented by Xerox Corporation and developed jointly by Xerox, Intel, and Digital Equipment Corporation. Ethernet networks use CSMA/CD and run over a variety of cable types at 10 Mbps. Ethernet is similar to the IEEE 802.3 series.

expectational acknowledgement Acknowledgement used by TCP where the ACK number is sent back to the source to indicate the next byte that the receiver expects to receive.

F

fiber-optic cable Physical medium that uses glass or plastic threads to transmit data. A fiber-optic cable consists of a bundle of these threads, each of which is capable of transmitting data into light waves.

File Transfer Protocol (FTP) Application protocol, part of the TCP/IP protocol stack, used for transferring files between network nodes. FTP is defined in RFC 959.

flash A removable component that has memory space for storage. Used on the router or switch for storing the compressed operating system image.

flow control The management of data flow between devices in a network. It is used to avoid too much data arriving before a device can handle it, causing data overflow.

Forwarding Information Base (FIB) A data structure that contains all routes known. Conceptually the FIB is similar to a routing table. A networking device uses the FIB lookup table to make destination-based switching decisions.

fragmentation The dividing of IP datagrams to meet the MTU requirements of a Layer 2 protocol.

G

gateway Normally, a relatively general term that refers to different kinds of networking devices. Historically, when routers were created, they were called gateways.

global configuration mode From the privileged mode, you can enter the device's global configuration mode. From global configuration mode, you can configure global parameters or enter other configuration submodes such as interface, router, and line configuration submodes.

goodput Application-level throughput. It is the number of useful bits per unit of time from a certain source address to a certain destination, excluding protocol overhead and excluding retransmitted data packets.

graphical user interface (GUI) User-friendly interface that uses graphical images and widgets, along with text, to indicate the information and actions available to a user when interacting with a computer.

H

header Control information added before data during the encapsulation for network transmission.

hexadecimal (Base 16) A number system using the digits 0 through 9, with their usual meaning, plus the letters A through F to represent hexadecimal digits with values of 10 to 15. The right-most digit counts ones, the next counts multiples of 16, then $16^2=256$.

Hextet The unofficial term used to refer to a segment of 16 bits or four hexadecimal values. For IPv6 addressing, each digit is a single hextet, 16 bits or four hexadecimal digits.

host address IPv4 address of a network host. When talking about host addresses, they are the network layer addresses.

I

initial sequence number (ISN) Randomly chosen number and is used to begin tracking the flow of data from the client to the server for this session. The ISN in the header of each segment is increased by one for each byte of data sent from the client to the server as the data conversation continues.

Institute of Electrical and Electronics Engineers (IEEE) An international, nonprofit organization for the advancement of technology related to electricity. IEEE maintains the standards defining many LAN protocols.

integrity The assurance that the information has not been altered in transmission, from origin to destination. Data integrity can be compromised when information has been corrupted—willfully or accidentally. Data integrity is made possible by requiring validation of the sender as well as using mechanisms to validate that the packet has not changed during transmission.

International Organization for Standardization (ISO) An international standards body that defines many networking standards. Also, the standards body that created the OSI model.

Internet The network that combines enterprise networks, individual users, and ISPs into a single global IP network.

Internet Assigned Numbers Authority (IANA) An organization that assigns the numbers important to the proper operation of the TCP/IP protocol and the Internet, including assigning globally unique IP addresses.

Internet Control Message Protocol (ICMP) As part of the TCP/IP Internet layer, ICMP defines protocol messages used to inform network engineers of how well an internetwork is working. For example, the ping command sends ICMP messages to determine whether a host can send packets to another host.

Internet Message Access Protocol (IMAP) Protocol that describes a method to retrieve email messages. Unlike POP, copies of the messages are downloaded to the client application but the original messages are kept on the server until manually deleted.

Internet of Everything (IoE) A reference to adding devices of all types onto the Internet. IOE brings together people, process, data, and things to make networked connections more relevant and valuable.

Internet Service Provider (ISP) A company that helps create the Internet by providing connectivity to enterprises and individuals, as well as interconnecting to other ISPs to create connectivity to all other ISPs.

IPv4 address A 32-bit number, written in dotted decimal notation, used by the IPv4 protocol to uniquely identify an interface connected to an IP network. It is also used as a destination address in an IP header to allow routing. As a source address, it enables a computer to receive a packet and to know to which IP address a response should be sent.

L

learning spaces An environment, physical or virtual, to promote collaborative learning.

limited broadcast A broadcast that is sent to a specific network or series of networks.

link-local address An IPv4 address in the range of 169.254.1.0 to 169.254.254.255. Communication using these addresses is used with a TTL of 1 and is limited to the local network.

Logical Link Control (LLC) The IEEE 802.2 standard that defines the upper sublayer of the Ethernet Layer 2 specifications (and other LAN standards).

logical topology A map of the devices on a network representing how the devices communicate with each other.

Loopback A special reserved IPv4 address, 127.0.0.1 and IPv6 address of ::1, that can be used to test TCP/IP applications. Packets sent to 127.0.0.1 (::1) by a computer never leave the computer or even require a working NIC. Instead, the packet is processed by IP at the lowest layer and is then sent back up the TCP/IP stack to another application on that same computer.

M

MAC address table On a switch, a table that lists all known MAC addresses, and the bridge/switch port out that the bridge/switch should use to forward frames sent to each MAC address.

Manchester encoding Line code in which each bit of data is signified by at least one voltage level transition.

maximum transmission unit (MTU) The largest IP packet size allowed to be sent out a particular interface. Ethernet interfaces default to an MTU of 1500 because the data field of a standard Ethernet frame should be limited to 1500 bytes, and the IP packet sits inside the Ethernet frame's data field. The Gigabit Ethernet standard supports "jumbo frames," which can be as large as 9216 including tagging.

Media Access Control (MAC) The lower of the two sublayers of the IEEE standard for Ethernet. It is also the name of that sublayer (as defined by the IEEE 802.3 subcommittee).

media independent The networking layers whose processes are not affected by the media being used. In Ethernet, these are all the layers from the LLC sublayer of data link upward.

mobile learning An environment supporting learning. This may be physical or virtual.

multicast Sending a message to selected hosts that are part of a group. A single packet is copied by the network and sent to a specific subset of network addresses. These addresses are specified in the destination address field. Compare with broadcast and unicast.

multicast client A member of a multicast group. Every multicast client in each group has the same IP address. IPv4 multicast addresses begin with 224.*.*.* and end with 239.*.*.*. IPv6 multicast addresses have the prefix FF00::/8.

multiplexing A process where multiple digital data streams are combined into one signal.

N

network address A dotted decimal number defined by the IPv4 protocol to represent a network or subnet. It represents the network that hosts reside in. Also called a network number or network ID.

Network Address Translation (NAT) Translation of IP addresses to different addresses. This is commonly used to translate RFC 1918 addresses that are not routed on the Internet to public domain addresses that can be routed on the Internet.

network infrastructure The architecture defining the connection within a network; refers to the physical hardware and connections used to transmit data.

Network Interface Card (NIC) Computer hardware, typically used for LANs, that allows the computer to connect to some networking cable. The NIC can then send and receive data over the cable at the direction of the computer.

network prefix This initial part of a Layer 3 IP address. The network prefix is used by routers to forward the packet to the proper network.

next hop The next gateway to which a Layer 3 packet is delivered, used to reach its destination.

nibble boundary A nibble is 4 bits or one hexadecimal digit. A nibble boundary is using nibble aligned for subnet masks. By borrowing bits from the interface ID, the best practice is to subnet on a nibble boundary.

nonreturn to zero (NRZ) Line code in which 1s are represented by one significant condition and 0s are represented by another.

nslookup A service or a program to look up information in the DNS (Domain Name System).

O

octet A group of 8 binary bits. It is similar to, but not the same as, a byte. One application in computer networking is to use octets to divide IPv4 addresses into four components.

Organizationally Unique Identifier (OUI) The first half of a MAC address. Manufacturers must ensure that the value of the OUI has been registered with the IEEE. This value identifies the manufacturer of any Ethernet NIC or interface.

overhead Resources used to manage or operate the network. Overhead consumes bandwidth and reduces the amount of application data that can be transported across the network.

P

packet switched Network architecture that routes packets along the path perceived as the most efficient and allows a communications channel to be shared by multiple connections.

peer-to-peer (P2P) In peer-to-peer networking each device serves as both a client and a server portion of an application. P2p also describes a small local network where hosts can play the role of client and/or server.

physical media The cabling and connectors used to interconnect the network devices.

physical topology The arrangement of the nodes in a network and the physical connections between them. This is the representation of how the media is used to connect the devices.

ping A troubleshooting tool used to verify network connectivity by sending a packet to a specific IP address and waiting for the reply.

port In networking, this term is used in several ways. With Ethernet hub and switch hardware, port is simply another name for interface, which is a physical connector in the switch into which a cable can be connected. With TCP and UDP, a port is a software function that uniquely identifies a software process on a computer that uses TCP or UDP. With PCs, a port can be a physical connector on the PC, like a parallel or USB port.

Post Office Protocol (POP) A protocol that allows a computer to retrieve email from a server.

power over Ethernet (PoE) The powering of network devices over Ethernet cable. PoE is defined by two different standards: IEEE 802.3af and Cisco.

prefix length In IP subnetting, this refers to the portion of a set of IP addresses whose value must be identical for the addresses to be in the same subnet.

private address Defined in RFC 1918, an IP address that does not have to be globally unique because the address exists inside packets only when the packets are inside a single private IP internetwork. Private IP addresses are popularly used in most companies today, with NAT translating the private IP addresses into globally unique IP addresses.

privileged executive (EXEC) mode An IOS administrative level mode that supports access to configuration and management commands.

proprietary One company or vendor controls the definition of the protocol and how it functions. Some proprietary protocols can be used by different organizations with permission from the owner. Others can only be implemented on equipment manufactured by the proprietary vendor.

protocol analyzer Network monitoring device gathers information regarding the status of the network and devices attached to it. Also known as network analyzer, or packet sniffer.

protocol data unit (PDUs) A generic term from OSI that refers to the data, headers, and trailers about which a particular networking layer is concerned.

protocol suite A delineation of networking protocols and standards into different categories, called layers, along with definitions of which sets of standards and protocols need to be implemented to create products that can be used to create a working network.

protocols Written specifications that define what tasks a service or device should perform. Each protocol defines messages, often in the form of headers, plus the rules and processes by which these messages are used to achieve some stated purpose.

public address An IP address that has been registered with IANA or one of its member agencies, which guarantees that the address is globally unique. Globally unique public IP addresses can be used for packets sent through the Internet.

Q

Quality of Service (QoS) A control mechanism that can provide different priorities to different users or data flows, or guarantee a certain level of performance to a data flow in accordance with requests from the application program.

queuing In routing and switching, a backlog of packets or frames waiting to be forwarded out an interface.

R

radio frequency interference (RFI) Radio frequencies that create noise that interferes with information being transmitted across unshielded copper cabling.

Random Access Memory (RAM) Also known as read-write memory, RAM can have new data written to it and can have stored data read from it. RAM is the main working area, or temporary storage, used by the CPU for most processing and operations. A drawback of RAM is that it requires electrical power to maintain data storage. If the computer is turned off or loses power, all data stored in RAM is lost unless the data was previously saved to disk. Memory boards with RAM chips plug into the motherboard

real-time traffic Data traffic that carries signal output as it happens or as fast as possible. Real-time traffic is sensitive to latency and jitter.

redundancy In internetworking, a network architecture designed to eliminate network downtime caused by a single point of failure. Redundancy includes the replication of devices, services, or connections that support operations even in the occurrence of a failure. *See also* redundant system.

reliable A characteristic of a protocol that uses mechanisms such as handshaking, timers, acknowledgement messages, and dynamic windowing to help ensure that data received is the same as the data received. Reliable protocols require additional overhead on the network in terms of much larger segment headers.

Requests for Comments (RFC) Series of documents and memoranda encompassing new research, innovations, and methodologies applicable to Internet technologies. RFCs are a reference for how technologies should work.

response timeout How long a service waits on a response before taking some action. How long service waits and what action is taken if a response timeout occurs are defined by the protocol.

Round-trip time (RTT) The time required for some networking PDUs to be sent and received, and a response PDU to be sent and received. In other words, the time between when a device sends data and when the same device receives a response.

routing The process by which a router receives an incoming frame, discards the data-link header and trailer, makes a forwarding decision based on the destination IP address, adds a new data-link header and trailer based on the outgoing interface, and forwards the new frame out the outgoing interface.

runt frame Any frame less than 64 bytes in length. These frames are automatically discarded by receiving stations. Also called collision fragment.

S

Secure Shell (SSH) A protocol that provides a secure remote connection to a host through a TCP application.

segment 1) A collision domain that is a section of a LAN that is bound by bridges, routers, or switches. 2) In a LAN using a bus topology, a segment is a continuous electrical circuit that is often connected to other such segments with repeaters. 3) When used with TCP, the term segment (verb) refers to the work TCP does to accept a large piece of data from an application and break it into smaller pieces. Again with TCP, used as a noun, segment refers to one of those smaller pieces of data.

segmenting In TCP, the process of taking a large chunk of data and breaking it into small-enough pieces to fit within a TCP segment without breaking any rules about the maximum amount of data allowed in a segment.

selective acknowledgement (SACK) Optional TCP feature that makes it possible for the destination to acknowledge bytes in discontinuous segments. With SACK, the source host would only need to retransmit the specific unacknowledged data rather than retransmitting all data since the last acknowledged data.

sequence number Information placed in a data header to ensure correct sequencing of the arriving data.

server Can refer to computer hardware that is to be used by multiple concurrent users. Alternatively, this term can refer to computer software that provides services to many users. For example, a web server consists of web server software running on some computer.

Server Message Block (SMB) An application level network protocol mainly applied to shared access to files, printers, serial ports, and miscellaneous communications between nodes on a network.

session A related set of communications transactions between two or more network devices.

shielded twisted-pair (STP) cable A type of network cabling that includes twisted-pair wires, with shielding around each pair of wires, as well as another shield around all wires in the cable.

Simple Mail Transfer Protocol (SMTP) An application layer protocol providing electronic mail services to transfer mail from client to server and between servers.

slash notation A method of expressing a network prefix. It uses a forward slash (/) followed by the network prefix, for example, 192.168.254.0 /24. This /24 represents the 24-bit network prefix in slash format.

socket a logical communications end point within a network device. A socket is typically represented by a Layer 3 address and a Layer 4 port number.

source The device that is originating the PDU.

source IP address The IP address of the originating host that is placed into the IP packet header.

spoofing A person or program that masquerades as another to gain access to data and the network.

standard An internationally recognized definition of technical specifications that ensure worldwide consistency.

stateful Tracking of actual conversations and their state of the communication session for a protocol, such as TCP.

Stateless Address Autoconfiguration (SLAAC) Plug-and-play IPv6 feature that enables devices to connect themselves to the network without any configuration and without any servers (like DHCP servers).

subnet A group of IP addresses that have the same value in the first part of the IP addresses, for the purpose of allowing routing to identify the group by that initial part of the addresses. IP addresses in the same subnet typically sit on the same network medium and are not separated from each other by any routers. IP addresses on different subnets are typically separated from one another by at least one router. Subnet is short for subnetwork.

subnet mask A dotted decimal number that helps identify the structure of IPv4 addresses. The mask represents the network and subnet parts of related IPv4 addresses with binary 1s and the host part of related IPv4 addresses with binary 0s.

subnetwork *See* subnet.

switch fabric The integrated circuits and the accompanying machine programming in a switch that allow the data paths through the switch to be controlled.

Switch Form-Factor Pluggable (SFP) Removal modules used in routers and switches to support a number of different network media.

switch virtual interfaces (SVI) Virtual interfaces for which there is no physical hardware on the device associated. An SVI is created in software. The virtual interfaces are used as a means to remotely manage a switch over a network. They are also used as a method of routing between VLANs.

T

Telecommunications Industry Association (TIA) An organization that develops standards that relate to telecommunications technologies. Together, the TIA and the Electronic Industries Alliance (EIA) have formalized standards, such as EIA/TIA-232, for the electrical characteristics of data transmission.

TelePresence Cisco multimedia products for business virtual meetings and collaboration.

Telnet A non-secure network service that supports CLI access to a remote host. It also can be used to verify the application layer software between source and destination stations.

terminal emulation Network application in which a computer runs software that makes it appear to a remote host as a directly attached terminal.

test-net address The IPv4 address block 192.0.2.0 to 192.0.2.255 (192.0.2.0 /24) that is set aside for teaching and learning purposes. These addresses can be used in documentation and network examples.

three-way handshake The process used by TCP to establish a session.

throughput The actual data transfer rate between two computers at some point in time. Throughput is impacted by the slowest-speed link used to send data between the two computers, as well as myriad variables that might change during the course of a day.

Time to Live (TTL) A field in the IP header that prevents a packet from indefinitely looping around an IP internetwork. Routers decrement the TTL field each time they forward a packet, and if they decrement the TTL to 0, the router discards the packet, which prevents it from looping forever.

topology The arrangement of networking components or nodes. Examples include star, extended star, ring, and mesh.

traceroute (tracert) A command on many computer operating systems that discovers the IP addresses, and possibly host names, of the routers used by the network when sending a packet from one computer to another.

traffic prioritization A process in Quality of Service (QoS) where frames are forwarded in priority order based on their marking.

Transmission Control Protocol (TCP) A Layer 4 protocol of the TCP/IP model, TCP lets applications guarantee delivery of data across a network.

Trivial File Transfer Protocol (TFTP) A protocol similar to FTP that provides the transfer of files from one computer to another over a network. TFTP is supported by UDP where FTP is supported by TCP.

U

unicast Message sent to a single network destination. Compare with broadcast and multicast.

unique local address IPv6 similar to RFC 1918 private addresses for IPv4. Unique local addresses are used for local addressing within a site or between a limited number of sites. These addresses should not be routable in the global IPv6 Internet. Unique local addresses are in the range of FC00::/7 to FDFF::/7.

unshielded twisted-pair (UTP) cable A general type of cable, with the cable holding twisted pairs of copper wires and the cable itself having little shielding.

unspecified address An IPv6 all-0s address represented in the compressed format as ::/128 or just :: in the compressed format. It cannot be assigned to an interface and is only to be used as a source address in an IPv6 packet. An unspecified address is used as a source address when the device does not yet have a permanent IPv6 address or when the source of the packet is irrelevant to the destination.

User Datagram protocol (UDP) A connectionless transport layer protocol in the TCP/IP protocol stack. UDP is a simple protocol that exchanges datagrams without acknowledgements or guaranteed delivery, requiring that error processing and retransmission be handled.

user executive (EXEC) mode The limited CLI mode where the commands available to the user are a subset of those available at the privileged level. In general, use the user EXEC commands to temporarily change terminal settings, perform basic tests, and list system information.

V

variable length subnet masking (VLSM) Ability to specify a different subnet mask for the same network number on different subnets. VLSM can help optimize available address space.

virtual classroom A logical classroom environment created as a collaboration space without physical restraints.

Virtual Local Area Network (VLAN) A network of end devices that behave as if they are connected to the same network segment, even though they might be physically located on different segments of a LAN. VLANs are configured through software on the switch and router (IOS on Cisco routers and switches).

virtual terminal line (vty) The reference to text based logical interfaces on an IOS device. These are accessed using Telnet or SSH to perform administrative tasks. VTY lines are also called virtual type terminal.

virtualization The creation of a virtual version of something, such as a hardware platform, operating system (OS), storage device, or network resources. As an example, a virtual machine consists of a set of files and programs running on an actual physical system.

Voice over IP (VoIP) Voice data encapsulated in an IP packet that allows it to traverse already implemented IP networks without needing its own network infrastructure.

W

window size As filed in the TCP header that is set in a sent segment, signifies the maximum amount of unacknowledged data the host is willing to receive before the other sending host must wait for an acknowledgement. Used for flow control.

wireless access point (WAP) A network device that provides connectivity of wireless clients to connect to a data network.

P

public IPv4 addresses, 416-417
pulse-coded modulation. *See* PCM
purpose
of data link layer, 198
of physical layer, 166-169
PUT message, 526
PuTTY, 67

Q-R

QoS (quality of service), 37-39, 562
queuing packets, 38
QuickTime, 518

radio frequency interference. *See* RFI
RAM (random access memory), 316
randomly generated interface IDs, 443-444
ranges
addresses, IPv4, 474
subnets, assigning addresses, 470
read-only memory. *See* ROM
real-time applications, small networks, 561
real-time traffic, 558
Real-Time Transport Control Protocol. *See* RTCP
Real-Time Transport Protocol. *See* RTP
reasons for subnetting, 467
reassembling
segments, 345
UDP datagrams, 380
reconnaissance attacks, 570
recovery, passwords, 611
redirection, ports, 571
redisplaying lines (Ctrl-R), 82
redundancy in small networks, 556
reference models, 137
benefits of layered models, 138
OSI, 139-142
TCP/IP, 140-142
registered ports, 359
reliability
low overhead, 379-380
of networks, 31
TCP, 353, 364, 373-379
transport layers, 347
UDP, 355
reload command, 97

remote communications, ARP, 256
remote devices, accessing, 87
remote hosts, 300
remote network routing table entries, 311
remote resources, accessing, 150-152
remote routes, 308
remote user connections, 25-27
representations
hexadecimal number systems, 428
IPv6 addresses, 429-431
networks, 18-21
Request for Comments. *See* RFCs
requests, UDP, 381
requirements
hosts, 487
networks, 488
small network protocols, 564
subnetting, 468-470
research, collaboration tools, 11
resequencing segments, 373
resources
availability, 5
local, accessing, 146-149
networks, 11
clients/servers, 13
P2P, 13-14
sizes, 12
remote, accessing, 150-152
response timeouts, 122
restoring IOS configuration files, 607-611
results, ping command, 583
RFCs (Request for Comments), 134, 143, 204
RFC 1918, 416
RFC 3330, 418
RFC 6598, 417
RFI (radio frequency interference), 174
ring topologies, 211, 214
Roberts, Larry, 129
roles
protocols, 125
of TCP, 353
of transport layers, 343
of UDP, 355
rollover cables, 183
ROM (read-only memory), 239
routed ports, 274-275

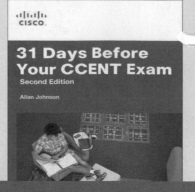